A History Of
The Georgia Baptist Convention
1822–1972

By

James Adams Lester

Commissioned By

The Executive Committee

The Baptist Convention of The State of Georgia

Searcy S. Garrison

Executive Secretary-Treasurer

DEDICATION

This volume is dedicated with love, affection and deep appreciation for and to:

Every Georgia Baptist, living and with Our Lord, who has had a part in the advance of the Kingdom of God through the Churches and Associations in fellowship with the Baptist Convention Of The State of Georgia, and:

To
SEARCY S. GARRISON

their dedicated servant and leader in the finest tradition of 150 years of fine leadership for our Lord.

TABLE OF CONTENTS

Chapters

A History Of The Georgia Baptist Convention 1822–1972

BY JAMES ADAMS LESTER

Introduction

Anticipating its one hundred and fiftieth anniversary, the Georgia Baptist Convention appealed to Georgia Baptists to make 1972 a year of thanksgiving, renewed commitment to Christ, and extraordinary achievement in Kingdom service. The Convention authorized the Executive Committee to proceed with plans and preparations for a worthy observance of the Sesquicentennial.

Publication of a definitive history of the Georgia Baptist Convention was one of the achievements anticipated by the History Committee and the Executive Committee of the Convention. Upon the recommendation of the Administration Committee, James Adams Lester was commissioned by the Executive Committee to prepare the manuscript of the history.

James Lester was well prepared for the service for which he was commissioned. He is a native Georgian, the son of a beloved Georgia pastor, Paul E. Lester, and a mother who in her widowed years served on the staff of the Georgia Baptist Children's Home. Lester is a graduate of three Baptist institutions—Norman College, Mercer University and the New

Orleans Baptist Theological Seminary. He wrote a history of *The Christian Index,* journal of the Georgia Baptist Convention, as his thesis for a Master of Theology degree at the New Orleans Seminary.

At the time Mr. Lester began work on the history, he had served as pastor, journalist, a member of the Executive Committee staff of the Georgia Baptist Convention for eleven and one half years, and had begun his work as editor of *The Baptist And Reflector,* journal of the Tennessee Baptist Convention. For more than twenty years, he has been a serious student of Baptist history in general and Georgia Baptist history in particular.

Those who read this history will find it an interesting account of the achievements of Baptists in Georgia through cooperative efforts to extend the Master's kingdom. Students of Georgia Baptist history will find the book to be a valuable guide and source of information, a worthy successor to earlier historical works by Ragsdale, Campbell, Sherwood, Mercer and Benedict.

Lester's manuscript was begun after approximately four years of careful research which carried him to numerous original sources as well as to the works of others. The history is carefully documented, which will serve serious students in their in-depth studies of the history of Georgia Baptists. The author has sought to be objective in his examination and report of the important events and developments in Georgia Baptist life. The author's method and purpose inspire confidence, and the numerous pictures and statistical reports add to the interest and value of the book.

An understanding of the past is essential preparation for a wise and successful life and service in the present. The Book of Deuteronomy presents Moses, the aged leader of Israel, preparing his beloved people for the time when he would be their leader no longer. Moses called upon Israel "to remember the Lord their God" and their convenant with Him, the way over which they had come, the commandments, and their mission. Moses sought to prepare

Israel for the future by reminding them of their history, and by calling upon the people to renew their faith in and commitment to the Lord their God.

This history of the Georgia Baptist Convention will serve Georgia Baptists well in reminding them of a worthy heritage of Christian faith and achievement. With appreciation for all who "made the history," and with expressions of gratitude to the author for recording the story faithfully yet sympathetically and with devotion, we commend *A History of the Georgia Baptist Convention* to Georgia Baptists and to their Christian friends and colleagues in witness and service.

It is my prayer that the recalling of a rich and inspiring heritage will prepare us for a more effective service today and more glorious achievements through the years to come.

Searcy S. Garrison
Executive Secretary-Treasurer
Executive Committee
Georgia Baptist Convention

A History Of
The Georgia Baptist Convention
1822–1972

By James Adams Lester

Foreword

The heritage of Baptists in the State of Georgia, their Christian witness for more than two hundred years, and their impact upon the cause of Christ and the ministries of Baptists within the state and in America is great. Their work through the Baptist Convention of the State of Georgia is a continuing monument of Christian service.

Baptist influence has been exerted in Georgia since earliest Colonial days, and in many ways the course of secular history has been influenced in large measure by Baptists, as individuals and as a Denomination within the state.

An idea in the minds of many since the mid-1950's, this history was commissioned by the Georgia Baptist Convention in 1969. The author has done study, independently, in this area for the past eighteen years, and wrote in 1954-1955 *A History Of The Christian Index.*

This volume was authorized as a part of the Sesquicentennial celebration of the organization of the Convention during 1972. This history is not intended as an exhaustive treatise, but rather a comprehensive, documented presentation of the life and ministry of this august body of Christians. There is available sufficient material dealing with Baptist bodies, individual Baptists, and their lives and ministries in Georgia, to fill many volumes.

Dr. Searcy S. Garrison, Executive Secretary-Treasurer of The Executive Committee of The Baptist Convention Of Georgia, exercised leadership in plans for preparation of this history, and it is the property of The Executive Committee.

The purpose of this volume is to present, in narrative fashion, the life and work of Baptists in Georgia as they moved across the pages of history from time into eternity, and to present documentation sufficient to substantiate the record.

It is the role of the historian to recount history. This is written, therefore, as an account of the thrilling movement of Baptists from Colonial Georgia to the present, without editorial commentary.

Appreciation is expressed to the many persons who gave of their time and interest in assisting in the typing, necessary proofreading and other labor involved in the preparation of a volume such as this.

The Author.

Background for the History

Sources available for use in this work were numerous. Several of the earlier histories about Georgia Baptists should be mentioned. They range from information on Baptists contained in *The Gazeteer* by Adiel Sherwood, published in two editions, 1827 and 1829, to the latest written history as such, the *Story of Georgia Baptists,* in three volumes, by the late B. D. Ragsdale, printed during the 1930's. In between these works, materials include: *A History of the Georgia Association,* by Jesse Mercer, published in 1838; *A History of Georgia Baptists, with Biographical Compendium,* published by the Index Printing Company in 1881; *Memoirs of Jesse Mercer,* by C. D. Mallary, published in 1844; *Memoir of B. M. Sanders,* by C. D. Mallary, published in 1854; and *Georgia Baptists: Historical and Biographical,* by J. H. Campbell in 1847. The late B. J. W. Graham published a three-volume biographical presentation of leaders in Georgia Baptist life, the last volume being published in 1923.

During the early 1960's, P. Harris Anderson, of Mercer University, Macon, compiled a mimeographed volume entitled *The Witness and Work of Georgia Baptists,* which is a useful book, designed for courses in Baptist ministries offered through the Extension centers of Mercer University.

The repository of the Georgia Baptist Historical Society, the "Museum" in the Stetson Memorial Library at Mercer University, Macon, contains a priceless collection of Georgia Baptist history, both in printed and manuscript form. When the Georgia preparation of the first edition of the *Encyclopedia of Southern Baptists* was undertaken in the mid 1950's under the direction of Dr. Spencer B. King, Jr., head of the history department at Mercer, a useful collection of manuscript material was added to the museum collection.

Countless pages of documented materials, prepared by numerous Georgia Baptist leaders upon assignment from King, remain unused from the necessary culling and reducing in quantity of this material for use in the Encyclopedia.

Additionally, since the early 1940's, and begun under the direction of the late Charles H. Stone, then Mercer librarian, the Mercer library has collected countless records from individual churches and associations, each of which has a bearing upon Georgia Baptist history, and is a contribution to this larger body of materials.

Minutes, many in detailed form, of the Georgia Baptist Association, first association in the state, shed light upon the overall picture of an emerging work. These minutes, together with volumes of *The Christian Index,* which has been published in Georgia since 1833, and detailed Minutes of the Georgia Baptist Convention, 1822-1971, offer a rather complete picture of Georgia Baptist life.

Numerous books, in manuscript and printed form, tell the story of various areas of Baptist life in Georgia. The late Spencer B. King, Sr., long-time treasurer and State Missions secretary for Georgia Baptists, wrote in 1928 a volume entitled *Georgia: A Mission Field. Youth's Fifty Years,* by Leslie S. Williams, is a history of Training Union in Georgia from the beginning of that movement until 1945.

The late Dr. Spright Dowell, president of Mercer University for 25 years, and two-term president of the Georgia Baptist Convention, wrote *A History of Mercer University, 1833-1953.* There is a separate volume, *His Story: In Georgia W.M.U. History* by Mrs. W. J. Neel, published in 1939. Another volume on Woman's Missionary Union is *Wrought of God* published in 1959.

The rather complete minutes of the Executive Committee of the Georgia Baptist Convention, and its antecedents, and the record of the proceedings of the Convention proper in annual session, provide an accurate panorama of Baptist work in this state. Additionally, the minutes of the Administrative Committee of the Executive Committee are excellent primary sources of information.

Baptists began to be history conscious in the years after the War Between the States, and in the earlier years of this century to a degree greater than at any time. Dr. James W. Merritt, former executive secretary-treasurer of the Executive Committee, during his tenure, helped to provide an accurate chronology of the events in Georgia Baptist life. Since the beginning of the administration of the current executive secretary-treasurer, Dr. Searcy S. Garrison, in 1955, probably as complete and precise a set of records of Convention and Convention-related actions has been kept as of any "body politic" in this country.

Examination of the printed records of proceedings of Committees and Commissions provides an accurate and concise accounting of the life of Georgia Baptists during one of their greatest eras of growth.

Throughout the years, material available has chronicled not only the statistical growth of Baptists, but also the occasional theological controversies; difficulties involved in dealing with the question of slave-holding; attitudes concerning the formation of the Southern Baptist Convention in 1845 in Augusta; and to a large degree, the impact which these and like matters had upon the total record of progress.

Sources dealing also with Georgia Baptists in broader scope, include Benedict's *History of the Baptists,* in which historian David Benedict made use not only of material he had gathered himself, but materials shared with him by Jesse Mercer and Adiel Sherwood. Armitage's *History of the Baptists,* in several editions, provides considerable material on Baptist life in Georgia. *The History of Baptists* in three volumes, by Isaac Backus, published by the New England Historical Society in 1871, provides information on Georgia Baptists, as well as the one-volume history of Backus, entitled *Church History of New England,* published in 1839.

Volumes and sources cited may be considered the major repository of material related to Georgia Baptists. There are many other—and countless—references in records of the state of Georgia as such, and in local and regional histories to Georgia Baptists. *Georgia Baptists, Organization and Division, 1772-1848,* a History of Primitive Baptists in Georgia, an unpublished thesis by Elder Emerson Proctor of Jesup [1970] sheds considerable light upon the controversy which deveolped between mission and anti-mission forces in the state, culminating in the split into two groups which was complete around 1837.

Finally, in this introductory statement, it must be noted that, without exception, references in and about the history of Georgia Baptists leave no doubt that the unifying and organizational strength of this denomination focused in missions and education in the early stages, and these emphases were the backbone of organized Georgia Baptist life as we know it today.

The Analytical Repository, published by Henry Holcombe, in Savannah during 1802 and 1803—though short-lived—was the first Baptist publication of its type, and to this source the author is indebted; especially for a clear delineation of Baptist organizational life in Georgia from the founding of the Georgia Association to the period during and after the Powelton conferences, 1801-1803. These conferences were the seed-bed for the emergence in 1822 of the Convention as an organized body. This paper contains the only known minute record of the second and third Powelton conferences.

Use of material in the *History of Georgia Baptists With Biographical Compendium* and the three-volume work by Ragsdale would have been far more extensive were it not for the fact that the material is largely undocumented. There is a mass of what obviously is primary source material, but there is insufficient documenting of the sources to use *except in the many instances where* this author was able to document by cross-reference to other documented sources, primary and secondary.

Having studied carefully Boykin's *History of the Baptist Denomination In Georgia,* [*History of Georgia Baptists With Biographical Compendium*] and subsequently primary sources, the author was able to authenticate the great majority of material prepared by Boykin. Most of the sources used by Boykin, were traced by the author in his own research.

Conclusions concerning the final organization of the volume remained largely unchanged from the original projection of the work to the Administration Committee of the Executive Committee, and the Convention's History Committee. Extensive use is made in this work of the author's earlier work on *The Christian Index,* and includes thesis materials, together with material accumulated in the process of research for this thesis.

With all the illustrious personages involved in the history of Georgia Baptists, it has been impossible to credit adequately their vast contribution. Biographical information on individuals has been used where that information sheds light upon some historical fact, or upon some stream of activity related closely to that individual. A compendium of several thousands of pages would be necessary to chronicle adequately the total contributions of the many thousands of the servants of God who have made their witness a part of temporal history and eternal memorial. The same is true of the vital role the District Association and hundreds of Georgia Baptist Churches.

The author's assignment was to write a comprehensive history of the Baptist Convention of the State of Georgia. This specific assignment, vast in scope of itself, precluded fuller presentation of Associations, Churches and individuals.

Quotations are reproduced exactly as they appeared in the sources, including spelling. This was done not only to retain accuracy, but to retain also the "flavor" of the vernacular.

xvii

CHAPTER 1

Political Background

When James Edward Oglethorpe embarked from England in November of 1732, on the ship Anne, he brought with him 114 colonists under charter of a corporation called "Trustees for establishing the colony of Georgia in America," issued by King George II.[1] Oglethorpe came to an area claimed both by Spain and England. Plans for the colony were begun in 1730 by Oglethorpe, at that time a member of the British Parliament, and Lord John Perceval, an English philanthropist.[2]

Original planning for the colony had included importation of persons from debtor's prisons and those who had been freed from debtor's prisons. Oglethorpe, after some two years, abandoned the idea of an entire colonial development by debtors, and "few debtors were accepted in the group."[3]

The group arrived at Yamacraw Bluff, now the site of Savannah, February 12, 1733, after a voyage of approximately three months. Carswell says that Baptists came with Oglethorpe, or "soon afterward," and included, "William Calvert of Lincolnshire, William Slack of Ireland, and Thomas Walker of Northampton."[4]

[1]Charter, Quoted in *Historical Collections of Georgia,* p. 2 [Note: For more detailed background, see *Historical Collections of Georgia,* Rev. George White, New York, Pudney and Russell Publishers, 1855] p. 2.

[2]*The World Book Encyclopedia,* Vol. VII, [Chicago: Field Enterprises Corporation, 1962] p.p. 130, 131.

[3]*Ibid.,* p. 132.

[4]Encyclopedia of Southern Baptists, Vol. I, [Nashville: Broadman Press, 1958] p. 532. Monograph by W. J. Carswell.

1

This account is probably the most accurate. Armitage states that two Baptists, Messers Campbell and Dunham[5] were in the original group to arrive with Oglethorpe. Cathcart says that William Calvert, William Slack, and Thomas Walker, and William Dunham were Baptists in the original group.[6] Morgan Edwards considered a primary source, and used by Carswell, identifies Calvert, Slack, Walker, and one Paul Hill as being in the first settlement of the Georgia colony.[7] The contingent aboard Oglethorpe's vessel arrived in a land which was home territory for the Creek Indians in the South and the Cherokee Indians in the Highlands of the present state boundaries. They came to an area which at that time extended westward almost to the Mississippi river.

This was an area across which Hernando de Soto had traveled—possibly the first white man to do so—nearly two hundred years earlier in his trek from Florida to the Mississippi river,[8] and an area where French explorers had established a settlement on the St. John's river in 1562.[9] This settlement on the St. John's had caused dismay on the part of Phillip II of Spain who had, in effect, claimed the territory for that country. In 1565 he had sent Petro Menendez de Avites to build forts along the coast, and during that period, Menendez had claimed what is now the Southeastern United States for Spain.[10]

England laid claim also to the same region as part of the original Carolina grant made by Charles I to Sir Robert Heath in 1629.[11]

[5]Thomas Armitage, *A History of the Baptists*, Vol. II, [New York: Bryan, Taylor, and Co., 1887] p. 770.
[6]William Cathcart, *The Baptist Encyclopedia*, [Philadelphia: Louis H. Everts, 1881] p. 441.
[7]Morgan Edwards: *Materials Toward A History of Baptists in Georgia.* Furman manuscript, p. 1.
[8]Lucian Lamar Knight, *Georgia's Bi Centennial Memoirs and Memories*, Vol. IV, p.p. 20, 21. See also 22-27. [and original sources] p. 28. Charter.
[9]*Ibid*, p. 31.
[10]*Ibid*, p. 14, and see also *World Book* Vol. VII, p. 131.
[11]*Ibid*, p. 35.

In 1717, Sir Robert Montgomery secured a grant of land between the Altamaha and Savannah rivers from the Lords Proprietors of Carolina. The grant was for settlements on the south side of the Savannah, but was never implemented.[12] "The English built a fort on the Altamaha River in 1721, but its expense caused them to abandon it in 1727."[13]

The charter granted permission to the trustees

> . . . to transport and convey out of our realm of Great Britain, or any other of our deminions, into the said province of Georgia, to be there settled, so many of our loving subjects, or any foreigners that are willing to become our subjects and live under our allegiance in the said colony, as shall be willing to go to inhabit or reside there, with sufficient shipping, armor, weapons, powder, shot, ordnance, munition, victuals, merchandise and wares, as are esteemed by the wild people, clothing, implements, furniture, cattle, horses, mares, and all other things necessary for the said colony. . . .[14]

Such provision implies that those who would settle in Georgia held some property or owned some goods.

An extract from the Minutes of the Trustees, April 11, 1733, said further: "Names of all those who go to Georgia paying their own expenses, shall be published in one of the newspapers."[15]

While the colony had a benevolent object to furnish freedom in the new world for debtors and those who felt oppressed, it is apparent that many came with some means.[16]

> The main-spring of the colony's existence was benevolence; and it was not to found a colony of jail-birds nor to purge the prisons of England. . . .
> Georgia was the only one of the English colonies to receive its birthright from an act of Parliament, though a charter, signed by George II followed in due course of time.[17]

[12]*Ibid*, p.p. 39-42.
[13]World Book, Vol. VII, p. 131.
[14]White, Historical collections of Georgia, Charter, p. 9.
[15]White, *Historical Collections of Georgia*, p. 15, Extracts from Minutes of the Trustees.
[16]Knight, p. 2.
[17]Knight, *loc. cit.*

The Royal charter was for a separate and distinct province between the Savannah and Altamaha rivers,[18] intended originally to be named Georgia.

Following embarkation at Deptford, near London, the group arrived in Charleston harbor January 13, 1733, and at Beaufort, South Carolina, January 20. Oglethorpe then selected a site for his settlement, which was the bluff upon which Savannah now stands. Upon their arrival, the colonists erected tents, and landed formally February 12, 1733.[19]

Activity by the Spaniards in Florida earlier in the eighteenth century caused concern upon the part of the residents of South Carolina; and, according to several sources, the settlement of Georgia as a colony originated in the minds of South Carolinians as a barrier between them and the Spanish settlement in Florida.[20]

It was, therefore, to an area claimed both by Spain and England, and defended adequately by neither, that Oglethorpe came in the winter of 1733. And during the 20 years that trustees for the crown controlled Georgia, they sent more than 1810 colonists, many of them Germans from Salzburg, and an additional 1000 other settlers came to the colony at "their own expense" during this time.[21]

DIFFERENT BACKGROUND EVIDENT

Facts indicated in this part of the political background are important because: Whereas come other colonies were settled by debtors who came to America a century earlier, bankrupt, and with a desire for physical as well as religious freedom, settlers in Georgia were somewhat different.

The character of the colonists must of necessity condition the character of the colony, and affect development in many areas. The composition of the colonists included many who

[18]*Ibid.*, p.p. 7, 8. Charter as reproduced.
[19]Knight, *loc. lit.*
[20]Samuel Boykin, *History of Georgia Baptists With Biographical Compendium* [Atlanta: James P. Harrison and Co., 1881], p.p. 3, 4.
[21]*World Book*, Vol. VII, p. 132. [Note: Data for the World Book was prepared by Albert Saye, perhaps the leading contemporary Georgia historian.]

paid their own way; and when they paid their way they came out of backgrounds of what would be termed working stock, having apparently earned their livelihood in their native lands. Additionally, the Salzburgers came with an intense appreciation for religious liberty, as well as an aptitude for many trades, and a reputation in their own Germany for industriousness.[22]

These facts are given because they contributed to a type of life and thought which helped set the stage in Georgia for Baptists as they grew numerically to place great emphasis not only upon a form of church government strongly democratic, but which helped to lay the foundations for what became a major and controlling interest in Baptist life from that time until the present in missions and education.

The colonists came to a land which stretched from the sea coast to elevations in the northern part of the state approaching 5,000 feet.[23] They came to a land with a climate boasting a mean annual temperature of 65 degrees fahrenheit,[24] and a state which was to become the last of the 13 original colonies, and the southernmost of the 13.[25]

BAPTIST BEGINNINGS

Thus, when Messers Campbell and Dunham, followed shortly thereafter by a Mr. Polhill,[26] came as colonists to Georgia, they came also as Baptists, Separatists, and with them came the germ for Baptist growth from the original colonial site. Historians have ascribed traditionally origins of Baptist work in Georgia to the settlement of Baptists from South Carolina, as they moved down the Atlantic coast from Massachusetts through Virginia, North Carolina, South Carolina, and into Georgia.

While it is correct to assert historically that Baptists have

[22]White, Historical Collections of Georgia, Extracts from Minutes of Trustees, p.p. 14-20.
[23]World Book, Vol. VII, p. 121.
[24]*Ibid*, p. 124.
[25]*Ibid*, p. 120.
[26]Armitage, Vol. II, p. 770.

been in Georgia since the earliest days of the settlement of the colony, it is not possible to assert definitely that a permanent Baptist work developed as a result of the work of these colonists. It is a fact, however, that their presence, and their identification as Baptists, provided a basis for Christian endeavors which helped to provide the foundations for permanent work.

Careful examination of the writings of historians including William Cathcart, David Benedict, Thomas Armitage, Issac Backus, Morgan Edwards and others provide ample documentation of the fact that Baptists, identifiable as Regular Baptists, did leave their mark upon Georgia Baptist work, establishing a permanency to it, as they moved from Pennsylvania, Massachusetts, and Connecticut into and through Maryland, into North Carolina, Virginia, South Carolina, and thence to Georgia.

Daniel Marshall, for example, who ranks as a pioneer Baptist leader in Georgia Baptist life, received probably the basic impulses for his life and work as a Baptist from Shubal Stearns, his brother-in-law. Stearns was born in Boston, Massachusetts, January 28, 1706, and was a minister among the New Lights, later called Separatists.[27] Stearns, after having been for six years a minister among the New Lights "as the converted Congregational communities were called," became a Baptist in 1751 at Tolland, Conn.[28] Stearns, "in what he conceived to be a Spirit-led move westward" moved from Connecticut to Virginia in 1754 with a few members of his congregation.[29] They stopped at Opeckon, Berkeley county, Virginia, where he met Marshall, who had married Martha Stearns in 1748.[30]

Marshall had been a missionary among the Indians, and upon his arrival at Opeckon became a Baptist.[31] From

[27]Robert B. Semple, *Semple's History of the Rise and Progress of the Baptists in Virginia*, revised by G. W. Beale, 1894, p. 12.
[28]Semple, *Loc. cit.*
[29]*Ibid.*, p. 13.
[30]Semple, *Loc. cit.*
[31]Semple, *Loc. cit.*

Opeckon, Marshall moved to Sandy Creek, Guilford county, North Carolina, and on November 22, 1755, he and his companions constituted the Sandy Creek church, calling Stearns as pastor. Marshall at that time was not ordained.[32]

Again, the ministries of George Whitefield throughout the colonies left a permanent impact upon Georgia Baptist life, although Whitefield was not Baptist.[33] He was licensed to come to Georgia as a Deacon in the Church of England.[34]

These and many others who left an indelible mark upon Georgia Baptist life will be discussed further.

The first seven years of the colonization of Georgia transpired with no apparent Baptist work of permanent nature. Colonization of the state moved rather slowly during that period, and in 1740, the war between Spain and England began. It was ended when Oglethorpe defeated the Spanish at the Battle of Bloody Marsh on St. Simons Island in 1742, and ended for a time the fighting in America.[35]

At the time of fighting between Spain and England, George Whitefield was in Savannah [1740], where his preaching left its mark in a move toward religious awakening. Whitefield had first been in Savannah May, 1738,[36] and laid the foundation for an orphanage,[37] returning to England in Sept., 1738 to raise money for the work.[38] He returned to America, sailing Aug. 14, 1739,[39] his orphange was begun, and he traveled throughout the New England states.[40]

The influence of religious thought moving directly from England into Georgia is demonstrated further in the life and ministry of Nicholas Bedgewood, [Bedgegood] who, probably was "the first Baptist minister who proclaimed the gospel in

[32]*Ibid*, p. 14.
[33]Historical Collections, p. 17.
[34]Extracts, Minutes of Trustees, Dec. 21, 1737; Historical Collections, p. 17.
[35]*World Book*, Vol. VII, p. 132. Also: Knight, p. 109.
[36]John Gilles, *Memoirs of George Whitefield*, [Middletown, Hunt and Noyer, 1838] p. 30.
[37]*Ibid.*, p. 32.
[38]*Ibid.*, p. 33.
[39]*Ibid.*, p. 42.
[40]*Ibid.*, p. 44.

Georgia." [41] A classical scholar, he came to Savannah apparently at the invitation of Whitefield to accept employment at Whitefield's Orphan House in 1751. According to Campbell, and other sources, Bedgewood led in the conversion of several persons who were employed at the orphan house,[42] and these he baptized, and later administered to them the Lord's Supper, "probably as an arm of the Charleston church".[43] This has been accepted as the first Baptist communion in the state.[44]

Bedgewood had been baptized by Oliver Hart in Charleston in 1757 upon embracing the sentiments of Baptists. [Armitage says Bedgewood was baptized in 1756.[45]] He later moved to Pedee, South Carolina, and subsequently was pastor of the Welch Neck, South Carolina, church.[46] Campbell says that Bedgewood was disowned by the Charleston Association because of accusations that he had a wife living in England when he married in this country.[47] While not a Baptist upon his arrival in Georgia, he undoubtedly had embraced Separatist views, at least by the time he followed Whitefield into the colonies.

Carswell differs from Campbell in declaring that the first observance of The Lord's Supper in Georgia was by a group of Seventh Day Baptists from South Carolina who settled near Tuckaseeking about 1759 in what is now Effingham county. The group of Baptists who gathered around Bedgewood apparently left no permanent church to their memory.[48]

Benedict makes evident that the dispersion of Baptist

[41]Campbell, Jesse H., *Georgia Baptists: Historical and Biographical*. [Richmond, Virginia: H. K. Ellyson, 1847] p. 26.

[42]Boykin, p. 11; *Loc. cit.*

[43]*Loc. cit.*

[44]*Loc. cit.*

[45]Thomas Armitage, *A History of the Baptists*, Vol. II [New York: Bryan, Taylor and Co., 1887] p. 770.

[46]*Loc. cit.*

[47]Campbell, p. 26.

[48]Encyclopedia of Southern Baptists, Vol. I, p. 532, Monograph by W. J. Carswell.

strength from around Whitefield's orphan house was to Whitefield's satisfaction.[49] The denomination still "existed in this region:" and, according to Morgan Edwards, as early as 1772 there were "in the low countries of this colony as many as forty Baptist families, in which were found about fifty baptized members, who had come hither from the mother country, or the other colonies." [50]

POLITICAL SITUATION CHANGING

While these developments were taking place among Baptists in Georgia, the political situation within the state was one of change. Oglethorpe, who came with powers of governor, permitted no liquor in the colony, and slave-holding was prohibited. Trustees for the colony in 1742 permitted liquor, and in 1749, the owning of slaves was permitted.[51] In 1752 Trustees of the then financially-troubled colony petitioned the British Parliament for money, which was refused on the ground that Georgia already had received more money than any other colony. In 1752, the Trustees returned their Royal Charter to the Crown, and for two years, the governmental structure continued until George II organized the colony as a Royal Province in 1754.[52]

Another look at the political situation in Georgia during the first decade of the colonial settlement is valid. When it became evident that the colonization plan was not altogether effective, the trustees, early in the 1730's, made proposals to "Highlanders from Scotland, who settled on the Altamaha in January, 1736, and built a town now known as Darien," [53] but called first New Inverness.[54] At "about the same time, one hundred and seventy Germans arrived, and

---

[49]David Benedict, *A General History of the Baptist Denomination In America*, etc., [New York: Lewis Colby and Company, 1848] p. 722.

[50]Benedict, *Loc. cit.* [quoting Edwards.]

[51]*World Book*, Vol. VII, p. 132.

[52]*Loc. cit.*

[53]Boykin, p. 4.

[54]Knight, p. 13.

joined the seventy-eight Salzburgers, from Salzburg, Bavaria, who had settled at Ebenezer, thirty miles above Savannah, in March, 1733." [55] If this account is correct, it indicates that by the first of 1736, there were over 600 white inhabitants in Georgia, one-third being Germans.

> Ten years after Oglethorpe settled at Savannah there were twelve or fourteen towns scattered throughout the territory, from Darien to Augusta, which had been settled in 1735, and was now advancing in wealth and population.[56]

BAPTIST MOVEMENT FROM SOUTH CAROLINA INTO GEORGIA

The permanency of Baptist work in Georgia owes a great debt to the ministries of Baptists in South Carolina where there was a Baptist work about 50 years before Oglethorpe arrived in Savannah.[57]

In 1683, William Screven [Scriven] emigrated from Kittery [Piscataway], Maine, "to a place forty miles from Charleston which he named Somerton." [58] Screven was a native of England, born about 1629. He settled at Piscataway, New Hampshire, [Maine] and under pressure because of his religious beliefs, he moved to South Carolina.[59] Benedict places Piscataway in Maine[60] and says that Screven fled "from the intolerant laws of the New England pedo-Baptists" with a "considerable number of his brethren." [61]

Relying upon the manuscript of Morgan Edwards, [Furman collection, examined by the author,] Benedict allows for a twenty-year error in Edwards' dating of the Charleston

[55]Knight, *Loc. cit.*
[56]*Loc. cit.*
[57]Benedict, p. 701.
[58]Joe M. King, *A History of South Carolina Baptists*, [Published by the General Board of the South Carolina Baptist Convention Columbia, S. C., R. L. Bryan Company, 1964] p. 10.
[59]Cathcart, p. 1036.
[60]Benedict, p. 701.
[Footnotes 58, 59, 60, have discrepancies in name and state but all references apparently to same place.]
[61]*Ibid.,* p. 702.

[Charlestown] church [1664] and says the church at Charleston was founded in 1683. Fourth pastor of the Charleston church was Oliver Hart, alluded to earlier, who served from about 1750 until about 1780.[62]

Again, with apparent reliance upon Edwards, Benedict says: "The foundation of this [Euhaw] church was laid in 1683".[63] It was the outgrowth of efforts of Screven and some members of the Charleston church. A group settled on Edisto Island ". . . where was the seat and centre of the community, which stood as a branch of the Charleston church".[64] About forty years later, some of the families moved to Port Royal, south of Edisto, and others to Euhaw, called Indian Island.[65] The Port Royal settlers eventually moved to Euhaw, and the first meeting house of the Euhaw church "was erected on the island of Edisto, in 1726".[66]

This relates to Georgia because of the fact that after being turned out of a common meeting house by "their overbearing brethren, the Presbyterians, . . ."[67] the Baptists constructed a church in 1751 in which George Whitefield preached, and the Euhaw Baptists constructed a meeting house on Hilton Head Island, not far from Savannah.[68]

It was the influence of the Charleston church, and the ministry of Oliver Hart, with Nicholas Bedgewood, which gave some Baptist organizational ties, loose though they were, to the Baptists in Georgia. While no permanent church resulted from these connectional influences, the spiritual ties with families of Baptists in the Savannah and Augusta areas were evident, laying the groundwork for later church development.

About the time the Euhaw church was begun, the political

[62]*Ibid.*, p.p. 702, 703.
[63]*Ibid.*, p. 703.
[64]Benedict, *Loc. cit.*
[65]Benedict, *Loc. cit.*
[66]Benedict, *Loc. cit.*
[67]Benedict, *Loc. cit.*
[68]*Ibid.*, p.p. 703, 704.

situation in Georgia was improving.[69] With the making of Georgia a Royal Province, in 1754,[70] and the allocation of lands in fee simple to settlers, the Colony began to prosper.[71] Immigration from states along the Eastern Seaboard increased, and: "During 1754 a large colony of Puritans, originally from England, moved from South Carolina and settled at Midway, Liberty county." [72]

Creek Indian raids, which had imperiled the settlers, began to diminish following placation of the Creeks and the Cherokees by the Colony's administration after 1754. ". . . For years the colony of Georgia embraced a territory only 150 miles long, and thirty miles wide, except in the extreme Southern portion." [73] In 1750, the Creeks could muster a fighting force of 3500 warriors, while the best the colonists could do was a force of less than 500.[74]

The second General Assembly of Georgia, meeting in 1758, established the Church of England as the official church.[75] This was a reversal from the original charter granted to the trustees which allowed freedom of worship except for papists.[76]

Again, the weight of South Carolina—the lower regions—made itself felt in the personage of Edmund Botsford, who came to Charleston around 1766, during times of political unrest as seeds of the American Revolution were being sown. Also an English emigrant, Botsford was "converted under the ministry of Oliver Hart," his conversion being termed by Botsford as "a day of light, a day of joy and peace." [77] He served for some 23 years as pastor of the church at George-town, South Carolina, and preached extensively in Georgia.

---

[69]White, Historical Collections, p. 20. Charter, The trustees resolved to surrender their charter Jan. 8, 1752.

[70]World Book, Vol. VII, p. 132.

[71]Boykin, p. 4.

[72]*Ibid.*, p. 5.

[73]Boykin, *Loc. cit.*

[74]Boykin, *Loc. cit.*

[75]Boykin, *Loc. cit.*

[76]White, Historical Collections, p. 10. Charter.

[77]Cathcart, p. 119.

Following the dispersion of the Bedgewood group around the Orphan House and Savannah, Benjamin Stirk, who had been baptized by Bedgewood, moved into Effingham county [Newington] in 1767, and started preaching at his own house, eighteen miles above Savannah, and at Tuckaseeking, about twenty miles farther north.[78] Stirk evidently led in constitution of a church as a branch of the Euhaw church, and died in 1770.

Upon the death of Stirk, Botsford, who had been licensed by the Charlestown church under Hart, visited the Euhaw church and received an invitation to come to Georgia and preach to the branch of the Euhaw congregation. Benedict says Botsford's first sermon at Tuckaseeking was June 27, 1771,[79] and Carswell, in his monograph in the *Encyclopedia of Southern Baptists,* said that in that same month he became pastor of the church, moving a year later to New Savannah and in 1773 established a church now "called Botsford church."[80]

Some forty years elapsed from the time of the first settlement under Oglethorpe to the sowing of seeds of Baptist work which would result in permanent establishment of churches, which would begin to multiply and exert considerable influence upon colonial government. Botsford, and the group among whom he exerted influence, were identified as Regular Baptists.

Thus three trends emerged: Dissenting Baptists, who came directly into Georgia from England; and Regular and Separate Baptists, who came into the state as the state lines were apparently crossed and recrossed during the period 1750-1770, and a third company described prosaically by Benedict in an introduction to them by writing:

> We are now prepared to give an account of the entrance of the remains of the New England New Lights in this then lowest Province of the American Union, after their various wanderings and sojournings, for

[78]Benedict, p. 722.
[79]*Ibid.,* p. 723.
[80]Encyclopedia of Southern Baptists, Vol. I, p. 532.

about fifteen years since they bid adieu to their distant home, and describe their incipient and succeeding movements which resulted in the founding of the great majority of the baptist churches, which in such rapid succession arose in this State. We have seen all along that their course was onward, that the propogation of the baptist faith was their Alpha and Omega, and that their evangelizing and proselyting efforts were always and every where attended with uncommon success.[81]

Had Whitefield been more of a Baptist persuasion, Baptist beginnings at the Orphan House could have resulted in a permanent work.

If a son's biographical account of his father is correct, Abraham Marshall, writing of his father Daniel, brings Daniel Marshall directly into Georgia for his ministry in this state from Beaver Creek church, in South Carolina.[82] Carswell dates Botsford's move into Georgia in 1771.[83] Relying upon Mercer's chronology and quoting evidently from Mercer, Benedict says that Marshall settled in Georgia "A little previous to Mr. Botsford's coming over to Tuckaseeking . . ." [84]

Again, the Whitefield influence is evident. Abraham says of his father Daniel: "He heard George Whitefield preach and caught his seraphic fire. . ."[85] Sometime around 1771 Daniel Marshall moved to Horse Creek, fifteen miles north of Augusta.[86] It was at Horse Creek that he was arrested for preaching the gospel.[87]

[81]Benedict, p. 723.

[82]Henry Holcombe, *The Analytical Repository*, Vol. I, No. 1, May and June, 1802, p. 25. Life of Daniel Marshall by his son Abraham Marshall.

[83]Encylopedia of Southern Baptists, Vol. I, p. 532.

[84]Benedict, p. 724.
[Carswell in his monograph on Georgia Baptists says that Daniel Marshall moved on January 1, 1771, Encyclopedia of Southern Baptists, p. 532.] Mosteller, A History of the Kickee Baptist Church, p. 113, uses the 1771 date for the beginning of Marshall's ministry in Georgia.
[Marshall, the Separate Baptist, and Botsford the Regular Baptist were good friends. Mosteller, p. 114.]

[85]Holcombe, p. 23.
[86]*Ibid.*, p. 25.
[87]See Campbell, p.p. 16-17 for fuller details.

Baptist Building, Georgia Baptist Convention Offices

This building, located at the corner of Peachtree and Baker Streets in Atlanta was purchased by the convention in 1943. It is the first and only building up to 1972 which the Executive Committee has owned for office use.

Old Kiokee Baptist Church, First Baptist Church in Georgia.

Botsford Baptist Church, Second Baptist Church in Georgia.

Old Kiokee Baptist Church, restored by the Georgia Baptist Convention, members of the congregation, and friends. The church is located near Appling, Columbia County.

Powelton Baptist Church, Hancock County, where the historic Powelton Conferences were held in 1801, 1802, and 1803, and where the Georgia Baptist Convention was organized in June, 1822.

THE PENFIELD CHAPEL
MERCER UNIVERSITY
ERECTED 1846
RESTORED 1949

THIS HISTORIC BUILDING - ONE OF THE
FINEST PATTERNS OF CLASSIC REVIVAL
ARCHITECTURE IN THE SOUTH - CHERISHED
BY GEORGIA BAPTISTS AS A SYMBOL OF THE
FAITH AND VISION OF THE FOUNDING FATHERS
WAS RESTORED AND REDEDICATED BY THE
GEORGIA BAPTIST CONVENTION AND THE
PENFIELD BAPTIST CHURCH ON NOVEMBER
17, 1949 ON WHICH OCCASION THE CLOSING
PERIOD OF THE 128TH ANNUAL SESSION OF
THE CONVENTION WAS HELD IN THIS BUILDING

FIRST SAMUEL 7:12

CONVENTION COMMITTEE	PENFIELD COMMITTEE
LOUIE D. NEWTON	E. A. KILGORE
SPRIGHT DOWELL	J. E. CAMPBELL
JAMES W. MERRITT	W. S. COLCLOUGH
CAREY T. VINZANT	S. S. ENGLISH
W. F. DUNWODY, ATECT.	T. H. McGIBONY

THIS PLAQUE PRESENTED BY
DRUID HILLS BAPTIST CHURCH

"OLD MERCER"

Actuated by a legacy from Josiah Penfield,
Mercer University was founded here in 1833
as Mercer Institute. After considering
several locations, the Trustees moved the
institution to Macon in 1871 and, in 1880,
transferred all holdings in Penfield to the
Georgia Baptist Association, except the
venerable Penfield Cemetery where Jesse
Mercer, Billington M. Sanders, Mrs. Sanders,
and other notable Mercerians are buried.
The chapel was given to the Penfield Baptist
Church, founded in 1839 with Rev. Adiel
Sherwood as pastor. The academy building
became the Penfield public school building.

The historic chapel for the Mercer University at Penfield, restored and now used as the Penfield Baptist Church, (upper left). (Above), Marker indicating restoration of the chapel in 1949.

(Left), State of Georgia Historical Marker indicating the Penfield site for Mercer University.

Entrance to Penfield cemetery, final resting place for many Georgia Baptist leaders. The cemetery was restored and rededicated in 1948.

(Photographs By Doyle Middlebrooks)

Jesse Mercer
1769-1841

First Moderator of the Georgia Baptist Convention, and a prime leader in the establishment of the Convention in 1822, as well as the establishment of Mercer University in 1833.

The American statesman Benjamin Franklin, in his auto-biography, noting the tremendous impact of Whitefield said:

> The multitudes of all sects and denominations that attended his sermons, were enormous, and it was a matter of speculation to me, who was one of the number, to observe the extraordinary influence of his oratory upon his hearers, and how much they admired and respected him by assuring them they were naturally half beasts and half devils. From being thoughtless or indifferent about religion, it seemed as if all the world were growing religious, so that one could not walk through the town in an evening without hearing psalms sung in different families of every street.[88]

Actually, Franklin counseled Whitefield to build his orphan house in Philadelphia, rather than solicit contributions there and elsewhere and bear the expense of transporting materials to Georgia.[89] Upon Whitefield's expression of his determination to proceed with the project at Savannah, Franklin said: . . . "I therefore refused to contribute . . .".[90] However, Franklin declared later that . . .:

> I happened soon after to attend one of his sermons, in the course of which I perceived he intended to finish with a collection, and I silently resolved that he should get nothing from me. I had in my pocket a handful of copper money, three or four silver dollars, and five pistoles in gold. As he proceeded I began to soften and concluded to give the copper. Another stroke of his oratory made me ashamed of that and determined me to give the silver; and he finished so admirably that I emptied my pockets wholly into the collector's dish, gold and all.[91]

SUMMARY

Baptists, therefore, moved into the state in three stages. The first stage was the immigration of some Baptists, who, though identifiable, left no permanent work. The second

[88]Autobiography of Benjamin Franklin [New York: the Macmillan Company, 1911] p. 103.

[89]*Ibid.*, p. 104.

[90]*Loc. cit.*

[91]*Ibid.*, p. 105.

was a stage of Baptist migration into the state from North and South Carolina, and the third group, Separate Baptists from South Carolina, who began settling around Augusta.

Out of this last wave of Baptists came the seeds of the establishment of a permanent work. However, efforts have been made to delineate the inter-relation between the several groups which was evident. Thus was laid the foundation for the beginnings of a work which grew from the 1760's until the present.

CHAPTER 2

The Stage Is Set For Baptist Growth

During the last thirty years of the eighteenth century, the climate in Georgia, as well as in all of the colonies, was one of change and political ferment. Growing dissatisfaction with the absentee lordship of the British Crown, together with increasing disenchantment with Crown representation in the Colonies, left Georgians unhappy and unsettled.

While the preaching of Baptist ministers was being heard in several areas of the state, particularly within a 50-mile radius of Augusta, rumblings of political discontent were heard even louder. During this period, as of 1790, there were in Georgia forty-two Baptist churches, with thirty-three ministers, thirty-nine licentiates, and 3,211 members.[1]

Following his settlement in Georgia in 1771, Daniel Marshall was instrumental in founding the Kioka [Kiokee] church, oldest extant church in the state, in the year 1771 [or 1772].[2] This was four [or five] years before the Declaration of Independence was signed, and a like period before the first major battle of the War of the Revolution occurred, the Battle of Bennington, in Vermont.[3]

The years between Marshall's move into the state, and

[1]John Asplund, *Annual Register of the Baptist Denomination in North America in 1791*, p. 52.

[2]James Donovan Mosteller, *A History of the Kiokee Baptist Church in Georgia*, [Ann Arbor, Michigan, Edwards Brothers, Inc., 1952], p. 71.

[3]*World Book*, Vol. 15, [Chicago: Field Enterprises Educational Corporation, 1962], p. 265.

the record of Asplund in 1790, were years filled with anxiety, poverty in many cases, hardship, and the inevitable decline in religion caused by internal political dissension. It has been estimated by various sources that about 75 per cent of the residents of the state were patriots, loyal to the cause of independence. Yet, they were living in a Royal Province.

While the original charter to the Trustees for the Colony of Georgia guaranteed religious liberty to all except papists [see Chapter 1, p. 12], the change in status to that of Royal Province in 1754 changed the religious picture also. The third session of the Second General Assembly of Georgia met in Savannah in January, 1758, and among other acts approved was one which was called:

> An act for constituting the several Divisions and Districts of the Province into Parishes, and for the establishing Religious Worship therein according to the Rites and Ceremonies of the Church of England; and also for empowering the Church Wardens and Vestrymen of the respective Parishes to assess Rates for the repair of churches, the relief of the poor, and other Parochial service.[4]

Thus during the fourteen years which elapsed between the enactment of this bill and the establishment of the church at Kioka, Baptists and other churches not of the establishment, came under the increasingly watchful eye of the established church. Consequently a local, weakening Royal government, in light of the impending Revolution, probably precluded more severe punishment of non-conformists than would otherwise have transpired.

The Indians continued to be a constant menace and, many, both Cherokees and Creek, were in friendly alliance with the Royalists.[5] In 1774,

> . . . the population of Georgia was 17,000 whites, 15,000 blacks, with only 2,828 militia scattered from Augusta to St. Mary's.

[4]Samuel Boykin, *History of Georgia Baptists with Biographical Compendium* [Atlanta: James P. Harrison And Co., 1881], p. 6.

[5]Kenneth Coleman, *The American Revolution in Georgia*, 1763-1789 [Athens: University of Georgia Press, 1958], p.p. 96, 238-241.

While at the same time,

> There were within the borders and along the frontiers of Georgia, 40,000 Creeks, Cherokees, Chickasaws, and Choctaws, of whom 10,000 were warriors, any number of whom could be brought against the colony.[6]

The advance, therefore, of Baptists, Presbyterians, Lutherans, and Wesleyan followers was not under the most ideal of circumstances; and it was against this background that Baptist organizational life began to emerge.

Daniel Marshall, the Separatist Baptist, visited in Saint Paul's parish [Augusta area] several times prior to settling at Horse Creek, fifteen miles north of that town. It was his custom to visit and preach in private homes, and

> . . . on the second or third of these, while in prayer, he was seized, in the presence of his audience, for preaching in the Parish of St. Paul, and made to give security for his appearance in Augusta, on the following Monday, to answer this charge. Accordingly, he stood a trial and, after his meekness and patience were sufficiently exercised, was ordered to come, as a preacher, no more into Georgia.[7]

Campbell's account, which is materially the same as other records of Marshall's arrest, indicates that upon giving security for appearance in court in Augusta on the following Monday, the preaching continued. Mrs. Marshall [Stearn's sister] remonstrated with those who arrested her husband to such a degree by quoting

> several texts of Scripture with so much force as to confound the opposers and convict several persons. . . . and after preaching, two persons were baptized.[8]

Marshall stood trial in Augusta, and was ordered to quit preaching in the province. Marshall's answer was: "whether it be right to obey God rather than men, judge ye." [9] Then

---

[6]Bokyin, p. 6.

[7]Henry Holcombe, *The Analytical Repository*, Vol. 1, No. 1, May and June 1802.

[8]Jesse H. Campbell, *Georgia Baptists: Historical and Biographical* [Richmond H. K. Ellyson, 1847.] p. 17.

[9]Campbell, *Loc. cit.*

followed the move to Kioka [Kiokee] and the organization in the spring of 1772 [1771] of the church, the mother church of Georgia Baptists.

The Kiokee church was later to send out as ministers Sanders Walker, Samuel Newton, Loveless Savidge, Alexander Scott and Abraham Marshall.[10]

BOTSFORD'S ITINERANT MINISTRY

During this same period, Edmond Botsford, a Regular Baptist, still not ordained, preached throughout East Central Georgia, into Burke county, and identified himself as the "flying preacher." [11] He was ordained by the church in Charleston March 14, 1773, "and by the middle of the following November he had baptized forty-five." [12] Of his travels, Botsford said:

> In the month of August, 1773, . . . I rode six hundred and fifty miles, preached forty-two sermons, baptized twenty-one persons, and administered The Lord's supper twice.[13]

Botsford was laying the groundwork for the development of churches soon to be organized. Botsford was a patriot in his sentiments, and incurred the wrath of the Royalists. He settled finally [so he thought] on Briar Creek, Burke county, where he purchased land, built a house, and with money from the people whom he served, and an inheritance from his brother in England, he lived apparently comfortably. He continued a ministry of itinerant preaching for some six years, until he was forced to flee the state because of his anti-royalist sentiments. According to Campbell, for the remainder of The Revolution.

> he had no very permanent abode—was a part of the time chaplain in the American army—the balance of it, in South and North Carolina, and in Virginia. He

[10]*Ibid.*, p. 18.
[11]*Ibid.*, p. 13.
[12]Campbell, *Loc. cit.*
[13]Campbell, *Loc. cit.*

settled finally in Georgetown, S. C., as pastor of the church.[14]

To Edmond Botsford must go major credit as a principal leader in the establishment of Baptist work in Georgia. Although he was forced to flee Burke county in haste, taking only two horses and a cart with a bed, blanket and sheet, the impact of his ministry remained.[15]

While Botsford carried the Baptist witness throughout the Southeast central part of the state, Daniel Marshall was building the church on the Kiokee into a permanent work, out of which would come many ministers who would themselves later become leaders prominent in the Baptist cause in Georgia.

Samuel Cartledge [possibly a brother of the constable who arrested Marshall], Loveless Savidge, and Silas Mercer were licensed by the Kiokee church.

Botsford's ministries continued to be evident as a result of the church established under his leadership at New Savannah in 1773, about 30 miles south of Augusta.[16] It was called later Botsford's old meeting house; and was the second oldest church in Georgia.[17]

DEVELOPMENTS AT KIOKEE

Because of the historic significance of Kiokee church, portions of the formal incorporation act of 1789 are reproduced.

> An act for incorporating the Anabaptist church on the Kioka, in the county of Richmond
>
> Whereas, a religious society has, for many years past been established on the Kioka, in the county of Richmond, called and known by the name of the Anabaptist Church on the Kioka . . .
>
> Be it therefore enacted . . . that the said Abraham Marshall, William Willingham, Edmund Cartledge,

[14]*Ibid.*, p. 14.

[15]*Loc. cit.*

[16]David Benedict, *A General History of the Baptist Denomination in America, etc.* [New York: Lewis Colby and Company, 1848], p. 723.

[17]C. D. Mallary, *Memoirs of Elder Edmund Botsford*, [Charleston: W. Riley, 1832], p. 47.

> John Landers, James Simms, Joseph Ray and Lewis
> Gardiner, and their successors in office shall be, and
> they are hereby declared to be a body corporate, by
> the name and style of the Trustees of the Anabaptist
> Church of Kioka . . .
> And be it further enacted . . . that the Trustees of the
> said Anabaptist church shall hold their office for a term
> of three years; and on the third Saturday of November,
> in every third year after the passing of this act, the
> supporters of the gospel in said church shall convene at
> the meeting house of said church, and there between
> the hours of ten and four, elect from among the sup-
> porters of the gospel in said church, seven different
> persons as trustees . . .[18]

James D. Mosteller, in *A History of the Kiokee Baptist
Church in Georgia,* published in 1952, has made a significant
and largely unrecognized contribution to the history of this
church by an intensively-documented study which both
raises and answers from primary sources questions concerning both the date of organization and the houses of worship.

In his volume, Chapter Three, dealing with the physical
history of the church Mosteller raises first the question of
date. The date accepted traditionally for organization of
Kickee Baptist Church is 1772. The first pages of the earliest
church book are not known to be in existence, and the first
reference to a date is on the title page of the second volume
which begins August 17, 1820. The title page says: "this
church was constituted in the year of our Lord 1772."
Asplund used this 1772 date, as did the minutes of the
Georgia Association, Benedict, Mercer, Campbell, Kilpatrick
and others.[19]

Mosteller says there is a strong possibility that the church
was organized a year earlier. As arguments for an earlier
date, he includes a statement of Abraham Marshall in the
Analytical Repository for 1802, in which Abraham Marshall
writes concerning his father, Daniel Marshall. Abraham
Marshall said:

[18]Mosteller, p.p. 96, 97. [copied by Lon Fleming, Attorney, from **Digest
of the Laws of Georgia** [1800]], p.p. 409-10, No. 424.
    [19]*Ibid.,* p. 71.

> . . . on the first of January, 1771, [Daniel Marshall]
> came with his family and took up his final earthly
> residence at Kioka; the following Spring the church
> here was formed . . .[20]

Mosteller says that if Marshall came to Kiokee in January,
1771, this would mean that he formed a church in the spring
of 1771. He concedes two objections may be urged against
the conclusion; one being that Abraham Marshall was using
the old style chronology and the year should be added to
make it coincide with the new style of dating.

> However, it seems clear that the younger Marshall was
> acquainted with the new system and was using it. For
> example, Styles gives 1705 as the date of Abraham
> Marshall's birth, but Abraham, without any explana-
> tion, gives the date as 1706. Since there is little reason
> to accuse either historian of error in this case, it is
> reasonable to conclude that Abraham in 1802 was using
> new style and added a year to his father's birth. Thus it
> is improbable that he would not use the same procedure
> in the dating of his father's move to Georgia. January 1
> would then be the dividing point, not March 25, and
> the following spring would be 1771 and not 1772.[21]

Mosteller adds that it was the precedent of the Separate
Baptists, based upon actions of Shubel Starnes and Daniel
Marshall at Sandy Creek, to organize a church immediately
upon settling at a location.[22]

While he concedes that in view of tradition and some
difficulties concerning 1771, it is better to conclude that
1772 is the latest date, nevertheless he suggests the strong
possibility of 1771.[23] Based upon the documentation of
Mosteller, and others, this author agrees a strong possibility
exists that Kiokee church was organized in 1771.

SIX HOUSES OF WORSHIP

Again, Mosteller has made a significant contribution to
Georgia Baptist history and to the history of the Kiokee

[20]Mosteller, *Loc. cit.*

[21]*Ibid.*, p. 71.

[22]*Ibid.*, p. 72. [Reference from the Repository taken, from Benedict, second
edition, p. 353.]

[23]*Ibid.*, p. 73.

Baptist Church when he deals in the same chapter with the houses of worship, which the Kiokee Baptist Church used during its history. His summary statement dealing with houses of worship will be amplified. It says:

> This chapter has isolated six houses of worship, and each of them was the result of prayer and careful planning, and each played its part in the extension of the Kingdom. . .[24]

Georgia Baptists have believed historically that there have been three principal houses of worship for the Kiokee Baptist Church, and that the Kiokee Baptist Church was established at what is now the site of Appling, Georgia. In 1950 the History Committee of the Georgia Baptist Convention erected in Appling a marker which says:

> Kiokee Baptist Church the oldest Baptist Church in Georgia constituted in the spring of 1772 by Daniel Marshall and served by him as pastor until his death in 1784 was originally located a few yards southwest from this marker as described in courthouse records of Columbia County. Church was removed in 1888 to brick building three miles away which still stands. Present church located in Appling. This marker erected in 1950 by Georgia Baptist Convention.[25]

This marker indicates only three houses of worship, and the location as being in Appling.

In his extensive research into courthouse records in Columbia County and into plat surveys of land, together with other information, as indicated in his concluding statement, Mosteller isolated six different houses of worship. Three of these have hitherto not been acknowledged generally by Georgia Baptists. If Mosteller's thesis is accurate, and this author follows Mosteller's line of reasoning as well as his conclusions based upon the research done, then the marker located in Appling is in error both as to number of churches and as to location.[26]

---

[24]*Ibid.*, p. 96.

[25]*Ibid.*, p. 75. Photograph of Historical Marker.

[26][Detailed documentation at this point may be found at the conclusion of chapter 3 of Mosteller's volume.]

Mosteller says that Abraham Marshall wrote a letter to Dr. John Rippon of London and the letter is headed Kioka, Georgia May 1, 1793. Marshall's son, Jabez, in his preface to the biographical memoirs of the late Reverend Abraham **Marshall** published in 1824, gives his address also as Kiokee, Columbia County, Georgia.[27] Mosteller's conclusions are, in essence, that the original building erected of wood by Daniel Marshall in 1771 was not situated in Appling, which at that time was still vacant land. The conclusion is that Appling probably grew into prominence *after* the American Revolution and was influential enough to become a county seat around 1790.[28] Further, courthouse records do not prove that the first building was in Appling.

> The courthouse records of Columbia County do not prove that the first building was in Appling, but instead show negatively it was not located there. Hence, it could not have been located 'a few yards southwest of the marker' erected in 1950 because there is no record of a meeting house on the lot donated by William Appling before 1792. The church minutes and Sherwood both prove a building was not erected in the village until many years afterward.
> 3. Daniel Marshall evidently built the church further east, somewhere 'on little Kioka' as Morgan Edwards stated. Possibly it was located at a community called Kiokee, at any rate nearer the center of the area where the Marshalls and their colleagues settled.
> 4. Some years after the death of Abraham Marshall it was agreed that a change of location was expedient, but some desired to move farther west than others; hence, two lots were presented as attractions in 1792.[29]

Kiokee's second house of worship was built on the lot given by a John Marshall sometime perhaps during the latter part of 1792.

> It will come as a surprise to many that such a building as designated ever existed [the names of these churches are used by the writer for convenience] for again tradition has obscured the church known vernacularly at the

[27]Mosteller, p. 83.
[28]Mosteller, *Loc. cit.*
[29]*Ibid.*, p.p. 83-84.

close of the eighteenth century as 'Marshall's Meeting house.' [30]

Mosteller says:

> the Kiokee congregation erected a second frame building [the brick building was a third, not the second] on the lot given by John Marshall, three or four miles from Appling, but the move was from a different original site, not from Appling. Further the church was built long before 1808. Proof for these statements is available.[31]

Enough question has been raised by two sources to give some indication that there was for a time a village of Kioka [Kiokee] and that this village of Kiokee was located where reference is made to Marshall preaching, which was north of Augusta, whereas Appling was about twenty miles west of Augusta.

The implication is clear that Marshall not only had a station at Quakers settlement but also at Kiokee while still in South Carolina.[32] From the first building then, the Kiokee congregation moved some point west after the death of Daniel Marshall. This westward point was *toward* Appling not from Appling, Mosteller concludes, as indicated earlier, that the church was built long before 1808.[33]

Concerning the second building there is indication "it could not have been built before July, 1792 for that was the date of John Marshall's deed to the church for its site." [34] The top limit would be October, 1793 based upon associational minutes for the Georgia Association for that year which specified meeting at the new Kiokee meeting house.[35] This would be designated as Marshall's Meeting House and the second meeting house for the congregation.

By July 1806, at a business meeting, Abraham Marshall declared that the meeting house was on the decline and in

[30]*Ibid.,* p. 84.
[31]*Ibid.,* p. 62.
[32]Mosteller, *Loc. cit.*
[33]*Ibid.* p. 84.
[34]*Ibid.,* p. 85.
[35]*Ibid.,* p. 87.

August of the same year it was agreed to build a new meeting house of brick.[36] At a conference of the church on January, 1808 a deed was produced and in February,

> the church ordered that the deed given by Daniel Marshall to the 'trustees of the big Kiokee meeting house for three acres of land be recorded in the church book'.[37]
> In 1838, 7 and ¾ acres were added around this lot from the estate of Jabez Marshall, making a total of eleven acres.[38]

There was a shift during the next twenty years westward toward Appling and

> . . . building a meeting house in Appling was seriously considered. While the church still had the lot donated in 1792, it had expended itself in the erection of the brick church, which could not be abandoned.[39]

There is a record then of further action:

> The trustees of the Baptist Church at the Kiokee and also trustees of the baptist meating house theat is to be built on the baptist lot at the villedg of Apling has subscribed $200 of the money theat theay received for lots theat wear belonging to the sead baptist church at the Kiokee.[40]

The conclusion is therefore there was a chapel of the Kiokee Church built at Appling around 1828. Sherwood dates completion of construction at 1828.[41] It was evidently a small chapel to be used only with the larger Kiokee Church,[42] was later used by Presbyterians but not sold to them by Kiokee Church. "After the civil war it was used by the Negro members of Kiokee for separate services." [43]

The church and lot site of the Appling Chapel, according to a diagram indicating lots being sold, places this property,

[36]Mosteller, *Loc. cit.*
[37]*Ibid.*, p. 89.
[38]Mosteller, *Loc. cit.*
[39]Mosteller, *Loc. cit.*
[40]*Ibid.*, p.p. 89, 90.
[41]*Ibid.*, p. 90.
[42]Mosteller, *Loc. cit.*
[43]*Ibid.*, p. 92.

the Appling Chapel, as being the fourth church for Kiokee. Apparently in 1875 a tornado demolished the Appling Chapel and

> While the minutes are strangely silent about the facts of this calamity, it is Robinson's belief that it was destroyed by this tornado in 1875. The church records assume the loss as common knowledge, for by that time the congregation was once again wrestling with that recurrent problem of shifting population. In September, 1881, 'A motion was made and carried that a committee of three look into the propriety of moving the organized body of Kiokee church.' In January, 1882, the church granted Mrs. Ella Bugg, 'the privilege of building on Kiokee Church lot at Appling, Ga.'

These items indicate that the lot was vacant at that time, and also that the congregation could not move back to Appling without building another church. Nothing was done, either about building or moving, for 12 years later, in 1894,

> The trustees were requested to meet at Appling on the Fourth Monday in the present month and suggest a plan as to the disposition of our house of worship to our next conference with a view to *rebuilding* at Appling.[44]

In essence, the fifth building of the Kiokee church was constructed in 1907,[45] and the sixth church, a brick structure, was constructed in 1937.[46]

Mosteller, therefore, places the first Kiokee church north of Augusta at some distance along a branch of the Kioka creek, indicating that it could not have been built where tradition has described the first location. Part of the problem is that there were three Kiokee creeks. One flowing east into the Savannah River, another, further north, called Kiokee creek, flowing northeast through Appling where it is joined by Greenbrier creek, and from that point to the Savannah it was called Great Kiokee. Thus; a little Kiokee creek, a Kiokee creek, and a Great Kiokee creek[47] are identifiable.

[44]Mosteller, *Loc. cit.*
[45]*Ibid.*, p. 93.
[46]*Ibid.*, p.p. 95, 96.
[47]*Ibid.*, p.p. 81, 82.

In summary, the first church was on Kiokee creek in 1771 or 1772; the second, known as Marshall's meeting house, which dates to 1792 approximately, certainly no later than 1793; the third one called new Kiokee Meeting House still out of Kiokee, west of Kiokee; the fourth the Appling Chapel in 1828, the fifth the brick building, and the sixth, the final building in 1937.

ORGANIZATIONAL GROWTH SLOWED BY WAR

After the defeat of Savannah in the Revolutionary War December 29, 1778, most of the ministers in the state left. Sunbury surrendered in January, 1709, and it appears that Daniel Marshall alone of ordained Baptist ministers remained with his church. Benedict so implies, declaring that the

> . . . intrepid Marshall stood his ground and never deserted his post; . . . [and] Assisted by a few licentiates, who remained on the field with him, the good work went on; the spirit of pure religion was progressive, and even in those times that tried men's souls, very many were converted to God.[48]

After the formation of Kiokee and Botsford churches [Briar Creek], at a later date came the formation of the Red Creek [Aberleen] church, Little Briar Creek Church in 1777; Fishing Creek church, 1783; and Greenwood church [Upton's Creek], 1784. These were the Baptist churches in existence at the time of the organization of the first Baptist Association, the Georgia, in 1784.[49]

Unsettled conditions occasioned by the War of the Revolution, together with the fact, as noted earlier, that Marshall alone was left of the ordained ministers, accounts doubtless for the almost complete lack of organized growth during this period. Twelve years passed between organization of Little Briar Creek [1771] and the organization of the Fishing Creek

[48]Benedict, p. 725.

[Author's note—Benedict is used extensively because of his access to papers of Campbell, Mercer and Sherwood, which constitute in most instances primary sources, and were extracted from his 1812-13 edition.]

[49]*Ibid.* p.p. 724-725. [Quoting Mercer's history]; Campbell, p.p. 191-192.

church in 1783. The stage was set during this period for the first steps in organized Baptist life out of which came the organization of Georgia Baptist Convention.

Earlier historians of Georgia Baptists declared without exception that during the War of the Revolution, the Baptist cause suffered in the state; both in the area of growth, and in terms of personal danger and hardship to Baptists.[50]

In 1773, after Kioka church was established, Edmund Botsford married Miss Susanna Nun, who lived in Augusta, and had been baptized by Daniel Marshall [51] and from the time of his marriage, Botsford traveled extensively throughout Georgia in what we would today term an itinerant evangelistic ministry.[52] During his ministry, and the ministry of Marshall at Kioka and in surrounding areas, Georgians were trying to determine their political allegiance. On July 4, 1775,

> The Provincial congress met again . . . [In Savannah] and elected three delegates to the Continental Congress. During its session a British schooner arrived at Tybee with 13,000 pounds of powder on Board. This was captured by a vessel commissioned by the Provincial Congress of Georgia, and 5,000 pounds of the powder were sent to Washington, and enabled him to drive the British out of Boston.[53]

When the Assembly met in January, 1776, the House decided to become free from British control, "and orders were given to arrest Governor Wright and His council." [54] Thus, by early 1776, Georgia was in open rebellion. On December 29, 1778, Savannah was captured; Sunbury falling on January 6, 1779, and Augusta by late January, 1779.[55]

It was about this time then, that Baptist ministers who had been loyal to the Colonial interests began to flee north-

---

[50]Benedict, p.p. 724-725, [Quoting Mercer's history.]

[51]Charles D. Mallary, *Memoirs of Elder Edmund Botsford* [Charleston: W. Riley, 1832], p. 47.

[52]*Ibid.*, p. 48.

[53]Boykin, p. 22.

[54]Boykin, *Loc. cit.*

[55]Boykin, *Loc. cit.*

ward. Botsford's departure has been noted earlier. "Silas Mercer, father of Jesse Mercer, went to North Carolina, accompanied apparently by Abraham Marshall." [56]

Of the Baptists, Boykin said:

> Espousing the cause of liberty from high and holy motives, they had an eye not only to the temporal interests of the land, but to the rights of conscience, the prosperity of their churches and the general interests of the Redeemer's Kingdom. It was because they were such ardent friends of liberty that Botsford and Silas Mercer fled . . .[57]

Indicated earlier was the fact that Daniel Marshall, alone of ordained Baptist ministers, remained with his church ". . . because he was such a staunch patriot and faithful minister . . ."[58]

Abraham Marshall, writing of his father Daniel, said:

> No scenes, however, from the commencement to the termination of hostilities, were so gloomy and alarming as to deter my estimable father from discharging the duties of his station. . . As a friend to the American cause, he was once made a prisoner and put under strong guard. But, obtaining leave of the officers, he commenced and supported so heavy a charge of exhortation and prayer that, like Daniel of old, while his enemies stood amazed and confounded, he was safely and honorably delivered from this den of lions.[59]

This is perhaps a better picture of the character of Daniel Marshall than the estimable picture conveyed by Benedict, quoting Mercer, and even more interesting in the light of the fact that the son who praised his father for remaining at his post, fled the state for fear of his own life!

One of the last major battles of the War of the Revolution was fought in South Carolina, Oct. 7, 1780, the Battle of King's Mountain, with 90 American casualties and 1,100 British casualties.[60]

[56]*Ibid.,* p.p. 22, 23.

[57]*Ibid.,* p. 23.

[58]Boykin, *Loc. cit.* [Citing *The Analytical Repository* [1802] and quoted by the author of the *History of Georgia Baptists* verified by the sketch in the Repository.]

[59]Boykin, *Loc cit.*

[60]*World Book,* Vol. 15, p. 265.

Thus, during the period of the organization of the churches which were to become the nucleus of organized Baptist life in Georgia, Georgia Baptists were engaged in a war which left them poor financially, but rich morally.

Those who labored in and from the Kiokee [Kioka] church, including Sanders Walker, Silas Mercer, William Franklin and Joseph Buisson, laid the groundwork, and a free, but poor Georgia Baptist ministry began to expand.

With this expansion came the period of expansion of Baptists, seeds of which had been planted nearly fifty years earlier, watered regularly by preaching and intermingling of Baptist pioneers, and emerging into fruition with the organization of the Georgia Association in 1784.

CHAPTER 3

The Beginning of Organized Work

In 1784, the principal ministers in Georgia were Abraham Marshall, Silas Mercer, William Franklin, Loveless Savidge, Sanders Walker, Peter Smith, and perhaps Alexander Scott.[1] Also in that year, Daniel Marshall died at the age of seventy-eight, and there were the following churches; Kioka [Kiokee], Botsford's [Briar Creek], Fishing Creek, Upton's Creek [Greenwood], and Red Creek [Aberleen].

Almost without exception, histories of Baptist life in Georgia up to this time, name these churches, and then assert they were the churches in existence when the first association, the Georgia, was organized. Jesse Mercer places the organizational meeting at Kiokee Church.[2]

Mercer says:

> It is most probable it [organizating association] took place at the Kiokee Church. This was the mother church and it would seem reasonable to suppose that the union was formed there.

Mosteller asserts Kiokee was site of the organization also.[3]

Usually, one can find a statement as to the purpose of any organization when it begins. In the case of the formation of the Georgia Association, no material known to this writer gives any clear-cut reason or motivation for the or-

[1]Jesse Mercer, *A History of the Georgia Baptist Association*, Washington, Georgia, 1838, p. 20.

[2]James Donovan Mosteller, *A History of the Kiokee Baptist Church in Georgia* [Ann Arbor, Michigan, Edwards Brothers, Inc., 1952], p. 245.

[3]Mosteller, *Loc. cit.*, citing Historical Table of Georgia Association Minutes.

ganization of the churches into a constituent body until 1832. The preface to the constitution, appearing first in the minutes for that year, says: We

> . . . are convinced from a series of experience, of the necessity of a combination of churches; . . .

for the preserving of a federal union amongst all the churches of the same faith and order. It then set forth a statement of faith and order, since

> . . . we are convinced, that there are a number of Baptist churches who differ from us in faith and practice; . . .[4]

It is clear that organization came about as Baptists began to grow in the state following the end of the War of the Revolution. It is evident from material, documented amply, that mission interests were central in the thinking of those involved in the organization. However, to find a concrete reason for organization, one has to look beyond the organizational period to a copy of the constitution of the Association which appears in the minutes of that body *listing* the year *1832,* although adopted evidently much earlier.[5]

In 1831 the Association authorized a committee to collect facts for a history to be submitted to the Association in 1832.[6] In 1832, citing difficulties, the Association voted to turn the matter of a history over to the moderator, under patronage of the association.[7]

Concerning the organization date, Benedict indicates that if the constitution of the Association were in 1785, in addition to the five churches named earlier, Phillip's Mill and Wheatley's Mills would be counted in the organization group.[8]

Considering the fact that Jesse Mercer's father, Silas, was

---

[4]*Minutes, Georgia Baptist Association,* 1832, p. 8.

[5]*Loc. cit.*

[6]*Minutes, Georgia Baptist Association,* 1831, p. 7.

[7]*Minutes, Georgia Baptist Association,* 1832, p. 5.

[8]David Benedict, *A General History of the Baptist Denomination in America,* etc. [New York: Lewis Colby and Company, 1848], p. 726. [Benedict's 1848 edition, thirty years after his first two-volume edition, and quoting Mercer's history.]

an early member of the Kioka Church, and had knowledge of the Baptist life in Georgia up to the time of the organization of the Association, it appears likely that the Association was formed in 1784, and that the first minutes of the body probably were under date of 1785, reporting on the 1784 meeting.

Again, Mercer in his history says:

> The Rev. Mr. Mercer [Silas] and the Rev. Mr. Smith, were received by the Charleston Association in November of that same year [1784] as messengers from the Georgia, then but recently formed.[9]

This is the strongest argument for the 1784 date.

Concerning the purpose for establishment of the Association, it must be recalled that Daniel Marshall was himself a missionary among the Mohawk Indians for three years and that Botsford identified himself as the "flying preacher" because of his mission activity.[10]

EMERGING LEADERS

Two dominant personalities were emerging into positions of leadership in the embryo formation of the organized life among Baptists; Silas Mercer and Abraham Marshall.

[9]Jesse Mercer, *A History of the Georgia Baptist Association* [Washington, Ga.: 1838], p. 20.

[Note: Addendum on date, Benedict, footnote 8, p. 726. "There is some difference of opinion between Mercer and Sherwood as to this date, which I find is thus given in my old work. I do not remember how this and some other facts were ascertained, but am confident that they were communicated by Mr. Abraham Marshall, as I spent some time with him at his own house at Kiokee, in 1810, where his venerable father died. He had then been in the ministry about 40 years.

Mr. Asplund visited Mr. Marshall twenty years before, to whom he gave the same account as to the date of this body, as appears by his Register for 1790.

Mr. Sherwood's arguments are plausible, and as there were no records to refer to, it would not be strange if Mr. M. was mistaken in a year. Again, as they met at first twice a year, and as old bodies formed as this was generally had preparatory meetings, and grew into an association in an informal manner—so it might have been in this case. . ."]

[10]Mercer, *Loc. cit.*

Abraham Marshall, son of Daniel, was born April 23, 1748, in Windsor, Connecticut. Cathcart and others indicate that he was probably the oldest son of Daniel by his second wife, Martha Stearns.[11] He united with the church at Horse Creek, South Carolina, about 1770, and was baptized in the Savannah River; and when he moved with his parents in 1771 to Big Kiokee Creek, he was licensed to preach, and was ordained May 20, 1775.[12] Daniel Marshall died November 2, 1784, and Abraham was called as pastor of Kiokee. Abraham Marshall left Georgia in May, 1786, to visit his native Connecticut to settle his father's estate, and returned to Kiokee in November, 1786. He preached almost every day while traveling on horseback to New England, and

> his sermons drew together vast crowds, some comparing him to Whitefield in the fervor and power of his eloquence.[13]

A revival, sparked by Marshall's preaching, was evident by the spring of 1787, and during that year

> more than 100 were baptized at Kiokee church alone, and the church membership soon increased to more than 300.[14]

Within a three-year period, churches in the Georgia Association increased from seven to thirty-one, and in seven years, to fifty-six, while during the same period the ministers had increased from six to thirty-six. Abraham Marshall's itinerant ministry and service as pastor at Kiokee upon his return to Georgia reaped large spiritual rewards.

In his *Register of the Baptist Denomination in North America* to the first of November, 1790, John Asplund says that the Association had two meetings yearly, the first on Saturday before the third Sunday in May, and the second on the Saturday before the third Sunday in October, and

---

[11]Cathcart, William, *The Baptist Encyclopedia*, [Philadelphia: Louis H. Everts, 1881], p. 749.
[12]Cathcart, *Loc. cit.*
[13]Cathcart, *Loc. cit.*
[14]Cathcart, *Loc. cit.*

met for three days. In his 1790 Register, Asplund says
that the Association had not at that time adopted a confession of faith but held Calvinistic sentiments, and that they
corresponded with the Charleston and Sandy Creek Associations by letter and sometimes by sending delegates.[15]

In his Register for 1791, Asplund said that the Association
had 47 churches, 32 ordained ministers, 45 licensed ministers, and 3,557 members [1791]. On pages 44 and 45 of his
Register, he listed 34 churches. Baptists were in Burke,
Chatham, Effingham, Franklin, Green, Richmond, Washington, and Wilkes counties; and he indicated that all were
General Baptists.[16]

Much of this growth is attributed to Abraham Marshall's
missionary efforts. The Kiokee pastor married a Virginian,
Miss Ann Waller, in 1792, had four sons, was pastor at
Kiokee for 35 years, and died August 15, 1819.[17]

Silas Mercer fled Georgia in 1777.[18] In the Memoirs of
Elder Jesse Mercer, by C. D. Mallary, printed in 1844, there
is included a sketch of the life of Silas Mercer, written,
according to internal evidence, by a half-brother of Silas.[19]
The memoir, perhaps as accurate as any, indicates that Silas
Mercer was born near Currituck Bay, North Carolina, in
February, 1745, and was for a time active in the Church
of England.

He was immersed about 1775 and became a member of
the Kiokee church following some apparent struggle in his
own mind with the matter of believer's baptism.[20] Ten
years later he is listed as one of the messengers from the
Georgia Association to the Charleston Association, and he

[15]*John Asplund, The Annual Register of the Baptist Denomination in
North America, 1791*, p. 52.

[16]*Ibid.*, p.p. 44-45.

[17]Cathcart, p. 749.

[18]Samuel Boykin, *History of Georgia Baptists with Biographical Compendium* [Atlanta: James P. Harrison and Co., 1881], History, p. 23

[19]C. D. Mallary, *Memoirs of Jesse Mercer,* [Philadelphia: American Baptist
Publication Society, 1844], p. 17

[20]*Ibid.*, p.p. 12-14.

served apparently as both a licensed and ordained minister during the ten-year period.[21]

Of his baptism by Alexander Scott, it is said:

> He rose from the water as it were, a minister of the gospel; for before he left the stream where he was immersed, he ascended a log and exhorted the surrounding multitude. Having been formally licensed by the church, he at once entered upon a course of ministerial labor, which was characterized by much zeal, ability, and usefulness.[22]

He returned to Georgia apparently in 1782 or 1783, and soon established a school[23] which his son Jesse attended as a young married minister.[24] Silas Mercer died in August, 1796.[25] He was a principal organizer of the Phillip's Mill Church in 1785.[26]

This background is given because of the interest Silas Mercer took not only in mission endeavor, but in education. He paid apparently for an instructor for his school, and preached more than 2,000 times during his six-year stay in North Carolina.[27]

Therefore, interwoven into the earliest history of Georgia Baptists is the thread of that which we today identify as state, home and foreign missions. Because to the Baptists of the late 18th century, a ministry among Indians was foreign missions, and so indicated; preaching efforts of Georgia ministers carried them up and down the Eastern Seaboard and into and out of North and South Carolina, and throughout the state of Georgia.

[21]Campbell, Jesse H., *Georgia Baptist Historical and Biographical*, [Richmond: H. K. Ellyson, 1847], p. 211.

[22]Mallary, p. 14.

[23]Mallary, *Loc. cit.*

[24]*Ibid.*, p. 29.

[25]*Ibid.*, p. 38.

[26]R. L. Duke, *History of Phillip's Mill Baptist Church*, from Church records.

[27]Mallary, p. 14.

THE POWELTON MEETINGS

A significant watershed in the life of Georgia Baptists was a series of conferences held at the Powelton church in 1801, 1802, and 1803. From the formation of the Georgia Association in 1784 to the first of three Powelton conferences, two additional associations were formed, the Hephzibah and the Sarepta. The Georgia continued to grow in numbers, churches, and in the number of ministers.

The Georgia Association in 1792 had fifty churches.[28]

Meeting at Powell's Creek [Powelton] in 1794, messengers agreed to divide the Georgia, with churches in the Southern portion of the Association forming a separate group, and on the fourth Saturday in September, 1794, delegates from eighteen churches met at Buckhead Davis' Church and formed the Hephzibah Association. In October, 1798, eight additional churches in the northern boundaries of the Georgia were dismissed to become the Sarepta Association. The churches held an initial meeting at Shoal Creek Church in May, 1799 and in October organized formally.[29]

From the organization of the Georgia Association in 1784 until at least 1790, the Association met twice each year. Beginning apparently in 1791 or 1792, they met annually.[30] Sometime around 1788, Abraham Marshall had ordained Andrew Marshall, a Negro, as pastor of the First Colored church in Savannah. Records are unclear concerning the early affiliation of this Negro church in Savannah with the Georgia or Hephzibah associations. However, a listing of churches in the Georgia Association Minutes for 1803 lists an African Baptist Church in Augusta as being a member of the Georgia Association, with 497 members, and 69 baptisms for the year. It is a matter of record, documented amply, that Negro slaves were listed as members of Baptist churches in the state.[31]

[28]Benedict, p. 727 (from manuscripts given Benedict by Abraham Marshall in 1810.)

[29]Boykin, p.p. 65-66.

[30]Benedict, p. 727, footnote and explanation.

[31]*Minutes, Georgia Baptist Association*, 1803, p. 5.

The Hephzibah Association was

> organized in 1794, with eighteen churches, which were
> dismissed from the Georgia community, and was the
> first colony which went out from that nursery of
> churches and ministers.[32]

The Hephzibah Association reported in 1803, 22 churches,
and 1,132 members—about the time of Powelton conferences
held within the boundaries of that association.[33] The Sarepta
held its first session at Van's Creek church in Elbert county
apparently late in 1799, and adopted the constitution and
decorum of the Georgia Association.[34]

Two additional associations were in existence when the
Georgia Baptist Convention was organized. They were the
Ocmulgee, constituted in 1810[35] with 20 of 52 churches then
reported by the Georgia Association, and the Savannah
River, constituted April 5, 1802, with three churches, includ-
ing the colored church then served by Andrew Bryan [t].[36]

ORGANIZED GROWTH

In the 17-year period between the organization of the
mother association of Georgia Baptists and the subsequent
organization of two additional bodies, Georgia Baptists had
begun a period of organized growth which was to lead directly into channels of cooperative, organized endeavor.

Powell's Creek Church was constituted July 1, 1786, with
26 members by a presbytery including Silas Mercer, John
Thomas, and John Harvey. Jesse Mercer became pastor at
Powelton [Powell's Creek] February 4, 1797.[37]

Mission interests were strong in the area of the Georgia
association prior to formal associational organization. As the
Hephzibah and the Sarepta associations were formed out of
the Georgia, Baptist work continued to grow, and with this

[32]Benedict, p. 731.
[33]Boykin, p. 66, minutes as listed therein.
[34]Boykin, *Loc. cit.*; Also, Benedict, p. 731.
[35]Benedict, p. 732.
[36]Boykin, p. 66.
[37]Mallary, p. 48.

growth came a continued mission emphasis, bolstered also by an emphasis upon education which resulted in the little school established by Silas Mercer.[38]

When the Georgia Association met in 1800 at Sardis Church, twelve miles northwest of Washington, two resolutions "evidently the composition of Jesse Mercer" were adopted which had as their purpose the unifying of the extant associations in their mission and educational endeavor.[39] The resolutions read:

> That, as a spirit of itineracy has inflamed the minds of several ministers, who are desirous to enter into some resolutions suitable to carry into effect a design of travelling and preaching the gospel, a meeting be, and is hereby, appointed at Powel's Creek, on Friday before the First Sunday in May next, for that purpose. That same day should be observed as a day of fasting and solemn prayer to Almighty God for prosperity in the design, and for a dispensation of every new covenant mercy in Christ Jesus.[40]

Two years earlier, in 1798, subscriptions had been taken to raise funds for a new meeting house at Powelton.[41]

William Rabun, later to become governor of Georgia, was a member of Powel's Creek. Boykin, referring to Mallary's *Memoirs of Jesse Mercer* and to original Sherwood manuscripts, indicated that Rabun helped to originate the idea of Powel's Creek conferences.[42]

However, Rabun's membership of the church would indicate that he probably did have an interest in, and was a party to, the formation of the conferences. He was clerk and chorister at Powelton in 1819.[43]

[38]Boykin, p. 66.

[39]*Ibid.*, p. 40, following records in *Analytical Repository*, and *Georgia Association Minutes.*

[40]*Ibid.*, p. 40.

[41]Paul E. Jernigan, *History of the Powelton Baptist Church*, Item 76, Georgia collection, Dargan-Carver library, Historical Commission, SBC.

[42]Boykin, p. 40.

[43]Mallary, p. 50. Also Julia L. Sherwood, *Memoirs of Adiel Sherwood, D. D.* [Philadelphia: Grant and Faires, 1884], p.p. 124, 125.

FIRST CONFERENCE, MAY, 1801

Therefore, in what evidently was a new meeting house, with Jesse Mercer as pastor, the first conference was held in May, 1801, the first direct organizational step in formation of organized Baptist life. There must have been a spirit of revival evident even at the time of the 1801 Powelton conference. Campbell says that in 1802 about 700 were baptized in the Georgia Association.[44]

While there is no evidence that Henry Holcombe attended the first conference at Powelton, he did attend, and in his *Analytical Repository,* recorded the proceedings of the second and third conferences, and provided by his record of the second conference, a brief picture of the first meeting.

The significance of the influence of Henry Holcombe in the organizational life of Georgia Baptists has perhaps not received proper attention. Holcombe was born in Prince Edward county, Virginia, September 22, 1762, and moved to South Carolina as a child. His formal education ended at the age of 11, and one of the greater minds and better writers in early Georgia Baptist life was largely self-educated.

The following biographical information concerning Holcombe is germain at this point because the thinking and leadership of this man was of great importance in the shaping of the second and third conferences at Powelton. His influence resulted not only in the beginnings of one of the earliest educational institutions by Georgia Baptists, but his theological and organizational concepts as expressed to the Powelton conferences helped in no small way to shape the final course of these conferences.[45]

Holcombe served as an officer in the fight against the British, and decided sometime around 1784 that his infant baptism as a Presbyterian was not sufficient.

> To pass softly over this tender ground, the result of my serious and reiterated inquiries into the materials, ordinances and government of the apostolic churches

[44]Campbell, p. 193.
[45]*Ibid.,* p. 29.

was the full conviction, that to follow the dictates of my conscience, I must be a Baptist; and not conferring with flesh and blood, I rode near twenty miles to propose myself as a candidate for admission into a Baptist church.[46]

Holcombe was licensed to preach upon his baptism, was invited to become pastor at Pike Creek, South Carolina, and was ordained September 11, 1785, the same day baptizing three men whom he had led to Christ.[47] Married at 24, he subsequently baptized his wife, brother-in-law, and mother-in-law; later baptizing his father also. He was a representative

in the convention of South Carolina which approved the Constitution of the United States . . .[48]

Holcombe preached in and around Euhaw and Beaufort, in South Carolina and moved to Savannah in 1799.

Four years earlier, Savannah Baptists, assisted by subscriptions from other Christians in the city [1795], had begun a meeting house. With no minister, they rented their meeting house in 1796 to the Presbyterians. In a rather unusual situation, Holcombe, when he arrived in Savannah, came at a time when the Presbyterians still occupied the Baptist meeting house, and there was no Baptist church as such.

The pew-holders of this building called Holcombe as their pastor and he served, Baptist pastor of a Presbyterian congregation, for nearly a year.[49]

Early in 1800, Holcombe and 11 others formed a Baptist church, and in September of 1800, he baptized by immersion

the first white person who had ever received that holy rite in Savannah,

and the Savannah Baptist Church was constituted November 26, 1800.[50]

---

[46]*Ibid.*, p. 31, quoting from the *Baptist Chronicle.*
[47]Campbell, *Loc. cit.*
[48]*Ibid.*, p. 32.
[49]*Ibid.*, p. 33.
[50]Campbell, *Loc. cit.*

A Negro Baptist Church had been organized in Savannah sometime around 1788 when Abraham Marshall baptized Andrew Bryan, who became pastor of the group.[51] This church was begun in loose organizational ties about the beginning of the Revolutionary War by George Leile [George Sharp] who went to Jamica

when the country was evacuated by the British . . .[52]

A second Negro Baptist Church had been formed in Savannah in 1803.[53] Bryan was respected highly in Savannah; and, when Baptist cooperative work began in Savannah, white and Negro churches worked together in early missionary endeavors.

Both Holcombe's ministry in Savannah and the strength of the Negro Baptist Church there were to have their influence upon the conferences of 1801, 1802, and 1803.

Again, when Abraham Marshall visited Savannah in 1788 and ordained Bryan,

he was accompanied on this trip by Jesse Peter, a Negro Baptist minister from Augusta.[54]

There is ample justification for the statement that when early Georgia Baptists began to think collectively about mission work, white and black were thinking in terms, primarily, of a mission witness to the Indians at this point in history, prior to the beginning of the mission efforts evident by 1813, and led in by Luther Rice.

BACK TO POWELTON

Details of the first Powelton conference are meager. Holcombe's account in the *Analytical Repository* of the proceedings of the second conference, by allusion, indicate some of the 1801 participants and their thinking. In the *Repository* for July-August, 1802, Holcombe wrote:

[51]Benedict, p. 740.
[52]Benedict, *Loc. cit.*
[53]*Ibid.,* p. 741.
[54]*Ibid.,* p. 740.

Taking into consideration the low, and languishing state of religion among the churches, generally, for whom they were concerned, a number of ministers and other leading characters, in Georgia, by mutual agreement, met to hold a religious conference, on the first Lord's day in May, 1801, at Powelton. Several days were profitably spent, it is hoped, in humble endeavors to strengthen the things that remained, and to form liberal and judicious designs of usefulness. The principal of these respected itinerant preaching through, and to the utmost boundaries of the state, and the formation of a Missionary Society, to support, if no more, a couple of pious, and suitably-gifted ministers of the gospel, in confining their labors to our dark and almost barbarous frontier, where, from a variety of obvious circumstances, there can be no standing ministry. To mature and contribute as much as possible to the execution of these plans, whose objects were to revive, and extend the influence of true religion, and, of course, to promote morality, good government, and every social blessing, another conference was appointed at the same place, the Thursday before the first Sunday in May, 1802.[55]

Boykin indicates that Jesse Mercer, John Robertson, Edmund Talbot, Adam Jones, John Harvey, Joseph Baker and Francis Ross were among those present for the first conference, and suggests that Abraham Marshall and Holcombe were present also.[56] Marshall probably was; Holcombe evidently not. For the second conference, the *Repository* carried apparent complete minutes, including the names of all present. We are indebted to the *Repository* for the only apparent extant primary records of the second and third conferences.

Present at Powelton on April 29, 1802, were Joseph Baker, Joel Willis, George Granberry, John Bott, Jesse Mercer, Francis Ross, John Robertson, John Harvey, Adam Jones, Benjamin Thompson, Miller Bledsoe, William Lord, William Maddox and Benjamin Maddox, all from different Baptist Associations.[57] Holcombe obviously was present also.

[55]Henry Holcombe, *The Analytical Repository*, [Vol. 1, No. 2, 1802], p.p. 55, 56.
[56]Boykin, p. 41.
[57]Holcombe, p. 56.

Following a sermon by Joseph Baker, preaching from Isaiah 35:8, a report of the meeting of the previous year was presented; apparently by several who had attended, as well as reports of preaching tours since the first conference. When the conference got down to business on Saturday morning, Jesse Mercer proposed a plan of union of Christians from different denominations; and, according to Holcombe, the proposal elicited general interest and approval. Ministers of other denominations were invited to sit in upon the second conference.[58]

As a result of this second conference, a Committee of three, Jesse Mercer, Joseph Baker and Henry Holcombe, was appointed to bring a report concerning prospects for a plan

> for promoting union and communion among all real Christians to be respectively submitted to the consideration of the Georgia Baptists, that should it be approved they may concur in a plan for action.[59]

The conduct of the second conference is of particular significance because it was evident there were sentiments in favor of a plan of inter-denominational cooperation at this point. Holcombe had himself served for a time as pastor of a Presbyterian congregation. Baker's sentiments were not as evident.

REPORT SETS THE DIRECTION

When the Committee of Three made its report, the tide of future Georgia Baptist organizational growth was turned toward a more strict denominational structure. The Committee reported that:

> . . . the number, and present situation of the Baptists of this state require a stricter and more intimate union among themselves, in order the most effectually to concentrate their powers for any particular purpose; that they conceive this more eligible state of the churches might be effected by a choice of delegates to represent

[58]*Ibid.,* p.p. 57-58, July-August, 1802.
[59]Holcombe, *Loc. cit.*

Georgia Baptist Children's Homes

Cottage Baxley Campus

*Chapel, Children's Home, Palmetto Campus,
newest campus of the Home's three branches.*

*Historic Arch,
entrance t o
old campus
for the Chil-
dren's Home
in Hapeville.*

Georgia Baptist Hospital Complex, Atlanta, including architect's drawing of new, $16 Million Addition.

Tabernacle Infirmary, Luckie Street, Atlanta, beginning site for present hospital ministries.

Mrs. Kathyrine Ransbotham, Director, School of Nursing, Baptist Hospital.

Baptist Village, Waycross

These photographs, showing two different views of Baptist Village, represent Georgia Baptists' first Home for the Aged, with a planned capacity of 300 residents.

Peachtree-On-Peachtree Inn, Inc., Atlanta, (upper left) given in 1966 by W. Fred Beazley, (lower left) as a home for the elderly. Valued in excess of $2 million, this property was the largest single gift by one person to the Convention. (Upper Right) Chapel at Peachtree-On-Peachtree. (Lower right) Dining area at the Inn.

each church, annually, in the associations to which they respectively belong, vested with power to elect three members from each association, to compose a general committee of the Georgia Baptists, which should meet annually, in some convenient, and, as nearly as possible, centrical part of the state, with liberty to confer, and correspond, with individuals, and societies, of other denominations, for the laudable purpose of strengthening and contracting the bonds of a general union . . .[60]

The Committee agreed to meet again in May, 1803, to form, if possible, a plan of mission activity and consolidate their thoughts about closer Baptist union. Prior to the meeting in 1803, the Savannah Association had been formed, April 3-5, 1802,[61] with three churches, the Savannah white church, the Newington church and the Savannah colored church.[62]

April 29, 1803, was the date for the opening session of the third conference at Powelton. There were 24 ordained ministers present together with numerous others. Holcombe was elected moderator and Jesse Mercer, clerk.[63]

The following minutes were recorded:

 I. A discourse was delivered at 10 o'clock a.m. by Brother Henry Holcombe, from John 17 and 1.
 II. Brother Holcombe was chosen moderator, and Brother Jesse Mercer, clerk.
 III. Ministers' names were enrolled, and arrangements made for preaching to the people.
 IV. Interesting accounts were received respecting the late progress of religion, the door now open for propagating the gospel, and the flourishing state of the churches.
 V. Discussed the plan more closely to unite among all real Christians as stated in the Georgia Analytical Repository.
 Adjourned til tomorrow 10 o'clock.
 April 30th. Met according to adjournment.
 I. Engaged in public exercises of devotion.
 II. On calling over the list, the ministers present were

[60]Holcombe, p. 58.
[61]*Ibid.*, p.p. 75-78.
[62]Boykin, p. 43. [An account of the organization of the Savannah Association may be found in *The Analytical Repository*, July-August, 1802, p. 75.
[63]*Ibid.*, p. 143, quoting Holcombe.

found to be, Miller Bledsoe, Henry Cunningham, a man of color, Charles Goss, Stephen Gafiord, William Green, Henry Holcombe, John Harvey, James Hiflin, William Lord, William Lovell, Abraham Marshall, Benjamin Mattox, James Mathews, Jesse Mercer, Robert Meginty, William Mattox, Francis Ross, John Ross, Benjamin Thomion, Edmond Talbot, Joel Willis, and Sanders Waller.

III. Chose a committee of twelve, to be known by the title of The General Committee of Georgia Baptists, to transact the business and pursue the objects of conference.[64]

H. Holcombe, moderator
Jesse Mercer, clerk

This was the formal establishment of the Committee of Twelve by the third Powelton conference. Those present had decided apparently well in advance that the proposals for unity made at the conference were sound. Records of those listed as present indicate that many of them had traveled at length throughout the state between the conferences, and whatever soundings of opinion they had made caused the third conference as such to be short-lived. By 3:00 p.m. on April 30, 1803, the third Powelton conference was history. Holcombe gave also the minutes of the General Committee of Georgia Baptists. These minutes are highly significant and are cited from the *Analytical Repository*.

I. At 3 o'clock, p.m., the Rev. Messieurs Miller Bledsoe, William Green, Henry Holcombe, Abraham Marshall, James Mathews, Jesse Mercer, Robert Meginty, Francis Ross, John Ross, Edmund Talbot, and Sanders Waller took their seats as members of the General Committee.

II. Brother Marshall was elected chairman, and Brother Holcombe secretary.

III. The ministers present, not of the committee, amongst whom was the Rev. Robert M. Cunningham, of the Presbyterian order, were invited to seats.

IV. Resolved, that the encouragement of itinerant preaching, the religious instruction of our savage neighbors, and the increase of union among all real

[64]Holcombe, Vol. 1, 1803, p. 281. [Full minutes of the third conference may be found Vol. I, 1803, p.p. 281-284.]

Christians, which were the leading objects of the late conference, shall be zealously prosecuted by this committee.

Adjourned 'till tomorrow 10 o'clock.

May 1st—Met conformably to adjournment.

I. Resolved, that this committee, appointed by as numerous a body of the Baptists of this state as it is reasonable to expect could be convened on any ordinary occasion, should, the more effectually to promote the general interests of religion, be rendered permanent, either by an annual delegation from the Georgia Associations, or otherwise.

II. Resolved, That while the committee encourage itinerant preaching, by their worthy brethren, the members should individually, practice it, as far as will (not) conflict with other, and indispensable duties.

III. Resolved, that the best endeavors of this committee shall be used, whenever circumstances will justify the attempt, to establish, *as the germ of a vital mission,* an English school among the Creek Indians.

Adjourned till 10 o'clock tomorrow.

Met pursuant to adjournment.

I. Resolved, that the circular address of the General Committee of Correspondence appointed by the Philadelphia Baptist Association, and republished in the Georgia Analytical Repository, has a strong claim to the persevering attention of all the Baptist Ministers, Churches and Associations in the United States.

II. The Committee had the honor to receive, immediately from a respectable Society in London, two volumes of excellent tracts, as a present for the state of Georgia; whereupon, Resolved, That publicity be given to such of these pieces as possess special merit, in the Repository.

III. Agreed on the matter of a circular address to the Baptist Associations, and all Gospel Ministers, of every other denomination, in this state; and requested the Secretary to prepare, and publish the name, with the preceding minutes.

IV. Appointed the next meeting of this Committee the Saturday before the first Sunday in May, 1804, at the Kioke—The introductory discourse be delivered by brother Holcombe, or, in case of failure, by brother Meginty. Adjourned.[65]

[65]*Ibid.,* p.p. 282, 284.

MISSIONS PRIMARY FUNCTION

The primary function of the General Committee, then, as they conceived of it, was to promote a mission ministry primarily among the Indians, and a ministry of itinerant preaching within the state of Georgia. The General Committee met for several years under its original plan and became later, in effect, trustees for Mt. Enon Academy.[66] By 1803, the boundaries of the settlements in Georgia extended from South Carolina to Savannah, and in a belt to the east and west some fifty miles.

Under Holcombe, *The Analytical Repository* was well on the way to being the semi-official voice of Georgia Baptists, the only paper at that time. However, only six issues were published; four in 1802, and two in 1803.[67]

The stated effort to establish a mission work apparently was not successful. Biographical sketches of the men who were members of the General Committee indicated that they did perform an itinerant mission ministry in addition to serving as pastors of one or more churches. However, it was not until 1815-1817 that a missionary to the Indians actually was employed, and then not by the General Committee, but by the Sarepta Association.[68]

Baptist efforts from the formation of the General Committee were concentrated primarily in the area of education. While the stated goal was the interest in mission activity, the first tangible evidence of a cooperative effort was in the establishment of the Mt. Enon academy.

Silas Mercer had established in 1793

> a classical school on his own premises, and continued it until his death in 1796. Here his own son, Jesse Mercer, then a married man and an ordained minister,

[66]Boykin, p. 58. [Largely concerned with Mt. Enon from 1807 on, the Committee was dissolved about 1810. [Boykin, p. 60, quoting Sherwood, Mss.]
[67]Cathcart, p. 532.
[68]Henry Thompson Malone, *Early 19th Century Missionaries in the Cherokee County*, Article in Tennessee Historical Quarterly, Vol. 10, No. 2, June, 1951, p. 133.

pursued a course of study in the languages which he had
commenced with Rev. Mr. Springer two years before.[69]

However, this was the work of one man.

Records of the history of Mt. Enon Academy are sketchy.
Holcombe was a leading force in the establishment of it.
When the General Committee met in 1804, they made plans
to establish "The Baptist College of Georgia.[70]"

Abraham Marshall, George Granberry, Holcombe, Joseph
Clay and _____ Moreton.

were appointed "to apply to the legislature for a charter
. . . "and determine upon a location.[71]

The Legislature refused approval of a charter, and the
General Committee, meeting at Bark Camp in 1805, heard
a report from Abraham Marshall that some fears expressed
by the Legislature had been removed.[72] A second committee
was named to seek a charter. To secure a charter, it became
necessary to drop the word "Baptist." Abraham Marshall,
Jesse Mercer, Joseph Clay, D. W. Lane and Thomas Polhill
were on the second committee.

Original refusal to grant the charter stemmed in part from
the fact that Baptists were growing rapidly in the state.[73]
It had not gone unnoticed that a proposal to make ministers
ineligible to serve in the General Assembly was defeated by
Jesse Mercer at the Constitutional Convention in 1798.
Mercer introduced an amendment to make doctors and
lawyers ineligible also, and the motion was withdrawn.[74]
Mercer was a member of that Constitutional Convention.[75]

These factors account, in some measure at least, for the
apparent fear upon the part of the Legislature that a Baptist

[69]Campbell, p. 195.
[70]Boykin, p. 56.
[71]Boykin, *Loc. cit.*
[72]Boykin, *Loc. cit.*
[73]Henry Holcombe, Excerpts from *The First Fruits,* in a series of letters,
[Philadelphia, printed for the author by Ann Cochran, 1812], p.p. 117-121.
[74]Campbell, p. 182.
[75]Campbell, *Loc. cit.*

college would become eventually a political power spot, and their

> . . . numbers and influence would be dangerous to the religious liberties of the state.[76]

Also, the University of Georgia [then Franklin college, 1801], had been established at Athens, and there was apparent fear that a second college would endanger the prosperity of the state institution. It is evident that an academy [grammar school] opened at Mt. Enon in September, 1807, with Charles O. Screven in charge.[77] The Legislature granted a charter in 1810 for

> The Trustees of Mt. Enon academy in the county of Richmond.[78]

Mt. Enon was located some fifteen miles south of Augusta on 102 acres of property donated by Henry Holcombe.

The General Committee met in May, 1806, at Clark's Station and approved the site. A prospectus for Mt. Enon Academy for the year 1808, in the Mercer University library, indicated a course of study which was of the academy or then high school level. The academy functioned for perhaps four years.

In December, 1805, Charles O. Screven was elected president of Mt. Enon. There were twelve trustees, including

> Jesse Mercer, Henry Holcombe, Lewis C. Davis, James Matthews, Abraham Marshall, Charles O. Screven, Thomas Rhodes and Benjamin Brooks.[79]

Mt. Enon began to decline with the removal of Holcombe from Savannah to Philadelphia in 1811, although minutes of a meeting of trustees of the then defunct school, around 1819, indicate that financial indebtedness incurred earlier

[76]Holcombe, *First Fruits,* p.p. 117-121.

[77]Boykin, p. 60; *The Hephzibah Association Centennial,* 1794-1894, W. L. Kilpatrick, p. 23.

[78]Abridgement, Act of Incorporation, W. P. A. transcript, De Renne Collector, University of Georgia library, Athens [State of Georgia] Acts 1810, p.p. 139-141.

[79]Boykin, p. 59.

still had not been paid.[80] Minutes of the academy trustees for 1817 [1818?] indicate that a quorum could not be assembled for business, and it was resolved

> as the disordered affairs of the institution require and justify something extraordinary; the boarding house, and apertinences thereof be sold, at auction, of the benefit of the institution on 22 May next; and that Jesse Mercer apply to absent members of the Board for their approval to the above resolved to render it valid. Present Jesse Mercer, Abraham Marshall, James Matthews. Agreed to Thomas Rhodes and Ed Shackleford.[81]

For October 28, 1818, records show in attendance at a trustee meeting William B. Johnson, [signed] Jesse Mercer, president; Board Members, Jesse Mercer, Dr. W. B. Johnson, secretary, J. A. Matthews, A. Marshall, B. I. Scriven. Some time around 1817, Holcombe had apparently made some type of financial claim upon the trustees of the then defunct institution, which claim the trustees denied.[82]

The first efforts of a General Committee, then, became a business failure, and the classical school which was intended originally to be a college, died within seven or eight years of its beginning. Holcombe had the idea, used later at Penfield, that tracts of land for residences could be sold around the academy, thus creating a community. A few lots were sold apparently.[83]

Therefore, from the formation of the General Committee in 1803, passing through several years when the General Committee functioned only in connection with Mt. Enon, until 1822, there was no formal organizational life. Missionary endeavors were carried out by individual associations.

However, from the Powelton conferences ending in 1803 until the formation of the Georgia Baptist Convention in

---

[80]Handwritten minutes of academy, trustees meeting, original, at Stetson Memorial Library, Mercer University, examined by author.

[81]*Loc. cit.*

[82]*Loc. cit*

[83]*Source Materials on Mount Enon Academy,* Carswell.

1822, there was a unique interest in missions manifested in every association in the state. The emphasis upon missions was a two-pronged one connected by the friendships and ministries of the pastors in the state who were, in effect, frequent itinerant missionaries.

MT. ENON ACADEMY

The author is indebted to W. J. Carswell, Savannah, for his research into primary sources on Mt. Enon Academy. In a mimeographed paper entitled *Source Materials on Mount Enon Academy*, Carswell has, from court records and official documents, traced the property at Mt. Enon from Holcombe's original purchase, through present ownership. He has included further the act incorporating the academy, which places the date three years later, by date of the legislative act, than historians have previously ascribed. While the academy began functioning evidently in 1807, the charter was not granted until 1810, and signed by David B. Mitchell, Governor, 15 December, 1810.[84] [Boykin is quoted concerning Mt. Enon because cross references to Carswell's primary information and Boykin's information coincide, and because Boykin indicates following a manuscript by Adiel Sherwood at this point, which coincides also with other accounts.] [85]

Holcombe had apparently purchased 102 acres of land prior to 1807 known as Mt. Enon, and on September 5, 1810, for $3,500 purchased 2,054 acres, less the original 102 acres, in the same area. [Deed recorded October 23, 1811, Realty Book "M", p. 94, Office, Clerk, Superior Court, Richmond County, Georgia.] [86]

Holcombe sold 2,000 acres the next year for $4,000.[87] He

[84]Augustin Smith Clayton, Esqr., *A Compilation of the Laws of the State of Georgia. Passed by the Legislature since the Political year 1800, to the year 1810, Inclusive, etc.*, Augusta Adams and Duyckinck, 1812, 666 p.p.

[85]Carswell paper, Items III, IV.

[86]Carswell paper, Item II.

[87]Carswell paper, Item V.

also sold his house and lot in Savannah at the same time.[88]
Holcombe deeded 102 acres to academy trustees for $10.00,
retaining two lots of land, February 18, 1813.[89] The academy
functioned as late as 1814.[90]

In the Southern portion of the state, the Savannah Asso-
ciation grew into a group of churches on both sides of the
Savannah River; and in 1806 the name was changed to the
Savannah River Association.[91] This brought into the sphere
of Georgia activity the vision and leadership of William
Theopholus Brantly, Sr., then living in Beaufort, South Carolina. His influence was to be felt in Georgia in many ways.
Born in Chatham county, North Carolina, January 23, 1787,
Brantly was named rector of Augusta's Richmond Academy
when he was twenty-two. This places him in Augusta in
1809 when no Baptist church existed there. Brantly preached
at the academy, and in 1811 became pastor of the church at
Beaufort, S.C. He returned to Augusta in 1819, again as
rector of Richmond academy, and led in the establishment of
a church which was dedicated May 6, 1821. Brantly, during
his time in Beaufort, was influential in affairs of the Savannah River Association and in the development of mission
interests there. His influence in the Hephzibah and the
Georgia were felt more directly at a later date. Brantly
served for a time as editor of *The Columbian Star* [*The
Christian Index*] when he was in Philadelphia as pastor of
the Baptist church there, succeeding Henry Holcombe at
the church.[92]

The second figure emerging as a force in Baptist life was
William B. Johnson, who succeeded Holcombe as pastor of
the church in Savannah. Johnson was born at John's Island,
South Carolina, June 13, 1782. Johnson had studied law,
and was a graduate of Brown University with the A.M.

[88]Carswell paper, *Loc. cit.*

[89]Carswell paper, Item XI.

[90]Wilbert W. G. Boogher, *Secondary Education in Georgia 1732-1855,*
p. 171, quoting from *Georgia Patriot,* March 3, 1814.

[91]Boykin, p. 76.

[92]Cathcart, p. 186; Boykin, p.p. 49-55; See also Campbell, p. 56, f.

degree. He was converted in 1804, and apparently began
to preach shortly thereafter. Johnson had the distinction
of being

> the only man who attended initial meetings of both the
> General Baptist Missionary Convention [1814] and the
> Southern Baptist Convention [1845], [and] was also the
> only man who served as president of each.[93]

With the arrival upon the scene of Georgia Baptist labors
of men like Sherwood, Johnson, and Brantly, a generation of
ministers with formal education began to be evident. Evident also were the close ties, especially of Sherwood and
Johnson, with early mission movements and mite societies
along the Eastern Seaboard.

And yet, no less evident was the mission interest on the
part of men with less formal schooling—the Marshalls, the
Mercers, Sanders Walker, and others.

It is important to note the backgrounds of these men.
Brantly, anxious enough to preach to leave Richmond Academy for the Beaufort pulpit, and Johnson, successor to Holcombe, were in Savannah when the association in 1812

> . . . employed Rev. Thomas Trowel as an itinerant
> missionary.[94]

This was done because money had been sent in by several
churches for mission work. The conversion to Baptist principles of Judson and Rice had an almost immediate impact.
Rice apparently was in rather close communication with
Johnson, in view of Johnson's attendance at the first meeting
of what was to become known as the Triennial Convention.
Rice visited and addressed the Savannah River Association
in 1813.[95]

[93]*Encyclopedia of Southern Baptists*, Vol. I [Nashville: Broadman Press,
1958], p. 709.

[94]Boykin, p. 76.

[95]Minutes Savannah River [S.C.] Association, 1813, p. 2, Item 9; p. 3,
Item 12.

Johnson was named by the Savannah River Association in 1812 to prepare a circular letter on

> "The Importance And Advantages Of Itinerant and Missionary Efforts."

He read this in 1813, Rice spoke, and in that year, the

> General Committee of the Savannah River Association for the encouragement of itinerant and missionary efforts,

was organized.[96] Following adjournment of the Association, a Baptist Foreign Mission Society was formed in Savannah also, with the same officers as the General Committee of the Savannah Association; William B. Johnson, Thomas F. Williams, H. W. Williams, C. O. Screven and William T. Brantly. Brantly was made corresponding secretary of the Foreign Mission Society; Johnson, president of the Savannah society.[97]

The Savannah society was

> the first Georgia associational organization for missionary purposes. There had been sent up by the churches $230.26

and $106.80 was held over from the 1812 meeting.[98]

Minutes of the Hephzibah Association of 1813 and 1816 indicate that

> A number of churches in our connection expressing in their letters a desire for the continuance of itinerant preaching, the ministers and preachers agreed to continue it in the usual mode . . .[99]

The Ocmulgee, in 1814, resolved that its members go out two by two as itinerant missionaries.[100] A mission society was formed in that Association in 1816-17.[101]

The Georgia Association, apparently taking note of the circular letter of the Savannah River Association of 1813, in 1814 recommended formation of a similar group, which

[96]Boykin, p.p. 76-77.
[97]Boykin, *Loc. cit.*
[98]*Ibid.,* p. 77.
[99]Boykin, *Loc. cit.*
[100]Boykin, *Loc. cit.*
[101]Campbell, p. 196.

was done at Powelton in 1815; a society was formed and in 1816 designated

> The Mission Board of the Georgia Association.

This board continued until 1825

> . . . when the business was turned over to the state convention.[102]

Organization of a mission society in the Sarepta was in June, 1816.[103] Campbell says either 1816 or 1817. If Malone is correct, the Missionary society in the Sarepta may have been formed as early as 1815; because, according to him, this association supported a missionary, William Standige, to the Cherokee Indians from 1815-1817.[104]

The Savannah River Association divided in 1817, with churches on the South Carolina side of the river keeping the name and records, and the Georgia group named themselves the Sunbury Association following a meeting at that place in November, 1818.

> In 1819, the missionary plan of the Savannah River Association was put into operation in the Sunbury Association . . .[105]

The Mission Board of the Georgia Association had become a "component member" of the Triennial Convention.[106]

In 1814, the Ebenezer Association was constituted at Cool Springs church, Wilkinson county, from churches out of the Hephzibah and Ocmulgee; and this association corresponded

> with the General Baptist Mission Committee in Philadelphia, and took an interest in "Indian Reform" among the Creeks.[107]

[102]Campbell, *Loc. cit.*

[103]Boykin, p. 77.

[104]Henry Thompson Malone, *Early 19th Century Missionaries in the Cherokee Country,* article in *Tennessee Historical Quarterly,* Vol. 10, No. II, June, 1951, p. 133.

[105]Boykin, p. 77; also Benedict, p. 710.

[106]*Ibid.,* p. 81.

[107]*Ibid.,* p.p. 88-89; Also, Benedict, p. 733.

In 1817, the Tugalo Association was formed from churches out of the Sarepta and some from South Carolina. The Piedmont was formed also in 1817, and by 1819 had

"voted to have nothing to do with missions." [108]

Therefore, in 1819, there were eight associations; Georgia, Hephzibah, Sarepta, Sunbury, Ocmulgee, Ebenezer, Tugalo and Piedmont—the Piedmont being the only one to voice openly anti-mission sentiments.

One other factor needs to be noted in the years just prior to the formation of the Convention. The Georgia and Ocmulgee Associations had expressed interest in a ministry to the Creek Indians. In 1819 Francis Flourney was sent from the Ocmulgee as agent to the Creeks; and, in 1820, this association heard a plan for a school for the Creeks. [109] In 1819, a committee was named by the Ebenezer to work with the Ocmulgee in a reform mission among the Creek Indians and this must have been an active ministry at least until sometime in 1822. [110]

The Mission Board of the Georgia Association continued in existence until 1825, at which time the affairs of this group were merged with the state convention. [111]

The situation then was ready for the formation of the Georgia Baptist Convention at Powelton in 1822.

The suggestion for the formation of this body appeared in the minutes of the Sarepta Association of October, 1820. [112]

[108]*Ibid.*, p. 89.
[Note: Additional material of historic interest on the mission activity of the associations in Georgia between 1813 and 1822 may be found in the *History of the Baptist Denomination in Georgia: With Biographical Compendium and Portrait Gallery of Baptist Ministers and Other Georgia Baptists; Georgia Baptists: Historical and Biographical* by J. H. Campbell; *Memoirs of Jesse Mercer,* C. D. Mallary; Mercer's *History of the Georgia Association,* and *Story of Georgia Baptists,* Volume One, Ragsdale.]
[109]*Ibid.*, p. 96; see also, Campbell, p. 196.
[110]*Loc. cit.*
[111]Campbell, p. 196, [In 1815 the association "resolved itself into a body for missionary purposes; . . ." Minutes, Georgia Association, 1815, p. 3., Item Seven.]
[112]*Ibid.*, p. 197; Sherwood's Memoirs, p. 182.

In 1821, the Ocmulgee agreed to the proposal which was to discuss "the propriety of organizing a General meeting of Correspondence." [113]

The Georgia Association in October, 1821, appointed messengers and named Powelton as the site for an organizational meeting in June, 1822.[114]

[113]Campbell, p. 197, Sherwood, Memoirs, p. 203.
[114]*Loc. cit.;* Sherwood Memoirs, p.p. 203-204.

CHAPTER 4

Formal Organization of The Convention

The Baptist Convention of the State of Georgia was organized June 29, 1822, at the Powelton Baptist church, following two days of organizational meetings. First name used by the body was "The General Baptist Association of the State of Georgia." This was the second state Baptist Body, the South Carolina Convention having been organized in 1821.[1]

Developments in mission activity during the years 1813 to 1822 by the associations had a direct bearing upon the formal organization. Creation of several missions societies in associations in existence between 1803 and 1822 provided a direct basis for cooperative endeavors. Affiliation of at least two associations—the Savannah River and the Georgia—with the General Convention formed in Philadephia in 1814, provided yet another link in pre-convention cooperative life. The General Missionary Convention of the Baptist denomination in the United States of America for Foreign Missions [Triennial Convention] was organized in Phila-delphia May 18, 1814, and was the first organized body of Baptists in America cutting across state lines.[2]

---

[1]Encyclopedia of Southern Baptists, Vol. II, [Nashville: Broadman Press, 1958], p. 1223.

[2]William Cathcart, *The Baptist Encyclopedia*, [Philadelphia: Louis H. Everts, 1886] p. 1164.

SHERWOOD ENTERS GEORGIA

The appearance of Adiel Sherwood in Georgia in 1818 provided yet another strong leader in early Convention life. Sherwood was born October 3, 1801, at Ft. Edward, N. Y.[3] He graduated from Union College, and studied at Andover Theological Seminary, making him perhaps the best educated minister in terms of formal training to come to Georgia during this period. He had toured New England to promote the Baptist Missionary Magazine, and form missionary societies. He served as city missionary in Boston in 1818,[4] and then went to Waynesboro because "my lungs were then very weak, and several persons advised me to seek a milder climate".[5]

Sherwood assisted in teaching at an academy in Waynesboro for some six months beginning in November, 1818, and preached "almost every Sabbath, either at Waynesboro, Brushy Creek, Rocky Creek or Buckhead churches." [6] He was licensed to preach at Brushy Creek.[7]

Apparently he formed a Sunday School and a Missionary Society at Trail Creek church near Athens July 4, 1819, and on July 13 in the same year he formed a Mite Society at the same church.[8]

Sherwood came to Georgia very mission-minded, and found much anti-mission spirit. Preaching at Providence Meeting House in Jefferson county in February, 1819, he tried to answer some objections to missions, and in his diary said: "never before had there been uttered from that pulpit a syllable in favor of missions. The people actually stared." [9]

[3]Julia L. Sherwood, *Memoirs of Adiel Sherwood D.D.* [Philadelphia: Grant and Faires, 1884], p. 34.

[4]*Ibid.*, p.p. 55, 77, 69, 87.

[5]*Ibid.*, p. 89.

[6]*Ibid.*, p.p. 102-104.

[7]Samuel Boykin, *History of Georgia Baptists with Biographical Compendium* [Atlanta: Jas. P. Harrison & Co., 1881], *Compendium*, p. 474.

[8]Sherwood, p.p. 130, 131, 136.

[9]*Ibid.*, p.p. 118, 119.

He was called as pastor of the Bethlehem Baptist church December 4, 1819, and on March 16, 1820, he consented to be ordained at the request of the Bethlehem church.[10] Bethesda Baptist Church, Greene county, was the site of his ordination March 20, 1820, during a meeting of the Mission Board of the Georgia Association.[11]

In April, soon after his ordination, he left Georgia for New York, and returned to Elbert county in October, 1820, to attend the session of the Sarepta Association October 21-24 at Van's Creek church.[12] These facts have a direct interest to Georgia Baptists. Out of his New England background, came his formal theological education and interest in missions. This missions interest was manifest during the time he spent in Georgia, and he apparently made a surprising number of favorable contacts during his first Georgia stay. It was this man, out of this background, who "drew up and, through Charles J. Jenkins, the clerk, offered the resolution" [13] to the Sarepta Association which was the direct organizational seed for the Georgia Baptist Convention.

The resolution, adopted by the Sarepta, said: "*Resolved,* That we suggest for our consideration and, respectfully, that of sister associations in this state, the propriety of organizing a general meeting of correspondence." [14]

The fact of his earlier contact with the Mission Board of the Georgia Association in March of that year apparently had given him some indication of interest in that association.

In a letter written in 1870, Sherwood said he introduced the motion through the clerk Jenkins ". . . as he was popular, and I was regarded as an *educated man;* which, you know, was considered an impediment, in the opinion of some in those early times." [15]

---

[10]*Ibid.,* p.p. 159, 170.

[11]*Ibid.,* p.p. 170-171.

[12]*Ibid.,* p.p. 182-192. [Sherwood's journal record indicates he read his circular letter to the Association on October 16.] Sherwood, p. 192.

[13]*Ibid.* p. 182.

[14]Sherwood, *Loc. cit.*

[15]*Ibid.,* 1820, p.p. 197-198.

This was the resolution which the Georgia Association heard October 15, 1821, and agreed to "concur in the suggestion and recommendation of the Sarepta and Ocmulgee associations in the formation of a General Meeting." [16] The Georgia appointed messengers at this session, and apparently named the place of meeting—Powelton.[17] The Sarepta, meeting in 1821, reversed its position of 1820 and said that there was ". . . no need for such a body." [18]

The resolution from the Sarepta in 1820 was sent to the Georgia, Ocmulgee, Hephzibah, and Savannah River associations.[19] Of this group, the Georgia acted favorably, the Sarepta in 1821 reversed its position, the Sunbury [old Savannah River, split in 1817] postponed action until 1822, and again, until 1823. The Hephzibah and Ebenezer associations sent no representatives.[20] The Ocmulgee concurred.

CLEAR PURPOSE FOR MEETING

From the minutes of the General Baptist Association for the state of Georgia for 1822, the purpose of the organizational meeting, which began on June 27, 1822, is outlined clearly.

> A desire to form a medium of general communication among the associations in this State, and thereby to draw more closely the ties of christian love, and to extend the operations of benevolence, induced the Georgia and Ocmulgee associations to appoint Delgates, at their last annual meetings, to assemble in convention, at a suitable time and place, in order to establish a plan by which the whole denomination might unite, if deemed expedient in purposes of common utility. In conformity with this appointment, delegates met at Powellton, on the 27th of June: . . .[21]

[16]Sherwood, p.p. 203-204.

[17]Jesse H. Campbell, 1807-1888, *Georgia Baptists: Historical and Biographical* [Richmond, Virginia: H. K. Ellyson, 1847], p. 197.

[18]Sherwood, p. 204.

[19]William Cathcart, *The Baptist Encyclopedia* [Philadelphia: Louis H. Everts, 1881], p. 534.

[20]*Minutes, Georgia Baptist Convention, 1822, p. 1.*

[21]*Loc. cit.*

[22]*Loc. cit.*

Cyrus White, Robert M'Ginty and J. M. Gray were to represent the Ocmulgee. Gray was absent on the 27th.[22] From the Georgia, Jesse Mercer, William T. Brantly, Winder Hillman, James Armstrong and J. P. Marshall were delegates. Mercer was elected moderator, J. P. Marshall, clerk, and W. T. Brantly, assistant clerk.[23] Of the group present, Brantly, Mercer, White and Armstrong were named as a committee to form a constitution and report to the session the next day, [Friday, the 28th]. Sherwood was selected to preach before the business on the 28th, and Posey after the business sessions.[24]

Beginning on Friday morning, June 28th,

> The constitution was first read and the grounds of each article briefly stated; after which it was again read, article by article, and adopted as far as the 5th specification and the 10th article.[25]

Beginning Saturday, June 29, at 9 a.m., discussion of the constitution sections not previously adopted was continued and then the entire plan was adopted. The group also "received and approved" an address prepared by the same committee.[26] At this point in the proceedings, Hillman and Mercer were named to present the actions of the group to the Ocmulgee; Brantly to the Georgia and to the South Carolina state convention, with a letter of explanation.

Compere and Perryman were asked to present to the Ebenezer the action of the General Association; Posey and Sherwood to the Sarepta; and Armstrong and Marshall in the Tugalo.[27] Those present on the 29th of June felt evidently that if the associations not represented at the sessions could be informed properly, and forcefully, that they would join the group within the year. Such, however, was not to be the case.

Other actions of the meeting included setting the next

[23]*Loc. cit.*
[24]*Ibid.*, p. 2.
[25]*Loc. cit.*
[26]*Loc. cit.*
[27]*Loc. cit.*

meeting place, Powelton, beginning on Thursday before the last Sabbath in June, 1823, and ordering 500 copies of the minutes with the constitution and address, to be printed. Brantly was given the task of having the minutes printed, which he did at the Advertiser office in Augusta.[28]

Between the time that delegates to the meeting on the 27th were named, and the time the constitution was adopted finally on the 29th, it appears from internal evidence in the constitution that J. M. Gray, absent on the 27th, arrived, because his approval is given also in the past tense in the preface to the constitution.[29]

FIRST CONSTITUTION

It is considered advisable to reproduce the entire constitution as printed in the minutes for 1822 in view of the fact that other copies of the constitution, appearing as direct quotations in other volumes, vary slightly in wording, and to a slight degree in intent because of the difference in wording.

CONSTITUTION: General Baptist Association for the State of Georgia
Whereas, it is highly expedient that a more close and extensive union among the churches of the Baptist denomination in the state of Georgia should exist, and that a more perfect consent and harmony with a good christian understanding should prevail betwixt the several Associations in the State: And whereas, this harmony and good understanding cannot be established without stated meetings of delegates of the several Associations, to confer together on subjects of general interest and plans of public utility; to devise and recommend schemes for the revival of experimental and practical religion; for the promotion of uniformity in sentiment, practice and discipline; for the extension of the gospel by missions and missionaries, by bibles and tracts, and for the fulfilment of that scriptural injunction, "provoke one another to love and to good works;" and since it hath seemed good to the Georgia and Ocmulgee Associations to make the first attempt to accomplish these important objects in the State of Geor-

[28]*Ibid.*, p.p. 2, 8.
[29]*Ibid.*, p. 3.

gia, and delegates being appointed from these bodies to meet in convention at such time and place as might be agreed upon, and these delegates, namely, Jesse Mercer, William T. Brantly, Winder Hillman, J. P. Marshall and James Armstrong, on the part of the Georgia, and Robert M'Ginty, J. M. Gray and Cyrus White, on the part of the Ocmulgee, having been appointed to convene at Powellton, June 27th, 1822, did accordingly assemble and adopted the following plan of operation:

1. This body is constituted upon those principles of Christian faith exhibited in Scripture, generally acknowledged and received in the Baptist denomination.

2. The constitutents of this body are the Baptist Associations in the State of Georgia, or as many of them as may think proper to accede to the terms of this convention.

3. It should be known and distinguished by the name of "The General Baptist Association for the State of Georgia," and shall form the organ of general communication for the denomination and throughout the state.

4. Each association may send not less than three and not more than five delegate[s] to represent them in this body, and all delegates shall hold appointments until others are elected to succeed them.

5. The officers of this union shall be a Moderator and Clerk, and Assistant Clerk, who shall be appointed by ballot at each annual meeting, and shall form a committee of the body during the recess of the meeting; but this committee may be increased as occasion shall require.

6. The Moderator shall perform the same duties that devolve on Moderators in the several Associations, and in addition to this, shall be authorized to call meetings of the committee in the interval of annual meetings, should he deem it expedient.

7. The Clerk, who shall likewise be treasurer, shall enter in a book all the transactions of this body. The Assistant Clerk shall take charge of all distant communications to or from this body, and shall write all the letters which it may require.

8. Questions of difficulty may be referred from any of individual Associations to the deliberation and advice of this body.

9. The acts and proceedings of this body shall be submitted from time to time to its constituents for inspection, and no decision shall be further binding upon any

Association, than the decisions of Associations are upon the Churches which compose them.

10. The following are the specific objects of this body:

1. To unite the influence and pious intelligence of Georgia Baptists, and thereby to facilitate their union and cooperation.

2. To form and encourage plans for revival of experimental and practical religion in the State and elsewhere.

3. To promote uniformity of sentiment and discipline.

4. To aid in giving effect to the useful plans of the several Associations.

5. To afford an opportunity to those who may conscientiously think it their duty to form a fund for the education of pious young men, who may be called by the Spirit and their Churches to the christian ministry.

6. To correspond with bodies of other religious denominations on topics of general interest to the Redeemer's kingdom, and to promote pious and useful education in the Baptist denomination.

11. It shall have power to form rules, make arrangements and appoint committees for the accomplishment of any and all the above objects, provided none of those rules and arrangements shall be inconsistant with the Scriptures and the known principles of the Associations.

12. Two thirds of the whole number of delegates shall form a quorum, and a majority shall decide a question.

13. The above constitution shall be liable to amendment or alteration by two thirds of the delegates present, provided the change may have been proposed by a member of the General Association at the preceding meeting.

Jesse Mercer moderator J. P. Marshall, clerk.[28]

There follows an address from the General Baptist Association of Georgia to the associations which compose it, and to other similar bodies in the state, sending Christian salutation. The address said:

It has always been a subject of regret among the friends of our religious persuasion, . . .[29]

that churches and the associations had so little contact with

[28]*Ibid.,* p.p. 3, 4.
[29]*Ibid.,* p. 5.

each other, and that because of this their Christian acquaint-
ance was confined and limited.

> No motive could be seen, and no reason could be al-
> leged, for the solitary aspect of a denomination, whose
> uniformity of belief and practice on one of the great
> sacraments of christianity, was regarded as a principle
> of union no less dear, than sacred.[30]

Actual formation of the Georgia Baptist Convention was
on the basis of formal representation of only two associations. And over a period of several years, efforts were made
by the Convention to elicit enough interest on the part
of the district associations to become affiliated with the
larger body; even to the point of sending representatives to
the annual sessions of the district bodies to encourage participation.

The circular address of the formative convention is of
interest to Baptists of the present day, this address "To
the Associations which compose it [General Baptist Asso-
ciation], and to other similar bodies in the state. . . ." [31]
presented motivation for the organizational structure which
has stood unchanged basically for 150 years.

During the period from the end of the third conference at
Powelton, until 1822, Georgia had grown numerically, financially, and was well on the way to the cotton economy which
was to dominate along with other farming interests for more
than a century. The invention of the cotton gin made possible expansion in farming operations. Population increases
were rather rapid from 1813 until 1822, and Baptist churches
were rising across the state because of interest in missions
and an itinerant mission ministry.

The Georgia and Savannah Associations had taken an
interest in the program of the General [Triennial] Convention in Philadelphia. Luther Rice continued to visit Georgia
regularly, and the Georgia Association had sent representation to the Philadelphia sessions. Out of this background,
and with sincere concern, the circulatory letter was designed

[30]*Ibid.*, p. 5. [Entire letter, p.p. 5-8.]
[31]*Ibid.*, p. 5.

to point out need for strong organizational ties. Also, by 1822, Luther Rice had formed Columbian College in the nation's capital, and his pleas for missionary support by 1822 were mingled with strong appeals for support of the proposed college, and these pleas were heeded by the Georgia Association.[32]

The circular letter cited also the fact that messengers had corresponded by letter, but that correspondence alone did not bring about desired unity, and there was need for discussion and comparison of views held by the churches and leaders in the different associations.[33] These and other reasons were given as to the thinking that it was considered vital to bring together the energies and wisdom of the churches and associations in an annual meeting to provide

> a mass of information and of matured observation, of solicitude for Zion's prosperity, and of the true spirit of love which, would flow back with augmented energy to the several points from which it eminated.[34]
> Viewing the known principles of independence upon which all Baptist churches are constituted, it is worse than idle to raise any alarms about the power and authority of a General Association. The idea of a spiritual judicatory does not exist in the Baptist denomination . . . Nay, such an idea cannot exist until the whole present system shall have been subverted, and a new one substituted in its place. Now, a General Association does not go one step out of the old track; it grows naturally and spontaneously out of those elements of order already established and recognized. It claims to be a member of the same family, the elder branches of which are so widely diffused and so well known.[35]

AUTONOMY STRESSED

Every apparent safeguard was taken, both in the Constitution and in the circulation of information concerning the formation of the association, to assure the independence and autonomy of the local church and to assure that the

[32]Campbell, p. 228.
[33]*Ibid.,* p. 5.
[34]*Minutes, Georgia Baptist Convention,* 1822, p. 6.
[35]*Ibid.,* p. 6.

general body had no intention of infringing upon the authority and rights of the district associations. Concern for revival was genuine and so noted [36] where the letter said:

> The revival of religion is one of the important objects which this new association will hold in anxious contemplation.[37]
> Again: Nor is it too much to hope that this General Association may be the instrument of calling forth more laborers into the Lord's harvest. The present small number of devoted laborers is rapidly becoming still more reduced. Within the last few years the interest of the Georgia Baptists has lost by deaths, removals, and otherwise, a large portion of its most distinguished and religious ministers. The names of Baker, Marshall, Sweet, Winn, Williams, Franklin and Boyd, Bateman and Willis. though embalmed in the dearest recollections of the Churches and brethren who knew and appreciated their worth, live in our memory only to tell us of the dismal vacuity which their removal from earthly scenes has caused.[38]

The letter was a basic and far reaching challenge; a flinging out of the gauntlet.

> To spend our time in unavailing regrets is not the right way to improve an afflictive bereavement. To sit down in forbidden repose, until the rust of inaction consumes our energies, is not the way to repair a breach. It is the Lord's work to qualify men with talents and grace for the holy employment of the ministry; but it is our work to pray for the sending forth of such, to watch the bruised reed that waves before the blast, and to prop it with seasonable succors, to fan the half suffocated spark of the smoking flax, and to run eagerly with those who have their faces set as if they would go up to Jerusalem to strengthen them in the way. But to speak without a figure, it is most evident that our Churches have only themselves to blame for the fewness of their ministers. And if the fault is chargeable upon them and not upon God, is it not time for them to be roused to a sense of their deficiency, and begin to do that which they have left undone? Let pious young men receive the aids of learning. Let their dormant faculties be drawn out by the light of science. Let the burden of poverty

[36]*Loc. cit.*
[37]*Ibid.*, p. 6.
[38]*Ibid.*, p.p. 7, 8.

be taken from the shoulders of those who already labor in word and doctrine. Let churches see that their ministers are freed from the oppressions of worldly care, and have their time devoted to the study of the Scriptures and the care of souls. Let concerts for prayer be punctually attended and devoutly observed. Let the slumbering energies of discipline be roused into wholesome action, and let all hearts beat in unison with the holy promises of final success, and with the coming glories of the Saviour's happy reign.[39]

The letter ended with the notation that the meeting had been "numerously attended" and that the end was an emotional scene.[40]

A third association, the Sarepta, was represented unofficially when the second meeting of the General Association convened, again at Powelton, June 26, 1823. Adiel Sherwood, Isham Goss and _____ David were received as corresponding messengers and admitted ". . . as constituent members of the General Association." [41]

With no fixed order of business, Sherwood, Armstrong and Brantly were named on the 26th to prepare an order of business for the following day. The minutes for that year included a recommendation on Saturday, June 28

that several agents in various sections of the state . . . use their exertions to promote the interest of this body, to travel and preach to the churches, to enlist the feelings of ministers and other influential members in our behalf, to establish family religion, and the establishment of Sabbath schools, to make particular enquiries among the brethren as to the expediency of establishing a Classical and Literary Seminary, to be under the patronage of the Baptists in South Carolina and Georgia, to receive such donations as may be offered, in aid of our general purposes.[42]

Another significant step in the emerging organizational structure was the agreement that the Georgia Association [general body] correspond with other state conventions.

[39]*Ibid.*, p. 8.
[40]*Loc. cit.*
[41]*Minutes, Georgia Baptist Convention*, 1823, p. 2.
[42]*Ibid.*, p. 4.

Efforts to encourage participation by the other associations continued in 1823, and in the circular letter, messages were addressed to associations by name. To the Hephzibah Association: . . .

> We again invite you to join with us in the common cause. Our proposition for a union of this sort you have once rejected, but we humbly trust you will be induced to reconsider the measure. We love you in the Lord with a genuine christian affection, and ardently desire that you might see as we see in this highly important concern. We have laid no snare for you, we meditate no hurtful plot against you, but offer you the same privileges and powers which are common to the Associations composing this Body. . . . we cannot feel contented that you should remain without the knowledge of that which you certainly would approve were you aware of its worth and importance. At least, make trial by sending up delegates, and if you are then discontented with us, you shall have our cordial approbation for withdrawing.[43]

In a message directed to the Sarepta Association, the letter approved of

> . . . the caution and circumspection with which you proceed in this business, and feel anxious that we should be thoroughly known before we receive the official testimony of your respect and concurrance. When you have examined with care, and have then united with us, your approbation will be worth something, as it will have resulted from an enlightened and honest conviction.[44]

The Sunbury Association was reminded that it was necessary to ". . . collect the strength of our denomination . . ." throughout the state, and the hope was expressed that the denomination might" . . . indulge the hope that we shall enjoy the company of your delegates at our next meeting." [45] In a word to the churches in the Ebenezer and Tugalo associations, the letter pointed out:

The plan of a General Association has already had a

[43]*Ibid.*, p.p. 6, 7.
[44]*Ibid.*, p. 7.
[45]*Ibid.*, p.p. 7, 8.

second trial, and is found, upon experiment, to possess all the advantages which were anticipated.[46]

The brethren of the Georgia and Ocmulgee were commended for that work done "in devising a more extensive" plan of union.[47]

By 1824, the Convention in session in Eatonton, had corresponding messengers from the Sunbury as well as from the Sarepta to meet with the member Georgia and Ocmulgee Associations.[48]

The guiding hands of Mercer, Sherwood, and Brantly especially are evident in the first sessions of the Association. These three were named in Eatonton to follow up on a recommendation in 1823 concerning a school of learning in cooperation with the South Carolina convention.[49]

By 1824 there appeared to be a decided plan to use a general agent for the entire Convention, and when "none could be procured," the group decided to employ several men from different areas of the state for service of three months each. Gray, Connor, White and Sherwood were named for the year, and Mercer, Haygood and E. Battle "were appointed a committee to consult with the agents, as to the field of labour, and give them credentials." [50]

The Convention heard reports of the formation of the General Baptist Tract Society at Washington, D. C.,[51] and mention was made of a lack of zeal ". . . in the promotion of practical religion and the spread of the gospel in the Ocmulgee . . ." [52] The Ocmulgee, like other associations, had churches which were anti-mission in sentiments.

TIES TO TRACT SOCIETY

Reference in 1824 concerning the formation of a General Baptist Tract Society, is of more than passing interest to

[46]*Ibid.*, p. 8.
[47]*Loc. cit.*
[48]*Minutes, Georgia Baptist Convention*, 1824, p. 1.
[49]*Ibid.*, p. 2.
[50]*Ibid.*, p. 3.
[51]*Loc. cit.*
[52]*Ibid.*, p. 4.

Georgia Baptists. This society was advocated in an editorial in *The Columbian Star* sometime in January, 1824, written either by Editor James D. Knowles, or Luther Rice, who founded the paper in 1822 which is now *The Christian Index.* Out of this editorial suggestion came a meeting on February 25, 1824, in Washington, D. C. attended by Rice and Knowles among others.[53]

From this organizational meeting, sparked by *The Star,* came the formation of The American Baptist Publication Society.[54] Therefore the leadership of the paper which was to come to Georgia nine years later under the editorship of Jesse Mercer in Washington, was instrumental in formation of a pioneer society to disseminate gospel tracts and lesson leaflets.

Of significance in the light of later developments in Georgia Baptist life is the notation in 1824 that some Sabbath Schools had been set up[55] and at least some "weekly and concert prayer meetings." [56] Thus, there is evidence that the mid-week service in Georgia Baptist churches is rooted almost as deeply in Georgia Baptist history as is the organizational structure.

There were evidences of revivals in the Georgia Association during 1824, especially at two churches, County Line, in Oglethorpe and Bethel in Wilkes, and in the entire association, 293 were baptized during the year.[57]

Only in its third meeting, the general body tabled a resolution which would have changed its name to the "Baptist Convention for the State of Georgia." [58] This was brought up again in 1827,[59] and no action was taken, but the name was changed in 1828.[60]

[53]Daniel Gurden Stevens, *The First Hundred Years of The American Baptist Publication Society* [Philadelphia: The American Baptist Society], 107 p.p., p. 4. Photograph of copy of issue of *The Columbian Star,* p. 4.
[55]*Minutes, Georgia Baptist Convention, 1824,* p. 2.
[56]*Ibid.,* p. 4.
[57]*Ibid.,* p.p. 4. 5.
[58]*Ibid.,* p. 5.
[59]*Minutes, Georgia Baptist Convention,* 1827, p. 3.
[60]*Minutes, Georgia Baptist Convention,* 1828, p. 1.

When the Convention met in 1825, still another association was represented, the Yellow River, listed along with the Sarepta as corresponding members. Member associations sending delegates were the Sunbury, the Georgia and the Ocmulgee.[61] However, delegates from the Sarepta and Yellow River were granted privileges of constituent members.[62]

The Yellow River Association was organized September 18, 1824 at Harris Springs church, Newton county, Georgia with seven churches dismissed from the Ocmulgee and six new churches not affiliated with any other associations.[63] The seeds of anti-mission movements were evident even in the earliest years of the denomination.

Additionally, at the 1825 session in Eatonton, then perhaps the strongest church in Georgia, "Ross and Steely," from the "Ebenezer Missionary Society" and "Kilpatrick and Key" from the Hephzibah Auxiliary Society" were invited to seats.[64]

The subject of a name change was discussed in 1825, and a decision was made to leave the name unchanged.[65]

Counting member bodies, representatives invited to seats, and those seated as corresponding members, seven associations were represented at the 1825 Convention which named J. M. Gray as a general agent for the Convention with a salary of $350.00 per year.[66] Basic function of the general agent at this time was to perform the work of an itinerant missionary, as well as to present the case for uniting with the general convention to those not yet committed. He was ". . . to travel and preach in the State, explain the objects of this Body, take collections, and form Auxiliary Societies . . ."[67]

First evidence of an Executive Committee for the de-

[61]*Minutes, Georgia Baptist Convention*, 1825, p. 3.
[62]*Ibid.*, p. 4.
[63]*Encyclopedia of Southern Baptists*, Vol. I [Nashville: Broadman Press, 1958], p. 555.
[64]*Minutes, Georgia Baptist Convention*, 1825, p. 4.
[65]*Loc. cit.*
[66]*Ibid.*, p. 8.
[67]*Minutes, Georgia Baptist Convention, 1824*, p. 3.

nomination appears in the minutes for 1825 when it was stated that "Brethren Brooks, Armstrong, White and Henderson were appointed . . ." to compose, with the officers, the Executive Committee of this body during the present year.[68] Although, in 1824, a Committee of Three was named to consult with the agents, which may have been the forerunner of the Executive Committee.[69] However, the original Constitution, Article Five, made of the officers of the General Association a committee between annual sessions. Also in that year, associations were allowed a maximum of eight "messengers"; up three from the previous maximum. The 1822 Convention ordered 500 copies of the minutes printed for distribution [70] and the 1825 session ordered 1,000 copies.[71] Following the preaching of a missionary sermon by Mercer, the 1825 convention raised $218.00 for missions,[72] and allocated $100.00 for the Withington Station mission.[73]

The Convention agreed to meet in Augusta in 1826,[74] and the minutes for 1825 carried the notice:

> As many Brethren, either of the Ministry or Laity, as shall be connected with the General Association, and all visiting Brethren may expect to find ample accommodations in Augusta, during the meeting.[75]

This was in answer to some apparent concern as to whether Augusta could accommodate the crowd expected for the sessions; although for Eatonton this apparently was a problem not worthy of mention!

By 1825, there were 260 churches, 110 ministers, 23 licentiates and 18,484 members including six South Carolina churches with 244 members. These were from ten associations; Georgia, Ocmulgee, Sunbury, Yellow River and

[68]*Loc. cit.*
[69]*Ibid.* p. 3.
[70]*Minutes, Georgia Baptist Convention,* 1822, p. 2.
[71]*Minutes, Georgia Baptist Convention,* 1825, p. 9.
[72]*Ibid.,* p. 7.
[73]*Ibid.,* p. 9.
[74]*Loc. cit.*
[75]*Loc. cit.*

Sarepta which sent delegates, and the Tugalo, Hephzibah, Ebenezer, Piedmont and Flint River, which sent no delegates.[76]

Formation of the General Baptist Tract Society, reported in 1824, stimulated interest in a tract ministry in Georgia, and sometime between 1824 and 1825, a series of tracts and messages which had been read before the General Association were compiled into tract form and printed in Augusta.[77]

BAPTISMS, LORD'S SUPPER AT CONVENTION

The fifth annual session of the General Association met in Augusta March 10-13, 1826, with five associations represented; the Sarepta and Yellow River still on a corresponding basis.[78] Among visitors seated and invited to deliberate with the group was Luther Rice, apparently making his first visit to the General Association, and the pastors of the Presbyterian and Methodist churches in Augusta. W. B. Johnson, Basil Manly, and J. Landrum came as official representatives of the South Carolina, and they, along with Abner Blocker, "were appointed Messengers to this body." [79]

The Augusta session was a busy one for the General Association. For the first time, they agreed that they would send "delegates" to the "General Convention of our denomination in the United States" when they were financially able.[80] Of significance is the acceptance of members of societies as messengers. It had become evident that several associations did not intend to join officially, so therefore the group:

> Resolved unanimously, That as several of the Associations in this state, have not concurred in the designs of the General Association, and as it seems now doubtful, when or whether they will concur, therefore the second article of our Constitution is so amended,

[76]*Minutes, Georgia Baptist Convention*, 1825, p. 10.
[77]Shown on Dargan-Carver Library, Nashville, microfilm of Georgia Baptist Convention between 1825 and 1826 Minutes.
[78]*Minutes, Georgia Baptist Convention*, 1826, p. 4.
[79]*Loc. cit.*
[80]*Loc. cit.*

*Adminis-
tration
Building, Mer-
cer University,
Macon, Con-
structed
in 1872.*

*Classroom Build-
ing, Old Mercer
campus, Penfield.*

(Photograph By Doyle Middlebrooks)

Home of Jesse Mercer in Washington, Georgia.

Jesse Mercer (Old Simon) Home, near Washington Georgia. Mercer lived here after marrying the widow of Abram Simon. ' (Photographs Copied By R. L. (Bill) Duke)

Nurses Home, Tabernacle Infirmary

Women Prominent In Early Baptist Life

Mrs. R. M. Seymore
Second President
Georgia WMU

("ole Miss")
Mrs. B. M. Sanders

Mrs. Stainback Wilson
First President, Second
Corresponding
Secretary, Georgia
WMU

Recitation Hall, Locust Grove Institute,
Locust Grove. A unique Georgia
Baptist Educational Institution which
was closed in 1929.

President
Claude Gray

Aerial view of the historic City of Savannah, and the Savannah River, where James Edward Oglethorpe landed at Yamacraw Bluff in 1733.

The First Baptist Church, Augusta, (Right) as it appeared when the Southern Baptist Convention was organized there in 1845.

Baptist Student Center, Athens, (Below) one of the many areas of State Missions Ministries of the Convention.

> that Auxiliary Societies may be admitted as component parts of this Body, on exhibiting their Constitutional Rules for our approbation: Provided, that in all cases when the Associations in which the societies shall be located, may manifest a wish to join our body, the said Auxiliaries shall be blended with the Associations in which they are located.
> The Brethren Key and Kilpatrick, were according to the above resolution, received as representatives of the Hephzibah Auxiliary Society.[81]

The Ocmulgee and the Georgia Associations turned over funds to the General Association "to be appropriated in such manner, for Missionary purposes, as it shall deem best".[82] The pattern was being set for operation in the years ahead, and the Ocmulgee

> having omitted to supply the delegates, she had appointed to the General Convention, with the amount requisite to ensure him a seat: It was resolved, That this Body appropriate one hundred dollars for the purpose.[83]

While no mention is made in minutes prior to this time of a fee or specific sum of money necessary for the seating of messengers, numerically set by the Constitution, it appears evident from this quotation that some type of informal agreement existed which involved the associations in sending $100.00 with each delegate. Wording of the quotation involves use of 'him' singular.

The same Convention which named Brantly to represent it in April, 1827, at the meeting of the "General Convention" in New York,[84] also adopted a resolution taking note of Brantly's imminent departure from Augusta for service as a pastor in Philadelphia.[85]

Of great significance was the resolution, approved, which called for the ". . . Executive Committee of this Body, [to] prepare a plan to provide a fund for purposes of Theo-

[81]*Ibid.*, p. 5.
[82]*Ibid.*, p.p. 5, 6.
[83]*Ibid.*, p. 6.
[84]*Loc. cit.*
[85]*Loc. cit.*

logical Education." [86] M. Reeves, B. M. Sanders, J. H. Walker and J. P. Marshall were named as the Executive Committee with authority to employ one or more itinerant ministers to ". . . travel, preach, and explain the designs of this Body." [87]

At the Augusta session, business was taken care of, sermons were preached, money was collected for missions and education, several were baptized in the Savannah River, by W. T. Brantly, and the General Association observed The Lord's Supper as a Convention! [88] "It was truly an affecting and precious season." [89] "The rules of decorum prepared for this Body, were read and adopted." [90]

The treasury of the General Association showed a balance of $1,998.49¼ for 1826, with a total of $892.91¾ expended, leaving a balance of $1,105.57¾. [91]

Of additional significance in the actions of the session in 1826 is the outline of a form of auxiliaries which would be admitted to membership in the General Association. The Constitution of 1822 made no specific provision for membership by groups other than associations. However, the General Association had as early as 1823 admitted corresponding messengers and by vote accepted them as constituent members. [92] Then, as indicated earlier, by 1826, [93] they accepted by Convention vote members of societies as representatives, and in that same year, the Convention printed what amounted to an outline form for auxiliaries defining the terms under which they would be admitted as ". . . delegates to this Body, and enjoy all its privileges." [94] The form actually was entitled a constitution. [95]

[86]*Ibid.*, p. 7.
[87]*Loc. cit.*
[88]*Ibid.*, p. 6.
[89]*Loc. cit.*
[90]*Ibid.*, p. 7.
[91]*Ibid.*, p.p. 14, 15.
[92]*Minutes, Georgia Baptist Convention*, 1823, p. 2.
[93]*Minutes, Georgia Baptist Convention*, 1826, p 5.
[94]*Ibid.*, p.p. 16, 17.
[95]*Loc. cit.*

Additionally, the suggestion was made that individual churches resolve themselves into auxiliaries,[96] which would have the net effect of making individual churches direct members of the General Association, by-passing the association, when the association did not choose to affiliate itself with the general body. The suggested form called for two things. Article I called for ". . . subscribers, cordially approving of the object and the Constitution of the General Association . . . do agree to form a Society. . .," and Article II indicated that "All persons paying one dollar or upwards annually, shall be Members of this society."[97]

In 1848, the Missionary Societies of the Macon and Dahlonega churches were admitted as constituent members.[98] In 1850, the Griffin Baptist Church Missionary Society, applied for membership as a church. The church was accepted following discussion and study by a special committee; after which steps were taken to insure that additional individual churches would not be admitted.[99]

Since by 1826 only five associations were represented as member bodies, the circular letter for that year said it was obvious some associations were fearful of having their independence and the autonomy of their local churches undermined. The letter declared therefore that:

> The feature in the Constitution of this Body which is odious to some is, that which proposes to afford the means of education to pious young men fitting for the Gospel Ministry. It is designed to establish a Seminary, where, not only candidates for the Ministry, but every child of the denomination, may be educated. Opposers think they discover something in this clause, which will by and by seek to 'lord it o'er God's heritage,—undermine the independence and liberty of the Churches, and introduce a host of imposters to corrupt the pure principles of Christianity.[100]

[96]*Loc. cit.*
[97]*Ibid.*, p. 16.
[98]*Minutes, Georgia Baptist Convention,* 1848, p. 4.
[99]*Minutes, Georgia Baptist Convention,* 1850, p. 6.
[100]*Ibid.*, 1826, p.p. 18-19.

This idea was refuted.[101]

In 1826, there were about 70 ordained and licensed ministers, and 11,500 members in the ". . . three Associations fully United . . ." with the General Association.[102]

Thus, through five general sessions, and as many years of organizational effort, the foundation was laid which was secure enough to have existed for a century and a half with basic goals, purposes, directions and methods unchanged.

The Convention had appointed missionaries, secured funds for Christian education, framed and circulated a Constiution which stood until 1919 basically unchanged, established doctrinal positions, and distributed information about the Convention across the state, with invitations to join extended both to associations and auxiliary societies formed in the associations.

CHAPTER 5

Continued Growth

The Convention met in Washington in 1827, and while the record does not indicate a specific request, the body voted to allocate $50.00 to the Executive Committee to purchase books for

> . . . our ministering brethren, who may stand in need of such assistance. A copy of Buck and Brown's Dictionary was directed to be purchased for each of the following brethren, viz: Benjamin Willson, John Reeves, Wm. Lacy and Joshua Hillman.[1]

The number present for the 1827 session in Washington, which was in the heart of the Georgia Association, was such that, on the Sabbath, not only were services held at the Baptist meeting house, but the Presbyterian church was filled, and services were held at the same time in the courthouse, also filled.[2]

Three associations were represented; the Georgia, Ocmulgee, and Sunbury, together with the Hephzibah and Flint River and Sarepta auxiliary societies.[3] As in previous years, and in subsequent years, ministers of other denominations were invited to assist in deliberations.[4]

A movement to start a weekly paper in South Carolina, to be called the *Southern Watchman* had been launched, and a prospectus for this publication was read to the group and

[1]*Minutes, Georgia Baptist Convention,* 1827, p. 5.
[2]*Loc. cit.*
[3]*Ibid.,* p.p. 3, 4.
[4]*Ibid.,* p. 30.

patronage of Georgia Baptists was encouraged, "should such a paper be commenced, . . ." [5] The same year, *The Columbian Star* was moved from Washington, D. C., to Philadelphia, Pennsylvania, and placed under the editorship of W. T. Brantly, Sr., who had moved from the Augusta church to Philadelphia, upon the death of Henry Holcombe, to assume Holcombe's pastorate.[6]

The Columbian Star had some evident circulation in Georgia from its beginning in 1822, and during Brantly's editorship, this circulation into Georgia continued to grow.[7] However, the Georgia Convention was willing to encourage the efforts of its sister convention to publish a paper.

Although implied in earlier years, when the Executive Committee was named in 1827, consisting of M. Reeves, B. M. Sanders, Armstrong and J. H. Walker, the appointment of domestic missionaries was committed to them specifically, and this move within less than a decade was to emerge as a specific program of state missions,[8] although not so named.

As further evidence of growing reliance upon the Executive Committee, that group was appointed also to prepare a plan for provision for monies for theological education, which recommended:

> . . . that each member of this Body, and the several ministering brethren within our bounds, be requested to use their exertions to advance this object by removing prejudices and showing the value of education to a pious ministry. There are in the State more than 20,000 members. Is there one of these who would be deprived of the privilege of giving 50 cents for so desirable an object? [9]

The need for theological education was felt strongest in the Georgia Association. There appeared to be some fluctu-

[5]*Ibid.*, p.p. 3, 4.
[6]James Adams Lester, "A History of *The Christian Index* 1822-1954," [unpublished Master's Thesis, 1955], Appendix A, p. 128, Appendix C, p. 134, p.p. 19, 20, 21.
[7]*Ibid.*, p. 25.
[8]*Minutes, Georgia Baptist Convention*, 1827, p. 5.
[9]*Loc. cit.*

ation from year to year in sentiments in the Sunbury, Flint River, and Sarepta Associations on the subject, and there is clear evidence that other associations were against ministerial education. The seeds of a later split into mission and anti-mission forces made itself felt as much at the point of theological education as at the point of missions.

Convention sessions were planned consistently so that one day would fall upon the "Sabbath" and the religious services lasted from early morning throughout the day, and into the evening, as part of the Convention program.[10]

By 1827, the Convention was making direct appropriations to students for advancement of their education in state institutions. As an example, the treasurer was authorized to pay J. Lumpkin and S. Borders

". . . any sum not exceeding 50 dollars to aid in the support of brother Thomas Walsh the present year. And we recommend that he enter the College at Athens, a regular student, and continue there till he shall be graduated." [11]

Terms for grants to students for "ministerial aid" were definite, rather strict, and the assistance could be withdrawn if the student failed to do good work.

Aid was not at this time paid directly to the student, but in this case to two well-known pastors, who would pay as necessary. This was the beginning of a pattern which was to continue for many years, even after the establishment of Mercer Institute at Penfield. Since this was the first year such action was taken, the Executive Committee was instructed to draw up rules ". . . by which this body shall be governed in receiving beneficiaries." [12] Objects of financial interest included Furman Academy, Whittington Station, the Burman mission, as well as the support of missionaries within the state.[13]

The Convention in 1825 approved an amendment to the

[10]*Loc. cit.*
[11]*Ibid.,* p. 6.
[12]*Loc. cit.,* item 24.
[13]*Ibid.,* p.p. 7, 8.

Constitution dealing with numerical representation of delegates.[14] In 1826, the Convention added a provision for sending delegates to the General Convention to the Constitution. It changed the Constitution further to make provision for membership by auxiliary societies.[15] The revised Constitution is given.

CONSTITUTION OF THE GENERAL ASSOCIATION AS ALTERED AND AMENDED

1. This body is constituted upon those principles of christian faith exhibited in Scripture, generally acknowledged and received in the Baptist denomination.

2. The constituents of this body are, the Baptist Associations in the State of Georgia, or as many of them as may think proper to accede to the terms of this convention; and also two delegates each from such auxiliary societies as contribute annually to our funds, whose constitution may be approved.

3. It shall be known and distinguished by the name of "the General Baptist Association for the State of Georgia," and shall form the organ of general communication for the denomination throughout the state.

4. Each Association may send not less than five, and not more than eight delegates to represent them in this body, and all delegates shall hold their appointments until others are elected to succeed them.

5. The officers of this union shall be a Moderator and Clerk, and Assistant Clerk, who shall be appointed by ballot at each annual meeting, and shall form a committee of the body during the recess of the meeting; but this committee may be increased as occasion shall require.

6. The Moderator shall perform the same duties that devolve on moderators in the several associations, and in addition to this, shall be authorized to call meetings of the committee in the interval of annual meetings, should he deem it expedient.

7. The Clerk, who shall likewise be Treasurer, shall enter in a book all the transactions of this body. The Assistant Clerk shall take charge of all distant communications to or from this body, and shall write all the letters which it may require.

8. Questions of difficulty may be referred from any of

[14]*Minutes, Georgia Baptist Convention*, 1825, p. 4.
[15]*Minutes, Georgia Baptist Convention*, 1826, p.p. 4, 5.

the individual Associations to the deliberation and advice of this body.

9. The acts and proceedings of this body shall be submitted from time to time to its constituents for inspection, and no decision shall be further binding upon any Association, than the decisions of Associations are upon the Churches which compose them.

10. The following are the specific objects of this body.

1. To unite the influence and pious intelligence of Georgia Baptists, and thereby to facilitate their union and co-operation.

2. To form and encourage plans for the revival of experimental and practical religion in the state and elsewhere.

3. To promote uniformity of sentiment and discipline.

4. To aid in giving effect to useful plans of the several Associations.

5. To afford an opportunity to those who may conscientiously think it their duty to form a fund for the education of pious young men, who may be called by the Spirit and their Churches to the Christian ministry.

6. To correspond with bodies of other religious denominations on topics of general interest to the Redeemer's kingdom, and to promote pious and useful Education in the Baptist denomination.

11. It shall have power to form rules, make arrangements and appoint committees for the accomplishment of any and all the above objects, provided none of those rules and arrangements shall be inconsistent with the Scriptures and the known principles of the Associations.

12. Two-thirds of the whole number of delegates shall form a quorum, and the majority shall decide a question.

13. The above Constitution shall be liable to amendment or alteration by two-thirds of the delegates present, provided the change may have been proposed by a member of the General Association at the preceding meeting.

14. When its funds will justify it, this body may send delegates to the General Convention of our denomination in the United States.[16]

In substance, changes included in the Constitution printed in 1827 were to permit expansion of the number of delegates

[16]*Minutes, Georgia Baptist Convention,* 1827, p. 11.

from a maximum of five to eight for each association, to provide for membership by societies or auxiliaries, and to provide for delegates to the General Convention.

SUPPORT FOR COLUMBIAN COLLEGE

Evidence of the support of Columbian College upon the part of Georgia Baptists exists in many writings. In this year, the Convention proper had a recommendation from Jesse Mercer as moderator, and Adiel Sherwood as clerk, that Georgia Baptists help provide $50,000 necessary to keep that college alive.[17]

In 1828, the Convention voted finally to name itself "The Baptist Convention For The State Of Georgia." [18]

After the amended Constitution of 1827 had made provision for sending delegates to the General Convention as funds were available, in 1828 Adiel Sherwood was named to attend the General Convention, and $200.00 was appropriated to the General Convention.[19] Brantly was named as a delegate for 1827, but he was moving to Philadelphia anyway.[20]

The itinerant missionaries reported their

> . . . belief that the churches are becoming more and more impressed with the importance of the objects of this Body,—that prejudice is fast losing its influence and christians (are) feeling that they 'are not their own' but (are) 'bought with a price'.[21]

Some evidences of revival in Georgia had been reported as early as 1812-1813. Campbell said: "Many dated their awakenings from the shocks of earthquakes felt in 1812. The Lord's ways are not as our ways." [22] Sometime during 1827, a revival of some consequence broke out in the neighborhood of Eatonton. "Upwards of fourteen thousand were

[17]*Ibid.,* p.p. 11, 12.

[18]*Minutes, Georgia Baptist Convention,* 1828, p. 1.

[19]*Ibid.,* p. 2.

[20]*Minutes, Georgia Baptist Convention,* 1826, p. 6

[21]*Minutes, Georgia Baptist Convention,* 1828, p. 2.

[22]Jesse H. Campbell, *Georgia Baptists: Historical and Biographical.* [Richmond: H. K. Ellyson, 1847], p. 193

brought in during its progress," [23] in the state. Adiel Sherwood was pastor of the Eatonton church at that time. He had been interested in ministerial education for some time, and at the 1826 session:

> A proposition in writing was handed in from the Eatonton Church and other Brethren in Putnam (county), wherein they offer to afford instruction and support for one year to any of our young ministering Brethren, who are desirous of improvement. Cordial thanks were voted for this kind expression of desire to have all our young Brethren 'workmen that need not be ashamed.' Brother Mercer at Washington, is the Chairman of the Committee to examine applicants for admission into said School.[24]

Emphasis for a manual labor school came probably from Sherwood's educational background as well as the revival emphasis. Of the revival of 1827, Sherwood said:

> In July, 1827, we had a meeting of __ [sic] days, at Eatonton, and I baptized seven on Monday, and in a few weeks several more—in all about one hundred persons. This was the commencement of the great revival, exceedingly increased by the meeting of the Ocmulgee Association; for the work spread to that Association and then swept over most of the state, and before the gracious influences had ceased more than sixteen thousand persons were baptized.[25]

Sherwood attributed the revival to ". . . a ladies' prayer meeting, which had been faithfully observed by a few pious members of the church." [26] Also, during 1825, Sherwood had taught school ". . . in the neighborhood of my plantation, in Greene county, and preached also to the churches at New Hope, Oglethorpe county; Freeman's Creek, Clarke county, and Greensboro." [27]

Sherwood said

At the convention of 1828, I made a proposition from

[23]*Loc. cit.*

[24]*Minutes, Georgia Baptist Convention,* 1828, p. 2.

[25]Julia L. Sherwood, *Memoir of Adiel Sherwood D. D.,* [Philadelphia: Grant and Faires, 1884], p. 226.

[26]*Loc. cit.*

[27]*Ibid.,* p. 225.

the Eatonton church, to instruct all the young ministers
who would apply, the church at Eatonton promising to
provide for their board. This proposition was accepted; one commenced to study that spring and two
the next year.[28]

Author of Sherwood's memoirs, his daughter Julia L.
Sherwood, said of this effort, approved by the 1828 Convention:

> "This little school of the prophets was the first syste-
> matic effort to bestow a theological education among
> the Baptists of Georgia, and was really the very be-
> ginning of Mercer University." [29]

While this may appear to overemphasize the importance
of the Eatonton educational effort, when consideration of
an institute at Penfield came to the serious discussion stage,
the Convention did ask Sherwood, in 1832, to discontinue
the school at Eatonton, which he did.[30]

First evidence of the Southerly direction of the *Columbian
Star (The Christian Index)* appearing in the Convention
minutes, was in 1828 also, when the group voted ". . . that
we exert our influence in behalf of the *Columbian Star,* and
recommend it to the patronage of our friends." [31]

Background of the paper is given. It was called first *The
Columbian Star,* later *The Columbian Star and Christian
Index, The Index and Southwestern Baptist,* and, *The
Christian Index,* and was referred to by all of these names.

Luther Rice returned to the United States from Burma
in September, 1813, afire with missionary zeal. In May,
1814 he was instrumental in the formation of the "General
Convention of the Baptist denomination in the United
States for Foreign Missions", and its subsidiary, "The Baptist
Board for Foreign Missions". Sometime in June or July of
1817, after having been appointed by the mission board as
its general agent, he suggested "the plan of issuing under

---

[28]*Ibid.,* p. 232; *Minutes, Georgia Baptist Convention,* 1828, p. 2.
[29]*Loc. cit.,* Sherwood.
[30]*Minutes, Georgia Baptist Convention,* 1833, p. 9; Sherwood, p.p. 237, 238.
[31]*Minutes, Georgia Baptist Convention,* 1828, p. 2.

the patronage of the board, a quarterly publication, the object of which should be to diffuse information on the subject of missions." [32]

A general circular of the Baptist Board of Foreign Missions, dated October, 1817, said:

'The consideration alone that the terms of that valuable work, [The American Baptist Magazine, published in Boston] forbid its effusion through the West and Southwest without incurring a positive expense to the Board, has induced the latter to propose another work, . . . to be denominated *The Latter Day Luminary*.'
In an address accompanying the fourth annual report of the Board in May, 1818, it is stated, that the Board have commenced a periodical publication, entitled *The Latter Day Luminary*. The annual letter of the agent, Mr. Rice, present at the same time, contains a circumstantial account of the origin of the *Luminary*. . . .[33]

This periodical met evidently with early success, for in a letter dated October 24, 1817, Rice, speaking of *The Luminary*, said:

The good hand of the Lord has been upon me ever since parting with you. . . . You will perceive by the foregoing proposals, that the plan of a quarterly publication, on account of which my late visit to Boston was undertaken, has succeeded; this of course will be an object of much attention and labour with me. . . . The arrangements of the business will require me to visit Philadelphia once a quarter, and to spend, perhaps, rather more than a fourth part of my time in that city. . . .[34]

The Luminary actually was a predecessor to *The Star*. Rice was instrumental several years later in establishing a college for ministerial education. Columbian College, located in the National Capital, Washington, opened its doors. in January, 1822.

An important object which about this period engaged the attention of Mr. Rice, was the origination and circulation of a weekly periodical, entitled *The Columbian*

[32]James B. Taylor, *Memoir of Rev. Luther Rice*, [Baltimore: Armstrong and Berry, 1841], p. 163.
[33]*The Columbian Star*, October 21, 1826.
[34]Taylor, p. 163.

Star. It was published in Washington, under the editorial management of the Rev. James D. Knowles, and subsequently, Rev. Baron Stow.[35]

During this formative period in Baptist history, Rice was a frequent visitor to Georgia, and was a good friend of Jesse Mercer, with whom he visited often. This was, probably, one contributing factor to Mercer's later ownership of the paper.

The Star's first offices were located on the campus of Columbian College, and these offices became the first Baptist tract repository, The Baptist General Tract Society was organized at the *Star* offices February 25, 1824, with Rice as first treasurer. Out of this tract society came The American Baptist Publication Society in less than two decades.[36]

MOTIVE DEFINED CLEARLY

The first issue of *The Columbian Star* appeared Saturday, February 2, 1822, a month after Columbian College began operation. A report of the Board of Missions of the Triennial Convention presented at the eighth annual meeting held in Washington April 24, 1822, after referring to *The Latter Day Luminary,* said: "An additional work has recently been commenced denominated *The Columbian Star.* About eight hundred subscribers are already obtained." [37] It is therefore evident that within a period of three months, the circulation had grown rapidly.

As late as 1830, when the Convention met at Bethesda, in motivation behind founding of the paper.

> Published every Saturday by Anderson and Mechan
> . . . Terms, Three dollars per annum, payable before
> the first of May, Four dollars if payment is deferred
> to a subsequent period.
> To our patrons. After a delay . . . we have this day the
> pleasure of presenting to its readers the first number of
> the *Star,* and trust that nothing will prevent its regular
> appearance hereafter. . . . Our main design is to render
> the paper an authentick repository of Missionary and

[35]*Ibid.,* p. 174.

[36]Edward B. Pollard and Daniel Gurden Stevens, *Luther Rice: Pioneer In Missions and Education* [Philadelphia: The Judson Press, 1928], p. 50.

[37]*The Christian Index,* January 2, 1851.

other religious entelligence, as well as a medum for
inculating sound theological doctrines, and pure moral
precepts. We shall, also, present to our readers a com-
pendious summary of the passing tidings of the times;
inform them of the progress of the sciences, and all
those liberal and useful arts, which embellish society,
and meliorate the condition and economy of life, and
we shall be pleased, if our *Star* shall be able to throw an
occasional beam upon the path of classical and elegant
literature.
With politicks we wish to have no concern. . . .
All theological discussions will, we trust, be conducted
with the fairness and humility becoming an earnest inquiry after truth.
The religious principles which will guide our conduct
are those which are maintained by the Baptist church.
. . . While we hope to render our paper worthy of the
patronage of Christians generally, it is principally to
our brethren of the Baptist communion that we look
for efficient co-operation and supports.[38]

A survey of news content in the first editions revealed that
theological, scientific, missionary, news summary, editorials,
news of Congress, obituaries, poetry and miscellaneous news
and advertisements were featured. This basic pattern of
news coverage was to be followed to a large degree for many
years. Whatever profits were made were "devoted to the
cause of the gospel." [39]

As indicated previously, the *Latter Day Luminary* and
The Columbian Star had a close inter-relationship.

It may be proper . . . to observe that the *Luminary*
and *Star*, although edited by different persons, are designed to proceed in concert, and to make up, together,
the complete scope to which they are devoted. . . . The
same matter, therefore, is seldom published in both.[40]

Although devoted to "religion and science", this phrase
being carried over the name of the paper, the *Star* covered
almost every type of news the first year. Congressional coverage was rather complete, and members of Congress were
supplied the paper at the special price of one dollar during

[38]*The Columbian Star*, February 2, 1822.
[39]*Ibid.*, undated supplement issued after October 25, 1822, and before
November 9, 1822.
[40]*Loc. cit.*

the session. During the first year there was little evidence of polemical writing. The paper was very well edited, even by modern standards, although there was some repetition from week to week.

After the headquarters of the Board of Missions had been transferred to Boston, *The Columbian Star* was moved to Philadelphia in 1827.[41] Apparently in addition to desiring a change after the Mission Board had been removed from Washington, some of the "Triennial Convention" leaders wanted to try a more Northerly location in the hope of increasing circulation of the paper.

When the *Star* was moved to Philadelphia, it was "placed under the editorial management of the Rev. W. T. Brantly, Sr." [42]

Holcombe, after leaving Savannah, became pastor of the First Baptist Church in Philadelphia, and upon his deathbed in May, 1824, was asked by his congregation to recommend a pastor for them. He suggested Brantly. The congregation called Brantly, and he moved to Philadelphia.[43] He had not long been in Philadelphia when "the editorial department of the *Star* was confided to his care. . . ." [44]

Brantly went to the Philadelphia church at a substantial reduction in salary. The $1,600.00 a year was less than half what Richmond Academy paid him, excluding his salary as pastor of the Augusta church, and he opened a classical school in Philadelphia in order to help make a living before he took over the *Star*. Therefore, when he became editor of the *Star*, that was his third "full-time" job.[45]

In spite of the multiplicity of duties, Brantly evidently rendered satisfactory service in behalf of the paper.

> How this trust was discharged is well known, since several thousand copies of the paper were circulated in different parts of the union. In its columns, during this

[41]Lester, p. 134.
[42]*The Christian Index,* January 2, 1851.
[43]Lester, p. 74.
[44]Campbell, p. 67.
[45]Lester, p.p. 21-22; [quoting Boykin, *History of Georgia Baptists*], p.p. 53f.

period, may be found, we think, some of his ablest writings. . . .

Shortly after taking charge of the *Star*, Dr. Brantly became acquainted with a young man, then unknown to fame, with whom he was so much pleased, that he associated him with himself in the conduct of the paper. This young man was afterwards well known as Willis Gaylord Clark, who has written some of the sweetest of American poetry.[46]

In 1829 also, Brantly, "desirous that its name should indicate its religious character, . . . called it '*The Columbian Star and Christian Index.*'"[47] With the issue of Saturday, January 1, 1831, the name of the paper became *The Christian Index*, changed evidently by Brantly on his own authority.[48]

The paper under Brantly was a quiet, conservative publication, very pro-temperance, and with a marked increase in news from and about Georgia. In 1830, names of eighty eight Georgians were listed as being agents for *The Star and Index* . . . . well over one third of the total number of agents. This was another sign that *The Index* was gravitating rapidly toward Georgia. An increasing amount of secular news was noted toward the close of Brantly's tenure as editor, and the writings of Jesse Mercer were used with increasing frequency. During 1830, woodcuts were used for illustrations for the first time, and after he reduced the size of the paper, Brantly printed it in sixteen-page form.

In 1833, *The Index* carried the interesting note:

> The Charlotte [N. C.] Journal states, on the authority of the Post-Master at that place, that a pair of India rubber shoes passed through that post office, a few days since, franked by a member of Congress as "Public Documents.'[49]

Thus, carrying everything from profound theological discussions to the lighter side of the news, the *Index* under Brantly, with a circulation of "several thousand," became an established and respected Baptist newspaper.

[46]Lester, p. 22; quoting Campbell, p.p. 67-68.

[47]*Loc. cit.;* [quoting *The Columbian Star,* January 2, 1851.]

[48]*Ibid.,* p.p. 22-23; [quoting *The Columbian Star,* February 10, 1833]

[49]*Ibid.,* p. 23; [quoting *The Columbian Star,* March 2, 1833.]

The committee on the state of religion for that year said concerning conditions:

> . . . that it is more flattering in Georgia than it ever was before. On the Ocmulgee, Flint river, Yellow river and Georgia Associations, the Lord has poured out his spirit in rich profusion and many have been added to the churches. From the Ebenezer and Tugalo Associations, we have nothing very encouraging. The spirit of opposition to missionary efforts in the Hephzibah association, seems to be giving way. From the Sunbury Association, a member of this Convention, we have some encouraging prospects. Nothing special is heard either from the Piedmont, Sarepta, or Chattahoochee Associations. From a part of the Ministers present, the committee obtained the number they had Baptized since the first of August—1960. The probable number however throughout the state in that time is 2,500,150.

The Convention had sent Jonathan Toole to the University at Athens, and appropriated $150 for his support, and provided support for Joseph Hand to attend school at Eaton-ton.[51] Rules set up by the Convention for beneficiaries of educational grants included the requirement that each person produce

> . . . a regular license from the Church of which he is a member to preach the gospel in her bounds, accompanied by a certificate of his good acceptance among his Brethren and of his good report in the community at large.[52]

Additionally, the beneficiary was to undergo an examination and receive approval of the Executive Committee concerning the call to the ministry, gifts, talents, etc., and with regard to the course of study he should pursue. The recipient was to submit to the direction of the committee and preach as much as possible.[53]

PENFIELD LEGACY

At the meeting of the Convention in Milledgeville in

[50]*Minutes, Georgia Baptist Convention,* 1828, p. 3.
[51]*Loc. cit.*
[52]*Loc. cit.*
[53]*Loc. cit.* [Full list of rules for beneficiaries is on p. 16, minutes for 1830.]

1829, principal item of interest was information presented concerning a legacy of Josiah Penfield, of Savannah, which provided for $2,500 as an educational fund if the Convention would raise an equal amount.[54]

Sherwood said:

> . . . before the session took place I had heard of Mr. Penfield's death in Savannah, and had become acquainted of the conditions under which he had left the Convention a legacy for educational purposes. Before leaving home for the Convention, I had accured the pledges of some friends, to make up the equivalent, viz.: $2500, as that was the condition on which the legacy was to be paid. Ere the close of the session I called up the business, and we raised the sum in a few minutes. In those days this was a large sum to make up, as we had not then learned to do things on a large scale, as we do now.[55]

The Convention minutes stated that a committee was named to "devise some plan" to raise the $2,500.[56] The committee reported back the next Monday with the recommendation that the amount of $2,500 be

> . . . immediately raised by this body, and such friends as feel the importance of the subject. The sum was promptly subscribed and notes given to the Treasurer, the interest of which is to be paid when the legacy becomes available, and the principal when called for by the Convention.[57]

Sherwood, however, could well have secured some of the pledges in advance.

It was at the Convention in Milledgeville that the Executive Committee for the first time made a formal report of their activities to the Convention which consisted largely of reports of itinerant mission work, educational beneficiaries, and authorization of books for agents.[58] From this year, the role of the Executive Committee assumed increas-

[54]*Minutes, Georgia Baptist Convention,* 1829, **p. 4.**
[55]Sherwood, p.p. 235, 236.
[56]*Minutes, Georgia Baptist Convention,* 1829, p. 4.
[57]*Loc. cit.*
[58]*Ibid.,* p. 5.

ing importance, and by the following year, 1830, that body was itself incorporated.[59]

The Committee on the State of Religion, in 1829, gave information which indicates that the effects of the revival which began around Eatonton in 1827, and spread northwest through the area around Greene County, still were being felt.

> The Committee on the state of religion, beg leave to report: That in the bounds of these associations hitherto unfriendly to the views and objects of this convention, there is considerable change. Some partial revivals have taken place, family altars have been erected, weekly prayer meetings constanly kept up in many churches . . .
> In the bounds of those associations, who have united with this Convention, there have been many Bible, Tract and Sunday School Societies formed; and very great accession of members by experience and Baptism; nearly 8,000 were baptized during the last assocational year, . . .[60]

It was the custom of the Convention from early days to request various ministers to prepare dissertations or addresses upon assigned subjects for presentation the following year. Subjects covered the range of doctrinal issues, and after a request in 1827 that an address be prepared on the prerequisites to ordination,[61] Jesse Mercer finally presented his dissertation in 1829. Principle points in his comments upon prerequisites to ordination included for the minister the following:

1. He must be regenerated and born of God.
2. He must be of good report both in and out of the church.
3. He must be called of God to the work.
4. He must have gifts suitable to the discharge of the duties of the office.[62]

While little has been said directly concerning the ministries of Jesse Mercer, it must be understood that since 1822

[59]*Minutes, Georgia Baptist Convention*, 1831, p. 7.
[60]*Minutes, Georgia Baptist Convention*, 1829, p. 5.
[61]*Minutes, Georgia Baptist Convention*, 1827, p. 5.
[62]*Minutes, Georgia Baptist Convention*, 1829, p. 13.

he had been moderator of the Convention, and in this role had guided unquestionably the growth of Georgia Baptists to a degree which could be accorded no other single individual. Mercer was author of many of the circular addresses sent out by the General body, and as a member of the Executive Committee, by virtue of this office, exercised great influence upon every level of organized life among Georgia Baptists.

As late as 1830, when the Convention met at Bethesda, in Greene county, only two associations—the Georgia and the Ocmulgee—were represented as associational entities. The Sunbury was not represented every year, and other associations were represented on a corresponding member basis.[63] The main strength of the Convention through 1830, and beyond, was in the strength of the Georgia Association. Auxiliary societies continued to be admitted, including in 1830, the Rocky Creek and McDonough groups.[64]

In 1829 a proposed amendment to the Constitution was tabled and called up in 1830. The proposed change, which was adopted, indicated the growing importance of the role of the convention treasurer.

> The proposition made last year in order to amend the Constitution, was called up and it was agreed that the words 'and treasurer' be inserted after Assistant Clerk in the 5th article; that the sentence, 'who shall likewise be treasurer,' be erased from the 7th, and that the following be the 8th article of the Constitution: the treasurer shall take charge of all monies, specialties and property of all kind belonging to the body—giving sufficient security for the amount in his hands—report the state of the funds from time to time, as the Convention may direct and hand over to his successor in office all its monies, property, etc.[65]

And, in a move which in present-day Baptist life would be a bit unusual, the Convention ordered ". . . That the several persons indebted by note to this Convention be in-

[63]*Minutes, Georgia Baptist Convention*, 1830, p. 3.
[64]*Loc. cit.*
[65]*Ibid.*, p. 4. [This change was incorporated in the Constitution printed in the Minutes for 1830, p.p. 14, 15.]

formed that payment will be expected on the first day of January next." [66]

The rise of educational institutions in the state is evidenced by the report of the Executive Committee that assistance had been given to Jesse Moon for study at Crawfordville, and the Shiloh church was supporting a student at Wrightsboro.[67]

Mission and anti-mission sentiment was reflected almost annually in the listing of those associations represented. In 1831, Sunbury was represented, but the Ocmulgee was not. The Sarepta stayed on the fringes of full membership for a decade. During the 1831 session, the Hephzibah [Hepsibah] sent several men ". . . as a visiting committee, to look closely into our order . . ." [68]

On the second day of the meeting at Buckhead church in 1831, report was made of a letter received from the Ocmulgee Association indicating that the Association was withdrawing from the Convention.[69]

This was the first association to withdraw formally from the group, as the minutes indicated, because of ". . . unhappy divisions among them, . . ." [70]

The subject of education continued to occupy the interest and much attention of the Convention at each session. In 1831, the Convention adopted a proposal:

> That as soon as the funds will justify it, this convention will establish, in some central part of the State, a classical and theological school, which shall unite agricultural labour with study, and be opened for those only preparing for the ministry.
> Resolved further, that the Executive Committee, be requested to devise some plan to raise $1,500, by the 1st day of December next; and if so that a school be opened as soon as practicable.[71]

[66]*Ibid.*, p. 5.
[67]*Ibid.*, p. 8.
[68]*Minutes, Georgia Baptist Convention,* 1831, p. 3.
[69]*Ibid.*, p. 4.
[70]*Ibid.*, p. 9.
[71]*Ibid.*, p. 5.

In the report of the Executive Committee, was the statement: "The act of incorporation for this body was passed at the last session of the Legislature." [72]

Following is "An Act To Incorporate the Baptist Convention of the State of Georgia." [73]

> Section 1st, Be it enacted by the Senate and House of Representatives of the State of Georgia, in General Assembly met, and it is hereby enacted by the authority of the same, That from and after the passing of this Act, Jesse Mercer, Moderator, Adiel Sherwood, Clerk, J. P. Marshall, Assistant Clerk, James Armstrong, B.M. Sanders, Jonathan Davis, and Thomas Stocks, who composed the present Executive Committee of said convention, and their successors in office, shall be, and they are hereby declared to be, a body Corporate, by the name and style of the Executive Committee of the Baptist Convention of the State of Georgia, and by the said name and style, shall have perpetual succession and power to use a common Seal, to alter and amend Bye-Laws of the same, provided such Bye-Laws be not repugnant to the laws and Constitution of this State or the United States.
>
> Section 2nd, And be it further enacted by the authority aforesaid, That the Executive Committee aforesaid, and their successors in office, elected agreeably to the Constitution of said Convention, shall have full power and authority, under the name and style of the Executive Committee of the Baptist Convention of the State of Georgia—by which name they shall sue and be sued in any Court of Law or Equity in this State, and to take, hold and enjoy any real or personal property; to sue for, and recover all sum or sums of money now due, or that may hereafter become due to said Convention, at any court of law or equity in this State, or at any tribunal having jurisdiction thereof, and the rights and privileges of said Convention to defend in any tribunal whatever; also, to receive any bequests, or donations whatever; made to said convention; and they shall be vested with all powers, privileges and advantages of a Society incorporated; any law, usage or custom to the contrary notwithstanding.
>
> Asbury Hull, speaker of the House of Representatives. Thomas Stocks, President of the Senate. Assented to Dec. 22, 1830, George R. Gilmer, Governor."

[72]*Ibid.*, p. 7.
[73]*Minutes, Georgia Baptist Convention,* 1838, p. 26.

Affairs of the Executive Committee had grown as the Convention each year had added additional burdens and responsibilities to the group.

Increasing divisions were evident when the Convention met at Powelton in 1832. Only one association, the Georgia, was represented as such, although there were representatives from several auxiliary societies.[74] And, ten years after Convention organization, the Sarepta was still sending letters of correspondence, but had not united as a full member with the Convention.[75]

The concept of Christian education, out of which Mercer University was to emerge, came a step nearer to fruition when the Convention heard a report that $1,500 had been subscribed toward the purchase of land for the contemplated school with about half paid. The committee was directed by the Convention to purchase a site eight miles north of Greensboro[ugh,] with plans to have the school in operation by the first of January, 1833.[76]

A careful analysis of the treasurer's report for the first decade of operation by the General Association reveals that funds each year were made available for ministerial education.[77]

There is little internal evidence reflected in Convention minutes on the subject, but enough to indicate the strong influence which the Eatonton church exerted in the interest of Christian education under the leadership of Adiel Sherwood. And, the influence of Luther Rice upon the mission concerns of Georgia Baptists still was evident as that year the Convention agreed to appropriate all foreign mission funds in hand for the Burman mission.[78] Another interesting pattern which had been evident from 1830, was the consistency with which the report of the Executive Commit-

[74]*Minutes, Georgia Baptist Convention,* 1832, p. 2.
[75]*Ibid.,* p. 3.
[76]*Loc. cit.*
[77]Treasurer's reports, *Minutes,* 1823-1832, *Georgia Baptist Convention.*
[78]*Minutes, Georgia Baptist Convention,* 1832, p. 3.

tee was broken down to reflect a complete picture of the domestic [state] mission endeavors in Georgia.[79]

Careful planning upon the part of the Executive Committee for a formal school was evident in its report for that year.

> The committee beg leave to submit to the Convention, for their consideration, a few of the outlines of a plan devised by them for the operations of the contemplated School; hoping, at the same time, that, as the scheme is yet with them to be a matter of experiment, they will be left at liberty to alter or amend as expediency may seem to require.
>
> The plan, in essence, called for "The ultimate and conclusive direction of all the interests and operations of the institution to be in the executive committee, as agents for the Convention. There shall be five trustees near the institution, who shall be Baptists, in full fellowship, and not under 25 years of age, who shall make by-laws for its detailed operations, supervise its interests, and decide in all differences between the teachers and steward. With their consent the principal teacher may expel from the institution any student guilty of immoral conduct, or disobedience of the by-laws; but in all cases an appeal may lie from them to the executive committee. They shall be appointed by the committee, and shall report the state of the institution . . ." to the executive committee. No debts shall be contracted by the committee or trustees on the credit of the institution, without funds in hand to pay—otherwise, in every such case, it shall be on their own individual responsibility.
>
> There shall be a steward appointed by the committee, who shall be a Baptist in full fellowship, of industrious habits, and fair reputation; who shall take charge of the farm, tools, provisions, stock, and other appendages, and be accountable for the faithful use or return of all that is put into his charge. He shall direct the pupils in their labor, and labor himself, devoting his whole time to the interest of the institution, being subject in all his operations to the direction of the trustees.[80]

The report continued with a statement of conditions under which teachers should be named and students should be admitted. All students "shall be required to labor at

[79]*Ibid.*, p.p. 5, 6.
[80]*Ibid.*, p.p. 6. 7.

the rate of three hours each day. The time of labor to be arranged between the teacher and the steward—teacher having preference." [81]

GEORGIA ASSOCIATION STRONG LEADER

Thus was evident the considerable care and planning which the Executive Committee had expanded in long-range efforts to establish a permanent school. Evident also was the influence of the pattern of the manual labor school at Eatonton, which had Convention approbation.

The strength of the Georgia Association in forming the full-blown Convention structure must be noted by the fact that even in 1833, this Association was the only one represented officially; along with several auxiliary societies.[82] And some five months after the Convention met, *The Christian Index* came to Georgia.

Southern sentiment was reflected in the columns of *The Christian Index* to an ever-increasing extent during its publication in Philadelphia. In May, 1831, Brantly wrote Jesse Mercer a letter outlining his plan to move *The Index* from Philadelphia.

> I have, of late, thought much of the state of things in South Carolina [he served for some years as pastor at Beaufort, S. C.,] and Georgia, in reference to *The Index.* The time has come when a southern paper of the kind that I am editing, will be required for Carolina, Georgia and Alabama. As mine is already taken there, and the difficulties of mail transmission are many, I have thought it probable that it would be acceptable to the brethren in that region to encourage the idea of an entire removal of the *Index* to some central point in one or the other of the two states.[83]

One point was not clear. Though maintaining, evidently, nominal ties to the "Triennial Convention," yet Brantly apparently was the sole figure of authority for *The Index*

[81]*Ibid.,* p. 7.
[82]*Minutes, Georgia Baptist Convention,* 1833, p. 2.
[83]James Adams Lester, [A History of *The Christian Index* 1822-1954 unpublished master's thesis] 1955 p. 25; quoting Boykin, p. 199.

during his editorship, and he evidently had the authority to sell, move, or give the paper away . . . which he exercised.

The Index had trouble with credit subscriptions all through its history until the 1930's. Brantly, writing just before *The Index* removal to Georgia declared:

> Some individuals have received this paper six years without the payment of one cent. Some have had it four years, others three, others two, some one, and very many, fractional parts of a year. . . without making any payments.[84]

Writing in June, 1833, Brantly said:

> This No. closed the 8th vol. of *The Christian Index.* As soon as the necessary arrangements can be made, it will be transferred to Washington, Wilkes Co. Georgia, where its publication will be continued under the editorial directon of the Rev. Jesse Mercer. Meanwhile the 9th volume commencing with July 1st, 1833, will be begun and published here; so that there will be no interruption to its weekly appearance whilst the transfer is being made. The time during which it may be printed here, will be from one to two months, or whilst the preparations are going on for its reception in Georgia. But it should be understood that the Southern *destination* of the *Christian Index* commences with the next No. Its Southern *location* will follow as soon as possible. . . .[85]

Brantly was sincere apparently in the belief that the paper should be in the South, and there was no evidence he was motivated by any desire simply to absolve himself of the responsibility of editing *The Index*. Moreover, he had high respect for Jesse Mercer, to whom he planned to give the paper.

> . . . In such hands as those into which it is about to be committed, it will certainly acquire a claim upon Southern readers far beyond its present pretensions; at the same time its real value to such will be greatly enhanced.[86]

With the issue of August 3, a change in format was evi-

[84]Lester, p. 26; [quoting *The Christian Index,* April 20, 1833.]
[85]*Loc. cit.;* [the *Index,* June 29, 1833.]
[86]*Loc. cit.*

dent, indicating that although it was still printed in Philadelphia, Brantly had changed printers. Additionally, to the name he had added the words *and Miscellany,* calling it *The Christian Index and Miscellany.*

Details of the transfer to Georgia were sketchy. *The Index* was printed by contract while in Philadelphia.

One of Mercer's biographers, C. D. Mallary, writing in 1844, said that

> the purchase of an office, of a new press and suitable type, subjected him [Mercer] to the expense of between two and three thousand dollars. . . .[87]

It was thus rather certain that Brantly simply transferred the name, good will and subscription list of *The Index* to Mercer at no apparent financial increment to himself, and Mercer assumed all expenses involved in setting up a printing plant in Washington, Georgia. On Saturday, September 14, 1833, the first Georgia edition of *The Christian Index* was published at Washington, with Jesse Mercer as editor and proprietor.

Mercer's view of his trusteeship of *The Index* for the promotion of the Baptist cause was indicated clearly when he said *"The Christian Index* is not a private paper, but one in which the denomination has a common stock . . .", although he owned it in its entirety.[88]

Circulation suffered some in the transfer to Georgia. Mercer indicated in the first issue he published that *The Index* had lost many Northern subscribers.[89] Although Brantly had in mind South Carolina as one of the reasons for removal of *The Index* from Philadelphia, by 1835 a good number of South Carolina patrons had dropped their subscriptions. By 1836 Mercer was warning Georgia Baptists that *The Index* must look increasingly to them for support as other states began to acquire their own denominational papers.

[87]Lester, p. 27; [quoting C. D. Mallary, *Memoirs of Elder Jesse Mercer,* p. 110.]

[88]*Ibid.,* p. 30; [quoting *The Christian Index,* December 24, 1833.]

[89]*Loc. cit.*; [*Index,* September 14, 1833.]

Delegates to the Convention which met that year at McDonough were informed that extra expense had been incurred because the well fell in shortly after the site for the planned institution was purchased. The Executive Committee had, in the meantime, contracted for improvements on the property and with a gift by Jesse Mercer of $1,000, contract had been let for a house 46 by 36 feet, two stories high with chimneys, complete for $1,500.[90]

> The report of the Executive Committee said that: The school has opened under very favorable auspices; 39 students are receiving instruction in it, all boarding on the premises but three; the utmost harmony abounds among them, and the prospect of the success of the enterprise equals fully the anticipations of its friends. The Institution has been denominated the 'Mercer Institute,' by the unanimous voice of the Committee present [except brother Mercer himself] and with the concurrance of all the trustees. . . .[91]

The activities of the Executive Committee in planning for the institute are important because plans for the school and actual opening were the major activities in the Convention between the 1832 and 1833 sessions.

The Executive Committee reported in 1833 that in the fall of 1832, Sherwood was requested to discontinue his school

> . . . lest it should leave the appearance of an opposition to the Institution of the Convention,—but as said institution cannot receive half the applicants for admission into it—we think it best to revoke said request.[92]

When the Convention met in 1834 at Indian Creek in Morgan county, it approved a recommendation for the formation of a Baptist Sunday School Union, declaring that Sunday Schools were opposed by many Baptists because of their connection with the American Sunday School Union.[93] This action was to be followed in subsequent years by an emphasis upon Sunday Schools which culminated in 1873

[90]*Minutes, Georgia Baptist Convention,* 1833, p. 9.
[91]*Loc. cit.*
[92]*Loc. cit.*
[93]*Minutes, Georgia Baptist Convention,* 1834, p. 5.

with formal approval of a Sunday School department in the Convention.

While Georgia Baptists were growing organizationally, the anti-mission sentiment within the state was becoming more pronounced. And, organizationally, Georgia Baptists, through their Convention, were expending major interest upon affairs at Mercer to the extent that the Executive Committee even attended the examinations of the institute at the close of the first term on July 4, 1833.[94]

With the concern evident upon the part of the Convention for missions within the state, reports of mission activity for the first decade were not encouraging and a major problem was in the securing of missionaries. Salaries offered to itinerant missionaries varied from $16 per month to $20 per month.[95] Mission activity had spread fairly well throughout the state, with mission work in South Georgia, in Lee, Sumpter, Baker, Dooley and other counties in Central and North Georgia.[96]

An interesting trend in Baptist giving was noted. In 1834, the Convention balance sheet showed a credit to domestic missions of $852.77; foreign missions, $357.93; education fund, $913.36; general purpose fund, $319.84; Permanent fund, $7,619.98; farm account, $17.18, for a total of $10,081.06. With a carry-over, there was a total of $12,137.31.[97]

Several observations are valid: 1-For the first decade of Convention life, emphasis upon mission activity within the state was strong, and drew considerably more support than did foreign missions—from the convention proper. 2-The Convention's education fund reflected generous concern for preparation of ministers who would preach while studying. 3-Primary financial, as well as organizational, support still was coming from the Georgia Association. For the years 1832, 1833, 1834, and 1835, only the Georgia was represented

[94]*Ibid.*, p.p. 5, 6.
[95]*Ibid.*, p. 7.
[96]*Loc. cit.*
[97]*Ibid.*, p. 12.

as an association, and in 1831, only the Georgia and the Sunbury were present as associations.[98]

Throughout the 1830's, the Convention continued to receive societies from throughout the state as auxiliary members. In 1835, Mercer Institute was received as an auxiliary society to its own parent body! [99] This afforded opportunity for complications inasmuch as delegates from auxiliary societies had voting powers in the Convention sessions by virtue of the terms of the constitution. They had fewer representatives, but the representatives had equal voting powers.

Of interest in terms of long-range planning is the fact that by 1835, two years after the beginning of the institute, the Executive Committee was authorized to have the property of ". . . the Institute insured, if the policy can be effected. . . ." [100] It was in that year that formal action in terms of a goal for foreign missions was first made when the Convention agreed to raise $3,000 of a $100,000 goal for "missionary purposes set up by the United States Baptist Convention for Foreign Missions." [101]

The Convention was moving well organizationally, with an expanding membership of auxiliary societies. Foreign missions had begun to occupy increasingly the interest of Georgia Baptists. Mercer Institute was occupying the time and energies of the Convention to an increasing degree. Despite the impending split of mission and anti-mission forces within the state, the delegates were, apparently, optimistic about the future of Georgia Baptists. *The Index* had come to Georgia where it was to be useful in uniting the Convention, and was to serve as a continuing medium of information.

---

[98]*Minutes, Georgia Baptist Convention,* Respective Years.
[99]*Minutes, Georgia Baptist Convention,* 1835, p. 3.
[100]*Minutes, Georgia Baptist Convention,* 1827, p. 11.
[101]*Minutes, Georgia Baptist Convention,* 1835, p.p. 5, 6—item 29.

Presidents, Georgia Baptist Convention

J. D. Mell
1912-1928

B. M. Sanders
1841-1846

S. Y. Jameson
1909-1911

T. H. Stocks
1847-1856

Jesse Mercer
1822-1840

W. J. Northen
1896-1908

P. H. Mell
1857-1871 &
1878-1887

D. E. Butler
1872-1877

A. J. Battle
1888-1889

J. H. Kilpatrick
1890-1895

Convention Presidents

This page of presidents of the Georgia Baptist Convention represents more than a century of service by 10 presidents and leaders among Georgia Baptists.

Convention Presidents Continued

John E. White
1929-1930

J. Ellis Sammons
1931-1933

T. F. (Snap) Callaway
1934-1935

Aquila Chamlee
1936-1938

Ellis A. Fuller
1939-1941

Frederick S. Porter
1942-1943

J. C. Wilkinson
1944-1945

Columbus Roberts
1946-1947

Spright Dowell
1948-1949

Convention Presidents Continued

Louie DeVotie Newton
1950-1951

Searcy S. Garrison
1952-1953

James White Merritt
1954-1955

James Pickett Wesberry
1956-1957

Howard P. Giddens
1958-1959

Dick H. Hall, Jr.
1960-1961

Convention Presidents Continued

J. Thornton Williams
1962-1963

Monroe F. Swilley
1964-1965

J. Robert Smith
1966-1967

Walter L. Moore
1968-1969

Robert Jackson Robinson
1970-1971

CHAPTER 6

Years of Consolidation

Concern upon the part of Georgia Baptists was for a spiritual ministry to all people, one which was genuine, of long standing, and without evident external pressure. Abraham Marshall had been instrumental in the establishment of Negro churches in Savannah and Augusta. Earliest Convention minutes reported congregations by race, and there were Negro members of the great majority of early Georgia Baptist churches.

Concern for Christian education for Negroes was expressed first formally in the 1835 session when the Convention approved a resolution recommending ". . . to all our brethren a due consideration of the best method of affording religious instruction to the black population among us, and that such facilities be afforded for this instruction, as in their best judgment may be deemed most expedient." [1]

Little internal evidence exists in the Minutes of the Convention concerning the struggle which was under way during this period between missionary and anti-missionary; education and anti-education forces within the state.

Elder Emerson Proctor of Jesup has made a significant contribution to this vacuum in his unpublished thesis *"Georgia Baptists, Organization and Division, 1772-1840."* Proctor traces, from the Primitive Baptist background, the differences which culminated in open division by 1837.

Rumblings of discontent were evident when the Conven-

[1]*Minutes, Georgia Baptist Convention,* 1835, p. 6.

tion met at Shiloh church in Greene county in 1835. Internal evidence of the discontent is evident by the fact that at this session the Convention voted to amend the 5th, 10th and 11th articles of the constitution. Background for the amendments is found in the statement:

> Whereas, it has been agreed that this Convention, by a construction of her constitution, may assume an absolute control over the churches, and thereby infringe on, or even destroy, their rights, independence and sovereignty: therefore
> Resolved, That this Convention disclaims all power by which she can exercise any dominion over the Faith, or control the Discipline of the churches, or in anywise coerce them to do, or contribute, any thing whatsoever, contrary to their own sense of propriety and duty.[2]

The Constitutional amendments are as follows:

> 5. The officers of this union shall be a Moderator, a Clerk and Assistant Clerk, and a Treasurer, who shall be appointed by ballot at each annual meeting, and shall form a committee of the body during the recess of the meeting; but this committee may be increased as occasion may require; and have authority to fill any vacancies which may happen, and also that of the Treasurer.
> 10. The acts and proceedings of this body shall be submitted, from time to time, to its constituents for inspection; and none of its decisions shall be binding on the associations or auxiliaries.
> 11. The following are the specific objects of this body, viz:
> 1. To unite the influence and pious intelligence of Georgia Baptists, and thereby to facilitate their union and cooperation.
> 2. To form and encourage plans for the revival of experimental and practical religion in the State and elsewhere.
> 3. To aid in giving effect to useful plans of the several associations.
> 4. To afford an opportunity to those who may conscientiously think it their duty to form a fund for the education of pious young men, who may be called by the Spirit and their churches to the Christian Ministry.
> 5. To correspond with bodies of other religious de-

²*Loc. cit.*

nominations, on topics of general interest to the Redeemer's Kingdom, and to promote pious and useful Education in the Baptist denomination.[3]

Two other significant actions emerged from the 1835 session of the Convention; one which was the forerunner of an active stewardship promotion program still evident; and one which was short-lived. A special committee was named to study Matthew Henry's commentary, which it did and reported full endorsement of the commentary, saying the committee subscribed to the orthodoxy and excellence of doctrinal character, and did ". . . most cheerfully commend it to the patronage of Southern churches." Jesse Mercer was chairman of this committee,[4] apparently the first such to be asked to study and recommend or disapprove the "orthodoxy" of a given book.

The second action that year, which was to have lasting consequences, was the request in the circular letter that all Georgia Baptists give three per cent of their income. If this were done, the letter said, it would provide enough monies to support all ministers in the state at the rate of $500 per year, provide $5,959 for missions, and leave $10,000 for the institute [Mercer]. The letter declared if this were done for ten years, the principle and interest of the amount for Mercer would

> . . . place the Institute on a footing not equalled by any similar institution in the Southern states. It would render further appropriations unnecessary, so that all the energies of the friends might be directed to missionary operations; and carrying out this system, in twenty years the glorious benefits of the Gospel of Peace would be realised by thousands and tens of thousands, who are now blinded by the grossest Idolatry, through the instrumentality of the Georgia Baptist Convention.[5]

The circular letter ended by saying

> . . . should this rate be adopted, more will be accomplished in one year than is now done in fifteen . . . We

[3]*Ibid.*, p.p. 23, 24.
[4]*Ibid.*, p. 20.
[5]*Ibid.*, 1835, p.p. 20-22.

leave you, Dear Brethren, to decide upon the merits of these calculations, with a hope that you will act out the honest dictates of your conscience.[6]

The letter pointed out that if every Georgia Baptist tithed they would have available $111,170 each year for their Convention ministries.[7]

If not the forerunner of present-day stewardship emphases in fact, it stood in spirit as such.

Perhaps the Convention in 1836 was not in itself as important as a meeting which followed some two months later in Forsyth. At the session in 1836, the Georgia and the Central Associations were represented, along with sixteen societies. The Sarepta Association was received as a constituent member.[8] Shortly after the Convention, the Central Association apparently withdrew and found it necessary to print a tract entitled "History-Faith, Views, Plans, etc., of the Central Association," embracing the whole ground of difference between her and those associations from which she was separated.[9]

However, the Central, if it withdrew, did so for a short time only, because Minutes for 1837 show a delegation from that association.[10]

THE INDEX IS RECOGNIZED

Although *The Index* had been removed from Philadelphia to Washington, Georgia, in 1833, it was not until 1836 that any mention of the paper was made in Convention records, when the Convention:

> Resolved: That we feel a deep interest in the success and general circulation of the *Christian Index,* regarding it as a useful medium of religious instruction and intelligence: and that the determination of the Editors to exclude all inflammatory and personal pieces from

[6]*Ibid.,* p. 22.
[7]*Loc. cit.*
[8]*Minutes, Georgia Baptist Convention,* 1836, p. 3.
[9]*Minutes, Georgia Baptist Convention,* 1837, p. 3.
[10]*Loc. cit.*

its columns meets the highest approbation of this body.[11]

Also in 1836, repositories were authorized for Augusta, Macon, and Columbus for Sabbath School books.[12]

In this year,

> ... A division in the Baptist denomination in Georgia often voiced became a reality in 1836. A wide breach existed between the Old School Baptist and the Missionary Baptists, and the Old School Baptists made no effort to retain fellowship with the advocates of the missionary movement.
>
> One last effort was made to avert a division. A call from ministers in ten different associations was made through *The Christian Index* for a meeting of all the Baptist ministers in the state 'to Discuss the divided condition of the churches'. This meeting was held in Forsyth, Georgia in July of 1836, and a second one was held later during the year. However, the efforts were initiated primarily by the Missionary Baptists and had little chance of success. The Old School Baptists looked on the efforts with suspicion and most declined to attend.[13]

Proctor's summation of differences is stated well:

> One of the most important factors causing dissension was the fundamental difference between Missionary Baptists and Old School Baptists in the conception each had toward the function of the church. The Old School Baptists believed that the church as it existed before the development of the organizations which supported the missionary movements conformed most closely to the ideal system outlined in the New Testament. The Baptist denomination in Georgia was established by the method of evangelism employed under this system. They believed this general system should be perpetuated and carried on without change. Consequently, they looked upon any deviation from this system as a departure from the recognized faith of Baptists.
>
> The Missionary Baptists held a more flexible view of change in the church. They believed that change was

---

[11]*Minutes, Georgia Baptist Convention,* 1836, p. 5.

[12]*Ibid.,* p. 6

[13]*The Christian Index,* Vol. IV. No. 16, April 28, 1836, p.p. 241-242 [about ministers meeting, p.p. 451-453]. Emerson Proctor, *Georgia Baptists Organization and Division, 1772-1840,* Georgia Southern College, unpublished thesis, 1969. [p. 119]

inevitable and that some adjustments should be made to meet that change. Jesse Mercer supported the idea that opposition based on resistence to change was unfounded . . .[14]

This, together with differences of opinion concerning the role of the association with relation to the local church in matters of discipline, doctrine, etc., and a great difference of opinion concerning education for ministers were basic in the split between the missionary and primitives. Proctor's statements are as concise from the Primitive Baptist point of view as any available.

Basic Primitive Baptist opposition to theological education is expressed in the minutes of the Towaliga Baptist Association for 1838 which said:

> We believe that Theological Seminaries are calculated to aid, and abet, in the corruption of the church, by offering inducement to designing characters to seek after and obtain the advantages derived from the same; and through their exertions as false teachers, corrupt the church, of whom our Lord bids us beware.[15]

Internal evidence of a lack of co-operation consisted primarily and almost exclusively of a listing of associations by identification non-missionary or anti-missionary in the lists published as folded inserts in Minutes of the Convention at irregular periods.

Proctor says also that:

> The Hephzibah Association was completely controlled by the Old School Baptist advocates during the period 1819-1825. This association went so far in 1825 as to insert an article in its decorum to prevent the subject of missionary activities from being brought before the association.[16]

It read,

---

[14]*Proctor*, p. 87, quoting Charles D. Mallary, *Memoirs of Elder Jesse Mercer* [New York: John Gray, 1844], p.p. 193-197.

[15]Proctor, p. 92, quoting *Towaliga Primitive Baptist* Association Minutes, 1838.

[16]*Ibid.*, p. 104.

> This association shall have no right to correspond by
> letter, or messenger with any general board; any brother
> moving either of the above subjects in this body shall
> be considered in disorder and therefor reproved by the
> moderator . . .[17]

This analysis of the "Old School" point of view is important because for years many of the associations were not members of the Convention, but they were represented by auxiliary membership, indicative of divisive opinions within the associations upon the subject. Under these circumstances it was indeed a mark of progress that the Convention was able to move as rapidly and as effectively as it did in the areas of mission activity and theological education.

Allen, for the year 1836, listed 24 associations, of which twelve were missionary, five Old School and six neutral. His Register for that year listed a total of 572 churches and 42,949 members.[18]

The Mission—Anti-Mission controversy in Georgia was long, bitter, and left scars which took many years to begin healing;[19] never healing completely. Differences concerning authority of the associations were evident also. In 1833, the matter was of sufficient importance for a dissertation "on the resemblances and differences between church authority and that of an association" to be printed in the minutes instead of the regular Circular Letter.[20]

The apparent split in 1836 between missionary and anti-missionary forces was to prove healthy for the Georgia Baptist Convention. In that year, four associations were represented, and that number increased consistently through the ensuing years. The Georgia, Central, Sarepta and Sunbury were represented when the Convention met in Ruckersville in 1837.[21]

[17]Minutes, *Hephzibah Association,* 1821-1822, quoted in Proctor, p. 104.

[18]Allen, I. M., *The Triennial Baptist Register,* [Philadelphia: Baptist General Tract Society, 1836], p. 203.

[19][The anti-mission movement is treated at some length in Boykin,] *History of Georgia Baptists,* Chapter XIV, p.p. 161-174.

[20]*Minutes, Georgia Baptist Convention,* 1833, p.p. 10-12.

[21]*Minutes, Georgia Baptist Convention,* 1837, p. 3.

SOUTHERN BAPTIST COLLEGE PROPOSAL

Despite the activity which centered around the Mercer Institute north of Greensboro at Penfield, emphasis upon a plan for a southern Baptist college in Washington was pushed to a great degree by the Georgia Association during 1835-36, including an offer from the town of Washington of $35,000 as an inducement to establish the college there. There was agreement that a college not be begun until $100,000 had been subscribed.[22] This was to come primarily from Washington residents. The concept behind this proposal was that since the South Carolina Convention planned to establish a theological school, Georgia Baptists would co-operate with that venture, and ask the South Carolina Convention to co-operate with Georgia Baptists in the development of a Southern Baptist college.[23] The first proposal came as a recommendation to the Convention from the Georgia Association.[24]

Funds for the proposed college were solicited. The Convention went so far as to name several agents to seek monies and the Executive Committee secured a charter and appointed a Board of Trustees[25] but the college never began operation.

While efforts were being made to set up a Southern Baptist College during 1835-37, efforts were being made also during the years 1836-37 to establish a female school on the campus of the Mercer Institute.[26] And, by 1837 the Hephzibah, which had for a time been anti-missionary, was admitted as a constituent member of the Convention, along with the Apalachy [Apalachee] Association.[27] For the first time a

[22]*Minutes, Georgia Baptist Convention*, 1836, p.p. 6, 8, 9.
[23]*Ibid.*, p. 6.
[24]*Ibid.*, p. 8; *Minutes, Georgia Baptist Convention*, 1835, Report E.
[25]*Minutes, Georgia Baptist Convention*, 1837, p. 8.
[Note: See Appendix D, p. 789 f. for complete background on the Washington College proposal.]
[26]*Ibid.*, p. 5.
[27]*Ibid.*, p. 4.

minister, Edward A. Stevens, was ordained at a Convention session at the request of the Sunbury church.[28]

Of great significance was the correspondence during this time between the South Carolina and Georgia Conventions on respective purposes of the college proposed for Washington, and the theological institution proposed for South Carolina, for therein lay the apparent seed for the later establishment of what was to become Southern Baptist Theological Seminary. A committee named to confer with the president of the South Carolina Convention brought a report in 1837 indicating the necessity of making clear that the objects proposed were different; one being literary, and the other theological [Furman], ". . . yet such is the intimate connection between science and religion, that a friendly intercourse must result in mutual benefit." [29]

How the proponents of the proposed Southern Baptist college in Washington reconciled their need for it without seeing any danger to the Mercer Institute, which they supported, or conflict of interest with it, was not clear. One apparent answer lay in the stress upon identity as Southern Baptist institutions, with different functions at Washington and in South Carolina as the 1837 report said:

> The Seminaries are not *State* but *Southern* Seminaries, and this fact being affectionately, and *publicly* recognized by their respective officers, will induce a similar recognition on the part of the friends of the Institutions in the different States which may be interested in their success.[30]

Evident disagreement upon the site of the proposed college was reflected during 1837, as Talbotton sought, apparently actively, to secure the proposed institution for that town should it be established. An offer of $120,000 in subscriptions by Talbotton proponents—$20,000 more than the Washington proponents—was rejected finally as the committee named to consider the matter reported negatively.[31]

[28]*Ibid.*, p. 6.
[29]*Ibid.*, p. 9.
[30]*Loc. cit.*
[31]*Ibid.*, p. 14.

Their report said that the matter was in the hands of the trustees who had been named for the college; and that a charter had been obtained for such an institution in Washington, with conditions by which the trustees were to prepare for such a school being fulfilled [raising of $100,000 in subscriptions and cash] and

> . . . to suspend a collection with a view to change a location, might be considered by many, as dissolving their obligations, and at the present pressure of the times, it would be inexpedient to give up a certain subscription for one not yet raised.[32]

The committee said further that they could not deal with the Talbotton group on the basis of the $120,000 offer without giving Washington an opportunity to raise $120,000 ". . . and it would engender strife, . . ." so they left it as planned.[33] [See Appendix D, p. 789 for full background on this college proposal.]

By the mid 1830's each Convention session heard committee reports almost without end, including also an ample supply of sermons and addresses. Interestingly enough, by this time, when stated committees brought their report, the report was referred routinely to a special committee to study and report on the report to the Convention. This included the report of the Executive Committee, and created a double-check on major reports. Also, it was not unusual for committees to be named to deal in advance with specific sections of a given report, and not the entire report itself.

Leaders in the Convention during the 1830's had a clear idea of the direction they felt Baptists in Georgia should pursue, and by committee organization and structure keep the Convention moving in this direction. There can be little doubt that the Georgia Association and leaders in that association kept a firm rein upon the direction of the Convention.

While the names of committee members reflect inclusion of members from member associations and constituent

[32]*Loc. cit.*
[33]*Loc. cit.*

bodies, these committees, none-the-less, reflected a substantial number from the Georgia Association. This would not have been unusual, considering the fact that this Association was for several years the only Association, as such, represented at Convention sessions.

Of interest in 1838 is the fact that the Convention resolved to request not only editors of *The Christian Index,* but the publications, *Signs of the Times,* and *Primitive Baptist* to print the act incorporating the Convention, together with the amendment passed by the Legislature, incorporating Mercer University.[34]

Evident also from proceedings of the Convention during the 1830's and the 1840's was the emergence of the treasurer as a leading silent force in the convention. The treasurer began to be elected separately, by ballot, and would in a few years be placed on a salary basis for his work, although no other Convention officer, nor any officer of the Executive Committee during this period was paid. Further steps to safeguard the Convention's investment in Mercer were taken during this 1838 session at Monroe when the group requested the Executive Committee

> . . . to petition the next Legislature to amend the charter or act of Incorporation of the Mercer University, so as to authorize the Convention, to elect the Board of Trustees of said University, once in three years, and also to require said Trustees; to make an annual report of their proceedings to the convention.[35]

MERCER'S FUTURE ASSURED

In 1838, with interest in Mercer growing rapidly, the demise before birth of the Southern Baptist college in Washington was reported by the Executive Committee. This committee's report included a resolution ". . . adopted by the late Board of Trustees of the Southern Baptist College . . ." in which they said they decided it was not expedient

[34]*Minutes, Georgia Baptist Convention,* 1838, p. 5.
[35]*Ibid.,* p. 6.
[36]*Ibid.,* p. 15.

". . . to undertake the building of a college under present circumstances."[36] The committee cited, among other things, the embarrassment of the times, the differing views of the brethren with regard to plans proposed, and the inadequacy of the means in hand.

The Executive Committee decided that it had the authority under its charter to do what they considered ". . . the only hopeful alternative, viz: the connecting of a Collegiate Department with the Mercer Institute."[37] They believed they had power to do this inasmuch as ". . . the ultimate and conclusive direction of all the interests and operations of the Institution had been vested in the Executive Committee, as agents for the Convention, . . ."[38]

In essence, what happened was that out of funds raised or pledged for the proposed Southern Baptist college; "Between fifty-five and sixty thousand dollars of the old subscriptions have been transferred, and twenty-eight thousand dollars in new subscription have been obtained, . . . about fifty thousand dollars [of] the subscription have been taken up in notes."[39] This was to be channeled into the Mercer Institute, with the elected trustees of the institute to take control of the funds and management.[40]

The Institute was occupying a major interest of the Convention at this time, and reports of the Convention and the Executive Committee reflect the emphasis in detail, including reports concerning sale of town lots in Penfield. And, during 1838, plans for the establishment of a female seminary at Penfield were made. During the early part of that year a school for small children was in operation; all as a part of, or to be a part of, the Mercer Institute.[41]

What developed, therefore, was that Penfield became, perhaps next to Athens, the second seat of learning in Georgia, with classes for age groups from what we now con-

[37]*Loc. cit.*
[38]*Loc. cit.*
[39]*Ibid.*, p.p. 16, 17.
[40]*Ibid.*, p. 16.
[41]*Ibid.*, p.p. 17, 18.

sider elementary school through college, with theological preparation at the Institute. This emphasis upon education for all ages was to be reflected in ensuing years as associations were organized. Many of these associations undertook as a major initial emphasis the establishment of schools, seminaries, or institutes—in essence basic educational centers— in the areas where the associations were organized.

The Convention itself scheduled the organizational meeting for the Board of Trustees of Mercer for the ". . . Tuesday after the 2nd Sabbath in July next (1838) at 9 o'clock a.m. . . ." at Penfield.[42]

Minutes for the 1838 Convention session contained the first printed act of incorporation of the Executive Committee, although the Committee was incorporated eight years earlier. If by inference, one is to draw a conclusion, during the years since the Committee was incorporated, its responsibilities had increased annually, and with the increased business related to Mercer Institute, it was felt in order to remind the constituency of the limits and boundaries of Executive Committee authority.

Subscription notes for Mercer Institute were coming due, and the section dealing with powers of the Executive Committee to sue for funds may have had more than passing interest to those who signed pledges.

In 1837, to deal with legal and organizational problems related to establishment of Mercer, an act to amend the act of incorporation of the Convention was approved by the State Legislature. The amendments specified clearly the relationship between the Convention and the institution, which served as the basis for organization of Mercer, as well as relationships with educational institutions which were to be formed in later years.

The act is as follows:

> An act to amend an Act entitled an Act to incorporate the Baptist Convention of the State of Georgia.
> Section 1st. Be it enacted by the Senate and House of

[42]*Ibid.,* p. 25.

Representatives of the State of Georgia in General Assembly met, and it is hereby enacted by the authority of the same, That if by the Act entitled an Act to incorporate the Baptist Convention of the State of Georgia, said Convention, or their Executive Committee, are invested with taxing power, all such power is hereby annulled and made void.

Section 2d. And be it further enacted by the authority aforesaid, That the Executive Committee of the Baptist Convention of the State of Georgia shall have power to establish and endow a Collegiate Institution, be known by the name of the MERCER UNIVERSITY, on the premises owned by said Convention, in Greene County; and said Committee are hereby authorized to make all necessary bye-laws and regulations for the government of said university, provided they be not repugnant to the Constitution or Laws of this State or the United States, until a Board of Trustees shall be appointed by the aforesaid Baptist Convention.

Section 3d. And be it further enacted, That the Baptist Convention of the State of Georgia, may at its next meeting, or at any subsequent meeting, elect a Board of Trustees for the said Mercer University, consisting of not less than fifteen, nor more than thirty one, in number, who shall, or their successors in office, be a body politic and corporate by the name of the Trustees of the Mercer University, and as such, they shall be capable of, and liable in law, to sue and to be sued, plead and to be impleaded, and shall be authorized to use a common Seal, to hold all manner of property, both real and personal, for the purpose of making a permanent endowment, of said Institution, and to raise funds for the support of the same, and for the erection of buildings, or to confer literary degrees, and to exercise such other power not inconsistent with the laws of this state or the United States, as the aforesaid Convention may see fit to vest in their hands.

Section 4th. And be it further enacted, That the aforesaid Convention shall be authorized to determine the manner in which said Board of Trustees shall be perpetuated, and the character of the individuals from whom they may be chosen.

Section 5th. And be it further enacted, That upon the premises now owned by the Baptist Convention of the State of Georgia, in Greene County, or that may hereafter come into their possession, no person shall by himself, servant or agent, keep, have, use, or maintain a gaming house or room of any description, or permit with his knowledge, any house or room occupied or owed by him to be used by any person whatever as a gaming place, nor shall any person, upon the premises aforesaid, by himself, servant or agent, keep, employ or allow, with his knowledge, to be kept or employed on the premises he may occupy, and Faro table, Billiard Table, E. O. Table, A. B. C. Table, or any other Table of like characater, nor shall any person by himself, servant or agent, upon the premises now owned by the aforesaid Convention, in Greene County, or that may hereafter come into their possession, to be allowed to sell Ardent Spirits, Wine, Cordials, Porter, or any other intoxicating drinks whatever, nor permit the same to be done with his or her knowledge or approbation, on the premises which he or she may occup, provided, however, that the Trustees of the Mercer University may have the power to authorize any individuals to sell Ardent Spirits, Wine, etc. upon their premises for medical and sacramental purposes. Any person violating the prohibitions contained in this section, shall be liable to be indicted for a misdemeanor before the Supreme Court, and on conviction, shall be fined in a sum not less than one thousand dollars for each and every offence.

Section 6th. And be it further enacted, That the Executive Committee of the aforesaid Convention, in executing Titles for Lots which they may sell from time to time, shall have power to insert such conditions as may tend further to defend the premises aforesaid from the nuisances specified in the foregoing section of this Act.

Joseph Day, Speaker of the House of Representatives, Robert M. Echols, President of the Senate, assented to, 22d Dec. 1837 George R. Gilmer, Governor.[43]

Thus management of the institute was to be channeled into a Board of Trustees, relieving the Executive Committee of what had become a difficult task in overseeing even the minute details of the organization of a school of learning. The Convention did not take steps to make of the Mercer Institute a University until the proposal or a Southern Baptist College at Washington was disposed of finally.

[43]*Ibid.,* p.p. 27, 28.

CONSOLIDATION CONTINUES

The structure of representation at the 1839 Convention is of interest. It is a pattern. The Georgia, Central, Sunbury, Apalachee, Sarepta and Hepzibah Associations were represented, and the Columbus and Rehoboth Associations were received as component members, together with societies representing other areas of the state, including South Georgia. Organized Convention structure still was in the heartland of the organizational area, but Convention strength was gaining across the state, and full support was felt increasingly from associations West, South, and North.[44] Efforts to elicit support were evident annually as delegates were appointed from the Convention to associations not in full fellowship with the Convention.[45]

And in efforts to present major emphases of the moment, in 1839, the sermon on education was dispensed with in order that a sermon be preached on foreign missions.[46] There was continuing intercourse between messengers [delegates] of the Georgia Convention and Conventions in neighboring states.[47]

Georgia Baptists have never been without concern for the education and spiritual welfare of Negroes. With emphasis upon Christian education at a peak because of plans surrounding Mercer University, the Executive Committee in 1839 was instructed

> . . . to make enquiry respecting the practicability of affording oral religious instructions to the colored people in our state, and to make such arrangements as their means and information will permit.[48]

Background for the stricture on taxing powers by the Convention as indicated in the Amended Act of Incorporation [see p. 124] centered apparently around the unique structure of Penfield.

[44]*Minutes, Georgia Baptist Convention,* 1839, p. 3.
[45]*Ibid.,* p. 4.
[46]*Loc. cit.*
[47]*Loc. cit.*
[48]*Ibid.,* p. 6.

Following the amendments to the Convention charter in December, 1837, An Amended Act of Incorporation for 1838 was passed by the Legislature in December of that year. In essence, this amendatory act was to authorize trustees of Mercer University who lived at Penfield or in Greene county

> . . . to make such by-laws and regulations for the government of the Village of Penfield, and the premises above named, as may be proper and necessary to carry out the design of the said Baptist Convention . . .[49]

This act is of significance because it gave a religious body, Georgia Baptists, through their Convention, power to govern and make laws for governing, a community in conjunction with the operation of a religious-owned institution. And, with the period 1838-1839 in the background, Mercer University was on its own, with trustees and all funds from the Convention for Mercer were in the care of Mercer trustees. Thereafter the University was largely self-governed through these trustees, with annual reports submitted to the Convention, and trustees being named by the Convention. B. M. Sanders was elected first president, on a temporary basis, and Sherwood became professor of Sacred Literature and Moral Philosophy.[50]

A look at the mission activities of the Convention as recounted in the report of the Executive Committee is valid at this point. In the report for 1839, the Committee said it had

> . . . been deeply affected with the destitute conditions of many parts of the state and have prosecuted . . . the supplying of such sections with the preaching of the Gospel.[51]

Missionary Chastain had been named to labor in the northern part of the state, but was ill and failed to accomplish much. A Brother Phillips reported 100 days of service; a Brother Pearson 70 days labor preaching 70 sermons, aiding in the constitution of one church, baptizing three persons,

[49]*Loc. cit.*
[50]*Ibid.*, p. 7.
[51]*Ibid.*, p. 12.

helping to ordain several deacons, and for this effort was paid $46.70. Joshuah Mercer, ministering as an itinerant missionary in the Southern part of the state, reported 162 days labor, travelling 1,855 miles, preaching 107 sermons, baptizing 31 persons, aiding in the contribution of one church, for which he was paid $162.00.

> Bro. Mercer [Joshuah] states that he met with a family in this State, in which there were two children 14 years old, who had never heard a sermon before, and that all the younger children had never been to a meeting. On one occasion a lady with a small child, walked 8 miles to a night meeting. He represents the destitution as vastly distressing.[52]

This report was typical of those submitted by the Executive Committee to the Convention on missionary activity during the 1830's and into the 1840's when mission activity was to be accelerated. As a pattern of future concern, and future operations, it is significant that money for books for students was being allocated, expenses being paid for a delegate to attend the Triennial Convention, and additionally, a report of the payment of $160 for the support of two youths who were orphans of indigent Baptist ministers; the first recorded support for orphan children.[53]

For the first time since constitutional amendments were approved in 1835, the Amended Constitution was reproduced in the entire text in 1839, and is as follows:

> Constitution of the Baptist Convention for the State of Georgia, as Altered and Amended.
> 1. This body is constituted upon those principles of Christian faith exhibited in Scripture, and generally acknowledged and received in the Baptist denomination.
> 2. The constituents of this body are the Baptist Associations in the state of Georgia, or as many of them as may think proper to accede to the terms of this Convention; and also two delegates from such auxiliary societies as contribute annually to our funds, whose constitutions may be approved.
> 3. It shall be known and distinguished by the name of "The Baptist Convention for the State of Georgia,"

[52]*Loc. cit.*
[53]*Ibid.*, p. 13.

and shall form the organ of general communication for the denomination throughout the State.

4. Each association may send not less than five, and not more than eight delegates to represent them in this body; and all delegates shall hold their appointments until others are elected to succeed them.

5. The officers of this union shall be a Moderator, a Clerk and Assistant Clerk, and a Treasurer, who shall be appointed by ballot at each annual meeting, and shall form a committee of the body during the recess of the meeting; but this committee may be increased as occasion may require; and have authority to fill any vacancies which may happen, and also that of the Treasurer.

6. The moderator shall perform the same duties that devolve on Moderators in the several associations, and in addition to this, shall be authorized to call meetings of the committee in the interval of annual meetings, should he deem it expedient.

7. The Clerk shall enter in a book, all the transactions of this body. The Assistant Clerk shall take charge of all distant communications, to or from this body, and shall write all the letters which it may require.

8. The Treasurer shall take charge of all monies, specialties, and property of all kinds, belonging to the body—give sufficient security for the amount in his hands—report the state of the funds from time to time, as the convention may direct—and hand over to his successor in office all its monies, property, etc.

9. Questions of difficulty may be referred from any of the individual associations, to the deliberation and advice of this body.

10. The acts and proceedings of this body shall be submitted, from time to time, to its constituents for inspection; and none of its decisions shall be binding on the associations or auxiliaries.

11. The following are the specific objects of this body, viz: — 1. To unite the influence and pious intelligence of Georgia Baptists, and thereby to facilitate their union and cooperation. 2. To form and encourage plans for the revival of experimental and practical religion in the State and elsewhere. 3. To aid in giving effect to useful plans of the several associations. 4. To afford an opportunity to those who may conscientiously think it their duty to form a fund for the education of pious young men, who may be called by the Spirit and their churches to the Christian Ministry. 5. To correspond with bodies of other religious denominations, on topics

of general interest to the Redeemer's kingdom, and to promote pious and useful Education in the Baptist denomination.

12. It shall have power to form rules, make arrangements, and appoint committees for the accomplishment of any and all the above objects: accomplishment of any and all the above objects: *Provided,* none of those rules and arrangements shall be inconsistent with the Scriptures and the known principles of the Associations.

13. Two-thirds of the whole number of delegates shall form a quorum, and a majority shall decide a question.

14. When its funds will justify it, this body may send delegates to the General Convention of our denomination of the United States.

15. The above constitution shall be liable to amendment or alteration by two-thirds of the delegates present, provided the change may have been proposed by a member of the Convention at the preceding meeting.[54]

REGULATIONS FOR BENEFICIARIES

In 1828, the Convention had adopted a set of regulations for receipt of educational funds by beneficiaries. They were reprinted from time to time for more than a decade and are cited.

1. Every person proposed to participate in this benefit, shall produce a regular license from the church of which he is a member, to preach the gospel in her bounds, accompanied by a certificate of his good acceptance among his brethren, and of his good report in the community at large.

2. He shall undergo an examination by and receive the approbation of the Executive Committee of the Body, as to his call of God, to the Gospel Ministry, his gifts and talents commending him to this grace, his destitution of the means to acquire an education, and the fellowship of the church to which he belongs, with the associate churches around her.

3. He shall put on that course of study and degree of improvement which, all things considered, he and the committee shall mutually approve.

4. He shall be required to submit to the direction and government of the Convention and to preach during his studies as much as practicable.

[54]*Ibid.,* p.p. 21-22.

5. He shall forfeit the confidence and aid of the convention, on apostasizing from the orthodox faith, or becoming immoral in practice, or unworthy in any wise in the public estimation.[55]

It was to the 19th anniversary meeting of the Convention at Penfield, in 1840, that Jesse Mercer offered to give to the Convention: "The Institution of the Christian Index, having been transferred to me by the Board of Foreign Missions, for publication in the south . . ." [56]

In this author's *A History of The Christian Index, 1822-1954,* there is quoted a letter written in May, 1831, by W. T. Brantly, Sr., to Jesse Mercer, in which Brantly, then publishing *The Index* in Philadelphia, outlined his plan for moving the paper from that city.

I have, of late, thought much of the state of things in South Carolina and Georgia, in reference to *The Index*. The time has come when a southern paper of the kind that I am editing, will be required for Carolina, Georgia, and Alabama. As mine is already taken there, and the difficulties of mail transmission are many, I have thought it probable that it would be acceptable to the brethren in that region to encourage the idea of an entire removal of *The Index* to some central point in one or the other of the two states.[57]

The letter is quoted in the light of Mercer's statement in his offer of *The Index* to the Convention that it had been transferred to him by the Board of Foreign Missions. Although *The Index* maintained nominal ties to the Triennial Convention under Brantly's editorship, internal evidence made clear the fact that Brantly was the sole figure of authority, with the right to give, sell, or otherwise dispose of *The Index* as he chose. It was moved to Georgia in 1833.[58]

[55]*Ibid.,* p. 22.

[56]*Minutes, Georgia Baptist Convention,* 1840, p. 5.

[57]James Adams Lester, *A History of The Christian Index, 1822-1954,* [Unpublished Master's Thesis, 1955,] p. 25, quoting Samuel Boykin, *History of Georgia Baptists with Biographical Compendium* [Atlanta: James P. Harrison Co., 1881], p. 199.

[58]Lester, p. 28.

It is from this background therefore, that some six and one half years later, Mercer was to offer to give the paper to the Convention. After some deliberation, the Convention accepted unanimously a report of a special committee named to study the matter under the following conditions:

> 1. That said proposition be accepted, embracing all the operations of the department from the 1st January, 1840.
> 2. That the Convention regard this proposition as another expression of Bro. Mercer's liberality toward this body; and it is hoped that he will accept our thanks for his generous offer; and receive our assurance that the feelings which prompted him are highly appreciated.
> 3. That the management of the Institution, be turned over to the Executive Committee, to be controlled by them, as shall in their judgment most successfully secure the object of the revered Donor.
> 4. That the Executive Committee be requested to relieve the Senior Editor from unnecessary labor for the balance of the year, by obtaining additional assistance.
> 5. That the institution be removed to Penfield by the 1st January, 1841, if practicable, and the property in Washington be disposed of to the best advantage.[59]

Thus the Convention accepted the paper, about which the Executive Committee was to say some 16 years later, in proposing sale of it, that no other single item had been more vexatious or a source of perplexity than operation of the paper.[60]

Finding an apparent loophole in the Convention Constitution, the group in 1840 approved amending the Constitution to assure that delegates who were regular members of Baptist churches only should be seated. Reason for the action is found in a report which said

> . . . That although no other than regular members of Baptist Churches, have ever taken their seats as delegates in this body, yet as persons of a different character are not expressly excluded; we deem it proper, and all the more effectually, to guard the body against injurious suspicions. . .

[59]*Minutes, Georgia Baptist Convention*, 1840, p. 6, item 6.
[60]*Minutes, Georgia Baptist Convention*, 1856, p. 20.

such action should be taken.[61] The Constitution, Article Two, was amended to read:

> And also two delegates, who shall be members of regular Baptist Churches, from such auxiliary societies as contribute annually, Sc.[62]

One of the more interesting items in the report of the trustees to the Convention included the notation that during the past summer, a faculty member, Dr. Tolefree, had spent $1,100 in New York ". . . . for a philosophical apparatus . . ." for the university.[63]

With the inclusion of *The Index* in the official Convention family, there began to appear annually in the minutes reports of a publication committee, which included not only remarks concerning the paper, but other publications. This publication committee was in later years to indicate loose ties with publication societies throughout the country, and especially the Savannah Baptist Publication Society; with Convention funds expended in support of various publication groups.

Publication or endorsement of other publications is implied in the report of this committee when it endorsed the Mother's Monthly Journal, and indicated that ". . . our own *Christian Index, Temperance Banner,* and *Southern Baptist Preacher,* merit much more patronage than they find." [64]

SUMMARY:

In the period 1822 through 1840, the Georgia Baptist Convention was to place itself in position for ministries both in actual operation and in prototype patterns. These formative years put the Convention in "running gear," carried it through the worst period of mission and anti-mission dissension, and served as a time for the establishment of policies and procedures upon which the Convention was to build in successive years. During these years a constitution was

[61]*Minutes, Georgia Baptist Convention,* 1840, p. 7.
[62]*Loc. cit.*
[63]*Loc. cit.*
[64]*Ibid.,* p. 13.

adopted—and amended several times; an Executive Committee was established; a university was conceived and placed into operation; provision for ministerial education was made; attention was directed toward missions—state, home and foreign—and an atmosphere of co-operation in all areas of the convention's ministry was established.

No single person emerged during these years of organizational life as forcefully as did Jesse Mercer. No single association presented as united and progressive front for advance as did the Georgia. Next to the Georgia, the Savannah area, under the names of the Savannah River Association until 1818, and the Sunbury Association after 1818, produced a large share of Convention leadership, and much of what the Convention was to accomplish in later years was based upon the stature of men in these areas, as well as to organizational ministries at the associational level.

The influence of Adiel Sherwood was felt to a large degree as a "front-runner" favoring an educated ministry as well as his activities as an itinerant minister-missionary.

These years saw also the establishment of a state paper, as well as emphasis upon Sabbath schools, a tract ministry, a book depository and colporteur ministry. Missionaries and field agents covered the state in behalf of Convention interests.

It can be said with justification that the year 1841 marked a turning point in Georgia Baptist life with the death of Jesse Mercer, and the influence of a more diversified leadership into Convention life.

And, the Convention needed all the strength it had gained by this time. Emerging into a positive, non-apologetic missionary stance, the Convention was soon to become immersed in difficulties which were to lead in a little more than four years to organization of the Southern Baptist Convention. Influence of Northern abolitionists upon the several boards of missions, and upon national Baptist life in general, was to create difficulties which Georgia Baptists, along with other Southern states, were to face.

However, the foundation was laid, and solidly. Theological positions on many issues had been clarified in circular letters, and the strength of the Separatist, partially-Calvinistic position which was to mark those who identified themselves as "members of regular Baptist churches", and who cooperated in the work of the Georgia Baptist Convention, was quite evident.

CHAPTER 7

1841 to The Edge of War

The years 1840 to 1860 were years of increasing internal dissension within the United States; particularly upon the subject of slavery. Growing abolitionist strength in the Northern states was beginning to be evident in actions and attitudes of the Triennial Convention. In turn, these sentiments were reflected in the state Conventions as the Conventions' delegates returned to the Southern states with reports of activities and events at the Triennial Convention. As early as 1841, at the session in Thomaston, the report of the Executive Committee said: ". . . that this Convention highly approve the stand taken by said Committee towards the Board of Managers of Foreign Missions, on the subject of abolition, . . ." [1] The stand of the Board of Managers was reflected in the report of the delegates to the Convention, which said that in the election, ". . . all known abolitionists were left off the Board of Foreign Missions." [2]

The Georgia delegates, in their report, declared they had expressed their disapproval of a move to introduce new tests of good standing in fellowship in the Convention, they

> . . . deem it their duty and privilege to record their full conviction, that no new tests unauthorized by the Scriptures, and by the established usages of the great body of churches, should be suffered to interfere with the harmonious operation of these benevolent Associations. . . [3]

[1] *Minutes, Georgia Baptist Convention*, 1841, p. 6.
[2] *Ibid.*, Appendix 1, p. 7.
[3] *Loc. cit.*

The associations referred to were the Baptist General Convention of the United States; The American Baptist Home Missionary Society, and the American and Foreign Bible Society.[4] Thus, 19 years before the actual outbreak of the War Between the States, rumblings of discontent upon the subject of slavery were being felt in the Georgia Baptist Convention.

By this year, *The Christian Index,* accepted by the Convention during the 1840 session, had been removed to Penfield.

> A large and commodious building has been erected for it, 60 feet by 24, and two stories high, at a cost of $1429.25; and the first number of the ninth volume was published in Penfield, 1st January, 1841.[5]

Jesse Mercer purchased the old building in Washington in which *The Index* had been printed for $400,[6] and in the settlement with Mercer, ". . . for the paper last year, it appears to have saved $103.37 over all its expenses." [7]

Support of foreign missions had begun to suffer because of changing sentiments concerning slavery. Several associational meetings the preceding Fall had decreased substantially their contributions for Foreign Missions.[8] The report to the Convention on the decline in giving said

> . . . the principles cause alleged, was the interference of Northern brethren with our domestic relations, and apprehensions entertained by many of the brethren here, that members of the Foreign Board were themselves more or less concerned.[9]

Internal evidence at this point indicates some discussion concerning the turning over of Georgia funds to the treasurer of the General Convention. Referring obviously to slavery, the Foreign Board informed the Georgia Committee that

> in these matters they were neutral in their official capacity, leaving us to infer, that in their individual capacity they might be guilty.[10]

[4]*Loc. cit.*
[5]*Minutes, Georgia Baptist Convention,* 1841, p. 8.
[6]*Loc. cit.*
[7]*Ibid.,* p. 9.
[8]*Loc. cit.*
[9]*Loc. cit.*
[10]*Loc. cit.*

The money was paid despite some apprehension.[11] However, during the months preceding the meeting of the Convention, the Foreign Board had felt it necessary to send H. Lincoln, their treasurer, to discuss with the Georgia Convention Executive Committee the matter of funds for foreign missions, and the attitudes of Board members.[12]

The Georgia delegates, B. M. Sanders and Thomas Stocks, said of their attendance at the Baltimore Convention:

> From a ten days intercourse with our Northern brethren in private and in public we can confidently say, that we see no reason to apprehend any future disturbance of the most cordial cooperation of the North and South in the grand design of evangelizing the world.[13]

A financial decline in mission giving made itself felt in parallel ways also. "Tight" money had forced by this time a reduction in room and board for Mercer students to $7.00 per month, and the labor of the students was being paid for at the rate of 5¢ per hour.[14]

The Mississippi Baptist Convention was organized in 1836.[15] Sometime around 1838, a Southwestern Baptist Home Mission Society was formed at Columbus, Mississippi, by R. T. Daniel, of North Carolina. This Society died apparently sometime in 1841 after the Georgia Convention had held its annual session.[16]

In the report of the Committee on Publications for that year, in citing the need for presenting the claims of Sabbath school Bible class instruction, the Committee said:

> It is known to some of our brethren that some little time since there was organized at Columbus, Mississippi, the Southwestern Home Mission Society, for the purpose of sustaining missionary labor in destitute regions in the South and west. It has been thought by some that it might be highly beneficial to modify and extend the

[11]*Loc. cit.*

[12]*Loc. cit.*

[13]*Minutes, Georgia Baptist Convention,* 1841, p. 8.

[14]*Ibid.,* p. 12.

[15]*Encyclopedia of Southern Baptists,* Vol. II. [Nashville, Broadman Press, 1958] p. 885.

[16]*Ibid.,* p. 886; *Minutes, Georgia Baptist Convention,* 1841, p. 5.

plans of this society, or to form some new organization which should concentrate more fully the energies of the entire south upon the cause of home missions. Such a society might, with great propriety, embrace in their plans the religious instruction of our more destitute colored population, and the new and interesting field of the Texian Republic.[17]

Again was evident some fear, upon the part of at least some members of the Convention, that the American Baptist Home Missionary Society might fall into the hands of abolitionists.

By 1842, the Convention was in correspondence with the Hearn Manual Labor School at Cave Spring [18] which was to result in that school becoming in 1844 [19] a member of the Convention family, and its second educational institution for male students. It was found necessary for the Convention in this year to affirm that control of the female institution at Penfield was in the hands of the Convention and not of the Mercer trustees.[20] There was some apparent move, not clear in the minutes, to place this institution under the Mercer trustees.

Jesse Mercer had died in 1841. The man who in life loomed so large upon the horizon of Georgia Baptist expansion, in death was the object of Convention discussion and action. The Board of Trustees of Mercer University, in that year, said that since Mercer had died during the year, and since he

. . . had outlived his nearest relatives, and had devoted his useful life to the interest of the church and his country, and in his death had bequeathed his earthly substance to benevolent objects, his final burial may properly be considered at the direction of his brethren. The Board would ask the counsel of the Convention in relation to the place, the time and the manner of his final interment.[21]

[17]*Minutes, Georgia Baptist Convention,* 1841, p. 15.
[18]*Minutes, Georgia Baptist Convention,* 1842, p. 6.
[19]*Minutes, Georgia Baptist Convention,* 1844, p.p. 6, 7.
[20]*Minutes, Georgia Baptist Convention,* 1842, p. 6.
[21]*Ibid.,* p. 9.

Mercer, who died near Indian Springs September 6, 1841,[22] left his money to Mercer University in the following manner.

> In the disposition of his effects, after liberal bequests to various benevolent societies, he devised $12,500 in bank stock to this institution, and to the Theological Department of it, $10,000 in bank stock, and a residuary legacy that may be worth 20 or $25,000. We regret the necessity of adding that his relatives have thought proper to endeavor to overturn the will and thus frustrate the execution of his benevolent designs.[23]

And, beginning with the minutes of 1842, there was a report on deceased ministers by a committee which was not formed until the death of Mercer. The Convention requested the trustees of Mercer to make ". . . arrangements for the final interment of his remains, and for the erection of a plain substantial monument over his grave," requesting also that some individual be named to prepare Mercer's memoirs.[24]

And, long before the days of Alcoholics Anonymous, there was a committee report noting

> . . . with gratitude and thankfulness to God, the great success which has attended the efforts of the society of reformed drunkards which originated at Baltimore not two years sence. . .[25]

Active participation in the Convention by the associations continued to increase. By 1843, the Georgia, Central, Columbus, Hephzibah, Coosa, Rehoboth, Flint River, Apalatchee, Sunbury, Sarepta, Western, and Washington Associations, twelve in all, were represented, along with several missionary societies.[26]

The Convention, in 1843, passed as an apparent routine motion, one allocating $40 for the printing of a catechism for children [27] and heard also that because of the loss by fire of the main College building in January of that year,

[22]Charles D. Mallary, *Memoirs of Jesse Mercer,* New York: John Gray, 1844, p. 384.

[23]*Minutes, Georgia Baptist Convention,* 1842, p. 9.

[24]*Ibid.,* p. 16.

[25]*Ibid.,* p. 12.

[26]*Minutes, Georgia Baptist Convention,* 1843, p. 3.

plans for final burial of Jesse Mercer were still incomplete.[28]

For the first time since its founding 10 years earlier, Mercer University was in trouble financially. Citing inability to collect interest due from funds on deposit by the Institution, the trustees reported to the Convention they were behind a year's salary to the faculty.[29] As a consequence of this report, the Convention instructed that group to issue a circular informing holders of notes that suits for collection would be instituted if the interest were not paid.[30] This threat to sue for interest due was the first time that the Convention made any move to use the legal authority which its Executive Committee had in a court of law.

The situation at Mercer during 1842 and 1843 apparently was severe enough for all officers of the institution to offer their immediate resignations in December of 1842; which resignations were not accepted because of a lack of a quorum of trustees present.[31] However, sometime shortly before the Convention met in 1843, the trustees did meet with a quorum, and accepted the resignations of the faculty and made plans to elect a new group in July of that year.[32]

Declines in giving affected not only Mercer and mission causes, but the underlying concern over the direction of the American Baptist mission societies was evident annually. The Executive Committee in 1843 said:

> That, as our confidence in the integrity and judgment of the Board of Foreign Missions, in their management of the important concerns committed to their charge, remain unabated; we earnestly recommend to our brethren that they send up liberal contributions for foreign missions, that that body may be enabled to fulfill existing contracts. . .[33]

[27]*Ibid.*, p. 8.
[28]*Ibid.*, p. 9.
[29]*Ibid.*, p. 8.
[30]*Ibid.*, p. 9.
[31]*Loc. cit.*
[32]*Loc. cit.*
[33]*Ibid.*, p. 11.

State Mission Secretaries

J. H. DeVotie
1877-1891

John G. Gibson
1891-1900

S. Y. Jameson
1900-1906

J. J. Bennett
1906-1914

Arch C. Cree
1915-1930

James White Merritt
1930-1954

(Photographs Copied By Doyle Middlebrooks)

(Photograph By James A. Lester)

Searcy S. Garrison
Executive Secretary-Treasurer
1955

Servants of the Denomination.

(Left to right) Edmund D. Keith, Searcy S. Garrison, Miss Dorothy Pryor and Julian T. Pipkin. Each of these has served from 15 to 20 years.

Seated, left to right, Mrs. LaNette Callaway, Miss Alexine Gibson, Mrs. Mary Ellen Haralson, Mrs. Helen Goodwin, Miss Lona Dellenger Mrs. Catherine Belnap.

Standing, Earle F. Stirewalt, Jack U. Harwell, James F. Gray, O. Bruce Barbour. Each has served from 10 to 15 years.

Aerial View, Campus of Mercer University, Macon.

Georgia Baptist Hospital
Main Building

SOUTHERN EMPHASIS GROWS

While no overt mention of any body such as a Southern Baptist Convention is found in minutes of the Georgia Convention prior to organization of that group, there is enough internal evidence to indicate that what the brethren were not printing in the minutes, they were saying to each other. The earlier indication of communications between Georgia and South Carolina leaders concerning institutions with a "Southern" slant and emphasis has been noted.

Once again, in 1843, while closing out the subject of a cooperative effort between Georgia and South Carolina for a center for theological education, this emphasis was apparent again. Repeating that because of restrictions in the two states upon funds pledged, a union for such a school would cost South Carolina between $20,000 and $30,000 and Georgia, between $50,000 and $70,000, a study committee none-the-less said:

> While however, they thus believe, they deeply feel the solemn consideration, that under present arrangements these difficulties can never decrease, but will continue to augment—and that posterity must receive at our hands a fettered system of effort in behalf of Theological Education, and they cannot but think that, if all the Southern states would heartily unite in this great object, the benefits resulting therefrom would be such, as amply to repay any necessary sacrifice on the part of the different individual States in question.
>
> They therefore most respectfully submit to the Convention, and through their minutes to our brethren of the other States, whether this desirable object may not be worthy of most serious consideration and effort—whether such a union of all the Southern States may not be formed for this purpose, as may well recompense very great losses in our present funds. [Signed in behalf of the committee by J. G. Binney] [34]

This appears to be ample evidence of growing sentiment upon the part of the Georgia brethren for union with other Southern states in education. Earlier references to possible approaches to other mission groups such as the Southwestern Baptist Home Mission Society, continued expressions of con-

[34]*Ibid.*, 1843, Item F., p.p. 11, 12.

cern, and the necessity of assurances that monies sent by Georgia were being handled satisfactory to the interests of the Georgia brethren, all served as a barometer to the thinking concerning some type of southern union of conventions. And, to read other than the seeds of the present Southern Baptist Theological Seminary into this particular report, would be inaccurate.

The character of the Minutes, reflecting a change in the character of the conduct of business upon the floor of the Convention, was evident following Mercer's death, although this *could* have been incidental to the change. The Minutes began to reflect Convention procedure whereby reports of various committees were called up, and referred to committees to study the reports of the standing committees, and then referred back to the Convention for action. The evident guiding hand of Mercer upon the committees was absent. They appeared to function more independently. This was a fixed pattern until the 1860's.[35] Little Convention business dealing with reports was transacted until brought back to the Convention floor following special study by committees named at the current sessions of the Convention.

Also for a few years, beginning with 1843, there appeared in the Convention Minutes paragraph reports dealing with the state of the several associations.[36] As the number of participating associations increased, this practice was discontinued.

With the 1844 session, preceded by some discussion during 1843, the Convention agreed to accept officially the Cave Spring School from patrons of that school with the statement:

> Resolved, that this Convention are willing to take said institution under their control, and to recommend to the patrons that when they transfer the power of electing a Board of Trustees, the transfer be made to the

[35]*Minutes, Georgia Baptist Convention,* years 1842-1863.
[36]*Minutes, Georgia Baptist Convention,* 1843, p.p. 12, 13.

Executive Committee of the Baptist Convention of the state of Georgia.[37]

Including Mercer, the female institution at Penfield, and the Hearn Manual Labor School at Cave Spring, the Convention was sponsor and operator of three institutions of learning. Additionally, the Convention was providing funds regularly for ministerial education at small schools or academies which were beginning to spring up in towns across Georgia.

It was not until that session that the Mercer trustees were able to report that:

> A decree of the Court in the county of Wilkes has been obtained for the payment to the Treasurer of the entire legacy bequeathed to the Institution by the Rev. Jesse Mercer in his last will, and a part of it has already been paid over. His library has also been received and added to the Library of the institution.[38]

Of particular significance to the long-range history of Georgia Baptists is the fact that in that year also there was a move to have standing committees appointed by the Convention to superintend some of the work of the Convention which has been entrusted to the case of the Executive Committee. A special committee named to study the matter said:

> They conceive however desirable the appointment of such committees might be in itself, for the purpose of dividing the arduous labors which now rest upon the hands of the Executive Committee, that it would be difficult so to organize them as to secure extended, permanent and efficient action. The appointment by the Executive Committee of efficient Agents, to travel extensively in the State, and present the claims of the leading benevolent objects of this body, would probably be the wiser course.[39]

Such a proposed dilution of the authority of the Executive Committee in terms of active operation of the Convention's programs was not to occur again in this fashion; the authority

[37]*Minutes, Georgia Baptist Convention,* 1844, p.p. 6, 7. The Convention met in Cave Spring that year. [1844, p. 1.]

[38]*Ibid.,* p. 11.

[39]*Ibid.,* p. 12.

and functions of the Executive Committee being well enough established by this time to show not only its usefulness, but the apparent necessity of the pattern of operation then in use.

The break between the North and South in the denomination the next year was foreshadowed in 1844 when a report from the Georgia delegates to the Triennial Convention said:

> It is not to be disguised that there is a considerable party among our Northern brethren, with whom the great cause of Foreign and Home missions has lost much of its interest, in their absorbing concern for the colored people of the South. Some of these infatuated individuals were bitter in spirit—uncourteous in expression and unsparing in their denunciations. . . .

However, the delegates declared:

> . . . We take great pleasure in believing that an overwhelming majority of our brethren in the free States, are men in whom 'an excellent spirit' prevails. These are willing to leave domestic slavery where the scriptures leave it, where the constitution of our country leaves it, and where the constitutions of all our great benevolent institutions leave it, viz: with those involved in it.[40]

SOUTHERN CONVENTION ORGANIZED

The Southern Baptist Convention was organized in the Baptist church, Augusta, May 8-12, 1845.[41]

There was growing awareness of the need for Sabbath schools during the 1840's, with reports concerning this need appearing almost annually. The committee which made the report on Sabbath Schools for 1844, outlined a plan which basically is evident today in Sunday School structure. It submitted a plan which called for a superintendent to open the school with reading and exposition of the Scriptures, and closing with singing ". . . in which all the scholars and children shall join." [42] The plan outlined called also for an assistant superintendent, and teachers, and along with the Sabbath school a Bible class to meet ". . . at the same or

[40]*Ibid.*, 1844, p.p. 13-14.
[41]*Encyclopedia of Southern Baptists*, Vol. II, p. 1244, [Background for organization of the Convention is documented amply in this work.]
[42]*Minutes, Georgia Baptist Convention*, 1844, p.p. 14, 15.

another hour and which should differ from a class in the Sabbath school, only by requiring all who join it to be able to read; and also in the use of Question book. . ."[43]

Interest in curtailing the use of alcoholic beverages in the state continued evident upon the part of Georgia Baptists, and the Convention gave apparent approval to the report of a Committee on Temperance [which made irregular reports] that during a recent session of the Legislature,

> . . . there was not a solitary Tavern in Milledgeville which kept a public bar during the session . . . last winter, and that very few members kept ardent spirits in their rooms.[44]

This, the committee took to be a sign encouraging to the temperance movement.

Reports of the activities in the associations indicated that suggestions to educate Negroes had been followed at least in the Sunbury [Savannah area and northward], with the Sunbury reporting for 1843 there were 302 members received by baptism ". . . mostly blacks."[45] The report declared there had been a missionary serving that association among the blacks along the Savannah for a year, and for about six months, one serving blacks along the Altamaha.[46]

Only four days after the Southern Baptist Convention was organized in Augusta, the Georgia Baptist Convention convened at Forsyth, in Monroe county, some 100 air miles west southwest of Augusta. The time and location are significant because in less than a week after formation of the larger convention, the Georgia Convention "Resolved, That all monies contribute for Foreign Missions be paid over to Dr. W. B. Johnson, the agent for the F. M. Board of the S. B .C."[47]

Concurrent with formation of the Southern Baptist Convention, had been formation of the Foreign Mission Board

[43]*Ibid.,* p. 15.
[44]*Ibid.,* p.p. 15, 16.
[45]*Ibid.,* p. 18.
[46]*Loc. cit.*
[47]*Minutes, Georgia Baptist Convention,* 1845, p. 7.

of the Southern Baptist Convention, as well as the Home Mission Board, known as the Southern Baptist Domestic Mission Board. The record does not indicate that funds intended for the foreign mission interests of the Triennial Convention had been withheld previously. However, the record does indicate that funds intended for the American Baptist Home Mission Society during 1844 and early in 1845 had been withheld from that society by the Executive Committee.

When the committee to study the report of the Executive Committee for 1845 made its report, that body approved, and suggested approval by the Convention, of the withholding of the funds until the 1845 meeting, and the Convention instructed the Executive Committee ".... to pay over the same to the Southern Baptist Domestic Mission Board at Marion, Alabama." [48]

It followed almost as a logical conclusion that the Georgia Convention would endorse the organization of the Southern Convention; so recommended by the Executive Committee which must have drafted hastily a portion of its report between May 12 and May 16. The study committee for the Executive Committee report, in its statement to the Convention said:

> The Committee appointed to report on the article of the report of Executive Committee relating to the Southern Baptist Convention, submit the following:— While this body deeply regrets the necessity of separating from our Northern brethren, we highly approve the action of the late meeting in Augusta; and earnestly recommend our churches and brethren throughout the State to support this southern organization, with liberal benevolent contributions. Therefore,
> Resolved, That this Convention become auxiliary to the Southern Baptist Convention, and proceed to elect five Delegates to represent us in the meeting of that body to be held, Thursday before 2d Lord's day in June 1846. A. Williams chairman.[49]

The apparent tensions which developed during 1843-1845

[48]*Ibid.*, p. 11.
[49]*Loc. cit.*

between Georgia Baptists and the leadership in the Triennial Convention were evident in mission giving. During 1844, for example, the Executive Committee reported that for the entire year, they had received only $83.38 for domestic missions, and that had it not been for help from the Georgia Association, the Convention could not even have sustained one missionary. However, and this is of significance in emerging patterns of Convention and Associational structure, the report revealed that:

> For a few years past nearly all the Benevolent Churches send up their funds for the object to their own Association, many of which are now actively engaged in Domestic Mission labor.[50]

And, minute reports for the associations, as appearing in the digested report of the Committee on Domestic Missions for several years, especially in the early 1840's, support this statement. Once organized, the associations, as soon as possible, started missionary activity within their own boundaries, supported by churches in the associations.[51]

"SEPARATE" BENEVOLENT ORGANIZATIONS

By 1845, trustees of Mercer felt certain enough of the future, of the institution to contract for a chapel [currently in use as the Penfield Baptist church] to cost $7,000, and to be of brick 58 feet by 75 feet with an 11-foot projection in front to be supported by six large pillars.[52]

The manual labor department of the institution was suspended that year, and trustees reported three students for theological education, twenty-three in the collegiate department, and forty-fiive in the "academical" department, for a total of 71 students.[53]

At the 1846 session in Macon, it was necessary also in the eyes of the delegates for the Convention to go on record:

That [in] the opinion of this Convention, it is expedient

[50]*Ibid.*, 1845, p. 12.
[51]*Minutes, Georgia Baptist Convention,* 1840-1845.
[52]*Minutes, Georgia Baptist Convention,* 1845, Item K, p. 14.
[53]*Ibid.*, p.p. 14, 15.

for the Southern Baptist Convention to adopt such a
course at their meeting in Richmond as will unequivo-
cally separate the South from the North in all the
general organizations for Christian benevolence.[54]

Constitutional amendments had been proposed in 1845
dealing with representation from associations and auxiliary
societies. The proposed amendments included deletion of
authority to send delegates to the General Convention and
including associations not in the State of Georgia.[55]

The application of the Florida Baptist Association in 1846
for membership in the Georgia Baptist Convention, was
made in 1846 and approved subject to constitutional
change.[56] Alterations appear in an amended and altered
constitution approved by the 1846 Convention. The Constitution, as approved in 1846, is as follows, and is reproduced, as are others, in order to indicate the changes, however slight, which occurred in the official document of the
Convention:

Constitution of the Baptist Convention of the State of Georgia as altered and amended.

1. This Body is constituted upon those principles of
Christian faith exhibited in Scripture, generally acknowledged and received in the Baptist denomination.
2. The constituents of this Body are the Baptist associations in the State of Georgia, or as many of them as may
think proper to accede to the terms of this Convention,
and such Auxiliary Societies as contribute annually to
our funds, whose constitutions may be approved.
Associations and Societies located out of the State may
be received into the Body, when their peculiar location,
and other circumstances, may in the judgment of this
Convention, render it desirable and important.
3. It shall be known and distinguished by the name of
"The Baptist Convention for the state of Georgia."
4. Each auxiliary society shall be entitled to two delegates to represent it in this body, and each Association
to any number not exceeding ten; all delegates shall
hold their appointments until others are elected to

---

[54]*Minutes, Georgia Baptist Convention,* 1846, p. 7.
[55]*Minutes, Georgia Baptist Convention,* 1845, p.p. 15-17.
[56]*Minutes, Georgia Baptist Convention,* 1846, p.p. 3, 4.

succeed them. The delegates to the body shall be orderly members of regular Baptist Churches.

5. The officers of this union shall be a Moderator, a
Clerk and Assistant Clerk, and a Treasurer, who shall
be appointed by ballot at each annual meeting, and
shall form a committee of the Body during the decess
of the meeting, but this committee may be increased as
occasion may require; and have authority to fill any
vacancies which may happen, and also that of the
Treasurer.

6. The Moderator shall perform the same duties that
devolve on moderators in the several Associations, and
in addition to this, shall be authorized to call meetings
of the committee in the interval of annual meetings,
should he deem it expedient.

7. The Clerk shall enter in a book, all the transactions of this Body.—The Assistant Clerk shall take
charge of all distant communications, to or from this
Body, and shall write all the letters which it may require.

8. The Treasurer shall take charge of all moneys,
specialties, and property of all kinds, belonging to the
body—give sufficient security for the amount in his
hands—report the state of the funds from time to time,
as the Convention may direct—and hand over to his
successor in office all its moneys, property, etc.

9. The acts and proceedings of this Body shall be submitted, from time to time, to its constituents for inspection; and none of its decisions shall be binding on the
Association or Auxiliaries.

10. The following are the specific objects of this body,
viz:

1. To unite the influence and pious intelligence
of Georgia baptists, and thereby to facilitate their
union and co-operation.

2. To form and encourage plans for the revival
of experimental and practical religion in the State
and elsewhere.

3. To aid in giving effect to useful plans of the
several Associations.

4. To afford an opportunity to those who may conscientiously think it their duty to form a fund for
the education of pious young men, who may be
called by the Spirit and their churches to the
Christian Ministry.

5. And to promote pious and useful Education
in the Baptist denomination.

11. It shall have power to form rules, make arrangements, and appoint committtees for the accomplishment of any and all the above objects; Provided, none of these rules and arrangements shall be inconsistent with the Scriptures and the known principles of the Associations.

12. Two-thirds of the whole number of delegates shall form a quorum, and a majority shall decide a question.

13. When its funds will justify it, this Body may send delegates to the Southern Baptist Convention.

14. The above Constitution shall be liable to amendment or alteration, by two-thirds for the delegates present, or at any of its annual meetings.[57]

An early prototype of present-day pastoral aid practices appeared with the 1846 Convention, when there was recommendation from the Executive Committee for the group to consider a proposition for establishing pastors in towns, finding 50 persons who would pay $20 annually for five years; 100 persons who would pay $10 each, and 200 who would pay $5 each for a total of $3,000 annually to aid destitute churches in towns and villages in supporting pastors on the condition that the churches raise monies themselves, with no one church receiving more than $300 annually.[58]

The suggestion called for these pastors to be considered missionaries of the Convention, reporting regularly to the Executive Committee, and allowing them the privilege of some other work which would not interfere with their pastoral ministries. The Executive Committee suggested that a general agent be appointed to obtain subscribers to such a plan.[59]

When implementation of this specific proposal does not show clearly from the record, it is a fact that from about this time until the War Between the States erupted, the Convention did allocate funds for construction of churches in strategic areas of the State, as well as giving some monies for erection of the houses of worship in cities outside of

[57]*Ibid.*, 1846, p.p. 8, 9.
[58]*Ibid.*, p. 12.
[59]*Loc. cit.*

Georgia. And, the pattern of support for domestic missionaries continued.

For several years, the Convention had used Turpin's Drug Store in Augusta as a Bible and tract depository, with the store selling Bibles for the Convention which had been purchased from the Bible societies in the North. For the year reported in 1846, sales up to April 27 had amounted to $453.44, with $198.76 worth of books on hand.[60] However, the Executive Committee in 1845 had refused a request from the American Baptist Publication Society to send to Georgia a representative; and they were now in favor of the formation of Southern boards for publishing religious literature.[61] This was a rather clear indication that the Georgia Convention sought, as much as possible, to sever all ties with Baptist organizational work which remained linked with Northern interests. Out of this background was to come later the several publication societies.

One problem in Baptist life which has vexed administrative personnel is indicated as far back as the year 1846 when the clerk for the Convention stated that although many churches were giving liberally to missions, the custom had been to report only that which was sent directly to the Convention. Thus, sums contributed directly to agents and others were never counted. The association and church clerks were requested to report all monies sent directly or given to agents in order that a clear picture of mission giving might be indicated.[62]

A summary paragraph for the year 1845 is in order as indicative of Convention growth, and also because the minutes for 1846 were the first in which an attempt was made to present a clear statistical table giving all pertinent information on the work of the churches and the associations. For that year, there were 46 associations, 971 churches, with some 58,388 members.[63] For 1845, there were 4,561 baptisms

[60]*Ibid.,* p. 14.
[61]*Ibid.,* p.p. 14, 15.
[62]*Ibid.,* p. 20.
[63]*Ibid.,* p. 27.

reported, with 464 ordained ministers, and "Number of licentiates incomplete 142".[64]

There were many times in the history of Georgia Baptists when that which was not said in the minutes was perhaps as indicative of trends as that which was recorded. While much emphasis had been placed upon the Sabbath school movement during the late 1830's and early 1840's, when the committee on Sunday Schools was to make its report in 1847, they reported succinctly that they were ". . . unable to obtain any facts of interest connected with Sunday Schools." [65]

A request by the Southern Baptist Publication Convention to the Georgia Baptist Convention, meeting in Savannah May 14-17, 1847, for the Convention to regulate its sessions to give the publication group opportunity for another meeting, indicates that that body was in session in Savannah at the same time.[66]

This was a publication agency designed to serve Southern Baptists, but with no organic connection with the Southern Baptist Convention. It grew out of some dissatisfaction on the part of some members with the decision of the Southern Baptist Convention in 1846 not to undertake any enterprise involving publishing and selling books.

Interested persons in the Southern Convention met in Savannah at the session of the Georgia Baptist Convention, to consider formation of a publication society. Representatives attended from Alabama, South Carolina, Virginia and Georgia. At the session, granted the group by the Georgia Convention, a constitution for a Southern Baptist Publication Society was adopted and Charleston, S. C. was chosen for headquarters.[67]

Following organization of this group,

> The various Southern organizations that had been auxiliary to the American Baptist Publication Society

[64]*Loc. cit.*
[65]*Minutes, Georgia Baptist Convention,* 1847, p. 4.
[66]*Ibid.,* p. 4.
[67]*Encyclopedia of Southern Baptists,* Vol. II. p.p. 1266-1267.

became auxiliary to the Southern Baptist Publication Society. The former society, having been organized by Southern men and largely supported until 1845 by the South, and not being a party to the controversy that forced the formation of the Southern Baptist Convention, wished to continue as the publication society for the South. However, without passion or prejudice, Southerners decided that they should have their own organization.[68]

The first publication issued by this group was the work of a Georgia pastor and denominational leader, C. D. Mallary and was a sermon entitled "The Advancement of Sabbath School Instruction," a booklet printed in 1848.[69]

This society is not to be confused with a society bearing the same name and organized in 1870 under the leadership of J. R. Graves at a meeting of the Big Hatchie Association in Tennessee. This society was in effect a stock company of Baptists.[70]

The Southern Baptist Publication Society ceased operations either late in 1863 or early in 1864.

> During its existence it received gifts of more than $100,000 for its work. It printed more than 80 different books and booklets, and sold in excess of 230,000 copies. It did much to develop Southern Baptist authors, and made a lasting contribution to Southern Baptist life.[71]

Information about this society is given because it reflects a clear pattern of strength for Baptist work in Georgia which made Georgia Baptists cooperative with plans and ideas which would advance the work of the denomination through the Southern Convention. Strong Baptist leadership in the Savannah-Charleston areas made Savannah a logical place for organization of this south-wide group.

For the first time, at an afternoon session of the Georgia Baptist Convention in 1847, it was necessary for the body to adjourn for lack of a quorum.[72]

[68]*Ibid.*, p. 1267.

[69]*Loc. cit.*

[70]*Encyclopedia of Southern Baptists,* Vol. I [Nashville, Broadman Press 1958], p. 579.

[71]*Encyclopedia of Southern Baptists,* Vol. II, p. 1267.

[72]*Minutes, Georgia Baptist Convention,* 1847, p. 7.

With a circulation of 2,700, and debts outstanding of $6,467, the Convention, accepting a recommendation of a year earlier, agreed to farm out *The Christian Index* to J. S. Baker for him to publish on his own responsibility. Terms of the arrangement are of interest.

> They [Executive Committee] therefore, entered into arrangement with brother J. B. Baker, to publish the paper, from the beginning of the present year, on his own responsibility; and for the paper, with the office and furniture, he agrees to pay $400 a year, and $1 for each of the net[t] gain of new paying subscribers yearly; to collect, as far as possible, and pay over quarterly, the amounts due to the Index, at a discount of 10 per cent for his trouble; to publish all the Committee documents free of charge; to furnish the Committee one column for advertisements, and not to fill more than four columns with paying advertisements. The paper to be printed on a sheet 24 by 36 inches . . . The contract is to run as long as both parties are content; and six months' notice is required to be given by either party before dissolution.[73]

Of the $5,988.02 appropriated by the Executive Committee during the previous year [1846] $1,043.50 went directly to the Foreign Mission Board and $603.76 to the Domestic Mission Board.[74]

And in an interesting sidelight to history—and there are many—the report of the Mercer trustees indicated that a committee named to prepare an inscription for the monument to Jesse Mercer reported acceptance of the inscription, and preparation of a slab to cover the tomb was contracted for. The slab was prepared, shipped as far as Greensboro, where it was broken, and a new slab had to be prepared.[75]

The late 1840's were "good times" for Georgia Baptists. Within a single year, four associations had been added, bringing the total to 50,[76] and for 1846, there were 1,004 churches, and at least 59,467 members. And, in the statistical tables for 1846, printed in the 1847 minutes, while the

[73]*Ibid.,* p. 15.

[74]*Ibid.,* p.p. 16, 17.

[75]*Ibid.,* p. 23.

[76]*Minutes, Georgia Baptist Convention,* 1846, p. 27.

Georgia Association did not report the number of white members, the Association did report 3,382 blacks; the Rehoboth reporting 1,229 whites and 507 blacks and the Sunbury reported 485 whites and 3,764 blacks on membership rolls.[77]

Two significant actions occurred during the 1848 session of the Convention meeting in Griffin. The Convention passed a resolution "That the Domestic Mission Fund of this State take the name of State Mission Fund." [78] And, the Convention adopted a revised and amended constitution, which made provision for an expanded Executive Committee

> . . . consisting of at least seven members, . . . whose duty it shall be to attend to the business of the Convention during its recess. This committee shall have power to fill all vacancies which may occur, and also shall appoint a Treasurer in case of a vacancy in that office.[79]

The constitutional change reflected another significant factor; that of distance, and the necessity of frequent meeting on the part of the Executive Committee. For, when the constitution was altered in 1848, it did not include the convention officers as being a mandatory part of the Executive Committee structure on the grounds that it was

> . . . necessary for the committee to be convenient to each other to facilitate their frequent meetings; but such necessity does not exist in relation to the officers of the Convention, who meet but once a year.[80]

The revised constitution of 1848 differs only in articles five and six, with six actually a new provision. This made a total of 15 articles. The amendments are given. Otherwise the Constitution is identical to the one approved in 1846, which had several changes. [See earlier this chapter.] It was recommended to the Convention by the Executive Committee that the changes be made.[81]

[77]*Minutes, Georgia Baptist Convention,* 1847, statistical tables, end of minutes, abstracts, p.p. 32, 33 unnumbered.
[78]*Minutes, Georgia Baptist Convention,* 1848, p. 17 .
[79]*Ibid.,* p. 8.
[80]*Ibid.,* p. 24.
[81]*Ibid.,* p. 7.

5. The officers of this union shall be a moderator, a clerk, and assistant clerk, and a treasurer, who shall be appointed by ballot at each annual meeting.

An Executive Committee, consisting of at least seven members, shall be chosen at each annual meeting, whose duty it shall be to attend to the business of the Convention during its recess. This Committee shall have power to fill all vacancies which may occur, and also shall appoint a Treasurer in case of a vacancy in that office.[82]

Following the change in the designation of Georgia Missions to the State Mission Fund, and beginning with 1849, there appeared a full report on State Missions, not structurally different, basically, from similar reports to be presented a century later.

Financially, the Convention exhibited during the 1840's a steady but conservative growth. The treasurer's report in 1849 reflected a balance of $40,071.11, and the report was divided into a general purpose fund, a state mission fund, a foreign mission fund, an indigent orphan fund, a mission purpose fund, a female academy fund, permanent mission fund, Baptist tract fund, Domestic [Home] mission fund, Bible cause fund, Indian mission fund, Town lot fund, and so on.[83]

State boundaries were not important in Georgia Baptist organizational structure in earlier days. For example, it has been noted earlier that the Savannah River Association until 1817 comprised churches both on the Georgia and South Carolina sides of that river. With the separation of that body, churches on the Georgia side took in 1818 the name Sunbury Association. [q.v.] Also, the Florida Association had for some years been a member of the Georgia Baptist Convention. As the first half of the 19th century ended, the Georgia Convention reported three churches and 47 members in Alabama; ten churches with 266 members in Florida; seven churches with 154 members in Tennessee, and five churches with 89 members in Alabama; [c.q.] six

[82]*Ibid.*, p.p. 19, 20.

[83]*Minutes, Georgia Baptist Convention*, p.p. 24-29.

churches with 191 members in South Carolina and three churches with 83 members in North Carolina, for membership in seven states, including Georgia.[84]

Until 1850, the Convention included consistently as constituent members missionary societies of individual Baptist churches. However, by that year, there were enough societies with representation to cause the naming of a special committee to study the matter of representation following application of the Griffin Baptist church Missionary Society. The special committee concluded:

> . . . that said Society, under the existing provisions of the constitution of the Convention, are entitled to membership and representation in said body—and therefore recommend, that said Society be received accordingly.[85]

The committee asserted that

> your committee would beg leave, further to recommend, that the constitution of the Convention, be so modified, as hereafter to exclude all auxiliary societies from direct representation, in this Convention.[86]

Thus the time had come for the Convention to begin to limit membership to Associations to provide more evenly for representation. Mission societies continued to grow, and the attitude of Georgia Baptists to missions, and especially foreign mission interests, is expressed well in a letter written May 20, 1850 by Eli Ball, an agent for the Foreign Mission Board to the moderator of the Georgia Association. Ball said:

> . . . I came almost a stranger into this State, one year ago, and, although I have traveled more than 5,000 miles among the churches, visited more than eighty congregations and preached more than two hundred sermons, I have never failed to meet a cordial reception. All have aided me, to some extent, in the objects of my mission, and some have done nobly. About $5,000 have come into the Treasury of the Foreign Mission during the year that has just now closed, from those whose piety and zeal in the Saviour's cause I shall ever delight to call to my recollection. I am, dear brother,

[84]*Minutes, Georgia Baptist Convention,* 1849, Statistical Summary, end of published Master's Thesis, 1955] p. 58.

[85]*Minutes, Georgia Baptist Convention,* 1850, p. 6.

[86]*Loc. cit.,* 1850, p. 6.

yours truly, Eli Ball.[87]

The continued interest in education was reflected at the Convention in 1850 when General Duff Green spoke upon the subject of education, and offered $20,000 to endow two institutions, a male and a female school at Dalton, provided others would contribute an additional $20,000.[88] This proposal was presented to the same Convention which rejected a proposition to move Mercer University to Griffin.[89] The Green proposal, referred to a committee for study, was reported back to the Convention. The report included the statement

> . . . that a Society called the Southern Education Society has been organized at Dalton in this state. This Society has obtained from the Legislature, acts incorporating the Society and granting charters for a Female College and University, and it is understood that the 'Dalton City company' are willing to appropriate, as part of an endowment, to each of these institutions, the sum of ten thousand dollars upon condition that other individuals, societies or associations will contribute a like sum for that purpose.[90]

In rejecting the proposal, the Committee said:

> The objects, however, of this Society, are so multifarious, and their accomplishment depends upon so many contingencies, that this Convention, at its present session, cannot act understandably upon them. . .[91]

Following the War Between the States, there was established in Dalton an institution which listed as trustees those who were for that year listed also as trustees for Mercer University, then located in Macon. However, there was no apparent organic relationship discovered between the two.[92]

Three years after the establishment of the Southern Baptist Publication Society, the Convention adopted [1850] a plan of colportage in connection with that society, with men

[87]*Ibid.,* p. 9.

[88]*Ibid.,* 1850, p. 8.

[89]*Ibid.,* p. 11.

[90]*Ibid.,* p.p. 11, 12.

[91]*Ibid.,* 1850, p. 12.

[92]Descriptive brochure, Dalton Institute, "Museum," undated. Stetson Memorial Library, Mercer University, Macon.

selected as agents to be approved by a Convention committee
and by the Society for appointment, with the rate of compensation to be set by the state Convention.[93]

MOVE TO SAVANNAH SOUGHT FOR *THE INDEX*

In an interesting move in 1851, the Savannah Baptist
Publication Society made a two-fold request of the Convention. They asked that ". . . books and money hitherto applied by this convention to the Publication Department,"
be conveyed to them, and urged that *The Christian Index*
be moved to Savannah.[94]

Agreement of the committee named to study the proposal
on funds and books transfer apparently made the Savannah
society a semi-official representative of the Georgia Convention in this area. The proposal to move the state paper
to the Coastal city was studied and referred to a select Committee, and this group approved the books transfer.[95]

It suggested that the question of moving *The Index* be
referred to the Executive Committee with instruction to
negotiate ". . . Provided that the property and ultimate
control remain in the Convention."[96] The proposal of an
Index move to Savannah was only one of many suggestions
concerning location, ownership and publication responsibility which apparently plagued the Convention and its
Executive Committee for more than 20 years; until the paper
was sold finally in 1861.[97]

On July 8, 1851, there had been scheduled in Marietta a
meeting for the purpose of organizing a state Education Convention which would seek to establish ". . . an improved
and universal system of Education, for the people of the
commonwealth."[98] Therefore, the report of the Conven-

[93]*Minutes, Georgia Baptist Convention*, 1850, p. 13.
[94]*Minutes, Georgia Baptist Convention*, 1851, p. 6.
[95]*Ibid.*, p. 11.
[96]*Ibid.*, p. 12.
[97]Lester, James A., A. History of *The Christian Index*, 1822-1954, [un-
published master's thesis, 1955] p. 58.
[98]*Minutes, Georgia Baptist Convention*, 1851, p. 13

tion's Committee on Education for 1851, delivered in May, took note of the role of secular education; declared that it did not consider itself [committee] out of bounds in recognizing the validity of a school system; cited with pleasure the efforts to establish an improved system of education; and then recommended that the Georgia Baptist Convention appoint three delegates to the proposed organizational meeting of the state Education Convention.[99]

Thus, the Convention did not consider it improper to participate, as a religious body, in plans for the formulation of a state-wide educational system. Attitudes in the area of church and state which might be looked upon as unusual today, were taken for granted and accepted as normal by 19th century Georgia Baptists.

Other examples of this attitude were to be seen in the operation of the town of Penfield by the trustees of Mercer University. Neither was it unusual for Convention funds to be allocated to students to attend a state or private institution. Willingness to accept funds from municipalities for the location of Baptist institutions also was a standard pattern; to be exploited fully in the removal of Mercer University to Macon, Georgia in 1871. Also, offers were received from both Washington and Talbotton for the proposed Southern Baptist College, and an offer was received—and rejected—from Griffin for removal of Mercer to that city in the late 1840's.

The phrasing of an agreement in 1850 for a missionary, reported in the 1851 minutes, is significant. The Convention, through its Executive Committee had for many years used the plan of itinerant missionaries, often in cooperation with the associations. Sometimes this cooperation involved the use of a person part-time. At other times, a person would be employed for a period of three months, six months, or longer. However, in the report of the Executive Committee for 1851, it was stated, concerning a missionary, that

> Upon the earnest application of the brethren in the Northern part of the State, we agreed to furnish $150

[99]*Loc. cit.*

> per annum, toward the support of bro. E. Hedden, pro-
> vided they would furnish an equal amount, which they
> agreed to do;[100]

Thus emerged, even clearer, the pattern of co-operation with the associations in a ministry by an associational missionary.

The towering interest in education upon the part of Georgia Baptists was reflected in many ways. Not only was there constant concern for Mercer, the Hearn school, and other institutions—by name—but by 1851, the permanent education fund of the Convention had grown to $30,938.67; out of a total in the treasurer's report for that year of $51,559.75.[101]

Mercer University in the meantime was doing well, reporting for 1850, 130 students,

> eighteen with the ministry in view, admitted during the
> previous year, six in the theological seminary, sixty-five
> in the college classes, eleven into the highest academic
> class, and forty-eight into the lower classes.[102]

As reflected in this and other reports, evident for many years was the fact that about half of the enrolment at Mercer, not including attendance at the "off and on" female academy, was in the lower section—or elementary level. In the same year, Mercer reported a permanent fund of $121,565.38.[103]

Not in apparent boasting, the statistical tables did, however indicate growth rates by mission and anti-mission associations. In the 1851 abstracts of records, 57 associations were reported, with 1,183 churches and 71,879 members. Baptisms for 1850 were 5,579, and the gain in membership among Convention associations was 1,900; the gain in membership in anti-mission associations thirty-nine, the gain in "neutral" associations, 238, and the gain in "United Baptist" associations, forty-eight, for a new increase of 2,225 in the state. There were listed 615 ordained ministers and 296 licentiates.[104]

[100]*Ibid.*, p. 17.
[101]*Ibid.*, p.p. 20, 24.
[102]*Ibid.*, p. 25, Report C.
[103]*Loc. cit.*
[104]*Ibid.*, statistical tables, end of minutes.

The increasing importance of the office of treasurer for the Convention was evident. In 7850, the salary of the treasurer was increased to $400 per year.[105] By 1852, at the session in Columbus, with T. J. Burney elected treasurer, the Convention:

> Resolved, That the salary of our Treasurer be adjusted by the Executive Committee in consultation with the Trustees of Mercer University on motion of brother Crawford,
> Resolved, That the Executive Committee be instructed to pay the salary of the Treasurer proportionally out of the several funds in his charge.[106]

Although the Cherokee Nation had been forced westward some 20 years earlier, the Convention, as late as 1852, still considered ". . . our Indian tribes as a very inviting field for missionary labor, which should be cultivated without delay."[107] Continued emphasis upon missions was reflected in the 1851 giving, as reported in 1852. The Foreign Mission Board was allocated $2,615.19; the Domestic Mission Board, $1,614.34, and $382.50 to state missions.[108] Interest in work among the Indians was reflected also in the fact that $1,052.54 was allocated to that work, and the Southern Baptist Publication Society was allocated $476.27; with $86.30 going to the Southern Bible Board in Nashville, and $11.00 to the American Bible Union.[109]

The Convention, meeting for the first time in Atlanta in 1853, heard from its Committee on Education a report that there were:

> Not less than seventeen Collegiate Seminaries or Institutions of a high order, and containing on an average some twenty-five hundred young ladies are now in active and successful operation; . . .

in Georgia.

> But as a Baptist State Convention, this body has one grand object which legitimately demands our best atten-

[105]*Minutes, Georgia Baptist Convention,* 1850, p. 17.
[106]*Minutes, Georgia Baptist Convention,* 1852, p. 7.
[107]*Ibid.,* p. 11.
[108]*Ibid.,* p. 16.
[109]*Ibid.,* p.p. 14, 15.

tion. The College and Theological Seminary of Mercer University are the united product of the efforts and prayers of many hundreds of our brethren, and of our fathers in the ministry. . .[110]

This report set the stage, apparently, for a report later during the Convention session from the special committee studying the Executive Committee's report which called for the Convention to turn over to the town of Penfield the female academy,[111] in the light of the fact that other educational institutions for women were beginning to spring up in communities around Georgia, and ". . . for several years, [the Penfield Female Academy] has been little more than a local institution . . ."[112]

Further evidence of the quasi-official connection with the Savannah Baptist Publication Society in Savannah lies in the fact that the Convention began to receive annual communications from this society, and named a special committee to study and report upon the work, suggesting in 1853 that:

> . . . We recommend to the several Associations, which have direct communication with Savannah, to instruct their Home Missionaries to avail themselves of the advantages which this fund affords them, for supplying their mission circuits with religious books.[113]

The same year, the Convention authorized transfer of the Bible Committee at LaGrange to Savannah, with the convention authorizing the Savannah Society to ". . . receive the funds and documents now in the hands of the Committee at LaGrange."[114]

The year 1853 was one of some importance to Georgia Baptists. They faced for the first time in several years, and in more depth, the problem of Sunday Schools, and what to do about them. It was brought to the attention of the Convention that there were few Sabbath schools, not because

[110]*Minutes, Georgia Baptist Convention,* 1853, p. 8.
[111]*Ibid.,* p. 12.
[112]*Ibid.,* p. 20.
[113]*Ibid.,* p. 14.
[114]*Loc. cit.*

of a lack of interest or opposition, but because Georgia Baptists failed to appreciate the importance of them. Other factors involved included distances, travel difficulties, and the fact that many churches had

> . . . the unscriptural practice of meeting but once or twice a month for the worship of God.
> Besides, many churches, located in remote regions, are embarrassed for the want of suitable books. These difficulties, though serious, are not insurmountable; and, if your body can devise a plan which will meet the case, and remove the difficulty, you will have rendered a signal service to the cause of Christ.[115]

This report to the Convention called upon churches to set up a fund for the purchase of Sabbath School books ". . . at publishers prices."[116] As interest in the Sabbath School movement was intensifying, growth among Georgia Baptists continued. With sixty associations, 1,242 churches, 77,962 members and 6,114 baptisms the previous year, [1852], Baptists were beginning to both appreciate their past record over a thirty-year period, and also look ahead to an expanded ministry with the state.[117]

Indian Missions continued to occupy a stronger interest among Georgia Baptists than is perhaps indicated in the minute record of their activities. The Convention continued, in 1854, to send delegates to various Indian mission groups, including two to the Indian Mission Association in Memphis, Tennessee, during 1854, with expenses paid out of the Indian Missions fund.[118]

The Convention followed still the policy of sending delegates directly to the Southern Baptist Convention,[119] and as it had done upon previous occasions, adopted a resolution to permit delegates named to the 1855 Southern Con-

[115]*Ibid.*, p. 50, [Including a report on the sessions of the Sunday School Convention.]
[116]*Ibid.*, p. 51.
[117]*Ibid.*, statistical tables, end of minutes.
[118]*Minutes, Georgia Baptist Convention*, 1854, p. 7.
[119]*Ibid.*, p.p. 6, 7.

vention, fill any vacancy which might occur in their own number.[120]

Slight constitutional changes were approved in 1854 which reflected concern on the part of the Convention for proper and adequate representation from the associations, and reducing representations from societies, as well as delineating more clearly the basis upon which membership in the Convention was to be established.

Articles adopted included the following in place of the 2d, 3rd, and 4th articles of the then existing Constitution.

> 2. The constituents of this Body shall be the Baptist association in the State of Georgia, or as many of them as may accede to the terms of this Convention, and whose constitution shall be approved by the Convention; and such auxiliary Societies as shall contribute annually to our funds according to the terms hereinafter prescribed and whose constitutions shall be approved. Associations and Societies, located out of the State, may be received into the Body, when their peculiar location and other circumstances may, in the judgment of this Convention, render it desirable and important.
> 3. It shall be known and distinguished by the name of "The Baptist Convention of the State of Georgia."
> 4. Each Association shall be entitled to four delegates, and to one additional delegate for every five hundred members; provided the number of delegates for any one Association shall never exceed fifteen. Each auxiliary Society contributing annually fifty dollars to the funds of the Convention, shall be entitled to one delegate; and to one additional delegate for each additional hundred dollars contributed as aforesaid, not to exceed three delegates for any society. All delegates shall hold their appointment until others are elected to succeed them. The delegates to the body shall all be orderly members of regular Baptist churches.
> The committee further recommend to strike out the 7th article; and also, in the 13th article, to insert the word "present' after the word 'delegates'.[121]

There was underlying concern also about the identity of the churches as "regular" which identified at that time

[120]*Ibid.*, p. 7.
[121]*Ibid.*, p. 8.

churches which in essence supported missions, and the causes fostered by the denomination. It apparently did not carry the connotation in their minds of theological distinctions, i. e. Regular and General as the term Regular Baptist has been used.

Constitution of the Baptist Convention of the State of Georgia, as amended [in 1854.]

1. This Body is constituted upon those principles of Christian faith exhibited in Scripture, generally acknowledged and received in the Baptist denomination.

2. The constituents of this body shall be the Baptist Associations in the state of Georgia, or as many of them as may accede to the terms of this Convention, and whose constitutions shall be approved by the Convenvention; and such Auxiliary Societies as shall contribute annually to our funds according to the terms, hereinafter prescribed, and whose constitutions shall be approved. Associations and societies, located out of the State, may be received into the Body, when their peculiar location, and other circumstances, may, in the judgment of this Convention, render it desirable and important.

3. It shall be known and distinguished by the name of "The Baptist Convention of the State of Georgia."

4. Each Association shall be entitled to four delegates, and to one additional delegate for every five hundred members; provided the number of delegates for any one Association shall never exceed fifteen. Each Auxiliary Society, contributing annually fifty dollars to the funds of the Convention, shall be entitled to one delegate, and to one additional delegate for each additional hundred dollars, contributed as aforesaid; not to exceed three delegates for any Society. All delegates shall hold their appointments until others are elected to succeed them. The delegates to the body shall be orderly members of regular Baptist Churches.

5. The officers of this union shall be a Moderator, a Clerk and Assistant Clerk, and a Treasurer, who shall be appointed by ballot at each annual meeting.

6. An Executive Committee, consisting of at least seven members, shall be chosen at each annual meeting, whose duty it shall be to attend to the business of the Convention during its recess. This Committee shall have power to fill all vacancies which may occur, and also

shall appoint a Treasurer in case of a vacancy in that office.

7. The Clerk shall enter in a book all the transactions of this body. The Assistant Clerk shall take charge of all distanct communications, to or from this Body, and shall write all letters which it may require.

8. The Treasurer shall take charge of all monies, specialties and properties of all kinds belonging to the body—give sufficient security for the amount in his hands—report the state of the funds from time to time, as the Convention may direct, and hand over to this successor in office all its monies, properties, etc.

9. The acts and proceedings of this body shall be submitted, from time to time to its constituents for inspection; and none of its decisions shall be binding on the Associations or Auxiliaries.

10. The following are the specific objects of this body, viz:—

  1. To unite the influence and pious intelligence of Georgia Baptists, and thereby to facilitate their union and co-operation.

  2. To form and encourage plans for the revival of experimental and practical religion in the State and elsewere.

  3. To aid in giving effect to useful plans of the several Associations.

  4. To afford an opportunity to those who may conscientiously think it their duty to form a fund for the education of pious young men, who may be called by the Spirit, and their Churches to the Christian Ministry.

  5. And to promote pious and useful Education in the Baptist denomination.

11. It shall have power to form rules, make arrangements and appoint committees for the accomplishment of any and all the above objects; Provided, none of these rules and arrangements shall be inconsistent with the Scriptures and the known principles of the Associations.

12. Two-thirds of the whole number of delegates present shall form a quorum, and a majority shall decide a question.

13. When its funds will justify it, this Body may send delegates to the Southern Baptist Convention.

14. The above Constitution shall be liable to amendment or alteration, by two-thirds of the delegates present, at any of its annual meetings.[122]

[122]*Ibid.,* p. 17.

STATE MISSIONS IDEA WELL DEVELOPED

The operations of the State Missions department [for the first time so identified in 1854][123] was limited by growing mission activity within the local associations as the committee on Missions was forced to note and explain. The concept of a state missions program at this point, was well developed, but hampered financially at the state Convention level by the fact that:

> The several Associations connected with the Convention are, to some extent, engaged in supporting missionaries in their own bounds, and an increasing impression prevails among them, that this department of benevolent enterprises has high claims on the patronage and support of the churches.[124]

In the light of historic developments in the states indicated, it is of interest to note that even prior to the War Between the States, the report on Domestic Missions [in this instance missions operated under the Board at Marion] stated that there were requests from Florida, Texas and California for both prayer and more assistance in the form of missionaries.[125] This has importance with regard to California, for example, because notice of missions needs came less than five years after the great gold rush of 1849 had begun to open up that state for settlement; and in Texas, because of unsettled territorial conditions of that period.

Some insight into a situation which apparently plagued Georgia Baptist forefathers from earliest days in the area of Christian education, and was a situation which was to last until well into the 20th century, may be found in the report of the committee on Education for 1854.

While Mercer University had in most instances been all that the founding fathers had anticipated, there was one area in which their aspirations never were really accomplished; the theological department. One reason apparently was that the trustees continued to believe that a theological seminary would one day develop as a part of Mercer Univer-

[123]*Ibid.*, p. 9.
[124]*Loc. cit.*

sity. Mercer, as one of the chief interests of the denomination since its inception, occupied a major share of concern at the annual Convention sessions. There was no particular complaint concerning the activities of the University as such, [collegiate department] and the Committee on Education could report:

> Our numerous institutions for male and female education have been well attended, and they are so conducted as to merit the confidence and patronage of our families in every part of the State. A fair trial only is needed to convince any that nothing can be gained in an education by sending pupils to other States, or to other denominations in our own State. The time has come, when Baptist families will find it for their own interest to patronize Baptist institutions of learning. In these remarks, we would particularly include the Collegiate department of our University at Penfield.[126]

However, theologicial education was another matter.

> In one respect, your Committee are pained at the review. Theological Education has not received the encouragement which has been extended in other departments. . . Let us properly endow this department—let us provide every facility for the most thorough Theological education of our young men, called of God to the Gospel ministry—and, having thus brought our tithes into the storehouse, see if God will not favor us with a corresponding blessing in the number and character of those who are to have the care of souls in our State.[127]

Nineteen years after its organization,

> The Foreign Missionary Board of the Southern Baptist Convention held its annual meeting in connection with the session of the Convention . . .[128]

This is indicative of the strong influences exercised by Georgia Baptists upon the activities of the Foreign Mission Board.

By 1854, the Executive Committee had four state missionaries under its employment. In the light of existing conditions, with regard to transportation, the reports which

[125]*Loc. cit.*
[126]*Ibid.*, p. 10.
[127]*Loc. cit.*
[128]*Ibid.*, p. 16.

these four submitted to the Convention are of interest. J. R. Miller has traveled 3,020 miles, preached 115 sermons, delivered 33 exhortations, attended four prayer meetings, baptized 33 persons, aided in constituting three churches, and in ordaining five deacons at a salary of $300. J.H. Cowart, for that same period, traveled 2,068 miles, preached 92 sermons, delivered 21 exhotations, visited 111 families, attended four prayer meetings, baptized seven persons, and aided in constituting three churches and in ordaining two deacons at a salary of $240.

E. Hedden traveled 1,567 miles, preached 122 sermons, delivered 167 exhortations, visited 294 families, baptized 55 persons, established several Sabbath Schools, and delivered four temperance lectures. His salary was raised from $150 to $200. S. Sick, reported 154 days of service, traveling 1,299 miles, preaching 116 sermons, giving 68 exhortations, visiting 169 families, baptizing 26 persons, and distributed 60 Bibles and testaments, at a salary of a dollar a day "while laboring"[129]

By 1855, twenty-one Associations, and four Societies were represented at the Newnan Convention.[130]

The Board of Trustees at Mercer felt it important to report to the Convention that not only did the library consist of 3,500 volumes, but that "the cabinet of minerals contained 1600 specimens."[131]

In 1853, the Bible Committee of the Georgia Baptist Convention was organized. The committee was evidently a type of loose-knit auxiliary to the Convention; met at the time of the Convention; and reported its sessions in the Conventions minutes. By the third meeting, in 1855, at the end of two years of organization, the committee had general agents who served as colporteurs, tract distributors, and also as itinerant missionaries; thus, to a degree duplicating the work of the State Missions program.[132]

[129]*Ibid.*, appendix, p.p. 19, 20.
[130]*Minutes, Georgia Baptist Convention*, 1855, p.p. 3, 4.
[131]*Ibid.*, 1855, p. 22. Five hundred Volumes had been acquired for the library during the year; *Minutes, Georgia Baptist Convention*, 1854. p. 23.

It is a matter of continuing interest that from earliest days of Convention organization, churches of different denominations in the host city invited representatives or delegates to the Convention to supply pulpits on Sunday. At Savannah, delegates filled the pulpits of the First Baptist Church, Second Baptist church, Trinity Methodist, Wesley Chapel, Lutheran, Independent Presbyterian, First Presbyterian, First Colored Baptist, Second Colored Baptist, Third Colored Baptist, and Andrew chapel.[133]

The particular interest manifested by the Savannah white Baptists for the interests of the Negro churches was evidenced in the representation for the Sunday services. This spirit of co-operation between white and Negro Baptists in Savannah had been evident from the beginning of the 19th century, and had produced a strong Baptist witness, white and colored, in the port city.

Out of a discussion in 1856 concerning location of *The Christian Index,* or possible sale, came the appointment of a Committee to determine upon a new location for the paper. A move to sell *The Index* to private interests was countered with the proposal for a change in location. With authorization for the Executive Committee to name a Committee to select a location, the paper subsequently was moved to Macon prior to the 1857 session of the Convention.[134]

Georgia Baptists never lost sight of the needs of their Negro brethren; neither did they cease to develop means of presenting a Christian witness to them. This is illustrated well in a request from the Sunbury Association to the Convention in 1856 for assistance from the Convention to support a missionary among the Negroes. At the Savannah session, the Sunbury presented a memorial in behalf of the colored population, reporting that

> In view of the peculiar conformation of the territory, and of the distribution of the population in the six seaboard counties of Georgia, there is a special necessity

[132]*Ibid.,* p.p. 28-30.
[133]*Minutes, Georgia Baptist Convention,* 1856, p.p. 7, 8.
[134]*Ibid.,* p.p. 9, 10; *Minutes, Georgia Baptist Convention,* 1857, p. 18.

for the Baptist denomination in assuming this field as a missionary ground.[135]

Declaring that the Association extended from the Savannah river to the St. Mary's river, and included ". . . to some extent the second tier of counties lying interiorly from those on the seaboard" [136] the problems of the Association were then presented to the Convention. The report said that the Association ". . . embraces in its membership about 6,500, less than eight hundred of whom are white members . . ." [137]

The Sunbury claimed peculiar attention, in their view, because they said that while few white persons were influenced by Baptist life and thought, ". . . the whole colored people are readily inclined to receive the gospel from Baptist ministrations." [138] At that time, the Sunbury supported one missionary, A. Harmon, and in cooperation with the Domestic Mission Board supported a second missionary, John W. Turner, and still,

> It is made evident to your committee, that the Sunbury Association have now more on their hands than they can adequately manage; and it is a plain case in the judgment of your committee, that the denomination should make an appropriation for the support of another missionary in this field.[139]

Thus, one association, large in geographic territory, was in 1856 being served by two missionaries, and approval being sought—and granted,—for permission to employ a third missionary, with the principal endeavors of all of them being among the Negro population!

For all practical purposes, the Savannah Baptist Publication Society ceased to function in 1856 by virtue of a motion authorizing Convention transfer of all assets of that society to the Southern Baptist Publication Society.[140] Again, this in indicative of trends which had been followed

[135]*Minutes, Georgia Baptist Convention*, 1856, p. 10.
[136]*Loc. cit.*
[137]*Loc. cit.*
[138]*Loc. cit.*
[139]*Ibid.*, p.p. 10, 11.
[140]*Ibid.*, p. 11.

Index Editors

W. T. Brantly
1827-1833

Jesse Mercer
1833-1840

Baron Stow
1824-1827

Joseph Walker
1858

J. F. Dagg
1850-1856

William H. Stokes
1840-1843

Joseph S. Baker
1843-1848

Billington M. Sanders
1849-1850

Index Editors

S. Shaver
1867-1874

David E. Butler
1874-1878

Samuel Boykin
1858-1861

B. J. W. Graham
1901-1920

I. J. Van Ness
1896-1900

Henry Holcombe Tucker
1878-1882, 1885-1892

J. C. McMichael
1892-1895

T. P. Bell
1896-1915

Editors of The Christian Index, *1920-1972*

Louie DeVotie Newton
1920-1930

Osceola Pinckney Gilbert
1930-1947

John Jeter Hurt, Jr.,
1947-1966

Jack U. Harwell
1966-

Earlier and present-day servants of the Convention. Upper left, Spencer B. King, Sr., long-time Office Manager and State Missions Secretary. Upper middle, B. D. Ragsdale, Convention Recording Secretary for 49 sessions, and Convention historian.

Upper right, H. R. Bernard, Convention Auditor, Acting Executive-Secretary for one year, and author of the "Bernard Plan" for financial support. Left center, Buren C. Smith, long-time office manager for the Executive Committee.

(Left to Right) Servants with more than 20 years of service to the Denomination include, seated, Mrs. Charlie Mae Pearson, Mrs. Mary Weaver, Mrs. Emma Barbour, Mrs. Norris Nasworthy, Mrs. Joyce Bannister. Lower inset, Miss Ruth Davis. Standing, Paul McCommon, Aubrey L. Hawkins, Bernard D. King, W. A. Anderson, and Spencer Tate.

since 1845, and were to be followed in subsequent years. When agencies or groups under Southern Baptist Convention sponsorship, directly or indirectly, were organized, Georgia Baptists transferred their support and directed their ministries through the South-wide agencies.

A problem which was to be a recurrent one, begun to be evident during the 1850's as schools of various types, under Baptist sponsorship or endorsement, developed. With the development of an educational system came the fear expressed in the report of the Committee on Education which said, in part:

> While they [the committee] are thankful for the widespread benefits of our numerous denominational schools and colleges, they cannot but express the fear that the great multiplication of so many institutions, some of which are competitors for public favor, may cause the rivalry between them to degenerate into a strife for numbers, and where the endowments are meagre, for bread.[141]

The report continued:

> There is a point at which this increase should be arrested, and it may be indicated, whenever the means for the highest mental culture are not afforded. Expansion beyond capital, whether monied or literary, is invariably attended with failure, when it cannot meet the demands made upon it. There should be no tinkering where mind is concerned. The influence, the strength, and the glory of a State are the well-trained minds of its sons and daughters.[142]

At the session in Americus, April 23, 24, and 26, 1958, with the nation nearing a point of divisive war, the Convention still expressed major concern in the area of missions. The report of the Committee on Missions for that year said

> Your committee feel that it is too late in the nineteenth century, to attempt an argument to prove, that the cause of Missions is the cause of God. The success which has attended the enterprize in all its departments, is sufficient proof that it is God's plan to diffuse the knowl-

[141]*Minutes, Georgia Baptist Convention*, 1857, p. 8.
[142]*Loc. cit.*

edge of His glorious Gospel, and subjugate the nations
to Messiah's sway.[143]

And in this year the Convention began to carry a summary
report of the work of the Foreign Mission Board.

A recapitulation of mission expenditures for 1858 is of
interest, and included: $1,682.38, foreign missions; $520.07
domestic missions; Central African missions, $533.55; Bible
Board, $131.30; Indian Missions, $401.79; General purposes,
$407.00; Southern Baptist Publication Society, $45.00; China
Missions, $8.78; Bible Board of Georgia and Colporteur
Society, $318.80; Domestic mission board for Athens mis-
sions, $158.00; Domestic mission Board to build House of
Worship at Athens, $134.00; African missions, $116.29; mission house for Brother Hogue, $70.40; for a total expended
for mission purposes $4,527.36.[144]

The Convention received also a report on the background
of the college proposed for Washington in 1835. Essence of
the report prepared by C. D. Mallary, of New Albany, appeared to be that the Presbyterians in Washington had
made tentative plans for establishment of a college in that
city. The Baptists in that city, led apparently by Jesse
Mercer, decided that if the Presbyterians could establish a
college in that town, so could they.[145]

Mallary, who was unofficial Convention historian, and
upon occasion the official writer of histories for that body,
said in the report it was in a meeting of the trustees at Washington, [apparently 1835 or 1836]

> . . . [I think it was in June,] the venerable Mercer
> manifested more feeling than I recollect ever to have
> witnessed in him. He opposed the discussion of the
> question of change. He said they had been appointed
> under the charter to perform a certain work, and if any
> could not agree to help in carrying it forward, it was
> their duty at once to resign and give place to others.
> Still, the discussion went on, till Brother Mercer become
> so much warmed up, that he left his seat as Chairman

[143]*Minutes, Georgia Baptist Convention*, 1858, p. 8.
[144]*Ibid.*, p. 26.
[145]*Minutes, Georgia Baptist Convention*, 1858, p.p. 27-33. [For complete
statement by Mallary, see Appendix D, p. 789.]

and refused to preside. Cooling at length, and kindly urged by his brethren, He went back to the chair.[146]

The change in location under discussion was an offer from Talbotton to subscribe funds to secure the proposed college.[147]

In view of the fact that Mallary had worked closely with and observed Jesse Mercer in his position as presiding officer over many Baptist bodies during Mercer's lifetime, this provided an interesting insight into the loyalty which Mercer the Baptist statesman felt for his community, and his determination to provide a college in that city, if at all possible.

Mercer's determination to establish a college in Washington so soon after establishment of Mercer Institute at Penfield perhaps indicates also some frustration upon his part that Mercer Institute was not established in that city. However, his backing of the college at the likely expense of the Institute at Penfield, which institute he had in large measure fathered, is difficult to understand, and there is no internal evidence to explain the situation.

By 1859, the Convention, in a policy switch from previous years, voted

> That no appropriation be made to defray the traveling expenses of our delegates to the Southern Baptist Convention.[148]

The delegates approved also a motion by C. D. Mallary

> That in appointing Delegates to the Biennial Convention, we be not restricted to the members of this Convention, but to the bodies represented in this Convention.[149]

Another unusual move at the Columbus meeting was for the Convention to go on record asking

> That a Committee consisting of one from each association represented here, be appointed to nominate Delegates to the Southern Baptist Convention.[150]

[146]*Ibid.*, p.p. 28-29.
[147]*Ibid.*, p. 28.
[148]*Minutes, Georgia Baptist Convention,* 1859, p. 6.
[149]*Loc. cit.*
[150]*Loc. cit.*

The Committee on Missions included a summary report on gifts to missions by Georgia Baptists from 1845 to 1859, indicating that the Convention had contributed to domestic missions $42,461.09 since organization of the Domestic Board, and Indian Missions had benefited to the extent of $12,587.06 during the same period.[151]

On the eve of the War Between the States, Georgia had

> . . . six chartered Colleges with over 600 students, and not less than 30 Female Seminaries, where the learned languages are studied and degrees conferred. All these, except the State Institution, have sprung into existence in less than a quarter of a century; an irrefragable proof of the progress of the age and enlightenment and liberality of our people.[152]

The report of the Committee on Education declared further that:

> The three male, and most, if not all the Female Colleges under our denominational supervision, are in a highly prosperous condition.[153]

The three male colleges were Mercer University, Cherokee College, and Marshall College.[154]

Interesting because of phraseology as well as import, the report said:

> We have lived to see the old odium expire, 'the Baptists are unfriendly to education.' Requiescat in pace. It had a tedious burial and rather ludicrous funeral sermon; its chief pall bearers were the 500 ministers, that have, in the first half of the nineteenth century, opened their eyes to new but important truths taught in the New Testament, and yielded obedience to their majesty. It is to be hoped that the grave, like that of Moses, has been dug so deep that it can never be found. Respectfully submitted, Adiel Sherwood, ch'n.[155]

Georgia Baptists felt by this time, and perhaps correctly so, that the long fight against anti-mission and anti-education forces among Baptists in the state had been won. And the

[151]*Ibid.*, p. 13.
[152]*Ibid.*, p. 15.
[153]*Loc. cit.*
[154]*Loc. cit.*
[155]*Ibid.*, p.p. 15, 16.

treasurer's recapitulation for that year indicated a balance of $50,169.95,[156] an average for the Convention for about a decade.

In a final survey of Georgia Baptist Convention life prior to the beginning of the War Between The States, the report for 1859 listed 64 associations, with 89 churches located in adjacent states, for a total of 1,406 churches which were members of the Convention.[157] There were 93,447 members in the churches, with 7,759 baptisms reported for the year [1858] with 769 ordained ministers in the state and 211 licentiates.[158] The tenor of Georgia Baptists, as indicated officially, right up to the beginning of the war, was one of optimism, prosperity, increasing interest in the causes of missions, and a forward look. The Convention recognized in 1859 the great mission responsibility which had fallen upon Southern churches after 1845.[159]

Nothing was indicated in the minutes of 1859 concerning internal political conditions; no note of caution was sounded; Rather, the Convention looked ahead, paying no attention, officially to political circumstances which were to bring about drastic changes in the life of the convention, and in the personal lives of most Georgia Baptists for the following four years in a direct manner, and for many years thereafter indirectly.

Actually, no word or official note of the impending war was taken by the Convention, even in 1860. It was still "business as usual" when the delegates met at the Baptist church, [First] Macon, April 20, 21, and 23. Discussion centered around parliamentary procedure, requests for assistance in building churches from congregations at Ringgold and Brunswick, and a major item of interest was presentation by Josuah Mercer to the Convention of a walking cane belonging to Jesse Mercer, his brother. The request from Josuah was that the cane be entrusted to the care of

[156]*Ibid.*, p. 28.
[157]*Ibid.*, p. 45.
[158]*Loc. cit.*
[159]*Ibid.*, p. 11.

Mercer University, and by Convention vote, the cane was received by the University president.[160]

Lack of internal evidence concerning political conditions is stated because an era of great growth upon the part of Georgia Baptists was drawing to a close. It must have been obvious to Georgia Baptists, and their official bodies, that political conditions were changing rapidly; yet no note was taken by the Convention, and no evidence of any advance planning in the event of possible strife was recorded.

However, *The Index* Committee of the Convention gave indication that a strong undercurrent to sell the paper to private individuals still existed, but they did not recommend such a sale, leaving the matter to the judgment of the Convention.

[160]*Minutes, Georgia Baptist Convention,* 1860, p.p. 5-7.

CHAPTER 8

Years of Uncertainty

The year was 1861. The War Between the States was a fact. And, for the first time, at the session in Athens April 26, 27, 28 and 29, the Georgia Baptist Convention took a strong political stand, declaring unswerving allegiance to the Confederacy.

The Convention, adopting a report of a special committee on the "present political crisis," [1] said:

> Whereas, the state of Georgia, in the legitimate exercise of her sovereignty, has withdrawn from the Confederacy known as the United States of America; and, for the better maintenance of her rights, honor and independence, has united with other States in a new Confederacy, under the name of the Confederate States of America; and whereas, Abraham Lincoln, the President of the United States, is attempting by force of arms to subjugate these states in violation of the fundamental principles of American liberty; therefore,
>
> 1. Resolved, by the members of the Baptist Convention the State of Georgia, that we consider it to be at once a pleasure and a duty to avow that, both in feeling and in principle, we approve, endorse and support the Government of the Confederate States of America.
>
> 2. Resolved, That while this Convention disclaims all authority, whether ecclesiastical or civil, yet as citizens, we deem it but a duty to urge the union of all the people of the South in defence of the common cause; and to express the confident belief that, in whatever conflict the madness of Mr. Lincoln and his government may force upon us, the Baptists of Georgia will not be behind any class of our fellow citizens in maintaining the independence of the South by any sacrifice of treasure or of blood.

[1] *Minutes, Georgia Baptist Convention*, 1861, p. 5.

3. Resolved, That we acknowledge with devout thankfulness to Almighty God, the signal favor with which up to this time, He has blessed our arms and our policy; and that the Baptist churches of this State, be requested to observe the first and second days of June next, as days of fasting and prayer, that God will deliver us from all the power of our enemies and restore peace to our country.
4. Resolved, That the Confederate Government be requested to invite the churches of all denominations within the Confederacy, to unite in observing said days of fasting and prayer.
5. Resolved, that copies of these resolutions be sent to President Davis, the Confederate Congress, the Governor of Georgia.

N. M. Crawford, chairman,[2]

To further solidify Convention approval behind the measure,

. . . the congregation were invited to express their opinion on the sentiments of this report. The whole assembly rose to their feet in testimony of their unanimous approval. On motion of Bro. Campbell, the Moderator called upon Brother Mallary to lead in prayer.[3]

Even the report of the trustees of Mercer University reflected an unusual spirit of optimism, declaring that the affairs at the University were

. . . in a far more prosperous condition than at any previous period of its history. There were in attendance last Fall Term 130, the present term 125.[4]

And there was a gain in total membership of 3,422, in 65 associations, with $21,180.89 contributed for missions.[5]

However, by 1862 the picture of Georgia Baptist life had begun to change. Only fourteen associations were represented at the First Baptist church in LaGrange, and concern was expressed at that meeting that in so far as possible, national [Confederate] affairs be shaped in such manner that violation of the Sabbath in the discharge of official

[2]*Ibid.*, p.p. 5, 6.
[3]*Ibid.*, p. 6.
[4]*Ibid.*, p. 8.
[5]*Ibid.*, p. 3.
[6]*Minutes, Georgia Baptist Convention*, 1862, p. 7.

duties be prevented as much as possible.[6] An awareness of responsibility for a ministry to Confederate troops was apparent by 1862.[7] This awareness was to continue through the war. With the suspension of the "Southern Bible Board" [apparently the Southern Baptist Publication Society in Charleston,] ". . . by the invasion of the enemy",[8] funds which would have been sent to it were turned over to the Georgia Baptist Bible and Colporteur Society to purchase Testaments, religious books and tracts for distribution to the soldiers.[9]

Apparently a war-time measure, none-the-less, the Convention expressed appreciation to the governor for his ". . . recent judicious and patriotic action. . ." in the suppression of distilleries in the state.[10]

And, Georgia Baptists took some satisfaction in their belief that the Indian tribes still in the state were ". . . in cordial and active sympathy with us in the revolution which is now in progress." [11]

The Convention in 1862 went on record as reasserting sentiments "so far as applicable to the present circumstances, of the resolutions on the state of the country, passed at the last session of this body," and

> Resolved, That while profoundly feeling that our cause is just, we nevertheless have great reason to humble ourselves before Almighty God, and to acknowledge his chastening hand in our late reverses.[12]

Believing profoundly in the cause of the Confederacy, the Convention supported it by declaring:

> That we find in the present circumstances of the country no cause for discouragement; that God, our heavenly Father, often chastens most promptly those whom He most loves; and that, trusting in Him with the whole heart, we are more and more determined, by His bless-

[7]*Ibid.*, p. 6.
[8]*Ibid.*, p. 8.
[9]*Loc. cit.*
[10]*Ibid.*, p. 6.
[11]*Ibid.*, p. 10.
[12]*Ibid.*, p. 12.

ing, to oppose the invader of our soil by every means placed in our power and to the last extremity.[13]

While no mention was made in 1862 of other institutions operated by the Convention, it was evident that effects of the war were felt at Mercer, with enrolment in the college dropping for the 1860-1861 year to 112.[14] At this point, the Mercer trustees were determined, in so far as possible, for

> . . . the Faculty to be preserved in its entirety, and all the exercises of the Institution be continued without alteration or modification; provided that can be done without bringing the University in debt.[15]

By the 1862 session, J. H. Campbell, who by then had been long identified with missionary endeavors within the state, was reported as serving ". . . as colporteur among our soldiers on the coast." [16]

After the end of a year of war, the treasurer's report for 1862 indicated a sounder financial picture for the Convention than the previous year. This was due in part to the fact that communications between the Georgia Convention and the Foreign and Domestic Mission Boards had been limited, and some of the funds listed were those which normally would have been transmitted to these boards.[17]

In 1863, the Convention met in Griffin, and for the first time had proceedings of the sessions provided in a paper printed in Griffin, and also for the first time, on motion of J. H. Campbell, "Newspaper reporters were invited to seats on the floor." [18] Again, the treasurer's report indicated an increase in funds, from $53,231.38½ in 1862 to $55,508.18 in 1863.[19]

The statistical tables for 1862 and 1863 reflected an increasing difficulty in communications throughout the state. Many were figures which extended back to 1861 and some

[13]*Loc. cit.*
[14]*Ibid.*, p. 15.
[15]*Ibid.*, p. 16.
[16]*Ibid.*, p. 18.
[17]*Ibid.*, p.p. 21, 26.
[18]*Minutes, Georgia Baptist Convention*, 1863, p. 2.
[19]*Ibid.*, p. 22; *Minutes, Georgia Baptist Convention*, 1862, p. 26.

of them remained unchanged until the end of the war.[20]

Perhaps as good an index to Georgia Baptist strength available is that evidenced by the fact that in 1864, when the South was beginning to feel the turning tide, and prior to Sherman's march through Georgia, and the burning of Atlanta, representatives from fifteen Associations and five missionary societies were able to assemble for the Convention.[21]

The list of areas represented is of value in determining Baptist strength. Associations represented at the session meeting with the Second Baptist church in Atlanta, included the Apalachee, Bethel, Central, Ebenezer, Flint River, Georgia, Hephzibah, Mount Vernon, Middle Rehoboth, Sarepta, Sunbury, Stone Mountain, Washington and Western. Societies represented were the Augusta, Antioch, Atlanta Second church, Madison Baptist church and Bairdstown.[22]

In a time of crisis—and really occasioned by it—the Convention made its first move to establish any type of orphan's home when a resolution was adopted which called for a Committee of Seven to

> . . . take into consideration the propriety and practicability of establishing within the bounds of this Convention an orphan house or asylum for the education and support of destitute and helpless orphan children residing in the state of Georgia, said asylum to be under the patronage and direction of the Georgia Baptist Convention.[23]

The Committee named to study the proposal reported:

> That they are deeply and favorably impressed with the importance of attempting such an enterprise, but are of opinion that it would be better not to connect it with the Convention. Some brethren entertain doubts whether it would come properly within the objects for which this Body was formed, and we all think that the

[20]*Minutes, Georgia Baptist Convention*, 1862, p.p. 30, 31; *Minutes, Georgia Baptist Convention*, 1863, p.p. 24, 25.
[21]*Minutes, Georgia Baptist Convention*, 1864, p.p. 3, 4.
[22]*Loc. cit.*
[23]*Ibid.*, p. 5.

connection would injuriously incumber both institutions. A voluntary association, however, might be
formed, whose sole object should be the care for
orphans; and we hope that brethren will be found who
will carry on the work.[24]

The report continued by encouraging establishment of a
home, declaring that:

We, therefore, recommend that an opportunity be afforded to the friends of such an enterprise to establish such an organization as they may deem best calculated to accomplish the result proposed.[25]

Concern had been expressed in previous years for orphans,
and war casualties heightened this concern. However, this
brief investigation of the proposal in 1864, in a Convention
session at the Second Baptist church, Atlanta, apparently was
the seed thought for what was later to emerge as the Georgia
Baptist Orphans' home. This home was created largely
through the efforts of women in Atlanta churches, and
women in the Second Baptist church occupied a place of
leadership in the establishment of the home.

General John B. Gordon had addressed a letter to the
1864 session of the Convention, stating that Baptists had
done very little to strengthen the religious welfare of the
Army of the Confederacy.[26] There were, apparently, other
similar expressions in view of the fact that a committee of
three men was appointed ". . . on General Gordon's letter
and similar documents."[27] Life in Georgia was affected by
the war in every way by 1864. This session was the first
which heard addresses by Army officers, including Colonel
Edwards, of the 47th Regiment, who "made an interesting
address on the religious wants of the army."[28]

Out of expressed needs concerning an increased ministry
to soldiers, several interesting trends in Georgia Baptist
life and thought were to emerge.

[24]*Ibid.*, p. 7.
[25]*Loc. cit.*
[26]*Ibid.*, p. 6.
[27]*Loc. cit.*
[28]*Loc. cit.*

1. Funds were made available through the Domestic Mission Board for the support of ". . . any ministers who were willing to go to the army." [29]

2. The Convention took an official position concerning ministers who were serving in the ranks, but not as chaplains, by adopting a resolution as follows:

> Resolved, That the Baptist State Convention of Georgia appoint a committee of three to memorialize his Excellency President Davis upon this subject of appointing ministers who are serving as soldiers to be chaplains, when, in the opinion of their regiment, their services would be more valuable in the latter capacity than the former.[30]

However, that resolution was reconsidered later the same day it was passed with adoption of another as a substitute which placed a new concept upon the military chaplaincy by Georgia Baptists.

The Convention went on record finally requesting President Davis

> . . . to pass an order directing the discharge from military service any ordained minister of the gospel whose services are asked by any regiment or separate battalion in service, *or by any church as a pastor*.[31] [author's italics]

This proposal, adopted by the Convention, placed Georgia Baptists on record as urging separation from military service of any minister who was called by a church to become pastor while serving with armed forces.

3. A third aspect of the discussion concerning military chaplains, linked to the second, reflected an early concern at the level of separation of church and state. The Convention memorialized further the Confederate government, declaring that they did

> . . . not approve of the principle of appointing chaplains for the army to be paid out of the public treasury, and we pledge ourselves as a denomination to do all in our power to support all ministers of our de-

[29]*Loc. cit.*
[30]*Ibid.*, p. 10.
[31]*Ibid.*, p. 11.

nomination discharged and permitted to attend as missionaries upon regiments or battalions which may petition for their services.[32]

FREE TUITION OFFERED

Mercer's trustees reported to the 1864 Convention they had taken action to allow disabled Georgia soldiers or soldiers who might be disabled in the services of the Confederate states or the State of Georgia to attend the University without paying tuition.[33] Of funds expended and reported in 1864, nearly $4,000 went for support of missionaries among soldiers, and $124.93 was used to provide *The Christian Index* to the troops.[34] While no time span was indicated, the Board of Missions reported that it had expended for missions to the Army and to the churches 20 men and about $50,000.00 of all funds received by the Domestic Board, Georgia Baptists had contributed over one third of the amount.[35]

A final survey of 1864 is contained in the report of a committee on the state of the country, which said, in essence, that after three years of hardships and desolations,

> . . . we find ourselves unchanged in our feelings and principles, as respects the endorsement and support of the cause of the Confederate States of America.
> While we recognize the hand of God in the reverses of the past year, and acknowledge that the chastisement was justly administered, we take courage from the fact that, to some good extent, these judgments have been sanctified, and that the spirit of prayer and dependence upon the Divine Assistance is more than ever manifest.[36]

The Convention had been scheduled to meet in Columbus in 1865. During the time scheduled for the meeting, Columbus was occupied by Union troops, and no session was held.[37]

When the first Convention session met following the end

[32]*Loc. cit.*
[33]*Ibid.,* p. 13.
[34]*Ibid.,* p. 17.
[35]*Ibid.,* p. 18.
[36]*Ibid.,* p. 25.
[37]*Minutes, Georgia Baptist Convention,* 1866, handwritten note, flyleaf. Microfilm copy, Dargan-Carver Library, Nashville.

of the war, in 1866, fifteen associations were represented, and about the most the Convention was able to ascertain concerning missions was contained in the statement ". . . that very little has been done for the cause of Missions during the past year".[38]

It was perhaps out of the selection of a meeting place for the 1866 Convention, that the idea of expanded authority for the Executive Committee developed. That committee reported to the Convention in 1866 that while it did not have authority, they considered themselves not out of order in "the unforeseen emergency" to make arrangements for that session.[39] The Executive Committee said that the Constitution of the Convention made no provisions for the selection of places of subsequent meetings since the officers and the committee were "appointed" or "chosen" at each annual meeting, with no specified powers to hold over, until the appointment of their successors.[40]

However, although the Executive Committee suggested ". . . that the Constitution be so amended as to provide for future contingencies of this kind,"[41] the amended Constitution for that year did not expand the authority of the Executive Committee.[42]

Doctrinal differences with other denominations, elaborated upon rarely, were studied in the first Convention session following the War Between the States, and Georgia Baptists passed a resolution:

> That, in the judgment of this Convention, the differences in doctrine between the Baptists and Campbellites are such as to render any attempt to effect a union between the two Denominations undesirable and pernicious.[43]

Additionally, the Convention, with no minute evidence indicating the reason, approved a resolution declaring:

[38]*Ibid.*, p. 6.
[39]*Ibid.*, p. 19.
[40]*Loc. cit.*
[41]*Loc. cit.*
[42]*Ibid.*, p.p. 28-29.
[43]*Ibid.*, p. 14.

> That the Georgia Baptist Convention testifies its entire
> disapprobation of church members dancing, playing
> cards, even for amusement, visiting theatres and circuses,
> and drinking spirituous liquors as a beverage.[44]

The Convention did adopt a revised Constitution in that
year,[45] changing the name officially to "The Georgia Baptist
Convention of the State of Georgia." The changes were in
Article Five and Article Six, which articles, in revised and
approved form, are reproduced:

> Article 5.
> The officers of this union shall be: A Moderator, a
> Clerk, an Assistant Clerk, and a Treasurer, who shall be
> appointed by ballot at each annual meeting, [and who
> shall hold their offices until their successors are elected,
> in case, from any cause, an election shall fail to take
> place at the proper time.]
> Article 6.
> An Executive Committee, consisting of at least seven
> members, shall be chosen at each annual meeting, whose
> duty it shall be to attend to the business of the Conven-
> tion during its recess. This Committee shall have
> power to fill any vacancies which may occur, and also
> appoint a Treasurer, in case of a vacancy in that office,
> [and shall hold their offices until their successors are
> elected, in case, from any cause, an election should fail
> to take place at the proper time.] [46]

These changes came apparently when the Convention, as a
result of the hiatus created by the war, failed to meet annually to fill constitutional requirements for election of
officers.[47]

BRIEF ADVANCE IN WORK

For a brief time after the War Between the States, Baptist
life in Georgia advanced. This was before the full impact
of the reconstruction policies of the Federal Government
made itself felt. The Convention met finally in Columbus
in 1867, with fifteen associations and representation from the

[44]*Loc. cit.*
[45]*Ibid.,* p. 5.
[46]*Ibid.,* p.p. 28, 29; changes in the Constitution of 1854 are indicated by
brackets.
[47]*Minutes, Georgia Baptist Convention,* 1866, handwritten note, Flyleaf.

Greensboro Female Missionary Society in attendance.[48] And, it was at this session that J. H. Campbell reported that he was preparing a new edition of his *History of Georgia Baptists,* and requested that a committee be appointed to examine the work upon completion.[49]

The entire text of the Constitution approved in 1866 is reproduced to indicate guidelines under which the Convention was to operate for the next several years.

Constitution of the Baptist Convention of the State of Georgia As amended in 1866

1. This body is constituted upon those principles of Christian Faith as exhibited in scripture, generally acknowledged and received in the Baptist Denomination.

2. The constituents of this body shall be the Baptist Associations in the state of Georgia, or as many of them as shall accede to the terms of this Convention and whose Constitution shall be approved by the Convention and such Auxiliary Societies as shall contribute annually to our funds, according to the terms hereinafter prescribed, and whose Constitutions shall be approved. Associations and Societies located out of the state may be received into the body, when their peculiar location and other circumstances may, in the judgment of this Convention, render it desirable and important.

3. It shall be known and distinguished as "The Georgia Baptist Convention of the State of Georgia."

4. Each Association shall be entitled to four delegates, and to one additional delegate for every five hundred members; provided, the number of delegates for any one Association shall never exceed fifteen. Each Auxiliary Society, contributing annually fifty dollars to the funds of the Convention, shall be entitled to one delegate, and to one additional delegate for each additional hundred dollars contributed as aforesaid; not to exceed three delegates for any Society. All delegates shall hold their appointments until other are elected to succeed them. The delegates to the Convention shall be orderly members of regular Baptist Churches.

5. The officers of this union shall be: A Moderator, a Clerk, an Assistant Clerk, and a Treasurer, who shall

[48]*Minutes, Georgia Baptist Convention,* 1867, p. 3.
[49]*Ibid.,* p. 4.

be appointed by ballot at each annual meeting, and who shall hold their offices until their successors are elected, in case, from any cause, an election shall fail to take place at the proper time.

6. An Executive Committee, consisting of at least seven members, shall be chosen at each annual meeting, whose duty it shall be to attend to the business of the Convention during its recess. This Committee shall have power to fill all vacancies which may occur, and also appoint a Treasurer, in case of a vacancy in that office, and shall hold their offices until their successors are elected, in case, from any cause, an election should fail to take place at the proper time.

7. The Clerk shall enter in a book all the transactions of the body. The Assistant Clerk shall take charge of all distant communications to or from this body, and shall write all letters which it may require.

8. The Treasurer shall take charge of all monies, specialties, and properties of all kinds belonging to the body—give sufficient security for the amount in his hands—report the state of the funds from time to time, as the Convention may direct, and hand over to his successor in office all its monies, properties, etc.

9. The acts and proceedings of this body shall be submitted, from time to time, to its constituents for inspection, and none of its decisions shall be binding on the Associations or Auxiliaries.

10. The following are the specific objects of this body—viz:

    1. To unite the influence and pious intelligence of Georgia Baptists, and thereby to facilitate their union and cooperation.

    2. To form and encourage plans for the revival of experimental and practical religion in the State and elsewhere.

    3. To aid in giving effect to useful plans of the several Associations.

    4. To afford an opportunity to those who may conscientiously think it their duty to form a fund for the education of pious young men, who may be called by the Spirit and their churches to the Christian Ministry.

    5. And to promote pious, useful education in the Baptist denomination.

11. It shall have power to form rules, make arrangements, and appoint committees for the accomplishment of any and all the above objects: Provided, none of these

rules and arrangements shall be inconsistent with the Scriptures and the known principles of the Associations.
12. Two-thirds of the whole number of delegates present shall form a quorum and a majority shall decide a question.
13. When its funds will justify it, this body may send delegates to the Southern Baptist Convention.
14. The above Constitution shall be liable to amendment or alteration by two-thirds of the delegates present at any of its annual meetings.[50]

And, evidence of the increasing tempo of religious life was in the fact that representatives from the Domestic Mission Board, The Foreign Mission Board, the Sunday School and ten men from the Alabama Convention were received at the 1867 session.[51]

All Georgia Baptist interests suffered financial losses when the Confederate economy failed. A recommendation by a committee which examined the report of Mercer University, called for action to place that institution in such financial condition that it would be above future contingencies. The committee suggested also that action be taken to restore losses sustained by the failure of the Confederacy. A recommendation calling for approval of an additional agent to solicit $100,000 in endowment in shares of ten dollars each, was approved for Mercer.[52]

The Domestic Mission Board reported to the Convention that nearly $40,000 had been paid into its treasury during the year,[53] and the committee reporting on education indicated that: "The Hearn school is doing a good work." [54] And, despite the recommendation brought by the committee studying the Mercer report, the Education Committee reported that the University was beginning to make progress following the end of the war.[55]

The cause of Christian education rested heavily upon the

[50]*Minutes, Georgia Baptist Convention,* 1866, p.p. 28, 29.
[51]*Minutes, Georgia Baptist Convention,* 1867, p. 4.
[52]*Ibid.* p. 7.
[53]*Ibid.,* p. 8.
[54]*Ibid.,* p. 9.
[55]*Loc. cit.*

minds and hearts of Georgia Baptists and the Committee on Education said:

> In view of these facts, it becomes us as good citizens, looking forward to a prosperous future for our country, and as faithful Christians who desire the purity of Zion, to bestir ourselves not only in behalf of High Schools, Colleges and Universities, but to put forth every exertion in behalf of Common Schools, in which thousands of the poor and ignorant of our people may be fitted for usefulness in Church and State. Let us remember that it is the few educated men in a community who give character to the political and religious institutions of a country.[56]

And, from this springboard, as will be indicated later, Georgia Baptists were in the forefront of support and leadership in the state's creation of a public school system.

Henry Holcomb Tucker has been named to work out a plan for the instruction of ministers who were currently preaching, and in his report on ministerial instruction, a one month school was suggested for Penfield, beginning the 15th of November, 1867. Tucker and John J. Brantley were to be instructors and J. H. Cuthbert, Augusta, was to assist them. There was to be no expense by the instructors for board or travel and the instructors were to make no charge for their services.[57]

J. H. Cuthbert, who had been identified with efforts to train Negro ministers, made a motion, adopted by the Convention,

> That we recommend to our brethren in the ministry to aid by counsel and instruction, as far as may be practicable, all colored ministers, licentiates and ordained, who may desire to receive instruction at their hands.[58]

The report of the Mercer trustees for 1867 was in the form of a personal report by President Tucker.

APPRECIATION FOR VETERANS

With continued concern expressed by Georgians for their

[56]*Loc. cit.*
[57]*Ibid.*, p. 10.
[58]*Ibid.*, p. 12.

soldiers, Tucker's statement was in keeping with the times, when he spoke of veterans who had enrolled at Mercer.

> On the whole, I may say that a more docile, gentle, tractable, and dutiful body of young men I have never seen. A number of these young men were soldiers in the late Confederate army; and I desire to put it on record as one of the remarkable facts of the times that these war-worn veterans—veterans in arms, though young in years—who served the whole or large part of the war, are not only among the best students that we now have, but among the best we have ever had. It is touching to contemplate the almost incredible combination of heroism and gentleness. They were lions in battle—at home they are lambs. I need not say that it is a luxury to teach such noble youths, and an honor and a privilege to prepare them for their future career.[59]

Post-war difficulties were revealed also in the Mercer report Tucker declared:

> The Faculty have been placed in a most embarrassing position by the act of the Legislature which nominally provides for the education of maimed and indigent soldiers.
> The act provides that the several colleges named—Mercer University being one of them—shall furnish these students with board, clothing, tuition, and books, and that as a compensation for all this they shall receive $300 per year, payable not in currency, but in State bonds, of an inferior grade and of a character which I am sure must make them entirely unmarketable. For the last three years we have been offering, and we still offer to give tuition gratis to this class of students, but it is entirely impossible for us to furnish board, clothing and books gratis, or to furnish them for unmarketable bonds, which amounts to the same thing. I received a number of applications from disabled soldiers, asking to be received into this University under the provisions of the aforesaid act. A copy of the letter which I sent them in reply is herewith submitted, marked Doc A. The substance of the letter is, that we are not prepared to receive them at present on the terms proposed, but that we hoped that some satisfactory arrangements might be made in future.
> Subsequent to this, Governor Jenkins informed us that

[59]*Minutes, Georgia Baptist Convention*, 1867, p. 15.

he would pay for the first quarter in currency, but that he could promise no more. On this, I wrote to the applicants for admission that we would receive them if they came, but that in my judgment the nature of the provisions made for them, and the situation of public affairs were both too precarious to justify them in abandoning their present pursuits, and leaving their homes, to which in a few months or weeks they might be obliged to return, having lost time and expended money to little or no purpose. I then wrote to the Governor, and asked him whether, in his opinion, I had given the young men good advice, and whether, on the whole he approved my course. I received a reply, herewith submitted, marked Doc. B., in which His Excellency is pleased to say in substance, that he approves of my course in every particular. In case there should be any severity of criticism on what I have done, I shelter myself behind the impenetrable aegis of the approbation of the wise, benevolent, and patriotic statesman who occupies the gubernatorial chair.[60]

A summary of Tucker's apparent distaste for the law was evident in his concluding statement:

There are three young men in Penfield pursuing their studies under the provisions of the Legislative act, not one of whom is in College, and only one of whom is taught by the Faculty.[61]

Still engrossed with matters pertaining to education, the 1868 Convention, upon motion of David E. Butler, approved of a plan calling upon Georgia Baptists to contribute to Southern Seminary funds sufficient to support one professor.[62] In that year, the Committee on Education declared:

Let our people unite as one man to secure from our law makers a system of education, call it by what name you choose, as will meet the exigencies our present new and unorganized condition of affairs demands. If we cannot all become teachers, we can at least occasionally visit the school house, and by our sympathy hold up the hands and cheer the spirits of the much neglected instructors of our youth.[63]

J. H. Kilpatrick was chairman of a special committee in

[60]*Ibid.*, p. 17.
[61]*Loc. cit.*
[62]*Minutes, Georgia Baptist Convention,* 1868, p. 5.
[63]*Ibid.*, p. 10.

1868 which responded to the report in which trustees affirmed their decision for Mercer University to remain at Penfield. Taking note of what they believed to be the prevailing sentiment of Georgia Baptists, the committee submitted three resolutions dealing with the University, which were approved by the Convention. The resolutions, in effect, affirmed as ". . . expressing the sense of this body upon the whole subject, . . ." [64] the following:

1. A belief that the location was not to blame entirely for any lack of prosperity which the university might experience.

2. The belief that continued agitation concerning removal of Mercer was injurious to the interests of the university, and

3. A request that the Convention instruct the trustees, considering the subject of moving settled, to place the buildings and grounds of the institution in

> . . . A state of complete repair as soon as practicable, and, indeed, take all necessary steps, looking to the permanency and efficiency of the University.[65]

An implication in the 1868 minutes was that Mercer's refusal to accept disabled veterans had created displeasure among some Georgians, and the Convention adopted a motion that Mercer take such steps as might be necessary

> . . . . to continue their efforts to render available this appropriation, [for soldiers] and that they not earnestly strive to place Mercer in the same relation to disabled soldiers that sustained by like institutions in the State.[66]

Mercer apparently was the only private institution in the state which was called upon by the state to provide the free education for veterans.

And, in the report of Mercer's president, [the report of the trustees] Tucker referred again to the course the university had pursued. By the time the Convention met in 1868, Governor Jenkins had been removed from office, and;

> On the removal of Governor Jenkins from office, I wrote to General Meade, inquiring whether the State

[64]*Ibid.*, p. 11.
[65]*Loc. cit.*
[66]*Ibid.*, p.p. 11, 12.

appropriation for the education of disabled soldiers would be continued.

A copy of General Meade's reply is herewith submitted. The substance of it will appear in the following extracts from the minutes of the Faculty:

Whereas, in regard to the education of soldiers under the act of December 18th, 1866, General Meade has prescribed conditions involving the following particulars—to-wit: 1st that Negroes shall be received on a footing with the whites; and 2d, That Federal soldiers shall be received as well as Confederate; and whereas, this was not the intention of the Legislature in passing this act; nor is it in accordance with our own sense of duty or propriety; therefore,
Resolved, That we decline to receive students on the terms proposed.[67]

The issue ceased to exist when the State Legislature refused to appropriate funds for the education of soldiers.[68]

In 1868, the Convention heard a report that:

A number of brethren, some of whom had been in the ministry for twenty years, responded to the invitation. . .[69]

for a preacher's school, at Mercer in November, 1867.[70]

While the Kilpatrick report on Mercer's location was approved by the Convention, a report of an investigation to determine possible legal barriers to removal was given to the Convention. Essence of several legal opinions was that only a charter change with regard to location would be needed in case the Convention should desire to move the Institution.[71]

Setbacks to Baptist work were evident in the report of the Committee on The State of Religion and Religious Destitution in Georgia, which was presented to the Convention when it met in Cuthbert in 1869. This standing committee said:

[67]*Ibid.*, p. 15.
[68]*Minutes, Georgia Baptist Convention*, 1869, p. 1, Appendix.
[69]*Loc. cit.*
[70]*Minutes, Georgia Baptist Convention*, 1867, p. 10.
[71]*Minutes, Georgia Baptist Convention*, 1868, p.p. 16, 17.

In northeastern Georgia, east and north of Athens, there is not a minister who is supported while preaching the gospel . . .

In what is called Cherokee Georgia, there is a most interesting and promising field for missionary labor. The Cherokee Baptist Convention is dissolved; the Cassville College gone; and the building burned . . . in this portion of the State there is a general deficiency in the supply of preaching and Sunday schools. One minister for instance is supplying six churches. There is a low state of spirituality, and a far too general use of intoxicating drinks. . . .

In middle Georgia, there were churches without preaching, and general demoralization . . .

From the neighborhood of Newnan there is the report of a dearth of religious revivals . .

In Southwestern Georgia, Starkville is destitute.

The report continued,

Above Augusta, for twenty miles, there is much need of preaching. Belair and Groves' churches are unprovided for. The colored people of Augusta and vicinity are accessible to the ministry of white men. . .[72]

In the report of the Executive Committee, dated April, 1868, three suggestions were made. One, calling for Tucker to be ". . . invited to take the field to enlist the denomination more generally in support of Mercer University," was perhaps expected. The other two were to have far-reaching significance. One called for the Convention to ". . . commit to the Executive Committee or to a separate committee, the work of State Missions," the third suggestion was

That some plan be adopted by the convention for relieving the necessities of aged and infirmed ministers of our denomination in the State.[73]

The influence of J. H. Campbell is evident in the fact that these three suggestions were made by him in a letter to the Executive Committee and passed along to the Convention.[74]

With what had become almost a perennial question appearing again, the Convention, meeting in Newnan in 1870,

[72]*Minutes, Georgia Baptist Convention,* 1869, p. 9.
[73]Appendix, 1869, *Georgia Baptist Convention.*
[74]*Loc. cit.*

voted finally 71 to 16 in favor of moving Mercer University, with no specific site suggested.[75] Pursuant to the vote for removal of the university, the Convention adopted a resolution calling for Mercer's trustees, together with a committee comprised of one delegate from each association represented at that session, to

> . . . select a new location for Mercer University, after fully investigating the claims and advantages of each locality; . . .[76]

By 1869-1870, there were twenty-seven associations in fellowship with the Convention. In addition, there were forty-one other Baptist associations including fifteen not members of the Convention; twenty-one anti-missionary; three Negro; and two not otherwise identified. The associations co-operating with the Convention claimed 706 churches with 37,560 white members and 9,705 colored members, as well as 487 ordained ministers and 108 licentiates.[77] Five years after the end of the War Between The States, there were still nearly 10,000 Negroes who were members of white Baptist churches in associations affiliated with the convention.

[75]*Minutes, Georgia Baptist Convention,* 1870, p. 9.
[76]*Loc. cit.*
[77]*Minutes, Georgia Baptist Convention,* 1870, Statistical table, end of minutes.

CHAPTER 9

Forging Ahead

The decade of the 1870's was a watershed in development of Baptist life in Georgia in every area. Progress was not to be without hardship, but it was to be of a permanent nature. This decade could well be identified as one of re-grouping and forging ahead.

The interests of Home and Foreign Missions, Christian Education, and increasingly State Missions, were stressed, promoted, preached about and implemented. Many who served in capacities of leadership at Mercer University were in the forefront of denominational life, especially during this decade. These men, many of them, had been leaders in Georgia Baptist life prior to their election to the several positions at the University.

Mercer was a step nearer the move to the present location in Macon with specific approval by the 1870 Convention of a committee to study possible new sites and make recommendations in 1871.[1] After considerable discussion, the 1871 Convention adopted two reports dealing with the proposed removal of Mercer from Penfield. One was the report of the Board of Trustees, which report outlined plans for the move, and a second report, that of a special committee to recommend a site.[2]

Macon was selected as the site for the new location,[3] and the Convention agreed with a special committee that Mercer

[1]*Minutes, Georgia Baptist Convention,* 1870, p. 9.
[2]*Minutes, Georgia Baptist Convention,* 1871, p.p. 16, 17, 18.
[3]*Loc. cit.*

trustees retain control and management of the Penfield property until all questions of litigation could be resolved.[4] This carried the proviso that if litigation were dropped, Mercer trustees would

> . . . establish at Penfield a 'Mercer High School,' provided no draft be made on the present funds of the University for this purpose.[5]

Macon, Forsyth, Griffin, Atlanta, Newnan, Marietta and Gainesville had offered inducements to secure the University. The most attractive offer was by the City Council and citizens of Macon. The basic agreement was that Macon would pay to the Mercer trustees $125,000 in City of Macon bonds, and provide a site to cost not over $25,000.[6] The site chosen was the present one adjoining Tattnall Square, and the trustees reported that prior to acceptance of bonds and deeds, a contract had been entered into with the mayor and council and their successors. This contract amounted to a permanent guarantee from Macon that no effort would be made to coerce Mercer into being anything but the Baptist University which it was at Penfield.[7]

In addition to the inducements offered by Macon, friends of the university in Macon agreed to raise $30,000 to endow a new professorship, and at the time the report of the trustees was prepared for the 1871 Convention, $8,000 of the $30,000 had been subscribed.[8]

The special committee chose to make a point of the fact that money and land from Macon was ". . . conveyed to us not as a donation, but for a valuable consideration." [9] The obvious valuable consideration being that location of Mercer in Macon would bring growth to the Macon area, although it was not so stated specifically.

Henry Holcombe Tucker, and others, had tried for

[4]*Ibid.,* p. 10.
[5]*Loc. cit.*
[6]*Ibid.,* p.p. 16, 17.
[7]*Ibid.,* p. 17.
[8]*Loc. cit.*
[9]*Ibid.,* p. 18.

several years to secure either a branch line of the Georgia railroad to Penfield or a rail horse carriage from Greensboro to Penfield, but the efforts were not successful. Internal evidence indicates that Tucker's was a strong voice in favor of removal of Mercer. Residents of Penfield had instituted litigation to keep Mercer there, and the move was fought all the way to the Supreme Court of the State of Georgia by residents of Penfield. On Nov. 15th, 1870, Mercer trustees had appointed a committee to secure from the Superior Court of Bibb county an amendment to the charter. Although the application was granted January 14, 1871, the trustees had to declare that:

> We cannot, therefore, resume our usual college-work until the case is finally settled, as to the amendment.[10]

In effect, Mercer University was out of business for a short time following the end of the 1871 term and the conferring of degrees upon seniors who were to graduate.[11] The special committee to work out details of the move to Macon presented a resolution for Convention approval which said:

> Resolved, That sympathizing with our beloved Faculty in their temporary relief from the active duty of teaching in said College, we earnestly hope that the period of such interruption will not be long, and that Providence will kindly open to them some means of temporary livelihood, until we can again claim their services.[12]

In the area of missions, 1871 was an important year also.

> Twenty-four missionaries have been under appointment during the past year, through your arrangement with the Domestic Board of the Southern Baptist Convention.[13]

The cost for these twenty-four was $8,177.47.[14] "Of this

---

[10]*Ibid.*, p. 19.
[11]*Ibid.*, p.p. 19, 20.
[12]*Ibid.*, p. 20.
[13]*Ibid.*, p. 13.
[14]*Loc. cit.*

amount, the sum of $794.99, is in excess of that paid the Domestic Board by the State of Georgia." [15]

JOINT MISSIONARY SUPPORT

The report on State and Domestic Missions reflected agreements with the board in Marion, Alabama, for joint missionary support, which pattern has continued in varying degrees to this day.[16] Marion was the first home for the Domestic Board.

Behind the scenes of emphasis upon State Missions was the idea, near implementation, of a board of some type to supervise State Missions work in Georgia.

By 1871, Georgia Baptists were ready to move into yet another area which had been discussed during the War Between the States, and which had lain dormant since 1864; the establishment of some type of child-care ministry for orphan children. In 1871, the Convention adopted a resolution which said:

> Believing as we do that one of the most pressing duties now demanding the attention, prayers, labor and money, of Georgia Baptists, is the establishment of an Orphan's Home; therefore,
> Resolved, that a committee of seven be appointed to devise a plan, select a location, and proceed at once to raise funds for its establishment.[17]

With all the plans being made during that important year, the Convention had not gotten beyond the $27,000 figure in its treasury both for income and expenditures.[18] Therefore, new measures would have to be devised to provide funds for advance.

Georgia Baptists, historically, were never a people to dally when suggestions for programs were made. They simply, routinely, and almost universally appointed a committee, comprised either of three, five or seven members to explore,

[15]*Loc. cit.*
[16]*Loc. cit.*
[17]*Ibid.,* p. 16.
[18]*Ibid.,* p.p. 26, 27.

study, and report back to the Convention. And, the committee method appeared to work effectively.

The Convention approved unanimously a resolution stating

> That we reaffirm the principles asserted by the State Convention of our brethren, held in the city of Macon in 1866, in relation to the theatre, the opera, the modern dance, and card-playing, to-wit: that we deem a voluntary participation in them to be inconsistent with a proper Christian walk.[19]

A proprietory interest in the Southern Baptist Convention was evident when the Convention did

> . . . most heartily deprecate the agitation of the subject of removal, or abolition of any of the Boards of the Convention, and hereby enters into its solemn protest against these attacks. . .[20]

This was an apparent response to a debate at the 1868 session of the Southern Baptist Convention as to whether or not the Domestic Mission Board should continue to function,[21] and sentiments evident earlier concerning retention of Boards.

When the Convention met in Macon in 1872, two important committees were named. Georgia Baptists had been seeking, almost from the beginning of Mercer University, to establish a theological seminary in the state. The concept of such a seminary as an adjunct to Mercer, separate from Mercer, and Mercer as a seminary were at times discussed. In 1872, James P. Boyce, of South Carolina, spoke to the Convention and dealt with the proposed relocation of the Southern Baptist Theological Seminary. Following the address by Boyce, the Convention adopted a resolution dealing with the proper location and endowment of the seminary, declaring that

[19]*Ibid.*, p. 9.

[20]*Ibid.*, p. 7.

[21]Rutledge, Arthur B. *Missions to America,* Nashville: Broadman Press, 1969, p. 37.

> . . . we feel anxious, if possible, to secure its location
> within the State of Georgia, and if not, as near her
> borders as possible.[22]

A committee was appointed to confer with Boyce, and to
consider also the matter of uniting the endowment and funds
of the theological department of Mercer with the seminary.[23]

In its own version of a minister's retirement plan, the Convention in 1872 adopted a lengthy report of a Committee
on Aged and Infirmed ministers which declare that:

> . . . the class of Ministers of the Gospel contemplated
> in this report are not objects of charity, but are soldiers
> of Christ, entitled justly and rightly to their support
> from the citizens of Christ's Kingdom, as a fair re-
> muneration for past services. They are older brothers
> of the family who have worn themselves out in planting
> seed for the younger members to reap.
> In view of the righteousness of their claims, your com-
> mittee offer the following resolutions:
> 1st, that the Treasurer of the Convention open an ac-
> count upon his books to be called the Baptist Minis-
> ter's Savings Fund.
> Resolved, that the Deacons of every church within
> the limits of this Convention, and the offices of every
> Society in connection with this Convention, be requested
> to make or cause to be made a quarterly collection in
> such a manner as to bring the matter before all their
> church members during the year, . . .[24]

The proposal called also for assistance to the families of
deceased ministers who were in indigent circumstances.[25]
While the concept was laudable, and in keeping with historic
Convention interest in ministerial relief, it failed in efforts to
secure support from laymen!

There had been discussion for at least two years concerning establishment of a Baptist school in Dalton prior
to a formal proposal in 1872. In that year, G. A. Lofton presented a proposal to the Convention from the citizens of
Dalton and the Baptist church of that city. The proposal

[22]*Minutes, Georgia Baptist Convention,* 1872, p. 11.
[23]*Loc. cit.*
[24]*Ibid.,* p.p. 12.
[25]*Ibid.,* p. 13.

Administrative Staff

Ernest J. Kelley
*Administration-
Cooperative
Missions*

Searcy S. Garrison
Executive Secretary-Treasurer

A. Judson Burrell
*Annuity Programs-
Stewardship*

Bruce Barbour
Office Manager

Lawrence Webb
Public Relations

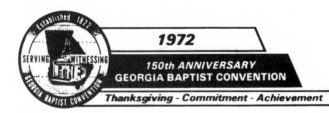

Established 1822
SERVING WITNESSING
GEORGIA BAPTIST CONVENTION

1972

**150th ANNIVERSARY
GEORGIA BAPTIST CONVENTION**

Thanksgiving - Commitment - Achievement

Heads of Educational Institutions
Georgia Baptist Convention

Rufus Carrollton Harris
Mercer University

Robert W. Jackson
Tift College

Randall H. Minor
Shorter College

Warner Earle Fusselle
Truett-McConnell College

J. Theodore Phillips
Brewton-Parker College

Leaders In Benevolent Ministries, Auxiliary

O. Leonard Pedigo
Children's Homes

Edwin B. Peel
Georgia Baptist Hospital

Cecil T. Underwood
Peachtree-On-Peachtree Inn

Charles C. Duncan
Georgia Baptist Foundation

Harvey R. Mitchell
Baptist Village

Miss Dorothy Pryor
Woman's Missionary
Union

Leaders In State Missions Programs

Julian T. Pipkin
Sunday School

O. M. Cates
Evangelism

Waldo Woodcock
Church Training

Aubrey L. Hawkins
Student Work

Bernard D. King
Brotherhood

Paul McCommon
Church Music

Earle F. Stirewalt
Program of Negro
Work

Clifton A. Forrester
Georgia Baptist
Assembly

Roy W. Hinchey
Pastor-Church
Relations

Garnie A. Brand
Norman Baptist
Assembly

offered $10,000 in Dalton city bonds payable at 7 per cent
interest semi-annually for 20 years, for construction of a
building and purchase of equipment if the Convention would
establish an institute in the city. The offer included land
for a site for the building, a condition that the property
would revert to the city and original owners if the Convention failed to carry on an institute, and called for at least
two teachers. The proposal called for establishment of such
a school through the Mercer Board of Trustees. The Convention adopted the resolution, referred it to the Mercer
trustees, and authorized the trustees to accept and act as they
saw fit.[26]

Pursuant to the action taken by the Convention in 1871
with regard to an orphan's home, a report was given in 1872
that trustees of the home had accepted a tract of 300 acres
of land about two miles from Marietta on the Western and
Atlantic Railroad,

> . . . where we hope, under the blessing of God and by
> the liberality of Georgia Baptists, soon to begin to
> establish our enterprise on a permanent basis. This
> property was donated to us for this purpose by the
> citizens of Marietta.[27]

Despite the glowing report of activities in behalf of the proposed home, difficulty developed in acquisition of the property, which was never deeded in accord with the earlier
promise.[28]

OPERATION BEGUN IN 1871

After the 1871 session, the trustees for the orphan's home
took the initiative in beginning operation of a small home,

> . . . a house having been furnished us free of rent for
> a year by a lady of this place. . .[Atlanta][29]

Thus in less than a year's time following the 1871 Convention, a small home had been opened in Atlanta, promise of

[26]*Ibid.*, p. 13.
[27]*Ibid.*, p. 14.
[28]*Minutes, Georgia Baptist Convention,* 1873, p. 13.
[29]*Minutes, Georgia Baptist Convention,* 1872, p. 14.

300 acres given, and cash receipts in hand of $4,791.25. With expenses for an agent's salary and home expenses of $2,119.11, there was a cash balance of $2,672.14. Additionally, there were notes on hand in the amount of $9,981.50, and $1,000 in Atlanta 8 per cent bonds, for a total of $13,653.64 accumulated in a year's time.[30]

With financial and organizational affairs in Georgia improving, the brethren began to turn their attention to doctrinal matters, which had been placed to some degree in a secondary position since the death of Jesse Mercer. An example of this is found in a resolution dealing with Baptist doctrine offered by S. G. Hillyer, and adopted unanimously by a rising vote of the Convention in 1872. The Hillyer resolution said:

> Whereas, It has been the custom of associated Baptists to reaffirm their views in regard to their distinctive doctrines and ordinances, whenever in their judgment it was necessary;
> And, whereas, a few of our brethren have recently given expression to opinions not fully in accordance with those now held and practiced, as they ever have been, by our churches on this Continent;
> Therefore, Resolved, That we maintain the following propositions in regard to the doctrine of Baptism and the Lord's Supper, to be scriptural, and in conformity with the view and practices of our churches, viz:
> 1. That baptism is the immersion of a believer in Jesus Christ, by an authorized administrator, in the name of the Trinity.
> 2. That such a baptism is an indispensible pre-requisite to church membership and to admission to the Lord's Supper.
> 3. Unbaptized persons, not being church members, cannot be clothed with authority to administer the ordinances; and, therefore, immersions performed by such persons are null and void.
> 4. That the sincerity of the subject cannot supply the want of authority in the administrator.[31]

Evidently the Mercer high school at Penfield began shortly after the 1871 session of the Convention, because the report

[30]*Loc. cit.*
[31]*Ibid.*, p. 15.

of the Committee on Education in 1872 indicated the existence and operation of the school

> . . . lingering yet in the groves whence have issued the faithful preacher and the devoted missionary, . . .[32]

The committee commended also the Augusta institute

> . . . for the education of colored brethren in the ministry, . . .[33]

This institute was not mentioned previously in Convention minutes.

The Convention, as indicated earlier, expressed keen interest in securing the Southern seminary, and following remarks by Boyce and others, adopted a recommendation which authorized the Convention to propose to Southern's trustees that the Convention would raise between $150,000 and $200,000 in endowment for the seminary and provide also

> . . . such sum as may be given by the city or local authorities of the place which may secure the location, on condition that it be located in the State of Georgia.[34]

The second part of the resolution concerning the Seminary indicated that it was not deemed

> . . . advisable for the Convention to take any action on the question of transferring the funds and securities belonging to the theological department of Mercer University to the Southern Baptist Theological Seminary.[35]

Indicative of the final disposition of legal matters connected with the removal to Macon, it was reported that the endowment of the University had been increased more than $25,000 ". . . since the settlement of the difficulties of removal. . ."[36] The Convention authorized further that any expenses which developed in operation of the Mercer high school be taken out of the general fund.[37]

The report of the Mercer trustees for 1872 was a fast-

[32]*Ibid.*, p.p. 16, 17.
[33]*Ibid.*, p. 17.
[34]*Ibid.*, p.p. 17, 18.
[35]*Ibid.*, p. 18.
[36]*Ibid.*, p. 20.
[37]*Loc. cit.*

paced account of progress made in the construction of a new campus. Highlights of the report included the fact that $60,000 had been allocated for the building committee by the Board of Trustees as required for building purposes, and that the offer from Macon's First Baptist church for use of their facilities until construction was completed was accepted.[38] As of the 1872 Convention, assets of Mercer, in cluding the $125,000 from Macon, were $291,411.28, with $13,144.95 in income for the past year.[39] The Penfield property was valued at $30,240.00.[40]

CORRESPONDENTS TO NEGRO CONVENTIONS

For the first time, in the minutes of the 1873 Convention, there appeared sample forms for use in bequests to the several interests of the Convention, including the Baptist Minister's Savings fund.[41] In 1873, the Convention received Wilks Flag as a correspondent from the Middle Georgia [colored] Association, and J. Milner, from the New Hope [colored] Association.[42] There was still a continuing pattern of interest in the education welfare and evangelization of the Negro in Georgia which had been a characteristic interest of Georgia Baptists. In 1873, the Convention still was appointing correspondents to several conventions including the colored convention in Georgia.[43]

The Orphan's Home was in difficulty in 1873. Although a small unit had been opened in Atlanta,[44] the proposed site at Marietta had not been delivered.

During the year, a dispute had arisen between the home board of trustees and the city of Marietta. The trustees indicated their belief that the city had not lived up to its initial promises and agreements. They reported that it

---

[38]*Ibid.*, p. 25.
[39]*Ibid.*, p. 26.
[40]*Loc. cit.*
[41]*Minutes, Georgia Baptist Convention,* 1873, p. 6.
[42]*Ibid.*, p. 9.
[43]*Ibid.*, p. 11.
[44]*Ibid.*, p. 14.

appeared the proposed property, which was at the foot of Kennesaw Mountain, would not be suitable for an Orphan's Home.[45] The special committee on the report of the home trustees recommended that, if possible, a site in or near Marietta be selected, and if this was not possible, then the board of trustees was authorized to make a permanent location for the home as they deemed wise.[46]

Fourteen missionaries had labored in Georgia between the 1872 and 1873 Conventions under the Domestic Mission Board.[47] Finally, at the 1873 session, meeting in Rome, the report of Sunday School work, delayed two days as unfinished business, was discussed. The discussion was spirited apparently because the brethren were limited to five minute speeches, and the report was referred finally to the "committee on state missions." [48] Significance of this was that the report of the committee on Sunday School work, in effect advised that this work

> . . . be made a regular department in the routine of business of this Convention. The plan of operations which we suggest is, to work through the regular and usual channels of Baptist ideas and methods of organization and labor—namely: for the Convention to excite or instigate the Associations, and for the Associations to encourage, animate and advise the individual churches.[49]

The report said further:

> We suggest the appointment of a Sunday School Executive Committee for the State of Georgia, responsible to this body, which shall encourage and promote the Sunday School Work in our denomination, and report to this convention annually. It shall have power to elect a State Superintendent of the Sunday School Work, with an adequate salary, who shall give his whole time to the work of organizing and promoting the Baptist Sunday School Work of Georgia.[50]

[45]*Minutes, Georgia Baptist Convention,* 1873, p. 13.
[46]*Loc. cit.*
[47]*Ibid.,* p. 15.
[48]*Ibid.,* p. 17.
[49]*Loc. cit.*
[50]*Loc. cit.*

This report was referred, as indicated, to the committee on state missions, and no action was taken by the Convention. The seeds of an identifiable program of State Missions were evident. Immediately following the end of the War, the Georgia Convention had done what it could not only to strengthen the missionary activity in the state, but at the same time to undergird the work of the Domestic Mission Board, as that Board sought to regain its own strength. Now, the Convention was beginning to feel that it was ready to better organize and supervise, at the state level, mission activities within the state.[51]

The most significant action of the Convention in 1873 was the initial step made for the formation of a State Mission Board. The Convention:

> Resolved, that the Moderator appoint a committee of five, to take into consideration the propriety of organizing a State Missionary Board, and propose a plan or organization for conducting the work so as to accomplish the greatest amount of good, and at the same time develop the habit of beneficence among our brethren, and report at the next meeting of this body.[52]

The Convention that year went on record as expressing strong dissent with a proposal that would have made all colleges in the state, including Mercer, a part of a state-wide university system.[53] During January, 1873, evidently, an outbreak of meningitis occurred in Macon which apparently claimed the lives of several Mercer students and kept the school closed until March 3, 1873.[54] The trustees reported

> . . . the Angel of Death, in the form of meningitis, invaded the precincts of our loved and cherished University, and claimed for his own many of the best spirits among our young men, . . .[55]

At the session in Americus in 1874, the Convention took

[51]*Ibid.,* p.p. 12, 14.
[52]*Ibid.,* p. 14.
[53]*Ibid.,* p. 18.
[54]*Ibid.,* p. 26.
[55]*Ibid.,* p. 25.

cognizance of the need for better relations between the Convention and the Associations, to strengthen the work of the Denomination. A committee was named to report to that Convention session some means of accomplishment.[56] This committee, recognizing the Constitutional purposes of the Convention, said:

> We lay down, first, then, as a general principle, that there should be some worthy and scriptural object on which all the Baptists of Georgia may unite, [as in the State Mission and Sunday School work.]
> Second, the organization of some scheme or plan which will lead to general union and co-operation. [Such as the establishment of a State Board, with instructions to carry out the common object and effect general co-operation.][57]

The report called for "official correspondence" with all Associations; to have one or more Convention representative at the annual meeting of every Association; to use the press to inform Georgia Baptists; to secure a State Evangelist; and to seek from each Association an annual statement of objects, statistics, and condition.[58]

> . . . to effect this end, it is necessary to take some steps now, not in practical operation . . .

The report suggested:

> that the clerk and Executive Committee be instructed to take proper steps, in accordance with this report, to carry out the objects of the resolutions considered and adopted.

Samuel Boykin was chairman of the committee, and the report was adopted by the Convention.[59]

It is evident from the minutes that a major part of the Convention sessions at Americus were devoted to studies of organizational structure. Left unresolved in 1873 was the suggestion for the establishment of a Sunday school department. This, together with interest in establishment of

[56]*Minutes, Georgia Baptist Convention,* 1874, p. 17.
[57]*Ibid.,* p. 24.
[58]*Loc. cit.*
[59]*Ibid.,* p.p. 24, 25.

a State Board of Missions became the object of the 1874 discussions. The record does not indicate why oversight of the state missions program was not granted automatically to the Executive Committee. From the first noted discussion, an alternate separate board, apart from the Executive Committee, was in the background. The subject had, however, become touchy.

On the final day of the Americus session the special committee studying the State Board of Missions and Sunday School work made its report. The report was tabled with the exception of the Sunday School work. This section was adopted and set in motion ground work for establishment of a Sunday School department. In its report, the committee said:

> They believed that the appointment of a Sunday School Superintendent, who should also be an Evangelist, thereby increasing his service and his usefulness, would widen the field of Christian effort in this department, and greatly add to its efficiency.[60]

The plan, contained in the report, provided for

> the appointment of a Sunday School Committee of five . . . who shall take charge of this work, and secure as early as practicable, a suitable man for the place. The plan of operations, and its details, should be left to the Committee and the Superintendent. It is understood that the Superintendent shall raise his salary, the amount of which shall be agreed upon between the committee and himself, upon the field, and in no case shall any indebtedness against this body be increased.[61]

This committee was located in Atlanta.[62]

FIRST SUNDAY SCHOOL SECRETARY

June 10, 1874 was a significant day in the life of the Georgia Baptist Convention, because it marked the appointment of T. C. Boykin as general superintendent and evangelist for the Sunday School ministry; the first in a long

[60]*Ibid.*, p. 21.
[61]*Loc. cit.*
[62]*Ibid.*, p. 23.

succession of organizational developments as a full-fledged State Missions program was structured. Boykin was paid a salary of $125 a month and traveling expense. He began his work September 1, 1874.[63] Long identified with Georgia Baptist life, he had edited in Macon a magazine called *Kind Words* which was read widely in Georgia and adjacent states.

While the report of a proposed board of missions was tabled, as indicated, the Convention ordered that it be printed in order to provide full information to Georgia Baptists concerning the proposals under study. In essence, the proposition which had been under consideration was that the Convention at each annual session appoint a Board of Missions, with a chairman, recording secretary, etc., for a total of seven members, and that this Board would have responsibility for the direction of all agencies in the collection and disbursements of funds from the churches and associations.[64]

A significant part of the report tabled included, in section three, the statement:

> That as co-operation is indispensible to success, the Associations be invited to commit the Missions now conducted by them, within their own bounds, to the State Board, [reserving, if they so please, the right to nominate the missionaries in their several districts] and to pay into the treasury all funds collected for Domestic and Indian missions.[65]

Of importance also is the portion of the report indicating:

> That twenty five per cent of the net collections of the State Board be paid to the Marion board, no part of which shall be claimed for work within the state; *provided*, that in consideration of this arrangement the Marion board shall leave with the state board the collection of funds from their field.[66]

[63]*Minutes, Georgia Baptist Convention,* 1875, p. 52.
[64]*Minutes, Georgia Baptist Convention,* 1874, p. 21.
[65]*Loc. cit.*
[66]*Loc. cit.*

A minority report was submitted which called for election of a board comprised of seven members, a majority of whom should live in the same community.[67] This report appeared to give a proposed Mission Board broader internal authority.[68]

The matter arose again in 1875 with presentation of a paper with reference to a State Board.[69] A committee to study the paper reported that ". . . in their judgment it is inexpedient, under existing circumstances, to make any movement in the matter. . ." [70]

The 1873 proposal concerning establishment of a high school in Dalton, approved and turned over to the Mercer trustees, had been implemented prior to the Americus session. The establishment of the Crawford High School in Dalton under the superintendence of William C. Wilkes, was reported in 1874, and agitation continued for creation of a college or university for women.[71]

For the first time, of record, the Milledgeville Convention in 1875 approved a change in procedure for sending messengers or delegates [as they were referred to interchangeably] to the Southern Baptist Convention. J. H. Kilpatrick, White Plains, submitted a resolution, approved which said

> that we recommend to our churches and associations that hereafter they appoint their delegates to the Southern Baptist Convention.[72]

Prior to this delegates to the Southern Convention had been elected by the Georgia Convention.

A list of high schools under the maintenance or control of Baptists included the Hephzibah High school, Richmond county, the Hearn High School, Cave Spring, and the Kirkwood High school, near Atlanta.[73] Directly under Conven-

[67]*Ibid.*, p. 22.
[68]*Loc. cit.*
[69]*Minutes, Georgia Baptist Convention,* 1875, p. 13.
[70]*Ibid.*, p. 15.
[71]*Minutes, Georgia Baptist Convention,* 1874, p. 27.
[72]*Minutes, Georgia Baptist Convention,* 1875, p. 13.
[73]*Ibid.*, p. 25.

tion control was the Mercer High school, Penfield, and the Crawford High school, Dalton.[74] References continued to be made to the institute for colored ministers in Augusta.[75] By the 1870's, the report of the Executive Committee had been reduced to reports on the condition of schools other than Mercer University and the distribution of ministerial aid.[76]

Significant also at the Milledgeville Convention was the meeting for the first time of a Pastor's Conference at which is was agreed: "That all white Baptist ministers in good standing in the State of Georgia, be entitled to membership. . . ." and a meeting was slated for 1876 in connection with the Convention at Thomasville.[77]

The Convention was near agreement upon the subject of a Board of Missions of some type when it met in Thomasville in 1876. Twenty-five Associations and ten societies were represented.[78] Discussion upon the subject was lengthy. There is merit in reproducing the rather full notation of the proposal at Thomasville, which, with changes and modifications, was adopted in Gainesville in 1877.

The special committee on the subject of Missions and Sabbath School called for election annually of a committee of missions to be located in Macon, composed of seven members, to hold office until their successors were appointed. This committee would have no power to appoint missionaries, but would be charged with the duty

> . . . of arousing the spirit of missions among the churches, securing, as far as practicable, the adoption by the churches of plans of systematic contribution, and effecting, to the full extent of their influence, the co-operation of the Baptists of Georgia in the great work of missions.[79]

The committee, as conceived, would have authority to appoint a single agent, who would receive an adequate salary

[74]*Ibid.,* p. 26.
[75]*Loc. cit.*
[76]*Ibid.,* p.p. 34, 35.
[77]*Ibid.,* p. 54.
[78]*Minutes, Georgia Baptist Convention,* 1876, p.p. 9-11.
[79]*Ibid.,* **p.p.** 17, 18.

to be pro rated from the contributions to the different boards. Another provision would place responsibility of Sabbath School work, as a part of the work of missions, under the Committee, giving that group leeway to ask the Home Board to name a Sabbath School evangelist whose salary would have been paid by that board from funds contributed through Georgia churches for that purpose. The Missions Committee would be responsible for securing contributions from the churches to pay for the evangelist. And, the suggested plan called for the Home Board to appoint only such missionaries as would be recommended by the State Board.[80]

The Thomasville report appears to reflect what in different character had earlier been evident; evidence of differing ideas concerning the role the Domestic Mission Board would have in Georgia Baptist Convention life. Immediately after the War Between the States, Georgia supported to an intensive degree the work of the Domestic Board, as that Board sought, in effect, to re-establish itself. By the early 1870's, it appears there were many influential Georgia Baptist leaders who wanted Georgia leadership to have more control over funds raised in Georgia for home missions purposes.

When the Convention met in Gainesville in 1877, J. H. Campbell made a motion that the Executive Committee, then located in Macon, be removed to Atlanta, and that management of Domestic Missions and Sunday school work in Georgia be committed to that Committee. Campbell's motion died when the Convention adjourned that session.[81]

When the Convention reassembled, it suspended the order of business to hear the Report of the Committee on Missions ". . . which was adopted . . ." after a rather thorough study of the mission situation in Georgia, and matters indicated in the Thomasville discussion of 1876.[82]

With adoption of this report, the Georgia Baptist Conven-

[80]*Ibid.*, p. 18.
[81]*Minutes, Georgia Baptist Convention*, 1877, p.p. 13-14.
[82]*Ibid.*, p. 15.

tion had created for the first time a vehicle for permanent organizational and promotional work in the state, and thus laid the foundation for nearly a century of progress, marred only by the effects of the Depression in the 1920's and 1930's.

The Convention had come a long way. In the 55 years since the Convention's organization in 1822, that body had survived anti-missionary spirit, opposition, war and depression. Not only had the Convention survived, it, for the most part, experienced continuous growth. Without a Mission Board as such, and with an Executive Committee whose powers had through the years diminished, the Convention in annual session had in reality hammered out its course of progress and maintained that course. Convention interests in missions, education, and a benevolent ministry in the Orphan's Home had been manifest during this period with solid accomplishments in each area, although at this time, the Orphan's Home project still was in a state of embryo growth.

CHAPTER 10

A State Mission Board Is Formed

Importance of the subject of organization of a Board of Missions was evident when the Convention, in 1877 at Gainesville, suspended the order of business to hear and adopt a report of the Committee on Missions. The report, which was approved, said:

> Resolved, That this Convention appoint a Committee to be located in the city of Atlanta, and consisting of brethren A. T. Spauldin, D. W. Glenn, J. H. James, J. M. Wood, J. H. Campbell, W. L. Goldsmith, and S. T. Jenkins, which shall take charge of Missionary and Sunday School work in the State of Georgia, and that they be authorized to employ Missionaries and Sunday-school workers, raise funds and expend them, using such agent or agents as they may deem necessary.[1]

In this succinct manner, the Convention launched a program of State Missions, leaving its Executive Committee in Macon, with no enlarged duties.

The Convention in Thomasville, as indicated, adopted the proposal looking toward establishment of a Board of Missions. The implementation of the board concept obviously was left unclear, and it remained for the 1877 Convention to formalize by resolution the actual procedure to be followed in setting up the board and delineating the areas of authority. Evidence of the rather vague status of the board between 1876 and 1877 is found in the 1877 minutes, when the State Missions Committee reported:

[1]*Minutes, Georgia Baptist Convention*, 1877, p. 16.

> Immediately after the close of your last session, the committee organized, and took the steps necessary to carry out your instructions. The Foreign and Home Mission Boards were requested to withdraw their agents from the State, and the whole work of collecting funds was placed in the hands of brother C. M. Irwin, as organizing agent. The Home Mission Board was requested to appoint brother T. C. Boykin as Sunday-school Evangelist for the State, which was done.[2]

The special committee on Missions had in 1876 called for a committee of missions, with no appointive authority. This committee was to seek to arouse ". . . the spirit of missions among the churches, . . ."[3] It was to be responsible for Sabbath School work, with the Home Board to employ the worker.[4] There was in this Committee on Missions the intermediate role leading to establishment of the Mission Board the next year.

No concrete evidence exists which would explain the phasing out of the Executive Committee in this manner. There is some evidence, by past history, that the Executive Committee's existence and continued function in Macon was, to a degree, because Mercer University was located at Macon. The first and primary activities of the Executive Committee centered around the founding and development of Mercer University.

In 1872, after Mercer University was moved to Macon, the Executive Committee, in its report, said:

> Owing to the removal of the University from Penfield to Macon, the necessity arises of locating a majority of the Committee at the latter place.[5]

This is indicative of the Executive Committee's concept of its functions.

Minutes of the Executive Committee during the 1830's and 1840's were devoted primarily to this matter. An auxiliary area of responsibility, related, was ministerial edu-

---

[2]*Ibid.*, p.p. 31, 32.
[3]*Minutes, Georgia Baptist Convention*, 1876, p.p. 17, 18.
[4]*Loc. cit.*
[5]*Minutes, Georgia Baptist Convention*, 1872, p. 24.

cation. Inasmuch as the Convention, in session, dealt in large measure with the Domestic Mission Board after formation of the Southern Baptist Convention, in areas related to work with missionaries, the Executive Committee had little to do with this area. Actually, the Executive Committee was *empowered* to act in areas in which there is little indication that it acted. By the 1870's the Executive Committee was comprised mainly of Macon area men. Some evidence of prevailing sentiment toward the Executive Committee is noted in the fact that when the Campbell motion [chapter 9, p. 218] was presented concerning removal of the committee to Atlanta, it died without action.[6]

Officials of Gainesville took advantage of the Convention meeting in their city to submit a proposition to Georgia Baptists concerning establishment of a female seminary "of high order" in that city.[7]

Gainesville offered the Convention six acres of land and $25,000 in city of Gainesville bonds with interest at eight per cent per annum from the time ". . . that said college shall be located, and building commenced . . ."[8] The city officials expressed further their belief that $20,000 would be raised by voluntary subscriptions.[9] At this point in the Convention proceedings C. D. Campbell made a motion which in effect changed the college proposal. The offer from Gainesville was for property and money for the establishment of a seminary. The Campbell resolution declared

> . . . that we take under our control the institution of learning for girls, which the city authorities of Gainesville, and the citizens thereof and vicinity, propose to build, and which they so generously tendered this body, . . .

and that in acceptance of this proposition from Gainesville the Convention ". . . did not disparage the claims of any similar institution. . ." and did ". . . not assume any financial

[6]*Minutes, Georgia Baptist Convention,* 1877, p.p. 13, 14.
[7]*Ibid.,* 1877, p. 18.
[8]*Ibid.,* p.p. 17, 18.
[9]*Ibid.,* p. 18.

liability whatever." [10] The resolution said further that the Convention was

> . . . ready to accept and adopt any institution of learning which may be tendered us: provided said acceptance does not involve any financial liability whatever.[11]

The resolution gave the Executive Committee authority to proceed by contract with proper authorities in steps to carry out the resolution.[12] The school was in operation by 1880.[13]

Citing the action of the 1877 Convention in regard to a proposed Female Seminary at Gainesville, the Convention in 1878 voted to accept tender of the Monroe Female College upon the same terms.[14]

A final item of interest for 1877 was the report of the trustees of the Orphan's Home which declared that the home was caring for 25 children; receiving fourteen during the year, finding homes for nine, with one death. The trustees reported that they were feeding, educating and training the children for usefulness ". . . and for heaven." [15]

Georgia Baptists had not been without interest in the preservation of history. J. H. Campbell had written *A History of Georgia Baptists,* C. D. Mallary had written the *Memoirs of Elder Jesse Mercer,* and *Memoirs of B. M. Sanders.* Jesse Mercer had written a valuable *History of The Georgia Association.* J. H. Kilpatrick had written on Baptist doctrine, and others had written minor works. However, it was to the 1878 Convention at LaGrange that credit must go for a new interest in Georgia Baptist history. W. L. Kilpatrick offered a resolution in LaGrange asking:

> That a committee be appointed to report to this body some plan looking to the preservation of facts connected with the history of our denomination in this State.[16]

[10]*Ibid.,* p. 19.
[11]*Loc. cit.*
[12]*Loc. cit.*
[13]*Minutes, Georgia Baptist Convention,* 1880, p. 22.
[14]*Minutes, Georgia Baptist Convention,* 1878, p. 15.
[15]*Minutes, Georgia Baptist Convention,* 1877, p. 42.
[16]*Minutes, Georgia Baptist Convention,* 1878, p. 11.

A committee was named.

It was not unusual for a delegate to offer a resolution at a session prior to a report upon the same subject. Such was the case apparently with the Kilpatrick resolution. The report of the Committee on the History of the Baptist Denomination was a special order for consideration, and that report, which was adopted, declared that the committee felt it

> . . . of the utmost importance that steps be taken at once for accomplishing the purpose above indicated, and recommend that brethren who desire to aid in this work, form a society having no organic connection with this Convention, yet at the same time looking to it for moral support: That this society be permanent in its character and self perpetuating.[17]

The History Committee looked also toward securing ". . . if possible, a room in the building of Mercer University for depositing the materials collected;" and urged annual meetings of the society in conjunction with Convention sessions.[18]

Concern for the religious welfare of Negroes in Georgia continued to be a topic of interest. Samuel Boykin, reporting to the group said:

> We are forced to the observation, that, amongst the colored people, there is great need of correct evangelical preaching and sunday school works; and we earnestly invite the attention of the Convention to this subject. Their churches and schools need the benefit of white training and instruction. We heartily commend the State Mission Board and its operations, and urge a generous support of it and its missionaries. At the same time, we remind you that various associations maintain their own missionaries, and some more than one.[19]

The latter part of Boykin's report alluded to what must have been a rather touchy subject from time to time. There was no expressed disagreement with the concept of the associations having their own missionaries. Rather, the tenor was one of concern lest associations of Missionary Baptist

[17]*Ibid.*, p. 18.
[18]*Loc. cit.*
[19]*Loc. cit.*

churches concentrate too much attention upon their own locality to the hurt of the overall missionary endeavor.

WOMEN'S WORK SANCTIONED

First official Convention sanction to organized work among Baptist women in Georgia was expressed in LaGrange, as the brethren:

> Resolved: That being deeply sensible of the growing importance of the work of woman's mission to woman, we earnestly commend it to the sisters in Georgia, and urge the formation by them of societies in the various churches for the furtherance of this work.[20]

This was a change from action in 1874 when the Woman's Mission to Woman Society petitioned for membership as a society, and a committee appointed to study the application reported:

> Resolved, that in accordance with the true meaning of the Constitution, we feel compelled to decline to receive the Society . . . of the Second Baptist Church of Atlanta.[21]

Women in Georgia had been active in mission work since the beginning of the 19th century. They had contributed liberally over the years, but it was not until this Convention session that "official" encouragement was given for organization in the local churches.

While the Convention was moving to consolidate forces, Mercer University, in the new location at Macon, had not been idle. As of the June, 1877, commencement, the institution reported 114 students.[22]

The first annual report of the State Mission Board revealed that J. H. DeVotie had been selected unanimously as corresponding secretary, completing organization work for the board just two and one half months after the Convention had ended. A. T. Spalding, president of the Board, served without compensation until DeVotie's election.[23]

[20]*Ibid.*, p. 27.
[21]*Minutes, Georgia Baptist Convention*, 1874, p. 23.
[22]*Minutes, Georgia Baptist Convention*, 1878, Appendix, p. III.
[23]*Ibid.*, p. V.

With a reminder that the Board required the missionary to raise his own salary, there was a report that to June 12, 1878, $6,537.90 had been received for state missions and $1,376.00 for building houses of worship for a total of $7,913.90.[24]

The report showed also that during this year, T. C. Boykin, Sunday school evangelist, had visited 190 churches and 45 associations, written 1,038 letters, preached 145 sermons, delivered 313 addresses, aided in nine "protracted meetings", organized 58 Sabbath schools, visited in 19 Sabbath-school Conventions, sold 447 Bibles and books, distributed 1,217 tracts and papers, added 1,414 scholars on Sunday-schools and traveled 7,231 miles.[25]

It was not long after the State Mission Board was created and began functioning, that it became obvious there was a considerable loss in the collection of money as agents for various enterprises made seperate appeals. Out of this concern, there was adopted in Columbus in 1879 a motion which said:

> Whereas it has become imperatively necessary to curtail the expense of collecting funds for our missionary operations, therefore, Resolved
> 1. That we respectfully request the Southern Baptist Convention to instruct both the Home and Foreign Boards, in raising funds in Georgia, to work through our State Mission Board.
> Resolved,
> 2. That the State Mission Board be instructed to put itself in direct communication with the pastors throughout the State, urging them to bring the subject of Missions directly before their churches, and to make collections at stated times during the year.
> Resolved,
> 3. That the Clerk of this Convention be instructed to furnish the Southern Baptist Convention, at its approaching session, with a copy of so much of the above preamble and resolutions as concern that body.[26]

The request that pastors keep causes of missions before their people was consistent with historic missionary emphases

[24]*Ibid.*, Printed insert in Appendix between pages VI and VII.
[25]*Ibid.*, p. VI.
[26]*Minutes, Georgia Baptist Convention*, 1879, p.p. 14, 15.

among Georgia Baptists. And, the direct link between the State Board and the pastor of the local church, as the key to denominational growth, recognized from the beginning, was to be a basic part of the Mission Board's approach to organizational unity and growth.

The Convention at the annual sessions kept the cause of missions before the messengers with addresses by representatives from the Home and Foreign boards. Emphases on the State Missions ministries were constant also.

One feature of the Columbus Convention which was to provide a temporary setback in one phase of Georgia Baptist work, dealt with the Orphans' Home. The Convention, apparently without much discussion, adopted the following resolution:

> Whereas, the Baptist Convention of the State of Georgia was organized for the purpose of prosecuting the work of missions and of education, and, whereas the establishment and maintenance of an Orphans' Home, and the providing of funds for the relief of aged ministers, are objects not embraced in the design of its organization, and consequently divide the time, labor and means of the Convention from the true objects; therefore,
> Resolved, that a Committee of five be appointed, whose duty it shall be to confer with the Board which has these matters in hand, and in conjunction with them, to devise such plans as shall dissolve the relations at present existing between these objects and the Convention, and report their action, through the Boards, respectively, to the Convention at its next meeting.[27]

The move was not to displace completely the aid for ministers, nor to affect permanently a ministry to orphan children. It did, however, delay for several years establishment of a permanent Orphans' Home under the sponsorship of the Convention.

The second annual report of the State Mission Board showed 24 missionaries, including the Sunday School evangelist and corresponding secretary in service,[28] with twenty

[27]*Ibid.*, p. 21.
[28]*Ibid.*, p. 28.

associational Sunday School conventions organized.[29] Baptist strength in the state increased gradually. By 1879, Georgia Baptists numbered 210,900, with 152,015 Methodists, 10,000 Presbyterians and 5,000 Episcopalians in the state.[30]

Following action concerning the Orphans' Home, a committee reported in 1880 that after conferring with the trustees of the aged ministers fund, the trustees had agreed to relinquish the work and leave the matter in the hands of associations in which ministers needing help resided. With regard to the Home, the committee recommended that it be placed in the hands of John H. James, Jos. E. Brown and H. H. Tucker with instructions to wind up all affairs of the home and turn over proceeds of the sale, and other assets, to the trustees of Mercer university.[31]

During this period, *The Index* was published, and apparently owned, by the James P. Harrison and Company printers in Atlanta. Published as a business venture by the Harrison Company, the paper still was considered very much the organ of Georgia Baptists with the 1874 and 1875 Conventions endorsing it, as well as other sessions. Advertising was not selective, and one advertisement was for a pistol, with the admonition that everyone should go armed.[32]

At this time Henry Holcombe Tucker was serving as editor for the second time, and *The Index* was publishing *The Index Bible Book* or the *Parents' and Teachers' Assistant* which contained Sunday school lessons for each week. The Convention considered the material of sufficient worth to commend use of it to the churches.[33]

STATUS OF INSTITUTIONS

In the report of the Committee on Education for 1880, a summary of the status of institutions under Baptist control

[29]*Ibid.,* p. 29.

[30]*Ibid.,* p. 50.

[31]*Minutes, Georgia Baptist Convention,* 1880, p.p. 16, 17.

[32]*The Christian Index,* Jan. 8, 1874, [quoted in James A. Lester, A History of *The Christian Index* 1822-1954 [Unpublished Master's Thesis, 1955] p. 69.

[33]*Minutes, Georgia Baptist Convention,* 1880, p. 20.

and patronage included: Southern Female college, La-Grange, with 12 teachers, 150 students; Shorter Female College, Rome, 140 or 150 students and nine "preceptors"; Perry Female College, Perry; Georgia Female College, Madison; Monroe Female college, Forsyth; Georgia Baptist Seminary, Gainesville with 107 pupils and eight teachers; Hephzibah High school, belonging to the Hephzibah association, four teachers and fifty pupils; the Hearn school, "prosperous"; Crawford High school, Dalton, belonging to the Convention; Mercer High school, Penfield, "both objects of pride; and the institution for education of colored ministers located in Atlanta." This institution was under the patronage of the American Board of Home Missions, and ". . . deserves our sympathy and most cordial co-operation." [34]

By 1880, it was estimated that there were 755 white Sunday schools in the state with 3,750 officers and teachers, 22,550 scholars, with 1,550 scholars baptized.[35] The same report showed 720 colored schools with 2,880 officers and teachers, 21,600 scholars and 1,440 baptisms.[36]

DeVotie, during 1879, had prepared a list of over 500 pastors in the State and had written letters and distributed circulars to them presenting the cause of missions in Georgia. DeVotie received a good response to this promotion, reporting to the Convention in 1880 that over 200 pastors had responded, promising ". . . to advocate the cause of missions before their churches and congregations . . .".[37] And there was a larger number of contributors as indicated by the record, with 650 churches reported as taking collections for missions either in cooperation with the Board or through their Associations.[38] The warning of the previous year concerning need to reduce the cost of collections was effective,

> . . . and a larger amount of funds have been obtained
> than under the Agency system, while the expense of

[34]*Ibid.,* p.p. 21, 22.
[35]*Ibid.,* p. 24.
[36]*Loc. cit.*
[37]*Ibid.,* p.p. 38-39.
[38]*Ibid.,* p. 39.

collections has been reduced from over thirty per cent to ten, saving for direct mission work a large amount.[39]

It was evident earlier that promotion through the Associational Executive Committees was not effective, and with the State Board making appeals directly to pastors for mission support, the work grew rapidly.

Fortunately for the child care ministry, the Woman's Missionary Society of the Second Baptist church in Atlanta, expressed willingness to take over operation of the orphans' home, assist in winding up affairs, and in the meantime look after the children. At that time, there were 12 children, four of them helpless. Of the twelve, one was blind, one paralyzed, one "weak-minded" and one on crutches.[40]

The Convention had from time to time gone on record as opposing the sale and use of alcoholic beverages. This opposition had been expressed in resolutions without apparent opposition by any Convention delegate. However, when the 1881 session agreed to petition the Legislature asking for a curb on the sale and use of alcoholic beverages, five men, including a former editor of *The Index,* asked that their dissent be noted in the record. In citing their dissent, the five, led by David E. Butler, the former editor, gave as their reason historic emphasis upon:

> Liberty of conscience, freedom of speech, and religious liberty; . . . cardinal principles, which Baptists have maintained in all ages, . . .

and that when the Georgia Baptist Convention, without authority upon the subject, [presumably from the churches,] agreed to petition the Legislature on the sale of liquor it was departing from basic and historic Baptist principles.[41]

For the first time in 1881, the Convention heard the annual report of woman's work in Georgia.[42] Finally, in 1881, seeking to dispose of the Orphans' Home matter, hanging for two years, the Convention agreed to appoint John H. James

[39]*Loc. cit.*
[40]*Ibid.,* p.p. 44, 45.
[41]*Minutes, Georgia Baptist Convention,* 1881, p.p. 16-17.
[42]*Ibid.,* p.p. 17-18.

of Atlanta as sole trustee to wind up sale of the property, incurring no debt to the Convention.[43]

During 1880 there were 3,965 baptisms among churches in the 36 associations connected with the Convention or constituent members of the Convention, and carried in the report of the Committee on the State of Religion, was the notice that in nine associations not affiliated with the Convention there were 1,130 persons baptized.[44]

The Christian Index had figured so prominently in the life of Georgia Baptists since 1833, that it is difficult to realize that there were many other papers published in the state under Baptist auspices of one type or another.

In the report of the Committee on Education was a description of other papers.

> The list is long: we cannot particularize at length. But in our own State we cannot forbear to mention *The Christian Index,* with that wonderfully gifted, versatile, trenchant defender of the faith, the venerable Dr. H. H. Tucker, at the helm; The *Baptist Banner,* a gem of a flag, held steadily in the breeze by the still strong arm of the patriarch, Rev. J. M. Wood; *The Baptist Sun,* that from the summits of its Roman hills sheds the light of Nunnally's brilliant intellect far and wide throughout the land; and dear, *Kind Words,* sent forth by our beloved brother, Samuel Boykin, a gentle missive of love and peace, to heart and mind, of young and old, in Sunday-school and home, all over the fairest State beneath the skies.
> Brethren, let us educate.[45]

Other publications issued in Georgia for a time included the *Gospel Expositor,* published at Elberton, and the *Baptist Reporter,* published at Guyton.[46] The *Central Georgia Baptist,* and the *Standard Expositor.*[47]

In the 1881 report of the Committee to report on the Mission Board's report, there is the first clear delineation of the Board's work.

[43]*Ibid.,* p.p. 18, 19.
[44]*Ibid.,* p. 19.
[45]*Ibid.,* p. 23.
[46]*Minutes, Georgia Baptist Convention,* 1888, p. 21.
[47]*Minutes, Georgia Baptist Convention,* 1889, p. 17.

The Board promotes the following objects:
1. The formation of Woman's Mission Societies.
2. The collection of funds for aged and indigent ministers.
3. The work of forming and increasing the efficiency of Sunday-schools by their Missionary, T. C. Boykin.
4. The distribution of the Bible.
5. The collection of funds, and the employment of missionaries.[48]

The report emphasized the value of the work of the Mission Board and pointed out that:

It should be especially remembered that the diversified work of the Board has been accomplished at expense of about nine per cent.[49]

In 1881, in the minutes of the Georgia Baptist Historical Society, attached to the minutes of the Convention, Samuel Boykin is identified as writer of the Historical section of the *History of Georgia Baptists With Biographical Compendium*.[50]

In research into Georgia Baptist history over a period of 20 years, this is the only positive reference to authorship of a work which since 1881 has been a primary source of information on Georgia Baptist life.

Mercer University realized $3,848.62 from the sale of the orphans' home property,[51] and the still young Mission Board was enlarged to 15 members

. . . of whom not less than five shall be brethren who are not engaged in the ministry. It is not supposed that there can be any objection to this request of the Board itself, and therefore the special committee content themselves with merely directing special attention of the Convention to it, with their hearty approval.[52]

The proposal apparently was at the suggestion of J. H. De-Votie. A second proposal concerning the Board, which was presented to the session at Americus, called for the Board

[48]*Minutes, Georgia Baptist Convention*, 1881, p. 26.
[49]*Loc. cit.*
[50]*Ibid.*, p. 89.
[51]*Minutes, Georgia Baptist Convention*, 1882, p.p. 18-19.
[52]*Ibid.*, p.p. 29, 30.

to enlarge its work to embrace colportage. The Board's report noted that this did not originate from the Board itself but rather from a need expressed within the Associations for such assistance. It was the belief that by leaving books in the associations there would be an increased witness.[53]

A comparison of the report of the State Mission Board and the report of the Executive Committee, revealed the increasing importance of the role of the State Mission Board and the decreasing responsibility of the Executive Committee during the 1870's and the 1880's. What in essence was to become the present-day Executive Committee was emerging out of the activities of the Mission Board. The then existing Executive Committee had been reduced in responsibility to presenting annual reports on funds allocated for ministerial education and funds supplied for ministerial relief.

The real base for the strength of the State Mission Board's departmental activity is found in the 1874 Convention at Americus when approval was given for the creation of a Sunday School department with a secretary who must also be an evangelist.[54]

Doctrinal issues did not occupy much time at the Convention sessions during the 1880's. Rather, the energies were devoted at the sessions to organizational steps. However, this was not to the discredit of the Convention, because there were leaders in the Convention, strong in doctrinal devotion, who expressed themselves on issues of the day and doctrinal stance through the pages of *The Christian Index* as well as occasional books and pamphlets. However, one sentence in a report to the Convention in 1883 in Griffin said that:

> As the distinguishing difference between us and other denominations is the requirement of a regenerate church-membership, we should keep this constantly revolving before the minds of the people.[55]

By 1883, a force of 26 missionaries was in the employ of the State Board, and positive action to work with Negro

[53]*Ibid.*, p. 30.
[54]*Op. cit.*, Minutes, Georgia Baptist Convention, 1874, p. 21.
[55]*Minutes, Georgia Baptist Convention*, 1883, p. 25.

ministers was indicated in the report of the Board to the Convention:

> The uninstructed condition of the colored preachers in Georgia, the main dependence for the religious teaching of five hundred and twenty thousand Baptist freedmen, induced the Board, in connection with Home Board of the Southern Baptist Convention, to appoint Dr. Wm. H. McIntosh, theological teacher to the colored preachers of this State. He commenced his work January 1st, 1883 . . . We deem this work equal to any other work in which we are engaged.[56]

Thus 18 years after the end of the War Between The States, Georgia Baptists still considered it a prime responsibility to provide education for Negro ministers.

In praise for DeVotie, it was indicated that he had

> . . . discharged the constant and varied duties of the position assigned him. Has written not less than 1,800 letters and communications, kept the accounts of the Treasury, and distributed the books of the colportage department, given some attention to the missionary department in *The Index,* visited officially 15 Associations, preached 32 sermons, delivered 35 addresses, traveled 6,038 miles.[57]

Another fact of interest to Georgia Baptists emerges as a constant pattern from the beginning of the State Mission Board: The Convention historically has held in high esteem the Mission Secretary, or Executive Secretary as he was called later, and followed in a good spirit the leadership of their chosen leader. And, notice of the work of the secretary, together with praise for that work, was frequent in the minutes.

From January 1, 1882, to January 1, 1883, Georgia Baptists gave for Convention causes a total of $31,294.69. Of this, $13,240.37 was for State Missions; $1,943.19 for Associational missions; Mercer endowment orphans' fund, $2,800; Ministerial relief, $473.84; Support of theological students at

[56]*Ibid.,* p.p. 39-40.
[57]*Ibid.,* p. 40.
[58]*Ibid.,* p. 41.

Mercer University $2,125; Foreign missions, $5,988.69; and Home and Indian missions, $4,723.60.[58]

ADVERTISING IN MINUTES

In an unusual step, which was not to last long, the Convention in 1883 permitted the use of advertising in the minutes to help defray cost of printing. In this year, advertisements included those from Vassar college, the Watch Tower Baptist paper from the Watch Tower Publishing Company, and, of all items, "the common sense milk bucket" manufactured by the Southern Milk Bucket Co., Rome. The advertisement was complete with picture of the bucket with stool and funnel leading from the cow! [59]

The Crawford High School in Dalton, for a brief time was identified as the Joseph E. Brown University, and in 1884 boasted 119 students.[60] By 1885, the school had been transferred to the Dalton Baptist church.[61]

Under the sponsorship of the State Mission Board, Women's missionary societies had expanded in 1884 to 76 units.[62] On a seven-year basis, $137,000 had been raised for various Convention objects.

> During the last five years, in which the raising of funds for the Boards of the Southern Convention has been entrusted to your Board without their agents, twenty-nine thousand dollars has been contributed for Foreign Missions, and twenty-one thousand for the Home Board, the annual contributions being larger than before, the expense having been diminished more than one-half.[63] ished more than one-half.[63]

Since the Sunday School ministry was identified as a Department of work under the State Board, it is of interest that the identification "department" was used also with regard to work with Negroes when, in 1885, the Board's report stated:

[59]*Ibid.*, p.p. 88-93.
[60]*Minutes, Georgia Baptist Convention*, 1884, p. 20.
[61]*Minutes, Georgia Baptist Convention*, 1885, p. 33.
[62]*Minutes, Georgia Baptist Convention*, 1884, p. 51.
[63]*Ibid.*, p. 48.

This department of labor promises great results, and
we may safely anticipate the favor of God upon this
undertaking . . . The Home Board of the S. B. C. co-
operates with us in this work.[64]

Negro Baptists were moving increasingly into cooperation
with their own state conventions. This further justified, in
the mind of the Convention, the need for a ministry to the
leaders of the Negro churches.

A detailed analysis of giving by Georgia Baptist churches,
in 1886, indicated

It appears that there is a large number of Baptist
churches in Georgia, which are constituents of this
Convention, who give nothing, and of these the contributions are made by less than half;

and the further statement:

striking and approximates the truth is that less than
25,000 persons, the members in those churches, contributed the past year all of the $26,000 collected in our
denomination for the support of all the Christian enterprises in our hands. If these are facts, they call loudly
and earnestly upon every Baptist preacher here, and
at home, to awaken out of their slumbers and consecrate
themselves afresh to the service of God in this behalf.
This committee believes that the State Board of Missions, as now operated, is a most successful and effectual
mode of raising funds, conducting your missionary operation in Georgia, and uniting and controling our
churches in these things. And, although it is true that
25,000 only of our boasted 185,000 Baptists in Georgia
give all the money we get together, it is nevertheless
true that your State Mission Board has lifted up the gifts
of these 25,000 donors to a larger amount than ever
before.[65]

Less than half the churches in Georgia, in fellowship
with the Convention, were contributing to Convention
causes. Out of nearly 1,400 churches in 1886, only 560 contributed to Foreign Missions, 450 to Home Missions, 440
for state work and about 50 for Associational Missions.

From this it appears that not more than 625 churches,
all told, together with the contributions of the Women's

[64]*Minutes, Georgia Baptist Convention,* 1885, p. 41.
[65]*Minutes, Georgia Baptist Convention,* 1886, p. 32.

Missionary Societies and individuals, give the entire amount expended by Georgia Baptists for the cause of missions in all departments.[66]

By 1886, the Mercer campus had been enlarged to include a main college building, three dormitories and students' hall, and a new preparatory school building, with accommodations for 75 boarders.[67]

The manner of Convention representation was changed by revision in 1886 of Article IV of the Constitution to read:

Each Association shall be entitled to four delegates, and to one additional delegate to every five hundred members; provided, the number of delegates for any one Association shall never exceed fifteen. Each church and auxiliary society contributing annually $50 to the funds of the Convention shall be entitled to one delegate, and to one additional delegate, to each additional hundred dollars contributed as aforesaid; provided, that the representation shall not exceed three delegates for any church or society, and that in no case shall two organizations, whether churches or societies, obtain representation upon the same funds. All delegates shall hold their appointment until others are elected to succeed them. The delegates to the Convention shall be orderly members of regular Baptist churches.[68]

This Constitutional Amendment was a step in insuring that the larger churches would not dominate the Convention by sheer weight of numbers and size of contributions.

Sometime in late 1886 or early 1887, the Ebenezer college was begun at Cochran under auspices of the New Ebenezer Baptist Association.[69] This was one of many schools begun by an Association, later to meet financial difficulty and either be turned over to municipal governments for public common schools or sold to independent groups who operated them for profit.

That the work of the Mission Board was meeting with approval upon the part of the Convention is evidenced by

[66]*Ibid.*, p. 48.
[67]*Ibid.*, p. 33.
[68]*Ibid.*, p. 7.
[69]*Minutes, Georgia Baptist Convention*, 1887, p. 20.

Georgia Baptist Assembly, Toccoa

Entrance to Assembly.

Camping site.

Royal Ambassador Camp

*Class,
Conference
Rooms.*

*Main
Building,
Georgia
Baptist
Assembly
Toccoa.*

*Lounge,
General
Assembly*

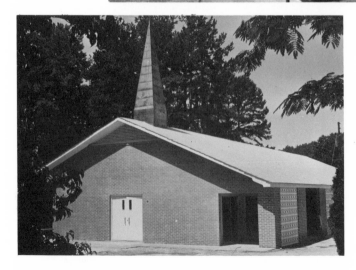

Garrison Chapel

Aerial View of Norman Baptist Assembly, Norman Park. Norman College was operated upon this site from 1900 until June, 1971, either as a Convention-owned or Convention-endorsed institution.

Administration-Classroom Building, Norman Baptist Assembly.

Early Convention Leaders

Henry Holcomb   Adiel Sherwood   W. T. Brantly

P. H. Mell   C. D. Mallary   J. H. Kilpatrick

William B. Johnson   Samuel Boykin   Joseph E. Brown

the endorsement given it in a Convention resolution which declared that

> . . . this Convention has undiminished confidence in the plan adopted by the Convention for raising funds for missions and our Mission Board is directed to continue the policy unchanged.[70]

The paper, *Kind Words* was a favorite in Georgia for many years. It was referred to occasionally from the Convention floor. By 1887, the paper was being published in Atlanta by the Home Board, and with it was being published three graded Quarterlies and a Baptist teacher.[71]

The report on Literature for that year reported the beginning of a new paper, *The Baptist Reporter,* published at Excelsior, Georgia, and the Committee on Literature had praise for the Commentary on Matthew by Dr. John A. Broadus; one of the few times that a book had been endorsed by this or any other committee. That "non-Baptist" literature was a problem with some churches is deduced from the fact that the same committee took occasion to ". . . report our grave doubts of the use of undenominational literature in our Sunday Schools." [72]

As the time drew near for observance of the Centennial year of the Georgia Association, the Convention became "Centennial conscious." The Convention at that time placed the centennial year for the Georgia Association as 1785. In their original planning in 1884, the Convention decided to request financial goals for the entire state. In 1886, a request to continue the centennial efforts was renewed, and the plans were projected again, directed toward observance of a "Semi-Centennial" for Mercer, several years [four] past the institution's 50th anniversary.[73] What appears obvious from a study of the planning for the Centennial and other like celebrations, was that Georgia Baptists discovered in these special observances an opportunity to increase gifts,

[70]*Ibid.,* p. 23.
[71]*Ibid.,* p. 25.
[72]*Ibid.,* p. 26.
[73]*Ibid.,* p. 30.

and they used the occasions to accomplish this purpose. In 1884, the Mercer trustees had reported that in connection with the Centennial of the Georgia Association, they planned to try to raise $100,000 for the endowment of the University.[74]

The 10th annual report of the Mission Board contained a summary of the progress which the Convention enjoyed under this plan of operation.

> We are constrained to acknowledge with humble gratitude and thankfulness God's direction and aid in bringing this Board through the first ten years of its existence to a degree of usefulness and successfully realizing the expectations of its most sanguine friends at the time of its creation. He gave his people a mind to work, and from the beginning he has constantly granted tokens of his gracious favor and has crowned their efforts, in obedience to his great commission to give the gospel to all men, with richest blessings. . .
> The plan adopted by the Convention was to us new and untried. Results indicate its wisdom and the Divine approval. It has united, the friends of missions and created harmonious action in its workings. One of its excellencies is economy in the expenditure of the gifts of God's people, which cannot fail to commend itself to all.
> In the year 1877, the year of this new departure at Gainesville, the entire amount contributed by the denomination in Georgia for Foreign and Home missions of the Southern Baptist Convention amounted to $10,087.13, about 25 per cent of which was paid for agents and expenses . . .
> There has been a gradual advance during the decade from $10,087.13 to over $30,000.00; as the Treasurer's report will show for this year, the entire expenses of collection not exceeding 10 per cent. The number of converts baptized by the State missionaries during this period is 3,037 . . . Twenty houses of worship have been erected at important localities, costing not less than $20,000, eight being at county sites.[75]

Thus, the earlier commendation by the Convention of the plan of operation had justification in fact. The leadership of

[74]*Minutes, Georgia Baptist Convention,* 1884, p. 40.
[75]*Minutes, Georgia Baptist Convention,* 1887, p. 37.

the Mission Board had been conscious from the beginning of the cost of securing monies under the agent system.

By 1887, a clear trend was developing in the report of the State Mission Board. It consisted of a report of building done with the aid of state funds, a report on Sunday School work, and emphasis upon instruction of colored preachers. Boykin exhibited more than usual pride in his work when he said in the 1887 report:

> When I commenced the Sunday-school work in Georgia, I was informed by my predecessor that there were only 400 Baptist Sunday-schools in the State. I am satisfied that there are not less than 1,000, perhaps more. I have organized, by my own agency, not less than 500.[76]

INCREASED EMPHASIS UPON WMU

Woman's Missionary Union was receiving increasing emphasis at the annual sessions of the Convention. In 1888, a special committee was named to report on the part of the Mission Board report which related to Woman's Missionary Societies, indicating growing interest in the potential for organized woman's work.

> Your committe recognizes with pleasure and devout gratitude to God the growing interest in missions and all benevolent work on the part of the sisters in our churches.
> The enlarged contributions of our consecrated sisterhood is becoming a tower of strength in our mission work. Your committee believes that it is well for this Convention to perpetuate and increase the friendly relations now existing between itself and the Women's Missionary Societies in the State; therefore,
> Resolved, 1st, that the Georgia Baptist Convention invite the earnest and continued co-operation of the Women's Missionary Societies in our various churches. 2nd, That we invite them to represent themselves in this Convention upon the following conditions; 1st, That they select such brethren as they may see fit to represent them; 2nd, That they be entitled to one delegate for the first fifty dollars contributed to the funds of the Convention, and to one additional delegate for each additional hundred dollars contributed

[76]*Ibid.*, p. 39.

as aforesaid; provided no society shall have more than three delegates.[77]

Not only did the interest of the women in missions become important, they were beginning to be a financial force in Georgia Baptist life. For, however small individual gifts might be, the sum total of their giving became an impressive addition to the amount of funds raised for Mission causes. However, the welcome mat to the women still was extended vicariously; the women were to make their report, but through men whom they would select. They were not to have access to the Convention floor to speak for their work!

Communications came to be a key word among Georgia Baptists. They were far ahead of their time in techniques. The concept of mass communication by letters, and the use of brochures was, for the 1880's an advanced type of promotion. In the report of the board in 1888, this was indicated when the Convention was informed:

> The secret of its [State Mission Board] success, practically considered, lies in the increased amount of information among the masses of our people, resulting from the plan we are operating. Fulfilling the obligation devolving upon them, by virtue of the very plan, many of our pastors have informed themselves and instructed their people respecting the grace of giving and the condition and needs of the cause.
> Our conclusion, therefore, is that our scheme of operations is eminently wise and practical, only needing to be energetically, systematically, and persistently pushed to attain the very highest results.[78]

An enlarged concept of the role of a Missionary Baptist Church is expressed further when the report declared:

> Our churches must be taught to regard themselves as Mission colonies, each planted in the earth by God's own hand, not to drag out a miserable existence in hum-drum performances, but to promote the glory of the Triune God in the salvation of the lost.[79]

The need for increased instruction in theology for minis-

[77]Minutes, Georgia Baptist Convention, 1888, p. 20.
[78]Ibid., p. 22.
[79]Loc cit.

ters in Georgia was expressed by the Committee on Education. In its report, the committee said:

> In many of our Associations there have been held from time immemorial what are known as Ministers and Deacons' meetings.[80]

These were the early forerunner of later pastors conferences. In observing the fact that the conferences had been held, the committee urged that such meetings be continued for a week or two instead of a day or two.[81] The Convention called also for a committee to prepare a condensed form of

> . . . our Articles of Faith, appending the Scriptures sustaining each article, and send them out to each Association, recommending these bodies to set them forth to the world in their minutes, that others may know where we stand and our reasons for it.[82]

As a result of activities of the Mission Board, there were reported 9,144 baptisms for the report year ending with the 1888 session. The Board announced with pride that gifts from Georgia could support 25 "first class" foreign missionaries, 25 in the Home, Indian and Cuban fields, and 43 state missionaries—for a total of about 90 missionaries, assuming the average home board salary of $500 and foreign board salary of $600.[83]

The reference to Cuban fields is of significance because Southern Baptists exhibited a peculiar and historic interest in Cuba which dates back to the 1880's. Georgia Baptists showed especial interest in this field of labor, and, as much space was devoted to the report of the work among colored ministers as anything else in the State Mission report.[84] By this time, there were about 150 Women's Missionary Societies.[85]

One cannot read the record of the 1880's without sensing the accomplishment which was exhibited with each annual

[80]*Ibid.*, p. 24.
[81]*Loc. cit.*
[82]*Ibid.*, p. 35.
[83]*Ibid.*, p. 39.
[84]*Ibid.*, p.p. 40-41.
[85]*Ibid.*, p. 42.

report of the work of the State Mission Board. Georgia Baptists made no apologies for their pride in this work which they believed to be of God. By 1889, the goal for giving was increased to $60,000 after the Convention heard a report that their goal of $50,000 for general objects had been exceeded.[86] During this period, Georgia Baptist women raised $14,255.89 for mission causes, an increase of over $4,000 over 1888. The work had grown to 216 white societies in 36 associations with reports from 160 of the societies.[87]

Following Convention recognition of women's work, societies grew rapidly, with 66 new societies in one year.[88]

In 1888, at the close of the Convention sessions, a request by the Committee on Education for a revised form of Articles of Faith was considered hastily in the adjournment shuffle. At the 1889 session, W. L. Kilpatrick offered a resolution which in effect killed the proposal of the previous year. It was rejected on the grounds it was considered

> . . . impracticable, in that Associations are called upon virtually to publish two distinct 'Articles of Faith', [their own or those furnished by the Convention] or else to suppress their own and give place to those furnished, And
> Whereas, The sending of 'Articles of Faith' to Associations and thus indirectly to the churches bears somewhat the appearance of dictation, . . .

The Committee believed therefore ". . . such action to be unscriptural and hence contrary to Baptist principles."[89]

Specific details of the arrangement with the Home Board for support of Negro ministers is found in 1889 when the State Missions report revealed that:

> Ten of the most pious, intelligent and useful negro ministers have been in the service of the Board since the first of July ten months. This arrangement was made in accordance with the recommendation of the Convention at Brunswick, at an expense of $4,000 per

[86]*Minutes, Georgia Baptist Convention,* 1889, p. 20.

[87]*Ibid.,* p. 21.

[88]*Minutes, Georgia Baptist Convention,* 1888, p. 42; *Minutes, Georgia Baptist Convention,* 1889, p. 21.

[89]*Minutes, Georgia Baptist Convention,* 1889, p. 28.

annum, of which the colored convention pays one-half. The Home Board appropriates $1,000 to the State Board, which also pays the same amount. A large part of the $2,000 which the colored convention was to contribute as agreed upon in the plan of cooperation, has been raised.[90]

T. C. Boykin, in his report on Sunday Schools indicated there were 1,375 Sunday Schools, with 8,250 officers and teachers, and 40,250 scholars. Boykin estimated that about $10,000 had been contributed through Sunday Schools for all purposes, with about $3,000 for mission causes.[91]

It must be admitted that financial considerations held prominent place in Convention consideration consistently. However, the Convention was aware that to finance an expanding program, an effective stewardship concept must be developed. And, it was realized that:

> One great hindrance in missionary progress is the credit system under which our Boards are compelled largely to operate.[92]

Many churches were taking weekly collections; others took offerings monthly.

> There is evidently a new departure tending in this direction. The adoption of the Gospel plan would remove the whole difficulty, and enable us to pay as we go.[93]

By 1889, there were 58 state missionaries in service,[94] with 5,514 baptisms in "Convention" Associations.[95] In 1890, there were 74 missionaries.[96]

At the Washington Convention in 1890, the Moderator, A. J. Battle, was absent, having been ". . . detained by the death of Brother W. H. McIntosh, . . ."[97] McIntosh was the leader of the Convention's work among Negroes. Conven-

[90]*Ibid.*, p. 37.
[91]*Ibid.*, p. 38.
[92]*Ibid.*, p. 39.
[93]*Loc. cit.*
[94]*Ibid.*, p. 37.
[95]*Minutes, Georgia Baptist Convention,* 1890, p. 51.
[96]*Ibid.*, p. 37.
[97]*Ibid.*, p. 12.

tion representation was growing rapidly. There were 36 associations which sent delegates, along with delegates from 43 churches and Mission Societies.[98]

PRAYER FOR FOREIGN MISSIONS

Because Georgia at that time had only one missionary serving on a foreign field, the Convention voted to set aside the first Sunday in June to pray for Foreign Missions, and to ". . . ask the Lord to impress more of our young brethren and sisters to go to the foreign field. . ." [99].

In 1891, the Constitution of the Convention was amended to provide relating to officers of the convention, changing Article 5:

> The officers of this Convention shall be a President, four vice-Presidents, a Secretary, Assistant Secretary and Treasurer.[100]

The Convention began actually to aid actively in the construction of houses of worship when the following resolution was adopted:

> Resolved, That the work of our Mission Board be enlarged so as to include building houses of worship. Resolved further, That we instruct said Board to pay $400 of the interest to accure for the year 1891 upon the debt due for the house of worship of Brunswick Baptist Church.[101]

That the Convention was not against the organization of regional conventions at the time appears evident, by the report of the Committee on Missions, in the section on State Missions, which said:

> In our own State we have cause for special thanksgiving. The report of our State Board was gratifying. In the recent organizations in the Northern and Southern sections of the State, co-operating with the Georgia Baptist Convention, we see signs of progress, for the

[98]*Ibid.*, p.p. 11-13.
[99]*Ibid.*, p. 18.
[100]*Minutes, Georgia Baptist Convention*, 1891, p. 14.
[101]*Ibid.*, p. 17.

entire State seems now about to be reached and aroused . . .[102]

The report on Education stated that Mercer had enrolled 345 students, with 40 preparing for the ministry. The report said further that the South Georgia Baptists were to be commended ". . . upon the prospect of having an institution for higher education at Cordele, . . ." which institution apparently never was organized.[103] The Hiawassee High School, later to be listed as a part of the Georgia Baptist Convention family, was indicated as being under the direction of the North Georgia Convention.[104]

The year was crucial in terms of general acceptance of the Orphan's Home. The committee on the home presented the following report which was adopted and a letter accompanying the report was ordered printed in the minutes. The report and the letter are:

> The Committee to whom the communication of the Georgia Baptist Orphans' Home was submitted, beg leave to offer the following:
> We rejoice that God has put it into the hearts of these noble Christian women to organize such a needful beneficent institution; therefore
> Resolved, 1st. That the thanks of our people are cordially extended to brother Jonathan Norcross for his handsome and liberal gift.
> 2d. That we commend the work of our people throughout the State for their sympathy, prayers and contributions, and that our churches be requested to give effect to this purpose in having an orphans' day in which to present the claims of the Georgia Baptist orphans, and secure contributions for its support; and that this day be indicated by the managers of the Home.[105]

While this did not give Convention approval to the concept of owning the home again at this time, it did pave the way for later acceptance of the home as support for it was encouraged officially in the churches.

[102]*Ibid.*, p. 20 [See Appendix E for additional information on sectional conventions.]

[103]*Ibid.*, p. 22.

[104]*Loc. cit.*

[105]*Ibid.*, p. 23.

The letter accompanying the report is little known to most Georgia Baptists.

To the Georgia Baptist Convention:

> Dear Brethren—We wish to bring to your attention the 'Georgia Baptist Orphans' Home,' in Atlanta.
>
> This had its origin in the gift of 20 acres of land in 1888, by brother Jonathan Norcross, for the establishment of such an institution. This land is in the suburbs of the city, and has been deeded to the Baptist women of Georgia. This land is valued at $10,000, and while it is not regarded as a suitable site, yet the deed allows its sale and the property to be used in buying a more eligible location or in the erection of suitable buildings. Through the earnest labors of some of the good Baptist women of Atlanta, and by our concurrence, a house on Stonewall street was rented and furnished by donation, a matron secured March 9th, 1890, and the Orphans' Home was opened, and begun work with three inmates. Finding that the location was not central, in September last these sisters rented No. 50 Capitol avenue, a comfortable brick house near our beautiful capitol, and moved into it, for which they pay $20.00 per month. The number of inmates have gradually increased until ten are now cared for. These came from different parts of the State . . . The current expenses during the past year have been $710.69, or about $59.00 per month. They have received $1,115.03 since May, 1890, and they had raised before that $631.75, making a total of $1,746.78, deducting current expenses, $710.69, leaving $1,036.09 and of this $945.45 are in notes at interest, and $60.64 in Treasury.
>
> The expenses of the Home have been borne by the city churches and friends in Atlanta, and the money received from the State has been put at interest, to be used as a building fund.
>
> The Georgia Baptist Orphans' Home Association is a regularly chartered institution, and properly organized with its officers, and authorized to hold property and to run an 'Orphans' Home' in all its necessary departments. Any one can become an honorary life member by the payment of $50, or annual members by the payment of $1.00. There are now 5 life members, and 317 annual members.
>
> It is the purpose of the Association in due time to sell the 20 acres of ground, and by purchase or by donation secure a proper site, and erect proper buildings for permanent use. While the Atlanta sisters were busy in

organizing and carrying forward the work, many of the
noble sisters in the State have come to their assistance,
and contributed liberally in excellent quilts, pillows,
boxes of clothing and other useful articles.

Now, we do not ask this Convention to adopt this
Home as a part of its work, but we simply desire to
bring it before you, and ask your active cooperation and
help, your prayers and your help, your prayers and your
sympathy, as pastors and Christian workers. Other
States have sustained an Orphans' Home in Louisville,
with several hundred inmates. North Carolina Baptists
have one in admirable trim at Thomasville, N. C., Virginia, South Carolina, Missouri, Maryland and Texas,
and perhaps other States, are moving in this matter,
and shall the great Baptist brotherhood of Georgia lag
behind? Will they not arise in their strength and hear
the cry of the fatherless and motherless, and help?

May our hearts be filled with the spirit of the Master,
and move all to join in this noble work. Advisory committee, George Hillyer, A. D. Adair, J. T. Pendleton,
B. F. Abbott.[106]

It is probable that this letter, as much as any single item,
helped to consolidate the thinking of the Convention concerning its involvement in the orphans' home.

Concern for persecution of Christians in other areas of
the world has been expressed by Georgia Baptists on many
occasions. First record of such was in 1891 when the Convention approved a resolution offering a protest

. . . against the spirit of persecution which is now exhibited by Russia, a professed Christian nation, against
the Jews in that country, . . .[107]

At the same time, the Convention protested the opening of
the World's Fair in Chicago on a Sunday.[108]

J. H. DeVotie died February 16, 1891. He had been a
strong leader in Alabama, had served as president of the
Domestic Mission Board at Marion, exhibiting wise judgment there. Later he served as pastor at Columbus First

[106]*Ibid.*, p.p. 23, 24.
[107]*Ibid.*, p. 33.
[108]*Loc. cit.*

Baptist church, Griffin First Baptist, and from 1877 until his death as Georgia's first state missions secretary.[109]

A native of Oneida county, New York state, DeVotie never moved his residence from Griffin. He served as a chaplain during the War Between The States, and led in the establishment of The *Alabama Baptist* and Howard College. [Now Samford University.] [110]

Under his leadership, the Georgia Baptist Convention made solid gains through the state mission board, and De-Votie strengthened the cause of Christian education, as well as mission causes.

The Convention took steps in 1891 to tighten organizational lines. There were in Georgia at that time three conventions of white associations and churches. The Baptist Convention of the State of Georgia, the Baptist Convention of North Georgia, and the General Baptist Association of South Georgia

> . . . with constitutions, objects and offices very similar to those of the Baptist Convention of the State of Georgia, covering in part the same territory and composed in part of the same constituency and all independent of each other.[111]

The State Mission Board was organized to strengthen the work in Georgia and also to curtail expense of collection of funds for missionary causes. The report spelled out rules to control what apparently had been a problem when it suggested:

> 1. That this board allow no draft upon its treasury to pay the salaries of officers of other organizations.
> 2. That in appointing the missionaries, the policy which has been pursued by your board be continued, viz., that the appointment be made in view of the destitution of the field, its necessities and hopefulness, and not because of the connection the appointee may sustain to any other organization; that the appointee, by virtue of his appointment, becomes the missionary of

[109]Encyclopedia of Southern Baptists, Vol. I, p. 361.

[110]*Loc. cit.*

[111]*Minutes, Georgia Baptist Convention,* 1891, p. 44. [See Appendix E for additional information on these conventions.]

the board; that he must hold a commission from this board, and report as required, an account of his services before he shall receive from your treasury the promised compensation; that this policy does not forbid the making of such agreement with other organizations as to the field, missionary and payment of the missionary as may be satisfactory to all parties.

This was adopted by the Mission Board at its meeting February 24, 1891.[112]

The statement left no doubt that the Convention expected from its missionaries an accounting of their work if they expected to receive payment. Neither did it leave room for doubt that the Georgia Baptist Convention had no intention of paying salaries for men employed in the name of other conventions, unless there was some type of co-operative arrangement.

The death of DeVotie marked the end of an era in Georgia Baptist life, and the beginning of a second stage of growth in organized denominational life. During the period of DeVotie's service, the Convention placed much emphasis upon the newly-created State Mission Board, and Christian education, while not neglected, did not claim the paramount interest for this period which it had in earlier years. For 14 years, Baptists were led by a man who assumed his duties at what is now considered retirement age, and who led in a vigorous program until his death in his 78th year.

[112]*Ibid.*, p.p. 44-45.

CHAPTER 11

Education, Missions Emphasized

The committee on the State of Religion, reporting to the 1892 Convention, took its work seriously. And to that committee must go credit for what evidently was the first survey of Baptist work on a systematic basis, by mail, in Georgia.

With the assistance of a grant from the State Mission Board for postage, the committee mailed report forms to 736 pastors in the state, all listed in the minutes of the Convention.[1] Not so surprising is the fact that the response to the questionnaire was that which might be expected today. The corresponding secretary of the State Board, John G. Gibson, approved a list of questions covering three departments of church work under the headings of Material, Spiritual, and Sunday School statistics. The forms were mailed in the summer of 1891, and the pastors were requested through the pages of *The Index*, and *The Watchman* to respond. Editors of the publications

> . . . not only joined in the request, but tendered their sympathy to your committee, for which we feel grateful. We have learned that Baptist preachers do not answer questions unless they want to.[2]

Response from the pastors was disappointing, but considered useful.

Only 76 out of 736 pastors, or 10 per cent, answered;

[1]*Minutes, Georgia Baptist Convention*, 1892, p. 19.
[2]*Ibid.*, p. 20.

and reported for 192 churches, or a little over 15 per
cent, of the churches constituent to the Convention.[3]

However, on the basis of material submitted, the following
calculations were made concerning the state of religion
[Baptist] in Georgia.

Of the 192 churches reporting [many pastors had more
than one church] 115 were in the country, and 77 in towns
and cities.

The average distance of the country churches from the
railroad was seven miles. The value of 190 church buildings
was set at $455,000 or an average of $2,370 per church with
the best house of worship worth $50,000; the poorest, $25.00.

Pastors' homes had a cumulative value of $14,700.00 for
a value of $1,837 each for those reported. However, 91 per
cent of the pastors reported they were in their own home,
or rented. The churches paid 87 pastors $42,309.60 in salary,
an average of $486.31 per pastor. The pastors of 54 churches
did not know the value of property owned by their members. However, 138 churches reported their members owned
property valued at $8,305,400.00 or some $60,000 per
church, ". . . making $618.00 per member, the churches
averaging 97 members each. And yet some Baptists complain
of poverty." [4]

The average pastorate lasted 4 and 8/9 years, and it was
". . . worthy of emphasis that the best report of all of those
received came from the church of the longest pastorate." [5]
This was the White Plains church where J. H. Kilpatrick,
the convention president, had served 37 years at the time.[6]

The statistics gathered from the reports of pastors proved
interesting. "Careful estimates for the denomination. . ." on
the basis of reports were that there were 1,088 ordained
ministers in the state, with 827 serving churches, and 261
ordained ministers idle. The average age of pastors was
over 47; there were 1,074 married ministers, 14 single, with

[3]*Loc. cit.*
[4]*Ibid.,* p. 20.
[5]*Loc. cit.*
[6]*Loc. cit.*

the average number of persons in the pastors' families set at over five, with average years in the ministry estimated at 18.[7] Of the pastors who reported,

> half were educated in college, and half in the country, but we know this proportion will not hold out when applied to all the ministers in the denomination, for not more than one-third, if that many, were educated in college.[8]

The survey revealed the average value of the pastor's library was $153.00, with the best library being worth $3,000.00 and the poorest reported at $2.00.

> Average value of property owned by preachers, $3,255.00. The wealthiest reports $20,000 and the poorest $30.00. About 81 per cent of the pastors are natives of Georgia, and 75 per cent, supplement their salaries by some secular work, principally farming, giving only one-third of their time to pastoral work. Sixteen of 76 pastors live in rented houses, at which rate about 21 per cent of our pastors have no home, 9 live in pastors' homes and 70 per cent live in their own houses.[9]

While one is able to detect some discrepancies in the report, it is a reasonably accurate portrayal of church strength. In the same report, the committee said

> . . . there is great destitution in different parts of the State, principally in South and North Georgia; the greatest and most needy being in the great and rapidly growing section known as the pine belt in the southern part of the State.[10]

And the report of an offer by the American Baptist Education Society to give Mercer University $10,000

> . . . Provided the Baptists of Georgia would raise $40,000 in interest bearing notes and subscriptions has been complied with, and the $10,000 promised has been secured.[11]

Although work of the Convention between annual sessions had been assumed by the State Mission Board for 15 years,

[7]*Ibid.*, p. 22.
[8]*Loc. cit.*
[9]*Loc. cit.*
[10]*Ibid.*, p.p. 22, 23.
[11]*Ibid.*, p. 25.

the Executive Committee continued to make the report of the Hearn school at Cave Spring, for this year reporting 53 males and 66 females.[12]

The Orphans' Home had been encouraged by the action of the 1891 convention and reported in 1892 feeling

> . . . peculiar gratification in reporting its growing pros-
> perity and promising future outlook. There are now
> twenty five inmates who receive the tender motherly
> care of sympathizing and ever watchful godly women.[13]

With re-establishment of Convention interest and implied sponsorship, though not ownership in 1891, the Home was assured a permanent place in the interest and support of Georgia Baptists.

Other indications of continued growth are contained in the report of the State Mission Board for 1892. John G. Gibson had succeeded DeVotie in 1891, upon the death of DeVotie. It was under his supervision, and probably coincident to his becoming corresponding secretary that the survey of Baptist life was prepared. The 1892 mission report is the first full one for which Gibson had administrative responsibility. During the time between Conventions, 1891-1892, women of the state had contributed over $18,000 to mission causes, and T. C. Boykin reported 42 associational Sunday School conventions ". . . in good working order. . ."[14] Emphasis continued upon the Convention's support of work with Negroes, with the note that special instruction had been given to 100 colored preachers and 77 deacons during the year.[15] Forty six associations were carried as constituent members of the convention in 1892.[16]

In 1893, the Convention met in Dawson, and by then, representatives from many State and Southern Convention interests were presenting their causes at the annual sessions.

Names remembered in Baptist life, present at Dawson, in-

[12]*Ibid.*, p. 41.
[13]*Ibid.*, p. 43.
[14]*Loc. cit.*
[15]*Ibid.*, p. 44.
[16]*Ibid.*, p.p. 62, 63.

cluded F. H. Kerfoot, representing Southern Seminary; J. M. Frost, representing the Sunday School Board; W. B. Harvey, of the *Western Recorder,* Kentucky; J. M. Green, and W. J. Northen, representing the Orphans' Home; John William Jones, assistant secretary of the Home Mission Board; E. C. Huguenin, treasurer of Mercer University, J. F. Edens and J. C. McMichael of *The Christian Index,* and D. H. Parker of the *Texas Baptist Herald.*[17]

Emphasis upon Christian stewardship was placed increasingly before Georgia Baptists, both as a Biblical necessity and as a means of supporting Baptist work. A new idea was advanced in 1893; that of a Committee of Co-operation to encourage gifts from churches which were not contributing. The Convention was informed that

> . . . a patient, intelligent and repeated presentation of the principles and facts of Christian missions—the facts as well as the principles of Christian missions—will certainly and irrestistibly enlist every regenerate heart in the joyful and practical support of this cause. Whatever other means are available for this purpose, we believe there should be a faithful use of postal facilities and missionary literature. We recommend, therefore, that a committee of co-operation be annually appointed by this body, whose duty it shall be to ascertain from your State Board of Missions the names of churches that contribute little or nothing to the various enterprises of this Convention, and use all proper means to develop the liberality of these churches.[18]

Of significance further is action of the Mercer trustees, endorsed by the Convention, in recommending

> . . . that the Board of Trustees elected during the present session of this body be authorized to donate the ground applied for by the members of the Tattnall Square Baptist Church on which to erect a house of worship, the lot thus donated to be used by the Tattnall Square Baptist Church.[19]

There is nothing in the original wording of the Trustee, and

[17]*Minutes, Georgia Baptist Convention,* 1893, p. 14.
[18]*Ibid.,* p. 18.
[19]*Ibid.,* p. 19.

subsequent Convention, authorization which hints at any
type of reversionary clause.

BALANCED EMPHASIS

Following the era of intense emphasis upon the State
Mission Board during the 1880's, the shift in emphasis began to move toward a more balanced one upon both missions and education during the 1890's. This balanced emphasis was to continue and to include increasingly the work
of the Orphans' Home. In the same year that land for Tattnall Square church was authorized, the committee bringing
the Report on Education wrote:

> The interest taken by Georgia Baptists in the great
> cause of education may be accurately gauged by the
> work done in and for our schools, whether academy,
> college or university. The number, patronage and suc-
> cess of these schools tells the state of education in our
> denomination in the state . . . We desire to commend
> the work of our associational schools, and to lay stress
> upon the importance of such institutions. With money
> which would be contributed to nothing else and which
> nothing else would call forth, by men whom nothing
> else would draw out, our country is being dotted with
> commodious, substantial [and many of them handsome]
> school buildings, filled generally with able, pious, pro-
> gressive teachers, under the supervision of Baptist Asso-
> ciations. . . . In these schools Georgia Baptists have
> property aggregating approximately $100,000; are giving
> employment annually to not less than 75 good teachers,
> giving instruction annually to not less than 1,500 stu-
> dents, and permeating the country with a good, whole-
> some Baptist sentiment. We are not sure but that we
> have in these schools an auxiliary more potent than in
> a great school where many could not go.[20]

This emphasizes the sentiment behind the organization of
many common or high schools by associational groups during
the latter part of the 19th century. They believed that even
an elementary or high school education under Baptist auspices would prove beneficial not only to the students but to
the cause of the denomination in the state. By 1893, Tift

[20]*Ibid.*, p. 21.

college, then called the Monroe Female College, at Forsyth had 118 students.[21] Shorter at Rome, Georgia Female Seminary, Gainesville, and Southern Female College, LaGrange were continuing to be operated under Baptist auspices.[22]

The Georgia Convention was told that:

> The Southern Baptist Theological Seminary, at Louisville, with its over $700,000 of endowment and property, belongs in part to Georgia Baptists. This session there are 250 students at our school of the prophets, under six professors.[23]

The committee on the State of Religion continued to provide valuable information concerning Georgia Baptist life, citing in the 1893 report that more than 1,200 churches had only monthly services, and that only about 15,000 members led in prayer, with 800 churches not holding prayer meetings. The report said also that 130,000 members of Baptist churches never read a Baptist paper, and in 300 churches, the members read no religious paper at all, and over 250 churches were without Sunday schools. The summary note was succinct:

> With those statistics we are not surprised at the meager contributions from those brethren.[24]

Between 1892 and 1893, the Orphans' Home in Atlanta

> received some large donations, thereby securing a lot and house with twelve rooms at a cost of eleven thousand dollars, nine thousand dollars of which has been paid. There are at present twenty-five inmates. Nine have been admitted this year, and four have been legally adopted by good, worthy people.[25]

Between 1893 and 1894 something new was being added to Georgia Baptist life which was to leave a permanent mark.

For the first time, in 1894, the Convention heard a report on the "Young People's Movement." [26] From this point on, interest in work with young people was to grow, and to

---

[21]*Loc. cit.*
[22]*Ibid.,* p. 22.
[23]*Loc. cit.*
[24]*Ibid.,* p. 28.
[25]*Ibid.,* p. 38.
[26]*Minutes, Georgia Baptist Convention,* 1894, p. 16.

result in 1913 in the establishment of a department of work with youth in Baptist churches.

The Convention in 1894 set guidelines for the movement when it adopted a report indicating that there was no apparent ". . . necessity for a State Convention of such as favor such work. . ." [27]

> The organization of our young people for training is earnestly recommended under the following condition:
> 1. All unions shall be strictly Baptistic, not inter-denominational.
> 2. They shall be in and under the control of the local churches.
> 3. All contributions of the union shall be through the local churches to the Boards fostered by the churches.
> 4. All matters of detail and of affiliations shall be left where they belong, with the local churches in which the unions exist.[28]

The conditions for organization of the movement provide a clear indication of the Convention's alertness to any situation which might cause it, or one of the causes it fostered, to become affiliated with either another denomination or an independent movement.

By 1896, the Baptist Young People's Union of Georgia lisited a slate of officers in the minutes, together with an Executive Committee. Thus, despite the fact that the 1894 Convention's wish was that there be no state young people's convention, election of a slate of officers and an Executive Committee paved the way for what was to become a state Training Union Convention in later years.[29]

The Hearn school remained for many years something of an enigma in Georgia Baptist life. There were references from time to time to the inability of the Convention to secure information concerning operation of the school. One source of the difficulty, reported in the minutes for 1894, indicated:

> That the right and duty of the Executive Committee of the Georgia Baptist Convention to appoint the

[27]*Ibid.*, p. 42.

[28]*Ibid.*

[29]*Minutes, Georgia Baptist Convention*, 1896, p. 8.

trustees of the Hearn School, though exercised only three times in forty nine years, is unimpaired and complete.[30]

It was reported to the Convention that its action on May 20, 1844 and the action of the school's patrons on July 3, 1844, was considered to be a complete transfer, management and control of the institution, with its premises, to the Executive Committee.[31]

It was unclear who was dissatisfied with the Hearn school or for what reason. It was evident that some group within the Convention believed strongly that all was not well. The Executive Committee, addressing itself for the second straight year to the school, decided finally that although they had authority to elect trustees, that to avoid any appearance of any undue assertion of authority, and also to avoid any friction which might have resulted if an entirely different Board of Trustees had been selected,

> . . . agreed to elect the existing trustees.[32] It was discovered among other things, that over $1,600 of the school's funds had been loaned to various parties, including some Trustees of the school.[33]

The Convention adopted a resolution in 1894 which called for organization of the Southern Baptist Convention

> . . . upon a numerical basis, and that its membership should aggregate not more than six hundred.[34]

The sessions heard also of the election of J. B. Gambrell as president of Mercer,[35] and the enrolment of 195 students at the University in all departments.[36]

The Executive Committee decided in 1894, finally, that

---

[30]*Minutes, Georgia Baptist Convention*, 1894, p. 26. [Full report on the relations between the school and the convention are related in the minutes of the Convention for 1894, p.p. 24-30.]

[31]*Loc. cit.*

[32]*Ibid.*, p. 47.

[33]*Ibid.*, p. 48.

[34]*Ibid.*, p. 41.

[35]*Ibid.*, p. 43.

[36]*Ibid.*, p. 44.

a change should be made in the years-old plan for aiding ministerial students.

> The committee thinks that it would be better to aid the students to the amount of one-half of their board instead of all of their board, as at present.[37]

This was to mark a change of procedure which had existed from the beginning of the ministerial aid fund.

CO-EDUCATION SUGGESTION
SURPRISES DELEGATES

A suggestion that Mercer University be co-educational was presented to the Convention at the Waycross sessions in 1895. The suggestion caught some of the delegates off guard. The matter was referred to the 1896 convention to allow

> . . . free discussion and mature thought on the part of the churches, associations, and brethren generally.[38]

The committee named to study the suggestion did not, evidently, wish to be caught in a cross fire on the subject, so it placed the matter before the Convention by saying:

> Concerning the question of co-education at Mercer University, your committee, without expressing their opinion, present to the Convention for its consideration the following question: Ought Mercer University to be opened to women who have full diplomas from female colleges of first grade? [39]

The original proposal was made by President Gambrell to the Trustees of Mercer.[40]

The group adopted also a resolution declaring

> That it is the sentiment of this Convention and we hereby recommend the same, that Mercer University be placed by our churches on the same plane as the Mission Boards, for annual contributions to her endowment and support.[41]

The Committee on Education reported the opening in

[37]*Ibid.*, p. 46.
[38]*Minutes, Georgia Baptist Convention,* 1895, p.p. 20-21.
[39]*Ibid.*, p. 20.
[40]*Ibid.*, p. 42.
[41]*Ibid.*, p. 20.

the fall of 1864 of the Southern Baptist College for Young Women at Manchester.[42] It suggested that churches, through the associations,

> . . . follow the noble example of the churches of the Hephzibah, the Washington, and Tunnel Hill Associations, and establish high schools to bridge the gap between the common schools and the college.[43]

Each year, as in 1895, the work of the Mission Board was studied and praised, and the Board was commended for inaugurating institutes for preachers.[44]

T. C. Boykin was withdrawn from the field due to lack of funds prior to the 1895 convention, and the Board had hoped that pastors would give special attention to Sunday School work and compensate for lack of a man on the field.[45]

Delegates from the Female College at LaGrange came to the Cedartown Convention in 1896 with an offer of that college to the Convention. A resolution offered to tender the management and control, with the request that the Convention appoint a Board of Regents, one-half of whom would be women.[46]

A special committee, named to study the proposal, reported unanimously their decision that:

> It would not be wise just now to accept any school that would rely upon the Convention or its constituents for any financial assistance. While the offer of the Board of Trustees does not now, perhaps, carry with it any request for financial aid, yet in the nature of things, if the school should become the property of this Convention, there would be implied in its very acceptance the right of its representatives to canvass churches and associations of this Convention for financial support. Its acceptance would necessarily imply financial obligations for its support.
> Again, we do not believe its acceptance would be wise just now, because of certain complications as to the ownership and right to the name and history of the

[42]*Ibid.*, p. 19.
[43]*Loc. cit.*
[44]*Ibid.*, p. 26.
[45]*Ibid.*, p. 46.
[46]*Minutes, Georgia Baptist Convention*, 1896, p. 27.

'Southern Female College'. We believe it would be unwise to express any opinion, either directly or indirectly, upon the merits of this question which has been brought before the public through the press and through the courts.

Again, we believe it would be unwise to make any discrimination in favor of any one of the several excellent female colleges that are now in different ways under the fostering care of the Baptists of Georgia.[47]

J. C. McMichael had been associated with *The Christian Index* apparently since 1888.[48] He became half owner of the paper in 1890, and apparently became sole owner in 1892.[49] McMichael died in October, 1895,[50] and upon his death, T. P. Bell, secretary of the Sunday School Board, with headquarters in Nashville, Tennessee, bought *The Index* for $11,010 at public auction. He brought with him to Georgia I. J. Van Ness who was at the time pastor of the Immanual Baptist church, Nashville.[51]

In 1896, Mercer formed a voluntary military company headed by "our Brother Colonel E. D. Huguenin." [52] Mercer was later to have military training units both in World War One and World War Two.

B. D. Ragsdale was elected secretary of the Convention in 1896, a position he was to hold through the 1943 session, the longest tenure of any Convention secretary. Ragsdale in 1896 was devoting his full time to the promotion of Bible institutes in the state.[53] He was later to be named Convention historian, placed on a stipend for his services in that capacity, and to write a three-volume history of the Convention.

Mrs. J. B. Gambrell, corresponding secretary of the

[47]*Ibid.,* p. 28.

[48]*The Christian Index,* September 27, 1888.

[49]James Adams Lester, A History of *The Christian Index,* 1822-1954 [Unpublished Master's Thesis, 1955,] p.p. 78, 81, 82.

[50]*Ibid.,* p. 82.

[51]*Ibid.,* p. 83.

[52]*Minutes, Georgia Baptist Convention,* 1896, p.p. 52-53.

[53]*Ibid.,* p. 57.

Georgia Baptist Woman's Missionary Union, reported that she had traveled 1,200 miles, written 2,000 letters, distributed 10,000 Christmas envelopes and 500 State Missions circulars, 8,000 Foreign Mission Board circulars and 4,000 Home Mission circulars.[54] The State Mission Board was authorized to ". . . assume such expenses of the [Woman's Missionary] Union as they may deem wise and legitimate, . . ."[55] By 1896, there were 35 children in the Orphans' Home, and the children were attending public school two blocks from the home.[56] The home was being operated at a minimal cost. There were increased contributions of goods

> . . . which we appreciate and know it has reduced our grocery bills so that each child has only cost us in cash about 3 cents per day.[57]

Following through on an earlier suggestion for a standing committee, the 1897 Convention heard the report of a Special Committee which outlined a plan calling for a five-member standing committee to be known as the Committee on Co-operation.

> The duties of this committee shall be as follows:
> 1. To labor in all commendable ways to induce all churches in associations not now doing so to co-operate with the Convention in every department of its work.
> 2. To promote among the churches now affiliated with the Convention, a wise plan of systematic and proportionate giving. By systematic giving is meant the giving by each church represented in the Convention at least once a year to every object indorsed by the Convention, to wit: foreign missions, home missions, State missions, ministerial education, Indigent Ministers' fund, Orphans' Home and endowment of Mercer University. By proportionate giving is meant giving to each object of the Convention in proportion to its needs as expressed by the board having the matter in charge.
> 3. To prepare and present to each Convention a budget setting forth what sums of money the various objects of the Convention will require for the following Con-

[54]*Ibid.*, p. 114.
[55]*Ibid.*, p. 46.
[56]*Ibid.*, p. 115.
[57]*Loc. cit.*

ventional year, and in general to study and suggest improvements in denominational methods.

4. The Committee on Co-operation shall be authorized to draw on the Treasurer of the Convention for necessary expenses up to the limit of $100 per annum.[58]

The work of this Committee over the years was to solidify further the Convention and create a climate favorable to growth in Christian stewardship as well as to lay the groundwork for the relative success of Georgia in meeting its obligations later in the $75 Million Campaign. Furthermore, efforts of this Committee, and the groundwork laid by it, provided the base for Georgia's almost immediate and effective support of The Cooperative Program nearly 30 years later.

Georgia Baptists had managed their business affairs efficiently and honestly over the years. There had been few occasions when it became necessary for a Convention to rectify any mistake or oversight by a previous Convention. However, in 1897, the Convention approved a resolution endorsing the action of the Executive Committee when the Executive Committee, on December 31, 1878, deeded property of the Georgia Baptist Seminary for young ladies at Gainesville, to a local board of trustees. There was no record of this transaction in the minutes of the Convention prior to this time. Therefore it was resolved,

> That the Georgia Baptist Convention, in regular session assembled, does hereby confirm said sale of said property, and hereby relinquishes any and all claim which it may have had to said property.[59]

The Gainesville group paid $1,000 to the Executive Committee for the property.[60]

Upon motion of B. D. Ragsdale, the Convention approved unanimously in 1897 appointment of a special committee of J. H. Kilpatrick, W. J. Northen and Lansing Burrows to

[58]*Minutes, Georgia Baptist Convention,* 1897, p.p. 28, 29.
[59]*Ibid.,* p. 30.
[60]*Loc. cit.*

rewrite and revise the Constitution and report to the 1898 Convention.[61]

In 1895, there were 55 Associations, with 1,527 churches in the Convention, and 26 of the Associations reported 583 Sunday Schools. By 1896, for comparison, there were 57 Associations with 1,558 churches, and 859 Sunday schools.[62]

STRONG PROHIBITION STAND

A particularly strong stand was taken in 1897 for prohibition when the delegates went on record as favoring a state law which would end the open saloon, and requested a state law which would provide for teaching a course in temperance in the public schools. The Convention asked also:

> That we urge our pastors and people to preach and sing, write and pray, practice and vote temperance with every opportunity, recognizing the fact that the Georgia saloon exists by consent of the Christian people of our state.[63]

The Convention meeting in Augusta in 1898 adopted a revised Constitution [64] by a vote of 210 for, none against.[65]

This 1898 Constitution was amended in 1900 and to it was added a set of by-laws by the 1904 Convention.[66] The by-laws were not printed with the Constitution until 1906.[67] The 1898 revision and by-laws follow:

Constitution
Revised in 1898

> I. This body is constituted upon those principles of Christian faith generally acknowledged and received in the Baptist denomination, and shall be known and distinguished as the Baptist Convention of the State of Georgia.

[61]*Loc. cit.*
[62]*Ibid.*, p. 37.
[63]*Ibid.*, p. 41.
[64]*Minutes, Georgia Baptist Convention*, 1898, p.p. 9, 10, 11.
[65]*Ibid.*, p.p. 20, 21.
[66]*Minutes, Georgia Baptist Convention*, 1904, p. 30.
[67]*Minutes, Georgia Baptist Convention*, 1906, p. 8.

II. The general object of this Convention is to facilitate the union and co-operation of Georgia Baptists in the great work of upbuilding Christ's Kingdom in the world.

Its more specific objects are:

1. To form and encourage plans for the promotion of experimental and practical religion in the State, or elsewhere.

2. To foster the missionary spirit in our churches, and to bring about larger and more systematic contributions to Christ's cause.

3. To co-operate with individual associations and churches in supplying the destitution in their own bounds.

4. To afford an opportunity to those who may conscientiously feel it to be their duty to form a fund for the education of pious young men who may be called by the Spirit and by the churches to the Christian ministry.

5. To promote pious and useful education in the Baptist denomination.

III. It shall have power to form rules, make arrangements, and appoint committees, for the accomplishment of any or all of the above objects, provided none of these rules and arrangements shall be inconsistent with the Scriptures and the known principles of the churches and the associations.

IV. The constituents of this body shall be:

> 1. The Baptist associations of the state of Georgia which shall accede to the terms of this Convention and whose constitution shall be approved by the Convention.
>
> 2. Such churches as shall contribute to our funds is hereinafter prescribed.
>
> 3. Such Sunday-schools and young people's unions and mission societies composed in whole or in part of members of churches in our fellowship, as shall contribute on the same terms.

Associations, churches, Sunday-schools, unions and mission societies, located out of the State, may be received into this body, when their peculiar location or other circumstances shall, in the judgment of the Convention, render it desirable.

V. Each association shall be entitled to two delegates, and to one additional delegate for every five hundred members, provided the number of delegates for the one association shall never exceed ten.

Each church contributing annually fifty dollars to the funds of the Convention, shall be entitled to one delegate, and to one additional delegate for each additional hundred dollars thus contributed; provided, that the representation shall not exceed three delegates for any church.

Each Sunday school, young people's union, or mission society contributing annually fifty dollars to the funds of the Convention, shall be entitled to one delegate. In no case shall two organizations obtain representation upon the same funds.

All delegates shall hold their appointment until others are appointed to succeed them, and all of them shall be orderly male members of regular Baptist churches, and shall present satisfactory evidence of their appointment by the bodies which they represent.

VI. The officers of the Convention shall be a President, four Vice-Presidents, a Secretary, and a Treasurer, who shall be elected by ballot at each annual meeting, and who shall hold their offices until their successors are elected.

VII. It shall be the duty of the Secretary to write a minute of the proceedings of the body, and superintend the publication and distribution of the same, together with such statistical information as he may be able to gather from the minutes of the associations and other sources. The Secretary shall have the privilege of selecting an assistant to render him such help as he may need during the sessions of the body.

VIII. It shall be the duty of the Treasurer to take charge of all moneys, specialties, and properties of all kinds belonging to this body, give sufficient security for the amount in his hands, report the state of the funds from time to time, as the Convention may direct, and hand over to his successor in office all its moneys, properties, etc.

IX. An Executive Committee, consisting of at least seven members, shall be chosen at each annual meeting, whose duty it shall be to attend to the business of the Convention during its recess. This committee shall have power to fill any vacancies which occur in its own number, and also any vacancies in the offices of the Convention.

[Amendment adopted in 1900] Whenever it becomes necessary or expedient in the opinion of the Committee, at any time, between sessions of the Convention, to sell or exchange real or personal property of the Convention, it shall have power to do so.

X. There shall be chosen at each annual session a Board of Missions, of twenty five members, whose special duty it shall be to take charge of mission work in the bounds of the State, including the collection of funds, appointment and payment of missionaries, the building of houses of worship, etc.

In addition to this special work, this board shall be charged with the special duty of seeing after the collection and forwarding of funds to the Home, Foreign, and Sunday-school Boards; also, the collection and disbursement of funds for destitute ministers and their widows.

This board shall have power to elect its own officers, fill any vacancies occurring in its membership, to make its own by-laws, to appoint its own Corresponding Secretary and Treasurer, both offices to be in the same man; also an Auditor, both of whom shall be ex-officio members of the Board of Missions.

The auditor shall be the joint-officer of the Board of Missions, and the Committee on Co-operation. This Board shall report annually to the convention.

XI. There shall be chosen by the Convention at each annual session a Committee on Co-operation, of as many members as there are interests fostered by the Convention; one for each interest.

This Committee shall make annual estimates of amounts of money for needed work, upon which estimates, all authorized agents and secretaries may make appeals to the churches and other bodies. It shall also prepare and publish suitable schedules for the guidance of agents and secretaries making appeals for funds. All that part of the work outlined by the Committee affecting the enterprises of the churches operating through the Convention, for each ensuing year, shall be submitted in report to the Convention, before the same becomes operative.

This Committee shall have power to elect its own officers, except that of Secretary, who shall be the same man as the Auditor of the Board of Missions, and who shall be elected jointly by that Board and the Committee on Co-operation.

This Committee shall report to the Convention annually.

XII. This body shall appoint delegates to the Southern Baptist Convention, and in accordance with the terms prescribed in the Constitution of that body.

XIII. This Constitution shall be liable to amendment at a regular annual session only, and at that time, only by the vote of two-thirds of the delegates actually enrolled; but for the transaction of any other business, a

Campus, Mercer University, Macon.

Aubrey Estes, Director, Mercer Extension Department.

Forsyth Campus View

Tift College,

Aerial View

of Campus

Upshaw Hall
Tift Landmark

Campus, Shorter College, Rome.

Administration Building, Shorter College, Rome.

Fountain at entrance, president's home, Truett-McConnell College, Cleveland.

Harry V. Smith, Sr.,
Long-time Convention
Servant

Arch, entrance to campus,
Brewton-Parker College,
Mt. Vernon

majority of the votes cast by those present on the floor shall be sufficient.

This text includes one amendment in 1900, so indicated, Articles IX, and XI included in 1906, along with changes in Article X.[68]

BY-LAWS

1. At each annual meeting of this Convention the president shall appoint a committee of ten, whose duty it shall be to nominate to the Convention all Boards, Commissions and Committees chosen by the Convention.
2. All Boards, Commissions and Committees reporting to the Convention shall cause to be embraced in their reports of finance the usual "Balance Sheet" employed by bookkeepers.
3. The Boards and other like bodies belonging to the Convention and under its control shall have their Treasurers placed under bond. Every Auditing Committee of a Treasurer's account shall report as to the validity of his bond.
4. No recommendation shall ever be embodied in any reports made to this Convention by any agent, secretary, or other officer of any Board or like body, which, if received and adopted, will modify or amend any item of the Constitution, By-Laws or Standing Resolutions of the Convention.
5. These By-Laws may be altered at any annual meeting by a majority vote of the members present and voting.[69]

These By-Laws were adopted in 1904.[70]

A comparison of this Constitution with the previous one reveals several things. One, it indicates the growing strength of the Sunday School and Young People's Movement. Two, it indicates the growing strength of the position of auditor, later to become a problem calling for change. Three, the revised Constitution provided a basis for an even stronger Executive Committee. This is interesting in view of that Committee's continuing diminishing function. The Board of Missions was strengthened further also.

[68]*Minutes, Georgia Baptist Convention*, 1906, p.p. 25, 27; also Chapter 13, p. 323.
[69]*Minutes, Georgia Baptist Convention*, 1907, p.p. 5, 6, 7, 8.
[70]*Minutes, Georgia Baptist Convention*, 1904, p. 30.

The report on State Missions for 1898 began with a statement of missionary policy of the Southern Baptist Convention, which said:

> The plans of the fathers were wisely projected and as wisely executed. The work of half a century has abundantly vindicated their wisdom. . . .
> The organization of State-Boards was a logical result out of the practical and wise management of the general board.[71]

The report declared that with increases in population, multiplication of facilities of travel, changing social and economic conditions, there developed a need for the State Boards to be in direct contact with the churches! The report then defined the mission, work, responsibility and possibilities of the State Board by stating:

> The mission of the State Board is fundamental. It seeks to supply the regions of destitution in Georgia, to reinforce the churches that are weak, and to effect a more thorough organization for practical work in all of the churches. In the accomplishment of these ends, it is in thorough harmony with the original plan of the Baptists of all the States of the South when they assumed the work of the evangelization of this region.[72]

The report thus indicated the belief of Georgia Baptists that the State Mission Board was the logical and necessary outgrowth of progress among Baptists following organization of the Southern Baptist Convention.

Tensions of the Spanish-American War were evident in a motion on religious liberty presented by B. F. Riley and adopted unanimously. The resolution said:

> Whereas, Religious freedom is a principle dear to every true American, and especially to every Baptist, therefore,
> Resolved, That this Convention respectfully requests the President of the United States and others in authority, that in the adjustment of the political affairs in the island of Cuba, they use every proper endeavor

---

[71]*Minutes, Georgia Baptist Convention*, 1898, p. 23.
[72]*Loc. cit.*

to secure equality of religious right to every inhabitant of that island.[73]

Moving steadily into the hearts of the Convention, the Orphans' Home was given a place in the established order of Convention business at the 1898 session. The home had been emphasized, and actually given time to present its needs, but the Convention was now taking official recognition of the place of the home in the Georgia Baptist Convention family. This was at the suggestion both of the Committee to report on the State Mission Board report and the Co-operation Committee.[74] The report said in part,

> . . . we recommend that it be more closely related to the Convention; and receive a place in the established order of business.[75]

The Co-operation Committee was making its influence felt when it suggested further that an effort be made ". . . to enlarge our Associations and merge the smaller ones into more powerful and influential ones, . . ." believing that

> . . . this would enable the servants of the Convention more nearly to cover all our territories. If they could be arranged, both as to number and time of meeting, so as to permit our servants to visit all of them, it would result in great good, we think.[76]

ASSISTANCE FOR CORRESPONDING SECRETARY

Gibson felt the increased burdens of office, and the Convention, noting his responsibilities, adopted unanimously a resolution declaring:

> Whereas, The great success of our State Board of Missions is adding, year by year, to the multitudinous burdens of our Corresponding Secretary, making it clear that he may need additional assistance at some period during the coming year, be it,
> Resolved, That the Convention instruct the Board to

[73]*Ibid.*, p. 24.
[74]*Ibid.*, p. 32.
[75]*Loc. cit.*
[76]*Ibid.*, p. 33.

exercise its discretion and afford the secretary all reasonable relief.[77]

The report of Young People's Work included the fact that the state convention for young people would meet in Macon, and be held during Mercer's commencement week so that B. Y. P. U. members could attend the commencement and brethren and friends attending commencement could also enjoy the B. Y. P. U. convention.[78]

The "dispute" between the Hearn school trustees and the convention continued. In 1898, the committee to study the report of the Executive Committee said the difficulties had

> . . . been satisfactorily arranged, and that all parties are entirely willing to abide the settlement of all disputed points as contained in the report of a special committee made to this Convention in 1894 which report fully sets forth the relation of Hearn School and adopted by it in the year to this Convention, . . .[79]

In the report of the Hearn School trustees for that year, dated Cave Spring, March 30, 1898, and signed by T. W. Asbury, secretary, was the succinct notation: "Hope to have the sympathy and co-operation of your body." [80]

The phrasing, which included the words "your body", indicated a rather clear lack of feelings of close relations to the Convention on the part of the Hearn trustees.

A significant step was made by Georgia Baptists when they accepted the offer of the Monroe Female college at the 1898 session. A proposition from the trustees was offered which, in effect, was a proposal to

> . . . tender to the Baptist Convention of the State of Georgia all of the above property absolutely unencumbered, and with the sole restriction that it be used for school purposes and forever controlled by the Baptist denomination.[81]

The tender cited the physical layout of the college and

[77]*Loc. cit.*
[78]*Ibid.*, p. 42.
[79]*Ibid.*, p. 47.
[80]*Ibid.*, p.p. 70, 71.
[81]*Ibid.*, p. 52.

the facilities available.[82] The committee named to study the proposal recommended acceptance, and also that the Convention at that session elect 15 trustees, five of whom would be from Forsyth and 10 from the state at large. The proposal called for the trustees elected to incorporate and following that to execute to themselves and their successors in office title to the property. Recommendation was made that the term of office be three years, and at the expiration of this time a new Board should be elected by the convention.[83]

A key factor in the proposal included the statement:

> That in accepting this proposition from Monroe Female College, we do not disparage the claims of any similar institutions which are now in existance, or may hereafter be established, neither do we give this college priority in its claims upon the denomination. And we recommend that this convention shall take under its fostering care all similar institutions upon the same terms on which the Monroe Female College is received.[84]

Thus, the terms were constructed upon which future acquisitions would be made by the Convention. At the same time, the recommendation sought to insure that no new institution would receive priority over those established already and functioning as a part of the Convention family.[85]

With education occupying major interest at this Convention, two other related matters were dealt with. One was:

> That the whole matter of the co-relation of both male and female education in the State be referred to the Committee on Schools and Colleges, to be appointed under the report of the committee on Bernard resolutions.[86]

The "Bernard" resolution was one which dealt at length with the subject of free tuition at state universities, public versus private higher education, and what could be done

[82]*Loc. cit.*
[83]*Ibid.,* p. 53.
[84]*Loc. cit.*
. .[85]*Loc. cit.*
[86]*Ibid.,* p.p. 53, 54.

in the area of private religious education to counter-balance this to strengthen denominational institutions in the light of growing interest in public higher education.[87]

Another resolution, offered by B. D. Ragsdale, and adopted unanimously, resolved:

> That the State Board of Missions of this Convention be authorized to procure for itself a charter in accordance with the provisions of the Constitution of this Convention, or that it be authorized to procure such amendment to the charter of this Convention as shall give to the State Board of Missions of this Convention corporate powers and rights to buy, sell, hold, or exchange such property as may facilitate its work of establishing and building up churches, schools and other benevolent enterprises.[88]

Ragsdale's work as secretary was evident in the statistical information in the minutes where ministerial changes, removals from the state, removals by death, gains by ordination were carried as well as listings of new meeting houses with their style of architecture. The year 1898 was one for building churches identified included Americus, Athens, Bainbridge, Conyers, Cuthbert, Dahlonega, Fairburn, Iron City, Loco, in Lincoln county, Kite, Marietta, Ohoopee, Pine Forest in Decatur county, Pine Grove in Decatur county, Sasser in Terrell county, Shadner, Campbell county, and Woodville, DeKalb county. Listed in process of construction were Atlanta Sixth, Elberton, Jackson Hill, Atlanta, Newnan Central, Tattnall Square, Macon, Valdosta, and West End, Atlanta.[89]

The Orphans' Home was still seeking to define its place as a part of the Convention, as evidence by its report in 1898 which said:

> This institution, while not under the control of the Convention, is directed and fostered by the Baptist women of Georgia, and properly falls under the scope of your board's report. [Mission Board] It is a question

---

[87]*Minutes, Georgia Baptist Convention,* 1897, p. 31, *Georgia Baptist Convention,* 1898, p.p. 27-31.

[88]*Minutes, Georgia Baptist Convention,* 1898, p. 54.

[89]*Ibid.,* p.p. 63, 64.

which has arisen in the minds of some thoughtful brethren, whether the orphange might not accomplish larger and better results if it were to become more closely related to the Convention and receive a place in the established order of business.[90]

At that time, R. H. Smith was financial agent for the home and he reported $5,036.01 cash collected.[91] Woman's Missionary Societies were doing a commendable work. They collected in cash and "boxes" for the year ". . . $14,458.71 for missions and other works of benevolence." [92] Smith had been employed jointly by the Orphans' Home and the Sunday School board [department]—a first such joint sponsorship—and preached 108 sermons and addresses and gave 185 ". . . talks on Sunday School literature and work." [93]

There was no apparent conflict in an agent being sponsored jointly by a Department of the State Mission Board and an institution which was run primarily by Baptist women in Georgia; principally women in the Atlanta area.

By 1899, some line of authority was established between the Orphans' Home and the Convention. J. L. White, B. M. Callaway, J. M. Brittain, and T. W. O'Kelley

> . . . were nominated for election as trustees in the Georgia Baptist Orphans' Home Association to fill the first vacancies occurring which are to be filled from among those nominated by this Convention.[94]

Out of the growing interest in the Orphans' Home, the Convention had agreed at last to elect some members to the Board of Trustees of the home! [95]

MISSION BOARD IN DEBT

By 1899, the Mission Board was in debt! Indebtedness was not new to the Convention. The manner in which the need was met is of interest in that the Convention, in finan-

[90]*Ibid.*, p. 77.
[91]*Loc. cit.*
[92]*Loc. cit.*
[93]*Loc. cit.*
[94]*Minutes, Georgia Baptist Convention*, 1899, p. 21.
[95]*Loc. cit.*

cial difficulty or under duress of other type, acted with considered judgment. In this instance, a committee named to study the financial condition of the State Board, reported assets of $750.00, and liabilities of $6,641.26. The Convention had for years taken an offering at each annual meeting. Estimates for the 1899 Convention were that $1,000 would be raised, leaving a net deficit of $4,891.26 the Board owed. The report indicated further that $3,033.05 had been borrowed from the DeVotie fund and did not have to be repaid immediately, with the State Mission fund paying interest over to the Indigent Ministers fund, in the amount of $181.98. By the committee's figuring, this left $1,858.21 to be made up.

After consideration of the situation, the report, adopted by the Convention, made three suggestions. One, that no immediate effort be made to pay back to the DeVotie fund monies borrowed, but to do so gradually. Two, that no special collection be made at the Convention for the funds. Key to the entire recommendation was in the third proposal calling for the Board to send a circular letter to all the churches stating financial needs, and request churches to provide gifts for past and present needs.[96]

Thus, the pattern of promotion and providing information to Georgia Baptists was established and functioning. The Committee, and evidently the Convention, believed that the churches would respond to the needs of the Board, to which they had given their continuous and generous approval over the years.

The pattern of election of delegates to the Southern Baptist Convention had continued unchanged for many years. Lansing Burroughs, in 1899, made a motion, approved, that

> . . . it is the sense of this Convention that delegates elected to the Southern Baptist Convention have not the right to appoint proxies, but that all vacancies shall be filled by the committee and in the way this Convention appoints.[97]

[96]*Ibid.*, p.p. 23, 24.
[97]*Ibid.*, p. 25.

Thus was ended the pattern whereby delegates, elected by the Georgia Baptist Convention, and unable to attend, could themselves name their proxies.

Growth of Convention work is indicated in the increasing list of standing committees appearing in the Convention minutes. Committees for 1899 included those on Education, State Missions, Home Missions, Foreign Missions, State of Religion, and Amount of Destitution, Work of Sunday-School Board, Young Peoples' work; Temperance, Deceased Ministers, Nominations, Representation in the Southern Baptist Convention, Time and Place, Printing and Distribution of Minutes, for a total of thirteen committees appointed for the 1900 convention.[98]

A committee had been named in 1898 to confer with the Orphans' Home association concerning enlargement of the home.[99] Following conferences, the committee reported:

> . . . we find an entirely agreeable disposition to harmonize upon plans for the enlargement of the Home and extending its sphere of usefulness, so as to make of it a denominational institution of great power and for the accomplishment of much good and also a corresponding disposition to seek the aid and fostering care of the Convention.
>
> Upon the following propositions we believe there will be no difficulty in an agreement being perfected, and we recommend the adoption of the same by the Convention, leaving final action thereon by the Association to be taken when the Convention shall have acted, and that a committee of four shall be appointed by the Convention with full power and authority to act with said Association, or any committee named by it to carry said agreement into effect, vis:
>
> 1. The Baptist Orphans' Home now located in the city of Atlanta shall be moved to a farm in the county of Fulton, said farm not to consist of less than fifty acres of land, such removal to take place when ever in the judgment of the Board of Managers of said Association the same shall be deemed feasible and advisable.
>
> 2. In the event of a determination for the removal of said Home to any other place in Atlanta, or in Fulton

[98]*Ibid.,* p. 31.
[99]*Ibid.,* p. 56.

County as above contemplated, the real estate in or near Atlanta now owned by said Association, or trustees for it, shall be sold as soon as practicable, and the amount realized from said sale shall be invested in the lands and buildings necessary for said removal.

3. The present trustees of the Association shall be continued in office until the expiration of their respective terms, the vacancies caused by such expirations to be filled as they occur by election of the Association from among such names as may be recommended therefor by the Convention, or any committee appointed by it, until the Convention shall have thus secured the election from among its nominees of nine of said trustees, and at the expiration of the respective terms of office of the nine trustees so nominated and chosen their successors shall thereafter continue to be elected by the Association from among persons similarly nominated by the Convention or its said committee.

4. Said Association shall make annual reports to the Convention of the work that has been done, of all amounts received and disbursed, and generally of the condition and affairs of the Home, and said convention shall co-operate with and aid said Association in carrying out the purposes of its creation. At the annual meetings of the Convention said Association shall be entitled to representation by two representatives eligible to membership under the constitution and laws of this Convention.[100]

This report was adopted by the Convention,[101] thus bringing the Home under official Convention control.[102]

Within a year following acceptance of the college at Forsyth, the trustees of Monroe Female college reported they had compiled with their instructions, and the trustees elected by the Convention to manage the affairs of the college found the property to be free of debt and worth at least $25,000. Under the new charter, the institution was known as "Monroe College—A Normal And Industrial School for Women." [103]

For educational purposes, $26,215.70 had been raised,

[100]*Ibid.*, p.p. 56, 57.
[101]*Ibid.*, p. 21.
[102]See also, *Minutes, Georgia Baptist Convention*, 1900, p. 15.
[103]*Minutes, Georgia Baptist Convention*, 1899, p. 63.

with $90,770.78 as the grand total for missions and edu-
cation.[104]

Baptist women in Georgia had been handicapped by their
inability to report directly to the Convention. When reports
were first accepted on their work, it was through the Mission Board.

In a communication to the Convention, the ladies declared:

> Dear Brethren:
> Heretofore we have reported to your body indirectly
> through Dr. J. G. Gibson, the Corresponding Secretary
> of the State Mission Board. We however, now ask to
> report directly to the convention, and desire that each
> year the Woman's Baptist Missionary Union be per-
> mitted to present through some brother selected by
> them, a report of their work directly to the Conven-
> tion.[105]

The Convention's action on the Woman's Missionary Union
report omitted any reference to this request,[106] but the request apparently did not go unheeded. They still were
unable to report directly, as women were not allowed to
address the Convention, but they had the satisfaction from
this time on of selecting their own spokesman.

The women did report 436 societies, 84 Sunbeam bands,
with contributions of $13,404.38 for the year and boxes for
the frontier valued at $3,251.49. There was in 1899 no
salaried officer except an organizer, paid $25 each month,
$10 of which was for travel expense.[107] And, the Georgia
Baptist Historical Society, dormant for several years, was
reorganized April 3, 1899, during the Convention's annual
session, and it received permission to meet with the Convention.[108]

[104]*Ibid.*, p. 72.
[105]*Ibid.*, p. 74.
[106]*Ibid.*, p.p. 22, 23.
[107]*Ibid.*, p. 75.
[108]*Ibid.*, p. 100.

END OF A CENTURY

With the final session of the Convention during the 19th Century in Savannah, a recapitulation of Baptist life is in order. During that century, Baptists had grown numerically in the state until they were in a dominant position, sizewise, and in influence. They had established a creditable program of State Missions, a ranking university, together with sponsorship or support of numerous colleges and other schools. Georgia Baptists had given leadership to, and support for, the organization of the Southern Baptist Convention, as well as continuing support through the years since 1845.

They had adopted and revised several times a Constitution and adopted a set of By-Laws. Patterns of organizational and departmental work were established which were to continue, essentially, to the present. The format of Convention programs, Minute reports, and methods of operation was well established, as was the program of Associational Mission work.

While efforts to establish a seminary failed, Georgia Baptists believed that in Mercer University they had facilities for theological education which were superior; although they supported generously the Southern Baptist Theological Seminary.

During this slightly over half of the Convention's organized life, it had learned to work as a unit with churches bound together in common purpose. Ministerial support, support for aged ministers and their families, help in building churches and establishing mission points had been integral phases of the Convention's operations.

Theologically, the Convention remained conservative in character, with overtones of Calvinism still evident. Well ahead of its time in promotion techniques, the Convention had, through its state paper, *The Christian Index,* and through direct mail and personal promotion, presented its causes and witness throughout the state.

Politically, the Convention left its impact upon the state as it memorialized the Legislature upon several occasions in areas of civic and moral interest.

In the field of education, Georgia Baptists, through their Convention, and as individuals had played an important role in the establishment of a public school system in the state.

With 1,758 churches, 66 associations, and 167,559 members, Georgia Baptists looked with optimism toward the 20th century.[109] There were 12 Associations, with 226 churches and 16,346 members friendly to the Convention, but not members.[110]

[109]*Ibid.*, p.p. 77, 78.
[110]*Ibid.*, p. 79.

CHAPTER 12

A New Century

The year was 1900, and the meeting place was Griffin, Ga. The time for sessions of the Georgia Baptist Convention had been set for March 29-April 1, in the sanctuary of the First Baptist Church in Griffin. It was the turn of the century and a spirit of optimism prevailed among Georgia Baptists as new ideas were being tried, and as the program of work continued to grow. S. Y. Jameson had been named corresponding secretary-treasurer of the State Mission Board.

A native of Towns County, Jameson had served as the first pastor of the West End Baptist Church in Atlanta, going from that church to the State Board position. Later to serve as president of Mercer University, Jameson was in his 41st year when elected to lead Georgia Baptists. And, during his leadership, mission gifts were to increase from $44,848 in 1900 to $110,065 in 1905.[1]

A native of Towns County, Jameson had served as the first Little is said about him in Convention minutes during the nine years he served as Corresponding Secretary. It is to Ragsdale's *Story of Georgia Baptists,* Volume III, that we are indebted for some information concerning him. When the Mission Board had been established in 1877, Gibson had been offered the position as corresponding secretary. A throat "affection" caused him to decline the post, and following DeVotie's tenure, Gibson was elected again in Hawkins-

[1]Encyclopedia of Southern Baptists, [Nashville: Broadman Press, 1958] Vol. I, p. 696.

ville in 1891, to succeed DeVotie. He accepted the second election.[2]

Called by some of his friends the "Spurgeon of Georgia," Gibson was elected to the Mission Board post at the first Convention he ever attended in Georgia.[3]

Gibson declined re-election in 1899 because of ill health. The Mission Board elected him Honorary Secretary with a salary of $500 and no specific duties.[4] He died Feb. 15, 1900.[5]

Two names were submitted as a successor: B. D. Ragsdale, Convention recording secretary, and S. Y. Jameson, pastor of the West End Baptist Church in Atlanta. Ragsdale was elected, but declined because of his position at Mercer as Bible professor. Jameson was then elected.[6]

Following Gibson's administration and his rather strong emphasis upon education, Jameson stressed both missions and education, and in his first report to the Convention, he said: "We can not afford to neglect our base of supplies." [7] Two recommendations by the Committee to review the report of the Board of Missions for that year were:

> 1. That all money raised in the State for Home and Foreign missions be sent through our State Secretary
> 2. That all mission work in the State be done through our State Board.[8]

Jameson who had been a merchant in Westminster, S. C., at the age of 16,[9] sought early in his administration to insure continued channeling of funds through the State Board for all mission causes. Evident also was the intent of the Convention that all mission work done in the state be

---

[2]B. D. Ragsdale, *Story of Georgia Baptists,* Atlanta, the Executive Committee of the Georgia Baptist Convention, 1938] Vol. III, p.p. 124, 125.

[3]*Ibid.,* p. 125.

[4]*Ibid.,* p. 128, quoting *The Christian Index,* April 13, 1899.

[5]*Ibid.,* p. 127.

[6]*Loc. cit.*

[7]*Minutes, Georgia Baptist Convention,* 1900, p. 20.

[8]*Ibid.,* p. 21.

[9]Encyclopedia of Southern Baptists, Vol. I, p. 696.

under the direction of the State Board. Jameson led the Board to suggest further to the Convention:

> That it is the sense of this Convention that Georgia Baptists should increase their contributions to missions twenty five per cent the ensuing Convention year.[10]

For the first time in 1900, there was printed along with the Minutes of the Convention, minutes of the Preachers' And Workers' Conference.[11] Evidently in 1899, G. W. Garner had suggested

> . . . That the preachers and other Christian workers of the State meet in conference the day previous to the assembling of State Convention for the purpose of discussing certain questions of vital interest to the churches, which could not be properly discusssed in the Convention. . .[12]

Subjects discussed at that first "Pastors' Conference" were not unlike those discussed over the years, and included *Organization In Church Work,* as well as *To What Extent the Baptist Ministry Discuss from the Pulpit Secular and Political movements?* Other items were *The Essential Elements of Pastoral Success,* the *B. Y. P. Union as the Pastor's Helper,* and *The Reciprocal Influence of Missions.*[13]

Boosting the Orphans' Home ministry before the Convention was a move which brought all the children from Hapeville to sing and present recitations, after which James B. Taylor, home superintendent, addressed the Convention.[14] Free transportation for the children was provided by the Central of Georgia Railway; duly thanked for its courtesy.[15] Following Taylor's address, the Convention adopted a resolution pledging co-operation with the trustees of the home ". . . . in raising money at once to erect such a building

[10]*Minutes, Georgia Baptist Convention,* 1900, p. 22.
[11]*Ibid.,* p. 10.
[12]*Loc. cit.*
[13]*Loc. cit.*
[14]*Ibid.,* p. 14.
[15]*Ibid.,* p. 16.
[16]*Ibid.,* p. 14.

or buildings as in the judgement of the Trustees the institution needs." [16]

Following acceptance of the Monroe Female College, other
colleges, including the one at LaGrange, sought to become
a part of the Convention family, and upon LaGrange college
trustees' indicating their desire to be heard on the Convention floor, the Convention adopted a motion reaffirming the
statement which it adopted in 1898, indicating willingness to
hear claims of other colleges.[17]

A motion by B. D. Ragsdale was adopted as an amendment to the Constitution which defined more fully the
authority of the Executive Committee. The sentence added,
to follow section nine of the then official Constitution, read:

> Whenever it becomes necessary or expedient, in the
> opinion of the committee, at any time between sessions
> of the Convention to sell or exchange real or personal
> property of the Convention, it shall have power so
> to do.[18]

In the report of the Committee on the Report of the
Trustees of Mercer, was a reaffirmation of the purpose for
Mercer:

> Your committee recognize the fact that the fundamental
> idea which brought Mercer University into existence,
> was the great need of an educated ministry, moving the
> hearts of our fathers; and this object has been steadily
> kept in view.[19]

A significant step by the Convention in 1900 was the
creation of a Board of Education, consisting of twenty-four
members. To some degree, this board was the forerunner of
the present Georgia Baptist Foundation. It was to be located
in Macon, meet at least once each year, and upon call by the
president, and was to be charged with the creation of new
endowments and increasing existing funds the Board was
to ". . . collect and disburse all funds for ministerial education in Georgia or abroad, donors being at liberty to give

[17]*Ibid.*, p. 17.
[18]*Loc. cit.*
[19]*Ibid.*, p. 19.

special directions to their contribution for same." [20] The Board was to gather and distribute up-to-date information on education, and would operate under a charter to hold and expend funds committed to it for educational purposes but was ". . . in no wise to incur any debt involving property or funds committed to its care." [21]

The Board of Education was to act also ". . . as a bureau of information to bring graduates of our denominational institutions, and other competent persons desiring to teach, into communication with schools seeking teachers." [22] Allowed to elect its own officers, fill vacancies, prescribe duties, fix remuneration and make its own by-laws, the board was set up with considerable authority.[23]

The Board was instructed to secure a charter, and granted further the ". . . power to petition the General Assembly of the State of Georgia, whenever it is deemed necessary, against any existing or threatened legislation adverse to our educational interests." [24] This board, as is obvious from assigned duties, assumed some of the responsibilities here-to-fore held by the Executive Committee. This action, together with the creation of the State Mission Board twenty-three years earlier, sounded the death knell for the Executive Committee as it was then structured in terms of effective authority by that Committee.

By 1900, Mercer had 260 students, and the Monroe Female College, 150 students, 64 of whom were boarders, with a new dormitory under construction.[25] A definition of the Convention's interpretation of State Missions is found in the report on State Missions, and is a definition which has remained accurate basically. The report said:

> In its broadest sense, State Mission work includes all efforts to extend and establish Christ's kingdom within the State's bounds, but specifically and especially it

[20]*Ibid.*, p. 24.
[21]*Loc. cit.*
[22]*Loc. cit.*
[23]*Loc. cit.*
[24]*Loc. cit.*
[25]*Ibid.*, p. 39.

refers to supplying the destitute with the gospel. And by the destitute we understand not only those who are out of the reach of present gospel ministrations, but all whom the gospel does not actually reach.[26]

By this year also, the B.Y.P.U. was referred to as ". . . a legalized and an integral part of the Baptist State Convention, . . ." [27]

STRONG BELIEF IN MISSION OF BOARD

Without apparent attempt to sound officious, the report of the Mission Board, its twenty-third, indicated the solemnity with which ministries in Georgia were approached.

> Georgia occupies a unique place among the sisterhood of States in the sunny South. Early God gave to her the talent, the temper and the traite, that lifted her in the prominence and let her fall just in the niche she was ordained to fill. And leadership has always been her place, and always will be. In her leadership she has opportunities, and consequently responsibilities, enjoyed by few and surpassed by none. . .
> Religiously as goes Georgia, so goes the South, and as goes the South, so goes America, and as goes America, so goes the world, are to many high-sounding words with little significance, and such they may prove to be, but who would be so bold as to say that we have not come to the kingdom for such a time and such a purpose as these words set forth. . .[28]

From October, 1899 until the Convention in the latter part of March, 1900, the Orphans' Home had become a citizen of Hapeville with ownership of a 50-acre farm, with all attachments, two dwellings, a number of outhouses, and 450 feet of frontage on the Central railroad.[29]

At the beginning of the 20th century, the effects of the Industrial Revolution were beginning to be felt in the lives of Georgia Baptists, and for the first time, at the Convention in Valdosta in 1901, some attention was paid to needs of a ministry among those Georgians who worked in cotton mills.

[26]*Ibid.*, p. 41.
[27]*Ibid.*, p.p. 48, 49.
[28]*Ibid.*, p. 59.
[29]*Ibid.*, p. 64.

In that year, a committee named to study mission work at these mills, reported:

> This work can be accomplished without money. It is not so much financial aid that these people need as it is kind attention and sympathy, especially in times of sickness and distress. . .

> As the mills in Georgia become more numerous, the operatives become more and more in demand, and as they become skilled in their work, the more anxious the mills become to retain them and not have them move away to other mills. Nothing will do so much to cause cotton mill help to be contented and happy as good church and school advantages. The cotton mill with no church, no Sunday-school and no common school, can not long retain its help. They have found this out and are not only too anxious to encourage them by building churches and paying the preachers.[30]

For a number of years after 1901, the Convention continued to give especial attention to the needs of millworkers, and later was to employ mill evangelists as a part of the program of state missions. In a move toward further consolidation, the Convention adopted unanimously a resolution in 1901:

> That there be omitted from the list of Standing Committes the three committees on these subjects [State, Home, and Foreign Missions], it being understood that special committees on these items of the Board's report shall be allowed, when thought desirable, to go beyond the matter of the Board's report in presenting facts, suggestions, or recommendations.[31]

To further indicate Baptist strength in Georgia, the Board's report said that from five thousand to six thousand Baptists in 1800, that body of believers had grown to over 400,000 in 1900.[32] The report of Jameson's work as Corresponding Secretary for the year is impressive. He had attended thirty-four associations, traveled 18,300 miles, preached eighty-seven sermons, delivered 109 addresses and issued

[30]*Minutes, Georgia Baptist Convention*, 1901, p. 24.
[31]*Ibid.*, p. 28.
[32]*Ibid.*, p. 65.

> . . . not less than two thousand and seven hundred re-
> ceipts and eight hundred bank checks.[33]
> Each contribution requires that the name of the con-
> tributor and his church shall be written four times and
> the amount entered five times. Four thousand letters,
> including appeals, were prepared and mailed.[34]

The Missions report stated that the co-operative work with
colored people would terminate January 1, 1902. This had
been a joint effort of the State Board, the Home Mission
Board, the Negro Educational Society, and the Home Mission Society of New York. The three-year plan, nearing the
end, involved $1,050 in Georgia funds.[35] This program
ended primarily because Negro Baptist groups in Georgia
were having difficulty in working together, and there were
two separate conventions.[36]

Interesting not only because of then current trends, but
because of historic antecedents, was the statement in 1901
indicating the method of dividing expenses of the operation
of the State Mission Board.

> The expense of the Board, according to the custom
> which has prevailed for years, is divided equally between
> the State, Home and Foreign Mission. No other funds
> passing through the Treasurer's hands are touched. The
> expenses are: salary of Secretary and Treasurer, $2,000;
> office assistant, $300; room rent, $150; books, stationary,
> postage and traveling expenses, the Corresponding Secre-
> tary, $325. These are fixed amounts.
> In addition, the Board pays the expenses of the W.M.U.
> incurred in prosecuting their work.[37]

By this time, it was estimated that of the 2,000 churches in
the Convention, about 1,500 contributed to ". . . at least one
of the objects fostered by the Convention." [38] Within two
years of Convention acceptance of the Orphans' Home, there
were ". . . eighty-three inmates in the Home, including the

[33]*Ibid.*, p. 66.
[34]*Loc. cit.*
[35]*Loc. cit.*, p. 66.
[36]*Loc. cit.*
[37]*Ibid.*, p. 71.
[38]*Loc. cit.*

Housekeeper, two matrons, two teachers, and a foreman." [39]
Approximate cost of operating the home was $550 per
month.[40]

An interesting development in the legal status of Mercer
University was reported to the Convention at the 1902 session in Rome. A committee had been appointed at Valdosta
in 1901 to compile in pamphlet form all of the charters of
the convention and its Boards.[41]

In its effort to comply with the Convention directive, the
committee discovered that the original charter dealing with
the removal of Mercer University to Macon had never been
recorded, and had been lost. The Charter Amendment had
been granted, but the original was missing from the files of
Bibb Superior Court. A thorough search of the records and
files of the court was made, and it was determined that
almost every person involved in preparation of the amendment had since died. The committee reported:

> . . . Through the accurate memory of Judge Thomas G.
> Lawson, together with many contemperaneous facts,
> your committee have been enabled to prepare a copy, in
> substance, and which they have set on foot measures
> to have established under the law in lieu of said lost
> original.
> Grave doubts exist as to whether the courts at that time,
> namely, 1870, had authority to grant or make an amend-
> ment to an existing charter; because at that time the
> Legislature had not delegated such power to the courts.
> Afterwards, however, the Legislature did grant that
> power in ample terms; and the amendment in question
> having been acted on and treated as valid in all re-
> spects from then until now, your committee conceive
> that, if in establishing a copy of such lost amendment
> the order of the court be so framed as to declare the
> provisions of said amendment valid and legal, the same
> will thus be made legal, whether it was technically so in
> 1870 or not. They have accordingly drafted and pub-
> lished a petition in Bibb Superior Court to reach these

[39]*Ibid.*, p. 78.
[40]*Ibid.*, p. 79.
[41]*Ibid.*, p. 19.

ends, and which, as before stated, they herewith submit.[42]

Thus, the charter amendment under which Mercer University transferred to Macon, as recorded finally in 1902, was one drafted from memory. Subsequent Charter changes then, were made upon the basis of this redrafted document, largely the work of the memory of one man, more than thirty years after the original action!

In endeavoring to secure the charters, the Committee found it necessary to request the State Board of Missions

> . . . for its aid touching a charter for that body. Said Board promptly took the proper steps and procured a charter, granted under order of Fulton Superior Court, . . .[43]

The information included in the pamphlet, which pamphlet apparently no longer is in existence, was the following:

> 1. Act incorporating the Baptist Convention of Georgia under the name of its executive committee, assented to Dec. 22, 1830.
> 2. Amendment to above Act which also incorporates Mercer University, assented to December 22, 1837.
> 3. Amendment enlarging powers of the Convention and of Mercer University, assented to December 28, 1838.
> 4. Amendment enlarging powers of Convention and Mercer University assented to December 28, 1842.
> 5. Amendment to charter of Mercer University, granted in Bibb Superior Court, October term, 1870, which having been lost as above stated, is to be established and rendered valid in the form herewith presented.
> 6. Amendment to charter of Mercer University granted in Bibb Superior Court February 24, 1875.
> 7. Amendment to charter of Mercer University, granted in Bibb Superior Court, July 1, 1879.
> 8. The Constitution of this Convention, as revised in 1898, and printed in the minutes of 1891, p. 1.
> 9. The charter of the Mission Board of Georgia Baptist Convention, granted in Fulton Superior Court, January 11, 1902.
> 10. The Charter of the Georgia Baptist Orphans' Home, granted in Fulton Superior Court, September 8, 1888.
> 11. An amendment to the charter of the Baptist Convention of Georgia which providing for the election of

[42]*Minutes, Georgia Baptist Convention,* 1902, p. 21.
[43]*Ibid.,* p. 22.

one-third of the number of trustees of Mercer University each year, instead of the whole number once in three years.[44]

Your committee are of the opinion that the charters, with amendments, of Monroe College, and other such Female Colleges authorized by law to confer degrees as are fostered by the denomination, and as the Convention may specify, should likewise be printed in said pamphlet. And, the committee recommend to be included under this head, Shorter College at Rome, Southern Female College at LaGrange, Cox College at College Park and Hearn School.[45]

STATISTICS ON INSTITUTIONS

The 1902 Committee on Education did a valuable service to Georgia Baptists for its day and for the present when it,

. . . after writing scores of letters and examining many catalogues and year-books, make the following report of work being done by Baptists in Georgia in the matter of education. In making a list of the schools, we place Mercer University first and arrange the others alphabetically:

Mercer University, Macon, Ga. P. D. Pollock, A.M., Ll.D., President, Organized at Penfield, Ga., 1837; moved to Macon, 1871; trustees elected by Georgia Baptist Convention; value of buildings and grounds $175,-000; endowment $250,000, $115,000 of this raised during the year; 11 in faculty of liberal arts and 4 in the faculty of the Law School; 220 students pursuing Literary Course, 50 in the Law Department.

Bethel College, Cuthbert, Ga., A. E. Kesse, A.M., D. D., President. Organized 1857; buildings burned and brick structure erected 1901, cost $12,000; trustees elected by Bethel Association; 5 teachers, 115 students.

Cherokee Baptist Institute, Adairsville, Ga., George W. Tribble, A. B., Principal. Organized 1901; brick buildings, cost $4,500; trustees elected by Middle Cherokee Association; institution co-educational; 5 teachers, 215 students.

Cochran College, Cochran, Ga., A. W. Jackson, President. Organized 1885, as the property of the New Ebenezer Association, now owned by private parties; valued at $15,000; 7 teachers, 211 students; co-educational.

[44]*Ibid.*, p.p. 22, 23.
[45]*Ibid.*, p. 23.

Ebenezer High School, Dudley, Ga., O. A. Thaxton, A. B., Principal. Co-educational. Organized 1901; building of wood, cost $1,500; controlled by Executive Committee of Ebenezer Association and a local board; 3 teachers, 98 students.

Hearn Institute, Cave Spring, Ga., L. B. Cornelius, President; co-educational. Organized 1839; brick buildings for school purposes, frame dormitory; value of property, $30,000; endowment $12,500; trustees self-perpetuating; 3 teachers, 80 students.

Hiawassee High School, Hiawassee, Ga., A. B. Greene, B. A., Principal. Organized 1886; frame building, cost $1,500; title in the heirs of W. R. McConnell; self-perpetuating board of trustees; 4 teachers, 230 students.

Hightower Institute, Cumming, Ga., Rev. J. J. S. Callaway, Principal.

Houston High School, Arabi, Ga., Lawson E. Brown, A. B., Principal. co-educational. Organized 1895; frame buildings cost $4,000; trustees elected by Houston Association; 7 teachers; 189 students.

John Gibson Institute, Bowman, Ga., J. A. Hunter, B. L., President, co-educational. Organized 1892; brick building, valued at $15,000; trustees chosen by the Sarepta and the Hebron Associations; 8 teachers, 200 students.

Hephzibah High School, Hephzibah, Ga., J. H. Sanford, A. B., Principal; co-educational. Organized 1861; frame buildings, cost $6,000; trustees elected by Hephzibah Association; 6 teachers, 175 students.

Locust Grove Institute, Locust Grove, Ga., Claude Gray, A. B., president; co-educational. Organized 1893; frame buildings, cost $6,500; trustees elected by Flint River Association; 7 teachers, 250 students.

Monroe College, Forsyth, Ga., C. H. S. Jackson, A. M., President; for girls. Organized 1849; brick buildings, valued at $40,000; trustees elected by Georgia Baptist Convention; 15 teachers, 170 students.

Norman Institute, Obe, Ga., P. A. Jessup, A. M., D. D., President; co-educational. Organized 1901; brick buildings, valued at $25,000; trustees elected by Mell association; 9 teachers, 200 students.

North Georgia Baptist College, Morganton, Ga., Rev. S. Emmett Stevens, president; co-educational; organized 1898; brick building, valued at $3,000; trustees; 8 teachers, 257 students.

Perry-Rainey College, Auburn, Ga., Rev. J. M. Pirkle, President; co-educational. Organized 1890; frame buildings, cost $4,000; trustees, 3 teachers, 140 students.

Shorter College, Rome, Ga., T. J. Simmons, A. M., President; for girls. Organized 1877; brick buildings, cost $140,000; endowment $45,000, self-perpetuating board of trustees; 19 teachers, 200 students.

Southern Female College [Cox College], College Park, Ga., C. C. Cox, A.M., Ph.D., President. Organized 1842; brick buildings, valued at $75,000; private ownership; 22 teachers, 200 students.

Southern Female College, LaGrange, Ga., G. A. Nunnally, A. M., D. D., President. Organized 1842; main buildings brick, valued at $50,000; self-perpetuating board of trustees; 20 teachers, 173 students.

Tugalo Institute, Carnesville, Ga., J. W. McFarland, B. A., President; co-educational. Organized 1900; buildings brick, cost $4,000; trustees; 4 teachers, 272 students.

The aggregate shows 20 institutions of learning, employing 195 teachers and enrolling 3,603 students, school property valued at $570,000, with an endowment of $307,000.

In the preceding paragraphs we give a list of the schools in Georgia under the control of the Convention, Associations, Churches and Baptist Boards of trustees.[46]

This lengthy list is important historically. It details clearly the intense interest exhibited by Baptists in Georgia in the area of education. Several things should be noted. *One,* many of these institutions developed around the turn of the century. *Two,* despite repeated "clarification" of the Hearn School, the status as listed by the committee revealed that the school still considered itself to be self-controlling in that the trustees were self-perpetuating. *Three,* most of the institutions were co-educational. *Four,* an evaluation of the location of the institutions indicates clearly that the interest in education was state-wide, not confined to one area. *Five,* the Convention exhibited strong interest in the institutions although many were owned by Associations or private groups. The interest was mutual. The institutions under private ownership and Association ownership, desired to be identified with the program of Georgia Baptists. However, as the report indicates, the multiplication of the institutions was causing problems which the committee felt should be dealt with by the Convention in some positive manner. The com-

[46]*Ibid.*, p.p. 24, 25, 26.

mittee referred back to the 1901 report of its counterpart which said:

> Educational enterprises are undertaken upon which local pride takes hold and carries to a partial success; but cooler judgment when it comes into play, does not sustain them, and they fail of full accomplishment and money, time, and much else are lost.[47]

Continuing its evaluation, the 1902 Committee said:

> Again, local liberality is exhausted, local dissensions spring up, bickerings and personal strife engendered, debts are incurred, and the prosperity of the school is not only prevented, but not infrequently the school is destroyed or abandoned, or purchased for a small sum by some other denomination and henceforth owned and controlled by them. Within the bounds of this Convention we can find many such wrecks, which stand as monuments to the folly of our Baptist people or as towers of strength contribute to the prosperity of other religious denominations.
> Not a few of the schools named in this report are today in the meshes of the net and are so entangled that they cannot make progress and are in danger of being entirely lost to our denomination.[48]

Thus the stage was set for a recommendation which would bring about the creation of an Education Committee, which was to occupy the attention and interest of Georgia Baptists for many years, and perhaps serve as the eventual means of preserving the institutions during the depression years which were to follow.

The recommendation of the committee said:

> The advantages of Conventional control of school property and of the adjustment of all these schools into a consistent, progressive and harmonious system are evident. Such relation of this Convention to these schools would secure for each school in the system a wider sympathy from the denomination and a closer fellowship between the schools. It would guarantee to contributors the safety and wisdom of investment, and appeal to the benevolence of Christian people everywhere. It would insure perpetuity to the schools and give greater confidence to patrons in the merit of the institutions. . .

[47]*Ibid.*, p. 26.
[48]*Loc. cit.*

Therefore, in view of all these facts and to meet the
necessities of our educational enterprises and to put all
our schools on a firmer foundation, we recommend the
following:

That this Convention appoint a committee of twelve,
four for one year, four for two years, and four for three
years, and as their terms expire the vacancies be filled
by appointments for three years—these, with one from
each school that may come into the system as hereinafter provided, shall constitute 'The Georgia Baptist
Education Commission.' This Commission shall be
charged with the duty of conferring with any duly ac-
credited representative of any recognized Baptist school
in Georgia and said Commission be clothed with authority to negotiate for the ownership or control of said
schools; provided, that in no wise shall they involve this
Convention in any financial obligation.

That they be instructed to fix the grade and rank of
each school into a general system; assist in relieving
said schools of any indebtedness that may be on them;
advise the local board to make such improvements
as to them seem wise; appeal to the denomination
for such aid as may in their judgment be needed for the
best interest of Christian education; to employ such
agencies as may seem best calculated to accomplish
these ends; to adopt such regulations for their own
government as will best conserve the management of
the business entrusted to their care.

This commission shall make reports to this Convention
of the work done and the progress made during the
year, and preliminary to such work all schools in the
State under Baptist control are cordially invited to
co-operate with the commission upon the terms herein
set forth with the distinct declaration that the non-
acceptance of this invitation on the part of any school
shall not be construed as antagonistic to the Convention,
nor allowed to reflect upon nor to disparage such school
in any respect whatever.[49]

The report, significantly, was adopted unanimously by the
Convention without discussion.[50]

As anticipated, the Convention was notified in 1902 that
the co-operative agreement for work among the Negroes had
been terminated after having been prosecuted ". . . for three
years with great patience and diligence, and for the most

[49]*Ibid.*, p. 27.
[50]*Ibid.*, p. 24.

part, with gratifying success." [51] Reason for the cessation of the plan was

> . . . owing to a division among the colored brethren in their organized work, the Board deemed it impracticable to continue its labors with them. It is hoped, however, that our colored people may yet be able to unite their forces and make it possible for the Board to renew and prosecute more successfully its work among them.[52]

With a growing organization, and an increased quantity of minute records, the Executive Committee, following instructions of the 1901 Convention, came up with a plan for sharing the cost of printing the minutes, which was approved by all parties concerned. The plan apportioned the expense 60 per cent to the Board of Missions, 20 per cent to the Trustees of Mercer, 10 percent to the Trustees of Monroe College, and 10 per cent to the Georgia Baptist Orphans' Home Association.[53]

A first was established in 1902 when the Convention met twice in the same calendar year, the second time in November in Americus. The first 1902 session was in Rome. No internal evidence indicated the reason for the change. The report on time and place had been tabled until the last session of the Convention, and the November meeting was approved 225 to 25 ". . . after lengthy discussion by various brethren. . ." [54] From this time, annual sessions were held either in November or December. At this second session of the year an amendment to the charter of the Convention was reported. This amendment, affecting Mercer University, gave the Convention the right to elect a total of 31 trustees, 10 for one year, 10 for two years, and 11 for three years, and as the terms expired, their successors would be elected by the Convention for three-year terms.[55]

[51]*Ibid.*, p. 37.
[52]*Loc. cit.*
[53]*Ibid.*, p. 58.
[54]*Minutes, Georgia Baptist Convention*, 1902 A, p. 28.
[55]*Minutes, Georgia Baptist Convention*, 1902 B, p.p. 23, 24.
[1902-A, 1902-B are used to delineate two sessions of the Convention held that year. A—Rome; B—Americus]

Mission work had not been neglected, and from about 1880 well into the 1900's, a great deal of emphasis was placed on mission work in South Georgia. Jameson, in the report of the Mission Board at the second 1902 session said:

> South Georgia is conceded by all the most rapidly developing part of the State . . . Your Board is of the opinion that it could wisely expend its entire income in South Georgia alone. What is done in that most promising area of the State must be done quickly.[56]

In the decades before and after the turn of the century, the Young People's movement began to grow rapidly. It was not without some opposition among the older leadership among the Convention, who had taken precautions to keep the movement from becoming an organized entity; but to little avail.

In a message to the Atlanta City Union in 1902, F. C. McConnell said:

> When the Ecclesiastical History of the latter half of the 19th century comes to write its annuals, he will have to note as among the most remarkable phenomena, the rise and development of the Young People's Movement in Evangelical Christianity. It came into existance in response to a need. Churches realized that they had within themselves much unused and undeveloped strength. Following close upon the heels of this thought was the further realization that they owed their undeveloped members the great duty of training them for service.[57]

The movement was to some extent interdenominational to begin with, and in the second 1902 session, it was recommended that the courses given in "The Baptist Union," published at 324 Dearborn Street, Chicago, the official organ of the B. Y. P. U. of America, be used by B. Y. P. U. in Georgia.[58]

In 1902 and in 1903 two actions were taken by Georgia Baptists which continued to positionize the Convention in

[56]*Ibid.*, p. 67.

[57]Lesile Spencer Williams, [Atlanta; Baptist Training Union Department of Georgia Baptist Convention, 1945] p. 14.

[58]*Minutes, Georgia Baptist Convention*, 1902 B, p. 35.

the area of church-state relations. One dealt with a situation in England, and the Convention approved a resolution declaring:

> We, the members of the Baptist Convention of the State of Georgia, assembled in session November 20-23, note with interest and admiration the dignified and earnest stand our Baptist brethren in England have taken against the unjust and oppressive education bill now pending in the British Parliament. We rejoice in the heroic and martyr-like spirit expressed by our English brethren in their declared purpose, should the bill become a law, to meet it at every point with passive resistance. 'taking joyfully the spoilation of their goods,' and seeking in all honorable ways to secure the repeal of the bill. We take this occasion to express to our English Baptist brethren, in whose magnificent struggle for the separation of church and state, history is repeating itself, our deepest sympathy and assure them of our prayers, and, if the occasion should arise, of our readiness to contribute to a fund to relieve the distress of such of our brethren as may suffer persecution for consciences' sake.[59]

The second action followed the lengthy structuring of the Education Commission in 1903. The Convention, acting upon a matter tabled the previous session, declared in substance, on the matter of state aid to denominational schools that they had studied the matter and were of the opinion that the adoption by the Convention of the policy outlined by the Education Commission set forth the position of the Convention sufficiently.[60] This report said that no state funds of any type would be accepted for a Baptist college.[61]

MERCER UNIVERSITY SOLIDIFIES STRENGTH

Mercer was solidifying its strength with endowment of $268,829.82,[62] and raising scholastic requirements.[63] The report of the Trustees cited the fact that:

> The scholarship requirements for entrance have been

[59]*Ibid.*, p.p. 39, 40.
[60]*Minutes, Georgia Baptist Convention*, 1903, p. 203.
[61]*Minutes, Georgia Baptist Convention*, 1902 B, p.p. 39, 40, esp. p. 78.
[62]*Ibid.*, p. 57.
[63]*Ibid.*, p. 58.

reasonably increased, and a larger per cent than usual of those who desired to enter College this year have been advised to attend some of our Baptist preparatory schools another college year.[64]

In the seven-month report of the Board of Missions, emphasis continued to be placed upon the matter of stewardship growth, with the statement:

> Your Board has tried to impress upon every member of our brotherhood the duty of regular, systematic and proportionate giving. By proportionate giving we mean contributing to every object of the Convention according to that ratio prescribed by the Committee on Co-operation. We could wish that our churches would abandon the habit into which some of them have fallen, making a specialty of some one object to the neglect of others. Intelligent principle and not impulse should guide us in meeting all our obligations as stewards of the Lord. All of the objects fostered by our Convention are alike dependent upon the generosity of its constituents; but the amounts of money to be given to these objects in one year ought to be determined by the Convention itself, and not by the partiality of the donor for that object in which for some reason he is more interested than in others.[65]

And, it was in reality the pioneer efforts in the teaching of proportionate and systematic giving, which placed the Georgia Baptist Convention in a position to grow through the years.

In recommendations of the Mission Board, Jameson indicated again a pattern of operation which was to continue through the years when he said:

> We beg to acknowledge that we have been able according to the wish of the Committee on Co-operation heretofore expressed, to apportion among the associations and churches of every association the proper amounts they ought to raise during the year for the purposes of the Convention. We need a connecting link between our offices in Atlanta and the eighty associations of the state. Wherever the association has an executive committee we consult with them, and usually act on such advice as they may see fit to give in regard

[64]*Loc. cit.*
[65]*Ibid.*, p.p. 64, 65.

to work within their territory. In case the association has no executive committee, we have to do the best we can by communicating with well-known individuals and consecrated brethren upon whose judgment we can rely. We believe that there ought to be an executive committee in every association, and that they are the body who ought to be charged with the duty of making apportionments of the churches within their bounds. If it be the pleasure of the Convention to order your Board in connecting with the Committee on Co-operation to make appointments heretofore explained, we beg to suggest that we will seek to have one representative in every association in the State who will, either in connection with the executive committee where one exists, or after conference with leading pastors where an executive committee does not exist, co-operate with us in the discharge of this duty.[66]

The Georgia Baptist Convention's Committee on Co-operation was years ahead of its time. Some of the great strength found in Georgia in later years for the $75 Million Campaign and later for Co-operative Program work may be traced to the work of this Committee on Co-operation with the State Mission Board. Again, the roots of long-standing co-operation with association Executive Committees has over the years aided the Convention in its program of advance in missions, education and benevolences. It was to this partnership concept that the Convention's advance owed a great debt.

The idea of schools for training was expanding also, and as Sunday School work continued to grow, the Convention upon recommendation of the Committee on Co-operation, was ready to sponsor a school of methods in 1903 for pastors and teachers emphasizing Sunday School work and missions. The emphasis was deemed of sufficient value to plan for a 10-day school under leadership of the State Mission Board.[67]

There is sufficient historic value, to record the basis upon which the Education Commission was organized. At a meeting, its second, in Atlanta on May 7, 1902, the Commission set up rules and regulations which were to have a permanent

[66]*Ibid.*, p.p. 68, 69.

impact upon the educational life of Georgia Baptist institutions as well as upon the growth of the Convention itself.

The Commission set up grades of schools, curriculum and terms of admission, among other items.

I. Grades of Schools.
1. The system comprising such schools as may agree to the terms and accept the conditions prescribed for admission shall be known as the 'Mercer System of Schools.'
The several schools shall be grouped into three classes: the University, the Collegiate and the Academic.
II. Curriculum.
1. The University shall be equipped to maintain as high a standard of scholarship as that of any institution of learning in the State and will confer the several Bachelor Degrees and the Master's Degree.
2. The schools denominated Collegiate shall be equipped to do full-college work, conforming thier courses of study to the University literary curriculum, or its equivalent. These colleges may then confer the usual Bachelor Degrees and will be recognized by this Commission as of Collegiate rank.
3. Schools denominated Academic shall have a course of study that will prepare students for at least the Freshman Class of the University.
III. Terms of admission.
1. All schools desiring to become part of this system shall file with this Commission at the time of application, official and itemized statements of their assets and liabilities.
2. Schools accepted by the Commission shall have their charter so changed, when necessary, as to prevent any future mortgage or liability for debt on any part of their grounds, or building, or vested funds. And also, so that hereafter their Boards of Trustees shall be appointed by the Georgia Baptist Convention, said Trustees having been nominated by the associations or churches, or by the remaining active members of their boards in accordance with their present methods of election, as provided for by charter; provided, that not more than one-third of the Board shall be liable to change during the Convention year; also, that two shall be nominated for each vacancy, from whom the Convention shall choose.
On the foregoing fundamental principles of action and

⁶⁷*Ibid.,* p. 69.

terms of affiliation, this Commission undertakes:

1. To raise a fund to be called Emergency Fund, sufficient for the liquidation of all existing debts now resting upon the schools which enter into this system.

2. In addition to paying these debts, the Commission shall devote its energies to the raising of a fund to be known as the Improvement Fund, to be used in providing for the necessities of these schools in the way of repairs, equipments and enlargements.

3. The Commission will also raise a fund for the endowment of the University and other schools as the Commission may decide to be wise and practicable. While special effort is being made for some particular fund, it is not intended to direct contributions to that fund alone, but to encourage liberal giving to other funds, especially to the Improvement and Endowment Funds.

4. All special agents for the raising of funds for any of the correlated schools shall be appointed or endorsed by this Commission in conference with the Board of Trustees of said school.

5. Any detail of work under the proposed plan of affiliation, not sufficiently provided for in this instrument, may be arranged for at subsequent meetings.

6. Any school failing to concur in this plan shall lose representation on this Commission, and cannot participate in the material benefits which the Commission will endevor to dispence, but such action shall not disparage the merit of said schools, nor give the accepted schools priority in their claims upon the denomination for patronage and support.

7. The annual meeting of this Commission shall be on the day preceding and at the place of meeting of the Georgia Baptist Convention, but meetings may be had at other times and places as may seem fit to the Commission, and in all of the meetings seven members may constitute a quorum.[68]

The plan called for schools seeking admission into the system to file application with M. L. Brittain of Atlanta, Commission secretary. Less than a month after the May, 1902 meeting, the commission met again on the campus of Mercer University, and considered matters which had arisen, evidently, from previous meetings and decisions made at the earlier meetings. One, indicated earlier, was in answer to inquiries from representatives

> ... of two of our leading Baptist secondary schools, who were present to advise with us, as to the conviction of the Commission on the question of receiving State aid, and as to what the policy of the Commission would be in its relation to such schools. This inquiry was answered in the form of a resolution passed by the Commission as follows: 'All schools under this system shall be under the management of Baptists exclusively and absolutely separate from all direction by the State and not subject to State appropriations for support and maintenance.[69]

As the result of the ground work laid, and the extensive preparations which went into the setting up of the Education Commission, the following arrangements were agreed to by the end of 1902: Shorter College, Mercer University, Hearn Institute and Monroe college were under the rules and control of the Commission.[70] Shorter had been throughout its history something of an enigma in terms of its relationship to the Convention. Like the Hearn Institute, it sought to identify with the Convention organization, and remain under the sponsorship of the Convention, but it never really wanted to give up completely its independence in the form of the self-perpetuating board of trustees. They came into agreements, and then returned to a semi-independent status upon several occasions over the years. The Southern Female College at LaGrange ". . . was offered to this Commission . . . but owing to local complication . . ." was not accepted.[71]

One of the better arrangements in the early stages of the life of this Commission, in terms of Convention control, was that which placed Hearn Institute ". . . by agreement with the Trustees of Mercer University under the immediate and positive control of the Board of Trustees of Mercer University, and under the mediate control of this Commission." [72] And, until the institute finally folded, the Conven-

[69]*Ibid.*, p. 78.
[70]*Ibid.*, p.p. 80, 81.
[71]*Ibid.*, p. 80.
[72]*Ibid.*, p.p. 80, 81.

tion maintained better control that it had ever done during the early years of the school's existence.

BOOK OF CHARTERS COMPLETED

In 1901 in session at Valdosta, and in 1902 at Rome and again at Americus, the Convention had called for preparation of a Book of Charters of all institutions of the Convention. Finally, at the 1903 session in Athens, completion of this project, with the printing of 3,000 copies was reported. The Committee named to prepare the pamphlet recommended under the order setting it up:

> That the charter of this Convention and of Mercer University, and of all incorporate bodies and institutions fostered by the Convention, be so amended as to require the investment of endowment or permanent funds; either in good rent-paying real estate, or on note and mortgage, or title deed on property worth at a fair valuation at least 65 per cent more than the loan over and above incumbrances.[73]

The Convention, early in the 20th century, continued to make long-range plans to provide endowment for its institutions. The Committee went so far as to spell out suggested investments in city, county or state bonds which were considered good and well established, proposing a safeguard

> . . . expressly forbidding any such funds to be in any case invested in any new or experimental enterprise, or company; and that no officer or trustee shall in any case be a borrower, or surety, or in any way directly or indirectly interested in the property purchased, or on which the lien is laid, or the title given as security as the case may be.[74]

The proposals under which the institutions would come under the control of the Commission called for any charter amendments necessary to conform to the Commission's rules.[75]

With the change involving the Hearn school, came a change in name to "Hearn Academy; from Hearn Manual

[73]*Minutes, Georgia Baptist Convention,* 1903, p. 13.
[74]*Loc. cit.*
[75]*Loc. cit.*

Labor School," with the decision of the trustees that the Academy would be a preparatory school of four grades to prepare students to enter the sophomore class at Mercer. Attendance was limited to sixty, it was to be co-educational, with the minimum age of admission at 12 years and tuition to be $50.00 annually.[76]

Jameson, in his report to the Convention in 1903, revealed that Georgia lead all other states in gifts to foreign missions, giving a total of $33,658.00, $5,000 more than contributions of any other state.[77] J. Frank Jackson was "mill evangelist." [78] As indicated earlier, mission work among those employed in cotton mills in the State occupied much attention on the part of the Convention.

In his book, *Georgia—A Mission Field,* published in 1928, Spencer B. King, Sr., then superintendent of State Missions, went into considerable detail to point out peculiar problems which were presented to Georgia Baptists by the cotton mill communities. In the book, King estimated there were 300,000 [1928] people living in these communities, ". . . assuring a continual growth of this gigantic state mission problem." [79] Citing the problems, King included the fact that the workers, who lived in " 'Company' houses do not—can not—feel any ABIDING interest in the establishment and maintenance of a Baptist church".[80] These people ". . . will not attend services in the 'town church' no mattter how nearby it may be!" [81] Other factors noted by King were shifting population as the workers moved from mill to mill,[82] and the ". . . tendency of the people in mill villages to follow any 'ISM' which might come along." [83]

Thus, a quarter of a cetury after the first mill evangelist

[76]*Ibid.,* p. 55.
[77]*Ibid.,* p. 60.
[78]*Ibid.,* p. 62.
[79]Spencer King, *Georgia A Mission Field,* [Atlanta: Executive Committee, Baptist Convention of the State of Georgia, 1928] p. 60.
[80]*Ibid.,* p. 61.
[81]*Loc. cit.*
[82]*Ibid.,* p. 62.
[83]*Ibid.,* p. 63.

was employed, this continued to be considered a serious problem and a great mission opportunity for Georgia Baptists.

An interesting result of the 10-day mission rally held in Macon earlier in the year was that 160 preachers from throughout the state attended, and ". . . One country preacher who attended the meeting, collected from his churches $130.00 against $28.00 the previous year." [84]

Further implementation of the plans of the Education Commission were reported by 1903 when the legal status of Mercer, Shorter, and Monroe college was reported.

> *Mercer University:*
> The Board of trustees of Mercer University is elected by the Georgia Baptist Convention, and the ownership and control of the property and endowment, now estimated at half a million dollars, are fully and completely in the hands of this Convention, through the Board of Trustees of Mercer University elected by this Convention, and under the directive supervision of the Education Commission and the rules and regulations governing its work.
>
> *Shorter College:*
> The Board of Trustees of Shorter College is elected by the Georgia Baptist Convention, [see pages 79 and 80 in the minutes of the Americus Convention, November, 1902], and the ownership and control of the property and endowment of Shorter College, now estimated at $150,000, are fully and completely in the hands of this Convention, through the Board of Trustees of Shorter College elected by this Convention under the directive supervision of the Education Commission according to the terms of agreement which the Trustees of Shorter College accept as set forth in the general principles of organization of the Commission and the rules and regulations governing its work.
>
> *Monroe College:*
> The Board of Trustees of Monroe College is elected by the Georgia Baptist Convention and the ownership and control of the property and endowment of Monroe College, now estimated at $100,000, are fully and completely in the hands of this Convention. . .[85]

[84]*Minutes, Georgia Baptist Convention,* 1903, p. 66.
[85]*Ibid.,* p.p. 77, 78.

Final assurance of Convention control and support of the Orphans' Home, discussed for several years, was given with the action of the 1904 session of the Convention in Columbus. The Convention's action in 1899 was official and definite.[86] However, it was evident that many Georgia Baptists still did not understand fully the impact of this action. A recommendation from a special committee to study what to do with the home was adopted. It was an agreement to place the home under direct control and management of the Convention through a Board of Trustees, with the Convention to

> . . . own all properties hereafter added to the Home by gifts or other contributions and that the Georgia Baptist Orphans' Home Association is requested to have all deeds to property hereafter coming into its possession properly conveyed to the Trustees of the Home.[87]

The Convention rather than the Orphans' Home Association would elect trustees.[88]

The agreement called for a Board of Trustees to consist of 25 members, 14 women and 11 men, with a recommendation that the ". . . fourteen godly and consecrated women who are members of the present board be elected the women members of the new board." [89] Of the 25 members, seven women and five men were to be from Baptist churches in Fulton county, and the charter was to be changed to meet requirements of the resolution approved by the Convention ". . . and at the same time perpetuate the existence of said Association.[90] [Georgia Baptist Orphans' Home Association.]

The matter of church control of public education in England was still one of concern to Georgia Baptists, and perhaps is indicative of the deep-seated ties of interest with the Colonial Georgia of more than 150 years previous, and that English heritage, which still existed in the State. The earlier pages of this history sought to define the different

[86]*Minutes, Georgia Baptist Convention*, 1899, p.p. 21, 56, 57.
[87]*Minutes, Georgia Baptist Convention*, 1904, p. 16.
[88]*Loc. cit.*
[89]*Loc. cit.*
[90]*Loc. cit.*

type of heritage which Georgians had in colonization than did many of the other Colonial States.

Adopted at the 1904 session was a resolution which declared:

> Whereas, the Parliament of England, guided by the clergy of the Church of England, has passed a school law which puts public education in England under the control and direction of said Church; and whereas said Church causes to be taught in said schools doctrines that deny the faith and violate the consciences of non-conformist parents and their children; and whereas non-conformists must pay taxes to support said schools or be imprisoned, therefore be it
> Resolved
> 1. That in the judgment of this Convention this school law in England is contrary to the exercise of that religious liberty which God would have all his children enjoy—hence contrary to the true spirit of Christianity.
> 2. That we commend our Baptist and other non-conformist brethren, for their condemnation of and passive resistance against this law.
> 3. That we extend to them our sympathy and join with them in prayer to 'Our Father which art in Heaven,' that the day may soon come when this law shall be repealed, they be relieved of their burden, and Christianity be rid of this blot, which can have only an ill effect upon an enlightened world.[91]

The shifting emphasis from floor control of the Convention to Committee Control is indicated clearly by an amendment to the By-Laws which provided:

> 1. At each annual meeting of this Convention the President shall appoint a committee of ten whose duty it shall be to nominate to the Convention all Boards, Commissions and Committees chosen by the Convention.
> 2. All Boards, Commissions and Committees reporting to the Convention shall cause to be embraced in their reports of finance the usual 'Balance Sheet' employed by bookkeepers.
> 3. The boards and other like bodies belonging to the Convention and under its control shall have their Treasurers placed under bond. Every Auditing Committee of the treasurer's account shall report as to the validity of his bond.

[91]*Ibid.*, p. 21.

4. No recommendation shall ever be embodied in any reports made to this Convention by any agent, secretary, or other officer of any board or like body, which, if received and adopted, will modify or amend any item of the Constitution, By-Laws or Standing Resolutions of the Convention.[92]

Writing concerning this action [although two years off on the date] B. D. Ragsdale, in his third volume of the *Story of Georgia Baptists,* said:

So the Convention by this plan surrenders into the hands of a committee of ten a very responsible task, as their nominations practically amounted to an election. Had the plan provided for extra or alternate names to be balloted on, majority rights might have been better expressed and conserved. Yet the plan has been acquiesced in without open protest, and no calamitous results have been noted.[93]

Ragsdale commented further:

Very remote would be counted the possibility that any member of the Convention would from the floor oppose any name or names submitted by the nominating committee.[94]

Although some conscious bias by Ragsdale was evident more than 20 years after the by-law was approved, his comment is reproduced for two reasons: 1. For forty-eight years, he was Recording Secretary of the Convention, and 2. For about 20 years he was the official Convention historian, at an annual stipend, and was commissioned by the Convention to write his three-volume history.

With some of the same interest which elicited support of Georgia Baptists in the formation of the Southern Baptist Convention in 1845, the Convention in 1904 gave expressions of sympathy and interest in the proposal to hold a Baptist World Congress in London in 1905.[95] The secretary of the Convention was ". . . authorized to furnish credentials to those of our brethren who expect to attend the said

[92]*Ibid.,* p. 30.
[93]Ragsdale, Vol. III, p.p. 148, 149.
[94]*Ibid.,* p. 148.
[95]*Minutes, Georgia Baptist Convention,* 1904, p. 39.

Congress," but no provision was made for sending an official delegate.[96]

AID TO CHURCHES CONTINUED

Budgeting of Convention monies, and the setting of goals was a responsibility which grew annually as the Denomination grew and added programs of work. Four thousand dollars was expended during 1903 for assistance to 30 churches

> . . . in erecting houses of worship thus securing to the denomination, property valued at more than forty thousand dollars. Help is extended only to those who have first exhausted their own resources, and are unable, without help, to complete their houses. We contemplate making this a Loan Fund, taking non-interest bearing notes from the churches, to be paid as early as circumstances will allow.[97]

It is in order to note in connection with this 1903 report of assistance in building churches that a careful study of the minutes of the Convention, extant minutes of the old State Mission Board, Minutes of the Executive Committee— both the first such Committee and the present Committee— and minutes of the Administration Committee of the Convention reveal one fact of which few Georgia Baptists are aware.

In the history of the Georgia Baptist Convention, a conservative estimate based upon records of assistance as indicated in the preceding paragraph, is that perhaps as many as 1,000 churches in Georgia have been aided at one time or another either in the construction of their houses of worship, erection of pastoriums, or with direct assistance for pastoral aid. Amounts ranged as high as $20,000 to the First Baptist church, Hapeville, in the 1940's to a few dollars. The Ponce de Leon church, in Atlanta, for example, was granted $10,000 by the old State Mission Board with terms which permitted repayment in five years, at no interest, with the church being allowed to use one-half of its

[96]*Loc. cit.*
[97]*Ibid.*, p. 75.

contributions to State Missions in annual liquidation of the principle! [98]

Most of the larger churches in the state—including the largest—owe their beginnings to direct assistance from the Georgia Baptist Convention. The aid was not limited to a specific area, but was accorded churches in every section of the State, with many of the older Atlanta churches sharing in larger amounts of Convention monies for their programs. It is thus a fair statement to assert that the organization of the Georgia Baptist Convention and its program has never been a one-way street, drawing from the churches for cooperative efforts. Rather, it has been historically a two-way street, with assistance being rendered by the collective body to a large extent.[98a]

Effectiveness of the Committee on Co-operation was never in question. The budget projected for 1905, in the 1904 report, included the following apportionments; Foreign Missions, $50,000; Home Missions, $30,000; State Missions, $30,000, Orphans' Home current support; $12,000; Christian Education, Emergency Fund of Education Commission, $5,000; Ministers' Relief Fund $3,000; Ministerial Students at Mercer and the Seminary, $2,500.[99]

The Committee tried each year to lead the churches to a greater appreciation of the necessity for giving in such a manner that all members of the Convention family were provided for equitably. The Committee said in 1904:

> Of the two thousand and more Baptist churches in the State, the number contributing to Missions is constantly increasing, but it is still true that less than one hundred furnish one-half of the money received. Some churches are partial in their gifts, having one object of the Convention or two or three. Only a small proportion give to the seven objects commended last year.[100]

[98]*Minutes, Executive Committee, State Mission Board,* May 31, 1905.

[98a]*Minutes, Georgia Baptist Convention,* Irregular Years, Tables and Paragraph information listing churches aided in purchasing lots and construction from State Mission Funds.

[99]*Minutes, Georgia Baptist Convention,* p. 88.

[100]*Loc. cit.*

First evidence that the Convention ever adopted, formally or informally any hymn was found in the introductory paragraph to the minutes for 1905 when it was reported that: "The Convention hymn, 'How Firm A Foundation,' was sung, . . ." [101]

A growing attendance at the Convention sessions was responsible, in part, for a Constitutional Amendment in 1905. The amendment, to section five of the constitution, provided that it read as follows:

> That each association shall be entitled to two delegates, and to one additional delegate for every 500 members, provided the number of delegates for the one association shall never exceed ten. Each church contributing annually fifty dollars to the funds of the Convention shall be entitled to one delegate; and to one additional delegate for each additional $100 thus contributed, provided that the representation shall not exceed three delegates for any church. Each Sunday-school, Young People's Union, or Woman's Missionary Society contributing each annually $50 to the funds of the Convention shall be entitled to one delegate, provided in no case two organizations obtain representation on the same fund, and all delegates shall hold their appointment until others are appointed to succeed them, and all of them shall be orderly male members of regular Baptist churches, and shall present satisfactory evidence of their appointment by the bodies which they represent.[102]

Because the matter of entertainment had become a problem, the Convention voted further that:

> We recommend second, that the communities hereafter entertaining this Convention shall be expected to limit their free entertainment to the duly appointed delegates from the associations, churches, Sunday schools, Young People's Union and Woman's Missionary Societies.[103]

An apparent conflict in the agreement between the Convention, authorized in 1904, and the Georgia Baptist Orphans' Home Association with regard to the amended

[101]*Minutes, Georgia Baptist Convention,* 1905, p. 9.
[102]*Ibid.,* p.p. 18, 19.
[103]*Ibid.,* p. 19.

charter, resulted in 1905 in a clarifying resolution adopted by the Convention providing:

> That the charter of the Georgia Baptist Orphans' Home Association be further amended so that the alienation or conveyance of any part of the real estate of said Georgia Baptist Orphans' Home Association, hitherto or here-after acquired, shall be forbidden and held to be void unless a majority of the Board of Trustees of said Georgia Baptist Orphans' Home Association, appointed or elected by the Baptist Convention of the State of Georgia, shall by vote of said body lawfully assembled, assent to and join in the execution of sail alienation or conveyance and, also, unless the said alienation or conveyance shall be previously authorized or afterwards confirmed by the Baptist Convention of the State of Georgia.[104]

The Convention approved also the sale of 16 acres of land, known as the "Norcross land" with the proceeds ". . . to be sacredly devoted to the erection of what is known as the main building at the said Orphans' Home at Hapeville. . ."[105] Authority to proceed with completion of the main central building was given also.[106]

In an unusual recognition of a gift to the Convention, on motion of A. M. Foute, the appreciation of the Convention was expressed for a gift of five acres of land from a colored brother, not named, ". . . as a part of the site for the Baptist Union Institute near Ailey, Ga." [107] The man was William C. Crawley. In addition to the five-acre gift, ". . . he sold his other ten acres to the new school." [108]

Some years ahead of its time and conditioned probably by the fact that most Georgia counties at the turn of the century had a "county poor house", the Convention accepted in 1905 a report of a study committee named to explore the possibility of a home for needy women. The committee indicated it felt it to be the duty of the local churches to care

[104]*Ibid.,* p. 20.
[105]*Loc. cit.*
[106]*Ibid.,* p. 23.
[107]*Ibid.,* p. 24.
[108]Brief Manuscript History, Brewton Parker College, untitled and un-dated, furnished by College.

318 / A History of The Georgia Baptist Convention

for their own poor, and not a denominational duty, and leave it to the best interest of the local churches to keep their poor in their own midst. They said they did not believe that the bringing together ". . . of these aged unfortunates would be conducive to their personal happiness." [109] The committee felt that

> . . . the number of worthy, helpless women, who would be willing to live in such an institution, is so small that the expense . . . would be too great to authorize such an institution.[110]

The expressed purpose for the need of a dairy at the Orphans' Home in 1905 would come as a surprise to residents of the Children's Home in 1972. In the report of the Orphans' Home Association it was said that:

> Our pressing want at this time is a dairy. Only six cows are giving milk, and the yield is insufficient to supply our large family. It would be fine training for our orphan girls to build up a dairy in connection with our Home.[111]

An inventory of the home's animals and supplies is of interest in that a pattern of partial home support through the loading of trucks and railroad cars from Associations was for several decades an annual event in the life of the Home and of Georgia Baptists.

> In the agricultural department are 2 stout mules, 16 hogs, 8 cows, 21 loads of hay, 5,400 bundles of fodder, 300 bushels sweet potatoes, 400 bushels corn, 30 bushels peas, 2 acres turnips.[112]

Under Jameson's leadership, contributions to mission work continued to increase, with State Missions receipts for the year 1904-1905 totaling $31,962, which was $7,235 more than the previous year.[113]

The method of approach to the churches shifted after 1905. While the importance of the Associational executive

[109]Minutes, Georgia Baptist Convention, 1905, p. 27.
[110]Loc. cit.
[111]Ibid., p. 87.
[112]Loc. cit.
[113]Ibid., p. 78.

committee was recognized, and Jameson had indicated that approaches to the churches would be made through these, it became evident that the committees did not produce the degree of cooperation or the amount of monies needed. The Committee on Cooperation said that about 100 of the more than 2,000 churches furnished about half of the money received, and revealed that beginning with the next Convention year they would make direct contact with the churches.[114]

> "Now that the methods and plans of the Committee are pretty well understood by all the brotherhood, we feel safe in laying the responsibility for co-operation where it properly belongs, namely, on the pastors and churches, and in apportioning the sums required among these New Testament sources of supply in the Master's Kingdom.[115]

The Convention's expressed interest in prohibition of the sale of alcoholic beverages continued, as in 1906, a committee was named to work with other religious groups in petitioning

> . . . the General Assembly of the State of Georgia in the name of the Christian people of the State, in the name of humanity and of God, to enact such legislation as will be calculated to prohibit the sale, the manufacture and importation of intoxicating liquors within the State.[116]

The years of the administration of Jameson were years of consolidation and continued growth. Following the death of Mercer president Pinckney D. Pollock in 1905, Jameson was offered the presidency. He declined at the time and Charles Lee Smith was named president.[117] Smith resigned in June of 1906, at which time Jameson was elected again. He accepted the offer the second time.[118] Smith's tenure at

[114]*Ibid.*, p. 90.

[115]*Ibid.*, p.p. 90, 91.

[116]*Minutes, Georgia Baptist Convention*, 1906, p. 13.

[117]Spright Dowell, *A History of Mercer University*, 1833-1953, [Atlanta: Foote & Davies Inc., 1958].

[118]*Ibid.*, p. 237.

Mercer had been one of tension.[119] Jameson had proven himself an able and wise administrator, and during the seven years of service to Mercer, he restored the institution to an even keel and led in advances in every area.[120] With Jameson's move to Macon, and a new corresponding secretary, the stage was set for yet another era of growth among Georgia Baptists.

[119]*Ibid.*, p. 237.
[120]*Ibid.*, p. 238.

CHAPTER 13

New Ideas, New Horizons

J. J. Bennett was the fourth corresponding secretary of the State Mission Board. He was elected as secretary when 30 years old. Bennett graduated in 1895 from the ". . . State University, and went in the fall to be principal of Hearn Academy and pastor of the Cave Spring Church." He served later at Albany, Monroe, and Jackson Hill in Atlanta, coming as Corresponding Secretary of the State Mission Board from the position as pastor of the First Baptist Church, Griffin, in 1906.[1] He was characterized as a forceful speaker and leader in the field.[2]

Changes in leadership of the State Mission Board provide logical divisions of this history as the emphases changed slightly, and each secretary and administration left a distinct imprint upon the work of Georgia Baptists. This is the case because the Convention had rallied historically behind the general secretary and the plans he projected and promoted.

In an effort to correlate reports from the several educational institutions, and to spell out clearly the function of the Education Commission the Convention, in 1906, amended its Constitution, Section 11, unanimously, to provide:

> 11. There shall be chosen at each annual session one-third of the following boards, vis.: The Education Commission and the Trustees of the Institutions of learning

[1]B. D. Ragsdale, Story of Georgia Baptists, Vol. III, [The Executive Committee of the Georgia Baptist Convention, 1938] p. 131.

[2]*Ibid.*, p. 135.

321

under the control of this Convention, in accordance
with the provisions of their respective charters—Mercer,
Monroe and Shorter Colleges; and
It shall be the duty of the Boards of Trustees of the
several institutions of learning connected with this body
to have the respective reports of their fiscal year [to
which may be added any necessary supplemental mat-
ter], in the hands of the Secretary of the Education Commission at least one day before the meeting of this
Convention; and it shall be the duty of said Commission to digest and condense such reports on said day
before the Convention assembles, presenting in said
digest such matters as need to come before this body
for consideration—including 'Changes,' 'Improvements,'
'Needs,' 'Prospects,' and 'General Condition' of said institutions, with such 'suggestions' as may seem wise to
the Education Commission; and such condensed and digested report will constitute the 'Report on Education'
usually considered by this Convention.[3]

The State Mission report, Bennett's first, showed receipts
of $42,059.80, a balance of $8.54 over expenditures.[4]

The Convention amended also two other sections of the
Constitution to delineate clearly the function of the Committee on Co-operation, based upon a joint recommendation of
that committee and the Board of Missions, and to give the
Mission Board expanded authority.

1. There shall be chosen by the Convention at each
annual session a Committee on Co-operation of as
many members as there are interests fostered by the
Convention—one representing each interest.
This Committee shall make annual estimates of amounts
of money needed for the work, upon which estimates, all
authorized agents and secretaries may make appeals to
the churches and other bodies.
It shall also prepare and publish suitable schedules for
the guidance of agents and secretaries in making appeals for funds.
All that part of the work outlined by the Committee
affecting the enterprise of the churches operating
through the Convention, for each ensuing year, shall be
submitted in report to the Convention, before the same
becomes operative.
This committee shall have power to elect its own officers,

[3]*Minutes, Georgia Baptist Convention,* 1906, p. 25.
[4]*Ibid.,* p. 20.

except that of Secretary, who shall be the same man as the auditor of the Board of Missions, and who shall be elected jointly by that Board and the Committee on Co-operation. This Committee shall report to the Convention annually.[5]

Item 10, dealing with the Mission Board, was amended to permit the Board

To appoint its own Corresponding Secretary, who shall devote his whole time to the work of the Board, and who shall be ex officio, a member of the same,

was changed to read thus:

And treasurer, both offices to be in the same man; also an auditor, both of whom shall be ex officio members of the Board of Missions. The auditor shall be the joint officer of the Board of Missions and the Committee on Co-operation.[6]

It was obvious that the position of auditor was becoming a power base within the Convention. Ragsdale's appraisal appears justified in that Bennett, a speaker and leader, was aided by H. R. Bernard as an "inside" man.[7] These constitutional amendments, approved the year Bennett became Corresponding Secretary, made the auditor, also secretary of the Committee on Co-operation, a force in Convention life.

The Woman's Missionary Union, in its report, requested the Convention

. . . to approve the action of the Woman's Missionary Union in creating and combining the offices of Corresponding Secretary and Treasurer, with the understanding that all monies collected by such officer or other agency of said union be paid, as in the past, to the Corresponding Secretary and Treasurer of the Board of Missions of this Convention.[8]

After provision was made for an auditor for the Convention, a motion by B. J. W. Graham was approved which requested:

That, the churches and other bodies be and are hereby requested to send all their contributions for Ministerial

[5]*Ibid.*, p. 27.
[6]*Loc. cit.*
[7]Ragsdale, Vol. III, p.p. 135, 136, 137.
[8]*Minutes, Georgia Baptist Convention*, 1906, p. 28.

Education and current support of Mercer University, as well as for all other objects, to the Treasurer of the Board of Missions, that all our contributions may be entered upon the same set of books.[9]

In the 30th annual report of the Board of Missions, the first under Bennett's leadership, a new concept of the Board's function was presented.

The Board of Missions is but a standing committee appointed by the Convention, whose term of service ends with each conventional year. The duties assigned to your Board make it a unique committee. It is at once active and passive—an agency and a means. It is appointed on the one hand to stimulate the spirit of missions in the churches, and to seek State-wide sympathy and co-operation; on the other, to become the channel, the means through which and by which the denomination may move forward in a rational, organized and co-operative way in the cause of the Master. Actively, the Board represents State, Home, and Foreign Missions, Ministerial Relief, and the Orphans' Home. Passively, it is the means by which the missionary, the benevolent, the eleemosynary gifts of the churches, societies and other organizations reach and accomplish the purposes for which they were intended.[10]

Factually, the promotional aspects of the definition of the Mission Board were practical, and well in line with the method of operation in the past. The definition of the Board as a standing committee would be subject to challenge in the light of constitutional authority given to the Board and the fact that it was a legally-chartered entity for continuing operations, liable for continuing financial obligations, and with the right to sue and be sued, etc.

From the beginning of his administration, Bennett was often to give statistical comparisons, which comparisons provide information on giving patterns. Referring to the beginning of the board in 1877, the Board's report said:

The convention of 1877 was destined to become historic. Organization, co-operation and expectation were in the air. From the Board's first report until the present day, our gifts have responded to the law of geometrical pro-

[9]*Ibid.*, p. 29.
[10]*Ibid.*, p. 65.

gression rather than arithmetical retrogression, each ninth year showing almost a 100 per cent increase over the report nine years before.[11]

Gifts by years were: 1858, Home and Foreign Missions, $14,996; 1878, Home and Foreign Missions, $9,931; 1878, Home, Foreign and State Missions, $17,320; 1887, Home, Foreign and State Missions, $29,850; 1896, Home, Foreign and State Missions, $56,034; 1905, Home, Foreign and State Missions, $110,065.[12]

> For all objects fostered by your Board, Ministerial Relief and Orphans' Home, as well as State, Home and Foreign Missions, the amount contributed last year, $132,575.07.[13]

Total receipts for the same year were $146,620.74, with disbursements of $137,575.85, for a balance of $9,044.89.[14]

In 1906, the Orphans' Home reported 100 residents, with 31 having left, including one married, six adopted, ten returned to relatives, and others with positions. Thirty were taken into the Home.[15]

With the change in the Constitution, the Education Commission was renamed the Education Board,[16] and authority was granted to that Board to secure a charter, name a corresponding secretary at a fixed salary, with provision for travel expense, office, rent, and a stenographer. The corresponding secretary would be an ex-officio member of the Mission Board ". . . and of the Board of Trustees of each Institution in the system, without voting power." [17]

Despite the planned approach to the churches directly for funds for Convention causes, the Board began work for the year Nov. 1, 1907, with a debit of $5,652.90, representing the amount borrowed to add to $43,998.26 collected for

[11]*Ibid.,* p. 68.
[12]*Loc. cit.*
[13]*Loc. cit.*
[14]*Ibid.,* p. 78.
[15]*Ibid.,* p. 81.
[16]*Minutes, Georgia Baptist Convention,* 1907, p. 59.
[17]*Ibid.,* p. 62.

mission work. Expenses had been $49,651.16.[18] However, a total of $144,935 was collected by the Board for all causes, which represented an increase of $40,527 over the previous year.[19] By 1907, the Orphans' Home reported that: "The electric cars are now running to Hapeville, and bringing our friends and visitors in to our grounds." [20]

It was evident in 1907 that the action in 1906 which made the Convention a party with other denominations in fighting liquor sales was effective. The Report on Temperance in 1907 stated:

> The battle, royal, has been fought out in Georgia, and after January the first, 1908, the legalized dram shops will cease to exist.[21]

Members of the Mission Board believed, evidently, that the overall cause of Christ was progressing in the state. A comparison citing State Missions effectiveness revealed "ten years ago 944 were added by baptism, 3,773 this year." [22]

The comparison continued:

> Ten years ago 409 added by letter, against 2,411 this year. Ten years ago, added by restoration 139 against 97 this year. This shows a total of 1,461 to our denominational force ten years ago against 6,281 this year. Ten years ago there were 1,685 churches in the Convention: of this number 415 contributed to nothing. This year we have 2,050 churches with only 265 not contributing.[23]

UNIQUE HONOR FOR NORTHEN

Former Georgia Governor W. J. Northen had been elected president of the Convention in 1896. At the 1909 session in Dublin he announced his retirement as president.[24] Northen had been throughout his life, including his term of office as governor, an active Baptist layman, and had contributed

[18]*Ibid.*, p. 76.
[19]*Ibid.*, p. 78.
[20]*Ibid.*, p. 84.
[21]*Ibid.*, p.p. 17, 27-28.
[22]*Minutes, Georgia Baptist Convention*, 1908, p. 80.
[23]*Loc. cit.*
[24]*Minutes, Georgia Baptist Convention*, 1909, p. 11.

wise leadership to Georgia Baptists, with especial interest in the activities of the Orphans' Home. Upon the occasion of his retirement, he was honored with resolutions and the presentation of a gold watch; the first such honor for a retiring president recorded in the minutes.[25]

A statistical review at the latter part of the first decade of Baptist work in the 20th century indicated healthy progress. Sunday School work was advancing with 1,691 schools, 11,513 teachers, 119,878 pupils in the schools, and 2,614 in the home department for a total enrolment of 134,005.[26] Young People's work was growing rapidly, and in May, 1909, the Southern Baptist Convention had made this emphasis part of the ministry fostered by the Convention. Georgia Baptists thus considered that the Young People's Movement was set upon a firm and permanent basis. The Southern Baptist Convention action did away with any organic union with the B. Y. P. U. A., (Baptist Young People's Union of America) enabling the Georgia Convention, really, to place more support behind the movement.[27]

The report of the Education Board had come to be lengthy, a normal outgrowth of the combining of many reports in the field of education, and included much information concerning the Convention's educational institutions. By 1909, Mercer reported 415 students, with 280 in the Literary Department, 70 law students, 18 in the School of Pharmacy, and 47 ministerial students. The Board of Education's report to the Convention included information on Mercer, Bessie Tift, Shorter, Locust Grove, Hearn Academy, Norman Institute, Union Baptist Institute, Gibson-Mercer, Oak Lawn, and Perry-Rainey with the notation that three schools, Hiawassee, Cherokee Academy and Ebenezer had applied for admission. Hiawassee school was admitted at the 1909 session with the other two to be accepted when they had fulfilled requirements for admission into the system.[28]

[25]*Ibid.*, p.p. 20, 21.
[26]*Ibid.*, p. 24.
[27]*Ibid.*, p.p. 32, 33.
[28]*Ibid.*, p.p. 66-68.

The financial plan for operating the Education Board should be of interest in that a three-way division of expenses was allocated against the Board of Missions, the schools, and from direct contributions to raise funds to cover financial obligations of the Board.[29] The suggestion evidently was adopted by the Convention.[30]

With emphasis upon Christian education strong, Bennett, in the report of the Mission Board, said that:

> Christian education has been given a place in the minds and hearts of our people perhaps hitherto unattained. This is especially true of our denominational high schools. The representatives of these various institutions have held educational rallies at important centers throughout the State, with the result that the principles of Christian education have been more thoroughly elaborated, perhaps, than ever before during a single Conventional year.[31]

Again, a promotional emphasis ahead of its time, in the form of the educational rallies, did much to impress upon Georgia Baptists the cause of Christian education.

One fact concerning education, not hitherto underscored, is that which bears upon the role of Georgia Baptist laymen, and ministers in the development of the public school system. Here is to be found, evidently, some impetus for the continued emphasis upon Christian education.

As an example, W. J. Northen, who served as Convention president for 14 years, 1896-1909, a former governor of Georgia—established a private school at Mt. Zion, Hancock county, after his graduation from Mercer University.[32] In an article written by J. O. Martin, then State Supervisor of Public Schools, quoted a contemporary concerning Northen. " 'His greatest interest was in his life work—education' ".[33] Martin said further:

> The common schools were improved and the term was doubled in length and to secure more efficient teachers,

[29]*Ibid.*, p. 68.
[30]*Ibid.*, p. 18.
[31]*Ibid.*, p. 74.
[32]*The Christian Index*, June 1, 1922, p. 40.
[33]*Loc. cit.*

he urged the establishment of Normal Schools. Two
such institutions were established—the Georgia Normal
and Industrial College at Milledgeville and the State
Normal School at Athens. . .[34]

Writing in the *Convention Centennial* Number of *The
Christian Index*, Martin's article featured other Baptists
prominent in public education. M. L. Duggan, appointed in
1911 as one of three original State Supervisors of Schools,
did much to bring about the basis for the modern school
system in the state. Duggan served as clerk of the Washington Association and as a trustee of Bessie Tift College, each
for 20 years.[35] Earlier, P. H. Mell, a Convention president,
served as chancellor of the University of Georgia, 1878-
1888.[36] His son, John D. Mell was president of the Convention, and also president of the Athens Board of Education.[37]
M. L. Brittain, identified prominently with the creation of
the Education Commission, later Education Board, served
as state superintendent.[38] And, this continued into the 1960's.
M. D. Collins, long-time state superintendent of schools, was
a Baptist minister.

These, together with many others, created several generations of distinguished preacher-teachers, who led not only
in churches as pastors, but who served as responsible school
officials at the local, county and state levels. Acknowledge-
ment of this background provides additional basis for understanding the continued interest of Georgia Baptists in Christian education. Many of these leaders were helping to frame
a modern system of schools to provide public education for
all children. And, they saw, evidently, nothing wrong, and
much right, with Baptists promoting private schools in which
a distinctive Christian witness would be given as well as a
good education provided.

Thus, an understanding of the administrative abilities of a

[34]*Loc. cit.*
[35]*Ibid.*, p. 41.
[36]*Ibid.*, p. 42.
[37]*Loc. cit.*
[38]*Loc. cit.*

man such as M. L. Brittain in a position of state leadership, aids in understanding the reasons why the Education Board functioned as effectively as it did.

By 1909, in the report of the Mission Board, a clear division of the work of the state departments was indicated: Sunday School, WMU—three ladies employed whose salaries have been paid by the WMU of their respective associations—prison work, evangelistic department, associational missionaries with 28 employed, with 69 pastor-evangelists. Additionally, there was a church extension department, and a provision in the state mission funds for $2,500 to be used in the construction of church buildings at strategic points in the state.[39] The WMU work was referred to as a department, and 155 workers on the field were reported.[40]

Still growing numerically, the Orphans' Home received for that year from all sources $26,336.06, and had run about $3,000 in the red for the previous two years.[41]

Interest in denominational affairs on the part of laymen had expressed itself earlier in formation of the B. Y. P. U. organization. Although directed toward young people, the movement from its inception had aroused general interest. As the young people became adults, they retained their interest in church and denominational affairs. There had, however, been little activity on an organized basis among the laymen. As the 1907 session of the Southern Baptist Convention meeting in Richmond, Virginia, the Laymen's Missionary Movement of the Southern Baptist Convention was formed on the basis of a recommendation presented by W. J. Northen of Georgia and Joshua Levering, of Maryland.[42]

In November of 1907, the Laymen's Movement was recognized in Georgia, and organization of Laymen's Leagues

[39]*Minutes, Georgia Baptist Convention,* 1909, p. 84.

[40]*Ibid.*

[41]*Ibid.,* p. 101.

[42]*Encyclopedia of Southern Baptists,* Vol. I, [Nashville: Broadman Press, 1958] p. 196.

". . . in all of our churches . . ." was commended by the Convention.[43]

BROTHERHOOD FUNCTIONED
AS EARLY AS 1910

From 1907 to 1926, the movement continued to be known by this name, and in 1927 was called the Baptist Brotherhood of the South. In 1908, John T. Henderson was named Executive Secretary.[44] Although the *Southern Baptist Encyclopedia* indicates that the movement was well established in Georgia in 1916,[45] the movement actually was functioning efficiently in the state as early as 1910, when consideration of the Laymen's Movement was a part of the Convention program, and a committee, already established, reported that they had ". . . representative laymen from every section of the State." [46] The report said that

> . . . with few exceptions, we have seen active service, traveling over the state in our own time and at our own expense. We have held meetings with one hundred churches. We have visited seventy-one out of eighty-three Baptist Associations and have succeeded in having about seventy of these appoint laymen's committees within their bounds and the State is now fairly well organized.[47]

The method of operation laid before the Convention for laymen included:

> First—the committee elected—That the Convention continue this work, electing a chairman together with an executive committee of ten for that purpose, authorizing them to select the General Committee, making it as large numerically as they deem advisable.[48]

The plan would make 25 pastors ex-officio members, with missionary rallies to be held with the assistance of the Boards and pastors between November, 1910, and the 1911 meeting

[43]*Minutes, Georgia Baptist Convention,* 1907, p. 22.
[44]*Loc. cit.*
[45]*Encyclopedia of Southern Baptists,* Vol. I, p. 197.
[46]*Minutes, Georgia Baptist Convention,* 1910, p. 17.
[47]*Loc. cit.*
[48]*Ibid.,* p.p. 17, 18.

of the Southern Baptist Convention. The 1910 Committee recommended that the associations be visited again by the committee with special emphasis to be placed upon business methods in missionary offerings and weekly contributions to missions and upon tithing. Further, there was to be an emphasis upon missions in the Sunday Schools, with the committee co-operating with the State Board in creating a missionary atmosphere in the schools.[49]

In concluding, the committee said:

> . . . we must report that the majority of our churches are living a very guilty distance for the Divine plan. In many churches current expenses seem all important, while missions are regarded as a side issue, a mere optional charity.[50]

The enthusiasm of the Laymen's Movement was obvious from the first. The reports of the committee from year to year revealed a genuine interest in seeking to advance the overall cause of Christ in and among Georgia Baptist churches. While it must be noted that the enthusiasm was not always tempered with an exhibited knowledge of the deliberateness of denominational growth, yet the zeal was present. Later, the Movement was to become somewhat demanding in its reports to the Convention, leaving the impression that if the suggestions of the movement were not followed by the Convention, then the brethren had other, more important things to do.[51]

It must not be forgotten, however, that the Movement had ties, though not organic, to the growth of interest in the Young People's Movement. Heavy in its emphasis upon stewardship, the Movement was perhaps to render its strongest service in this area.

The year 1910 was an important year in Georgia Baptist life for several reasons. In addition to the emphasis upon the Layman's Movement, the Convention heard for the first time that year a report dealing with hospital work. The

[49]*Ibid.*, p. 18.
[50]*Loc. cit.*
[51]*Minutes, Georgia Baptist Convention,* 1913, p. 106.

Tabernacle Baptist Church in Atlanta had in 1901 begun an infirmary in connection with the church under the ministry of Pastor Leonard Gaston Broughton.[52] Broughton, a native of Wake County, North Carolina, was a graduate of the Kentucky School of Medicine of the University of Kentucky, and entered the ministry and was ordained in 1893 while practicing medicine at Reedsville, N. C.[53]

Broughton went to Atlanta in 1897 to become pastor of the Jones Avenue Baptist Church, and in that year led 200 members to secure a location in downtown Atlanta and establish the Tabernacle Church.[54] Favoring medical work under Christian sponsorship, he established the Tabernacle Infirmary, which opened in a rented house on Courtland Street in 1903.

> Broughton personally paid the first month's rent of $25, and a group of women from his church renovated and equipped the building with furniture from their homes. Two women who had been unable to secure aid from the community were the first patients.[55]

The Infirmary was soon to be moved to Luckie Street, adjoining the Tabernacle Church complex.[56] As the ministry of the infirmary grew, it came to the attention of Georgia Baptists. And, the Convention took recognition of the work of the infirmary at least two years earlier than is generally indicated.

At the 1910 session of the Convention meeting at Elberton, the group on a motion of E. Z. F. Golden, agreed unanimously to the following resolution.

PREAMBLE AND RESOLUTIONS
CONCERNING THE BAPTIST TABERNACLE
AND ITS INSTITUTIONAL WORK

Whereas, there is now a wide-spread and growing interest all over the country, in what is known as the

[52]*Encyclopedia of Southern Baptists*, Vol. I, p. 557.

[53]*Encyclopedia of Southern Baptists*, Vol. III, [Nashville: Broadman Press, 1971] p. 1624.

[54]*Loc. cit.*

[55]*Encyclopedia of Southern Baptists*, Vol. I, p. 557.

[56]*Ibid.*, p. 558.

Institutional Church; and

Whereas, Such interest is resulting, among other things, in the establishment of Christian hospitals for the care of the sick and the training of Christian nurses for home and foreign mission work; and

Whereas, We recognize that the Baptist Tabernacle of Atlanta, the pioneer church in our Southland in what is known as church institutionalism was also the first to attempt to provide such Christian hospital in our Southern States; and

Whereas, it now has in the Tabernacle Infirmary an up-to-date hospital and training school of nurses, which has been built up at a cost of something like $100,000, and which is now being maintained for rich and poor alike in the most up-to-date and scientific way, and at great expense; therefore, be it

Resolved, First, That the Georgia Baptist Convention now in session at Elberton give its endorsement to the general institutional plans being fostered by the Baptist Tabernacle;

Resolved, Second, That we commend especially, at this particular time, the hospital line of its work, being done by the Tabernacle Infirmary and Training School for nurses, as a long felt need, both in the care of the sick and in the training of our Baptist young women for the profession of trained nursing at home and for our great and growing hospital work in foreign fields;

Resolved, Third, That it is the sense of the Convention that a closer relationship, if possible, shall exist between the institutional work of the Baptist Tabernacle and the Convention, especially the two most conspicuous ones, the Tabernacle Infirmary and Training School for Christian nurses, and the Home for Working Girls;

Resolved, Fourth, That looking to this end a committee of five be appointed to suggest a plan to this session of the Convention, which will, if possible, secure such closeness of the relationship.[57]

The committee moved to study the proposal concerning the Tabernacle reported favorably to the Convention upon the idea of establishing an organic connection ". . . with the institutional work of the Tabernacle Baptist Church". The Convention approved this, together with the statement:

That this Convention enter upon such a relation upon the following conditions: [1] that deeds be executed

[57]*Minutes, Georgia Baptist Convention*, 1910, p.p. 21, 22.

transferring the title to all the property of the Infirmary, the Training School for Nursing, Working Girls' Home and such other institutions as hereafter may be projected to a Board of Trustees of not fewer than twelve nor more than twenty men; [2] that all trustees shall be elected by this Convention, one-half of which number shall be nominated by the Tabernacle Baptist Church.

A committee was appointed to confer with representatives of the Tabernacle Church and with trustees of the Infirmary.[58]

Thus began the official Convention interest in the Infirmary which was to result two years later in a proposal to purchase the Infirmary to be operated as a hospital by Georgia Baptists. The 1910 proposition was not to succeed on the terms proposed. But it was the beginning of the idea for a benevolent ministry, which from that time to the present, particularly through the 1950's, was to occupy much time and energy upon the part of Georgia Baptists, and to create some rather large financial problems for the Convention.

In 1910, a resolution was approved which sought some means to identify closely with the ministry of the Tabernacle Infirmary. In the absence of Broughton, Tabernacle pastor, from the country, and because he had been ill, the Committee to study the matter asked for another year in which to consider the matter, suggesting that the matter

> . . . be referred to the Board of Missions with instructions to confer with the Tabernacle brethren, carefully consider the whole situation and report to the Convention at its next meeting.[59]

It was therefore to be later, in 1912, before the Convention, meeting in Moultrie, was to take steps out of which came the ownership of the Infirmary under the name Georgia Baptist Hospital.[60]

General features of the Mission Board's report indicated two areas of concern. 1. That churches emphasize steward-

[58]*Ibid.*, p. 50.
[59]*Minutes, Georgia Baptist Convention,* 1911, p. 24.
[60]*Minutes, Georgia Baptist Convention,* 1912, p.p. 29, 30.

ship to a greater degree than before, and 2. There was the underlying fear that women in Georgia were not giving to missions as they could.

> We must beware of covetous evasion in some forms of so-called secret giving to the Lord, which is really secret stealing from the Lord. If the giving of the mere pittance in the sunday school is used to evade the larger duty in the church, expose the sin and the sinner and the system of cheating God and deceiving men. . .
> If in the Woman's Missionary Society the woman of means and covetous meanness evades the larger giving of the church offering by paying ten cents a month and one dollar for the special offering in the society let her know her sin and urge her to repent.[61]

Ministerial relief, always a concern among Georgia Baptists, continued to be a matter of interest, and the committee on ministerial relief said Georgia Baptists were spending about $325 a month, or about $3,600 a year in providing assistance to 37 ministers and 16 widows, with assistance ranging from five to ten dollars per month. With the report, was the suggestion that a group of five be named ". . . to consider the advisability and practicability of organizing a Ministers' Insurance Association. . ." [62] Also, the committee urged the Board to increase appropriations to the beneficiaries by 20 per cent if possible, and asked churches to increase their contributions to this cause by 25 per cent.[63]

Different plans for provision of ministerial relief had been proposed and followed through the years. This was the first time that the formation of any type of ministers' insurance group was proposed. The Convention's auditor also had suggestions that year which included fuller information on the disbursements of the board

> . . . especially as it relates to the payment of salaries, giving the number of indigent ministers, the number of evangelists, the number of all other missionaries and officers of the Board and the total amounts paid each group respectively.[64]

[61]Minutes, Georgia Baptist Convention, 1910, p. 27.
[62]Ibid., p. 28.
[63]Loc. cit.
[64]Ibid., p. 29.

The State Mission Board was authorized also to secure the services of one man to be known as a Young People's Evangelist who would spend full time with young people in the churches.[65]

In 1905, the Convention authorized a B. Y. P. U. Field Secretary. For about 18 months one was employed under this authorization. There was by 1910 some doubt whether the 1905 resolution was still in force, hence the new resolution.[66]

This proposal had an impact later in the organization of a B. Y. P. U. department of the Convention. In the same year, a resolution was approved by the Convention requesting the Mission Board to consider the advisability of employing a missionary for evangelistic work among Hebrews in Georgia.[67] The group agreed also for a study dealing with possible removal of Mercer University to Atlanta.[68]

A Georgia Baptist minister, Henry Holcombe, in a memorial to the Legislature at the beginning of the 19th century[69] presented a case for reform in the penal system which resulted eventually in a complete reform for the state. Interest in, and support of work with prisoners was nothing new to Georgia Baptists, and the matter arose again at Elberton when a committee reported on needed reforms in criminal laws, dealing at length with the number of lynchings which were occurring each year, as well as the number of legal executions.[70] The Convention expressed itself ". . . squarely in favor of REFORMS in the criminal law." [71]

Again, the Georgia Convention was the first apparently in the Southern Baptist Convention, to authorize the services of a press representative. As early as 1910, L. R. Christie

[65]*Ibid.*, p. 31.
[66]*Loc. cit.*
[67]*Ibid.*, p. 48.
[68]*Ibid.*, p. 49.
[69]See *Analytical Repository*, 1801.
[70]*Minutes, Georgia Baptist Convention*, 1910, p.p. 35-41.
[71]*Loc. cit.*

presented a resolution authorizing and advising the Board of Missions

> . . . to secure the services of a competent man whose duties it shall be to report for the press the proceedings of our next annual meeting, and to make suitable arrangements with the press for the publication of the same.
> Resolved, That the aforesaid press representative be allowed the privilege of employing such clerical assistance as may be necessary for the efficient performance of the services indicated; and that his compensation be provided by the Board from the various funds, as the Board may deem equitable and proper.[72]

The resolution said,

> That this action be, in no sense, a complaint or criticism of the press, which is always friendly and considerate in its attitude in this respect, and whose columns are always open to us for the presentation of our work.[73]

Caution was taken by the Convention to insure that the Board of Education, under its new construction retained a working relationship to the Board of Missions.

> Whereas, The relation of the Board of Education to the Board of Missions is fundamental; and
> Whereas, The agencies of the Board of Education are of material assistance to the Board of Missions in the development of missionary interests and liberality; therefore be it
> Resolved, That the Convention approve the action of the Board of Missions in assisting the Board of Education last year and hereby instructs the Board of Missions to continue the same assistance during the coming year and that the money sent up for schools, and colleges, be handled by the Board of Missions without charge.[74]

AWARDS TO ASSOCIATION CLERKS

And, well ahead of other such awards, prizes were awarded by H. R. Bernard for excellence in Association Minutes to Spencer B. King, clerk in Floyd county, and J. W. McWhorter, clerk of the Appalachee, and M. L. Duggan, clerk

[72]*Ibid.,* p. 49.
[73]*Loc. cit.*
[74]*Ibid.,* p. 53.

of the Washington.[75] Mention should be made of the work of Bernard. A native of Robertson county, Tennessee, he was auditor of the Mission Board and secretary of the Committee on Cooperation from 1906 to 1916. He set up what came to be known as the Bernard Schedule, a plan for regular support of Convention causes which allowed emphasis among the associations at regular times upon specific causes. Prior to becoming auditor of the Board, he was editor and publisher of *The Southern Advance* [1902-1905]. For a year, he served as acting secretary of the mission board [1914].[76]

While his contributions to the life of the Convention were not always such as to keep him in the limelight, he became a strong and influential figure in State Baptist life. He was superintendent of schools in Clarke county for 20 years, and field secretary for Mercer, 1896-1901.[77]

A delineation of schools owned by the Convention and those owned by Associations is indicated again in 1910: Institutions listed as being owned by the Convention included: Mercer, Bessie Tift, Shorter, Hearn Academy, Norman Institute, Cyrene Institute, Perry-Rainey Institute, Oaklawn Academy, Locust Grove Institute, Union Baptist Institute, Hiawassee High School, Cherokee High School and Gibson-Mercer Academy. Schools owned by Associations, and not included in the Mercer system, were Draketown Baptist Institute, Ebenezer High School, North Georgia Baptist College, Blairsville High School, Bunn-Bell Institute.[78]

During 1910, in the field of education, $3,119.38 had been raised for ministerial student aid; $325,000 in cash and pledges for educational purposes, and $260,000 was needed during the year 1911 to complete the half million dollars needed for Tift and Shorter. Funds needed to complete improvements to secondary schools and to provide support for ministerial students, $46,000, with $5,000 needed to pay on

[75]*Ibid.*, p. 54.
[76]*Encyclopedia of Southern Baptists*, Vol. I, p. 157.
[77]Ragsdale, Vol. III, p. 136.
[78]*Minutes, Georgia Baptist Convention*, 1910, p.p. 85-87.

old debts for the support of ministerial students.[79]

The Convention was expanding. Georgia Baptists were growing. But at the same time debts were increasing. It was unusual for the Convention to go in debt to pay for support of ministerial students. However, considering the priority which was placed upon ministerial aid, the Convention would have been, and evidently was, as willing to be in debt for this cause as for the construction of buildings, or mission work under another name.[80]

There were 84 associations, with 2,300 churches, 260,000 members, with church property estimated to be worth $4,500,000. Estimated value of all educational institutions including endowment, was $1,850,000. Taxable property of the denomination was estimated at 30 per cent of the wealth of the state.[81]

Even though the Laymen's Committee presented its report, the Mission Board, in its report, took occasion to approve the work, declaring:

> The organized laymen's movement in Georgia, is a sign that the brethren are determined to have a larger share in aggressive Christianity. Less of distraction and more of consecration is inevitable. Some of the most inspiring addresses delivered during the associational period this Fall fell from the lips of laymen without charge to the organized work.[82]

With other groups organizing, it was not surprising that in 1910 moderators, clerks and members of Executive Committees in associations should organize. They met at the Presbyterian church in Elberton Nov. 15, 1910, apparently at Bernard's request or call.

Bernard said the purpose of the meeting was to provide

> . . . a better understanding of the relationship of the Baptist Brotherhood [laymen, not the present organization] in Georgia and to obtain co-operation in the matter of securing statistics and the promotion of other interests for the advancement of our Lord's Kingdom.

[79]*Ibid.*, p. 87.
[80]*Loc. cit.*
[81]*Ibid.*, p. 89.
[82]*Ibid.*, p. 90.

The group was to meet annually, and at its organizational meeting adopted a constitution and set of By-Laws.[83]

Evangelism was a key emphasis in State Mission work from earliest beginnings, and by 1910, 14 men were listed as evangelists, either full or part-time. Areas of interest in which the men served were prisons, systematic benevolence, Sunday-school, state evangelists, special evangelistic work during the summer, and territorial.[84]

The Convention's first Social Service Commission was created by the 1911 Convention meeting in Rome. E. C. Dargen proposed a resolution which called upon the Convention to

> . . . establish a standing committee on Temperance, Law Enforcement and other social and moral reforms, to consist of five brethren near enough to each other for convenient conference. This committee shall be known as the Social Service Commission; it shall correspond with smiliar commissions appointed by other Baptist bodies and shall have in hand the study and presentation to this Convention annually in a suitable report such great topics of social and moral reform as in its judgment may be desirable. After this year the Committee on Nominations shall nominate the commission, but for this the following brethren are asked to serve: Geo. Hillyer, Len G. Broughton, W. J. Northen, C. W. Daniel.[85]

This was the beginning of a study-report group which was to both please and displease the Convention in its studies, coming back to the parent body from time to time for a redefinition of its responsibilities and areas of work. However, with the creation of this Commission, the Convention, through this group, began to speak annually in areas assigned by the organizational resolution; and occasionally in areas not confined strictly within the limits of the resolution.

Apparently allaying any suspicion that the Laymen's Movement would become either governmental or inde-

[83]*Ibid.*, p.p. 188, 189.
[84]*Ibid.*, p. 98.
[85]*Minutes, Georgia Baptist Convention*, 1911, p. 15.

pendent, a committee in 1911 took especial pains to point out that the Movement was keeping in close touch with the Southern Baptist Convention's Laymen's organization, and at the same time recognizing their responsibility to the Georgia Baptist Convention. They stressed also that they were not interested in multiplying organizations. "We have enough and to spare. Would God we had fewer organizations and more spirituality." [86] The laymen asked for the appointment of only one committee,[87] and noted emphases in three areas; associational campaigns, church campaigns and associational rallies.[88] Further, they made clear the fact that the purpose of the movement was not to exclude or supplant pastors, but to supplement their work. "We recognize the pastors; as leaders, divinely appointed. . . ." [89]

Women were recognized increasingly for their abilities to raise money for mission causes, and the Convention was informed at Rome that in 23 years, Woman's Missionary Union had contributed over $1,878,070, increasing their gifts in five years from $19,717.70 to $71,759.70, a total in five years of $226,134.93.[90] Their goal between the 1910 and 1911 conventions had been to raise $65,000. They raised $71,759.70.[91] The Orphans' Home during this period continued to grow, with 210 children by 1911.[92]

Even with efforts to consolidate the Convention program, the annual sessions still were considered overloaded so that it was requested, and approved:

> That a Committee of five be appointed to consider the general features of our Convention program with a view to the increased efficiency of our annual meetings, and make such recommendations as they may deem wise, at our next annual meeting. They may consider such items as number and character of items allowed place on program; character and form of reports from Boards

[86]*Ibid.*, p. 28.
[87]*Loc. cit.*
[88]*Ibid.*, p.p. 27, 28.
[89]*Ibid.*, p. 28.
[90]*Ibid.*, p. 32.
[91]*Loc. cit.*
[92]*Ibid.*, p. 38.

and permanent committees; function and scope of
special committees; proportionate measure of time and
emphasis alloted to the interests fostered or considered;
or any point pertaining to these general features. Recommendations of this committee agreed upon prior to our
next session and made manifest, may influence the work
of the committee on order of business in their usual
duties.[93]

The motion, presented by Ragsdale, was designed apparently to provide some specific direction to the Committee
on Order of Business and at the same time provide some
means of limiting what had become rather lengthy reports
which he, as secretary, dealt with. A major part of the
background of the 1910 authorization of a study committee
dealing with possible removal of Mercer University rested
in the reversionary clause on the Macon property. There
was, and had been, moreover, some pressure from Atlanta
to have Mercer located in that city. The report in 1911 left
the matter still unresolved. The proposal of the Committee
on Removal was rejected 49 to 121.[94] A substitute motion by
L. R. Christie, adopted unanimously, declared it to be

... the sense of the Convention that it is not wise denominational policy for our Convention institutions to
have real-estate holdings with reversionary clauses in the
title papers, thus preventing our owning in fee-simple,
not only the land, but the buildings and improvements
thereon.[95]
That it is the sense of the Convention that an entirely
new site in Macon or elsewhere is desirable and will
soon be imperative for Mercer University.[96]

The Christie substitute report placed the Convention in
sympathy with the concept that an entirely new site either
in Macon or elsewhere was desirable, and Macon and Atlanta
citizens interested in the matter were requested to submit to
a special committee of 12, to be named, proposals which
would deal with a new plant site.[97]

[93]*Ibid.,* p.p. 38, 39.
[94]*Ibid.,* p. 51.
[95]*Ibid.,* p.p. 51, 52.
[96]*Loc. cit.*
[97]*Ibid.,* p. 52.

Approval of the Committee report in 1911 probably would have ended the matter at that time. However, the Christie resolution fueled the discussion. Dowell said that the need for more endowment was used as an issue in 1910.[98] After the Christie resolution was adopted, offers for two sites in Atlanta complicated further the issue. And ". . . aroused such feeling as to preclude the possibility of any unbiased consideration of an invitation of removal to Atlanta, . . ." [99]

Sometime after the Rome sessions in 1911, Mercer's trustees approved a resolution endorsing the ". . . judgment of the fathers' in selecting Macon as a site for the college; . . ." [100] The trustees warned that agitation for removal was ". . . a dangerous experiment, . . ." [101]

Once again, the committee dealing with possible removal of Mercer came before the Convention at Moultrie in 1912 with the suggestion, adopted, which called for elimination of all locations except Macon,[102] and referring to the Board of Trustees of Mercer the proposition for working out details necessary for an amicable settlement.[103] Eventual result of this action was to be that the city of Macon amended the original action granting property to the university which amendment removed the reversionary clause.[104]

President Jameson had favored the removal of the University to Atlanta, and with the decision to remain in Macon, it was "uncomfortable for him" and this led to Jameson's resignation.[105]

Efforts to move Mercer, which resulted in the removal to Macon, and efforts to move Mercer again in 1910-1912,

[98]Spright Dowell, *A History of Mercer University 1833-1953*, [Atlanta: Foote & Davies, Inc., 1958.] p. 240.

[99]*Ibid.*, p. 241.

[100]*Loc. cit.*

[101]*Loc. cit.*

[102]*Minutes, Georgia Baptist Convention*, 1912, p. 14.

[103]*Loc. cit.*

[104]Dowell, 261, 265. [For further information, see Dowell's *A History of Mercer University*, p.p. 240-242.]

[105]*Ibid.*, p. 242.

probably created as much dissension within Convention ranks as any other single issue.

A fair example of a Convention groping for methods and means for providing mission funds is given in the report of the Mission Board in which Bennett said:

> It may be that there is something wrong in our conception of missions, of which this decrease is but a symptom.
> There has been and is a tendency among us to give to missions only in the spirit of benevolence. There are those who seem to feel that missions is not missions unless ever accompanied by great, physical, social or intellectual need. With them there must be something of a startling nature in an appeal before it is very effective. The mere fact that one is unsaved arouses little interest. There must be squaler and want besides. Hence, the well-to-do brother at our door who is without Christ is apt to create little concern. His wealth and social position place him beyond the pale of many of our prayers.[106]

October had been a month for emphasis upon State Missions, and during that month in 1911, Bennett reported that although there was a general increase in contributions, State Missions gifts dropped during the last ten days of the month at the rate of $700 a day.[107] A $10,000 deficit in State Missions from the previous year had not been reduced.[108]

DANIEL RESOLUTION TURNING POINT

Efforts between 1911 and 1912 to reach agreement upon any disposition of Tabernacle Infirmary were unfruitful, and the committee was discharged at the 1912 session. At that point, C. W. Daniel proposed a resolution, adopted, which said:

> Resolved, That this Convention look with favor upon the general policy of conducting a Christian hospital.
> 2. That the proposition from Atlanta Tabernacle Infirmary or other propositions to establish such institu-

[106]*Minutes, Georgia Baptist Convention*, 1911, p.p. 90-91.
[107]*Ibid.*, p. 90.
[108]*Loc. cit.*

tion be referred to the Board of Missions for full and careful investigation and with power to act.[109]

Ragsdale, Convention recording secretary during this period, said that the infirmary's affairs were ". . . seriously embarrassed by its financial burdens." [110] Dr. Ellis Fuller, writing in 1939 when he was chairman of the Hospital Commission, agreed also that the Infirmary was in financial trouble ". . . because of heavy expenses and debts." [111] Sometime prior to the 1913 Convention, Broughton had left the Atlanta Tabernacle to become pastor of Christ's Church, in London, England.[112] Fuller, in writing a brief history of the hospital for the Baptist World Alliance edition, takes Ragsdale's position [almost the same phrasing] that after the 1912 Convention, the Mission board had taken over the infirmary ". . . without a dollar paid on the purchase price or a dollar in hand to meet the expenses of its operation, which at the time amounted to about $3,000 a month." [113]

Ragsdale further indicated that the Board of Missions did not make a specific report on their actions.[114] However, the minutes of the 1913 Convention do not sustain the Ragsdale statements. The Board, in reporting on its action with regard to the hospital, said first that they had been given the "power to act" following a full and complete investigation.[115]

Therefore, the Board reported:

> Acting under authority of this resolution, your Board on March 15th, 1913, after full investigation and deliberation, bargained for and purchased the property referred to in the foregoing resolution known as the Tabernacle Infirmary and Training School for Nurses located on Luckie, Bartow and Nassau streets, Atlanta. The terms of purchase were as follows: The assumption by the Board of two mortgages on the property aggregat-

[109]*Minutes, Georgia Baptist Convention*, 1912, p.p. 29, 30.

[110]Ragsdale, Vol. III, p. 265.

[111]*The Christian Index*, June 15, 1939, p. 51.

[112]*Encyclopedia of Southern Baptists*, Vol. III, p. 1624.

[113]Ragsdale, Vol. III, p. 265.

[114]*Loc. cit.*

[115]*Minutes, Georgia Baptist Convention*, 1913, p. 75, [also, *Minutes, Georgia Baptist Convention*, 1912, p. 30.]

ing, $25,500, a cash payment of $8,000, $10,000 due on December 15th, 1913, $10,000 due on June 15th, 1914, $10,000 due December 15th, 1914, and $21,500 by December 15th, 1915, making a total of $85,000. In the judgment of some of the leading business men of the city, disinterested parties, the land alone, not including buildings, improvement and furnishings, estimated at more than $40,000, is worth the sum paid.[116]

The Board borrowed money, giving notes for deferred payments, and secured a charter, with a provision that

. . . this Convention shall be vested with the right of appointing the Board of Trustees to manage said institution. The number of trustees shall be twelve or more, one-third of whom appointed at the present session to serve for one year, one-third for two years and one-third for three years.[117]

J. S. McLemore was named to the secretaryship of the work, and the Board agreed that the hospital should have a regular place in the schedule of offerings ". . . along with the other great enterprises. . ." [118]

During 1912, the cost of the evangelistic department was $6,950.00, with $8,011.09 collected for State Missions, leaving a credit balance of $1,061.09.

The occasional references from year to year are considered a part of a continuous narrative in that they reflect a continuous growth of State Mission work, and reveal further that some of this work produced income for the Board which helped to sustain the programs.

When the newly-created Social Service Commission made its first report following authorization in 1911, catagories presented for study included Temperance, Law Enforcement, Vice, and rights of Negroes.[119]

Continuing to maintain historic interest in the welfare of Negroes in the state, the report said:

We earnestly desire that this Convention shall declare itself in no uncertain tones upon the importance of the

[116]*Ibid.,* p. 75.

[117]*Loc. cit.*

[118]*Ibid.,* p. 76.

[119]*Minutes, Georgia Baptist Convention,* 1912, p.p. 110-117.

churches and pastors becoming enlisted in the great needs of these people.[120]

In 1901, the Convention had called for publication of charters for all institutions of the conventions, boards, etc.[121] In 1903, publication of 3,000 copies of a pamphlet containing the charters was reported.[122] In 1913, the Board of Missions was authorized to revise the pamphlet and print 500 copies for distribution.[123]

Georgia Baptists were growing rapidly. They felt strong enough to pursue additional ministries, as exhibited by the action of the Mission Board in acquiring the Hospital property. By 1913, there were 2,400 churches, with 1,394 reporting some form of woman's work, and 272 new societies being formed.[124] This was a time of expanding interest in Foreign Missions in Georgia and throughout the Southern Baptist Convention. And, as the interest in Foreign Missions grew, and the work of the State Mission Board was promoted, the women's work in the churches expanded as they emphasized missions. As of June, 1922, 67 Georgians had gone out as foreign missionaries under the Foreign Mission Board.[125] Forty of these had been appointed to China alone[126] which explains historic interest Georgians maintained in China mission work.

The Education Board, in an effort to strengthen its own hand, and, as they believed, in turn to strengthen the hands of the Convention, concluded its 1913 report by calling attention to the fact that it was meeting increased difficulty in exercising authority over schools in the system. The Board asked, therefore, that it be recognized in the Constitution as other Boards were recognized.[127] The Convention adopted the report of a committee named to review the report of the

[120]*Ibid.*, p. 117.
[121]*Minutes, Georgia Baptist Convention,* 1901, p. 19.
[122]*Minutes, Georgia Baptist Convention,* 1903, p. 13.
[123]*Minutes, Georgia Baptist Convention,* 1913, p. 16.
[124]*Ibid.*, p. 37.
[125]*The Christian Index,* June 1, 1922, p.p. 94, 95.
[126]*Loc. cit.*
[127]*Minutes, Georgia Baptist Convention,* 1913, p. 68.

Education Board. The review committee called for preparation of a constitutional amendment for submission in 1914.[128]

The Education Board's problem was summarized in a resolution at the end of its report.

> Resolved, That in view of difficulties met by the Board of Education in the discharge of its general supervision over all institutions in the Mercer System, and in order to strengthen the hands of the Board and give it the confidence of the Convention's support in the work of maintaining the co-operation and unity of the schools within the Mercer System, that the Convention herewith instructs its Board of Education that the regulations agreed to when the schools were admitted into the Mercer System, shall be enforced, leaving to each school not complying the right to withdraw from the System, and to the Board the duty of dropping from the System such schools as do not comply with its regulations and requirements.[129]

Georgia Baptists heard plans for development of a statewide Assembly at the 1908 convention in Madison. Property was developed at Blue Ridge, and in 1909 an auditorium was dedicated during the B. Y. P. U. meeting held there that year.[130] While the Convention gave tacit endorsement to the Assembly ideas, and heard occasional reports, the promotion of the concept rested apparently with the Woman's Missionary Society. As Gainer E. Bryan, Sr., pointed out in an article for the Southern Baptist Encyclopedia, Volume I, in 1958, up to that time:

> The summer assembly program in Georgia functions largely in terms of organizations, and is not based upon any one central and highly developed assembly site. Although some attempts have been made to develop a central assembly, the various programs, organizations, and emphases have largely been promoted in independent meetings held at varying locations.[131]

By 1913, the Convention recognized the Georgia Baptist Assembly, stating:

[128]*Ibid.*, p. 35.
[129]*Ibid.*, p. 68.
[130]*Encyclopedia of Southern Baptists*, Vol. I, p. 86.
[131]*Loc. cit.*

This institution along with similar institutions in the South is destined to create denominational unity and enthusiasm if it receives encouragement from our people its merits would justify. J. P. Nichols, than whom there is no more loyal layman in the State to all our work, is now president and we prophesy increasing enthusiasm and prosperity.[132]

The Assembly was to be an on-again, off-again proposition for some years. The Mary P. Willingham School was operated on adjacent property.

Information on this arrangement is rather meagre. However, in the book *His Story In Georgia W. M. U. History*, By Mrs. W. J. Neel, published in 1939, there is some information by the author, a contemporary and a party to the matter, who wrote:

> . . . Mary P. Willingham School for mountain girls was established at Blue Ridge by Woman's Missionary Union. During the Annual Convention at Hartwell, 1909, Mr. E. G. Willingham, husband of the W.M.U. president, offered the women a tract of land and $1,000 as a nucleus for establishing at Blue Ridge, Ga., a school for mountain girls. The offer was gratefully accepted and twelve women appointed as trustees to cooperate with a like number of men to be appointed as trustees by the State Convention, asking the Convention's approval of the enterprise. The matter was referred to the Baptist Board of Education. Founding another school at that time seemed to the Board unwise as all Baptist schools were clamoring for more adequate support. The following year at the W. M. U. annual meeting in Dawson the Executive Board of W. M. U. submitted a proposition to the Union 'that we cooperate with Georgia Baptist Assembly in establishment of the proposed school'; Mr. Willingham increasing his offer to $5,000. This proposition was approved by the Convention. The Georgia Baptist Assembly donated thirty acres of land to the trustees. Mrs. H. H. Tift, responsive to every Kingdom call, donated $1,000 to be used in a foundation of Georgia marble. A building committee with Dr. B. J. W. Graham chairman, was appointed. The school was first chartered under name of 'Blue Ridge Industrial School for Girls,' but in 1911 the name was changed to 'Mary P. Willingham School

[132]*Minutes, Georgia Baptist Convention*, 1913, p. 77.

for Girls.' . . . After fifteen years of service . . . the
trustees felt the school had served its high mission and
should be discontinued. . .[133]
As was the case with many other such ventures, establishment
of a public school at Blue Ridge contributed to its demise.[134]

LEAVELL NAMED FIELD SECRETARY

Baptist Young People's work in Georgia received a strong
boost when Frank H. Leavell was named field secretary
during 1913.[135]

Leavell, a graduate of the University of Mississippi in the
class of 1909, had gone to California in that year to enter the
real estate business,[136] and by 1913 had come to Georgia as
a full time director of B. Y. P. U. work, beginning his work
in February of that year.[137]

The Trustees' report for 1913 indicated that already the
newly-acquired hospital had caused a financial problem. The
report showed $5,253.83 past due for salaries, food bills, and
other current items.[138] The balance sheet on the hospital
for that first year of operation showed expenses of $24,752.39,
credits of the same amount, with an operational balance of
$1,732.51.[139] From March 15 to Oct. 31, 1913, the hospital
under Convention ownership cared for 489 patients.[140]

Another survey of the ministerial relief fund was interesting. With 68 beneficiaries, 43 men and 25 widows, with 65
of the 68 living in Georgia, grants of from $5 to $10 except
in two cases where there were church supplements, were
being made. However, out of 91 associations, only 17 had
not contributed to the Relief Fund, and of the 74 associations represented, the amount was from 665 churches. The

[133]Mrs. W. J. Neel, *His Story in Georgia W. M. U. History*, W. M. U.,
Georgia Baptist Convention, 1939, p.p. 42, 43, 45, 46.
[134]*Ibid.*, p. 46.
[135]*Minutes, Georgia Baptist Convention*, 1913, p. 83; *op cit.*, Ragsdale, Vol.
III, p. 242.
[136]*Encyclopedia of Southern Baptists*, Vol. II, p. 781.
[137]*Minutes, Georgia Baptist Convention*, 1914, p. 31.
[138]*Minutes, Georgia Baptist Convention*, 1913, p. 100.
[139]*Ibid.*, p. 91.
[140]*Ibid.*, p. 99.

report noted further that in 33 of the churches failing to contribute anything to the relief fund, there were in the memberships of these churches recipients of assistance.[141]

The Orphans' Home in 1913 showed total expenses of $50,576.39, with disbursements to balance the sheet including liquidation of loans in the amount of $21,071.81 of the total $49,814.64 expended.[142] The Home, from Nov. 1, 1912 through Oct. 31, 1913, had borrowed $21,717.16 for current operations.[143]

Just two years after its creation, the Social Service Commission still was seeking to define its role and reason for existence. Its report said:

> Social service may be defined as active effort to improve the physical, intellectual, moral, civil, industrial, and spiritual conditions of human beings in their associations with each other. . . The reason why this Convention appoints a commission to study and report upon this subject is that, from the very statement of it, Christians both in their individual lives and in their associated bodies, . . . do and evermore must have an interest in human social welfare. If the phrase 'Social Service' is new, the thing it describes is certainly not.[144]

This basic definition, with some modifications in terminology, continued through the years to be an expression of Convention concern for human needs in a Christian concept of these needs. With increased cooperation in coverage of Baptist news by Georgia papers, the Commission achieved perhaps more "mileage" from its pronouncements through the secular press than from any other source.

Within six years of the organization of the Layman's Movement, in 1907, there arose a spirit which can be described only as aggressive on the part of some of the leadership within the state. Further, they were prone to stress not only the work which they did, but their own concept of their importance in their annual reports. As an example, the 1913 report declared:

[141]*Ibid.*, p. 94.
[142]*Ibid.*, p. 98.
[143]*Loc. cit.*
[144]*Ibid.*, p. 101.

We insist, however, that the Convention must make radical change in its financial methods if conditions are to be materially improved. And the Laymen's Movement will be successful in proportion as the pastors realize their relation to it and forward it in the local churches. . . The Laymen's Movement is antagonistic to spasmodic and high pressure campaigns, and insists upon the adoption of scriptural plans without reserve and without abandonment in seeming crises. . .

The Movement stresses the thought yearly. Every member canvass in the local churches, the introduction of the duplex envelope and the weekly system of giving. It also emphasizes tithing as the minimum of giving under grace, and offerings rather than collections.[145]

With this emphasis, no one could argue, and such a stress upon systematic giving was an aid to the churches as they gradually, and sometimes painfully, began to use offering envelopes.

However, beyond this, the aggressive spirit emerged as the Committee continued its report:

We are uncertain as to whether the Convention is ready to adopt the principles of the Movement, setting aside any plans in competition therewith. We have attempted no work this year in an organized capacity because of this uncertainty, although much has been accomplished by members of the Committee as individuals.

We respectfully suggest that this report be referred to a special committee, and that the Convention make some clear cut expression of its attitude towards the Laymen's Movement. We are men in active business, and our time is of value to us and can be used profitably to the Kingdom in other channels, and we earnestly request that the Convention relieve us of this responsibility unless it feels assured that the plans and principles of the Laymen's Movement are vital to the future financial progress of the Churches, and is ready to give these plans right of way.[146]

Laymen spearheading the movement were coming to grips with problems which experienced pastors and denominational leaders had long since learned, and to a degree learned to live with; that is, that the promotion of the Kingdom of

[145]*Ibid.,* p. 106.
[146]*Loc. cit.*

God upon earth could not be ordered as a business venture would be. The impatience of the laymen was evident.

A final aspect of the 1913 Convention which was to have a lasting impact upon the life of the Georgia Baptist Convention was the appointment of a committee to study Convention ownership of the denominational newspaper—*The Christian Index*. This Committee reported back to the Convention in 1914 at the session in Carrollton.

Actually, the Committee appointed in 1913 was to study a proposal made by B. J. W. Graham who had offered to be one of 25 men to purchase and present to the Convention the paper and all the holdings of The Index Publishing Company.

> These holdings include the *Index,* a four-story reinforced concrete building, with basement, and $45,000 equipment, $3,000 worth of books and the good will of the business. This represents a total investment of $130,000, with a net profit of $10,000 annually.[147]

Graham's offer therefore meant each contributor must put up $5,000. The Committee named at Gainesville in 1913, then, was ordered ". . . to consider this generous proposition . . ." and report to the Convention.[148]

Graham, a rather unique figure in Georgia Baptist life for many years, had been publishing the *South Georgia Messenger* at Cochran. At the beginning of 1900, he became field director for *The Index* with headquarters in Macon. The paper had been purchased at public auction in Atlanta in 1896 by T. P. Bell and I. J. Van Ness. Early in 1900, Van Ness left *The Index* to become Editorial Secretary for the Sunday School Board of the Southern Baptist Convention. He had come to Georgia from a position as pastor of the Immanuel Baptist church in Nashville, Tennessee. Following Van Ness' return to Nashville, Bell made Graham an associate editor sometime between 1900 and 1901. By the end of 1901,

[147]*Minutes, Georgia Baptist Convention,* 1914, p. 15.
[148]*Loc. cit.*

Graham had become a partner, with half interest in *The Index*.[149]

In 1906 and 1907, Graham was a moving force behind a business venture, which resulted late in 1906 in establishment of The Index Printing Company, a stock company with $10,000 capital, later increased to $67,000, to begin operation March 1, 1907.[150] Graham had gathered with him some leading Georgia Baptists in the business venture. For example, charter members of the company included E. G. Willingham [also a benefactor of the Mary P. Willingham school,[151]] M. G. Campbell, Graham, M. L. Brittain, T. P. Bell, S. Y. Jameson, B. D. Gray, J. J. Bennett, H. C. Robert and J. K. Pace.[152]

Thus, Graham had gathered together some of the most prominent Georgia Baptists of the day into this stock company. Then, *The Index,* owned by Bell and Graham, contracted with The Index Printing Company, managed by Graham, to print *The Index*.[153] This venture expanded until, by 1909, in addition to printing *The Index,* The Index Printing Company was printing also *The Wesleyan Christian Advocate, The Home Field* and *The Railroad Record and Common Carrier*.[154] In 1912, the close ties between *The Index* and the printing company ended in a merger, with the printing company buying *The Index* from Bell and Graham for $30,000.[155]

By this time, a statement of the financial condition of the printing company revealed that the firm, with a capital of $67,000, had paid dividends every year and accumulated a surplus of $45,956.74. This surplus was due largely to the rapidly-expanding value of the property located at Ivy and Ellis streets in Atlanta. At that time, the company had

[149]James Adams Lester, A History of *The Christian Index,* 1822-1954," [Unpublished Master's Thesis, 1955], p.p. 83, 84.

[150]*Ibid.,* p. 87.

[151]*Op. cit., His Story,* Neel.

[152]*Ibid.,* p. 87; Index, 1/24/1907.

[153]Lester, p.p. 87, 88.

[154]*Ibid.,* p. 88.

[155]*Ibid.,* p. 90.

machinery and appliances valued at $36,000, with stock at a book value of $168.59 a share selling at $100 a share, and with 68 stockholders.[156] Book value of the stock rose from $168.59 in 1912 to $178.69 in 1913, and the surplus had grown to $57,725.65.[157]

It was from this background, therefore, that Bell, on behalf of the Index Printing Company, made the offer to the Convention in 1913. Considering the total financial outlook, the price at which the company and the paper was offered to the Convention was not out of line with prevailing financial conditions. Further, the strength of the Index Printing Company in the eyes of Georgia Baptists rested not only with the paper itself, but certainly from those who had financial interests in the concern. The study committee in 1914 reported to the Convention:

> We, your Committee, now beg to report:
> 1. That we greatly appreciate the genuine Christian philanthropy manifested in Brother Graham's splendid offer, and recommend that the thanks of this Convention be tendered him.
> 2. Your Committee believes that a publishing house, as an enterprise of this Convention, under ordinary circumstances, is a practical idea, full of possibilities; that its utility will some day be conceded by Georgia Baptists with a mastering conviction; that it will be, sooner or later, a necessity; that this idea is inseparable from the Christian Index, as one of its normal concommitants; and that a corrallary cropping, out as an associated idea, is the growing sentiment, that the Georgia Baptist Convention ought to own and control its accredited organ.
> 3. But in consideration of the financial crisis and the difficulty of finding the 24 men necessary to make the offer hold good, we regret that it does not seem wise to recommend to the Convention that it accept the proposition.
> 4. Recognizing the worth of the *Index,* and its helpfulness in every department of Christian service, we recommend that the Committee on Co-operation, and the Board of Missions make an earnest effort to put a copy of the paper in the homes of every pastor, every Sunday School superintendent, every deacon, every officer of our

[156]*Ibid.,* p. 91.
[157]*Ibid.,* p. 92.

Woman's Auxiliary work, and our B. Y. P. U. leaders, and extend its circulation every way possible.[158]

Two factors are indicated by the Convention's overall condition which probably resulted in the negative report of the committee. One was that the Convention had just become involved in operation of a hospital, assuming a rather large financial obligation in the process. The second was that in view of the fact that every area of responsible Georgia Baptist life, including the general secretary of the Mission Board, the president of Mercer University and the Executive Secretary of the Education Board were stockholders, the Convention assumed evidently that the paper was, for the time being, in safe hands in terms of responsible service to the Convention.

APPEALS FOR PASTORS' HELP

Within a year of accepting the Tabernacle Infirmary as a part of the Convention family, a resolution was adopted that called upon pastors to present the matter of the hospital's indebtedness and current support needs to their churches. Pastors were urged to co-operate with the Board of Trustees in providing funds for liquidation of the indebtedness on the property in view of the fact that notes given by the Board of Missions the previous year would soon fall due.[159]

The resolution requested further:

> That the Trustees of the hospital be enpowered to sell the present plant when in their judgent it seems wise, and with the proceeds obtained therefrom purchase the new site and begin the erection of a new and up-to-date hospital, at the very earliest date possible. It being understood that no additional indebtedness be incurred by the Board of Trustees in the erection of a new plant without the consent of the Convention is first obtained. That we request all our Baptist people when in need of hospital attention to patronize our own institution, thereby giving it their moral as well as their financial support.

[158]*Minutes, Georgia Baptist Convention*, 1914, p.p. 15, 16.
[159]*Ibid.*, p.p. 19, 20.
[160]*Ibid.*, p.p. 20, 21.

> We note with pleasure that it is the desire of the Board
> of Trustees of the hospital, that every Baptist minister
> in Georgia engaged in regular church work should re-
> ceive his hospital attention free and we trust the day
> will soon come when this can be done.[160]

Again, indications of the need for a move of the hospital
were reported a year earlier than indicated by Ragsdale.[161]
Thus, after operation under Convention management for
only a year, the trustees were seeking already for a new site,
and on the basis of the resolution above were granted approval [162] to seek a site and actually to build if no indebtedness were incurred, or if indebtedness was involved, by
Convention consent only. However, the actual move was not
to be made until 1921,[163] and in the interim, considerable
expansions were made to the facilities on Luckie Street.[164]
From this 1914 report, dealing with indebtedness[165] until the
present time, as records will indicate, the hospital occupied
not only a large share of Georgia Baptists' concern, but required considerable effort on the part of the Convention to
keep it in operation. It was, apparently, never out of debt
from the time it was purchased, for one reason or another.

While it is unclear exactly when the policy expressed by
the trustees concerning free care for Baptist ministers went
into effect, it is a fact that for many years this policy was
in effect.

Evidences of financial crises were apparent in Georgia
Baptist life in 1914 in several areas. These evidences in-
cluded the inability to purchase *The Index,* the need for
funds for the hospital, and in the report of the Education
Board, the financial difficulties at Bessie Tift College.[166]
The Board of Education in 1914 made a special recommenda-
tion concerning the withdrawal of Shorter college from the
Mercer system with the assurance that it would always be a
Baptist college, and would not at any time demand the

[161]Ragsdale, Vol. III, p. 266.
[162]*Ibid.,* p. 19.
[163]*Encyclopedia of Southern Baptists,* Vol. I, p. 558.
[164]Ragsdale, Vol. III, p. 266.
[165]*Minutes, Georgia Baptist Convention,* 1914, p. 20.

direct assistance of the Convention. The action was covered in a resolution which authorized:

> That Shorter College be allowed to withdraw from the agreements entered into between it and the Convention at Americus, and that the present Board of Trustees, appointed by the Convention, be requested to acquiesce in this suggestion and to take such steps as are necessary to legally recover all the powers which lay with the Shorter Board under the terms of its original appointment.[167]

Bessie Tift received Convention approval for an appeal to the churches for $100,000 to pay off the entire indebtedness of the college, and at the same time called upon the College to make no further debts or mortgages on its property.[168]

The Convention noted also the completion of the first decade of service by the Sunday School department of the Convention. Established Sept. 1, 1904, enrolment had increased in a decade from 78,127 pupils to 162,635 pupils,[169] under the leadership of George W. Andrews.

Georgia Baptist women continued to provide mission monies in increasing amounts. They were during this period setting rather large goals, and actually exceeding them. The goal for 1913-1914 was $90,000. They raised $92,373.67 of the gross amount of $252,000 received from churches and societies in the state.[170]

Agreement was reached:

> That all denominational interests beyond our borders and all interests within our State not organically connected with the Convention shall be expected to first confer with the Committee on Co-operation before appealing to the churches in any sort of campaign for funds, and we advise the pastors and churches to participate only in such campaigns as have the approval of the Committee on Co-operation.[171]

A second resolution involving the Committee on Co-

[166]*Ibid.,* p.p. 24-25; 26-27.
[167]*Ibid.,* p. 23.
[168]*Ibid.,* p. 24.
[169]*Ibid.,* p.p. 29, 30.
[170]*Ibid.,* p. 37.
[171]*Ibid.,* p. 41.

operation authorized that committee ". . . to fix its budget of
appeal to the churches at $300,000 for the current Conven-
tion year." [172] Sometime early in 1914, J. J. Bennett had
been forced to retire because of ill health. During the last
three years of his service as general secretary, he had, apparently, been in ill health. Spencer B. King, in a brief
account of the Mission Board for the Centennial Number
of the Georgia Baptist Convention, stated of Bennett that:

> The nine years of his administration were strenuous
> years, resulting in largely increased contributions and
> results on the field . . . In the closing years of this period
> by the demands of Georgia Baptists for Mission work
> outstripping their gifts to State Missions and by the
> purchase of the Hospital, the burden of debt was added
> to the already burdened Secretary. On account of failing
> health, Dr. Bennett retired from the work early in 1914.
> For three years his condition was precarious, but . . . he
> has sufficiently recovered to re-enter the pastorate.[173]

He had what would be termed a nervous breakdown.[174]

In its report, the Board of Missions expressed appreciation
to H. R. Bernard for his service ". . . during the trying
days of the past year," and recommended that the Board of
Missions elect with as little delay as possible a new Corresponding Secretary.[175] Bennett had

> ". . . been barred from meeting with the Board and
> from performing the functions . . . of his office
> . . . on account of his physical disability produced [as
> we believe] on account of his zeal, anxiety, and extra-
> ordinary effort to accomplish great things for the Master
> and His cause among the Baptists of the State and else-
> where. . .[176]

It was resolved by the Convention, therefore, "That our
sympathies go out for him, and, as earnestly pray he may be
speedily restored to his former health and activities." [177]

The resolution continued:

[172]*Loc. cit.*
[173]*The Christian Index,* June 1, 1922, p. 47.
[174]*Minutes, Georgia Baptist Convention,* 1914, p. 44.
[175]*Ibid.,* p. 43.
[176]*Ibid.,* p. 44.
[177]*Loc. cit.*

That in view of the fact that this condition was brought
on him, and due to his great work in the interest of the
Lord's cause, in trying to imitate his Master while on
earth by doing all the good he could, that we think that
it is the duty of those in charge of the denominational
work to see that suitable provision be made for his
temporal needs as may be consistent with the general
interests of the cause.[178]

The Mission Board reported adoption of a set of By-Laws
after the 1913 Convention.[179] And, the amount of indebtedness ". . . for consideration of the new management . . ."
[Bernard] was $26,153.36, of which all but $1,767.88 had
been paid.[180]

The effort by the Mission Board ". . . to pay all bills for
State Mission work contracted for by the Atlanta Association . . ." had resulted in an indebtedness to the Board of
$4,561.48.[181]

For years, the Convention had received, in annual session,
motions to amend either the Constitution or By-Laws, which
either passed or failed on the spot. Finally, the Convention
agreed:

That all propositions to be presented to the Convention
providing for amendment to the Constitution and By-
laws, or standing resolutions meant to guide the Convention or any of its Boards, Committees, or officers,
shall be printed in the *Christian Index* at least four
weeks before the meeting of the Convention.[182]

Further, it was resolved:

That printed copies of such proposed amendments or
standing resolutions be furnished members of the Convention the first day of the meeting and that no action of
the Convention on same be taken earlier than on the
second day of the meeting.[183]

A 10-year summary of the work of the Education Board
revealed that at least $1,000,000 had been added to school

[178]*Loc. cit.*
[179]*Ibid.,* p. 75.
[180]*Loc. cit.*
[181]*Loc. cit.*
[182]*Ibid.,* p. 44.
[183]*Ibid.,* p. 45.

property during the life of the Board.[184] The Board declared
it believed its work would have been more efficient

> . . . if from the beginning the Convention had founded
> it on a solid basis of authority and support. It should
> have been given a place in the Constitution of the Con-
> vention alongside the Board of Missions, and its main-
> tenance should have been securely provided for in the
> regular contributions of the churches. During every
> year of its history, the Board has been embarrassed by
> two things—its inability to act with authority and a
> precarious financial support.[185]

The report continued:

> It is the conviction of the Board that it cannot grapple
> with the opportunities and needs of Christian educa-
> tion in Georgia without a guaranteed income of not less
> than $12,000.00 a year. We have been trying to do
> our work on the slender basis of contributions to 'schools
> and colleges' under the schedule. This has amounted
> to about $2,000 a year with a tendency to decrease.[186]

The Board then referred back to the concept of the Mercer
System in which everything was, in effect, to be a feeder
for Mercer and Mercer was to be the central point in the
Baptist collegiate system in Georgia. They declared: "We
believe that the time is now come for the recovery of this
ideal and plan of operation." [187]

> Therefore the Board recommends that the Education
> Board, in co-operation with the Trustees of Mercer Uni-
> versity, proceed to organize a scheme of relations for
> Mercer and the secondary schools which are associated
> with it under the Education Board, and that a plan of
> regular visitation be arranged, provided the Convention
> shall make the necessary financial provision for the
> Board, to enable it to pay the expenses of such co-
> operation.[188]

A statement of the financial condition for all schools was
presented to the Convention, along with a summary which
indicated that the evaluation of properties and endowments

[184]*Ibid.*, p. 65.
[185]*Loc. cit.*
[186]*Ibid.*, p. 66.
[187]*Ibid.*, p. 68.
[188]*Loc. cit.*

was $2,000,000, with $181,000 in unpaid subscriptions. There was an $85,000 debt on the colleges; a $46,000 debt on secondary schools and $47,000 had been collected on subscriptions and appeals for schools and colleges, with a total collected for educational purposes of $58,429.76.[189] On January 13, 1913, the Logen E. Beckley Institute at Clayton, Ga. had been tendered to and accepted by the Mission Board. It had been listed by the Home Mission Board as one of the Mountain System of schools, with the Home Board having put some $4,000 into the enterprise.[190]

For the first time in 1914, the beneficiaries of the ministerial relief fund were listed with monthly amounts paid,[191] as well as the salaries of servants of the Mission Board. Salaries for full time service to Georgia Baptists, on a monthly basis in 1914, ranged from $291.66 for Bennett, to $40.00 for a bookkeeper. Bernard received $175.00; Spencer King, $100; cashier, $65.00; stenographer, $65.00, bookkeeper, $40.00 per month. In field work, Andrews was paid $175.00; the evangelistic secretary, H. C. Buchholz, $175.00; Enlistment leader, W. H. Dood, $110.00; W. M. Dyer, Institute Leader, $100.00; T. A. Henry, evangelistic singer, $105.00; J. Frank Jackson, evangelist, $110.00; J. T. Kendall, Enlistment, $75.00; F. H. Leavell, $133.33; J. S. McLemore, Enlistment, $175.00; B. J. Smith, evangelist, $110.00; J. T. Williams, Evangelistic Singer, $105.00; and J. D. Winchester, evangelist, $110.00 per month.[192]

The report of the Orphans' Home listed 221 children, a school with four teachers and 204 pupils, with courses of study equal to that of the public schools, daily double sessions and eight grades. One girl was attending Locust Grove Institute, another Bessie Tift, and the boys rotated in school, attending in the afternoon to the farm chores. There was a class in telegraphy for twelve students

. . . under a skilled teacher with modern instruments.

[189]*Ibid.*, p. 72.
[190]*Ibid.*, p. 76.
[191]*Ibid.*, p. 88.
[192]*Ibid.*, p. 89.

> Thirteen have gone out from the Home into telegraph
> offices at good salaries and have given satisfaction. Two
> of the girls have married since going into business for
> themselves. . .[193]

And the hospital report revealed that for the year 823
patients had been admitted, 531 being surgical cases, 310
medical cases, with 551 operations performed during the
year.[194] The hospital ministry was growing fast, and with
the growth, came the increased interest upon the part of
Georgia Baptists.

This was the year World War One began. The economic
purse strings had been tightening on the economy. Although
it was to be two years before active involvement upon the
part of the United States, the American economy was already affected by indirect involvement with the Allied cause.
The Georgia Baptist Convention interests were beginning
to suffer financially. An era of leadership under J. J. Bennett
had been ended by failing health. Georgia Baptists were
next to go through a period of financial crisis out of which
came the Convention's involvement in the $75 Million Cam-
paign. This was to result in a few years of high optimism
and marked growth, to be followed by another period of
extreme financial difficulty as the nation entered into the
period known as the Great Depression.

[193]*Ibid.*, p. 97.
[194]*Ibid.*, p. 102.

CHAPTER 14

Groundwork For Expansion

The history of the Georgia Baptist Convention may be divided into administrative eras of the State Mission Board following creation of that Board in 1877. With each change in administration, there were new emphases, and new approaches to the problems of seeking to provide adequately for all Georgia Baptist interests, which included also interests represented through the Southern Baptist Convention.

Such was the case with the administration of Archibald Cunningham Cree, elected executive secretary-treasurer in March, 1915.[1] Cree's authorization to handle affairs of the Executive Committee was granted May 6, 1915.[2]

An explanation of the terms "Executive Committee" and "Mission Board" is in order. The first Executive Committee of the Georgia Baptist Convention was chartered in 1830. For over 40 years, this Committee was charged with responsibility for operation of Convention affairs between annual sessions of the Convention. During the period of active service of what will be called the First Executive Committee, there was an evolvement in responsibility. At first, this Committee functioned primarily to create and set in operation Mercer University, maintaining for many years close supervision of the University, although the institution from the first had a Board of Trustees. The Minute Book of this

[1] *Encyclopedia of Southern Baptists,* Vol. I, [Nashville; Broadman Press, 1958] p. 330.

[2] *Minute Book, Executive Committee, State Mission Board,* 1915, MSS.

Executive Committee for nearly two decades was filled largely with affairs of Mercer University and allocations for ministerial aid, and also ministerial relief. Additionally, this Committee did make recommendations in other areas of work, maintaining a nominal supervision over mission work in the state.

For a brief period of time when the Convention first owned *The Index,* this Committee supervised also the affairs of the denominational paper, following its gift by Jesse Mercer in 1840, at a meeting of the Convention in Penfield.[3]

Until 1877, and for many years thereafter to a lesser degree, the business of the Georgia Baptist Convention was taken care of on the Convention floor during annual sessions of the Convention. With the organization of the Southern Baptist Convention in 1845, and the creation of the Domestic and Foreign Mission Boards at the same time, support for Domestic and Foreign Missions was left in large measure to field agents for these Boards. The University had used field agents to help raise funds for many years. Actual business of the Executive Committee was limited, and to a degree advisory in scope; there being not much business between annual sessions.

In 1877, the creation of a State Mission Board was authorized. With this development, functions of the Executive Committee, situated in Macon, were limited even further; primarily to reports on Christian education, some oversight of Mercer University, and reports on disbursements of Ministerial Aid and Ministerial Relief funds. The State Mission Board was set up in Atlanta, and has functioned with that city as principal offices since its creation.

The War Between the States created a further vacuum when there was not much for the First Executive Committee to do for a period of some five years. Then, when that war ended, it fell to the Convention itself to regroup and strengthen Baptist work in the state, and again to remold

[3]James Adams Lester, *A History of The Christian Index,* 1822-1954 [Unpublished Master's Thesis, 1955] p. 34.

the work at the annual sessions of the Convention. Therefore, when the State Mission Board was formed, there was
a proliferation of field agents for all causes, and one of
the first and most important functions of that Board was
to seek to channel all monies for Georgia and Southwide
causes through it.

The active program of promotion by the State Mission
Board left the Executive Committee, still sitting—almost
literally—in Macon, with even less to do.

It is probable that had it not been for close, historic ties
both organizationally and personally between the First Executive Committee and the University, the Convention would
have done away with it upon formation of the Mission
Board. A careful tracing of the record indicates personal
ties between the Committee and Mercer and the Mercer
trustees which probably made the Convention reluctant to
abolish the Committee. It existed, therefore, in something
of a limbo through the remainder of the 19th century.

There are no minutes of the meetings of the State Mission
Board known to be in existence prior to 1905. Proceedings
of the Board, fortunately, were recorded at length and with
apparent accuracy, in the anuual report of that Board to
the Convention. Were this not the case, a valuable segment
of Georgia Baptist history would have been lost. A careful
search of possible repositories for these minute books proved
fruitless. However, despite its waning influence, throughout
the years there appeared annually a report from the Executive Committee, limited finally to Ministerial Aid and
Ministerial Relief after the Education Commission, and
its successor, the Education Board, began to make reports
for all educational interests.

Copies of the minutes of meetings of the State Mission
Board, then, are the only valid clue to the transferral of
terms which have caused some confusion in identification.
These records identify them, in most cases verbally, and
consistently in confusing sequence, as minutes of the *State
Mission Board,* and as *Minutes of the Executive Committee.*

However, in minutes of the State Mission Board, the term "Executive Committee" was used to apply to the Executive Committee of the State Mission Board, and not to the *First* Executive Committee. On many occasions, as the consolidation of authority into the Board and a smaller committee grew, the records were identified only as minutes of The Executive Committee;—but these were minutes of the State Mission Board.

In 1919, with reorganization of the Convention, and adoption of a new Constitution, the old Executive Committee died and was buried permanently. The State Mission Board, in turn, became the Executive Committee of the Baptist Convention of the State of Georgia, as it is now called. At this point, what had been referred to as the Executive Committee in Mission Board minutes, became, in essence what is now called the Administrative Committee of the Executive Committee.

This explanation is germain, because it was under the administration of Cree that the Convention was to revise its Constitution and set in motion a pattern of operation still identifiable in Georgia Baptist life.

However, as a prelude to the administration of Cree, the work of H. R. Bernard must be noted. As indicated, Bennett had been forced to retire early, in 1914.[4] Bernard had become a leading figure in Georgia Baptist life, and for about a year served as acting executive secretary-treasurer.[5] Thus Bernard helped to shape actively the affairs of the Convention in matters which were considered by the Convention in two sessions, 1914, and 1915. The Bernard Plan[6] for promotion of Convention interests was shaped by this man who had served as auditor of the Mission Board and secretary of the Committee on Co-operation from 1906 until 1916.[7] He died in 1916.[8] His "schedule" was approved by

[4]*Op. cit.*, Chapter 13, p. 360.
[5]*Minutes, Georgia Baptist Convention*, 1914, p. 43.
[6]*Encyclopedia of Southern Baptists*, Vol. I, p. 157.
[7]*Loc. cit.*
[8]*Minutes, Georgia Baptist Convention*, 1916, p. 44.

the Convention in 1895.[9] During this time, even the By-Laws of the Convention were changed in order to make the auditor an ex-officio member of the Mission Board.[10]

From his year of service as acting secretary, Georgia Baptists benefited not only from his business acumen but his Christian spirit. His insistence upon strict procedure in dealing with finances, was reflected in the auditor's reports.

Thus, when Cree assumed the general secretaryship, he followed a man who had kept the Mission Board moving forward.[11]

Cree, a native of Innerleithen, Pebbleshire, Scotland, had served churches in South Carolina, Kentucky, Tennessee, and Georgia. He had an earned doctor of philosophy degree, and from 1912 until his election in March, 1915, was enlistment secretary for the Home Mission Board of the Southern Baptist Convention.[12] Amendments to the By-Laws in 1914 reflected again the background of the leadership which Bernard exerted during this interim and even earlier. The amendments tripled the length of the By-Laws. Additions were:

> The Committee on Co-operation shall prepare for each Convention a complete budget of the affairs of all the interests fostered by the Convention, giving in detail the sums the Committee thinks should be raised by the churches during the coming year for each interest, and also, after consulting with the Executive Committees of the Associations, prorating among the different Associations what sums, in the Committee's judgment, the Convention should ask each Association to give for each cause. When the budget is adopted by the Convention, the Committee on Co-operation shall officially inform the Executive Committee of each Association what the Convention asks of that Association for each cause, and do all in its power to persuade the Association to formally adopt the request and instruct its Executive Committee to make a fair apportionment of these various

[9]B. D. Ragsdale, *Story of Georgia Baptists,* Vol. III, [The Executive Committee of Georgia Baptist Convention Atlanta, 1938], p. 136.
[10]*Minutes, Georgia Baptist Convention,* 1906, p. 27.
[11]*Minutes, Georgia Baptist Convention,* 1914, p. 75.
[12]Encyclopedia of Southern Baptists, Vol. I, p. 330.

amounts among the different churches of the Association.

8. The budget above mentioned shall not only contain
an itemized statement of the amount each interest except the Board of Missions asks the Convention to help
it raise, but also an itemized statement of how the
money is to be spent, that all of our contributors may
know in detail what is to be done with their money.

In order that the Committee on Co-operation may intel-
ligently make this budget, each interest except the Board
of Missions shall be required to file with it before the
budget is made an itemized statement of all money it
has received from any source during the previous year,
and what its expenditures have been; provided that
this section shall not apply to the Home and Foreign
Boards of the Southern Baptist Convention, the Convention having no authority to require such an itemized
statement from them. The Board of Missions shall file
with the Committee on Co-operation an itemized statement for its expenditures during the past Convention
year, and shall also recommend what sums shall be spent
by the Mission Board in its work during the coming
Convention year.

9. The committee on Co-operation shall print and distribute this budget among the messengers of the Convention on the first day of each session, and it shall be referred to a committee on the budget, which shall report
on the second day, at a time fixed by the Committee on
Order of Business, and when it is adopted by the Convention, no change shall be made in it by anyone until
the next Convention meets.

10. The committee on co-operation shall be composed of
those who have no official connection with any of the
interests fostered by the budget.

11. The Board of Missions, through its enlistment
workers, working in harmony with the Enlistment Department of the Home Mission Board, is directed to do
all in its power to secure contributions from the un-
enlisted churches in Georgia for all the objects fostered
by the Convention, and to develop these churches in
missionary activities.

This effort shall be made in conjunction with the Executive Committees of the Associations and the pastors of
the local churches, everything being done within the
power of the Board to persuade the local churches to
adopt and work under, in accordance with the schedule,

one or the other of the financial plans suggested by the Convention that met at Rome.[13]

CONVENTION CONTROL OVER FUNDS

Thus was provided a clear-cut financial plan which would give the Convention strict control over the monies it allocated to the several interests, and at the same time provide the constituency with full information concerning the financial activities of these institutions and programs. Financial records of the Convention had always been well kept. Promotional activities throughout the state were intensified with creation of the Board of Missions. The amendments were but another step to insure accuracy and effectiveness in the enlistment of the churches in support of the work.

This is emphasized further by a continuation of the By-Law changes.

> 12. The state Board of Missions is directed in the beginning of each Convention year to make a definite agreement with the different Boards and interests for which it collects money, as to what amount it shall charge each of these Boards and interests for collecting and forwarding its money.[14]
>
> 13. The Board of Missions is directed in the beginning of each Convention year, in the name of the Convention, to request all Boards and interests outside of the State, that collect money from our churches, to put their agents, while working in Georgia, under the direction of the Board of Missions, that the budget and schedule of the Convention may be effective.
>
> 14. No Board, or governing body shall expend during the year, or incur any liability for, any amount in excess of estimated income as set forth in the budget.[15]
>
> 15. The Committee on Nominations shall nominate at this session of the Convention, a committee composed of five members, three being laymen, and two being ministers, and all being of recognized business ability, whose duty it shall be to see to it that all boards appointed by the Convention, and their employees, and all other servants of the Convention, shall obey the laws

[13]*Minutes, Georgia Baptist Convention,* 1914, p.p., 10, 11.
[14]*Ibid.,* p. 11.
[15]*Ibid.,* p. 12.

and rules laid down by the Convention for their guidance.

Three of these five, one being the chairman, shall serve for two years and two of them for one year, and their successors, when appointed, shall serve in like manner, and none of the five shall have any official connection with any board or interest fostered by the Convention.

Should any of the said boards, or employees or said servants, violate any of the laws and rules of the Convention, this committee of five shall have authority to declare vacant the positions held by such members of said boards, or their employees, or said servants, and to fill the vacancies by other appointments to hold good until the next Convention.

It is the purpose and intention of this By-Law to give this committee of five, power to act between the sessions of the Convention, just as the Convention would have itself, if it was in session. But this power to act shall apply only to the enforcement of laws already made by the Convention, and shall not confer upon the Committee the power to make any new laws.[16]

The By-Law change, adopted by the 1915 Convention, was another step in the development of an organizational pattern which was to result in the formation of the Executive Committee in 1919.

By-Law amendments seven through fourteen are quoted from the Minutes for 1914, and are identified as amendments made in 1914, By-Law fifteen was approved by the 1915 Convention. Both of these Conventions were held during the time Bernard was acting secretary.

In the report of the Board of Missions there is the statement: "Since the Convention of 1913, the Board has adopted a code of By-Laws. . ."[17] In 1914, there were two Minute records of changes in By-Laws by the Convention. One was a reference to By-Law 5, which was amended by striking the words: "and a like number of those longest in service shall be retired."[18] The other two By-Laws, seven and fourteen, were the outgrowth of suggestions from a Workers' conference.[19]

This Workers' conference apparently was the same group organized in 1910, called the Conference of Association Officers, and formed, evidently, under Bernard's sponsorship. John D. Mell was named temporary chairman at that group's organizational meeting.[20] The resolutions from the Workers' Conference which led to the By-Law additions of 1914 were presented by John D. Mell.[21]

The 1915 Convention did approve addition of By-Law 15.[22] Thus, a section of the By-Laws of the Convention which dealt entirely with, and gave considerable authority to the Committee on Co-operation, did not, by minute record, show Convention approval.

The only item dealing with constitutional amendments in 1914 was recommitted for a report to the 1915 Convention, and dealt with the Education Board.[23]

Again in 1915, the functions of the Committee of Five were clarified by a resolution proposed by Mell, which gave to that committee the power and responsibility ". . . to look after the general welfare of our denominational affairs, to plan for it such undertakings as may, in their judgment, be beneficial to our work in all its phases, . . ." [24]

This resolution appeared to mitigate the authority of the Mission Board, and may have been a counter-reaction to the growing authority of both the Education Board and the Committee on Co-operation.

This 1915 By-Law gave considerable authority to the Committee on Co-operation, with enough force to insure effective operation, and, to a sense, a policing of the budgets of all agencies, institutions and programs of the Convention. The first Committee of Five—Supervision, was comprised of L. G.

---

[19]*Ibid.*, p. 43.
[20]*Minutes, Georgia Baptist Convention*, 1910, p. 188.
[21]*Minutes, Georgia Baptist Convention*, 1914, p. 43.
[22]*Minutes, Georgia Baptist Convention*, 1915, p. 29.
[23]*Minutes, Georgia Baptist Convention*, 1914, p. 23.
[24]*Minutes, Georgia Baptist Convention*, 1915, p. 32.

Hardman, Commerce; John D. Mell, Athens; Z. H. Clark, Moultrie; F. C. McConnell, Atlanta; and J. P. Nichols, Griffin.[25]

With the election of Cree as secretary of the Mission Board, the Convention was to begin a 15-year pattern of growth which consolidated it fairly well into the organizational structure and promotional pattern evident today. Cree was to lead Georgia Baptists through the $75 Million Campaign, the Depression, consolidation of organzation within the Executive Committee, and to a rather complete development of a program of State Missions.

Emphasis upon evangelism had been strong throughout Convention life. During this period in Southern Baptist life, with the advent of preachers such as George Truett, L. R. Scarbrough, etc., flames of evangelism were kindled anew. In Georgia, a committee recommended to the Convention plans for a state-wide revival which had been urged by the Board of Missions. The plan which was endorsed asked for each pastor to support the effort, advised the Mission Board to direct the effort and declared: "We recommend that by adopting this report, the Convention put itself decisively and earnestly back of this movement . . ." [26] This was the first state-wide revival effort promoted in Georgia.

Something of a reaction to the Education Board developed and was expressed in the 1915 Convention. The Board had requested an amendment to the Constitution which failed to pass by the required two-thirds majority.[27]

From the earliest days of ministerial aid, the Convention, through its [first] Executive Committee, had provided direct grants for students at Mercer and at state institutions. These grants were changed slightly over the years, but by 1915, the Convention decided that ". . . except for very unusual reasons, the Executive Committee shall not assist any minis-

[25]*Ibid.*, p. 2.
[26]*Ibid.*, p. 19.
[27]*Ibid.*, p. 20.

terial student unless his own church and association contribute one half of the amount needed by such student." [28] In that year also, the Convention decided that in view of the difficulty in obtaining information on deceased ministers as in previous years when a biographical sketch was published, that henceforth, there would be ". . . a memorial page in our minutes containing only the name of deceased ordained ministers, their place of residence at death, the place of birth and date and the time of death and place." [29]

POLICY ONE OF DEVELOPMENT

Cree, in his first report, said that the mission policy of Georgia Baptists must more and more be one of development. "With the exception of a few limited sections, the state is pretty well covered with Baptist churches . . . The need now is for the development of the fields and the forces already won." [30] This guideline was one which was to be followed in large measure from 1915 to the present.

The Committee on Co-operation in 1915 suggested that the associations change the dates of their annual meetings to times prior to October 31.[31] This was evidently to allow time for reports from the associations to be available by the time for the annual Convention in November.

Amendments to the Constitution in 1916 indicate again the firm hold which Cree took in leadership of the Board of Missions. Section 10 of the Constitution was amended, striking the 5th paragraph which read "This board shall report annually to the Convention".[32] Substituted for this phrase, was: "This Board shall have its books audited annually by an expert public accountant, and shall report annually to this Convention."

In Section 10, third paragraph, the following was stricken

[28]*Ibid.,* p. 45.
[29]*Ibid.,* p. 47.
[30]*Ibid.,* p. 86.
[31]*Ibid.,* p. 107.
[32]*Minutes, Georgia Baptist Convention,* 1916, p. 14.

beginning at end of second line: "To appoint its own corresponding secretary and treasurer, both offices to be in the same man; also an auditor, both of whom shall be ex-officio members of the Board of Missions." Added in place of the lines stricken was the phrase: "To appoint its own corresponding secretary and treasurer, both offices to be vested in the same man, who shall be ex-officio member of the Mission Board."

And in Section 10 the fourth paragraph, reading as follows, was stricken: "The auditor may be the joint officer of the Board of Missions and the Committee on Co-operation." In Section 11, beginning at the end of the first line of the third paragraph, the following was removed: "And its secretary may be the same man as the auditor of the Board of Missions. In such case, the Secretary shall be elected jointly by the Board of Missions and the Committee on Cooperation." For that paragraph, there was substituted "And its secretary may be an employee of the Mission Board. In such case, the election of the secretary must be approved by *the Mission Board*." [33]

There was yet a further change in the Constitution, in Section 10, beginning with the words in the second line of the second paragraph striking: "Seeing after the collection and forwarding of funds to the Home, Foreign and Sunday School Boards; also the collection and disbursement of funds for destitute ministers and their widows." The substitute was:

> Seeing after the collection and forwarding of funds for Home and Foreign Mission Boards and the Baptist Orphans' Home, Georgia Baptist Hospital, Ministerial Relief, Ministerial Education, Schools and Colleges and all other objects fostered by Georgia Baptists.[34]

Another change in the Constitution made the closing lines of Section 10, and of paragraph two, read: "Ministerial Relief, Ministerial Education, Schools and Colleges, and all

[33]*Ibid.*, p.p. 14. 15.
[34]*Loc. cit.*

other objects [not specifically provided for,] fostered by Georgia Baptists." [35] [Phrase in brackets is the one added.]

While the foregoing may seem complicated, it is important. In effect, these amendments to the Constitution approved the first full year of Cree's service, negated to a large degree the impact of the authority of the office which Bernard had held, and which had led to the auditor of the Mission Board assuming executive status almost at a level equal with the corresponding secretary. The Committee on Co-operation became a near-equal of the Mission Board in authority. At least, the Amendments in 1914 and in 1915 laid the groundwork of this to transpire. It took only a year under Cree's leadership for the Convention to reverse this trend by making certain that monies for all Georgia Baptist causes were channeled through the Mission Board.

The Convention made certain also that any person who served in any subsidiary capacity would be elected by the Mission Board, and be an employee of that Board.

During 1916, women in Georgia gave $95,935.25 for mission and benevolent purposes through their regular channels of giving; $44,034.93 for local work and $8,449.69 in boxes for a total of $148,419.69 for all purposes. [36] This is revealing in several ways. One, the women were giving for all causes about one half the amount of the total state goal for state causes, and were contributing through the Mission Board more than one third of the total amount for all causes.

First reference to an Orphans' Home day in the Bible School was in 1916, and it was considered wise to set a goal of $24,239.34, representing the total indebtedness of the Home. [37]

The Convention in 1916 took a stand on religious work in the Army, which called upon Georgia representatives in Congress to introduce measure to set up an investigation of the religious condition of the Army and Navy,

. . . particularly of any limitations upon bona fide

[36]*Ibid.*, p. 28.
[37]*Ibid.*, p. 36.

efforts of Evangelical church workers in army camps or elsewhere; or of any improper influence or partiality in the selection of chaplains or in the prescribing of religious services or ceremonies; . . .[38]

The Board of Education still was able to report growth, stating:

> When we began a year ago only two of our High Schools were recognized by the Southern Association of Colleges and Secondary Schools or by the Georgia Association of Colleges when it was formed in 1915. Now all except one are so recognized, and one enjoys a place in the highest rank of the standard schools of the South.[39]

The Committee on Co-operation derived some pleasure in the response of the churches to the promotional efforts of that Committee. The report for 1916, signed by Spencer B. King as recording secretary, said that in 1897, the total amount handled by the treasurer of the Mission Board for all objects was $37,552.60, and in 1916, contributions totaled $248,664.74.[40] Contributions recorded from time to time did not reflect the special and designated gifts *directly* to the institutions, the Orphans' Home, and Hospital. The comparative figures represent the 18 years of the existence of that Committee.

The Committee of Five laid the groundwork between the 1915 and 1916 sessions for a plan to reduce indebtedness of Convention-owned institutions. The responsibility for this campaign was to rest with the Committee of Five.[41]

The Committee of Five in turn recommended formation of a Commission of Seven, a chartered body, to hold title to all properties of all institutions.[42] The Committee submitted plans for a detailed campaign to raise $415,735.39 to pay all of the Convention's debts.[43] This report, adopted by

[38]*Ibid.*, p.p. 40, 41.
[35]*Ibid.*, p. 24.
[39]*Ibid.*, p. 69.
[40]*Ibid.*, p. 117.
[41]*Ibid.*, p. 63.
[42]*Loc. cit.*
[42]*Ibid.*, p. 65.

the Convention,[44] represented the first all-out, united effort by the Convention to raise funds for debt retirement.

One of the most significant developments in Georgia Baptist life, largely forgotten, was the creation therefore in 1917 of what came to be called the Committee of Seven or Commission of Seven. In that year, two years from the beginning of the $75 Million Campaign, Georgia Baptist interests were in debt, and this they did not like. Setting up of this Commission was designed to make of it, in effect, a Holding Commission—under which name it was later called—to hold title to all property belonging to any and every Convention interest. This was to include holding of ". . . legal title to all property, . . . both real and personal, including bonds, mortgages, notes and other evidences of indebtedness of every kind, . . ." [45]

NO DEBT TO BE CREATED

At the same time, the Commission was not to create any kind of debt on the properties.[46] The Commission would receive all properties to be donated in the future to institutions fostered by the Convention, or on the part of any institutions which would later become part of the Convention. There was to be no authority or power or control over the internal operations of the institutions, and no member of the Commission was to have any official connection with any institution. "The Holding Commission shall make annual reports . . ." to the Georgia Baptist Convention, with itemized statements of all the propety held for each institution. Further, the Commission was not to receive or accept title to any property of the institutions ". . . unless the same shall be clear of debt at the time of the transfer of title. . ." [47]

This was to have the effect of forcing the institutions to get their financial affairs in order, making certain that

[44]*Ibid.*, p. 24.
[45]*Minutes, Georgia Baptist Convention*, 1917, p. 18.
[46]*Ibid.*, p. 19.
[47]*Loc. cit.*

property deeded over to the Holding Commission would not be encumbered by debt. The Education Board reported in 1917, that it had not elected a full time secretary because of a lack of funds.[48]

Perhaps because of the lack of funds, or possibly to delineate more clearly functions of the Education Board and the Commission of Seven, John F. Purser proposed a Constitutional amendment in 1917, passed without objection, which defined clearly—and really again—the role of the Education Board. The amendment called for:

> An Education Board of fifteen members, none of whom shall be officially connected with any of the schools fostered by the Convention, shall be chosen by the Convention, five to serve for one year, five for two years, and five for three years, the vacancies, as the terms expire, to be filled by election for three years. In addition to the fifteen members chosen by the Convention there shall be an advisory committee composed of one representative from each school in the Mercer system. This advisory committee shall meet with the Board and take part in its deliberations, but shall not have the right to vote.
>
> This Board, acting in accordance with the plans of the Convention, shall have the oversight of all the schools in the Mercer system, and shall be charged with the duty of soliciting funds for these schools for enlargement and endowment, and in co-operation with the Mission Board for current support and ministerial education. It shall also be the duty of this Board to distribute all funds for our schools and for ministerial education.
>
> The Board shall have power to make its own by-laws and to enforce all its regulations which have been approved by the Convention. It shall make annual reports of its work to the Convention, and shall also be the medium through which the schools in the Mercer system shall make their reports.[49]

This amendment served to strengthen the Education Board.

With this arrangement, there were really three forces in a power structure within the Convention. None of the three

[48]*Ibid.*, p. 21.
[49]*Ibid.*, p.p. 23-24.

forces were, apparently, at odds with the other, but with the growth of the Convention, and the constitutional changes, there was being created a situation which would, within two years, necessitate an entirely new Constitution and a new structure of operation. While the constitutional revisions in 1919 were attributed by some to a "make ready" for participation in the $75 Million campaign, these revisions were well on the way before the $75 Million Campaign was conceived.

There was the State Mission Board, with authority over mission work in Georgia and authority for collection and disbursement of funds for Home and Foreign mission work, as well as responsibility for promoting these ministries. Additionally, the Mission Board was responsible, overall, for promotion of the work of the Convention, including, through trustees, the hospital and Orphans' Home.

The Commission of Seven, was responsible for holding title to all properties of all institutions and agencies except the hospital—and this was to be a disputed point later. And, the Education Board had responsibility for soliciting funds for the schools for enlargement and endowment ". . . and in co-operation with the Mission Board for current support and ministerial education, . . ." [50] creating, in effect, an overlapping of authority at three levels. During this time, the hospital was struggling with problems of expansion and the financing of this expansion, desirous all the while to move to a different location, which it would soon do.

A change in By-Laws in 1917 assured that: "The Convention shall hold its annual meeting on the first Tuesday after the fifth day of December each year." [51] For the first time also, the Convention approved a resolution calling upon every Baptist church in the state to place the name of the church on the building.[52] Cree, in dealing with the report of the Social Service Commission, proposed that copies of the

[50] *Ibid.*, p. 24.
[51] *Ibid.*, p. 28.
[52] *Ibid.*, p. 46.

report be furnished the press of the state for publication,[53] and the Convention adopted a resolution on asking the Board of Missions to consider the advisability of aiding the Blue Ridge Assembly Program both in money and in speakers.[54]

The lengthy outline of the authority and function of the Education Board approved by the Convention, on By-Law changes, gave it the authority needed to enable Georgia Baptists ". . . to present an orderly front to the world in education . . ." and to promote and direct ". . . movements which resulted in creating a strong educational foundation in the Baptist conscience".[55]

The Committee of Five thereupon assumed responsibility for making and executing plans for the payment of debts on the institutions owned by the Convention, which institutions were being transferred one by one to the Commission of Seven. This Committee of Five in 1917 had named C. J. Hood of Commerce ". . . as General Manager of the campaign to pay the debts of our Institutions." He would not accept any compensation.[56] The Committee of Five had been authorized by the Convention to obtain money from the Board of Missions for expenses, which Hood did not do, advancing his own subscription of $3,000 to pay expenses. Members of the Committee of Five also advanced out of their subscriptions all of their personal expenses during the campaign. Funds expended up to the time of the preparation of the report for the 1917 Convention included $3,618.06 for salaries and other expenses.[57]

To obtain a clear summary of Convention activity at this stage of development, the following statement is in order. These groups were at work during the same time in the same general area, but with different responsibilities: 1. The

[53]*Ibid.*, p. 44.

[54]*Ibid.*, p.p. 45, 46.

[55]Spright Dowell, *A History of Mercer University*, [Atlanta: Foote & Davies, 1958], p. 249.

[56]*Minutes, Georgia Baptist Convention*, p. 67.

[57]*Loc. cit.*

Education Board, with broad authority for the operation of schools in what by this time was referred to commonly as the Mercer System. 2. The Holding Commission [Committee of Seven] gathering together all titles to property, and seeking to secure funds for debt retirement. 3. The Committee of Five, charged also with responsibility for campaigns to pay indebtedness of Convention institutions. 4. The Mission Board, working with the Education Board in raising funds for ministerial education and current operational expenses for the institutions, and directing the program of State Missions. And, all the while, Georgia Baptists were seeking to consolidate their forces.

It was the Committee of Five which reported that total indebtedness at the Fitzgerald Convention [in 1915] as reported by the institutions, was $524,546.17. As of the 1917 Convention, the indebtedness had been reduced to $434,-415.66 making a total of some $90,000 placed on debt retirement in two years.[58] To correct an error, the amount of indebtedness on the part of the Board of Missions as of the Fitzgerald Convention was $42,000, not the $30,333.88 as reported.[59] Financial indebtedness on the part of the Orphans' Home was $20,000.00.[60]

In the 41st report of the Board of Missions, Cree stated that the Board's book showed a balance in resources of $20,121.74,[61] and further that all money borrowed by the Board had been at five per cent interest instead of the seven and eight per cent paid three years previously and the 1916 average interest payment was 6¼ per cent.[62] Seemingly unimportant and uninteresting, these items in the financial reports had behind them a history involving more than money.

The Mission Board bought the hospital on faith in Georgia Baptists to stand behind it in the purchase of the

[58]*Ibid.*, p.p. 67, 68.
[59]*Ibid.*, p. 68.
[60]*Ibid.*, p. 69.
[61]*Ibid.*, p. 98.
[62]*Ibid.*, p. 100.

property. The Board borrowed money to meet notes on the indebtedness. At the April 30, 1917 meeting of the Executive Committee of the Mission Board, the Committee adopted a resolution authorizing:

> . . . the corresponding secretary and treasurer . . . in the name of the Mission Board to rearrange the financial obligation of the Mission Board in the matter of the $50,000 mortgage on the Georgia Baptist hospital property, provided that in doing so the current obligations assumed do not exceed the present interest cost of $4,000 per annum and provided, further, that it be agreed by the Executive Committee of the Board of Trustees of the hospital when the proposed rearrangement has been cared for, that additional funds collected for the hospital and applicable to the obligations of the hospital and financing the property shall be applied, as needed, to the liquidation of the obligation of the Georgia Baptist Hospital to the Mission Board so as to relieve the Mission Board from embarrassment to its credit on financial operations.[63]

The report dealing with refinancing of Mission Board obligations, then, was the Board's method of dealing with hospital obligations, which it was committed to care for, in such a manner that the credit standing of the Board would not be endangered. Apparently this step was scheduled to pave the way for the Commission of Seven to assume title to the hospital property. At the same meeting of the Executive Committee of the Mission Board there was recorded an action which indicated further that Bennett, the former corresponding secretary, was not, apparently, competent for a time to handle his own affairs. At the meeting, it was reported:

> In view of the relation of Dr. J. J. Bennett to the Mission Board as a beneficiary of the ministerial relief fund, a special committee, consisting of Dr. C. W. Mynatt, president of the Mission Board, and Dr. Charles W. Daniel, chairman of the Executive Committee of the Mission Board, was appointed to look at a matter of Dr. Bennett's financial status for his protection and for the protection of the Mission Board.[64]

[63]*Minutes, Executive Committee, State Mission Board,* April 30, 1917, p. 43.
[64]*Loc cit.*

During 1917, Georgia Baptists, through their Board, expended for State Mission enterprises a total of $53,660.90.[65] Of this amount, only $8,083.48 was spent in administrative expense.[66] Earlier that year, at the January 9 meeting of the Board's Executive Committee, it adopted a policy designed to encourage the grouping of rural churches into compact fields with resident pastors. It was agreed that in making appropriations for pastoral aid or other assistance, that preference would be given to churches which had entered into joint fields of service. The Board's policy contained the provision that no rural church, which declined to enter into such an arrangement, would be eligible for aid of any kind except for special mitigating circumstances.[67]

NATION ON WAR-TIME ECONOMY

In evaluating financial reports for 1917, it should be remembered that America was on a war-time economy, and economic conditions were affecting the Denomination's program in many areas. The Committee on Co-operation asked for the 1917 budget year a total of $300,000.[68] For 1918, it was asking $260,000, with five per cent of the amount, $13,000, to go to ministerial education; schools and colleges were to get eight per cent, or $20,800; State Missions, $65,000; Foreign Missions, $65,000, Home Missions, $41,600; Orphans' Home, $31,200, Ministerial Relief, $8,800; and Hospital, $15,600.[69]

Scheduled to meet in Forsyth in 1918, the Convention changed the place of meeting to Macon because of a flu epidemic in Forsyth.[70] A five-year report on State Missions revealed that contributions had increased from $211,622.33 to $452,491.69,[71] and at the Macon Convention, George W.

---

[65]*Minutes, Georgia Baptist Convention,* 1917, p. 123.
[66]*Loc. cit.*
[67]*Minute Record, Executive Committee, Mission Board,* Jan. 9, 1917, p. 37.
[68]*Minutes, Georgia Baptist Convention,* 1916, p. 117.
[69]*Minutes, Georgia Baptist Convention,* 1917, p. 126.
[70]*Minutes, Georgia Baptist Convention,* 1918, p. 13.
[71]*Ibid.,* p. 22.

Andrews presented to the delegates a service flag representing 16,691 stars signifying the names in military service from Sunday Schools in the Convention.[72]

The Committee on Co-operation of future campaigns proposed in 1918 a United campaign, to last five years, and designed to produce $2,500,000 to be distributed to the Convention interests as collected, and in proportion.[73] At this point, C. W. Daniel, who was serving as chairman of the Board's Executive Committee, proposed an amendment that the Georgia member of the Southern Baptist Education Commission, the Secretary of the Board of Education, the Secretary of the Mission Board, the Superintendent of the Georgia Baptist hospital and the General Manager of the Orphans' Home be made an executive committee ". . . with full power and authority to project and conduct the united drive for $2,500,000 for the enlargement of the several interests and institutions included in the campaign." It was agreed also that the committee be ". . . empowered to create an advisory committee of fifty men, or one man for each $50,000 proposed to be raised." [74]

Attitudes on the part of Georgia Baptists to involvement in World War I never showed officially until the war had ended, when the Social Service Commission, said

> Baptists found no embarrassment in adjusting themselves to the spirit and movement of this universal contact. A war, which at first was simply revolting to the American people to whom the issues for a season were more or less obscure, gradually assumed new aspects until out of all the confusion and horror the real issue emerged, clear-cut and sharply defined—whether or not 'government of the people, for the people, and by the people, should perish from the earth.' [75]

Thus, in three wars which had been fought during the history of the Convention up to this time, the pattern repeated itself. In the War Between the States, the Spanish

[72]*Ibid.*, p. 28.
[73]*Ibid.*, p. 31.
[74]*Ibid.*, p. 32.
[75]*Ibid.*, p. 34.

American War, and World War I, there was evidence that Georgia Baptists were in sympathy with and supported the causes of their government [the Confederacy for the first war], but they did not make it an issue which occupied commanding attention at the session of the Convention.

To avoid last-minute changes in the Constitution, W. W. Gaines proposed a resolution, adopted, which removed Article 14, and in its place adopted a new article stating:

> This Constitution may be amended at any regular session by the vote of two thirds of the messengers present and voting at the time; provided, that no amendment shall be made later than the second day of the Convention.[76]

The Convention had a good year financially, despite predictions and indications otherwise.

Receipts totaled $452,491.69 on a 13-month basis.[77] Because of the good year, W. H. Major proposed that:

> In view of the unforeseen and unprecedented advance in the receipts of our Board, be it resolved that Article No. 7 of the By-Laws be suspended for this Convention year; and that the Committee on Co-operation be instructed to make a new apportionment with a minimum total of $500,000, apportioning the same directly to the churches, and giving such publicity to this action and the cause therefor as may be necessary.[78]

Another effort to have the Convention purchase *The Index* was made in a resolution by W. W. Gaines which would have authorized the Convention to purchase the paper. However, the motion failed to pass the Convention,[79] leaving it to the 1919 Convention to make the decisive move on the paper.

The Committee of Five reported that Hospital indebtedness at the end of 1915 had been $91,248, and of this amount $42,628 had been paid, leaving a debt of $48,628. "This, as

[76]*Ibid.*, p. 46.
[77]*Ibid.*, p. 101.
[78]*Ibid.*, p. 46.
[79]*Ibid.*, p. 47.

reported last year, will be cared for by Atlanta Baptists." [80]

In his account of the Hospital's history, Ragsdale said:

> In 1917 there had been paid on the property debt $19,890.64, the Smith mortgage loan had been cancelled and its claim refinanced, and the Atlanta Baptists had agreed to raise the full debt on the Hospital as their part in the combined debts of the several institutions." [81]

The Atlanta Association over the years had been given some leeway in deciding how Convention allocations for mission causes should be expended. Evidence of this is in an action of the Executive Committee when that committee approved division of appropriations

> . . . made to the Atlanta Association in accord with the wishes of the Executive Committee of said Association, provided said appropriation be within the amount already approved for the association.[82]

Additionally, a group of businessmen, evidently in Atlanta, "backed the building of a forty room annex to the hospital building, and in a year and a half the financial obligations on this structure were discharged." [83] This addition, completed in August of 1918, doubled the capacity of the hospital, and cost, with equipment, $65,000, and was paid for ". . . in about a year and a half." [84]

In the same year, the Education Board held meetings of Mercer alumni across the state with plans to set up local organizations looking toward financial support from these sources.[85] The situation at Mercer in 1918 is of interest. Attendance was 429 in the Literary Department, with 240 of these having been inducted into the Student Army Training Corps; Summer School enrolment was 82 with 13 students in the Law School for a total enrolment of 524. Mercer had been selected as a center for training for the

[80]*Ibid.*, p.p. 64, 65.

[81]Ragsdale, Vol. III, p. 266.

[82]*Minute Book, Executive Committee, State Mission Board*, Dec. 2, 1915, p. 18.

[83]*The Christian Index*, June 15, 1939.

[84]Ragsdale, Vol. III, p. 266.

[85]*Minutes, Georgia Baptist Convention*, 1918, p.p. 72-73.

military, and apparently the War Department was satisfied with the program operated at Mercer.[86]

During the war, over 700 Mercer men had been engaged actively in military service. Expenses of the army training corps exceeded by $18,500 the amount the government agreed to pay. However, the University reported assurances by the War Department that the funds would be paid.[87]

Recommendations concerning completion of the debt-paying campaign included 1. Completion of the campaign. 2. Recommendation of an effort to increase student enrolment by promotion ". . . through correspondence and personal solicitation; . . . the building up circles of alumni and former students, . . ." and organization of Societies of the friends of Christian Education, and 3. By presenting the five-year program of education of the Southern Baptist Convention.[88]

A report on Hospital operations indicated that in the slightly over five years of Convention operation of the Hospital, 7,361 patients had received treatment, with more than 600 treated without expense to them, and over 400 having paid only a portion of their expense. It was estimated that this service rendered by the Hospital during the five years was valued in excess of $70,000. During the same period, churches contributed for work $40,159.[89]

The 42nd report of the Board of Missions indicated that the board had involved itself and the Convention in service to the military.

> No service undertaken by the Mission Board has been of larger value and more thoroughly appreciated than our work among our soldiers. In the work the Mission Board has been helping in two ways; to-wit, in tent Evangel meetings supported wholly by State Mission money, and in support of camp pastors in co-operation

[86]*Ibid.*, p. 79.
[87]*Ibid.*, p. 80.
[88]*Ibid.*, p. 81.
[89]*Ibid.*, p. 95.

with the Home Mission Board of the Southern Baptist
Convention and the Northern Baptist War Work
Council.[90]

Additionally, in January, 1918, T. F. Callaway, a state evangelist at the time, was loaned to the YMCA for work at
Camp Wheeler in Macon, with the YMCA to pay half of his
salary, and the Board half for January, February and March,
1918.[91]

The Mission Board continued an active interest in and
support of aged ministers and their wives, with 34 ministers
beneficiaries and 31 widows of deceased ministers, with a
total expended for this purpose of $9,602.25,[92] and for the
same year, 26 churches had been aided in building programs
to the extent of $11,542.15.[93]

A significant action of the Convention was made in 1918
with regard to a retirement program. Earlier, the Convention had authorized investigation of some type of ministers
insurance program for retirement. Nothing came of this
recommendation. At the meeting of the Southern Baptist
Convention in Hot Springs, Arkansas, in May, 1918, that
Convention had adopted a comprehensive plan for the relief
and care of widows, orphans, ministers, missionaries, etc.[94]
Therefore, the Convention in session in Macon approved a
proposal by the Mission Board:

> That this Convention hereby approves the action of the
> Southern Baptist Convention in thus seeking to solve
> the problem of Ministerial Relief in the way and manner aforesaid, and hereby expresses its willingness to cooperate with the General Board, and authorizes the
> Mission Board, in conjunction with the Board of Ministerial Relief and Annuities of the Southern Baptist Convention, to work out all matters of detail as to cooperation.[95]

[90]*Ibid.*, p. 109.
[91]*Minute Book, Executive Committee, State Mission Board,* Jan. 3, 1918,
p. 52.
[92]*Minutes, Georgia Baptist Convention,* 1918, p.p. 115-116.
[93]*Ibid.*, p. 112.
[94]*Ibid.*, p. 116.
[95]*Loc. cit.*

An emphasis upon stewardship continued:

> Stewardship is one of the key-notes in kingdom affairs
> to-day. Biblical finance and tithing with systematic
> giving and proportionate distribution are being stressed
> by all departments of our organized work . . . As a re-
> sult of all of these efforts, the Georgia Baptist Tither's
> League has been inaugurated and 5,794 tithers have
> been enrolled.

Efforts were planned to make January "Stewardship
Month" and enlist

> . . . pastors and other leaders to teach and preach the
> great doctrines of Stewardship and to urge upon our
> people the wisdom of starting the New Year right by
> adopting some definite system of Stewardship based on
> the teaching of the word of God.[96]

Appearing in the report of Sunday School work was the
first indication of special days set aside for emphasis in the
Sunday Schools. These included six: State, Home and Foreign missions, Orphanage, Hospital and Educational Institutions. Special programs were used to promote these emphases, and remittances from the Sunday Schools to the
Mission Board for all objects totaled $66,370.10.[97]

A final summary for 20 years, from 1898 through 1918 indicated growth in churches from 1827 to 2487. This was
the 20th year of the work of the Committee on Co-operation,
and in the first year, total cash received for all purposes was
$40,274.02, and in 1918, $452,591.69.[98]

Much of the planning for erasing financial indebtedness of
Georgia Baptists was to undergo radical change prior to the
next Convention meeting. The start of the $75 Million
Campaign was to occupy much attention on the part of
Georgia Baptists during the next five years, with several years
of bright anticipation and activity, followed by years of declining gifts as the nation entered into the depression years.

These first four of Cree's 15 years a leader were years of
consolidation and progress. The stage was set for increased

[96]*Ibid.*, p. 120.
[97]*Ibid.*, p. 126.
[98]*Ibid.*, p. 140.

expansion. However, when Georgia began cooperation with the Southern Baptist Convention in the $75 Million Campaign, much of the elaborate work done by the Committee of Five in planning for the payment of debt was scrapped and included in the larger five-year plan to be adopted by the Southern Bapitst Convention, and to be promoted vigorously and effectively in Georgia.

CHAPTER 15

Georgia and The $75 Million Campaign

Three events of major importance transpired among Georgia Baptists during 1919. One action was the Convention's authorization to the Executive Committee to purchase *The Christian Index.*

A second major action was the adoption of a new Constitution which placed into operation the Executive Committee of the Baptist Convention of the State of Georgia.

The third major event was the birth of the $75 Million Campaign in Atlanta and Georgia's subsequent participation in it. The importance of this Campaign can never be under estimated in Baptist life both in Georgia and throughout the Southern Baptist Convention. It followed, in Georgia, almost as a logical step in the expanding program to raise money for payment of indebtedness on Georgia Baptist institutions. Further, this campaign, in a real sense, laid the groundwork for what was later to be called The Cooperative Program. The campaign was:

> . . . A five-year program 1919-24, which provided greatly increased support for all Baptist missionary, educational, and benevolent work in the States and Southern Baptist Convention and set a new pattern for Baptist cooperation.[1]

Meeting in Atlanta May 14-18, 1919, the Southern Baptist Convention projected this campaign after J. B. Gambrell,

[1]*Encyclopedia of Southern Baptists*, [Nashville: Broadman Press, 1958.] Vol. II, p. 1196.

Convention president, called upon Baptists ". . . to adopt a program of work commensurate with the reasonable demands upon us." Following this, a committee was named, including all the state secretaries, which met immediately to survey the task. Although there was obviously not time to perfect an organization, the committee did report back to the Southern Baptist Convention, prior to adjournment, that:

> . . . in view of the need of the world in this hour and . . . the numbers and ability of Baptists, 'that the Convention adopt a financial goal of $75,000,000, this sum to be subscribed at once, and paid over a period of five years.[2]

The plan was for a

> . . . committee of one member from each state 'to be named to plan for a simultaneous drive,' . . . the campaign being so arranged that the part to be raised each year shall be larger than that of the year before, and thus secure the largest part in the last year of the five.[3]

On June 4-5, 1919, a conference was held in Atlanta to map strategy for the campaign across the Southern Baptist Convention, with agreement which included, among other things, that the state secretaries would serve as directors in their own states. Georgia was asked to accept a goal of $7,500,000. In addition to Cree's participation at the south-wide level, Mrs. W. J. Neel, Georgia, was asked to co-ordinate the effort among Woman's Missionary Union.[4]

Following this June 4-5 meeting of the southwide committee in Atlanta, the Executive Committee of the Mission Board met June 27, 1919, in Atlanta, and adopted the following resolution:

> Whereas the Southern Baptist Convention Commission on the Baptist 75 million campaign has requested that the meeting of the Georgia Baptist Convention be moved back from December to November so as to precede the Baptist 75 million campaign, etc., Be it Resolved that this Board agrees to the chance 'but urges

2*Loc. cit.*
3*Loc. cit.*
4*Loc. cit.*

that the Georgia Baptist Convention authorize all of its interests and agencies to include in their published reports for the 1919 minutes all the receipts, disbursements, and records of work done in the balance of the month of November, so as to preserve the order of our fiscal year and actually close all records and books on November 30.[5]

Another resolution adopted at the same meeting said:

Whereas the information has reached us that there is a probability of the Southern Baptist Convention Commission on the Baptist 75 million campaign making a request that there be no State Mission campaign this Fall, and,
Whereas to accede to such a request would upset all our plans for the year's work within the state and place in jeopardy our state interest and to this extent handicap our participation in the Baptist 75 million campaign,
Be it Resolved, that the Mission Board of the Georgia Baptist Convention cannot accede to such a request but must press the usual campaign for the state work, in order to meet the heavy obligations already assumed.[6]

The Executive Committee resolved further that:

Whereas, the Southern Baptist Convention Commission on the Baptist 75 million campaign has solicited the co-operation and support of this Board in putting on the program in Georgia to the extent of the employment of several special helpers, . . . and the service of such of our regular forces which may be available consistent with the duties already upon them,
Be it Resolved: That the Mission Board of the Georgia Baptist Convention hereby authorizes and empowers the Executive Committee to co-operate with the Baptist 75 million campaign so far as in their judgment seems wise and to provide such extra helpers, salary and expenses as they may be necessary.[7]

In the 1919 report of the Executive Committee on campaign organization, it was stated:

In January, representing the Convention, we instructed the Committee on the State Drive for Education that

[5]*Minutes, Executive Committee, Mission Board, Georgia Baptist Convention,* June 27, 1919, p. 76.
[6]*Loc. cit.*
[7]*Ibid.,* p. 77.

they should be empowered to act in co-operation with
the Southern Baptist Convention . . .

This instruction in essence was repeated with regard to the
$75 Million Campaign begun in May, with the modification
that the organization suggested by the Southern Baptist Convention should take the place of the organization appointed
by the State Convention.[8]

The phrase which dealt with instructions to the Committee on the State Drive for Education to act in co-operation
with the Southern Baptist Convention is significant, and was
reflected in 1919 action of the Georgia Convention.

Writing concerning the inception of the $75 Million Cam-
paign, Cree said:

> The triumphant advance movement, which has thrilled
> and challenged Southern Baptists, had its inception in
> the forward-looking program presented by the Education
> Commission to the Southern Baptist Covention at Hot
> Springs, Ark., in May, 1918. In this program it was
> proposed to raise for educational enlargement and en-
> dowment $3,000,000 per year for five years, a total of
> $15,000,000. Georgia Baptists accepted the challenge of
> that great program when in the Georgia Baptist Con-
> vention at Macon in December, 1919, they voted unani-
> mously to do their part and more in the campaign for
> education.[9]

A further insight into the effectiveness of the campaign
was evident when Cree wrote:

> But other interests, the Georgia Baptist Orphans' Home,
> the Georgia Baptist Hospital, etc., stimulated by the
> movement for education and by the splendid victories
> and advance won by Georgia Baptists in all their work
> that year, proposed in their several reports to the Con-
> vention to launch campaigns for enlargement and en-
> dowment. A wise leadership persuaded the Convention
> to unify these enlargement programs in one great uni-
> fied effort. This unified program contemplated an ad-
> vance of 20 per cent per year for the current support of
> all causes and the raising of $2,500,000 in five years for
> enlargement and endowment—a program that in five
> years would total $6,900,000 for all Kingdom causes.

[8]*Minutes, Georgia Baptist Convention*, 1919, p. 62.
[9]*The Christian Index*, Dec. 25, 1920, p. 12.

> But our Lord had a higher goal and a larger task for Georgia Baptists. In co-operation with the Baptists of the South they were to undertake the greatest task to which any denomination ever set their hands.[10]

Because Cree served as director of the Campaign in Georgia, and was also Executive Secretary, his observations, written less than one year after the Campaign, are considered valid. Cree said further that there were four distinct stages of the campaign in Georgia. These he identified as: 1. The initiation of the idea and the forming of central, State and district organizations; 2. The anxiety of organization by associations; 3. Selling the idea to the people, and;[11] 4. The point of confident anticipation. Fears had been banished, and the Convention looked ". . . forward with confidence and assurance to the great drive in Victory Week, November 30-December 7." [1919.] [12]

Cree's analysis of the $75 Million Campaign in Georgia was written for the Centennial Edition of *The Christian Index,* published Dec. 25, 1920—and, incidentally, somewhat ahead of time since the first issue of *The Columbian Star,* predecessor to *The Index,* appeared initially on February 1, 1822! [13]

Cree said that the selection of good men eased the first anxiety, and that the point of concern about associational organization was relieved by the effectiveness of a workers' conference held in Atlanta the last of July, 1919.[14] Cree and others attributed much of the success of the Campaign, in terms of acceptance, to the fact that George W. Truett and L. R. Scarborough made a speaking tour through Georgia in in September, 1919. On Sunday, Sept. 26, Truett spoke to 3,000 people in the city of Rome, and Scarborough to 2,500 in Gainesville, and that night they both spoke at a meeting in the Convention hall in Atlanta, attended by 6,000 people. Meetings were held on the Truett-Scarborough tour at

[10]*Loc. cit.*

[11]*The Christian Index,* Dec. 25, 1925, p. 12.

[12]*Ibid.,* p. 31.

[13]James Adams Lester, "A History of *The Christian Index,* 1822-1954," [Unpublished Master's Thesis 1955], p. 8.

[14]*Index,* Dec. 25, 1922, p. 12.

Columbus, Waycross, Valdosta, Savannah, Augusta, Macon, Cordele and Albany.[15]

The quota assigned to Georgia was $7,500,000. About $10,000,000 was pledged. The campaign period was August-December, 1919, and Victory Week was Nov. 30-Dec. 7, 1919.[16] The final figure for Georgia contributions was to be $5,236,120.88. This was from May 1, 1919 to Dec. 5, 1924.[17]

Louie D. Newton, Director of Publicity for the campaign in Georgia said:

> A program of promotion was launched in the summer of 1919 which included every media of communication available—daily and weekly newspapers, circulars, billboards, *The Christian Index,* letters and cards, regional and associational mass meetings, with final emphasis within the local churches, seeking to reach every member of every church with this gigantic undertaking to raise the largest sum of money Baptists had ever given for the furtherance of the gospel.[18]

This was the greatest cooperative undertaking of Georgia Baptists up to this time. And, one of the remarkable aspects of the campaign in Georgia, and throughout the Southern Baptist Convention, was the speed and efficiency with which the Campaign got under way following Southern Convention approval in May, 1919. Most of the action transpired after the Southern Convention meeting, and *before* the meeting of the Georgia Baptist Convention in Macon Nov. 18-20 of that year.

Official Convention sponsorship of the project was done under authority of the Executive Committee [Mission Board] acting for the Convention and was followed through with apparent great enthusiasm upon the part of Georgia Bap-

[15]*Loc. cit.*

[For further Georgia organizational information, see, *The Christian Index,* December 25, 1920, p.p. 12, 31.]

[16]*Index,* Dec. 25, 1920, p. 13.

[17]Bruce Barbour, office manager, Executive Committee, Georgia Baptist Convention.

[18]*Encyclopedia of Southern Baptists,* [Nashville: Broadman Press, 1958.] Vol. I, p. 539.

tists. The apportionment of the Georgia share in the planned $75 million receipts and the amount collected 1920-1924 in comparison with amounts collected the previous four years, 1916-1919, are indicated in the tables below. Prepared by Ragsdale, at that time recording secretary of the Convention, the information is taken from his *Story of Georgia Baptists.*

For Foreign Missions, Home Missions, and other South-wide Objects, 50%.		$3,750,000
For Georgia Interests, 50% as follows:		
State Missions $1,000,000		
Orphans' Home	500,000	
Hospital	400,000	1,900,000
Mercer University	925,000	
Bessie Tift College	370,000	
Locust Grove Institute	67,500	
Norman Institute	47,000	
Brewton-Parker Institute	47,000	
Gibson-Mercer Academy	37,000	
Hearn Academy	37,000	
Piedmont Institute	36,599	
Chattahoochee High School ..	5,500	
Shorter College	185,000	
Mary P. Willingham School ..	67,500	
Ministerial Education	25.00	1,850,000
		$7,500,000

The report of Secretary Cree to the Convention in 1924 gave, by way of comparison, a summary of receipts for the five years preceding and the five years including the 75-Million Campaign which was as follows:

Receipts	1916-19	1920-24
State Missions ....$	383,281.95	$ 615,552.08
Home Missions	265,934.81	721,549.62
Foreign Missions	406,677.56	1,170,035.55
Orphans' Home	211,588.46	307,771.43
Hospital	119,879.36	246,213.42
Ministerial Relief	42,025.16	153,890.35
Schools and Colleges	416,037.00	1,343,958.67
Ministerial Education ...	54,275.94	57,646.40
Campaign Specials		320,156.41
Miscellaneous	48,317.00	138,870.84

Christian Index and Book Dept.		302,336.21
Undistributed, December 24, 1924 . . .		17,110.94
Total $1,948,017.24		$5,395,091.92[19]

INDEX PURCHASE AUTHORIZED

Another significant action in 1919 was Convention author-ization to purchase *The Christian Index*. The motion, offered by W. H. Major, said:

> Whereas, It is the sense of this Convention that *The Christian Index* should be owned by the Georgia Baptist Convention. therefore be it
> Resolved, That the Executive Committee be authorized in its discretion to negotiate a purchase of *The Christian Index*.[20]

The 1914 Convention had rejected an offer by Graham, submitted for the Index Publishing Company. No real effort to secure the paper by the Convention was made from that time until 1919.

The June, 1919, meeting of the Executive Committee had been occupied largely with plans for the $75 Million Cam-paign. When the Executive Committee met in September, 1919, the matter of purchase of *The Index* was a major item of business. The Committee at that meeting passed a resolution stating that it was of the opinion that Convention ownership of *The Index* was desirable. A Committee was appointed to confer with the editor, B. J. W. Graham.[21] Earlier, in 1916, T. P. Bell, with whom Graham had been associated, had told the *Index* Advisory committee that he could no longer continue as editor due to failing health. At that time, Graham had assumed full editorial control.[22] Graham was, therefore, the determining factor in 1919, rather than the larger group involved in 1914, for which group

[19]B. D. Ragsdale, *Story of Georgia Baptists*, Vol. III, [Atlanta: The Execu-tive Committee of Georgia Baptist Convention, 1938], p. 142; *Minutes, Georgia Baptist Convention*, 1919, p. 134.

[20]*Minutes, Georgia Baptist Convention*, 1919, p. 14.

[21]*Ibid.*, p. 63.

[22]Lester, p. 96.

Graham was the spokesman. Thus it was to Graham that the committee turned with a resolution stating:

> Resolved, that Committee, Brethren Weaver, Burnette, R. F. Willingham and B. E. Willingham, be requested to say to Dr. Graham that the Executive Committee is willing to recommend that the Convention purchase the *Christian Index* for $50,000, provided that a satisfactory adjustment to be made as to subscriptions from August 1, 1919 until the turning over of the paper to the Convention.[23]

The Committee reported that:

> Further conference has been had by Dr. Graham and the Chairman of the Committee, but no proposition has yet been agreed upon for recommendation. The Committee, therefore, reports these actions and findings to the Convention as information, with suggestion that if the Convention itself can purchase on a satisfactory basis, it is desirable to do so.[24]

Therefore, in the report of the Executive Committee [of the State Mission Board] to the Convention in November, 1919, the matter was placed back into the hands of the Convention, which body simply referred the matter back to the Executive Committee to confer with Graham.

Sometime between the end of the Convention, and the end of the year 1919, *The Index* was sold to the Convention, but not the Index Printing Company. "On January 1, 1920, The Index Printing Company sold *The Christian Index* to the Executive Committee of the Georgia Baptist Convention, the present owner." [25]

The minutes of the Executive Committee for March 18-19, 1920 indicated that $40,000 was paid for *The Index;* and the book department cost $4,312.99 at invoice price.[26]

Cree's report in 1920 gave cost of the book department as $4,812.99.[27] For the first time since 1861, when the paper had been sold to Samuel Boykin and Rev. C. M. Irwin of

[23]*Minutes, Georgia Baptist Convention,* 1919, p. 63.
[24]*Loc. cit.*
[25]*The Christian Index,* Dec. 25, 1920, p. 5.
[26]Minutes, Executive Committee, Mission Board, Georgia Baptist Convention, March 18, 19, 1920, p. 112.
[27]*Minutes, Georgia Baptist Convention,* 1920, p. 68.

Albany, for $2,200, the paper was back in the hands of the Convention.[28] Agitation to sell the paper had been strong for several years prior to its sale, and at the 1861 session of the Convention in Athens, that body instructed *The Index* committee to:

> . . . effect a sale of the *Index* with as little delay as possible, including all the outstanding dues and every other appendage connected with it; provided, that a suitable purchaser can be found who will pay a fair price and continue its publication in Georgia; [and that] proceeds of the paper [sale] be invested in a permanent fund, to be called the *Index* fund, the interest of which shall be used for missionary purposes, or aid in defraying the incidental expenses of this body.[29]

The resolution was not unanimous.[30]

After nearly 60 years, *The Index* was again the property of the Convention's Executive Committee. The transfer of the paper involved, as indicated, the expenditure of $40,000 for the paper, with a mailing list of 22,000 subscribers. Graham had offered to sell the paper, not including the printing company, to the Convention for $50,000. The counter offer of $40,000 by the Executive Committee was accepted.[31]

Graham said in *The Index* for December 25, 1919 that he sold the paper because ". . . of a conviction that the paper will become more useful to the denomination in the promotion of its enterprises." [32] This was apparently the case, because at the time of the sale, the Index Printing Company was an apparent successful financial venture. [q.v.] This statement indicates further that actual sale of the paper had transpired prior to that date. In 1920, reporting on purchase of the paper to the Convention, the editor said that:

> Of the 22,000 subscriptions at the time the paper was purchased, we have had to discontinue above 5,000. These were delinquent for two years and more, . . .
> It is a minimum estimate that we now have 11,000 sub-

[28]Lester, p. 59, quoting *The Christian Index*, Dec. 25, 1920, p. 4.
[29]*Ibid.*, p. 59.
[30]*Loc. cit.*
[31]*Ibid.*, p. 101.
[32]*Loc. cit.*

scribers in arrears. Our records as of November 30, actually show 11,280. . . This gives us more than $22,000 now due us for subscriptions.[33]

Following the purchase by the Convention, the Executive Committee let the printing contract to a firm other than the Index Printing Company. That company later sold its machinery to an Atlanta citizen who organized the Southeastern Printing Company, which company later went into receivership.[34]

The Executive Committee [newly-created] met in January, 1920, and set up a Department of Publicity for the Convention, naming Louie D. Newton, a former professor at Mercer, and publicity director for the $75 Million Campaign in Georgia, as head of the department. The Executive Committee then decided that *The Index* would be operated, at least temporarily, as a part of the new department and named Newton as managing editor.[35]

At the March, 1920 meeting, the Executive Committee received a report that its Administration Committee had elected Newton as managing editor, and was informed that the Board of Directors and the managing editor meet each Tuesday for consultation.

> For the present we know of no better way in which to advance the work of *The Christian Index* than by this same form or organization, i.e., this Board of Directors and managing editor.
> So, with this statement of our judgment in the matter, after the experience of more than two months, we leave this matter with the Executive Committee and await its instructions.[36]

The first temporary board consisted of F. C. McConnell, W. H. Major, Henry A. Porter, Charles W. Daniel, and Arch C. Cree. The Executive Committee, in naming Newton, cited his service as state director of publicity for the $75 Mil-

---

[33]*Minutes, Georgia Baptist Convention*, 1920, p. 69.

[34]Lester, p. 102.

[35]*Loc. cit.*, quoting *The Christian Index*, Jan. 8. 1920.

[36]Minutes, Executive Committee, Mission Board, Georgia Baptist Convention, March 18-19, 1920, p. 112.

lion Campaign as proof of his ability to handle the position of superintendent of publicity.[37]

The Convention in 1910, upon a motion of L. R. Christie, approved a plan for securing

> ". . . the services of a competent man whose duty it shall be to report to the press the proceedings of our next annual meeting . . ." [allowing] ". . . the aforesaid press representative . . . the privilege of employing such clerical assistance as may be necessary . . . and that his compensation be provided by the Board, . . ." [38]

The creation of a Department of Publicity in 1920, therefore, had its roots for authorization in the 1910 Convention.

SHORTER GIVEN RIGHT TO CAMPAIGN FUNDS

One interesting aspect of the $75 Million Campaign in Georgia dealt with Shorter College. In 1914, the Board of Education made a special recommendation concerning the withdrawal of Shorter from the Mercer system at Shorter's request.[39] Five years later, with the $75 Million Campaign in full swing, Shorter, through the Education Board, asked for admission to the Mercer system again.[40] At the same time, a special committee had been named at the Convention to deal with alleged unorthodox teachings at Shorter and on the part of Dr. A. W. Van Hoose, president. Shorter's orthodoxy was vindicated, but the special Committee took exception to the part of the Education Board's report dealing with Shorter's readmission.[41]

Outcome of the situation was that while Shorter was not then readmitted into the Mercer system, it did receive a guarantee of Campaign funds.

Shorter had made a strong plea to get into organic line evidently to participate in the Campaign contributions. It

[37]Lester, p. 102, quoting *The Christian Index,* Jan. 8, 1920.
[38]*Minutes, Georgia Baptist Convention,* 1910, p. 49.
[39]*Minutes, Georgia Baptist Convention,* 1914, p. 23.
[40]*Minutes, Georgia Baptist Convention,* 1919, p. 35.
[41]*Loc. cit.*
[42]*Ibid.,* p.p. 35, 36.

was decided finally, after lengthy discussion that since Shorter

> ... has sought earnestly to co-operate with the Convention and to that end she is entitled to participate in the $75-Million Campaign.
> We further find that Shorter College shall receive ten per cent of the funds of said Campaign as designated by the majority report of the Education Board.
> Provided, however, that such funds as may be allotted to Shorter College shall be considered and used only as endowment and that the same shall be held and invested by the holding commission of the Baptist Convention of the State of Georgia, and the proceeds only of the investments shall be paid to the trustees of Shorter College.[42]

Thus, the institution, though not recommended for re-admission to the Mercer system, was recommended to participate in its share of campaign funds on a basis as if it were owned by the Convention. The difficulty had arisen, apparently, with a resolution from the Mercer Association concerning orthodoxy, and as an apparent result of this, though the allegations were dismissed, the Committee reporting on the Education Board report felt that since the $75 Million Campaign was of paramount interest, and nothing must stand in its way, that Shorter should not come into the system.[41]

The agreement proposed for assumption of control of Shorter College by the Convention, declared that the college was:

> ... given, owned and operated by Baptists, and so designated by its founder, [and was] desirous of entering into a closer relationship with the Georgia Baptist Convention, that it may have the prestige, power, and influence of said Convention; . . .[44]

The problem at Shorter really was not with the president or questions of orthodoxy. This was secondary to the fact that the college had two types of trustees; members elected for life and members selected for a specified term. Under

[43]*Ibid.*, p. 35.
[44]*Ibid.*, p.p. 86, 87.

the 1919 proposal, the life members would have no successors, and the remaining members would have terms arranged to expire with provision for the Convention naming new trustees upon expiration of the terms of those elected with limitations.[45] There were personality conflicts apparent also.[46]

The report of the Special Committee, except that section dealing with Van Hoose, was tabled.[47]

After the report of the Special Committee was tabled until 1920, the Convention, upon Cree's recommendation, approved ". . . after spirited discussion . . ." making provision to hold funds for Shorter until the 1920 Convention took action.[48] Further, the Convention did direct that credit toward church and association quotas in the $75 Million Campaign, be made for gifts to Shorter.[49]

The Convention agreed in 1920 to a report by the Special Committee on Shorter which approved Shorter's participation in campaign funds as outlined in the 1919 Education Board report.[50] Shorter, after conference with the committee, withdrew, without prejudice, the request for entry into the Mercer system.[51]

Shorter's request in 1919 caused, evidently, some considerable disagreement within the Convention.

Efforts to establish a school of medicine at Georgia Baptist Hospital were left in the hands of hospital trustees ". . . to work out the details and project such a movement when they see that such a movement is practicable and wise." [52] Further, the Committee dealing with the report of the hospital trustees said:

> We heartily approve the suggestions of the report that a
> program be perfected looking to the establishment of

[45]*Ibid.*, p. 87.
[46]*Ibid.*, p. 10.
[47]*Ibid.*, p.p. 34, 36.
[48]*Ibid.*, p.p. 36, 37.
[49]*Loc. cit.*
[50]*Minutes, Georgia Baptist Convention*, 1920, p. 10.
[51]*Ibid.*, p. 11.
[52]*Minutes, Georgia Baptist Convention*, 1919, pp. 20, 21.

other hospitals in our large centers as early as means
with wisdom will permit.[53]

An air of growth and expansion prevailed. There was
optimism, with the Campaign pledges coming in well, that
Georgia Baptists would grow even more rapidly. Thus, the
hospital trustees were looking toward a system of hospitals
in the state, which idea was not forgotten for some years,
and the establishment of a medical college. The apparent
ease with which the Convention approved purchase of *The
Christian Index* in 1919 perhaps was related to the "new
prosperity" felt by Georgia Baptists.

The Convention even went on record "respectfully" requesting churches to consider raising salaries of pastors;
a Convention first.[54]

When the matter of the Inter-Church World Movement
arose, the Convention spoke firmly, calling upon Georgia
Baptists ". . . to refrain from aiding the Inter-Church World
Movement, or any other so called union movement, that
would sacrifice doctrine and practice as held by us." [55]

NEW CONSTITUTION ADOPTED

A final step taken by the Convention in 1919, with permanent consequences, was when the body approved a new
Constitution and By-Laws, simplifying the organizational
structure of the Convention, and doing away with what had
become an unwieldy set of By-Laws.

At a meeting of the Executive Committee [First] early in
1919, the secretary of the Education Board called attention
to the ". . . need for revision of the organic law of the
Convention." The Executive Committee then asked representatives of the Mission Board, the Education Board, the
Committee on Co-operation, the Holding Commission, the
Committee of Five, The Orphans' Home, Georgia Baptist

[53]*Loc. cit.*
[54]*Ibid.*, p. 37.
[55]*Ibid.*, p. 38.

408 / A History of The Georgia Baptist Convention

Hospital, Mercer University, Bessie Tift college and two men at large to work with the Executive Committee:

> ... to review with reference to revision the organic law and plan of work of the Convention. This enlarged Committee appointed a sub-committee, which drafted a short and simple constitution and by-laws. This was in turn referred with more or less formality to the different boards and committees affected and some suggestions gathered from them have been embodied in the proposed law. The whole was passed upon and approved by the Executive Committee at its last meeting before the Convention. It is herewith submitted with recommendation that the Convention adopt the same.[56]

This is the report of the [First] Executive Committee to the Convention:

"The Convention reviewed the report of the Executive Committee, and acted." Review of the . . . report was submitted. Concerning the constitution by R. L. Baker

> After minor points of explanation relative to the new Constitution proposed the vote was as follows:
> On adoption of the proposed new Constitution and the name was approved with objection.
> On adoption of the proposed new By-Laws and the same was approved without objection.
> On the adoption of the report submitted by R. L. Baker which was approved as below, the same carrying adoption of the full report of the Executive Committee. 'We, the Committee to review the report of the Executive Committee do recommend the adoption of the report as printed, with amendment to end of Article Six, Section one; 'No one connected in any way with any institution fostered by the Convention shall be eligible to membership on this committee.[57]

The Constitution and By-Law approved by the 1919 Convention follow.

CONSTITUTION OF THE
BAPTIST CONVENTION OF THE
STATE OF GEORGIA

I. Name and Object

Section 1. The name of this body shall be the Baptist Convention of the State of Georgia.

[56]*Ibid.*, p. 64.
[57]*Ibid.*, p.p. 13, 14.

Section 2. The object of this Convention shall be to furnish a medium of co-operation for the Baptist churches of Georgia in their divinely commissioned work of missions, education, and benevolence.

II. Membership

Section 1. This body shall be composed of messengers from regular Baptist Churches and Associations, in the harmony and co-operation with the work and purpose of this Convention.

Section 2. Each Church shall be entitled to two messengers and one additional messenger for each $50.00 contributed to the funds of the Convention; but in no case shall any Church be entitled to more than eight messengers.

Section 3. Each Association shall be entitled to five messengers.

III. Meetings

Section 1. The Convention shall meet at least once each year, the time and place to be fixed either by the Convention or the Executive Committee.

IV. Powers

Section 1. This Convention shall never attempt to exercise authority over any Church, but shall always cheerfully recognize and uphold the sovereignty under Christ of the Churches.

Section 2. All funds entrusted to the Convention or to any of its boards or agents, shall be strictly applied according to the expressed will and direction of the donors.

V. Officers

Section 1. The officers of this Convention shall be a President, four Vice-Presidents, a Secretary, and a Treasurer, who shall be elected by ballot at each annual meeting, and who shall hold their offices until their successors are elected. Their duty shall be those usually discharged by such officers.

VI. Boards and Commissions

Section 1. An Executive Committee of this Convention shall be chosen by the Convention, and shall consist of the officers of the Convention ex-officio and forty-five members from the State at large, one-third of whom shall be elected to hold office for one year, one-third for two years and one-third for three years. The vacancies, as the terms expire, shall be filled for terms of three years.

[Amendment: No one connected in any way with any institution fostered by the Convention shall be eligible to membership on this Committee.]

Section 2. The Executive Committee [or Board] shall have charge and control, except when otherwise directed by the Convention, of all work of the Convention, including Missions, Education, and Benevolences, in the interim between sessions of the Convention. No member of the Executive Committee shall have any official connection with any of the institutions whose work it fosters.

Section 3. The Convention shall appoint a Holding Commission, consisting of seven members, which shall hold in trust and manage all the properties, annuities, trusts, and invested funds of the Convention and of the different institutions fostered by the Convention, guarding well any legal points involved in the terms of bequests or special donations, making an itemized statement of all the property it holds for each institution, how it is invested, and what sums it has paid to each during the year. No member of the Holding Commission shall have any official connection with any of the institutions whose property it holds.

VII. Amendments

Section 1. This constitution may be amended at any regular session by the vote of two-thirds of the messengers present and voting at the time; provided, that no amendment shall be made later than the second day of the Convention, and further, that notice of the proposed change has been given in writing to the Convention or in the state paper ninety days before its meeting.

BY-LAWS

Section 1. At each annual meeting of this Convention, the President shall appoint a committee of ten, whose duty it shall be to nominate to the Convention all Boards, Commissions and Committees chosen by the Convention.

Section 2. All Boards, Commissions and Committees of the Convention shall cause to be embraced in their reports of finance the usual 'Balance Sheet', accompanied by an audit, and a budget of estimated income and expenditure for the ensuing year.

Section 3. The Boards and other like bodies belonging to the Convention and under its control shall have their Treasurers placed under bond. Every Auditing Committee of a Treasurer's account shall report as to the validity of his bond.

Section 4. No recommendation shall ever be embodied in any reports made to this Convention by any agent, secretary, or other officer of any Board or like body, which, if received and adopted, will modify or amend any item of the Constitution, By-Laws, or Standing Resolutions of the Convention.

Section 5. The Executive Committee is directed in the beginning of each Convention year to make a definite agreement with the different Boards and interests for which it collects money, as to what amount it shall charge each of these Boards and interests for collecting and forwarding its money.

Section 6. It shall be the duty of the Committee on Order of Business to provide for the consideration of any proposed amendment to the Constitution.

Section 7. These By-Laws may be altered at any annual meeting by a majority vote of the members present and voting, notice of the proposed change having been given in the state paper at least thirty days before the Convention.[58]

Because of the new Constitution, the Holding Commission of the Convention, would become ". . . the custodian and manager of the properties and endowments of the Convention's schools and colleges, thus unifying their fiscal control, . . ." the following resolution was approved.

> . . . That this Convention instruct its Executive Board to go thoroughly into the question of creating the office of chancellor of our system of Schools and Colleges during the coming year and to bring a recommendation regarding the same to the 1920 session of this Convention.[59]

The Convention instructed Cree to call a meeting of the new Executive Committee in the First Baptist Church in Atlanta, December 18, 1919, marking the first and historic organizational meeting of this body.[60]

The resolution on a chancellor was almost inevitable with the emphasis which had been placed upon Christian education during the preceding ten years among Georgia Baptists.

[58]*Ibid.*, p.p. 64-66.
[59]*Ibid.*, p. 40.
[60]*Loc. cit.*

The Committee of Five, when first appointed, was instructed to pay the debts on all institutions fostered by the
Georgia Baptist Convention. These debts, at the time,
amounted to $524,880.05,[61]

> . . . but, because of interest accruing since then, and
> because of new debts incurred by some of these insti-
> tutions, as well as several old debts that were not at
> first reported to the Convention, but were afterwards
> added, the amount necessary to pay all the debts has
> grown to be $676,339.40, which includes our expense
> account.
> We are glad to report that all the debts on all the in-
> stitutions have been paid to the creditors in each case
> by the Committee of Five, or by the brethren who had
> them in charge, except a balance on the debt of Mercer
> University, but the evidence of all debts paid are held
> by Brother Cree, our Treasurer, and the Convention
> now owns them.
> The following institutions report to us that they are in
> this manner now entirely free from debt: Bessie Tift
> College, Gibson-Mercer Academy, Hearn Academy,
> Hiawassee Academy, Brewton-Parker Academy, Norman
> Park Institute, Locust Grove Institute, Blairsville Insti-
> tute, Orphans' Home, State Board of Missions, Georgia
> Baptist Hospital, Ministerial Education Fund, Foreign
> Mission Fund and Home Mission Fund.

The total amount paid on all of these debts since the beginning of the campaign was $554,284.38.

> The following institutions freed themselves from debt
> during the campaign, by their own wise management:
> State Board of Missions, Orphans' Home, Ministerial
> Education Fund, Foreign and Home Mission Fund,
> while the others were assisted by the Committee of Five.
> The debt on Mercer University was $240,000.00. This
> was made up of $130,000.00 lost endowment, and $110,-
> 000.00 money borrowed from the banks. We have
> paid in Liberty Loan Bonds, and other securities,
> $72,945.18 on the endowment that was lost, which in-
> cludes the $21,822 now in the hands of Dr. Yates,
> ready to be turned over, leaving a balance of $57,054.82,
> still due to restore that fund. We have also paid to
> the banks $45,000 cash on these notes, and all interest
> up to date, leaving $65,000 still due the banks, on the

[61]*Ibid.*, p. 67.

principal of the notes, so that it will take $122,054.82 to pay both debts.[62]

Continuing the report of its stewardship in eliminating debts on Convention institutions, Boards and programs, the Committee of Five reported that:

> The Georgia Council representing the $75-million Campaign of Southern Baptist Convention, formally requested us to discontinue the campaign to raise the funds to pay the Mercer debt, on the ground that this matter was fully provided for in the $75-Million campaign.
> The Committee of Five agreed to this because we did not think it wise to have two organizations in the state at work on the same thing at the same time, and this is why the Committee had made no further efforts to complete the campaign for Mercer University. The unpaid subscriptions and pledges in the hands of the Secretary amounted in face value to $57,246.13, subject to various kind of loss and shrinkage. The Committee has directed its Secretary to turn over to the authorities in charge of the 75-million campaign in Georgia all the subscriptions and pledges in his hands that they may collect them and apply the money realized. As the donors have directed, these brethren having agreed to collect those subscriptions or to pay the amount of them, and the agreement being that all these subscriptions will count on the 75-million Campaign, and your Committee, believing that this would be the best solution of the matter.
> The total amount of the expenses of the Committee of Five, during the four years of its existence, is $19,675.98.[63]

The Committee of Five then made the following recommendations which were approved by the Convention.

> First, That the Holding Committee of Seven be instructed to proceed at once to acquire the title to all property . . . of all institutions, etc.
> Second, That the Board of Missions of the Georgia Baptist Convention, be directed to assume the balance of the debts now due the banks on the Mercer University notes, to wit, $65,000, or whatever sum is necessary to pay the notes . . .

[62]*Loc. cit.*
[63]*Ibid.*, p.p. 67, 68.

This will free Mercer University of debt so it can at once put the title of its property in the Committee of Seven.

> Third, That the State Board of Missions and the Georgia Council of the Southern Baptist Convention be directed to pay this indebtedness so assumed, and the balance of $57,054.82 due to restore the endowment fund of Mercer University . . .
> Fourth, As the general financial interests of our institutions . . . have been amply provided for . . . we recommend that the Committee of Five be discharged.[64]

Thus, requesting its own end, the Committee of Five had in four years written an almost unparalleled record of accomplishment in assisting the Convention in debt elimination, and marked the only time, really, that the Convention, with the exception of Mercer University, could report itself free of debt. With only one year out of five in the $75 Million Campaign, and the four-year record of this committee, Georgia Baptists were probably at their highest point of enthusiasm in Convention history up to this time.

Contained in the report of the Education Board was the background for the end of the school at Draketown in which local authorities at Draketown had proposed to purchase the equity of the Home Mission Board and secure the property for a local public common and high school. This proposition was accepted, and the Home Board expected the Convention to petition it for equity thus recovered to be used in the development of a strong school in northwest Georgia, with Draketown as a possibility.[65]

SCHOOL OF CHRISTIANITY ESTABLISHED

Mercer, growing following the end of World War I, had at the suggestion of President Rufus Weaver set up the School of Christianity, the School of Commerce, and a School of Journalism had been authorized by the trustees to begin

[64]*Ibid.*, p.p. 68, 69.
[65]*Ibid.*, p. 76.

with the winter term, 1919.[66] Further, there were reported 1,221 students in Georgia Baptist high schools in 1919.[67]

In a summary statement dealing with the Education Board being succeeded by the Education Commission it was indicated as the sentiment of Georgia Baptists that:

> The success of the combined movement has impressed all with the fact that the hope of Convention effort in Education as well as that of the Institutions is bound up with the original proposition that the Convention, through its Education Board, should secure the 'ownership or control of recognized Baptist schools.'[68]

As the shift in organization structure was being made, the Education Board observed:

> This year the 75-Million campaign brings us to a period in which it may be wise for our denominational organization and methods to be changed.
> First, the By-Laws should require that all the institutions in the future shall bring annual audits and budgets with their reports. Second, with the Executive Committee absorbing the functions of the Committee on Co-operation, . . .
> the Committee should include enough members representing various interests fairly to balance it, . . .
> Third, the functions of the Education Board will naturally go over into the Executive Committee.
> The duties and responsibilities of this Board [Education] is embodied in its fundamental laws, adopted in 1907 and confirmed in 1917, are so important that it should be understood that in its work attending to the business between sessions of the Convention, the Executive Committee be clothed with all the rights and duties now pertaining to the Education Board.[69]

During this year of achievement upon the part of Georgia Baptists, organizational life was being strengthened. The Orphans' Home reported an enrolment of 300, with 86 received during 1919, and 43 being sent out;[70] and the

---

[66]*Ibid.,* p. 82.

[67]*Ibid.,* p. 80.

[68]*Ibid.,* p. 85.

[69]*Ibid.,* p.p. 93, 94.

[Note: A rather complete history of the Education Board; its work and interests may be found in the 1919 Convention Minutes, p.p. 73-95.]

[70]*Ibid.,* p. 105.

women of the state, measuring their growth in terms of financial giving, reported total contributions of $152,083.42, an increase of $42,083.42 over their goal for the year.[71] The Department of Evangelism said that its Mid-Summer Evangelistic Campaign was becoming an annual feature, and during 1919 they had secured the services of nine preachers ". . . with evangelistic talent. . . ." [72] In 1917, the Executive Committee of the Mission Board had purchased two tents, one for $430.00 and one for $425.00 for a tent mission ministry.[73]

Baptists' ministry to soldiers had diminished as the war had ended and demobilization was in effect, until the work was confined to Camp Gordon, located in the Chamblee, Georgia area, with headquarters for the work at the Chamblee church, which was located in the heart of the camp.[74]

Because Frank Leavell had been asked by the Mission Board to lead in the ". . . experiment in denominational instruction, being made in Mercer University and Bessie Tift College, it was necessary to secure a competent associate for the B. Y. P. U. work, . . ." in the person of H. Lewis Batts, then at Brewton-Parker Institute.[75] The reference to Leavell referred to an arrangement whereby Mercer and Tift offered courses in denominational life for credit during 1919.

The planned denominational instruction at Mercer and Tift deserves further explanation. Under the heading "Denominational Instruction" in the Board of Missions report, the plan was explained.

> For some years, our Baptist people have been made to feel that our Schools and Colleges have not gone as far as they should in definite denominational instruction. With a view to making an experiment in distinctive Denominational Instruction your Mission Board, under the approval of this Convention and with the hearty

[71]*Ibid.*, p. 122.

[72]*Ibid.*, p. 119.

[73]Minutes, Executive Committee, Mission Board, Georgia Baptist Convention, July 6, 1917, p. 45; Sept. 13, 1917.

[74]*Minutes, Georgia Baptist Convention,* 1919, p. 123.

[75]*Ibid.*, p. 121.

co-operation of our education leaders, has effected an
arrangement whereby definite courses covering in detail
Baptist organization and operation is now being offered
to the students of Mercer University and Bessie Tift
College without cost of the schools. The principal
course in this program as outlined in the plan agreed
upon is a series of studies, which shall later be developed into a textbook, covering the following points:
[1] Define a Baptist, [2] A Baptist Church, organization
and operation, demonstration in classroom, [3] A
Baptist association, organization and operation, demonstration of the activities both of the Association and
the Executive Committee, [4] A Baptist State Convention, organization and operation, with all of its interests, institutions, and activities, [5] the Southern
Baptist Convention, organization and operation, with
all of its Boards, institutions, and activities . . .
Incidental to, but woven in throughout, the funda-
mentals of Baptist belief, polity and practice will be
taught and drilled. With all of the Baptist boys and
girls in our Baptist Schools and Colleges required to
take such a course of study, we would have returning
from these institutions to our churches each year a
splendid band of thoroughly intelligent and truly
trained workers, and within a single generation all of
our denominational interests and activities would receive such a competent leadership as would carry us
forward to a glorious realization of our brightest
dreams and highest aims.[76]

EXPERIMENT SHORT-LIVED

The classroom experiment was short-lived. It was not
until 1961 that a volume entitled *The Witness and Work of
Georgia Baptists,* with P. Harris Anderson, of Mercer University, as general editor, appeared. This volume is the nearest
work in line with the 1919 outline which had appeared,
and was prepared for use at the Mercer University Extension
Centers, operated by Mercer, and supported by the Georgia
Baptist Convention. This 140-page volume, had it been used
as the Convention indicated earlier for such a work, would
have filled the need which was indicated.

The report of the Mission Board, prepared prior to the

[76]*Ibid.,* p.p. 131, 132.

Constitutional change, recommended that December be designated as Stewardship Month, recognizing that some type of continued emphasis would be needed to sustain the interest in and support of the $75 Million Campaign.[77] Thus, in a year of activity without parallel, the Convention, in the closing period of the year, at the annual session, could agree with the Mission Board in the report which declared that:

> Within the past six months Southern Baptists have been stirred to the depths and moved mightily by the greatest and most challenging program to which any denomination has ever set its hand, the Baptist 75 Million campaign.
> This soul-stirring movement was born of God, fired by faith and prayer, kindled in the greatest gathering of Baptists in the history of the world, fanned by a series of the most remarkably spiritual conferences in the knowledge and experience of our leaders and is now sweeping through the hearts of our great Southern Baptist hosts like a wild fire blazing its way through a dry stubble field, consuming all before.[78]

The quota breakdown for Georgia, not in the information which Ragsdale listed [p. 399] included: Foreign Missions, $1,900,795; Home Missions $1,172,205; State Missions $1,000,000; Education $1,850,000; South-wide schools $300,-000; Ministerial Relief $250,000; Orphans' Home $500,000; Hospital $400,000; Balance Debt-Paying Campaign, $127,-000; for a total for five years of $7,500,000.[79]

Georgia leaders deserved recognition. They included: F. C. McConnell, SBC Campaign Commissioner; Arch C. Cree, Director; Ely R. Callaway, Associate Director; Mrs. Kate C. Wakefield, W. B. M. U. Director; Louie D. Newton, Publicity Director; John W. Jenkins, Organization Director; W. H. Major, Speakers' Director. There was an advisory committee, including the above and Rufus M. Weaver, John G. Harrison, B. J. W. Graham, J. M. Long, T. S. Scoggins, and Mrs. W. J. Neel.[80]

[77]*Ibid.*, p. 133.
[78]*Loc. cit.*
[79]*Ibid.*, p. 134.
[80]*Loc. cit.*

Final emphasis upon the Campaign in 1919 was in a postscript to the Minutes for that year which stated: "Before the minutes went to print, the great Victory was won, and the pledges of Georgia Baptists totaled TEN MILLION DOLLARS." [81]

The financially-troubled Tabernacle Baptist Church in Atlanta, struggling really since Broughton's departure in 1912 as pastor, was given $10,000 by the Executive Committee [First] to help pay the church's indebtedness. Campaign headquarters were located at the Tabernacle church.[82]

One of the more interesting features of an action of the Executive Committee in 1919 was the presentation by that committee of $100 in gold on behalf of Georgia Baptists to Miss Nell Wheeler, a secretary for the Mission Board, upon the occasion of her marriage to Buren C. Smith, long-time servant in the Sunday School department and as office secretary for the Executive Committee of the Convention.[83]

Georgia Baptists in 1919 were at a high water mark. Their past combined with the present to project for the future a Convention fully organized, working in the areas of Missions, Education and Benevolences with a zeal which they had not exhibited for many years. They moved therefore into the decade of the 1920's, the years of great Foreign Mission endeavor,—and years which were to feature a Depression which curtailed activities from this peak and brought some activities to a halt. Faith and a strong belief in their mission kept Georgia Baptists operating during some of the years during the decade ahead.

The strength of Baptists was summarized well in a significant emphasis made by George W. Andrews in the Sunday School report. It was that the development of Sunday School work during its history had

[81]*Ibid.*, p. 135.

[82]Minutes, Executive Committee, Mission Board, Georgia Baptist Convention, June 27, 1919, p. 77.

[83]Minutes, Executive Committee, Mission Board, Georgia Baptist Convention, July 4, 1919, p. 79.

. . . been projected and maintained strictly on a denominational basis [and] has demonstrated beyond all question the correctness of our position, which is, THAT NO ORGANIZATION, WE CARE NOT BY WHAT NAME IT COMES OR WHAT CLOAK IT WEARS, CAN DO FOR BAPTISTS WHAT BAPTISTS CAN DO FOR THEMSELVES. We stand or fall by this proposition. We believe it to be as secure as the eternal hills, and the ultimate outcome certain. If the Baptists survive the clamor for church union by those who have no denominational conscience, whose religious propaganda would associate in one fellowship for services in the King's business all who declare themselves Christians, regardless of their practices and doctrines, which is contrary to the plain teaching of God's book, THEY MUST STICK TOGETHER, THEY MUST BE LOYAL AND TRUE TO THEIR OWN ORGANIZATION. Inter-denominational co-operation in any line of church activity never has, and never will stimulate Baptist life.[84]

This concept that Baptists could do for themselves that which was wise and useful was borne out abundantly in the new wave of enthusiasm which accompanied the $75 Million Campaign.

[84]*Minutes, Georgia Baptist Convention,* 1919, p. 136.

CHAPTER 16

Surge of Enthusiasm

For the year 1920, the best year of the $75 Million Campaign, the Georgia Baptist Convention reported contributions of $1,774,399.74, [apparently through October 31] a million dollars "better than the best efforts heretofore." [1] During that year, Woman's Missionary Union had contributed $458,818.79, also a record. [2] And, the Baptist Young People's Union, by then officially a part of the Southern Baptist Convention's program of promotion, boasted 1,226 unions, with 52 of the 94 associations organized. [3]

"Uncle George" Andrews, long-time Sunday School secretary, had been given a purse from friends to cover the expenses of a vacation trip to Florida. [4] The Convention in session commended especially the creation of a "great book department" as a permanent feature of State Mission work. [5] The book store inventory had been purchased early in 1920 along with *The Christian Index*. [6]

The Executive Committee, like two porcupines, was trying to find its comfortable place between the Convention and the churches, in terms of responsible action. A point of order was raised concerning interpretation of the new Constitution, Article VI, Section 2, and a ruling of President

[1]*Minutes, Georgia Baptist Convention*, 1920, p. 19.
[2]*Loc. cit.*
[3]*Loc. cit.*
[4]*Ibid.*, p. 18.
[5]*Loc. cit.*
[6]*Op. cit.*

John D. Mell was ordered a part of the record. Interpretation of Article VI, Section II, Constitution, follows.

> The point of order having been raised as to whether the Executive Committee [or Board] has authority to legislate in any matter, or whether it is simply an Executive Committee to carry out the laws already enacted by the Convention, the President ruled that the Executive Committee could not in any event make any new laws, but that it could only carry out the laws given it by the Convention. In so doing, it has a wise discretion in arriving at the meaning of the Convention when it passed the laws, but it can only seek to ascertain the meaning of the Convention in each case and cannot pass any new laws itself or change any law that the Convention has passed.[7]

Further discussion concerning the Executive Committee led to defeat of two proposals; L. R. Christie proposed an amendment making the Committee to consist of 24 members. This was defeated, along with an original amendment proposed by T. C. Burrell which would make the Committee to consist of one member from each association,[8] a plan to be followed later in large measure.

Organization of the Holding Commission was reported, with Professor John G. Harrison being loaned by Mercer University as special agent to aid in securing the transfer of certain properties [not further identified.] A. W. Evans had been named chairman of the Holding Commission, and A. H. Stewart was named treasurer at a salary of $3,600 annually, with offices rented in Macon.[9] The purpose and objective of the Holding Commission was to hold title to all properties of all agencies and institutions of the Convention, and the original stipulations had included the concept that the Commission would not accept title and deed until all mortgages on properties had been satisfied and clear title to the property evident.

Of the Commission, Dowell said:

[7]*Ibid.,* p. 21.
[8]*Loc. cit.*
[9]*Ibid.,* p. 59.

As might have been anticipated, the Holding Commission was never generally popular, mainly because it was considered an encroachment upon the duties and authority of the trustees of the institutions and a reflection upon, if not an indictment of, the management of institutional finances. This explains in part the refusal of the General Education Board to give the institution help for endowment until full control of the Mercer holdings was restored to the trustees by the Convention.[10]

Dowell's own judgment of the Holding Commission, however, was that ". . . the principle and purpose underlying its creation and the service rendered by it proved of real value in restoring confidence and in establishing a policy of more careful budgeting and the avoidance of debt." [11]

Dowell's reference to the General Education Board of New York involved a request that Mercer University contemplated making to that Board for a grant of $300,000.[12] The Board had indicated that it would not extend a grant as long as the University did not hold clear title to the property.[13]

The reversionary clause in the deed to Mercer University had caused several problems. It was used as an argument earlier for removal of the university either to Atlanta or to another site in Macon.[14] Later it was a hindrance to transfer of title of Mercer property to the Holding Commission.

At the meeting of the Mercer trustees on January 26, 1920, Harrison, representing the Executive Committee of the Convention, explained the need for clear titles to all denominational property. Col. Thomas E. Ryals was then asked to explain to the mayor and council in Macon the need for the city to remove the reversionary clause.[15] This was accomplished, because at a meeting of the Mercer trustees in

[10]Spright Dowell, *A History of Mercer University*, 1833-1953 [Atlanta: Foote and Davies, Inc., 1958], p. 265.

[11]*Loc. cit.*

[12]*Ibid.*, p. 261.

[13]*Ibid.*, p. 270.

[14]*Ibid.*, p.p. 240-241.

[15]*Ibid.*, p. 261.

Atlanta, December 6, 1920, Ryals reported all of Mercer's bonds, stocks, mortgages, and notes had been transferred to the commission and that conveyance of title to the real estate was in process.[16] Action by the city of Macon was reported to the Convention at the 1920 session. The city had executed a quit-claim deed for its reversionary interest in seven acres of land.[17]

Out of a series of actions begun when the Convention established its Committee on Schools and Colleges in 1899, came the Mercer University System by 1919. It was designed to link together all Georgia Baptist educational interests at the academic level, making Mercer and Bessie Tift as the two institutions for which the other schools would serve as "feeders" providing students.[18] This system was developed into a concrete pattern during the early part of 1920, and the Education Board reported to the 1920 session that the Mercer System had been organized, with the president of Mercer University being Superintendent of Christian Education for the entire Mercer system; which title was changed later in the year to Chancellor of the Mercer University System.[19] Concerning the naming of the Mercer president to head the newly-created system, the Board said:

> This is proper and right, because it is indispensible to the efficiency of the system, and to its unification, . . . that there should be a definite head of management and responsibility. The logical person for this position is unquestionably the President of Mercer University.[20]

SIGNIFICANT EDUCATIONAL DEVELOPMENT

The reason for changing the title from superintendent to chancellor was that it was felt that the title superintendent was not ". . . a happy one, as it is not in keeping with the dignity and importance of the position, . . ." [21] Although

[16]*Ibid.*, p. 265.
[17]*Minutes, Georgia Baptist Convention,* 1920, p. 25.
[18]*Minutes, Georgia Baptist Convention,* 1919, p. 85.
[19]*Minutes, Georgia Baptist Convention,* 1920, p. 24.
[20]*Loc. cit.*
[21]*Loc. cit.*

the system was not to last long, it was a significant development in Georgia Baptist Christian education, and one which produced, in all probability, lasting results in terms of keeping the educational institutions working together with a sense of direction and unity. The Education Committee reported

> ". . . that every student in Mercer University is required to take at least one course in the school of Christianity, and that the Secondary Schools have adopted the teacher's training courses outlined by the Sunday School Board."

The committee concurred in the recommendation

> ". . . that every one of our schools should require all students to take sometime during their stay such course or courses as will enable them to have an intelligent understanding of the Bible and Christianity as we interpret it." [22]

Additional concern with the matter of religious education, this time at the level of secular schools, was evidenced in adoption by the Convention of a resolution which said:

> Whereas, the fundamental principles of our democratic form of government prohibits the teaching of religious doctrines in schools sustained by State or Federal taxation, and,
> Whereas, the State has definitely and permanently established a system of public schools, colleges and universities sustained by taxation, . . . , and,
> Whereas, the obligation of teaching religion and morality rests primarily on the churches and religious denominations.
> Therefore, be it resolved, that the Executive Committee of this Convention be, and is hereby directed, during the ensuing convention year, to investigate the feasibility and advisability of establishing a permanent system of independent denominational units for giving religious and moral instructions to the respective students at the State schools, colleges and universities; such units to be established and maintained by the respective denominations without expense to the State. [23]

[22]*Ibid.*, p. 26.
[23]*Ibid.*, p. 41.

The Executive Committee was instructed to make a study and report back to the 1921 Convention. This type of "released-time" concept of religious instruction, in the light of historic developments years later, was to prove again the foresight of Georgia Baptist leadership.

Georgia Baptists had, additionally, long envisioned establishment of a Seminary in the state. They had sought one almost from the formal beginnings of the Convention. Furthermore, in 1920, Mercer President Rufus Weaver, among others, envisioned Mercer as a great educational center of the South, and actually proposals were made to the Southern Baptist Convention offering Mercer as the focal point for such a proposed Southern Baptist University.[24]

Weaver had hopes that a seminary would be established in the Southeast, and recommended

> . . . that one member be added to the faculty of the Mercer School of Christianity and that a two-year course be offered comparable to the work being done at the Southern Baptist Theological Seminary in Louisville. He addressed a paper to the Baptists of Georgia urging the establishment of such a seminary. The suggestion was approved and he was authorized, along with some member of the Executive Committee of the University, to draft a suitable recommendation. This was done and the recommendation was adopted at the November meeting of the Board of Trustees.[25]

Thus, it was at the 1920 session of the Georgia Baptist Convention the Education Committee, in its report, said it was of the opinion that ". . . if a third theological seminary were established, it should be located in Georgia." [26]

For the first time, in 1920, the Georgia Baptist Hospital named a chaplain, John F. Eden.[27] Eden's election as chaplain for the hospital was not the only matter of concern relative to the hospital to occupy the interest of Georgia Baptists at this Atlanta session. The Holding Commission had been authorized to secure title to all property. The

---

[24]*Ibid.*, p.p. 111, 112, 119. [Background: Dowell p.p. 261, 262.]
[25]Dowell, p. 267.
[26]*Minutes, Georgia Baptist Convention,* 1920, p. 27.
[27]*Ibid.*, p. 30.

hospital wanted to build. To secure funds for construction loans, it was necessary for the hospital to retain title to the property as security. Earlier, the hospital had made an apparent poor investment in some property on Luckie street. Concerning this venture, Ragsdale's account is accurate in stating that a building adjacent to the hospital had been purchased from the Atlanta School of Medicine for $105,000. Two years later, it was sold at a loss to the hospital of $41,790.54. It was purchased with the idea of making it serve as a 75-bed addition to the hospital, for a total capacity of 210 beds. Evidently it had never been renovated for hospital purposes. In 1921 it was rented as the Bartow Apartments.[20]

A special committee to consider a section of the Holding Commission's report dealing with the hospital is of interest. The report, submitted by B. J. W. Graham, dealt with the matter of title transfer, not enlargement. The hospital wanted to build new facilities, as indicated. The Convention debated the issue at length, and adopted finally the report which suggested transfer of the title to the Holding Commission.[29]

> The debate on this report was of unusual vigor and warmth. Points of order and questions of personal privilege became numerous. At the close of the discussion all participants gave expression to courteous and gracious explanation and apologies and good fraternity and fellowship prevailed.[30]

The matter actually went back to 1915, and the establishment of the Committee of Five at the Fitzgerald Convention, and the subsequent establishment of the Holding Commission. It had made clear that each interest fostered by the Convention was to transfer title to all property to the commission. Any necessary charter amendments to make this legal were expected and anticipated. The particular

[28]B. D. Ragsdale, *Story of Georgia Baptists*, Vol. III., (Atlanta: The Executive Committee of Georgia Baptist Convention, 1932) , p. 267.

[29]*Minutes, Georgia Baptist Convention*, 1920, p.p. 32, 33.

[30]*Ibid.*, p.p. 30, 31.

phase of the committee study submitted by Graham dealt
with their duty to make a recommendation ". . . as to defer-
ring putting the title of the property of the Hospital in
Holding Commission." [31]

It was felt by some, perhaps many, that a breach of faith
with Georgia Baptists was evident in a recommendation to
defer transfer of any of the hospital's property, no matter
what the reason.

It was pointed out that the representatives of the Committee of Five and the pastors, in efforts to secure subscriptions and pledges for the payment of ". . . the debts on our
institutions, assured the subscribers most emphatically that,
when the debts were paid, then outstanding, no more could
be created, not even by the Holding Commission." [32]

The steps in creating the Holding Commission were
retraced.

> At the Commerce Convention this Holding Commis-
> sion was appointed. In 1917, at Newnan, the Holding
> Commission presented a charter, which was unanimous-
> ly approved. At the Convention in Macon, in 1918,
> the Holding Commission was directed to take proper
> steps for securing the titles to all the property of our
> Baptist institutions as rapidly as their debts were paid.
> At the Convention in Macon, in 1919, the Committee
> of Five made its final report, announcing that unpaid
> subscriptions to the Debt paying campaign would be
> turned over to the authorities in charge of the 75 mil-
> lion Campaign, and that the remainder of the debts
> would be paid out of funds realized from this new
> campaign.
> In accordance with the instructions of the Convention,
> the trustees of the various interests it fosters have
> vested the title of their properties in the Holding Com-
> mission, except the Georgia Baptist Hospital.
> The trustees of the Georgia Baptist Hospital have
> interpreted the report of the committee on the report
> of the Hospital to the Convention, in Macon, 1919, as
> giving them authority to proceed on its plan of enlarge-
> ment. Accordingly, additional property has been pur-
> chased, a nurses's home is in process of erection, and at

[31]*Ibid.*, p. 31.
[32]*Ibid.*, p.p. 31, 32.

the present time, according to the auditor's report of
the Georgia Baptist Hospital, its present liabilities are
$245,994.89, with total assets of $659,341.52. The
trustees, however, hold a title to the original plant of
the Hospital, as it has been enlarged and paid for, and
the property is free from mortgage.

The creation of a Holding Commission, and the assurance that no further debts could be created against
our Baptist institutions when the title was vested in
said Holding Commission, gave our Baptist people new
heart. They, therefore, subscribed liberally to the
Debt-Paying Campaign and also the Baptist 75 Million campaign.

Believing that the failure upon the part of the Hospital
trustees to deed this property to the Holding Commission at this time would mar the confidence of the
brotherhood, and in order to keep faith with the
brotherhood, we, your committee, recommend that the
title to the original and enlarged plant adjoining the
Baptist Tabernacle be vested in the Holding Commission. It is our opinion that such a transfer will not
materially affect the credit of the Georgia Baptist
Hospital, nor frustrate its present plans of enlargement. It is also our opinion that no serious injustice will
be done to the creditors who hold claims to the amount
of $245,994.89 by such a transfer. The other assets of
the Hospital, together with its present income, are adequate to make secure the creditors. It is the belief of
your committee that the Hospital itself will gain vastly
more by keeping faith with our Baptist constituency
than it will lose in a reduction of credit, if indeed there
be any, in the transfer of the original hospital to the
Holding Commission.[33]

EXPANSION PROGRAM APPROVED

The Convention then approved a program of Hospital
expansion. Evidently, Convention approval of expansion
killed for the time being the insistence that the Hospital
deed its property to the Holding Commission, despite the
Graham committee report.[34] The report relative to the
hospital and Holding Commission was made at a morning
session. At the afternoon session, a special committee on
enlargement of the hospital made a report through Graham

[33]*Ibid.*, p.p. 32, 33.
[34]*Ibid.*, p. 34.

which was discussed, amended and adopted, as outlined below:

> 1. We recommend the plan of enlargement of the trustees of this convention.
> 2. That the Convention approve the proposed issue of bonds for the enlargement and extension of the hospital to the amount of $1,500,000 to carry out its plan of enlargement and extension.
> 3. That the receipts from operation and the amount received from the Baptist 75 Million Campaign be used as a sinking fund for the retirement of these bonds, except as the funds received from the 75 Million campaign have been pledged to repay the advance of $25,000 made by the Executive Committee to the Hospital.
> 4. That as a given unit of the enlargement and extension is completed and paid for, title to the same be invested in the Holding Commission.
> 5. That the management of the Hospital safeguard the Commission's property in accordance with the provision of the charter of the Holding Commission.[35]

Thus the stage was set for a long period of involvement upon the part of Georgia Baptists in seeking to build a hospital during Depression years. It was to result, in 1922, with the Executive Committee being forced to assume control of and title to the Hospital property to save it from financial disaster.

One further proposal concerning the hospital, made in 1920, sheds light upon the ambitions of Georgia Baptists concerning a hospital ministry. L. G. Hardman, of Commerce, presented a resolution, approved by the Convention, that called for appointment of a Committee of Five to cooperate with the management of the hospital in taking over hospital property and organizations in different sections of the state.[36]

There had been considerable agitation on the part of leadership of the hospital both for hospital expansion and for the establishment of a system of hospitals. Writing in *The Index* Centennial edition for Dec. 25, 1920, J. M. Long, superintendent, in an article entitled "The Georgia Baptist

[35]*Loc. cit.*
[36]*Ibid.*, p. 41.

Hospitals", called upon Georgia Baptists to have ". . . two or more units located in different cities, all under the management of one board of trustees, one general superintendent, with a local executive committee." [37] Long declared further that there was but one way for Baptists to build immediately without violating agreements of the $75 million campaign. This was to:

> Issue one and one-half million dollars in bonds bearing seven per cent interest, interest payable semi-annually, bonds maturing in ten years, with the provision to retire at the will of the hospital trustees, at any interest paying period.[38]

Long, and many other Georgia Baptists, were quite sincere in believing, as Long indicated:

> This is an age of hospitals, more particularly Christian hospitals [39] . . . God forbid that we should in this, like many other fields of service, follow where others have led. May we be pioneers in this great field of Christain activity.[40]

In the same issue of *The Index,* a full page advertisement in behalf of the hospital called for provision to care for 20,000 sick each year, and for the training of 500 Christian nurses.[41]

The same year the Convention purchased *The Index,* its messengers rejected a proposal for a special *Index* Commission with adoption of the following resolution:

> Whereas, at the meeting of this Convention in Macon, November, 1919, the Executive Committee of this Convention was authorized, in its discretion, to negotiate a purchase of the *Christian Index,* and
> Whereas, pursuant to the instructions of the Convention, the Executive Committee reports that it has affected a purchase of the *Christian Index,* and
> Whereas, the Convention has made no pronouncement as to the management and editorship of the *Christian Index* as the property of the Convention,

[37]*The Christian Index,* Dec. 25, 1920, p. 78.
[38]*Ibid.,* p. 86.
[39]*Ibid.,* p. 79.
[40]*Ibid.,* p. 80.
[41]*Ibid.,* p. 81.

Therefore, be it resolved by the Georgia Baptist Convention, now assembled:
First, that the purchase of the *Christian Index* by the Executive Committee of this Convention be, and the same is, hereby approved.
Second, that the management of the paper be continued under the control and direction of the Executive Committee.[42]

The paper therefore remained in the control of the Executive Committee, which arrangement has continued to the present.

Action by the Convention concerning the Hospital was the only obvious motive behind a resolution proposed by W. W. Gaines which said:

[1] That all reports and resolutions presented to the Convention shall have attached thereto separate recommendations of all things they wish the Convention to adopt; and that where there is more than one recommendation in any such report or resolution, the vote shall be taken separately upon each recommendation. [2] That the adoption in the future of any report or resolution shall not bind the Convention to anything not clearly stated in the said recommendations.[43]

O. P. Gilbert, later to become editor of *The Index,* proposed also that the Convention authorize establishment of a summer assembly

. . . provided that it be found to be advisable and provided that the committee sees its way clear to finance such a prospect without involving the credit of the Convention or the Executive Committee beyond a reasonable annual appropriation for the operation of the assembly.[44]

This resolution was approved by the Convention. The Assembly [at Blue Ridge] had been tendered without cost to the Executive Committee, the holdings at Blue Ridge consisting of several cottages, an auditorium, and other improvements on 120 acres of land. The proposal indicated further that trustees of the Mary P. Willingham school would

[42]*Minutes, Georgia Baptist Convention,* 1920, p.p. 33, 34.
[43]*Ibid.,* p. 43.
[44]*Ibid.,* p. 42.

give rent free the use of their building on adjoining lots for dormitory purposes.[45]

No records indicating actual transfer of the property to the Executive Committee were found, either in Convention minutes, or minutes of the Administrative Committee or its parent body, the Executive Committee. The apparent tender was never accepted formally. The Blue Ridge assembly was used for years by Georgia Baptist Convention groups, and was called the Georgia Baptist Assembly.

Cree in his report to the Convention said that through careful handling of balances, he had earned enough in interest, $3,921.04, to pay nearly four-fifths of his salary.[46] He reported that total receipts for a six-year period, 1915 through 1920, had been $3,722,416.98. Prior to that total receipts for the previous thirty-six years, 1878 through 1914, had been $3,509,307.24.[47]

Election of Newton as editor took place at the meeting of the Executive Committee on Sept. 14, 1920.[48] He had served as acting editor since January, 1920.

ASSISTANCE TO CHURCHES

For 1920, 34 church buildings and three pastoriums had been constructed because of $43,174.50 in funds appropriated through the State Mission Board.[49]

Other facts of interest during 1920 included enrollment of 309 children at the Orphans' Home.[50] Provision for 102 beneficiaries for ministerial relief including 53 ministers and 49 widows of ministers with a total appropriation of $14,650.00.[51]

Rufus W. Weaver, in the Education Report, said that between 1833 and 1874, Mercer had enrolled 119 ministerial

[45]*Loc. cit.*
[46]*Ibid.*, p. 65.
[47]*Ibid.*, p. 64.
[48]*Ibid.*, p. 68.
[49]*Ibid.*, p. 75.
[50]*Ibid.*, p. 91.
[51]*Ibid.*, p.p. 90, 91.

students, 23 of them from outside Georgia. He declared that
during a period of over 40 years, Baptist churches of Georgia
furnished only 96 men to Mercer preparing for the ministry.[52] By comparison, as of January 1, 1920, there were 109
students preparing for the ministry at Mercer, 100 from
Georgia Baptist churches, and Weaver said that for the year
more men

> . . . have matriculated at Mercer University preparing
> themselves for the Christian ministry than entered that
> institution during the first forty-one years of its exis-
> tence from all the Baptist churches of the State.[53]

In co-operation with the Home Mission Board, plans were
projected to make the Hiawassee High School into a Junior
college by the Home board, in such a way as to provide for
the claims of other states, and at the same time keep the
school and integral part of the Mercer System. To this end,
the Convention was asked to authorize transfer of the school
property to the Home Board, ". . . should in the judgment
of the Executive Committee this course be necessary to the
highest interest of the school." [54]

Events had been shaping for several years the proposals
to make Mercer a great university under auspices of the
Southern Baptist Convention. Two matters were presented
to the Convention in session Dec. 7-9, 1921, at Savannah.
The Board of Education reported that the School of Christianity at Mercer had been expanded until there was at
Mercer ". . . a real theological seminary with eleven instructors and an enrollment of ministerial students exceeded in numbers only by two other Baptist Seminaries
in America." [55]

The Mercer trustees offered a memorial to the Convention, which was approved, paving the way upon the part
of Georgia Baptists to expand Mercer in co-operation with
the Southern Baptist Convention. The memorial said:

[52]*Ibid.*, p. 109.
[53]*Ibid.*, p. 110.
[54]*Ibid.*, p.p. 115-116.
[55]*Minutes, Georgia Baptist Convention*, 1921, p. 19.

Whereas, present conditions seem to be most favorable for the realization within this generation of this original purpose of the founders, the Board of Trustees request the authority of the Convention to tender to the Southern Baptist Convention the control of Mercer University whose assets at the end of this 75 Million campaign will be $2,000,000.00, and that the Southern Baptist Convention shall accept such transfer of control upon condition that Mercer University is made one of the two universities which shall be established by the Southern Baptist Convention, one east and the other west of the Mississippi River and that the theological seminary proposed by the Southern Baptist Convention shall be made a distinct department of the University, . . .[56]

We further request the authority to tender to the Southern Baptist Convention the amount which has been set apart in the permanent Educational Program adopted by this Convention in 1920, which devotes one million dollars for theological instruction, and $1,500,000.00 for post-graduate work in connection with Mercer University on condition that the Southern Baptist Convention will agree to raise during the same five year period for Mercer University $2,500,000.00 additional.[57]

The Convention authorized Mercer trustees to tender control of the institution on that basis.[58] A second resolution called for the School of Christianity to

. . . be made the Theological Department of Mercer University, and that all funds which have been given to this institution for theological instruction shall be kept separate and the income used for this purpose solely, and that the $1,000,000.00 which Georgia Baptists have agreed to raise for theological instruction shall be devoted to the development of this department . . .[59]

A third resolution proposed to and approved by the Convention provided that in the event the Southern Convention declined to join in development of such a university, the Board of Trustees of Mercer would be authorized to tender

[56]*Ibid.*, p.p. 24, 25.
[57]*Loc. cit.*
[58]*Ibid.*, p. 22.
[59]*Loc. cit.*

the School of Christianity—the theological department—to the Southern Baptist Convention upon terms which would be approved by the Georgia Convention.[60]

Covering events of importance for 1921, the Executive Committee report to the Convention indicated over 26,000 baptized in Georgia during the year, and over $1,000,000 ". . . raised for the seventy-five Million Campaign." [61]

The Convention during 1921 found itself in an embarrassing position relative to the Hospital when it became evident there were internal disciplinary problems, and that liens had been placed against some Hospital property which had not been authorized by the Convention.[62] The trustees were authorized ". . . to do all further acts necessary to straighten out its financial entanglements." [63] Apparently as a result of this, C. W. Daniel proposed an amendment to the Constitution, Article 6, Section 2, by adding two paragraphs:

[a] When an unforeseen emergency occurs in any of the affairs of the Convention, or in any of the interests it controls, that, in the judgment of the Executive Committee, requires action before the next session of the Convention, the Executive Committee in that case, shall have full authority to take such action as it thinks will be best in the interim, and all parties will be bound by its action, provided [1] that it must report to the next session of the Convention all the facts in each case and what action it took; and provided [2] that whatever action it takes in such cases will be binding only until the next session of the Convention; and provided [3] that nothing in this article shall be construed as giving the Executive Committee authority over any matters already committed by the Convention to any of its Board of Trustees, unless such boards decline to act.

[b] The Executive Committee shall have authority to fill all vacancies that occur in its membership between the sessions of the Convention from any cause, provided That those who are so elected by the committee shall hold office only until the session of the next conven-

[60]*Ibid.,* p.p. 25, 26.
[61]*Ibid.,* p. 27.
[62]*Ibid.,* p.p. 29-32.
[63]*Ibid.,* p. 32.

tion, when the vacancies shall be filled by the convention itself, in the manner provided by its laws.[64]

Daniel introduced this evidently at the instruction of the Administration Committee of the Executive Board which had named a committee to give proper notice through *The Index* of the proposed amendments.[65]

Following earlier studies concerning the transfer of mortgages, the Convention, upon motion of W. H. Faust, expressed commendation and appreciation of the work of Superintendent J. M. Long and the hospital trustees.[66] The Convention commended also the work of *The Index* and approved the course adopted by the Executive Committee in supplementing the income of the paper ". . . during the depressing financial period . . ."[67]

A long way from Atlanta, the Savannah Convention in 1921 took a strong stand against an ordinance proposed by the Atlanta city council which would regulate public religious worship by ". . . specifying to whom and upon what condition a minister may preach or a Christian worker may teach; . . ."[68]

CONVENTION CENTENNIAL PLANNED

Plans were made during this session for the Convention's centennial celebration in June, 1922, to be held in connection with commencement at Mercer and the evangelistic conference in Macon. It was believed that the celebration, linked with the already planned meetings, would bring more people together.[69]

The idea of a series of hospitals owned by the Convention continued to attract the interest of some Georgia Baptists. By 1921, L. G. Hardman, Commerce, had been named chairman of a committee to investigate the feasibility of establish-

[64]*Ibid.*, p. 33.
[65]*Ibid.*, p. 37.
[66]*Loc. cit.*
[67]*Loc. cit.*
[68]*Ibid.*, p.p. 33, 34.
[69]*Ibid.*, p.p. 34, 35.

ing or securing control of one or more hospitals in cities other than Atlanta. The committee had been at work during the year, and reported propositions from Thomasville, Americus, Albany, Valdosta and other towns. However, because of the financial condition of the country, the committee felt it was not wise to make any recommendation at that time.[70]

A committee was appointed in 1921, to consider with power to act in the matter of transferring the property of the Assembly to the Convention.[71] Again, as in 1920, the implication was that the property would be transferred, but there still was no record of the actual transfer.

On October 1, 1921, offices of the Executive Committee moved from the Flat Iron Building to 317-24 Palmer Building, a new structure,[72] which was to remain the home of Baptist offices until 1935.[73] The general balance sheet for the year showed total investments by the Holding Commission of $582,440.53; total institutional property, valued at $935,062.37; current assets, $2,773.26; for a total of $1,520,276.16.[74]

A breakdown of monies expended upon State Mission work in the field for the year 1921 reflected a continuing pattern of growing. Appropriations included:

For pastors leading missions, $42,462.29; Church Building, $19,877.90; Evangelism, $13,776.84; Enlistment, $26,148.55, for a total of $101,265.68. The sum of $48,805.44 was appropriate for organic State Missions work originating in the office, and was distributed as follows: Administration, $16,394.74; publicity, $3,457.61; B. W. M. U., $10,604.49; Sunday School Department, $10,470.44; and B. Y. P. U., $7,878.16.[75]

During the same period, the Book Department's financial

[70]*Ibid.*, p. 35.

[71]*Ibid.*, p.p. 48-49.

[72]*Ibid.*, p. 78.

[73]James Adams Lester, "A History of *The Christian Index*, 1822-1954," [Unpublished Master's Thesis, 1955,] p. 134.

[74]*Minutes, Georgia Baptist Convention*, 1921, p. 66.

[75]*Ibid.*, p. 79.

statement indicated sales paid for, $21,180.69; sales not paid for, on open account, $3,098.95, for total sales of $24,279.64; with an inventory of stock on hand set at $13,589.20 less invoices for goods received of $1,971.55 for a total inventory of $11,617.65, and a total evaluation of $35,897.29.[76] The Book Department had experienced rapid growth in the less than two years required to bring it to this evaluation from an inventory purchase price in January, 1920, of less than $5,000.[77]

Baptist Young People's Union was experiencing unusual growth also. There were 963 senior B. Y. P. U.'s with an enrolment of 30,000 members; and 389 Junior B. Y. P. U.'s with an enrolment of over 11,000 members.[78] Thus, during the two years following completion of the $75 Million Campaign in 1919, growth experienced by the Convention was not only financial, but organizational. In what was at that time a record allocation for that purpose, the Executive Committee reported to the Convention that $15,000 had been appropriated to *The Index* for preparation of the Convention Centennial number.[79] This issue, published under date of June 1, 1922, consisted of 96 pages.[80]

The beginnings of the present-day Georgia Baptist Evangelistic Conference as such extend to 1920. In 1921, the Report on Missions included information that: "The Mercer conference on Evangelism which brings together the Baptist preachers of the State for two days immediately following Mercer commencement. . ." was such a success that it was believed in order to make it a fixed, permanent meeting on the Georgia Baptist Calendar. The 1921 conference attracted 500 attendants.[81] Another phase of this conference was that more than 70 "echo conferences" were held in

[76]*Ibid.*, p. 83.

[77]Minutes, Executive Committee, Georgia Baptist Convention, March 18, 19, 1920, p. 112.

[78]*Minutes, Georgia Baptist Convention,* 1921, p. 82.

[79]*Ibid.*, p. 90.

[80]*The Christian Index,* June 1, 1922.

[81]*Minutes, Georgia Baptist Convention,* 1921, p.p. 94, 95.

more than 70 associations following the summer state-wide session.[82]

The final chapter in the matter of Hospital-Holding Commission relations was to be written in later years. One step further was indicated in the Hospital report. Deeds had been drawn on the hospital property at 92 Luckie Street for transfer to the Holding Commission, but were returned to the Hospital with the statement by the Holding Commission that their charter prohibited them from accepting the property in its present condition. The Hospital trustees took the position then that they had sought to act in good faith in endeavoring to carry out Convention instructions.[83] John F. Eden, named the previous year as hospital chaplain, reported 39,916 visits, and 28 conversions.[84] [This amounted to an average of 109-plus visits each day for a 365-day year.] In December, the Executive Committee appropriated $720 on Eden's salary.[85]

In line with an earlier request from the Administration Committee for a clearer definition of that Committee's authority, the Executive Committee on Sept. 13-14, 1921, at its meeting reported that

> ... the Administration Committee is appointed by this Board as a sub-committee of the Executive Board of the Georgia Baptist Convention with authority to direct the administration of the affairs of the Board in all matters pertaining to administration, missions, education and benevolence as may be directed by the Board and to act in such emergencies as may arise between sessions of the Board, which require immediate action, subject to the approval of this Board.[86]

Georgia Baptist hospital was headed for trouble in 1921.

[82]*Ibid.*, p. 95.

[83]*Ibid.*, p. 123.

[84]*Ibid.*, p. 128.

[85]Minutes, Executive Committee, Georgia Baptist Convention, Dec. 15, 16, 1921, p. 183.

[86]Minutes, Executive Committee, Georgia Baptist Convention, Sept. 13, 14, 1921, p. 164.

[Note: See page seven, Section II, *Georgia Baptist Convention minutes*, 1920, which defines the authority and duties of this Executive Board.]

The severity of the financial difficulty was evidenced by an apparent called meeting of the Convention's Executive Committee, May 4, 1922, in the Sunday School Auditorium of the First Baptist church, Atlanta; which meeting was requested by a committee of the Hospital Trustees. The trustees of the hospital reported to the Executive Committee there was a serious situation with a total indebtedness on the hospital of $154,770.51; cash in all banks of $27,588.51, and accounts due and payable of $30,769.61.[87]

Ragsdale's abstract from the hospital balance sheet for Dec. 1, 1921 indicated total assets of $799,022.88. Liabilities included $155,672.96 on the new lot and home for nurses, and obligations on Luckie Street property and current expenses of $190,712.14, for total liabilities of $346,385.10.[88] While the balance sheet for December, 1921, and the statement of indebtedness as of May, 1922 are not in complete agreement, the Trustees' report to the Executive Committee apparently did not include the Luckie Street property or current expense items. Ragsdale said that by April, 1922, outstanding liabilities of the hospital were $355,000 with a deficit of $1,000 per month.[89]

HOSPITAL, PROPERTY TRANSFERRED

At the May meeting of the Executive Committee, Cree presented to that body a proposal for the hospital which called for the trustees, should they so request, to turn over their entire trust, legally, to the Executive Committee, with responsibility for operation of the hospital to be a direct responsibility of the Executive Committee, which would hold title to all hospital property.[90] This was approved by

[87]Minutes, Executive Committee, Georgia Baptist Church, May 4, 1922, p.p. 195, 196, 197.

[88]Ragsdale, Vol. III, p. 267.

[89]*Ibid.*, p. 268.

[90]Minutes, Executive Committee, Georgia Baptist Convention, May 4, 1922, p.p. 195, 196, 197.

the Convention in approval of the report of the Executive Committee.[91]

Prior to the annual meeting of the Convention in Atlanta, in 1922, the Board heard from Cree a proposition presented by the citizens of Toccoa relative to the location of a Baptist encampment at the falls near Toccoa.

> It was moved that the whole matter of a Baptist encampment be referred to the Convention with recommendation to all subsidiary organizations [that] meanwhile no action be taken by any subsidiary organization until the Convention shall take action.[92]

When the Convention met in Atlanta Dec. 6-8, 1922, it was to hear a report on the Hospital situation as well as one concerning observance of the Convention Centennial held earlier that year on the campus of Mercer University— and elsewhere in the state. The meeting place had been changed from Monroe to Atlanta to accommodate an expected large attendance.[93]

The Convention did mark its Centennial celebration in appropriate sessions held during the summer of 1922. The first part of the occasion was June 3, with services at Kiokee; services at Powelton on June 4, with the closing day of the celebration at Mercer on Tuesday, June 6. The Kiokee part of the observance drew some 1,500 people; the Powelton celebration about 2,500, and at Mercer,

> the speaking was held in an arbor which provided seats for five thousand persons. It was estimated that when George W. Truett delivered his address at high noon that there were not less than five thousand people present. A bountiful dinner was served by Mercer University.[94]

During the first century of its history, the Georgia Baptist Convention had been presided over by ten presidents; eight ministers and two laymen. Thomas Stocks served ten years;

[91]*Minutes, Georgia Baptist Convention,* 1922, p. 74.
[92]Minutes, Executive Committee, Georgia Baptist Convention, Sept. 15, 1922.
[93]*Minutes, Georgia Baptist Convention,* 1922, p. 9.
[94]*Ibid.,* p.p. 10, 11.

W. J. Northen ". . . probably the most useful Baptist layman of his day . . ." served fourteen years,

> . . . and like Dr. P. H. Mell, was also President of the Southern Baptist Convention. Others who presided over our Georgia Baptist body were S. Y. Jameson, J. H. Kilpatrick, A. J. Battle, D. E. Butler and B. M. Sanders.[95]

Jesse Mercer was the first president,

> . . . lovingly called in his later years 'Father Mercer.' No man in his day received at the hands of Baptists so many honors . . . Though more than eighty years have passed since his death, the influence of Jesse Mercer still pervades Georgia.[96]

The Convention had grown from a formal gathering of two associations who covenanted together to draft the first constitution, to a Convention comprising 95 associations, 2,504 churches, with 368,481 members.[97]

During that first century, Georgia Baptists had led in many areas of Southern Baptist life. They had been far-sighted, and had sought as best they knew to do the will of God as they understood it. Georgia Baptists, during this first century, had pioneered in programs of associational missions; had led in the establishment of schools of all grades and ranks, out of which the public school system of Georgia must acknowledge at least some rather strong debt. They had pioneered in Hospital work at the state convention level; accepted finally the responsibility for an Orphans' Home which by 1922 had well over 300 children, and perfected an organizational structure which was to endure and provide room for expansion.

Baptists had been active in the interests of temperance; had accepted and made good use of a state denominational paper, either under private or convention ownership, and pioneered in programs of work with prisoners, and in programs which provided direct assistance to churches in their

[95]*The Christian Index,* June 1, 1922, p.p. 15-16.
[96]*Ibid.,* p. 16.
[97]*Minutes, Georgia Baptist Convention,* 1922, p. 296.

building programs and in programs of financial assistance to pastors.

From the first, the care of aged ministers and their widows had been a matter of continuing interest, and there was expressed always concern for ministerial students; a concern expressed annually in concrete financial assistance.

Theologically, the Convention had remained conservative in the historic usage of the word, indicating, even constitutionally, ties to the concepts of "Regular" Baptists. It had ministered to Indians and Negroes in their own state, and through the Domestic and Foreign Mission Boards after 1845 had participated actively in programs of missions beyond the state. Even prior to the formation of the Southern Baptist Convention, Georgia Baptists had, through the old Triennial Convention, supported the interests of foreign missions, and Home Missions had been the recipient of Georgia help through the old American Baptist Home Missionary Society.

Woman's work in Georgia had become a substantial factor in Kingdom advancement with the women not only giving as best they could through the local societies, but becoming an increasing force in denominational life at the state level; especially in leadership for the Orphans' Home.

Georgia Baptists were entering into their second century having missed only one annual convention meeting—that for 1865, scheduled for Columbus. Not only had Georgia Baptists been generous in their support for missions, they had contributed a generous share of missionaries for the Home and Foreign fields.

The years immediately ahead were to be decisive years, but at the beginning of this second century of organized work, the enthusiasm of the $75 Million Campaign, and increased income therefrom, provided a basis for optimism concerning the future.

CHAPTER 17

The Convention Retrenches
In Depression Years

Financial conditions worsened during 1922. The Georgia Baptist Hospital was in serious difficulty, and came as near being closed as it had ever been. Gifts to mission causes were on the decline. One area of interest, expressed occasionally earlier, was in the possibility of a merger between Mercer University and Bessie Tift college. In the report of the Education Committee to the Convention in 1922,— approved by the Convention—was the following proposal:

> We, the Trustees of Bessie Tift College and of Mercer University, petition the Georgia Baptist Convention to give its approval to plans whereby these two institutions in the interest of economy and efficiency may be brought closer together. It is the purpose of the two Boards of Trustees to so relate these institutions as to enable Bessie Tift College to secure at a very early date recognition and rating as a standard college.
> We are not prepared at the present time to recommend the legal relationship, but we request from this Convention the authority to carry on our investigations, to work out our plans, to prepare our contracts, to make changes in our charters and, if need be, in order to accomplish the end desired, to merge the two institutions upon terms acceptable to the two Boards of Trustees, and that these terms shall not become effective until approval has been given by the Executive Committee of the Georgia Baptist Convention. Notice of the terms of agreement shall be published ninety (90) days preceding the Convention.[1]

[1]*Minutes, Georgia Baptist Convention*, 1922, p. 19

Therefore, from a Convention perspective, authorization had been given for the two institutions to merge organically upon approval of the Board of Trustees and the Convention's Executive Committee. However, that was the closest that the institutions were to come to a merger.

A memorial from the Mercer trustees was approved in which the trustees petitioned the Convention to set aside $175,000 in addition to the amount then available, to be used for erection of a heating plant, two or more dormitories, equipment and purchase of two tracts of land, needed for future development. The trustees wanted to begin construction of the dormitories so that they might be ready for occupancy in the fall of 1923.[2]

The germ of the present Georgia Baptist Foundation is found in the report of the Holding Commission to the Convention in 1922. The Commission, among other items, declared that the General Education Board of New York, had given money $100,000 and more to Shorter, Wesleyan, Agnes Scott and the University of Georgia, with ". . . practically every Baptist institution of college grade in the south . . ." receiving large donations except Bessie Tift and Mercer. Investigation, including a visit to New York, revealed that the Education Board, under its charter, could not give money to institutions where title to and management of the property was not held by the institution. Out of this conference with the Education Board, and additional committee conferences with the Holding Commission, came a recommendation that the Convention authorize yet another committee to study the advisability of making necessary charter changes. Additionally, the committee would study ways of better carrying out the purpose of the Holding Commission. The Foundation idea was included with a statement that the committee would study

> ". . . the plan and operation of the Baptist Foundations
> established and in operation in North Carolina and
> Virginia and seek and recommend such conclusions

[2]*Ibid.*, p. 20.

therefrom as may promise help in the working out of our problems.[3]

Following the earlier meetings of the Executive Committee, especially the May session, with proposals to help the hospital, the Convention adopted a resolution by C. W. Daniel that it authorize sale of the Luckie Street hospital property and apply proceeds of the sale to the hospital.[14] Also, the Convention was informed that the Hospital had turned over its entire trust to the Executive Committee.

"Your Executive Committee, believing that failure to meet this situation would result in the loss of the Hospital, . . . has assumed this responsibility for the purpose of saving the Hospital and maintaining the integrity and credit of the Georgia Baptist Convention." [5]

The Index in 1922 was placed in the Convention's Standing Committee list and the Convention approved a motion by Louie D. Newton that reports of standing committees be limited to a maximum of 500 words.[6] Cree reported a unique all-Georgia motor tour held in the spring of 1922, in which 1,000 churches were reached, and 1,000 meetings held during a single week,[7] and as financial crises neared, Georgia Baptists continued business as usual.

The 1923 Convention sessions were held with the First Baptist Church, Macon. At this session, the cutback in denominational funds began to be evident. A minority report, submitted by C. W. Daniel as chairman of the Executive Committee, was an amendment to Item 6 in a Report on Future Campaigns providing that the basis for a division of funds between the Southern Baptist Convention causes and Georgia Baptist Convention causes be changed from 50%-50% to 60% Georgia and 40% Southern Baptist Convention.[8]

[3]*Ibid.*, p. 36 [A full resume of the Mercer System of Schools may be found in the Education Report for 1922, p.p. 154-158, *Minutes, Georgia Baptist Convention.*]

[4]*Ibid.*, p. 49.

[5]*Ibid.*, p. 74.

[6]*Ibid.*, p. 56.

[7]*Ibid.*, p. 70.

[8]*Minutes, Georgia Baptist Convention*, 1923, p. 14.

A report on future campaigns was adopted and when the Executive Committee met prior to the 1923 Convention, nearly an entire day was devoted to discussion which had resulted in changes in the recommendation of the denominational program for 1925. The provisions included commendation to Georgia Baptists of the present stewardship movement and urged pastors and other leaders to instruct their people in the principles of stewardship. The second recommendation dealt with promotion of Baptist work upon conclusion of the $75 Million Campaign, and called for plans for the denominational program to be made annually, year by year, following the campaign, at the same time holding before Georgia Baptists their goal of $7,500,000 for the five-year period. The report said: ". . . for we feel on the one hand that we should not lower our present standard and on the other hand that we can not raise it in the face of present conditions." [9]

A third proposal was: That the denominational program for the year 1925 be known as the "Georgia Baptist Kingdom budget for 1925; and that our goal be set to raise a minimum of $1,000,000 for missions, education and benevolence in that year."

Other recommendations have historic value.

They included:

> 4. That the Executive Committee seek the co-operation of the Baptists and Baptist churches of Georgia in making a simultaneous, every member canvass of the membership of our churches for the support of this Kingdom budget, said canvass to be conducted as far as possible during the week of November 30 to December 7, 1924, and the subscriptions to the budget, as far as possible, to be made payable on the weekly basis.
>
> 5. That the Convention suggest to the churches that they make their annual, every member canvass for local church support at the same time as the canvass for the Kingdom budget, . . .
>
> 6. That of this $1,000,000, 50%, or $500,000, be allotted to Southern Baptist Convention causes, and that 50%, or $500,000, be allotted to Georgia Baptist Convention state causes.

Ibid., p.p. 14, 15.

7. That we ask the Southern Baptist Convention, or its Campaign Committee, to advise our Executive Committee as to the distribution of the $500,000 among the causes fostered by the Southern Baptist Convention.
8. That the Executive Committee be authorized and empowered to make such adjustments as may in its judgment appear to be necessary to meet the needs of the several causes.
9. That the $500,000 for state causes be divided as follows:

> Christian Education: For Schools and Colleges, 40%, $200,000; for Ministerial Education, 4%, $20,000; Benevolences: Orphans' Home 13½%, $67,500; Hospitals 13½%, $67,500; Emergency Fund, 1%, $5,000; Missions, State Mission Work, including Baptist work in secular schools, 24⅔% or $123,333.34; Headquarters Building 3⅓% or $16,666.66.[10]

Here, in essence, was a rather complete plan for a Georgia "Cooperative Program," 18 months before such a program, under a different name, was to be adopted by the Southern Baptist Convention at the 1925 session in Memphis, Tennessee.

Between 1922 and 1923, a study of the Holding Commission's work resulted in a proposed Constitutional Amendment, approved, by adding to Article VI, Section 3, at the end of the following phrase:

> Provided, however, that the Holding Commission as a whole may be ex-officio a member of the Board of Trustees of the institutions whose property it holds, especially for the purpose of holding said property.[11]

In the recommendations concerning secondary schools, submitted by Homer L. Grice, the Convention was reminded again of the fact that Locust Grove Institute and Norman Institute were to be developed into standard junior colleges as rapidly as conditions would permit.[12]

The beginning of the present Department of Student Work is traceable to the 1923 Convention in two areas: One, in

[10]*Ibid.,* p.p. 15, 16.
[11]*Ibid.,* p. 19.
[12]*Ibid.,* p.p. 34, 35.

the 1925 allocation of the proposed budget which called for state missions work "including Baptist work in secular schools." [13] The second indication was a recommendation.

> . . . that steps be taken by the Executive Secretary of the Georgia Baptist Convention, subject to the approval of the Executive Committee, to do such religious work among Baptist students in the colleges supported by the state as will do justice to their spiritual needs and their development into more useful Christian workers.[14]

The Orphans' Home was pleased evidently to report 348 ". . . bright, clean, healthy, happy, promising children in our little haven at Hapeville. . . . We note with peculiar pleasure the hearty co-operation of our home and its constituency. . . ." [15] The hospital reported treating 3,295 patients from 14 denominations, nine states and six nationalities,[16] reflecting an annual growth in services rendered despite a financial crisis.

Again, the Convention spoke in the area of church-state relations when it approved a resolution ". . . pledging the favor and support of this Convention for bill now pending in Congress to prohibit any appropriations by Congress to Sectarian institutions." [17]

Although all property of Mercer University had earlier been reported as having been turned over to the Holding Commission, the auditor's report of November 23, 1923, indicated that Mercer records had charged to the Commission the holding of real estate, [campus and buildings] valued at $455,000 which had never actually been transferred by deed. Following the report, the deeds were executed to the Holding Commission,[18] indicating again the firm hand the Holding Commission exercised in seeking to follow Convention directives.

[13]*Ibid.*, p. 16.
[14]*Ibid.*, p. 37.
[15]*Ibid.*, p. 39.
[16]*Ibid.*, p. 40.
[17]*Ibid.*, p. 44.
[18]*Ibid.*, p. 58.

Indicative of the academic standing of Mercer was the fact that in 1923, of 84 faculty and staff members, 13 were listed in "Who's Who In America," five were former college presidents and three were former deans.[19]

Impact of the $75 Million Campaign continued to be felt in every area of life. A comparison of baptisms indicated that during the four years preceding the Campaign, 1915-1919, the total number of baptisms in the State was reported at 58,217. For 1919-1923, the total was 81,374. In 1920, church records indicated 330,307 church members; 1921, 349,009; 1922, 368,481; 1923, 382,641.[20]

With one additional year of the Campaign remaining in 1923, Cree reported to the Convention that from 1919 to 1923 there had been a minimum of Campaign organization and field forces except voluntary help. Plans were proposed for a cautious expansion of field forces during the final year and further, a "Clean-Up Re-Canvass" was being proposed for 1924. This involved securing subscriptions from all who had not pledged; giving opportunity for readjustment of losses due to death and disaster, and to provide opportunity for additional gifts.[21] It was evident by this time that Georgia would not meet the $7,500,000 assigned goal or the $10,-000,000 pledged barring most unusual circumstances. State Mission expenditures for 1923 were $113,682.99.[22] The Board, however, still was out of debt, with a balance of $2,396.92 despite the financial conditions and a slowing down of receipts.[23] Although the Campaign had been planned originally for the largest amounts to come in during the last years, by the 1923 Convention, the slowing economy was evident.

STATEMENT OF PRINCIPLES ADOPTED

The Convention meeting in Columbus in 1924 adopted

[19]*Ibid.*, p. 110.
[20]*Ibid.*, p. 62.
[21]*Minutes, Georgia Baptist Convention*, 1922, p.p. 65, 66.
[22]*Ibid.*, p.p. 63, 64.
[23]*Ibid.*, p. 62.

for the first time a basic statement of principles which was
to govern employment of all officers and leaders in any phase
of Convention work, and any who taught in Baptist colleges.
The statement of principles amounted in essence to a declaration of affirmation in historic Baptist theological principles.
The statement, as approved, included those then in service
to the denomination, or those in institutions we ". . . shall
hereafter create or foster." [24]

In reporting upon the Laymen's Missionary Movement,
the Convention was informed that during the year 1921-
1922 the movement had enrolled nearly 250,000 tithers—
and claimed some credit for the advance in home and foreign
missions.[25] Additionally, a Committee on Coordination of
State Mission work was set up to discuss ways to avoid overlapping of the educational work in certain agencies, with
instructions to report back to the Convention in 1925.[26]
The problem was related primarily to Sunday School,
B.Y.P.U., and Women's Work, occasioned by growth as these
areas of work emerged organizationally at both State and
South-wide levels.

The Executive Committee made several recommendations
concerning the Hospital's proposed building campaign, one
being that the Convention reconsider and rescind its action
of December 9, 1920, authorizing the hospital trustees to
negotiate a bond issue of $1,500,000 to erect a main hos-
pital building.[27] Since the initital resolution on a bond
issue, property of the Hospital had been transferred to the
Executive Committee along with management of that institution.

The Executive Committee then requested the Convention
to authorize negotiations for an issue not to exceed $500,000,
to erect a first unit of the hospital. In the event it was considered best not to sell the old property by the time remain-

[24]*Minutes, Georgia Baptist Convention*, 1924, p. 20.
[25]*Ibid.*, p. 15.
[26]*Ibid.*, p. 21.
[27]*Minutes, Georgia Baptist Convention*, 1920, p. 34; also *Minutes, Georgia Baptist Convention*, 1924, p. 27.

ing obligations were due in 1927, the Executive Committee sought authority to finance the balance due on current obligations. The Committee felt that it might get by with an issue of $300,000 for the building since at least two years' receipts form the denomination would be available. They believed further that construction should not begin until $100,000 was available in addition to the $300,000 proposed issue of bonds.

The Committee recommended that the Convention instruct the hospital trustees to convey to the Executive Committee all properties to permit the Executive Committee to negotiate legally for the bond issue.[28]

Moreover, the Convention was asked to take action so that during the life of the bonds, the Convention would provide an annual allocation in its budget (for 1925, $67,500) with instructions that this allocation be applied to payment of principle and interest on the indebtedness, with the Committee following a minimum schedule of liquidation.[29]

Cree proposed an amendment to the Orphans' Home report which provided for a guarantee of $5,000 per month out of the 1925 program, and distribution of other funds to be on a regular ratio, with the remainder of the Home allocation being paid only when and in proportion as the other causes received their allocations.[30]

Plans for expansion of the Convention's educational program continued with the report on the Committee on Five including in 1924 recommendations for location of junior colleges. The idea, which had been advanced earlier in conjunction with planning by the Education Board called for a college in Southwest Georgia, with Norman Park having preference as a junior college. Brewton-Parker and Piedmont institutes were being considered for a college in Southeast Georgia; and the committee was to discuss the matter with trustees of these two institutions. In Central and

[28]*Minutes, Georgia Baptist Convention*, 1924, p. 27.
[29]*Ibid.*, p.p. 27-28.
[30]*Ibid.*, p.p. 29, 30.

North Georgia, there would be another unit in the secondary school system. The committee was recommending that the present outstanding debt owed ". . . to others than Baptists by the Chattahoochee High School . . ." would be assumed by the Convention and paid to secure the title—the amount not in excess of $3,000.[31] Locust Grove Institute was considered and favored upon more than one occasion as a site for a college for Central Georgia, a part of the secondary system. At the suggestion of Claude Gray, president of Locust Grove Institute, the Convention directed that the appointment of trustees for the institution be referred to the Executive Committee with power to act;[32] a move to bring that Institute under closer control of the Executive Committee.

CAMPAIGN ENDS

The $75 Million Campaign closed November 30, 1924. Beginning on that date, a Sunday, Georgia and Southern Baptists launched a canvass in the churches for promotion of the 1925 budget ". . . Program of Southern Baptists." [33] For the year under consideration at Columbus, total receipts, December 1, 1923 to December 4, 1924 amounted to $942,-263.88 for all interests. Of this amount, $869,632.22 was received in the $75 Million Campaign. This was an advance of $114,751.04 over the previous year.[34]

In an effort to stimulate interest in Georgia Baptist life, during July of 1924 a series of eleven regional conferences were held with pastors and leaders from the associations invited. At these conferences, campaigns old and new were discussed.[35] This was the beginning apparently of the conferences later to be called the Regional Conferences on Denominational Ministries, lasting into the 1960's as these proved effective in helping Georgia Baptists understand better their program of work, and provided a means whereby

[31]*Ibid.*, p.p. 35, 36.
[32]*Ibid.*, p. 39.
[33]*Ibid.*, p. 57.
[34]*Loc. cit.*
[35]*Ibid.*, p. 59.

joint discussion of promotion plans and Convention ministries would elicit expanded co-operation. Concern that full
information be given all Georgia Baptists concerning their
work was historic and continual.

For the first time, in 1924, the Convention's Executive
Committee authorized a campaign to promote the Daily
Vacation Bible Schools, the beginning of a long and continuing interest upon the part of the Convention in the movement.[36] This was directed by James W. Merritt, later Executive Secretary-Treasurer, who pioneered actually in promotion of VBS work in the state.

In 1919, the value of all the institutions, property, equipment and investments, including Mercer, Tift, Locust Grove,
Brewton-Parker, Gibson-Mercer, Hearn, Norman, Piedmont
and Chattahoochee High School was $1,550,088.18. Assets
in 1924 were $3,020,718.20.[37]

In almost every area of Convention life, the "Great Campaign" cropped up. In 1924, it was said that

> . . . it is proper to say that the educational institutions
> owned and controlled by the Georgia Baptist Conven-
> tion have within the period of the 75 Million Campaign,
> doubled in actual value.[38]

By 1924, Mercer was prepared to award the degree Doctor
of Theology, limited to students who had completed four
years of college work, who had received the master of arts
and the bachelor of divinity degrees given by the Theological
Seminary.

> Before the Th.D. degree is conferred, a candidate must
> complete one year of residence work in which he will
> devote himself solely to research and graduate studies.
> The following year he must prepare a thesis exhibiting
> scholarship of a high order, based upon research work
> in which a contribution of genuine value will be made
> to the subject he discusses. The following three years
> will determine whether the degree will be conferred.

[36]*Ibid.,* p. 81.
[37]*Ibid.,* p.p. 110, 111.
[38]*Ibid.,* p. 111.

Should he prove himself to be a successful leader in religious work, he will receive the degree of Th.D.[39]

The unusual step of providing time on the Convention program for an open conference on "Our Baptist Situation in Georgia: Its Causes and Its Remedies" was taken at the Savannah Convention December 9-11, 1925. However, no minutes of the discussion were kept, and following discussion at an afternoon session of the Georgia situation, the evening session was devoted primarily to consideration of the challenge of the unified program.[40] The Convention was seeking ways to enlarge its program, combat financial crises, and retain the momentum of the $75 Million Campaign.

Between events recorded concerning the 1924 session of the Convention, and the open conference in Savannah, an unusual and far-reaching step had been taken by Southern Baptists which was to reflect increasingly and permanently in the life of Georgia Baptists.

> After the 75 Million Campaign, a Conservation Commission was set up [by the Southern Baptist Convention] to conserve the results accomplished by the co-operative work done in the campaign. This was succeeded by the Future Program Commission, which in 1925 recommended to the Southern Baptist Convention that 'from the adoption of this report by the Convention our co-operative work be known as ' "Cooperative Program of Southern Baptists." ' The Cooperative Program Commission was discontinued in 1927, on the following recommendation: 'We recommend that all the work now done by the Cooperative Program Commission be taken over by the Executive Committee.' [41]

Working closely already with the Southern Baptist Convention's campaign committee on the $75 Million Campaign, the action of that convention in Memphis in 1925 was to set in motion increased co-operation between the Georgia and Southern convention.

A. W. Evans presented a proposed constitutional amend-

[39]*Ibid.*, p. 115.

[40]*Minutes, Georgia Baptist Convention,* 1925, p. 15.

[41]Encyclopedia of Southern Baptists, Vol. I [Nashville: Broadman Press, 1958], p. 323.

ment, to delete the final paragraph of Section 3, Article VI, substituting the following:

> Provided, however, that the members of the Holding Commission may be ex-officio members of the Boards of Trustees of the institutions whose property they hold, especially for the purpose of holding said property.[42]

The Colquitt Hotel in Moultrie had been given to Norman Institute. By 1925, it was in need of considerable repairs. Norman had no funds to use in a renovation program for the hotel, so the Convention approved authority for the Holding Commission to either sell or lease the hotel as the Norman trustees deemed advisable, ". . . provided that the endowment shall be kept as such either in money or property in the hands of the Holding Commission." [43]

The pattern of nomination of trustees for Mercer was clarified in 1925 with adoption of a resolution submitted by the Committee on Nominations in which that committee indicated it felt that trustee selection should be with the ". . . greatest possible care both as to their fitness for the positions and their interest in the work of these Boards:" [44]

The resolution was:

> 1. That we recommend that, each year, the Board of Trustees of Mercer University shall submit to the Chairman of the Nominating Committee nine names, from which the Nominating Committee may select three to fill the places of those whose term of office is expiring.
> 2. We recommend that the Mercer Alumni Association shall submit to the Nominating Committee nine names, from which three trustees may be selected.
> 3. We also recommend that the same rule apply to the Trustees and the Alumni of Bessie Tift College.
> 4. We further recommend that the Secretary of each Board elected by the Convention shall furnish to the Chairman of the Nominating Committee, the individual records of attendance of all members whose terms of office expires during that Convention year.[45]

[42]*Minutes, Georgia Baptist Convention*, 1925, p. 17.
[43]*Ibid.*, p. 22.
[44]*Ibid.*, p. 23.
[45]*Ibid.*, p.p. 23-24.

The Executive Committee at its December 8 meeting, adopted a resolution which perhaps forestalled action at the Convention level when it suggested that leaders of several of the auxiliary organizations had expressed a desire to keep in closer touch with plans and policies of the Executive Committee. The Committtee invited

> ". . . the Executive Committee of the Woman's Missionary Union, the Executive Committee of the Baptist Young People's Union and the Executive Committee of the Georgia Baptist Sunday School Convention to each appoint two members of their Executive Committee to attend the meetings of the Executive Committee of the Georgia Baptist Convention." [46]

Inasmuch as the meetings were not closed sessions, this appeared to be simply an additional invitation for attendance, but not providing for membership on the committee by the auxiliary groups. This situation was to reappear with positive action including membership on an ex-officio basis, in later years.

Overtones of the growing strength and force exerted by the Auxiliary Conventions was in evidence at the same meeting of the Executive Committee when that body heard a report of a special committee dealing with the Baptist Young People's Union department, which, in essence, said that the Convention's Executive Committee would welcome conferences with officials of the B.Y.P.U. organization with regard to the B.Y.P.U. secretary and field workers. Further, the Executive Committee agreed that traveling expenses incident to the meetings of the B.Y.P.U. Executive Committee would be paid out of funds allocated to the B.Y.P.U. department, provided no more than four such meetings were held annually. The agreement further called for the B.Y.P.U. treasurer to turn over to the Executive Secretary-Treasurer, Arch Cree, all funds and fees collected at the regional conventions, and this money would then be paid out upon vouchers submitted. In the event of a deficit in expenses of the convention of B.Y.P.U., the secretary-treasurer of the Executive Committee would finance the same until a joint conference could work out a solution.[47]

It was becoming apparent that a danger existed that the children of the parent body could become strong enough, and independent enough financially, to provide some threat to the total program of the Convention. This situation could have been influenced also by the fact that during that year, a new department, the "Student Activities" department, had been created under the leadership of D. B. Nicholson.[48]

Georgia Baptists were upon lean years as 1925 ended. It was reported to the Convention that: "This has been one of the most unusual years in the history of this state." [49] Thousands of Georgia Baptists had suffered economically because of an extensive drought. ". . . and to these thousands of drouth stricken Baptists must be added other thousands of good Baptists who have migrated to Florida, during this year. Those items, together with the adverse economic conditions, which have existed through a series of years, . . ." [50] were matters of serious concern.

BUDGET ADJUSTMENTS

Included in the recommendations from the Executive Committee to the Convention was one which would instruct the Executive Committee to make adjustments in Convention work and to the budget as necessary to ". . . enable it to take care of the deficit next year and to conform its program to a budget not to exceed the expenditures of 1925." [51] The budget was to be in two sections; one covering a budget limited to the amount spent on State Missions in 1925, $89,196.27, and the second a potential budget consisting of the actual budget plus certain items which would be included only when contributions to State Missions during

[48]*Minutes, Georgia Baptist Convention,* 1925, p. 25.
[49]*Ibid.,* p. 26.
[50]*Loc. cit.*
[51]*Loc. cit.*

1926 would warrant it. Deferred items included the head-quarters building and appropriations for new church buildings. The deficit on the 1925 budget was to be the first item for the 1926 budget.[52] It was $21,566.25.[53]

The Mercer University System was to undergo yet another change. The Convention adopted a resolution presented by Cree which would call upon the Executive Committee to appoint ". . . immediately after the session of the Convention, a committee of three members . . ." and that this committee of three not be salaried officers of any schools or members of any faculty, ". . . except that the chairman of the committee shall be ex-officio a member of all the Boards of Trustees . . ." [54] This had the effect of abolishing the office of Chancellor of the Mercer System.[55] The proposed committee would be the official representative of the Convention and the Executive Committee in dealing with the schools, and would in turn represent all the schools to the Convention. The Committee of Three would, in effect, be

". . . an affectionate, friendly umpire, trying to harmonize all differences that may arise among all the schools, and having authority to see that all the institutions in the system obey the rules of the Convention.[56]

The chairman was to visit all the schools officially at least once each year.

Further, all funds appropriated for education by the Convention would be distributed through the office of the secretary-treasurer of the Executive Committee,

. . . and shall, upon the written voucher of the Chairman of the Committee of Three be sent directly each month to the institution to which it belongs, . . .[57]

It was to be the responsibility of the chairman to see that the funds were spent in accordance with the Convention

[52]*Loc. cit.*
[53]*Ibid.*, p. 58.
[54]*Ibid.*, p. 29.
[55]*Loc. cit.*
[56]*Loc. cit.*
[57]*Loc. cit.*

budget, and the same committee was to make a budget annually for the amounts to be apportioned to each institution in the system. The chairman was to be paid a salary of $600 per year and travel expenses, which would be deducted from the educational fund before distribution of any money to the institutions.[58] The Committee was named at the December meeting of the Executive Committee and consisted of W. T. Granade, J. C. Wilkinson and T. W. Tippett.[59]

In abolishing the office of Chancellor, the Convention said:

> It is not our purpose to break down, or weaken in any way, the great historical Mercer System, with Mercer University at its head. Our intention is to strengthen it, and make it more useful.[60]

Continuing further with the concerns of Christian Education, the same Convention heard the report of a Commission of Nine appointed in 1924 to make a survey of educational institutions. J. C. Wilkinson was named chairman of that committee. The Commission reported to the Convention declaring they believed that the expense of making such a survey would be prohibitive, and asked that the commission be discharged.[61]

To aid the Georgia Baptist Hospital in collecting claims against the government for treatment of former soldiers, the Convention adopted a motion going on record as believing that the government had a moral right to pay its bills whether all technical details had been complied with or not.[62]

Total assets of the Holding Commission in 1925 were $2,150,709.85.[63] This Commission, in a sense also the predecessor of the present Georgia Baptist Foundation, reported through Jesse B. Hart, secretary-treasurer, that it had col-

[58]*Ibid.*, p.p. 29, 30.
[59]Spright Dowell, *A History of Mercer University 1833-1953* [Atlanta: Foote & Davies, Inc., 1958], p. 284.
[60]*Minutes, Georgia Baptist Convention*, 1925, p. 30.
[61]*Ibid.*, p.p. 31, 32.
[62]*Ibid.*, p. 36.
[63]*Ibid.*, p. 56.

lected income of $6,000 over 1924, but that between $40,000 and $50,000 of investments were producing no income.[64] As of November 17, 1925, the Commission had investments totaling $295,379.40; $452,808.00 in real estate mortgages; $7,899.00 in notes receivable; $1,246,708.00 in institutional property; $143,354.37 in institutional equipment.[65]

And, while the Holding Commission could report some increases in income, the State Missions deficit, as indicated previously, was $21,566.25.[66]

During the years 1921-1925, Christian Education was in the forefront of Georgia Baptist thought—and support. Between 1916 and 1920, the first five years of Cree's administration, $570,332.22 was given for education causes in Georgia. During the second five-year period, 1920-1925, $1,038,-549.29 was given for educational causes. However, during the same period, State Missions gifts went from $546,865.47 for the 1916-1920 period down to $445,149.86 during the second period—a decline of about $100,000.00 in the midst of an expanding State Missions program. Home Missions suffered somewhat; Foreign Missions was ahead slightly; the Orphans' Home held its own, and the Hospital down slightly, but it was educational causes which received the largest gain.[67] From this time on, the cause of State Missions was to suffer at the expense of the causes of Home and Foreign missions to some degree.

BUDGET DEFICITS GIVEN PRIORITY

Another comparison is of interest. For the 10-year period 1906-1915, total receipts were $1,978,565.31. For the 10-year period 1916-1925, which period included the $75 Million Campaign, $6,687,984.83 was contributed for all causes.[68] The projection for the 1926 budget was the first year in which a deficit from a previous year was a priority

[64]*Ibid.*, p. 53.
[65]*Ibid.*, p.p. 55, 56.
[66]*Ibid.*, p. 58.
[67]*Ibid.*, p. 59.
[68]*Ibid.*, p. 60.

for the next year. This was not to be the last time. For several years, the Convention budget would be so structured.

Transition from the $75 Million Campaign to the United Kingdom Program during 1925 should not go unnoticed. Some worsening of the situation, even after the 1925 Convention, is indicated by the fact that the Executive Committee, meeting Dec. 17, 1925, recommended that within three months from that date, the Department of Enlistment be discontinued.[69] This included really the work of evangelism and enlistment. In a five-year period up to 1925, four secondary schools, Bleckley Memorial, Hiawassee, Blairsville Institute and Morganton Institute had been transferred to the Home Mission Board.[70] And, the Mary P. Willingham School, which did receive aid through the $75 Million Campaign, received sole support from Woman's Missionary Union.[71]

With strenuous cutbacks, the State Mission operation was in the black by the 1926 session in Valodsta. During the year, Spencer B. King, Sr., had been named superintendent of State Missions. Citing the fact that 1925 was the only year in eight that there had been a debt, the report reviewing the administrative work for the Executive Board said: "Ours is the only Board with such a record. All other state boards have had from a few thousands to hundreds of thousands each year."[72] One item involved in the cuts was ministerial education, and there was an appeal from the Mercer trustees stating that for two years there had been no specific appropriation for ministerial education.[73]

For the first time, in 1926, it was reported that: "Presentation of the claims of the Co-operative Program of the Southern Baptist Convention was brought in a message by A. J. Barton of Nashville, Tennessee.[74]

[69]*Minutes, Executive Committee, Georgia Baptist Convention,* Dec. 17, 1925.
[70]*Minutes, Georgia Baptist Convention,* 1925, p. 112.
[71]*Loc. cit.*
[72]*Minutes, Georgia Baptist Convention,* 1926, p. 13.
[73]*Minutes, Georgia Baptist Convention,* 1926, p. 17.
[74]*Ibid.,* p. 20.

In September of 1926, the Executive Committee

> In consideration of report of the committee on 1927
> program, W. H. Major moved to amend paragraph rela-
> tive to giving the Georgia institutions and interests
> embraced by the Cooperative Program the right of
> appeal to individuals for funds for endowment, etc.,
> by adding the words, 'this restriction not to apply to
> missions.' [75]

The quotations are significant in that although the Co-
operative Program was adopted by the Southern Baptist Convention in May, 1925, there is no use of that term in minutes
either of the Georgia Baptist Convention or its Executive
Committee prior to the above two citations. Extensive search
failed to disclose any specific action either by the Executive
Committee or the Convention in annual session which placed
either group as being on record adopting formally the Co-
operative Program.

A further reference is noted in citing the 1925 Convention action which was:

> At its last session this Convention authorized and in-
> structed its Executive Committee after conference with
> the Program Commission of the Southern Baptist Con-
> vention to set up the Cooperative Program and Unified
> Budget for 1927 in Georgia. Having conferred with the
> Southern Baptist Convention Program Commission and
> with the leaders of the several state interests involved,
> your Executive Committee, as per your instruction, has
> approved and authorized the promotion of the following
> budget and program for 1927, with a total goal for the
> year of $600,000, to be divided equally between state
> and South-wide interests.[76]

This citation is at variance with the wording of the 1925
Convention to which it refers and implies that it is a
quotation thereof. What the 1925 Convention said was: "4.
We recommend that the Executive Committee be authorized
by the Convention, in co-operation with the Southern Baptist Convention Program Committee, to set up the Unified

[75]*Minutes, Executive Committee, Georgia Baptist Convention,* 1926, September 27, 28, p. 321.

[76]*Minutes, Georgia Baptist Convention,* 1926, p. 55.

Kingdom Program and Budget for 1927." [77] The 1925 phrasing omits the word "Cooperative Program" inserted in the 1926 report of the 1925 action.

Recommendations of the Administration [Cree speaking for the Executive Committee], called for authority for the Executive Committee, ". . . in co-operation with the Southern Baptist Convention program committee, to adopt and set up the Unified Kingdom Program and Budget for 1928." [78] The recommendation said: "That there be adherence to the budget plan for raising funds for the Baptist Co-operative Program. [79]

Georgia went along, immediately and wholeheartedly, with the idea, and apparently by implication adopted the term.

A constitutional amendment was approved by an almost unanimous vote in 1926. Purpose of the amendment is self-explanatory. It was a substitute for Section 1 of Article 6 of the constitution and read:

> Article 6, Section 1. An Executive Committee of this Convention shall be chosen by the Convention, and shall consist of the officers of the Convention ex-officio and forty-five members from the state at large, one-fifth of whom shall be elected to hold office for one year, one-fifth for two years, one-fifth for three years, one-fifth for four years and one-fifth for five years. The vacancies as the terms expire shall be filled for terms of five years. No one connected in any way with any institution fostered by this Convention shall be eligible for membership on this Committee. No member of the Committee shall be eligible to re-election after the expiration of his term of service until he has been in retirement from the Committee for at least one year. [80]

Shorter College appeared to have a way of being a member of the Convention family and at the same time being independent. This was demonstrated more than once, and again, with approval of this amendment, the question arose

[77]*Minutes, Georgia Baptist Convention,* 1925, p.p. 26, 27.
[78]*Minutes, Georgia Baptist Convention,* 1926, p.p. 13-14.
[79]*Ibid.,* p. 14.
[80]*Ibid.,* p.p. 20, 21.

about interpretation. It was agreed by the Convention that the limitation on eligibility be limited to state or state-wide institutions, and later, upon a motion by Rufus Weaver, it was agreed that Shorter would not be regarded as being subject to the limitations.[81]

Occasionally relatively small matters became the focal point of a resolution. The matters at the time were not, apparently, regarded as insignificant. Arch Cree submitted a resolution based upon a question having been raised as to the propriety of passing or giving out any resolution proporting to express the judgment of the Convention when a small number of messengers were present and voting. A motion was made by C. W. Daniel, the Convention approved, and the motion called upon the number present and voting to be recorded when a resolution was passed in the name of the Convention.[82]

The resolution in question at the time was one which urged the Sunday School Board to increase its service in promoting all Sunday School and Young People's organizations, Bible stewardship, tithing and church and denominational budget, and ". . . that it give as many as four lessons a year in all its departments of its literature, with two or three lessons consecutively in the fall of the year as a preparation for the every member canvass, and the securing of our annual budgets . . ." [83]

Evidence of the resolution indicated possibly that Cree wanted the Convention to proceed with caution in asking the Sunday School Board to assume responsibility for promotion of stewardship throughout the Convention at a time when the Executive Committee of the Southern Baptist Convention was moving into this area upon SBC approval of the Co-operative Program.

COMMITTEE OF FIVE ENDED

The year 1926 saw the end of the Committee of Five with

[81]*Ibid.*, p. 21.
[82]*Ibid.*, p. 25.
[83]*Ibid.*, p. 26.

the recommendation that its work be committed to the Committee of Three and that the Executive Committee, upon recommendation from the Committee of Three, be given final authority for action. Among other items reported were that the places for the three proposed secondary schools that the Committee of Five had been instructed to locate, had been so located. They had agreed earlier that the school for Southwest Georgia be located at Norman.[84] They were now in agreement that the school for Central and North Georgia be located at Locust Grove and the school for Southeast Georgia be located at Brewton-Parker.[85]

Mercer President Weaver had already, at this Convention, made a motion that the Constitution of the Convention be so interpreted that an amendment not be applied to Shorter.[86] Weaver gave notice that at the next Convention he would propose an amendment to Article 6, Section 1 (same article and section already amended by 1926 session) to strike the phrase . . . "No one connected in any way with an institution fostered by this convention shall be eligible to membership on this Committee."[87] Instead, Weaver wanted the phrase to read:

> No member of this Committee shall be connected with more than one other Board, institution or agency to which money is given by the Georgia Baptist churches under an allocation to which this Convention agrees.[88]

An interesting sidelight in Convention history was the fact that in the summer of 1926, Dr. T. W. Ayers, well-loved Georgia Baptist missionary to China, had returned to his home state because of the illness of his wife. Cree secured permission from the Foreign Mission Board to use Dr. Ayers as an assistant in field work, which Ayers did for six months before going to Tift College as professor of missions.[89]

[84]*Ibid.*, p. 28.
[85]*Loc. cit.*
[86]*Ibid.*, p. 21.
[87]*Ibid.*, p. 29.
[88]*Loc. cit.*
[89]*Minutes, Georgia Baptist Convention,* 1926, p.p. 58, 59.

The December, 1925, meeting of the Executive Committee did away with the Department of Enlistment and Evangelism.[90] In 1926, Spencer B. King had been named Superintendent of State Missions.[91] Because of the fact that the field men on salary had been released from work, the Executive Committee proposed that King organize a voluntary force of pastors to supplement the work of the evangelists; actually take the place of, since they were not there to be supplemented.[92]

Having done away with the evangelistic department in March of 1926—90 days after the agreement to do so in December, 1925, the Executive Committee was now saying that in view of the many appeals for assistance they would like to employ four general evangelists to be located in and labor in four sections of the state.[93]

The Committee of Three, in its first report, in 1926, said that it had organized for duty in January of that year and that after numberless meetings were stressing endowment for the educational institutions as a major need. The Committee declared in its report that it had been difficult to stay "sweet" in the midst of difficult conferences.[94] In the first report, the group recommended proposals which the schools had for endowment; suggested that secondary schools be limited in their appeals for endowment to the geographical areas which they served (leaving Mercer and Tift free to canvass the entire state); and endorsed the concept that at least 75 per cent of all monies raised be set up as permanent endowment. Further, they recommended formation of a Commission of Seven to survey completely the educational program in Georgia and report back to the 1927 Convention with a definite educational program for the Convention and a definite educational policy.[95]

[90]*Minutes, Executive Committee,* Dec. 17, 1925.
[91]*Minutes, Georgia Baptist Convention,* 1926, p. 58.
[92]*Ibid.,* p. 72.
[93]*Loc. cit.*
[94]*Ibid.,* p. 113.
[95]*Ibid.,* p. 152.

The Executive Committee agreed to assume control of the hospital in May, 1922. Cree became general manager and treasurer of the Hospital Commission,[96] and for several years managed the Hospital in addition to the responsibilities as executive secretary-treasurer of the Executive Board. In 1924, Cree reported that debts were not the only problem at the hospital. The staff and nurses were "sadly disorganized," and there had been considerable effort expended to reorganize the internal operations of the hospital.[97] He reported also that

> . . . the heavy liabilities reported to us by the Board of Trustees when they turned the hospital over to the Executive Committee, have been so substantially reduced that we feel now that the institution is on solid ground, . . .[98]

The Executive Committee still had not in that year sold the old hospital property on Luckie Street. Previously valued at $150,000, it was in that year valued at $200,000 and when sold, Cree reported, ". . . the hospital will be in a condition to liquidate its indebtedness." [99] Because of this more hopeful prospect for the Hospital, the Executive Committee heard the Hospital Commission's proposals for construction and gave approval for building, recommending to the Convention approval of a $500,000 bond issue.[100]

On June 1, 1925, a bond issue of $450,000 was sold to the Whitney Central Trust and Savings Bank, New Orleans, at six per cent interest, to be repaid in 12 years. The remaining $40,000 needed for construction was to be provided from other sources.[101] Ground was broken for the new hospital surgical building in December, 1925; the cornerstone was laid in May, 1926, and the unit was dedicated October 31, 1926. It had a capacity of 120 patients, and cost $240,000.

[96]*The Christian Index,* June 1, 1922, p. 85; *Minutes, Executive Committee, Georgia Baptist Convention,* May 4, 1922.

[97]*Minutes, Georgia Baptist Convention,* 1924, p. 87.

[98]*Ibid.,* p. 88.

[99]*Ibid.,* p.p. 88, 89.

[100]*Ibid.,* p. 89.

[101]*Minutes, Georgia Baptist Convention,* 1925, p. 90.

With facilities in the old medical building, this brought the Hospital's capacity to 200 patients.[102] By 1926, the Hospital was self-supporting in its current work, and there was no debt on operations.[103]

The change in hospital control from the old Board of Trustees to the Commission named by the Executive Committee was effected after the May, 1922, Executive Committee meeting and prior to publication of the June 1, 1922, issue of *The Index*.[104] Writing concerning the hospital under new administration, Louie D. Newton, in the Convention Centennial number of *The Index* called upon Georgia Baptists to give ". . . the Executive Committee, the Hospital Commission and our Secretary our hearty and sympathetic support. These brethren are not responsible for the present embarrassing condition." [105] The first commission was comprised of Cree, Charles W. Daniel, J. P. Nichols, W. B. Willingham, and A. J. Orme.[106]

Cree was to have executive control of the hospital for a period of nearly five years, until May, 1927, when J. B. Franklin became superintendent of the hospital.[107]

The Education Committee in 1927, meeting in Augusta, recommended that responsibility for ministerial aid be placed with the Executive Committee, and that the Convention appoint a committee to plan an endowment campaign for educational institutions.[108]

The Commission of Seven, recommended in 1926 by the Committee of Three to define the Convention's educational policy, reported in four areas. One, objectives: two, administration; three, finances; and four, supervision. They said first that:

[102]*Minutes, Georgia Baptist Convention*, 1926, p. 89.
[103]*Ibid.*, p. 90.
[104]*The Christian Index*, June 1, 1922, p. 85.
[105]*Loc. cit.*
[106]*Loc. cit.*
[107]B. D. Ragsdale, *Story of Georgia Baptists*, Vol. III, [The Executive Committee of Georgia Baptist Convention, Atlanta, 1938], p. 270.
[108]*Minutes, Georgia Baptist Convention*, 1927, p. 14.

"(1) The Convention is morally and legally responsible for all financial obligations which the trustees of Convention-owned schools may create. The Convention recognizes its moral obligation to support the schools which it owns and controls." [109]

The Social Service Commission, reporting in 1927, declared that:

The doctrine of separation of church and state with its untold blessings must never be forsaken. But this doctrine grew out of the oppression of religious people in their conscience by the agencies of government. It was never intended to prevent them from giving their best thought and deepest loyalty to the cause of good government or wholesome social life. Churches and religious bodies should not become instruments for the advancement or hindrance of persons or parties in a partisan struggle for place.[110]

At the annual meeting of the Southern Baptist Convention in 1926, the Laymen's Missionary Movement was renamed Baptist Brotherhood of the South, a title under which the movement was to operate until 1950.[111] Therefore, at the August session, there was for the first time a report on Baptist Brotherhood—the first time the phrase had been used officially among Georgia Baptists. The report recommended that the Laymen's Committee be discontinued as such in the light of the fact that it had reorganized itself under the name of Baptist Brotherhood of the State of Georgia.[112]

The Laymen's Movement evidently lost some of its impact upon Georgia Baptist life in the early 1920's, and through the period from the early 1920's until the creation of a Brotherhood Department of the Georgia Baptist Convention in 1946,[113] that active participation by laymen in Georgia Baptist life diminished somewhat.

[109]*Ibid.*, p. 16 [Note: The full report may be found under this reference.]
[110]*Ibid.*, p. 30.
[Note: A rather full history of the Social Service Commission may be found on pages 28, 29, 30 of the 1927 *Minutes of the Georgia Baptist Convention.*]
[111]*Encyclopedia of Southern Baptists*, Vol. I, p. 198.
[112]*Minutes, Georgia Baptist Convention*, 1927, p. 35.
[113]*Georgia Baptist Digest*, Vol. 31, 1971, p. 48.

During the year 1927, the hospital treated 303 patients free, 267 part-free, with the note in the hospital report that over a 14-year period, free service had been extended to 4,218 patients at a total cost, including doctors' free service, of $813,287.02.[114]

Of historic value is a report in 1927 by a committee named to compile and codify such Standing Resolutions of the Convention as might have permanent force and value. Resolutions included were: One by the Committee of Five in 1916 out of which came the Commission of Seven.[115] Another, in 1917,[116] called for a name to be placed on each Baptist church. A 1920 resolution called for all recommendations accompanying a report to be voted upon separately, with no resolution to be binding unless so stated clearly.[117]

One resolution calling for the annual report on the Orphans' Home to contain a detailed statement on all food, clothing, and other items, with approximate value was included.[118] Others were: Discontinuance of the Committee on Resolutions;[119] Approval for the Executive Committee to sell hospital property on Luckie Street and apply proceeds to hospital;[120] On law observance and enforcement on the part of the citizenry, courts and newspapers;[121] Recommendation of the Education Board that $25,000 ". . . be paid annually to Bessie Tift College until such time as the income from endowment will take its place." [122]

That Mercer trustees present annually to the Nominating Committee nine names with three of the nine to be chosen as trustees. The Alumni association was to present nine names also, with the same procedure applying. The same

[114]*Minutes, Georgia Baptist Convention*, 1927, p. 32.
[115]*Minutes, Georgia Baptist Convention*, 1916, p. 63.
[116]*Ibid.*, p. 30.
[117]*Minutes, Georgia Baptist Convention*, 1920, p. 43.
[118]*Minutes, Georgia Baptist Convention*, 1921, p. 53.
[119]*Minutes, Georgia Baptist Convention*, 1922, p. 41.
[120]*Ibid.*
[121]*Minutes, Georgia Baptist Convention*, 1924, p. 39.
[122]*Ibid.*, p. 33.

policy was to apply to Tift College.[123] The one discontinuing the Chancellorship of the Mercer System in favor of the Committee of Three [124] and one by the Committee of Five recommending Convention election of all trustees in the Mercer System was included;[125] a resolution concerning annuities for the hospital;[126] The final resolution included making the president of Mercer University president of the Georgia Baptist Historical Society.[127]

These are listed because as Standing Resolutions they carried constitutional force until changed.

The year 1928 was scheduled to be a year of observance of the Jubilee of State Missions.[128] With the Convention in 1927, the State Mission Board, and its successor, the Executive Committee, marked 50 years of service, with especial emphasis in earlier years upon State Missions, and in later years, with expansion of responsibilities.

50-YEAR COMPARISON

As the Convention made plans to observe this Jubilee Year for State Missions, a report of receipts for the 50-year period was presented.

1877-1891, J. H. DeVotie, Secretary, State Missions gifts, $231,193.76; sum total for all causes, $444,834.38.

1892-1900, John G. Gibson, Secretary, State Missions gifts, $207,420.19; total gifts, $668,800.82.

1900-1906, S. Y. Jameson, Secretary, State Missions, $151,341.10; total, $553,315.89.

1906-1914, J. J. Bennett, Secretary, State Missions, $486,$689.40; total gifts, $1,853,356.15.

1915-1927, Arch C. Cree, Secretary, State Missions, $1,138,590.19; total gifts, $8,621,665.76.

[123]*Minutes, Georgia Baptist Convention,* 1925, p. 24.
[124]*Ibid.,* p. 29.
[125]*Ibid.,* p. 31.
[126]*Ibid.,* p. 37.
[127]*Minutes, Georgia Baptist Convention,* 1926, p.p. 31, 32.
[128]*Minutes, Georgia Baptist Convention,* 1927, p. 41.

For the 50-year period, 1877-1927, total given for State Missions work was $2,215,234.64; total gifts, $12,141,973.00.[129]

By 1927, baptisms had increased slightly over 1926; 16,502 for 15,767, for a gain of 735,[130] and book store sales for the year May 1, 1926-May 1, 1927 were $39,680.78, an increase of nearly 33 per cent over the preceding year.[131] By this year, the book store was owned jointly by the Executive Committee and the Sunday School Board of the Southern Baptist Convention.[132]

Some years prior to 1927, the Convention's Executive Committee had approved a plan of pastoral aid which encouraged churches to unite in fields. The goal of providing active programs in small churches was not forgotten.

As Superintendent of State Missions, Spencer B. King continued to encourage this concept, reporting that in Georgia there were 160 towns with populations ranging from 800 to 20,000, and there were five cities with more residents than all the 160 towns together. Not an unusual comparison, King however was making the point that there were too many country churches, with one country church in Georgia for every 32 square miles.[133]

However, in his book, *Georgia, A Mission Field,* published in 1928, King repeated in essence the statement that there were too many churches ill-located, and declared that there were too few churches in some areas,[134] with rural churches being

> . . . the richest possession of Georgia Baptists. It is from the rural churches that the great leaders of our denomination have come through the past years, and there is every reason to believe that the majority of the real leaders in the future days will come from rural churches.[135]

[129]*Ibid.*, p. 54.
[130]*Ibid.*, p. 55.
[131]*Ibid.*, p. 59.
[132]*Loc. cit.*
[133]*Ibid.*, p. 67.
[134]Spencer B. King, *Georgia, A Mission Field* [Atlanta: Executive Committee Baptist Convention of State of Georgia, 1928] p.p. 48-50.
[135]*Ibid.*, p. 51.

What King sought to emphasize was that there were too many churches not functioning adequately, which could disband, and their members serve to greater advantage in other churches. On the other hand, King, as a leader in State Mission work, felt strongly that there were many opportunities for mission work, including the establishment of new churches. He took the position, and with some basis, that:

> "Our people have not been judicious in locating their churches in past years, or, after the churches were located, changes in the community have taken place which leaves the building far out of the way." [136]

While it was considered a new service in the 1960's for the Sunday School Department of the Convention to work in co-operation with the Department of Church Architecture of the Sunday School Board, the Sunday School Department in Georgia, in 1927, was giving architectural service to the churches upon request.[137] Churches aided by this service during 1927 included Bull Street, Savannah; Capital View, Inman Park and Gordon Street, in Atlanta; and First Baptist, Waycross.[138]

Thomasville, in deep South Georgia, was host to the Convention when it convened on December 4, 1928. W. H. Major, chairman of the Jubilee Committee from the State Missions observance gave to Georgia Baptists encouraging news. The total amount received at "Baptist Headquarters" for the year was $511,648.73, an increase of $60,358.90 in new income for the year. Designated gifts were $211,240.72, a gain of $47,232.54, and distributable receipts were $300,-408.01, or $13,126.36 over the previous year.[139]

Arch Cree, the man, was unique. Arch Cree, the Baptist leader, was unique also in many ways. As his tenure was nearing an end (he resigned late in 1929), he rendered to Georgia and Southern Baptists a service unparalleled, per-

---

[136]*Ibid.*, p. 48.
[137]*Minutes, Georgia Baptist Convention*, 1927, p. 72.
[138]*Loc. cit.*
[139]*Minutes, Georgia Baptist Convention*, 1928, p. 11.

haps, in Southern Baptist Convention history. For a time
he served both as Executive Secretary-Treasurer of the Executive Committee of the Georgia Baptist Convention and
Acting Executive Secretary-Treasurer of the Home Mission
Board of the Southern Baptist Convention.

On August 15, 1928, the treasurer of the Home Mission
Board disappeared.[140]

"Clinton S. Carnes became treasurer of the Home Mission
Board during the convention year 1919-1920, . . ." Prior to
his coming to the Home Board, he had a prison record in
Atlanta, unknown at the time to the Board. With authority
to handle funds over his signature, and with authority to
borrow money from banks in different states, "He so manipu-
lated his financial dealings that his criminal acts were committed legally in different states."[141] When the totals were
accumulated, Carnes had stolen $226,126.86 from the Board's
Church Building Fund, and $683,334.14 from the General
Fund, for a total of $909,461.00, or better than an average
of $100,000.00 per year.[142]

Termed the worst financial calamity to hit any work of
the Southern Baptist Convention, the defalcation became
known in August of 1928. About one-third of the amount
was recovered from Carnes: a special Baptist Honor day
raised $389,164.35, requiring the Board until 1943 to pay
the remainder of the amount lost.[143]

It was in this crisis, that the Home Mission Board turned
to Georgia Baptists, requesting the Executive Committee to
"lend" Arch Cree to the Home Board.[144] Cree assumed
leadership of the Board on a temporary basis,[145] and he did
much to place the Home Board back on a sound financial
basis. W. W. Barnes, writing the monograph on the Carnes
defalcation in the *Encyclopedia of Southern Baptists,* said:

[140]*Ibid.,* p. 49.
[141]*Encyclopedia of Southern Baptists,* Vol. I, p. 232.
[142]*Loc. cit.*
[143]*Loc. cit.*
[144]*Minutes, Georgia Baptist Convention,* 1928, p. 15.
[145]*Ibid.,* p.p. 49, 50

> Under wise and efficient management the board carried
> on a greatly limited work, and succeeded in clearing all
> debts by 1943. Much credit is due to Archibald Cun-
> ningham Cree, who served briefly during the crisis as
> interim secretary, and later to Secretary J. B. Lawrence
> . . . in meeting the situation so successfully.[146]

Cree, therefore, during his administration, had not only
led the hospital through its major crisis, serving as superintendent for five years in addition to his regular responsibilities, but within two years of being relieved of the hospital responsibility, he served again in a dual capacity; this
time for nine months.[147]

The Home Mission Board had moved to Atlanta following approval by the 1882 session of the Southern Baptist
Convention for a move.[148] The Board had begun to lag in
its ministries at the Marion, Alabama, location. The Southern Convention decided to move to

> . . . a more prominent city and make a new start. It
> chose Atlanta, and the Board began afresh with a new
> slate of directors and a new corresponding secretary.[149]

Georgia Baptists therefore had an interest of long standing in
the Home Board, and the request for Cree's services was
acceded to quickly.

With the Fall enrolment at Locust Grove Institute in 1927
down to 122, 42 less than in 1926, it was evident that the
institute was in trouble.[150] By 1928 it was dead as a Baptist
institution. The "last words" said over the institute as a
Baptist school were in the minutes of the Administration
Committee for June 8, 1928, when the Committee approved,
subject to review by the Committee's attorney, a contract
for sale of the Locust Grove property for $20,000 to Locust
Grove Institute, Inc., a corporation chartered to run the in-

[146]*Encyclopedia of Southern Baptists,* Vol. I, p. 232.

[147]Arthur B. Rutledge, *Mission to America,* [Nashville: Broadman Press
1969] p. 60.

[148]*Ibid.,* p. 36.

[149]*Loc. cit.*

[150]*Minutes, Georgia Baptist Convention,* 1927, p. 131.

stitution as a boy's day camp.[151] From this point, it was to take several years to dispose of the property. The institute, which began in 1894 under sponsorship of the Flint River Association, had during its lifetime, one of the most unique records of accomplishment in Georgia Baptist educational history.

Ragsdale gives credit to B. J. W. Graham as instigator of the proposal to have an institute at Locust Grove when Graham served as pastor at Locust Grove for four years as a Mercer student, and upon graduation in 1894, for about 18 months as a resident pastor. The Institute, under the leadership of Professor Claude Gray from 1897 on, was to produce an unusual share of Georgia and Southern Baptist leadership.[152] More than 350 Locust Grove graduates went on to Mercer University.[153] Dowell, in his history of Mercer University, cited the close ties between the institute and Mercer.[154] Of the institute, Ragsdale said:

> No secondary school in the State developed so nearly a state-wide patronage. It has repeatedly been challenged whether any other preparatory school sent to college so large a percentage of its students, students so well prepared or of finer general type. Though the end of the school was full of pathos and of seeming tragedy, its career was one of high usefulness and of abiding and fragrant honor.[155]

On June 29, 1958 a reunion of alumni was held on the campus site, attracting more than 400 persons for a day-long celebration. It is doubtful that any other such institution in Georgia or elsewhere could claim the distinction of bringing together that many alumni more than 30 years after its demise.[155a]

[151]*Minutes, Administration Committee, Executive Committee, Georgia Baptist Convention,* June 8, 1928.

[152]*Ragsdale,* Vol. II, p.p. 335-345.

[153]*Ibid.,* p.p. 337, 338.

[154]*Dowell,* p.p. 266, 267.

[155]B. D. Ragsdale, *Story of Georgia Baptists,* Vol. II [Macon: Mercer University, 1935] p. 345.

[155a]Copy of Program, Locust Grove Institute, Memorial Service, Author's Possession.

GRAHAM'S UNIQUE MINISTRY

Few men accomplished as much in the interests of Georgia Baptists, with as little recognition during their lifetime or after death, as did B. J. W. Graham. From his days as a Mercer student, and Locust Grove pastor, Graham conceived the idea of the institute, published a Baptist paper at Cochran, became associated in 1900 with *The Index,* becoming associate editor, part-owner and owner, then leading in establishment of the Index Printing Company. He served as a field representative for the Orphans' Home, published a three-volume biographical series on Georgia Baptist pastors, published numerous other books of theological value, served as pastor of Georgia churches during his tenure with *The Index,* sold *The Index* to Georgia Baptists, and left a portion of his estate to Christian education.

Other Convention institutions were folding. Piedmont Institute had been closed, and Gibson-Mercer Academy, Bowman had been sold.[156] Brewton-Parker, still a high school, ". . . surrounded as she is by good State high schools, and a growing junior college is feeling the pressure of State competition acutely." [157]

In the Jubilee Year, there were 90 associations, 2,371 churches with a membership of 408,673; 15,062 baptisms, 237,008 enrolled in Sunday School, 1,534 B.Y.P.U.'s, 2,091 W.M.U.'s, with the value of all church property set at $16,598,472. Pastors' salaries for the year were $946,816.02 (cumulative) and other local contributions were $1,444,-226.88. Total gifts to Cooperative Program, $491,760.26; total B.W.M.U. gifts $228,013.87; miscellaneous items $19,-888.47, for a total in contributions of $2,902,691.63.[158]

For the first time, in 1929, the Convention heard a report from the Cooperative Program Committee[159] and with adoption of amendments to the charter of Mercer University,

[156]*Minutes, Georgia Baptist Convention,* 1928, p. 82.
[157]*Ibid.,* p. 106.
[158]*Ibid.,* final statistical page (p.p. 262-263).
[159]*Minutes, Georgia Baptist Convention,* 1929, p. 18.

placed that institution for all practical purposes under complete control of the Board of Trustees, ending control held through the Holding Commission, and thereby, indirectly by the Executive Committee.[160]

At the beginning of the depression, it was necessary for resolutions on the budget to be adopted with the note that the Convention year did not end until December 31, and it was not possible until that time to make a budget for 1930. The matter of the 1930 budget was therefore referred to a special committee which would in turn refer it to the Executive Committee.[161] Plans were made for all participating institutions and programs to present their budget needs to the Executive Committee by making presidents of the institutions members of the committee.[162]

It was unfortunate, and through no fault of his leadership, that during the final year of Cree's Administration the Convention found itself in worse financial condition than for many years. Cree had established a record of sound business management as executive secretary-treasurer for the Executive Committee, and looked after the interests of the Convention well.

Therefore, in his final report, a note of regret and disappointment is evident when he gave to the Convention a picture of its financial condition. He said that for the first time in 15 years, there was the necessity of reporting a heavy deficit.

> "This deficit is due, for the most part," Cree said, "to the fact that at the last Convention we broke away from the conservative, business management and safeguard of many years, namely, that the State Missions budget for the current year shall not exceed the cash receipts for State Missions for the previous year." [163]

Cree said further that the Convention had placed the Executive Committee in serious financial condition when it

[160]*Ibid.*, p.p. 27-30.
[161]*Ibid.*, p. 35.
[162]*Loc. cit.*
[163]*Ibid.*, p. 78.

placed upon that committee financial responsibilities which included school debts, and deficits in operation of *The Christian Index,* (at that time, $17,195.39). He commented that the Convention in Valdosta in 1926 had ordered the Executive Committee to provide $8,000 immediately for Mercer University for ministerial education, but had made no provisions at the time, nor since then, as to where the money would come from. The Committee, therefore, had been forced to carry this sum as an overdraft from other funds.[164]

The report said also that in authorizing the issue of debentures for schools and colleges, the Convention had declared that debts for all schools should be taken care of immediately by these debentures, but that the Convention at the same time declared that no debentures should be sold until a sinking fund had been sat up. He had, therefore, been forced to delay the remittance of some funds for educational purposes in order to lighten the loads of the educational obligations.[165]

Further, the Convention in Augusta, 1927, in spite of Cree's warning that the plan was not feasible as a banking proposition, had ordered the Executive Committee to assume the indebtedness of secondary schools and finance these through a period of years. In March of 1928, because of unwillingness of financial institutions to finance such a program, the Executive Committee was forced to reverse the action of the Convention.[166]

However, despite these circumstances, some obligations had to be met, and Cree said: "We therefore recommend that the Convention give immediate attention to the imperative necessity of providing funds for the payment of the indebtedness on these schools." [167]

Despite the financial situation in Georgia, Georgia Baptists still were determined to carry as best they could their

[164]*Minutes, Georgia Baptist Convention,* 1929, p.p. 78, 79.
[165]*Ibid.,* p. 79.
[166]*Loc. cit.*
[167]*Ibid.,* p. 80.

proportionate share of Southern Baptist expenses. The Executive Committee recommended that the Convention instruct the Committee and its treasurer to conform to the actions of the Convention concerning the forwarding monthly of all sums collected in the various states for south-wide objects.[168]

Baptist Bible Institute, New Orleans, was chartered October 8, 1917.[169] Shortly after it began operation, evidences of Georgia Baptist support were evident. And it was reported to the 1929 Convention that the Administration Committee of the Executive Committee had on October 22 of that year considered the emergency facing the Institute, and agreed to urge the Executive Committee to recommend to the Convention that Baptist Bible Institute be given the right of appeal to Baptists in Georgia during the month of January, 1930.[170]

When the Convention came to consider its budget for 1930, that consideration was in the light of some hard facts presented by Cree in the report of the Executive Committee. Consideration involved recognition of the fact that the fixed appropriation would have to be $150,000 and must be considered before distribution of funds on a 50-50 basis. These fixed appropriations were the result of the 1928 action authorizing the issuance of $1,500,000 debenture bonds for debt payment, and other commitments made in 1928.[171]

Funds from Woman's Missionary Union had been committed by promises of endowment to Tift and specific gifts to Mary P. Willingham school and for specific south-wide work, including the W.M.U. Training School at Louisville, Ky.[172]

These items, plus an estimated $25,000 for administration, promotion, Convention allocations to *The Index,* and interest

[168]*Ibid.,* p.p. 83, 84.

[169]*Encyclopedia of Southern Baptists,* Vol. II, [Nashville: Broadman Press 1958] p. 968.

[170]*Minutes, Georgia Baptist Convention,* 1929, p. 83.

[171]*Ibid.,* p.p. 84, 85.

[172]*Ibid.,* p. 84.

on the debenture bonds constituted the fixed amount of $150,000 which had to be a preferred item. The 1930 budget was projected upon the basis of this amount plus $450,000, which was to be divided equally between Georgia and South-wide causes.[173]

Cree left Georgia in March, 1930, and became pastor of the First Baptist Church, Salisbury, North Carolina, remaining until 1941.[174]

Ragsdale, listing some major features of the Cree administration, cited the following: The inauguration of the Debt Paying Campaign in 1915. The establishment of the Holding Commission. The Purchase of *The Index* by the Executive Committee. The revision of the Constitution of the Convention. The projection of the 75 Million Campaign, and the expansion of the hospital by additions on Luckie Street and then removal to the Boulevard Avenue site.[175]

And, after years of some advance despite financial hardship, Georgia Baptists entered the 1930's with most of that decade to be taken up with efforts to pay indebtedness, keep the operations of the Convention moving under difficulty, and seeking to promote Kingdom advance.

[173]*Ibid.*, p.p. 84, 85.
[174]*Encyclopedia of Southern Baptists*, Vol. I, p.p. 330, 331.
[175]B. D. Ragsdale, *Story of Georgia Baptists*, Vol. III, p. 140.

CHAPTER 18

The Depression Years, Continued

James White Merritt served Georgia Baptists first as a field worker in the Sunday School department from 1920,[1] beginning April 1, to 1925, including promotion of Vacation Bible Schools. From March, 1925 to April 1, 1930, he was business manager of *The Christian Index*.[2] On April 1, 1930, he assumed the office of Executive Secretary-Treasurer of the Executive Committee.[3]

From the beginning of Merritt's leadership until the present, Georgia Baptist history is, to a large degree, that which has not been written in permanent form. Ragsdale's Volume III of his *Story of Georgia Baptists* was copyrighted in 1938. However, there is little historical record of the Convention after the mid-1920's, and outside of brief mention of the election of Merritt, little is said of the years following to 1938 by Ragsdale.

Two eras of Georgia Baptist history, therefore, exist which are recounted in the remainder of this volume; the period 1930 through 1954 under the leadership of Merritt, and the period 1955 to the present [1972] under the leadership of Searcy S. Garrison, who was to succeed Merritt. During the years covered through 1971, 41 of them, Georgia Baptists—perhaps unknowingly—wrote in many ways their greatest

[1]*Minutes, Georgia Baptist Convention,* 1954, p. 89.
[2]Lester, James Adams, "A History of *The Christian Index,* 1822-1954" [Unpublished Master's Thesis, 1955], p. 108.
[3]*Minutes, Georgia Baptist Convention,* 1954, p. 89.

history as they have lived through these 41 years of revolutionary change in every walk of life.

Inasmuch as the history, as indicated earlier, falls logically into periods of administrative leadership of the Convention, the "Merritt Era" involved 25 years of activity.

Merritt was elected on Dec. 11, 1929.[4] In reporting to the Convention in Macon concerning the election, B. H. Hardy said that:

> When the Executive Committee went into the choice of a man for Secretary-Treasurer, Brother Merritt had just been re-elected as Business Manager of the Index. On the first ballot, which was merely a nomination of the various men in the minds of the members for the position, his name, not having previously been mentioned and no nominating speeches having been made, was first among the number of outstanding Baptists, in and out of Georgia. From that moment, during the morning and afternoon sessions, through about thirty ballots, when the utmost harmony prevailed in the committee, his name continued to appear among the leaders, until the two-thirds vote was recorded for him, which then resulted in his election by a unanimous vote.[5]

The Macon Session in 1930 was faced with the necessity of reshaping the Convention's program in such a way that the work could be carried on without financial disaster. L. R. Christie, in making a proposal to this end, said "The Co-operative Program seems too valuable and vital in principle to be thrown into the discard and to be deliberately scrapped, . . ." [6] He cited further the fact that the equipment and maintenance of all schools was such a distinct and enormous task that special methods of financing were necessary, and that the Convention had entered already into agreements with the institutions. And, upon the strength of these agreements, the institutions were projecting their present and future programs. Thus, his resolutions offered to the Convention, and adopted, outlined an eight-point program to serve as a guide. The resolutions said:

[4]*Minutes, Georgia Baptist Convention,* 1930, p. 68.
[5]*Ibid.,* p. 11.
[6]*Ibid.,* p. 24.

1. That we recognize all obligations which we have incurred as binding upon the Convention, and that we will not fail to do our utmost to see that the last item of obligation, expressed or implied, is faithfully discharged.

2. That we call upon the schools and colleges and the Hospital to initiate programs immediately to assist the Convention in taking care of these obligations for the year 1931. We recommend that the schools undertake the raising of $35,000.00 during the coming year, to be applied upon the debenture obligations, with the expectation that $40,000.00 be paid out of the Co-operative receipts . . .

3. That the Boards of Trustees of these several institutions are hereby notified that on and after January 1, 1932, they will be charged with the full responsibility of initiating and executing all their appeals and programs for the purpose of providing for the needs of these several enterprises. To each and all of them the right and responsibility will be accorded to carry on perpetual programs of efficiency and enlargement, with the hope that they will create and cultivate clienteles who will be sufficiently able and interested to provide the large sums necessary for these institutions. . .

4. That the Georgia Baptist Hospital be asked to initiate, through the wisdom of the Hospital Commission and the Trustees of the same, a program to appeal to those especially interested in the ministry of healing, so as to raise a fund of $20,000.00, if possible, to be applied on the bond obligations maturing in 1931, leaving $30,000.00 to be paid out of the Co-operative receipts. This is not meant to imply that the Convention seeks to evade its moral and legal responsibility for the entire $50,000.00 principle and interest.

5. That we urge upon the Hospital Commission and the Trustees that they use their best efforts and judgment to set up a hospital program, to become effective January 1, 1932, which will make it possible to relieve the Convention of the necessity of making any allocation to the Hospital out of the Co-operative receipts, . . . 'other than for charity.' We hope it may be practicable, after this year, for the Convention to appropriate something like $15,000.00 or $20,000.00 annually for strictly charitable service, and that the Hospital will not undertake any charity work on its own account beyond the amount being taken care of by the Georgia Baptist Convention, until the bonds against the Institution have been retired. . .

6. That a strong statewide effort be made to raise a sufficient sum for the orphanage in the annual December appeal to retire the outstanding indebtedness on that institution, and that it be expected to have the freedom of the field to make such appeal to churches and Sunday schools and Societies as may be necessary to take care of the inescapable needs of this extraordinary enterprise. We would urge that the institution give special attention, in its special appeals, to the non-contributing Baptist churches and Sunday schools of the state, and to such other churches and societies as may invite the Orphanage to present its cause and appeal. We would urge the Orphanage Trustees and management to expect appropriations from the co-operative receipts for 1931 not in excess of $35,000.00, and to project their supplementary plans to raise the necessary amount in excess of this as their judgment may direct.

7. That on and after January 1, 1932, the Co-operative Program shall include the following items: Foreign Missions, Home Missions, State Missions, Orphanage, Ministerial Education, Relief and Annuity, Hospital Charities.

8. That if any unforeseen contingency makes it utterly impractical to initiate this program on January 1, 1932, the Convention meeting a year hence may provide such reasonable extension as will protect an enterprise, but all these several agencies and institutions involved are urged to complete their arrangements to go on this permanent basis by the first day of January, 1932.[7]

In addition to making plans for the 1932 fiscal year, the 1930 Convention took into account the fact that the next year, 1931, would be one of difficulty also. A resolution by E. C. Sheridan made provision for an emergency effort to finance Convention business affairs. The resolution, citing inadequacy of receipts to meet the absolute needs of the work for years, and a decrease, with a great increase of debts resulting, and, no indications that the receipts during 1931 will meet the needs, called forth a resolution:

That we recommend to the Convention that an unusual organization be set up, which shall have the assistance of all institutions which participate in Co-operative funds, in leading Georgia Baptists in an Emergency Effort for the securing of as large a fund as necessary for

[7]*Ibid.,* p.p. 25, 26.

removing financial obstacles to orderly, successful effort in the future.[8]

Although this resolution passed, no steps, evidently, were taken to implement it, except for the rather extreme caution exercised in preparation of the 1931 budget.

Despite business conditions, the Holding Commission reported an income for its fiscal year of $41,734.96, an increase of $1,535.69 over the previous year.[9] The Holding Commission was conservative in its investments over the period of its lifetime, and this accounts for the fact that income was produced during a depression. It had past-due interest of $2,946.00 also.[10] As might be expected, Co-operative Program receipts were on the decline. From January through October of 1930, receipts were $221,858.95; a decrease of $8,442.53, and designated gifts were down $20,085.92, for a total decrease during the year of $28,528.45 in gifts.[11]

The 1929 Convention had authorized the Executive Committee to borrow $100,000 to pay past due obligations. Merritt reported that this was done in February, 1930,[12] with repayment at the rate of $10,000 annually, plus interest. Warning about the seriousness of the fiancial crisis, Merritt reminded the Convention that in authorizing the loan, the 1929 session did so with the restriction that no additional money could be borrowed until at least 50 per cent of the $100,000 loan was repaid.[13] This placed a further imperative upon repayment of the $100,000. The Administration had an accumulated deficit for State Missions of $11,165.94 carried over from 1929 and Merritt warned that by the end of 1930, the total deficit would be about $20,000.[14] This meant that in projecting the 1931 budget, the Executive Committee recommended that the State Missions phase of the budget be projected upon the basis of not exceeding the

[8]*Ibid.*, p. 27.
[9]*Ibid.*, p. 60.
[10]*Loc. cit.*
[11]*Ibid.*, p. 65.
[12]*Ibid.*, p. 66.
[13]*Ibid.*, p. 67.
[14]*Ibid.*, p. 66.

cash receipts for 1930, and that the 1931 budget would include as ". . . large an amount of deficit as seems wise." [15]

The restriction upon further loans was even more important in the light of the fact that it was anticipated that by the end of the calendar year [1930] an additional $60,000 would be needed to take care of deficits accumulated during that year.[16]

As Merritt assumed leadership of the Executive Committee, and Georgia Baptist administrative work, *The Christian Index* was undergoing a change in leadership also. Louie D. Newton resigned as editor of the Index in 1929 to become pastor of the Druid Hills Baptist church in Atlanta.[17] On Dec. 19, 1929, Dr. O. P. Gilbert, then pastor of the First Baptist church, Brunswick was elected editor. He assumed his duties January 15, 1930.[18] Inasmuch as Merritt was business manager of The Index and did not become executive secretary treasurer until April 1, 1930, Gilbert actually assumed editorial control on January 15, and management of the paper April 1, 1930.[19]

NEWTON ACTIVE AS LAYMAN

Newton had served as managing editor and then editor of *The Index* for a period of ten years. He had long been active as a deacon in the Druid Hills church. F. C. McConnell, first and only pastor of that church to 1929, died in January of that year. Newton was called as pastor, and on April 4, 1929, he resigned the editorship of the paper, but agreed to stay with *The Index* until a successor could be elected.[20] For most of the decade during which Newton was editor, because of general financial conditions, *The Index* operated with annual deficits. This was through no fault of Newton as editor, or Merritt as business manager. The high

[15]*Loc. cit.*
[16]*Loc. cit.*
[17]*The Christian Index,* June 15, 1939, p. 25.
[18]Lester, p. 111.
[19]*Minutes, Georgia Baptist Convention,* 1930, p. 76.
[20]*Lester,* p. 110.

cost of paper and printing, the large number of past-due subscriptions which Newton as editor had inherited, and increased overall living costs, all contributed to the situation. Another important factor was that Newton became more selective in his advertising content, bringing advertising more into line with articles and objects which would be of greater value use to a Baptist-oriented constituency.[21]

One interesting notation during Newton's editorship was that appearing in *The Index* January 19, 1928 when Editor Newton reported that *Index* editorials, advertising list, part of the cuts, some poetry and some obituaries for the issue of January 19 had been stolen from his automobile parked in a public parking lot in Atlanta.[22]

During his tenure, Newton was an able editor, and a strong supporter of Georgia Baptists interests. Respected widely, he exerted an influential impact upon Georgia Baptist life, which continues to the present. He was conservative in editorial policy and was alert to defend what he believed to be any encroachment upon religious liberty or upon principles of the separation of church and state.[23] Of all editors, his by-line in *The Index* has continued over a period of 51 years, to the present, by virtue of the fact that after leaving the post of editor in 1930, he contributed news, editorial comments, including the page, later a column, entitled "This Changing World." No other man had access to the ears and eyes of Georgia Baptists through the pages of their state paper for this long a period of time as did Louie D. Newton. Few men exercised the leadership in as many areas of Baptist life as did Newton, both at the Georgia and Southern Convention levels.

Gilbert continued, for the most part, the policies of *The Index* which Newton had adopted, and both Newton and Gilbert had rather full confidence upon the part of the Convention in supporting them editorially and the paper under their leadership.

[21]*Ibid.*, p. 107.
[22]*Ibid.*, p. 110.
[23]*Ibid.*, p. 111.

Agreement to sell Locust Grove Institute had been made two years earlier. As indicated, it was "sold" to be operated as Locust Grove Institute, Inc.,[24] to W. W. Williams and others.[25] During 1930, however, the property was turned back to the Convention under provisions of the contract.

> No payments were ever made on the property and the buildings and equipment appear to have suffered considerable damage. The property that is now idle is under the supervision of a responsible citizen of Locust Grove who is occupying one of the buildings. It is contemplated that this property will be sold if and when a satisfactory purchaser can be found, . . .

the Convention was informed.[26]

As statistical information, the report of Spencer King, dealing with State Missions, is of interest. King said that in 1930, there were over 900,000 Baptists in Georgia of all kinds, comprising nearly 65 per cent of the church membership in the state, with an average of 15.2 Baptists to each of the 59,132 square miles in Georgia.[27]

Spright Dowell, Mercer president, in reporting to Georgia Baptists, declared that to

> 'Allay any disposition to doubt institutional integrity of management' the faculty of Mercer University adopted a simple convenant and the Convention set forth a few principles not as a substitute for the New Testament. . . but as guides to procedure.

This was done, Dowell said because of general unrest during a comparatively recent period over what he termed unwarranted assumptions and alleged unscientific procedure of extremists.[28] He declared:

[24]*Minutes, The Administration Committee, Executive Committee, Georgia Baptist Convention,* June 8, 1928.

[25]*Minutes, Georgia Baptist Convention,* 1930, p. 67.

[26]*Ibid.,* p.p. 67, 68.

[27]*Ibid.,* p. 81.

[28]*Ibid.,* p.p. 112, 113.

[Author's note: Full text of Dowell's statement is found in the Convention Minutes for 1930, p.p. 109-113 and is a masterful statement of Christian education, its purposes, place in a democracy, and Mercer's commitment to its historic role.]

The Baptists of Georgia therefore may well seize the present opportunity to give Christian Education such consideration and support as will insure for Mercer an exalted and commanding place as a Christian University as she enters upon her second century of service in 1933.[29]

Extracts from Dowell's statement include:

As congregationalists Baptists will always have need to renew their historic positions in the light of change. Holding that conscience must be free from every trammel, they are both competent and in duty bound to engage in higher education. United by the pursuit and voluntary acceptance of the truth, they are in a position to make a contribution to the progress of thought that is possible only for the best type of individualists and congregationalists. Accordingly, their duty is not optional but obligatory. However difficult the task, they must transmit every value already acquired, and utilize every facility for further advance.

No review of past declarations and no pronouncements of new ones however solemn will present differences from time to time. Those in positions of leadership may be ahead or behind those they represent. . .[30]

NORMAN PROGRESS REPORTED

Although other Convention educational institutions were in financial difficulty during 1930, Norman reported that its indebtedness had decreased over 60 per cent, ". . . and the net profit in operation this past year was the largest in the history of the school." The debt upon the college was a capital one, and not for current operations. The school during 1930 had 252 students, including 80 in the junior college, and 112 in high school.[31]

The Regional Conferences held during 1930 as a part of the Executive Committee's program of promotion emphasized two items; the God's Acre movement, and an offering from every church during the month of April ". . . as a token of welcome to our new Secretary, Brother James W. Merritt." [32]

[29]*Ibid.*, p. 111.
[30]*Ibid.*, p. 112.
[31]*Ibid.*, p.p. 125-126
[32]*Ibid.*, p. 143.

First woman elected as a vice president of the Convention was Mrs. W. J. Neel, named at the 1931 Convention in Atlanta.[33] For Baptist women, this was an honor, and in turn, an honor to a woman who had served Georgia and Southern Baptists well in many ways, including long-time leadership of Georgia Woman's Missionary Union as well as a Southwide leader in the $75 Million Campaign.

While one might question statistical and comparative material, it is a matter of record that much of the progress, and difficulties, of Georgia Baptists has been reflected in those pages of the minutes dealing with the Convention's financial affairs. Times of prosperity and times of depression were evidenced statistically, and the mood of the Convention was mirrored in these reports.

For example, as finances tightened, support of Southwide causes began to be curtailed. Approval of a budget for 1932 set the figure at $600,000, with the allocations to be 60 per cent for State causes, and 40 per cent for Southwide causes, with the percentage of distribution to state causes to remain the same as 1931.[34] For the second straight year, the Convention approved the Supplemental Appeal Plan which paved the way for all areas of work to raise funds to supplement those allocated in the Co-operative Program. In requesting approval for continuation of the Supplemental Appeals Plan, the Executive Board felt this was in no way intended to diminish the effectiveness of the Co-operative Program, but rather to strengthen it.[35]

One of the first items of business of the 1931 Convention was an announcement by R. Q. Leavell of his intention to seek in 1932 a proposed Constitutional amendment limiting the terms of Convention presidents to two years. Immediately following Leavell's notice, the Convention approved a resolution saying that it was the ". . . sense of this body that the tenure of office of the President of this Con-

[33]*Minutes, Georgia Baptist Convention*, 1931, p.p. 9-10.
[34]*Ibid.*, p. 15.
[35]*Loc. cit.*

vention should not exceed two years." [36] J. Ellis Sammons, Macon, was elected president in 1931 and was to serve three terms.[37] Two others, Aquila Chamlee and Ellis A. Fuller were to serve three-year terms also,[38] the other presidents, to the present, were to serve two years.

Plans began as early as 1931 for the celebration of the centennial of the founding of Mercer University in 1833. The Mercer Centennial Committee reminded the Convention that in anticipation of the occasion the Thomasville Convention of 1928 agreed to launch a campaign to increase the productive endowment of Mercer to a $2 million minimum. This was confirmed by the 1929 and the 1930 Conventions.[39] At the Atlanta session, this Committee reported that actual beginning of the campaign was being delayed by the grave economic conditions, but would be launched as soon as possible.[40]

Reorganization of the Social Service Commission in 1927, indicated previously, paved the way for a series of lengthy reports which had come to be an annual survey of a wide range of conditions, religious, moral, economic, etc.[41]

During the Depression years, the Commission called upon Baptists to assist jobless through the Community Chest and other welfare agencies.

The churches were urged to give that Americans might not suffer.[42] A strong statement calling upon Georgia Baptists to observe the prohibition laws was given also.[43]

The rather tenuous position occupied by Norman Institute and Brewton-Parker Institute in Convention life is reflected upon more than one occasion when the Convention

[36]*Ibid.*, p. 10.
[37]*Minutes, Georgia Baptist Convention,* 1938, Historical Table, p. 270.
[38]*Minutes, Georgia Baptist Convention,* 1966, Historical Table, p.p. 429-431.
[39]*Minutes, Georgia Baptist Convention,* 1931, p.p. 28, 29.
[40]Dowell, Spright, *A History of Mercer University,* 1833-1953, [Foote and Davies, Inc., Atlanta, 1958, p. 299.
[41]*Minutes, Georgia Baptist Convention,* 1931, p.p. 31-41.
[42]*Ibid.*, p.p. 33, 34.
[43]*Ibid.*, p.p. 36-39.

appeared to consider these institutions part of the Convention family, and at the same time to disclaim, when necessary, financial or judicial responsibility. Again in 1931 this was reflected when the committee on nominations recommended that the trustees selected by the several associations ". . . whose names are to be supplied to the Secretary for insertion in the Minutes, be elected by this Convention as Trustees of these institutions." [44]

By the end of the fiscal year for 1931, Co-operative Program giving was down $33,610.72 to $188,248.23. This was a slump from $221,835.95 for the preceding year. However, designated gifts had increased $15,583.53 to $72,426.33.[45] As Cree had done before him, Merritt found it necessary to keep reminding the Convention that part of the financial problem was the necessity to assume fixed obligations from previous years.[46]

Seeking clarification of its power to call extra-ordinary sessions of the Convention, the Executive Committee asked for authority to call a special session prior to the 1932 Convention should one be needed, and then asked for a clarifying interpretation of the Constitution. The authority was granted.[47]

The Executive Committee recommended that the Convention interpret Article 3, Section 1, and Article 6, Section 2 [a] as granting such power to the Executive Committee.[48] This was spelled out in the Constitution in 1932.[49]

KING LEAVES STATE POSITION

Numerical growth was evident during 1930 and 1931 despite financial conditions. Baptists in churches and asso-

[44]*Ibid.*, p.p. 43, 44.
[45]*Ibid.*, p. 66.
[46]*Ibid.*, p. 67.
[47]*Ibid.*, p. 77.
[48]*Ibid.*, p. 70.
[49]*Minutes, Georgia Baptist Convention*, 1932, p. 7.
[50]*Ibid.*, p. 78.

ciations in fellowship with the Convention by 1931 numbered 2,494 churches with 426,307 members.[50]

After five years as superintendent of State Missions, and General Field Secretary, Spencer B. King resigned in September, 1931,[51] returning to a second term as pastor of the Blakely church until his retirement in 1945. King had rendered valuable service to Georgia Baptists from the time of his ordination in 1907. He came to Atlanta first in 1912 to serve as office secretary for the State Mission Board. He was secretary of the Committee On Cooperation 1914 to 1919, and after several pastorates, he served from 1926 to 1931 as a leader in the state mission work.[52]

During his leadership in the State Missions program, King did much to solidify a concept of State Missions which would reach effectively into every area of Georgia. Upon his resignation, his duties were, in effect, performed by Merritt as executive secretary in an economy move which left vacant King's place.[53]

Even with a $9,900 appropriation from the Sunday School Board, and $4,332 appropriations from co-operating agencies, primarily Georgia associations, the total budget for Sunday School work was down to $19,332 for 1931.[54] The number of persons employed by the Convention dropped from 98 in 1930 to 75 in 1931—a decline of 23 workers, with salaries down from $43,240.55 in 1930 to $35,368.65 in 1931.[55]

Such a serious matter was the continuance of Georgia Baptist work by 1932, that during the second day of the annual session in Macon, the Convention discussed openly the budget for three hours of the morning session, having debated it for three hours in the afternoon of the first day. Out of the six hours of discussion, a motion was made finally by Louie D. Newton that a Committee of Five be named

[51]*Minutes, Georgia Baptist Convention,* 1931, p. 69.
[52]*Encyclopedia of Southern Baptists,* Volume II, [Nashville: Broadman Press, 1958] p. 751.
[53]*Minutes, Georgia Baptist Convention,* 1931, p. 69.
[54]*Minutes, Georgia Baptist Convention,* 1931, p. 81.
[55]*Minutes, Georgia Baptist Convention,* 1931, p. 128.

to report at that session any possible economies which could be effected or any better method of carrying on Georgia Baptist work.[56]

The only apparent advantage of the work of the committee called for in Newton's resolution was a suggestion for providing an additional $7,000 to Mercer by transferring to Mercer $2,000 of the proposed $4,000 for promotion and by abolishing the office of Field Secretary of the schools, which was created by the Convention. This would allow Mercer to add her share [$2,500] of the expense for this secretary to its budget and then to give Mercer notes payable to the Executive Committee for $2,500, thus providing for the $7,000.[57]

Roland Q. Leavell, speaking for the Georgia Baptist Assembly, as president, reported on the condition of that Assembly to the Convention asserting that the Board of Control had met in Atlanta on Nov. 7, 1932 and discussed the future of the Assembly. As was the case in many instances, a clear picture of a given program or institution was garnered from summary reports rather than year by year reports. In this case, for the first time, a clear picture of the history of the Assembly was presented in the minutes of the Convention. This was, coincidentally, the year after the Mary P. Willingham School for Girls, on adjacent property, had closed its doors.

Leavell reported that the property was in poor condition, with no funds to use for repairs. Various organizations in Blue Ridge had presented resolutions to the Board of Control requesting that the property be deeded to the City of Blue Ridge. The petitions for the property cited the fact that the property was given originally by citizens of Blue Ridge and organizations in the city, along with $10,000 for construction of an auditorium and other improvements. The requests for deeding of the property to Blue Ridge were accompanied by proposals to insert in the deed a clause which

[56]*Minutes, Georgia Baptist Convention,* 1932, p.p. 11, 12.
[57]*Ibid.,* p. 25.

would specify that the buildings would be repaired, the grounds improved, the buildings kept repaired properly, and that the Georgia Baptist Assembly [in this case a group or groups, not a physical property] would have use of the buildings and grounds free of charge. Further, the city of Blue Ridge urged that the Assembly be maintained, and the deed would stipulate that the property would never be sold by the city of Blue Ridge, and would be used only for unquestionable and wholesome purposes. Leavell told the Convention that the Board of Control had accepted unanimously the proposition from the city of Blue Ridge, and execution of the deed was expected soon.[58]

From this time, assemblies by Convention-sponsored groups would be held at several colleges, primarily Tift and Mercer University, and at Lake Louise, until the Georgia Baptist Convention, in November, 1963,[59] authorized purchase of the Lake Louise Bible Conference Grounds as a Georgia Baptist Assembly; the first such to be owned by the Convention. The entire history of the Georgia Baptist Assembly at Blue Ridge, like the Hearn Academy, Shorter college, and some other ventures was one of evident financial ties, implied legal ties, moral commitments, but never really clear-cut decisions as to permanent ownership. This was to change for Shorter during the 1950's when it became a part of the official Convention family permanently. Evident especially was the nebuluous situation with regard to the Blue Ridge Assembly and its organic relationship to the Convention through the years.

The Committee of Three made its final report in 1932, declaring that as then functioning, the Committee should be discontinued. The Committee's report was embodied in the report of the Executive Committee.[60]

As amended finally, the budget approved for 1933 called for notes to be given by the Executive Committee to the

[58]*Ibid.*, p.p. 16-17.
[59]*Minutes, Georgia Baptist Convention,* 1963, p. 30.
[60]*Minutes, Georgia Baptist Convention,* 1932, p. 24.

schools for any unpaid balance on debenture claims from the 1932 program with the notes to be due and payable within the year 1934, and to be set up as preferred items in the 1934 budget.[61]

With the advent of 1933, Georgia Baptists would mark a century of service by *The Christian Index* with a Georgia location. The Convention approved therefore a resolution calling for ". . . a suitable celebration of the paper's arrival in Georgia in 1833; . . ." [62]

PROPERTY DISPOSAL A PROBLEM

The Convention in 1932 still was trying to make some profitable use of the Locust Grove property, and therefore gave the Executive Committee, through a motion made by L. R. Christie authority to act as follows:

> Whereas, The property of Locust Grove Institute at Locust Grove, Ga., is not being used . . . and
> Whereas, It has been suggested that there exists a need and an opportunity for a Home for semi-orphan children in this State where parents or friends would be willing to pay for the care . . . a service which cannot be undertaken at Hapeville, therefore be it
> Resolved That the Executive Committee be authorized in their judgment and discretion to permit the use of the property for the aforesaid purpose to suitable and responsible parties. . .
> Provided, That neither the Convention nor its property shall be involved in any expense or financial obligation of any sort on account of this proposal.[63]

While the proposal was never implemented, it was significant in concept; the first time in Georgia life that a child-care institution was proposed upon a basis of payment by relatives for the care of children.

Columbus Roberts had been named chairman of the Holding Commission, and the 1932 report indicated that collections were $3,780.84 less than the previous year, and this was accounted for by carrying over the sum of $8,726.03 in

[61]*Ibid.*, p. 25.
[62]*Ibid.*, p. 41.
[63]*Ibid.*, p. 42.

past due earnings.[64] Total income from investments was $35,786.43.[65] Consolidation of the Committee on Promotion and the Committee on the Co-operative Program was made in 1932 under one committee, the Promotion Committee. The committees had, since the advent of the Co-operative Program, been related and to a large degree overlapping.[66]

The decline in giving continued throughout the year 1932, and when the record for the fiscal year was in, receipts for the Co-operative Program were down to $156,258.07; a decline of $31,990.16 over the previous year. Designated funds were up, but only slightly, showing a $2,048.77 increase for an overall decline in giving of $29,678.54.[67]

As giving declined, the continuing problem of retiring deficits from previous years increased. During 1932, the Executive Committee had retired on State Missions $11,533.19; Hospital Bonds $21,855.44; School Debentures in excess of $43,053.07 for a total of $76,441.70 in the budget for retirement. Of this amount, all but $12,478.30 had been retired, and this was expected to be cared for by the end of the year.[68] This amount for retirement of previous deficits however, was proving to be an increasing strain upon the resources of the Executive Committee. This perhaps accounts as much as any single reason for the fact that at the September, 1932, meeting of the Executive Committee, the Committee acquiesced in a plan for the Georgia Baptist Orphans' Home to withdraw from the Co-operative Program. The Board of Trustees of the Home, at the September meeting, presented a resolution to the Executive Committee asking:

> "That the Georgia Baptist Orphans' Home be allowed to withdraw from the Co-operative Program and be allowed to go into the open field to solicit contributions for the maintenance of the home." [69]

[64]*Ibid.*, p. 54.
[65]*Ibid.*, p. 55.
[66]*Ibid.*, p. 60.
[67]*Ibid.*, p. 64.
[68]*Ibid.*, p. 65.
[69]*Ibid.*, p. 67.

The Executive Committee approved, and voted that the matter be referred to the 1932 Convention to name a committee of three to confer with trustees of the home and work out arrangements. The arrangements agreed upon called for the churches to cooperate with the Home in raising funds ". . . in whatever way may be consistent with plans and policies of the local churches, . . . " and "That remittances from churches, or their auxiliaries, or individuals may be made through the office of the Executive Committee, . . . or direct to the Home." [70]

Additional agreement called for the Home to pay for the maintenance of the office of the Executive Secretary-Treasurer, the printing of the Convention's minutes,

> . . . and such other items as are necessary to the work, a sum deemed equitable for the service rendered; the value of the service and the amount to be paid to be determined each year by the chairman of the Administration Committee and the chairman of the Finance Committee of the trustees of the Orphans' Home.[71]

After many years in the last part of the 19th century and the first part of the 20th century spent in efforts to become a child of the Convention, the action of the 1932 Convention marked the end of an era of partial support from budgeted Convention funds for the Home. However, the action accomplished two things. It relieved the Convention of the necessity of providing Co-operative Program Funds for the Home at a time when there were no funds available. Perhaps the largest accomplishment, was that it opened the door for the Home to make direct appeals to the churches for support. With the emotional appeal which the Home had, it was able to secure funds for operation of the Home in excess of that which could have been provided otherwise. During the 1960's, the late John C. Warr, General Manager of the Home from 1950 until his death in 1969, had indicated that a survey revealed at least three hundred churches in Georgia were giving to the Home

[70]*Loc. cit.*
[71]*Loc. cit.*

which otherwise gave to no Convention cause because they were on the "fringe area" of denominational co-operation.

When the matter of securing funds for the home through the Co-operative Program was studied during 1960, the situation was left as agreed to by the 1932 Convention as being in the best interest of all concerned.[72] At that time, the annual needs of the homes [by then three branches] were in excess of one million dollars annually. There would have been no way for the Convention, with a budget of about $5 million at the time, to absorb this amount into the Georgia share of Co-operative Program funds, because the net increase in giving to the Co-operative Program under this arrangement would not offset the amount needed by the Home.

During this year of change from some Co-operative Program help to an independent financial path, [1932] and in later years, B. J. W. Graham served the Home as a financial agent. For this year, salary of the general manager was $2,160.00; and Graham's salary, November through June [1931-1932] was $2,250.00.[73]

Baptist Young People's Union showed some gains in enrolment during the Depression years. There was a substantial gain in enrolment for the year ending April 30, with 68 per cent of the increase in the Southern Baptist Convention being made in Georgia.[74]

The hospital had earlier been instructed to do all in its power so that by January 1, 1932, it would not need an annual allocation.[75] When it reported on operations to the 1932 session, a net profit under Schedule 3, Profit and Loss statement, was set at $4,922.56.[76] A careful examination of the auditor's report for this year indicated that this profit, small though it was, was paced by what appeared to be rather

[72]*Minutes, Executive Committee, Georgia Baptist Convention*, March 15, 1960, p. 84.

[73]*Minutes, Georgia Baptist Convention*, 1932, p. 95.

[74]*Ibid.*, p. 82.

[75]*Minutes, Georgia Baptist Convention*, 1930, p.p. 25, 26.

[76]*Minutes, Georgia Baptist Convention*, 1932, p. 104.

generous write offs prior to setting a final new profit figure.[77]

The hospital then, by 1932 was paying its way without Co-operative Program funds. The Orphans' Home had been permitted to withdraw from the Co-operative Program. Thus, in the height of the Depression, the Convention's two benevolent ministries were out of the unified program of support, expenditures for missions had been curtailed drastically, and the cause of Christian education suffered.

Georgia Baptists during these crisis years left no doubt about their interest in their benevolent ministries. Neither did they abandon them. Rather, these particular ministries were better able to move forward apart from the Co-operative Program than were the educational and missionary endeavors.

A small glimmer of light was ahead on the horizon, but the rainbow had not yet appeared, and would not during the remainder of the decade.

[77]*Ibid.*, p.p. 101, 103.

CHAPTER 19

Institutions Are Preserved

The historic inter-relationship between the Georgia Baptist Convention and Mercer University was unique. Mercer was begun by Convention leaders. Mercer officials led in Convention affairs. Mercer's interests and Convention interests had, since the inception of Mercer Institute, been one in basic purpose. Further, Mercer University provided from its graduating classes leaders in all walks of life and therefore strength for Convention advance. One State Mission Board executive secretary, S. Y. Jameson, had gone from that position to the presidency of the University. Other educational institutions of the Convention, first by individual trustee group leadership, and then officially through the Mercer System, had followed Mercer's lead in shaping their own programs.

Therefore, it was not out of character for Mercer leadership in the person of Spright Dowell, president, to keep burning the flame of concern for Christian education during the Depression.

One thing which perhaps helped Georgia Baptists continue their strong historic emphasis upon education in the time of crisis was emphasis placed upon the subject at the Convention's annual sessions. And the man who charted as clear a course as any single person was Dowell, who kept reminding Georgia Baptists of the purpose of Christian higher education.[1] Of all Georgia Baptist educators, Dowell

[1]*Minutes, Georgia Baptist Convention,* 1932, p. 109.

was probably the most far-sighted in articulating Baptists' historic position on education and then interpreting this position in the light of current trends. That Dowell was heard is indicated in many ways, including his election as Convention president in 1948 and 1949 while serving as president of the university.[2]

In citing the Convention's historic interest in education, Dowell referred in 1932 to Adiel Sherwood, who he termed ". . . the most constructive Christian thinker among Georgia Baptists in those early days and one of the most constructive thinkers throughout the entire period of their history." [3]

> As he [Sherwood] well foresaw, Mercer University has been the leading ally of the Convention for one hundred years and its main source of supply of learning and of leadership for our Georgia Baptist life. Unquestionably the growth and the influence of Baptists in Georgia find explanation here in large measure and certainly the Convention is under lasting obligation to make this centennial year meaningful and memorable in strengthening the resources of Mercer University for the larger opportunities and responsibilities of the new century.[4]

Dowell said further that:

> In the midst of its financial embarrassment, it has been necessary for the Corporation of Mercer University to pledge the income from certain endowed funds for maintenance and from the debenture income in order to refinance the accumulated indebtedness of $100,000 and provide for its repayment over a period of twenty years.[5]

Information concerning some of the specific actions of Mercer University has been given from time to time, and other Convention-owned institutions have not been so treated. While Mercer's problems were larger by virtue of its size, the trends in growth and in depression years at

[2]*Minutes, Georgia Baptist Convention*, 1954, Historical Table, (1948, 1949), p. 364.

[3]*Minutes, Georgia Baptist Convention*, 1932, p. 109.

[4]*Loc. cit.*

[5]*Ibid.*, p. 111.

Mercer were much the same trends which the other institutions shared also.

One fact which is documented amply in minutes from 1930 to the present, and which had bearing upon Convention growth, should not go unnoticed. Nominating committees under the administrations of Secretary Merritt and later Secretary Garrison made certain that representation from every section of the state and every segment of Georgia Baptist life was included in the Convention's program. An examination of the report of the various nominating committees and a comparison of the residences of the men nominated sustains this statement. Therefore, the burden of responsibility for leading the Convention out of crisis was not sectional.

The Georgia Convention went back to Augusta in 1933 in search of answers in what had been a troubled year. Three sessions were devoted that year to discussions as to whether the Convention could continue to sustain its educational institutions, and if so, how.[6] Finally, after lengthy discussion, recommendations from the Committee of Seven were recommitted without adoption.[7]

A comparison of the report of the Committee of Seven, appointed in 1932,[8] and the Convention's action in the same area are of interest. The Committee of Seven recommended:

> First, That the Convention continue a program of Christian education.
> Second, That the Convention cannot carry on its present program of Christian education with the funds it was now receiving or may reasonably expect to receive, without further serious and unjustifiable handicap to other Convention activities than already exist.
> Third, That the Convention center its educational interest, activity and support at Mercer University, and that the Convention provide a minimum of $25,000 annually to Mercer University, same being the equivalent of a five per cent income on a productive endowment of $500,000.00.
> Fourth, That in the light of our present financial con-

[6] *Minutes, Georgia Baptist Convention,* 1933, p.p. 10, 12-13, 14-17.
[7] *Ibid.*, p. 14.
[8] *Ibid.*, p. 10.

dition, and in the interest of economy and educational efficiency, the Board of Trustees of Bessie Tift College be requested to choose one of the following three plans of operation:

> [a] Take over the college and run it independently, . . .
>
> [b] Negotiate for Bessie Tift College to be co-ordinated with Mercer University,
>
> [c] Make Bessie Tift a standard accredited junior college for girls.

The committee suggested further that Shorter College trustees take over the college and run it independently without expectation of financial support, and that the board of trustees of Norman be requested to choose one of the following two alternatives: a. negotiate for Norman Junior College to be moved to and named Norman College of Mercer University, or else, take over the college and run it independently without financial support from the Convention.

Also a recommendation that the Board of Trustees of Brewton Parker take over that institution and run it independently, with the Holding Commission authorized to return to the Brewton Parker trustees the property of the institute was presented.

Further, the committee called attention to all colleges of the fact that they had a right to campaign for funds for endowment.

Finally, the committee said:

> That for such of these colleges as continue to operate without financial assistance from the Convention we wish to express our grateful appreciation of their work and speak for them the continued good will of the denomination.[9]

The committee, through G. Gordon Singleton[10] urged that this plan became effective July 1, 1934.[11]

This was a far-reaching series of proposals, and one which would in effect put the Convention out of the business of educational support with the exception of Mercer University. The Committee was quite willing to lend its name, good will, and moral support, but believed that it could not go beyond that.

[9]*Ibid.*, p.p. 15-16.
[10]*Ibid.*, p. 10.
[11]*Ibid.*, p. 16.

Following the recommitting of the report to the Committee of Seven with some instructions, the Convention decided further that the same committee should serve as the Committee on Schools which had been called for by special recommendation of the Executive Committee to report on the debentures at the next Convention session.[12]

DETERMINED TO MAINTAIN EDUCATIONAL PROGRAM

Additionally, the Convention did adopt a statement which declared among other things: "That we state positively our purpose and determination, maintain an educational program . . . and to make our educational program thoroughly Christian." Emphasized also was the Convention's ". . . purpose and determination to provide for our girls educational advantages under denominational control . . ." Further, the Convention instructed the committee to seek ". . . in cooperation with the schools, to provide standardized education for both boys and girls, . . ." and instructed the Committee

> . . . to make to the Executive Committee and to the next Convention such supplemental report as they may deem as desirable; and that we further instruct this Committee on Schools to publish their findings and achivements at least thirty days before the next meeting of the Convention.[13]

Continuing a positive statement, the Convention instructed the chairman of the Committee of Seven ". . . to call a meeting of the school men and the members of his committee at the earliest convenient date to discuss together the whole educational situation." [14]

Including a deficit of $2,988.77 carried over from the current year, [1933], the Convention had a budget for 1934, including fixed state appropriations, of $143,170.15, and $21,000 for state missions, for a total of $167,158.92 for

[12]*Loc. cit.*
[13]*Ibid.,* p.p. 16, 17.
[14]*Ibid.,* p. 17.

Georgia. This was 80 per cent for Georgia causes, and the 20 per cent for Southern Convention causes was $44,789.73.[15]

In the report, there were guarantees for schools in the following amounts: Mercer, $29,000; Tift, $5,000; Shorter, $1,500; Norman, $1,500 and Brewton-Parker, $1,500.[16] H. M. Fugate, proposed an amendment which was accepted by the Convention and became a part of the 1934 budget, calling for a goal of $500,000.00 with the provision that when the budget was met, distribution be on a 50-50 basis.[17]

As had come to be the case, the Convention recommended that notes of the Executive Committee to schools and colleges, in the amount of $17,074.41, due in 1935, be set as a fixed appropriation in the State's part of the 1935 program. It was agreed further that any deficit in the program of State Missions for 1934 be made a part of the 1935 budget. *The Index* was instructed to keep expenditures for 1934 within budgeted allocations.[18]

The Convention had for several years supplemented any deficit in *The Index* budget, but this was a warning that for 1934, this could not be done.

First Georgia Baptist Convention approval for federal aid for an institution came in 1933.[19] The request was in the form of a report from the Mercer University trustees through President Dowell. Dowell suggested that there might be a possibility of securing a loan from the Federal government for making repairs and improvements to buildings and the campus. There was considerable discussion, and the matter was referred to a committee for overnight study and a report to the Convention on the next day.[20] Thos Committee was comprised of Ellis A. Fuller, H. M. Fugate, Spencer B. King, W. W. Gaines and J. B. Turner.[21]

[15]*Ibid.*, p.p. 17, 18.
[16]*Ibid.*, p. 18.
[17]*Ibid.*, p. 19.
[18]*Ibid.*, p.p. 18, 19.
[19]*Ibid.*, p. 19.
[20]*Ibid.*, p. 20.
[21]*Loc. cit.*

Reporting back to the Convention, the Committee said:

Whereas, It may be deemed desirable after a thorough investigation of the terms and conditions of such loans for other institutions of our Convention to seek similar loans, therefore,

Be it resolved:

1. That the President of the Convention appoint a committee of five from the State at large to study the proposition with the Mercer Board and with the official boards of such other institutions as may be interested in securing such a loan.

2. That this committee be instructed to study the proposition to determine if it sound as a business venture, that it in no way violates any of our present constitutional provisions, that it is not contrary to the established Baptist principle of separation of church and State, and that each institution incurring the obligations incident to such loan can work out a self-liquidating proposition to retire the loan during the period of amortization set by the terms of the loan.

3. That this committee be and hereby is clothed with full and complete power of authority to act for and on behalf of this Convention and in all acts necessary in the premises, and may do any and all things that this Convention might do were it in session.

5. That in the event it is necessary, the Convention hereby authorizes and instructs its Executive Committee or the Holding Commission to make such deeds or do any other act in the premises as might be necessary to meet all legal requirements.[22]

This was indeed broad authority for a Convention committee in such a matter, and reflected obvious endorsement of the concept by the Convention in approving the resolution. It was apparently never implemented. Significantly, Dowell, who completed his history of Mercer University during the years 1953-1957, made no mention of this request he made of the Convention some 20 years earlier.

LITIGATION OVER HOSPITAL TAXATION

A shortage of funds was not the only problem Georgia Baptists faced in 1933. Litigation concerning taxation of some of the property of the Georgia Baptist hospital ended

[22]*Ibid.*, p. 27.

with a decision by the Georgia Supreme Court that the hospital was not exempt from taxation, making taxes in the amount of $34,000 for the previous four years due and payable. Through an agreement with the city of Atlanta, Fulton county and the State of Georgia, the amount deemed due was reduced to 25 per cent of the original total. The Hospital Commission then was able to report that two-thirds of the liability had been paid, with plans made to pay the balance in monthly installments.[23] "A substantial part of this obligation . . ." was met by gifts by hospital employees.[24]

Merritt was ill for some time during the early months of 1933,[25] [Feb. 2-April 21] and the administration of Convention and Executive Committee affairs was placed in the hands of W. H. Major and J. Ellis Sammons, who assumed the main duties of promotion and administration.[26]

The composition of the Social Service Commission, and the nature of its reports were, as might be expected, related inasmuch as a Commission of this type would be expected to express opinions on current issues. This was understood by the 1933 Commission which recalled that the 1927 Convention approved reorganization of the Commission, at that time clothing it

> . . . with responsibility to speak the mind of the Convention as expressed in regular or recess sessions. It should study conditions and sound sentiment, and should help to crystalize opinion in accordance with the Christian religion.[27]

With this background for its role, it is understandable why, with the creation in 1957[28] of a Public Affairs Committee, that there was to be, for a time, some overlapping in responsibility and some misunderstanding concerning the role of the committee and the Social Service Commission.

Co-operative Program giving continued to decline during

[23]*Ibid.*, p. 25.
[24]*Loc. cit.*
[25]*Ibid.*, p. 69.
[26]*Ibid.*, p. 28.
[27]*Ibid.*, p. 40.
[28]*Minutes, Georgia Baptist Convention*, 1957, p. 42.

1933, perhaps the worst year of the Depression for many Georgians. January through October figures showed giving at $118,649.68; down from the $156,258.06 figure for the comparable period in 1932, and representing a decline of $37,608.38.[29]

Total receipts, January to October, were $211,616.70, a net decrease of $26,024.27. A special State Missions emphasis in October, with gifts of $9,852.85,[30] proved to be a life-saver for the State Missions program. The sum of $54,749.39 in deficits had been carried over from 1932, with most of the amount retired.[31]

Despite the financial crisis, the year had been a great one for Mercer University as that institution observed its Centennial year—the founding of Mercer Institute at Penfield. Special events were planned to coincide with the graduation ceremonies in May. About 1,000 Baptists made a pilgrimage to Penfield. Of the Penfield part of the event, Dowell said ". . . many of the old residents of the community declared it to be the greatest day in the history of Penfield since the removal of Mercer to Macon some 60 years before." [32]

Pageants, sermons, addresses by state and national figures, a joint celebration of the Mercer Centennial and the Georgia Bicentennial in Macon's City Auditorium, all were features of the four-day observance.[33]

Again, Dowell the denominational statesman, in reporting to the Convention on the Centennial, said:

> The current Convention year marks the one hundredth birthday of Mercer University and of *The Christian Index*. The growth and development of Baptist principles and peoples and the place which Baptists are filling in the life of Georgia today are due in large measure to Jesse Mercer, that eminent Christian statesman who sensed as no one else did the vital importance

[29]*Minutes, Georgia Baptist Convention,* 1933, p. 66.
[30]*Ibid.,* p. 67.
[31]*Loc. cit.*
[32]Spright Dowell, *A History of Mercer University,* 1833- 1953 [Foote & Davies, Inc., Atlanta, 1958] p. 302.
[33]*Ibid.,* 302-305.

of co-operation, the priceless value of leadership and the continuing necessity of the spread of intelligence.[34]

After reporting upon details of the celebration and Mercer's condition, Dowell ended his report in this crucial year for Georgia Baptists by declaring:

> In the midst of our general confusion in public affairs and in the midst of active competition that may tend to obscure spiritual values we do well to recall the faith of our fathers that evangelism and education are the inseparable means by and through which the kingdom is to be brought in. Other phases of our collective work are important but these are fundamental.[35]

Out of the difficult years, came the Baptist Hundred Thousand Club—an effort to enroll Baptists in the South, 100,000 strong, to contribute one dollar per month over and above their regular Co-operative Program gifts to help pay debts of Southern Baptist Convention causes.[36] Initially, the state conventions did not share in the proceeds of this effort.[37]

$58,000,000 GIVEN IN CAMPAIGN

The $75 Million Campaign resulted in $58,000,000 given finally. Merrill D. Moore, said that because of debts, ". . . morale was at the breaking point." [38] The Southern Convention's Executive Committee in April of 1933 considered the Southern Baptist Convention debt situation, and the plan for the Hundred Thousand Club, suggested by Frank Tripp, was adopted, presented to the Convention in May, 1933, and was on its way with the object of ". . . the liquidation of the present debt of all the agencies of the . . . Convention." [39] Upon adoption by the Southern Convention, therefore, and prior to the Georgia Convention, Georgia

---

[34]*Minutes, Georgia Baptist Convention*, 1933, p. 122.

[35]*Ibid.*, p. 123.

[36]*Ibid.*, p. 69.

[37]*Encyclopedia of Southern Baptists*, Volume I, [Nashville: Broadman Press 1958] p. 660.

[38]*Ibid.*, p. 659.

[39]*Loc. cit.*

Baptists were sharing in this plan,[40] and over its lifetime, contributed a high level of support for Southern Baptist Convention causes in this manner.

In 1935, the state secretaries presented a memorial to the Southern Baptist Convention Executive Committee requesting that the states be included in the Club plan. This was not done, however, until the 1937 session of the Southern Baptist Convention.[41] Out of this Hundred Thousand Club came a Director of Promotion for the Southern Baptist Convention Executive Committee for the Co-operative Program and the Hundred Thousand Club,[42] and out of this office came eventually the present Stewardship Commission of the Southern Baptist Convention.

The Hearn Academy, although dead, was yet to be buried. The Holding Commission prior to 1933 had reconveyed the deeds to the Academy to the trustees. The school later closed, in debt. The Convention's interests in the "Hearn legacy" were in jeopardy. In 1932, John G. Harrison of the Mercer faculty was requested to work out a settlement of some kind. The 1933 report of the Executive Committee revealed that through the efforts of Harrison and the assistance of philanthropist Columbus Roberts, all parties of interest had been satisfied. Essence of the action was that about $12,000, the equivalent amount of the legacy, had been saved for the school of Christianity at Mercer, with $4,000 for a scholarship fund, and $8,000 for endowment. The Convention, therefore, resolved ". . . that the Holding Commission be instructed to apply the income of all the funds of Hearn Academy for purposes aforesaid as is also directed in deeds by the Trustees of Hearn Academy . . ." [43]

Authorization was given to the Holding Commission to pay Mercer University $350.00 plus interest, to settle a

[40]*Minutes, Georgia Baptist Convention*, 1933, p. 69.
[41]*Encyclopedia of Southern Baptists*, Vol. I, [Nashville: Broadman Press, 1958] p. 659.
[42]*Ibid.*, p. 660.
[43]*Ibid.*, 1933, p. 70.

claim against Gibson-Mercer Academy out of funds held by the Commission in the name of the academy.[44]

Refinancing of the Hospital's bonds was a problem also during the year and agreement was reached finally with the Whitney Trust and Savings Bank of New Orleans to refinance $340,000 of the bonds with a moratorium on payment of the principles until 1937, and with the understanding that when payment of the principal was resumed, the Convention would obligate itself to pay a minimum of $33,000 each year for principal and interest, and from 1933 to 1937, $20,400 in interest was to be paid annually.[45] The amounts then were to become fixed budget items beginning in 1937.[46]

The recommendations of the Executive Committee to the Convention on the budget for 1934 are of especial significance in that a pattern was set which continues basically to the present. In a called meeting of the Executive Committee on Nov. 2, 1933, the budget was predicated upon certain deductions, and these deductions together with the wording behind them are of interest and of significance.[47] Point One in the explanation is quoted:

> 1st. We recommend, in keeping with agreement with the Southern Baptist Convention Executive Committee, that administration expenses [including Administration, Program Promotion, W. M. U. promotion, Publicity Index] in amount as shown above, $27,000.00, be deducted from the 1934 receipts before distribution of distributable funds is made.[48]

A new definition of pastoral aid was enunciated by Merritt in his report for the year when he said:

> While performing the manifold duties of pastors, the major task of the twenty-eight missionary pastors, in whose support State Missions shares through Pastoral Aid, is soul winning and reports indicate that the evangelistic efforts of these men have been successful. These

[44]*Loc. cit.*
[45]*Ibid.,* p.p. 70-72.
[46]*Ibid.,* p. 72.
[47]*Ibid.,* p. 74.
[48]*Ibid.,* p. 73.

twenty-eight missionary pastors have served for the full year.[49]

As early as 1933, the B. Y. P. U. report indicated that a monthly B. Y. P. U. program was being presented over Radio Station WRDW in Augusta, and that other radio stations in the state had occasional B. Y. P. U. programs.[50] Georgia was to exhibit a long and intense interest in the use of public communications media in presenting the ministries of the conventions and the churches. This was to reflect itself in what became the Radio Commission of the Southern Baptist Convention, led by Georgian S. F. Lowe, with first offices in Atlanta, in 1942[51] and in other ways.

Mercer University was a pioneer in use of broadcast media, having begun radio station WMAZ on the campus under the administration of President Rufus Weaver. The station had been constructed in the tower of the chapel building. WMAZ was Macon's first radio station, and one of the first owned by a college in the United States. The call letters stood for "Watch Mercer Ascend to Zenith," and was managed by Hillyer Straton, a student. At the May 10, 1926 session of the University's Board of Trustees, Weaver suggested that the station be leased to a group of local citizens which the Macon Chamber of Commerce would name.[52]

ANDREWS' APPRAISAL OF SUNDAY SCHOOLS

George Andrews had served as leader of Georgia Baptist Sunday School work for 30 years, to the time of his death April 28, 1934.[53] The first full-time secretary, Andrews had led in the organization of Sunday Schools, associational Sunday School organization, and Vacation Bible Schools during three decades of Georgia Baptist life. A pioneer in his field, Andrews had begun his work Sept. 1, 1904. Of his work, he said in 1922:

[49]*Ibid.*, p. 89.
[50]*Ibid.*, p. 96.
[51]*Encyclopedia of Southern Baptist*, Vol. II, [Nashville: Broadman Press, 1958] p. 1130.
[52]*Dowell*, p. 288.
[53]*Minutes, Georgia Baptist Convention*, 1934, p. 12.

My first objective was to study conditions of which I knew absolutely nothing. I found that the Church School idea was practically unknown. The Sunday schools, as a rule, were being organized and conducted as independent institutions. It is true the schools bore the name of the churches who owned the buildings in which they met, but that was about the extent of the relation between the two . . . I also found that the Georgia Sunday School Association was thoroughly organized from the mountains to the sea and that all of the information and inspiration our Sunday school workers received was obtained from this interdenominational organization. This too, it seemed to me, was not exactly as it should be, and so I began the organization of our forces by Associations. It was a hard up-hill job, practically all of our leaders had been trained in the school of inter-denominational co-operation and this, coupled with the prevalence of the independent school idea, made it very difficult to win our own people to our own Baptist organization. The effect of this early training is to be seen today and even now some of our best are luke-warm when it comes to strictly Baptist business. However, within five years, more than half of our Associations had Baptist organizations and others have been, and are being, led to our view point.[54]

The value of Andrews' work and the problems in Sunday School and Baptist Young People's Development are illustrated by Andrews' statement, because the situations were basically the same. Andrews did indeed have a difficult task in seeking to mold the Sunday School organizations in the local churches in Georgia into co-operating, integral components of the church program.

It was in this environment and among these attitudes of Sunday School life that James W. Merritt came in July, 1920, to develop the associational organization of Sunday schools.[55] In the nearly two years of Merritt's service at the time Andrews wrote, 78 of the 93 associations had Sunday School Conventions.[56] Two facts are evident. Merritt, through this contact with the Associations, became well known throughout the state, and Andrews' observations reveal what was a

[54]*The Christian Index,* June 1, 1922, p. 53.
[55]*Loc. cit.*
[56]*Loc. cit.*

difficult problem in shifting the Sunday School organization into a strong arm of the denomination.

ENCOURAGED USE OF SBC LITERATURE

Further, Andrews encouraged the Sunday School organizations in Georgia to use literature prepared by the Southern Baptist Sunday School Board. He had found, upon beginning work in Georgia, that the American Baptist Publication Society was furnishing most of the literature and other supplies for Georgia Baptist Sunday Schools. The society had existed for many years, and encouraged support for use of its materials by purchasing advertisements in the associational minutes.[57]

And, the American Baptist Publication Society not only had strong but friendly roots in Georgia. The Society had been formed by Luther Rice, who had launched *The Columbian Star,* later *The Christian Index,* along with James D. Knowles, who served as one of the first editors of *The Star.* The Society was formed February 25, 1824, and had, apparently, grown out of articles in *The Star* urging such an organization.[58] The birthplace of the Society was the home of *The Columbian Star,* at 923 and 925 E. Street, N. W., Washington, D. C.[59]

This background gives a clearer picture of the strength of the Society in Sunday School organization in Georgia, and the difficulty involved in getting the churches to change to Sunday School Board literature.

Andrews' death in 1934 marked the end of the longest period of continuous service to the Convention up to that time by a staff member.

Still dealing with the problem of Locust Grove, the Convention, upon motion of Marshall Nelms referred to the Executive Committee, with power to act, a resolution that

[57]*Loc. cit.*

[58]*The Columbian Star,* March 6, 1824, quoted in *The First Hundred Years of The American Baptist Publication Society,* p. 5.

[59]*Ibid.,* Prefatory page, photograph and text.

the property be donated to Bessie Tift College ". . . to use such materials from its wreckage as might be to their advantage." [60] And in that year, the report of the Executive Committee was amended to permit the observance of Hospital Day in Georgia Baptist churches upon any Sunday in May except Mother's Day.[61]

Approval of the budget for 1935 involved a total planned expenditure of $218,827.27,[62] a far cry from the $600,000 of some four years previous. The 1935 budget included only $21,000.00 for State Missions.[63] During the years of the 1930's, the Orphans' Home cared for an average of 300 children, with 299 indicated in the 1934 report of the home to the Convention.[64] Concern about meeting financial obligations was paramount during the 1930's. Comparative studies of expenditures of other states were made as part of the effort to determine if Georgia was doing the best possible work with the amount of money available. The 1933 Convention had ordered such a study and the report in 1934 declared that expenses of administration in Georgia "were 20 per cent less than that of a comparable state." [65] The report said further that:

> We found that, contrary to a wide spread impression, the costs of administration and promotion have been greatly reduced within recent years. In 1925 the total was $24,728.75; in 1930 the costs had been reduced to $20,345.98. . . and in 1933 the total was only $13,629.50.[66]

Merritt had gathered the information for the committee, which sought answers to many questions.

> We looked diligently to see if we could find a way to reduce costs. We could find no way . . .
> Since our present efficiency and economical administration have been brought about by the wise direction and

[60]*Minutes, Georgia Baptist Convention,* 1934, p.p. 18-19.
[61]*Ibid.,* p. 19.
[62]*Ibid.,* p. 21.
[63]*Loc. cit.*
[64]*Ibid.,* p. 23.
[65]*Ibid.,* p. 25.
[66]*Loc. cit.*

supervision of our Executive Committee and the secretaries whom they have elected, we see no need at this time of a special committee to continue these studies. It is then our recommendation that our Committee be discharged and the Convention leave this work with the Executive Committee until such time as it may appear that there is need of further work by a special committee.[67]

The Committee of Seven submitted what was in effect a supplemental report to the Convention, noting that it was set up to be continued as a co-ordinating committee with the duty of working with the schools in seeking to put into effect the general policies of their report as submitted earlier to the Convention.[68] The supplemental report called for the Tift trustees to take over the college and run it without financial support from the Convention, and for the Convention to approve a petition for changes in the charter and by-laws proposed by the Tift trustees to accomplish this purpose.[69] Further, the Committee suggested that Norman's trustees do the same thing—run the college independently. The Norman recommendation called for Norman to surrender to the Executive Secretary all debentures and coupons issued in favor of Norman. These debentures, worth $133,-863.04, were to be destroyed in the presence of the Executive Committee. Also, the Convention was to assume responsibility for the Holding Commission returning all property, endowment, etc., to Norman together with assumption of an itemized indebtedness not in excess of $11,600.00; the amount the Convention assumed in 1927 on a then-proposed dormitory for boys.[70] Similar proposals approved involved Shorter and Brewton-Parker.[71]

MERCER ONLY "OFFICIAL" INSTITUTION

Concerning Mercer, the Committee recommended first that the Convention continue its support of the University,

[67]*Ibid.*, p. 26.
[68]*Ibid.*, p. 31.
[69]*Ibid.*, p. 32.
[70]*Ibid.*, p. 33.
[71]*Ibid.*, p.p. 33, 34.

and reported that an agreement had been reached with the Corporation of Mercer University, providing that Mercer, through its proper officials, surrender to the Executive Secretary of the Georgia Baptist Convention all debentures issued and all coupons issued ". . . thereon in favor of Mercer University in possession of any and all of the officials of same and $633,492.73 worth . . ." dated August 15, 1929.[72] In turn, the Convention would pay Mercer at least $30,000.00 annually in monthly installments or quarterly installments until such an endowment for maintenance in the amount of $633,492.73 was paid.[73] This was a complex series of actions, involving several charter changes, which left Mercer University as the only institution of higher education to remain a part of the Convention structure officially.[74]

A constitutional amendment was adopted in 1934 which limited the term of presidents of the Convention to a maximum of three years. An amendment to Article 5, Section 1, it read: "No person shall serve as president more than three years." [75] However, a proposal for a revised Constitution by B. J. W. Graham was tabled.[76]

FINANCIAL GAINS BY 1934

Financial gains were evident in 1934, although slight. Gifts January to October, 1934, were $128,033.16 for the Cooperative Program, as compared with $118,649.68 for January to October, 1933, an increase of $9,383.48. Designated and miscellaneous gifts increased also for total receipts of $247,-941.87; an increase of $36,325.17.[77] Secretary Merritt reported that

> For the first time in a number of years it has been possible to operate so far this year without borrowing for

[72]*Ibid.*, p. 35.
[73]*Ibid.*, p.p. 35, 36.
[74]*Ibid.*, p.p. 18, 31.
[75]*Ibid.*, p. 38.
[76]*Loc. cit.*
[77]*Ibid.*, p. 72.

current operations which, of course, has resulted in a saving in interest charges.[78]

Even with the increase, the goal for distributable funds was held to $250,000, and the basis of distribution between state and southwide causes was set at 80-20. ". . . until $220,-000 of undesignated gifts has been received, and that for all undesignated receipts over and above that sum the basis of division be 50-50." [79] The 50-50 concept was never forgotten, although not adhered to during the Depression years.

During the year, the State Mission Department had rendered a special service to young men in the Civilian Conservation Corps camps throughout the state by distributing Bibles and other religious material secured from the Sunday School Board.[80]

As it had done upon previous occasions, the Convention, meeting in Atlanta in 1935, again made some effort to concentrate assistance upon the country churches, adopting a resolution which said that many were dead, dying ". . . or weakly trying to weather the storm of adverse conditions . . ." [81] The resolution called for the Executive Committee

> . . . to take steps to see if a plan by which the Baptists of Georgia can be enlisted to co-operate in an effort to save the weak and struggling churches; and if wise, to seek to re-establish those which have ceased to function, by extending the helping hand to our discouraged brethren out in the country." [82]

T. W. Tippett assumed the leadership of the Sunday School department on January 1, 1935.[83] [having been elected in December, 1934.] Searcy Garrison, a student, spoke in the interest of Mercer,[84] and Roland Q. Leavell presented a

[78]*Ibid.*, p. 74. [Note: In many instances the 10-month financial figure is used inasmuch as this was the amount which made its impact upon the Convention Session, and during this period, gifts for November and December were in line with the 10-month period.]

[79]*Ibid.*, p. 82.

[80]*Ibid.*, p. 96.

[81]*Minutes, Georgia Baptist Convention,* 1935, p. 12.

[82]*Loc. cit.*

[83]*Ibid.*, p. 14.

[84]*Ibid.*, p. 21.

resolution which called for appointment of a committee of six, of which he would be a member, to study the matter of ". . . a more concerted and aggressive policy in Evangelism for Georgia Baptists, . . ." with the direction to report to the 1936 Convention.[85] Out of this committee study was to come in 1936 a Department of Evangelism;[86] with W. H. Faust, secretary, assuming his duties March 1, 1937.[87]

The Holding Commission report for 1935 indicated total assets of $744,079.65, with $24,195.55 in cash, $158,583.20 in stocks and bonds: $413,351.96 in real estate loans, $147,303.85 in real estate acquired by foreclosure, and $645.09 in notes receivable.[88] The Commission called for a true declaration of the status of Locust Grove and Blairsville Institutes and Hiawassee High School, reporting that the Commission had on its books accounts for real estate, buildings and equipment of a considerable amount ". . . and it is our information that the equipment in each of these schools has been disposed of." [89]

A reduction in operational deficits was evident during 1935. Receipts for the Cooperative Program were gaining; January to October, 1935, $138,716.48, an increase of $10,683.32.[90] At the close of 1932, a deficit of $120,359.54 had existed; by 1934 this had been reduced to $33,500.00 and it appeared that by the end of the current year, 1935, this deficit would not exceed $15,000 to $18,000.[91]

Finally, unable to sell Locust Grove, use it for an orphans' home, give the materials to Tift college, or, apparently, any other purpose, the Convention in 1935, by approving the action of the Executive Committee, voted to give the property to the Locust Grove Baptist Church with the understanding that one of the buildings, the boys' dormitory, be given

[85]*Ibid.*, p. 26.
[86]*Minutes, Georgia Baptist Convention*, 1936, p.p. 25-26.
[87]*Minutes, Georgia Baptist Convention*, 1937, p. 20.
[88]*Minutes, Georgia Baptist Convention*, 1935, p. 56.
[89]*Loc. cit.*
[90]*Ibid.*, p. 66.
[91]*Ibid.*, p.p. 67, 68.

to Tift for removal or for whatever disposition the college might wish to make of it. The Executive Committee recommended, therefore, that the Holding Commission be instructed to transfer title of the Institute's property to the church.[92]

OFFICES MOVED TO MARIETTA STREET

Offices of the Executive Committee were moved in November, 1935 from the Palmer Building to a site at 22 Marietta Street, corner of Marietta and Broad, Atlanta. Frank A. Hooper, Jr., was chairman of a committee on headquarters space. Upon the recommendation of Hooper's committee, the Executive Committee agreed on Sept. 20, 1935 to move, leasing the old C and S Building at 22 Marietta for $4,000 a year, including light, heat, water, janitor and other office building service. An original recommendation of the Committee had called for a sum of money to be laid aside, looking toward provision for a permanent location. This part of the recommendation was stricken from the report.[93]

Offices of the Convention were to remain at the Marietta street location for nearly eight years, until purchase of the present offices, located at 291 Peachtree St., Atlanta, in 1943.[94]

Convention affairs were showing signs of returning to a more normal state during 1935. Georgia had a population of approximately 3,171,000[95] and Baptists were intent upon evangelizing as many of these as they could. When the Convention met in 1936, the Committee suggested by Roland Q. Leavell the previous year to study means of more intense evangelism gave its report. The report contained a recommendation adopted by the Convention, that a Secretary of Evangelism be elected by the Executive Committee at its

[92]*Ibid.*, p.p. 70, 71.

[93]*Minutes, Executive Committee, Georgia Baptist Convention*, Sept. 20, 1935, p. 184; *Minutes, Georgia Baptist Convention*, 1935, p. 71.

[94]*Minutes, Executive Committee, Georgia Baptist Convention*, Aug. 17, 1943.

[95]*Minutes, Georgia Baptist Convention*, 1935, p. 91.

annual meeting in December of 1936.[96] In 1931, there were 21,501 baptisms by Georgia Baptist churches; in 1932, 23,911; in 1933, 19,732; in 1934, 19,745; and in 1935, 17,636. The 1935 figure was a ratio of 1 baptism to every 27.40 members.[97] The number of baptisms had declined substantially since 1932.

DECLINES IN ENROLMENT

During 1935, Georgia Baptists had suffered some declines in Sunday School and Training Union enrolments. Sunday School was down 1,083, and Training Union was down 6,791.[98] It was believed that creation of this Evangelism Department would help in reversing the downward trend. In the recommendation to the Executive Committee, the plan called for a secretary, with the provision that

> ... he be provided with a salary and a budget which in the judgment of the Executive Committee will be sufficient for him and his expense account, and for the necessary expenses in promoting the work of this department. We recommend that all honorariums and income from meetings or pulpit supply which he may receive shall be applied toward making up this expense budget for his department.[99]

The Executive Committee was to name a committee of at least five to recommend a secretary for this department, and the committee report contained a job description for the position.[100] Thus, for the first time since 1926, Georgia Baptists were planning a specific departmental ministry, having been forced to close the old Department of Enlistment and Evangelism and do away with the field workers in that year because of lack of income.[101]

The emphasis upon evangelism was evidenced further in the report on State Missions. During the year [1936] ten conferences on evangelism, stewardship and missions were

[96]*Minutes, Georgia Baptist Convention*, 1936, p. 25.
[97]*Ibid.*, p. 24.
[98]*Loc. cit.*
[99]*Ibid.*, p. 25.
[100]*Ibid.*, p.p. 25, 26.
[101]*Minutes, Executive Committee, Georgia Baptist Convention*, Dec. 17, 1925.

held across the state, and were attended by 319 pastors who served 595 churches.[102]

And in an unusual move, a resolution asking for preparation in permanent form of the names of benefactors of convention Institutions was referred to the Executive Committee.[103] This was an apparent move by B. J. W. Graham to secure not only names of donors, but the use which had been made of their bequests.[104]

Along with the emphasis upon evangelism, there was a renewed emphasis upon work with laymen. Organization of a general workers' council in each association, was reported, together with the observance of Layman's Day in April, and the use of special offering envelopes in an effort to have ". . . widespread participation in the April ingathering on behalf of the Co-operative Program." The Every Member Canvass still was emphasized.[105] Additionally, the God's Acre plan and the 100,000 Club were propoted also,[106] and with the promotion of evangelism, missions and stewardship, and emphasis upon laymen, together with improved economic conditions, Georgia Baptists gave more during 1936 than they had in several years. For the period January-October, 1936, Cooperative gifts were $145,351.85; designated, $73,178.36, and miscellaneous, $109,801.50, for a total of $328,331.71. This was an increase of $56,265.51 over the $272,066.20 figure for the previous year.[107]

Designated and miscellaneous gifts outweighed the budgeted giving through the Co-operative Program. Many Georgia Baptists had fallen behind, or ceased to give to the $75 Million Campaign because of the economy. Others had made pledges to specific causes, and still others apparently were waiting for funds to give to a favored need, or one to which funds had been pledged. This is indicated by

[102]*Minutes, Georgia Baptist Convention*, 1936, p.p. 21. 22.
[103]*Ibid.*, p. 14.
[104]*Loc. cit.*
[105]*Ibid.*, p.p. 58, 59.
[106]*Ibid.*, p. 60.
[107]*Ibid.*, p. 61.

the allocations under the miscellaneous gifts, including $30,787.25 for the Orphans' Home, special gifts to Mercer of $32,677.32, and special gifts to Tift of $31,128.26,[108] these three alone amounting to $94,592.83.

The special State Missions emphasis in October had been more effective also. From a 1932 figure of $3,974.15, the figure was up in 1936 to $11,541.00.[109]

Used since 1925 largely as rooming houses and a hotel, the old hospital property on Luckie Street was sold in 1936 to the regents of the University System of Georgia for $60,000 cash, with the net proceeds, $58,000, being earmarked to retire outstanding bonds.[110] The old property had been under lease since 1925.[111] This sale left the hospital with all of its property grouped together around the Boulevard avenue building and nurses' home.

In his report to the Convention in 1936, Merritt revealed that when he took office April 1, 1930, the Convention's indebtedness amounted to $535,051.33. In a six and one-half year period, the amount had been reduced by $222,551.33.[112] An evaluation of this indebtedness, all valid, is indicated. In 1929, Cree scolded the Convention for what he termed unwise financial policies against the advice of the Executive Committee.[113] The Executive Committee had no debt of consequence in 1928 and the amount indicated by Merritt was created not because of overspending on State Mission program, but because the Convention, through its Holding Commission, had assumed some liabilities of the institutions, and the Executive Committee had obligations to meet as a result of the hospital crisis of a decade past. The financial report, however, was a noteworthy progress report in the light of the Depression years, and the necessity upon several

[108]*Loc. cit.*

[109]*Ibid.*, p. 36.

[110]*Ibid*, p. 63.

[111]*Loc. cit.*

[112]*Loc. cit.*

[113]*Minutes, Georgia Baptist Convention*, 1929, p.p. 78, 79.

occasions of deficit financing of even the State Missions program by carry-over of deficits into the next year's budget.

Georgia Baptists were strong supporters of the Hundred Thousand Club. In 1936, there were 2,990 Georgia members who had given $57,098.03, making the state third in gifts and fifth in membership in the Southern Convention.[114] It would appear, that the Hundred Thousand Club gifts, and the 80-20 budget allocation for the Cooperative program, about balanced out for several years in terms of Georgia support of Southwide interests.

Prior to the 1936 Convention, the Executive Committee, in September, took the unusual step of asking the Secretary-Treasurer

> . . . to have a sympathetic understanding with the incoming president of the Convention regarding expenses so as to relieve the president of any embarrassment in the matter of taking care of his expense and accepting invitations in the interest of work in the state.[115]

Aquilla Chamlee was to be elected two months after this recommendation, for a three-year period.[116]

HONORS FOR LUTHER RICE

Luther Rice died in 1836. He had meant much to Georgia Baptists. From his visit to the Savannah River Association in 1813, to his establishment of *The Christian Index* under the name, *The Columbian Star,* and Columbian College, Washington, D. C., until his death, he had been a frequent visitor in Georgia. His influence helped to shape Georgia Baptists' concept of foreign missions. He secured considerable sums of money from Georgia Baptists both for Columbian College, Washington, which he founded, and for Foreign Missions under the old Triennial Convention. Therefore, upon the occasion of the observance of the Centennial of Rice's death, the Executive Committee approved

[114]*Ibid.,* p. 64.

[115]*Minutes, Executive Committee, Georgia Baptist Convention,* Sept. 22, 1936, p. 209.

[116]*Minutes, Georgia Baptist Convention,* 1954, p.p. 363, 364.

participation by the churches of the state in the observance of this centennial, and Merritt represented Georgia Baptists at ceremonies at Rice's grave at Pine Pleasant Baptist Church, Saluda, South Carolina.[117]

The budget approved for 1937 provided for a total of $193,961.59, with a 70-30 ratio, an improvement of 10 per cent over previous years.[118] Sunday School enrolment stood at 272,809.[119] This enrolment meant that of a total of 629,191 enrolled in all Sunday Schools of all denominations in Georgia,[120] that Baptists had over 40 per cent of the total.

In his report on Training Union, Edwin S. Preston said that nearly 200,000 in Georgia were looking for assistance through the 2,138 unions.[121]

Miss Mary Christian was Corresponding secretary-treasurer for Woman's Missionary Union,[122] and the women had grown by 1936 to 1,082 societies, 1,934 Sunbeam Bands, Girl's Auxiliaries, Royal Ambassador Chapters and Young Women's Auxiliaries, for a total of 3,016 organizations reaching some 45,106 women and young people.[123]

In October of 1936, trustees of the Orphans' Home had elected Mr. and Mrs. E. J. White, of Atlanta, as managers of the Home.[124] The Whites succeeded Mr. and Mrs. W. P. Anderson, who had served for 14 years. Mrs. Anderson had been acting manager following Anderson's death July 9, 1936, until election of the Whites.[125]

And, during this year, the Hospital cared for 6,768 patients, with 4,361 operations performed, and 724 babies born. There were approximately 100 students enrolled in the School of Nursing.[126]

[117]*Minutes, Georgia Baptist Convention*, 1936, p. 66.
[118]*Loc. cit.*
[119]*Ibid.*, p. 81.
[120]*Minutes, Georgia Baptist Convention*, 1935, p. 91.
[121]*Minutes, Georgia Baptist Convention*, 1936, p. 85.
[122]*Ibid.*, p. 90.
[123]*Loc. cit.*
[124]*Ibid.*, p. 97.
[125]*Ibid.*, p.p. 97, 98.
[126]*Ibid.*, p. 103.

84 ASSOCIATIONS; 470,362 MEMBERS

As of 1936, there were 84 associations, and 2,407 churches with 470,362 members. Total gifts for all causes were $2,419,987.43, and church property was valued at $17,-128,081.00.[127]

A perspective of the Convention's concept of its relation to the Southern Baptist Convention is indicated when in 1937, Merritt reported that although the Southern Baptist Convention had acted favorably upon the request from "certain" states in the south that they be included in receipts from the 100,000 Club, Georgia would not do so. The Executive Committee had gone on record as declaring that it did

> . . . not desire that Georgia share in such gifts and recommends to the Convention that Georgia continue to participate in the Baptist Hundred thousand Club plan on the original basis, namely; that all gifts in Georgia for the Baptist Hundred thousand Club shall go in full to Southern Baptist Convention causes for the purpose of paying the debts on these causes, and no part of such Club funds shall be used within the State.[128]

Through 1937, Georgia had contributed $79,514.46 of the total of $737,844.00 given for the Hundred Thousand Club, being second in total gifts and fourth in memberships.[129]

A motion by Ellis Fuller to name a committee to consider doing away with the Holding Commission was approved and instructions to report to the 1938 Convention.[130]

The report of the Nominating Committee for 1937, with Arthur Jackson as chairman, had some long-range effect by the statements it contained. After his committee had studied, apparently very carefully that year, the composition of the various boards and committees, Jackson presented the following observations of his group:

> 1. That some of the Boards had a tendency to fill their membership with laymen to the exclusion of ministers.

[127]*Encyclopedia of Southern Baptists*, Vol. I, p. 545.
[128]*Minutes, Georgia Baptist Convention*, 1937, p. 65.
[129]*Ibid.*, p. 98.
[130]*Ibid.*, p. 13.

2. That in some instances certain persons were serving on several Boards.

3. That in a few instances a man and his wife were serving on Boards.

4. That one institution drawing support from all over the State was choosing too largely local members.

5. That the Executive Committee had too many ministers and too few laymen and women.

6. That the honors and responsibilities should be distributed to give general representation and secure maximum efficiency in service.

7. That while consideration should be given to wide distribution or representation, yet first consideration should be given to fitness and qualification for the responsible position in service.[131]

With adoption of the report, including these observations, future Nominating Committees were to heed the suggestions.

"BAPTIST HOUR" PROPOSED

A. C. Baker offered two significant actions during the 1937 session. One was a resolution calling for a committee to investigate the possibilities of putting a Baptist Radio Hour over Station WSB in Atlanta.[132] The Second Baker action was a motion approved, which established the Radio Commission of the Georgia Baptist Convention.[133] This action grew out of an overnight study of the resolution.

Baker reported for the Committee on Radio with the following resolution:

Resolved, That the Georgia Baptist Convention appoint a Radio Commission which will have as its purpose the definite encouragement of the use of radio for the presentation of Baptist messages and will arrange for such presentation of messages from time to time as may be possible without incurring financial obligation on the part of the Convention.[134]

Out of this Radio Commission was to come encouragement for the use of communications media in Georgia, and this reflected in the interest of S. F. Lowe, active in use of com-

[131]*Ibid.*, p.p. 24, 25.
[132]*Ibid.*, p. 15.
[133]*Ibid.*, p. 35.
[134]*Loc. cit.*

munications media. Lowe, a Georgia pastor, requested the Southern Baptist Convention, in May, 1938, to explore the field of radio broadcasting.[135] Out of this came the Radio Committee of the Southern Baptist Convention in that year.[136] This became, in 1946, the Radio Commission.[137]

Georgia again was a pioneer in concepts which resulted in establishment of a permanent Southwide work.

There was considerable discussion concerning the proposed budget for 1938, and the discussion centered around one item; the distribution of $1,400 to ministerial education. There had been, evidently, some effort to apply some of the allocation of aid funds to students at secular institutions. W. M. Marshall offered a substitute for the seventh recommendation of the budget which, in effect, kept the ministerial aid available to students in Baptist schools in Georgia only.[138] A motion to continue Shorter college in the Convention budget for another year with a $4,500 allocation, was approved by the Convention.[139]

The motion to allocate $4,500 to Shorter was not to go unnoticed. A motion was made to reconsider the amendment to the Executive Committee's budget. It was referred to the Executive Committee.[140] After several parliamentary maneuvers, Grover Tyner moved that:

> In fairness to all of our Baptist schools and in order that all may share alike, and in view of what the Convention did for Shorter College this morning, I move that Bessie Tift College be given $4,500 and that Norman Junior College be given $2,500 for the year 1938.[141]

This too was referred to the Executive Committee. Apparently the proposals were not acted upon for 1938.

W. H. Faust had begun work as secretary of the Department of Evangelism on March 1, 1937, and in November re-

[135]Encyclopedia of Southern Baptists, Vol. II, p. 1130.
[136]*Loc. cit.*
[137]*Ibid.,* p. 1131.
[138]*Minutes, Georgia Baptist Convention,* 1937, p. 19.
[139]*Loc. cit.*
[140]*Ibid.,* p. 34.
[141]*Loc. cit.*

ported contact in 45 associations, giving 353 sermons and addresses during the years.[142]

An annual ingathering for the Cooperative Programs had come to be an important means of securing needed funds for Baptist work. Success of the effort was indicated when Merritt reported that the ingathering was

> . . . a highly important factor in bringing the year's work to a successful close as will readily be seen in the fact that December's gifts last year totaled $90,087.05. December also registered the largest total of undesignated Co-operative Program gifts of any month in 1936.[143]

INCREASED EMPHASIS
UPON STATE MISSIONS

Sunday schools and Woman's Missionary Unions were placing increasing emphasis upon the observance of State Missions Day in October, with the result that increases were being made in gifts to the State Missions causes.[144]

This year marked the beginning of Convention participation in the present Georgia Temperance League when a special committee asked the Convention to appropriate $250 in cooperation with other denominations to aid in the employment of Nath Thompson as a field worker "to further the cause of temperance." [145]

Over the years, the Convention had provided funds, and handled funds in trust for specific objects, and in an effort to help the Woodbine church, sold property on Norwich street in Brunswick, a gift from an estate.[146] Not an isolated instance, but recounted because of its recurrence, the Convention year by year made as best it could, provision for churches needing funds for building purposes, or new mission work.

By the time for planning the 1938 budget of $198,692.00,

[142]*Ibid.*, p. 20.
[143]*Ibid.*, p. 63.
[144]*Loc. cit.*
[145]*Ibid.*, p. 34.
[146]*Ibid.*, p. 66.

the division of funds between Georgia and Southern Baptist Convention causes had shifted to a 65-35 ratio,[147] a steady move back to the original 50-50 goal. Continuing contributions of Woman's Missionary Union to Convention financial as well as Spiritual life should not be overlooked. In 1936, Baptist women in Georgia gave a total of $183,318.22; $9,399.55 more than in 1935, and of this amount, $111,761.34 was for the Co-operative Program.[148]

Georgia Baptists historically took firm stands when they believed their cause was right. Persecution of Jews in Europe by Germany was becoming a world issue by 1938, and one of the first items of business for the 1938 session of the Convention was to go on record as petitioning the Secretary of State of the United States to take urgent steps in voicing the protest of the American people against atrocities against the Jews in Germany.[149]

B. D. Ragsdale, for many years recording secretary of the Convention, had over the years prepared copy for a history of the Georgia Baptist Convention. For some years, he was carried in the minutes as Convention Historian, with an annual stipend for this service. The Executive Committee, at its meeting on Dec. 18, 1928, signed a contract with Ragsdale for the writing of a Convention history, calling for him to be on a salary of $1,200 a year, with current expenses not to exceed $600 a year.[150]

From that time, for a decade, he remained under this contract for preparing this history. The history appeared in three volumes, and was the property of the Executive Committee of the Convention. The first volume appeared in 1932, copyrighted by the Executive Committee. The second volume, was copyrighted by the author in 1935, and in 1938, J. Ellis Sammons made an appeal to the Convention ". . . for approval and substantial encouragement in publishing a

[147]*Ibid.*, p.p. 66, 67.
[148]*Ibid.*, p. 95.
[149]*Minutes, Georgia Baptist Convention*, 1938, p. 11.
[150]*Minutes, Executive Committee, Georgia Baptist Convention*, Dec. 18, 1928, p. 389.

third volume, . . ." which, Sammons reported was ready. Advance orders were taken for the book, and volume III, copyrighted in 1938 by the Executive Committee and published by the author, completed the long-term undertaking.[151]

The third volume, although published in 1938, carried little, if any, detail of Georgia Baptist life from 1932 on. Actually, although the third volume was designed as a general history of the Convention and its ministries, little was said from the beginning of the Merritt Administration in 1930. The first two volumes dealt primarily with Mercer and other educational institutions.

Another significant step in 1938 was Convention approval of a retirement plan for employees of the Executive Committee. In making the recommendation, a committee named in 1937 to study the matter, reported that the Executive Committee had in the past faced situations where they had to provide for certain employees without any help or contributions made previously by employees to help care for retirees. The committee said that one employee had been paid a total of $15,023.00 over a period of 15 years, and another $7,125 over a period of seven years. The committee made its report after consultation with Annuity Board officials.[152]

A supplemental report concerning retirement programs for Georgia Baptist pastors was approved also. Provision was made for members to pay three per cent of their salary, the Convention two per cent and churches whose pastors were participating, three per cent. The Executive Board was given power to inaugurate the plan as of July 1, 1939, and authority to promote it throughout the Convention.[153]

The death knell was sounded in 1938 for the valuable and important Holding Commission. The Convention voted with earlier return of all property held by the Commission to the institutions to dissolve the Commission.[154] At that

[151]*Minutes, Georgia Baptist Convention*, 1938, p. 11.
[152]*Ibid.*, p.p. 15, 16.
[153]*Ibid.*, p.p. 16-19.
[154]*Ibid.*, p.p. 27, 28.

time it had holdings valued at $1,681,322.15. Another step in 1938 was approval by the Convention of a five-year, $300,-000 enlargement program for Georgia Baptist Hospital. Permission was granted by the Convention to the Hospital Commission, with concurrent approval of the Executive Committee ". . . to begin the work of improving and enlarging the Hospital buildings and facilities as rapidly as funds are secured or guaranteed by good pledges." [155]

Giving by Georgia Baptists to the Cooperative Program continued to show slight gains during 1938,[156] and the budget for 1939 was projected at $216,565.70, on a 60-40 ratio for Georgia and the Southern Baptist Convention.[157]

The Executive Committee presented yet another resolution concerning Shorter college which was approved by the Convention. Although not owning the institution, the Convention approved a proposal that nomination of new trustees for Shorter hereafter be submitted to the Convention for approval or disapproval before final action by the Shorter Board of Trustees—at that time, and for most of the time, a self-perpetuating body.[158]

Gainer E. Bryan, Sr., was elected March 8, 1938 by the Executive Committee to succeed Edwin S. Preston as Training Union Secretary. Preston had resigned after 12 years in the position to become executive secretary of Shorter college.[159] Prior to Bryan's election, he had been a field worker in Sunday School for 14 years. Another change in leadership occurred that year when Aquilla Chamlee retired as president of Bessie Tift after 16 years, and C. L. McGintey was named to succeed him.[160]

Through the most difficult decade in its history, the Georgia Baptist Convention was beginning in 1938 to emerge victoriously. Little permanent damage had been done to the

[155]*Ibid.*, p.p. 12-13.
[156]*Ibid.*, p. 65.
[157]*Ibid.*, p.p. 71, 72.
[158]*Ibid.*, p. 71.
[159]*Ibid.*, p. 83.
[160]*Ibid.*, p. 134.

work, and in many ways, it had been a decade of accomplishment for Georgia Baptists; one of the greatest accomplishments being that they had learned to work together, suffer together, pray together, and in the midst of hardship, to stay together as a Convention united.

The beginning of brighter days for Baptists were evident as the war clouds were evident also on the horizon in Europe; clouds which were to bring other periods of testing and difficulty to the Convention and to the nation as a whole.

CHAPTER 20

The Rising Tide and The War Years

The year 1939 was a banner one for Georgia Baptists. They put their best foot forward, and from Saturday, July 22, through Friday, July 28, were hosts to the Baptist World Alliance, meeting in Atlanta. *The Christian Index* published a 178-page special edition in honor of the occasion, and in so doing advertised all the interests of the Georgia Baptist Convention in an unusually advantageous manner. Every agency and institution, and many churches in the Convention, presented stories of growth, together with advertisements from commercial firms in the Atlanta area.

Welcomes were extended by Georgia Governor E. D. Rivers, chairman of the Board of Deacons at the Lakeland Baptist Church,[1] and by Atlanta Mayor William B. Hartsfield, at that time a member of the First Baptist Church in Atlanta, through the Atlanta Chamber of Commerce.[2]

Louie D. Newton, at that time pastor of the Druid Hills Baptist Church, Atlanta, had been instrumental in bringing the Alliance to Atlanta, and in making arrangements for the sessions.

It was a year also of progress among the churches and in the Convention program. Meeting in Augusta, the Convention was given reports which indicated that the effects of the Depression years were beginning to dissipate, and new challenges for growth were being issued. Enrollment for the

[1]*The Christian Index,* June 15, 1939, p. 9.
[2]*Ibid.,* p. 7.

sessions reached 678, and Ellis A. Fuller, Atlanta, was elected president to succeed Aquila Chamlee.[8]

On March 1, J. L. Fortney became manager of the Orphans' Home,[4] beginning a new era of progress for the Home.[5] By October, 1939, there were 275 children reported as residents of the Home. The Alliance Committee had tendered a gift of $5,000 to the hospital, which was accepted and used together with gifts from Wiley L. Moore and others to renovate a building on the corner of Parkway Drive and East Avenue, purchased the previous October, as a home for interns.[6]

The gift from the Alliance was apparently the first offered to a Georgia institution, and was occasioned evidently by the meeting of the Alliance in Atlanta.

An Orphans' Home called the Southern Industrial Orphans' Home, south of Baxley, Ga., was offered to the Convention at the 1939 session. It was a tentative offer for control and management of the Home and on motion of W. A. Taliaferro, a committee was authorized to explore the possibility of acquiring the property. Text of the Taliaferro resolution was:

> Resolved, That this Convention receives with Christian sympathy the tender of the property of the Southern Industrial Orphans' Home near Baxley, and that a special committee be appointed to investigate the facts and report to the Convention.[7]

The Executive Committee earlier, on March 7, 1939, in response to a request from R. T. Russell, president of the group which at that time operated the Home, named a committee to study the proposed offer. This Committee reported to the Executive Committee on September 12, 1939, and the Executive Committee at that time received the report as information and recommended to the Convention further

[8]Minutes, Georgia Baptist Convention, 1939, p. 9.
[4]Ibid., p. 20.
[5]Loc. cit.
[6]Ibid., p. 21.
[7]Ibid., p. 26.

study which was embraced in the Taliaferro resolution.[8] The matter, however, did not come back to the Convention.

A report submitted by the Committee of Seven to the Convention in 1938 had been referred to the committee for further study and report to the 1939 session. This was done, and because of the far-reaching effect of the recommendations of this committee, the Convention devoted considerable time to discussion of the many proposals.[9] The Convention approved several sections of the report of the Committee of Seven.

One segment of the report called for an amendment to the Constitution of the Convention Article VI, Sec. I, Boards and Commissions which changed that article to read:

> An Executive Committee of this Convention shall be chosen by the Convention, and shall consist of the officers of the Convention ex-officio [the President of the Georgia Baptist Sunday School Convention, the President of the Baptist Training Union, the President of the Baptist Student Union, the President of the Woman's Missionary Union, and the President of the Brotherhood, ex-officio], and forty-five members from the state at large.[10]

The Convention rejected a recommendation which would have made the president of the Convention the president of the Executive Committee. Total vote on this particular recommendation was 204 for and against out of a total enrolment for the Convention of 678.[11]

With this recommendation concerning the president, recommendation eight in the report, eliminated, the Convention approved the remainder of the report in its entirety and voted to continue the Committee of Seven empowering that committee to set up what became the Christian Education Commission,[12] and upon organization of this Christian Education Commission and approval of same by the Execu-

[8]*Ibid.*, p. 78.
[9]*Ibid.*, p.p. 22, 23, p. 30 following.
[10]*Ibid.*, p.p. 30, 31.
[11]*Ibid.*, p. 31.
[12]*Loc. cit.*

tive Committee that the Education Commission of the Georgia Baptist Convention became operative.[13]

Creation of this Education Commission was designed in some measure to replace the impetus provided for Christian Education by the Holding Commission, and at the same time fill a vacuum left in the Convention structure by the dissolution of that Commission which, prior to that time, had made not only observations but recommendations in the area of Christian Education.

The report of the Committee of Seven, as adopted by the Convention, was far-reaching in several ways. Out of this report came the Program Committee of the Georgia Baptist Convention, which was designed to help strengthen the overall program of the Convention to build ". . . a comprehensive, co-ordinated program for 1941, . . ."[14]

With creation of the Program Committee there was the recommendation that consideration be given by the Executive Committee to changes in Evangelism and Stewardship conferences so that these regional meetings, which had become a fixture in Georgia Baptist Convention life, could be followed by associational meetings, with the idea that the denomination's promotion emphasis go from the Program Committee plans, to the Regional Conferences, and from the Regional Conferences to Associational Conferences. It was the thinking of the Committee of Seven that in this manner, the total denominational program could be carried from the association to every church in the state, enhancing the ministries of the denomination and strengthening the Convention's work.[15] In the proposals of the Committee of Seven it was recognized that if this program committee was to function effectively it would require the complete and full co-operation of every department and interest of the Convention to help promote the work in a unified manner.[16] The

[13]*Loc. cit.*
[14]*Ibid.*, p. 33.
[15]*Loc. cit.*
[16]*Loc. cit.*

Committee was to provide ". . . a working program for the following Convention year." [17]

UNIFYING AGENCY HELD NEED

Concern for Christian Education by the Committee of Seven, as expressed in the creation of an Education Commission, was that the institutions needed a unifying agency and that Christian Education was a direct responsibility of the Convention and "That Georgia Baptists need to be resold on Christian Education." [18] Even more far-reaching implications were embodied in the concept of the Christian Education Commission in that the Committee of Seven foresaw:

> That a central endowment foundation owned and controlled by the Convention with adequate financial income would have a wholesome influence with all our educational institutions and would safeguard their usefulness in service to the denomination. [19]

Therefore, embraced in the report of the Committee of Seven as adopted by the Convention, were the following resolutions.

In the section dealing with education:

> I. Christian Education Foundation—That it is the sense of this Convention that Georgia Baptists should create a Christian Education Foundation, the income from which is to be used in the promoting of Christian education within the Convention, and in such institutions as may be qualified for doing such work.
> II. Christian Education Commission—That it is the sense of this Convention that the Christian Education Commission shall be formed to create and administer the Christian Education Foundation in the interest of the Georgia Baptist Convention.
> III. Charter for Education Commission—That the said Christian Education Commission is hereby authorized and directed to apply for a charter under which to operate, and the Executive Committee of the Georgia Baptist Convention is hereby requested to co-operate with said Education Commission in securing said charter.
> IV. Membership of Christian Education Commission—

[17]*Loc. cit.*
[18]*Ibid.*, p. 34.
[19]*Ibid.*, p. 35.

That the Nominating Committee is hereby requested to nominate to this Convention the names of five [5] suitable persons hereafter to be known as THE GEORGIA BAPTIST CHRISTIAN EDUCATION COMMISSION. Two members of this Commission to serve one year; two members of this Commission to serve for two years; one member of this Commission to serve for three years. . . .

V. Ownership of Christian Education Foundation—That the funds raised for the Georgia Baptist Christian Education Foundation, except where otherwise specified by the donor, shall forever remain the property of the Georgia Baptist Convention, and only the income therefrom shall be used for current needs and shall not be diverted to any other purpose.

VI. Assets of Abandoned Institutions—That if and when any school of the Georgia Baptist Convention ceases to function as a Baptist institution, its assets shall automatically become the property of the Christian Education Commission unless otherwise provided by law.

VII. Investment of Funds—That such funds shall be invested in Federal Government, municipal, county or state bonds, and such other securities as are recognized by the state of Georgia as legal for the investment of trust funds. Any change in this class of investment to that of any other type of security can be made only by the recommendation of the Georgia Baptist Education Commission and the Executive Committee of the Georgia Baptist Convention.

VIII. We recommend further that the Education Commission make the best arrangement possible with some reputable financial institution maintaining an efficient trust department to aid them in the management of this endowment fund.

IX. Distribution of Income—That the income from the Christian Education Foundation shall be distributed by Georgia Baptist Christian Education Commission to the schools which qualify to receive such funds. The basis of qualification is that of operating the school in accord with the educational policy attached hereto and adopted by this Convention. Due consideration should be given to cost per student in the Junior and Senior colleges and the awards made proportionately.

X. The Duties of Christian Education Commission—
1. To build Education Foundation
2. To raise endowment
3. To invest or place in trust for investment all funds entrusted to it.

4. To distribute income to schools doing Christian work in accord with Christian Education policy adopted by Convention as set out in article XII.
5. To administer such educational affairs as the schools may voluntarily delegate to the Commission.
6. To have supervision of all Christian Education interests of Georgia Baptists that may not belong to any one school.
7. To seek to promote the interest of the whole program of Christian Education; to secure co-operation between the several Baptist schools, and to promote amity, good-will and harmony among all our educational interests.
8. To create an interest and build an atmosphere in which any and all of our schools may present their causes effectively.
9. To be a voice for Georgia Baptists on Christian educational matters, interpreting the schools to the Convention, and the Convention to the schools.
10. The Christian Education Commission is hereby authorized to employ the necessary agents and agencies to promote the above educational program and raise the proposed Educational Foundation. But they are prohibited from incurring any indebtedness upon the Convention or any agency of the Convention without being duly authorized.[20]

Actually, it was out of this specific recommendation that the Georgia Baptist Foundation came into existence, although its antecedents may be seen throughout previous years in the work of the Holding Commission, and actually in the historic emphasis which had been placed by the Executive Committee, its predecessor the State Mission Board, and especially by the trustees of Mercer University upon the need for continuing endowment to provide especially for educational institutions.

This proposal, as adopted by the Georgia Baptist Convention was to have far-reaching and permanent effects upon the cause of Christian Education, and it should be noted that item nine under section ten indicated that this Education Commission would be a voice for Baptists on Christian Education and would seek to interpret the schools to the Con-

[20]*Ibid.*, p.p. 34-37.

vention and vice versa. The wisdom of this particular phrase was to be evident in later years.

The Education Commission as structured then, would seek to provide understanding for college, university and Convention alike in areas of mutual interest and an affirmation of the Christian character of institutions owned by the Georgia Baptist Convention was intended to be understood clearly as a responsibility of this Education Commission.[21]

"PERMANENTLY" IN EDUCATION FIELD

In stating aims for the Education Commission, the Committee of Seven wanted it understood clearly "that Georgia Baptists are permanently in the business of Christian Education." [22] Students in the institutions were to be urged to identify themselves with Baptist Student Unions and organizations of the churches.[23]

The supplement to the report of the Committee of Seven contained suggestions of far-reaching impact in terms of Baptists' concept of the role for communications media in the days ahead. In the supplement, the Committee said:

> This is a day of great propaganda. The printed page and the radio reach the whole world today for both good and evil. It is our conviction that our churches and denomination should command the best possible publicity. We ought to do our best with the printed page and the radio. We believe that no more profitable thing could be done than to make a comprehensive and thorough study. . . .[24]

Embraced in the suggestions for future study were suggestions that the Convention improve publications which were already in use; investigate the possibility of a Baptist daily newspaper, explore the possibilities for radio broadcasts and the report suggested further that Georgia Baptists consider the possibility of a high-powered radio station and

[21]*Ibid.*, p.p. 37-39.
[22]*Ibid.*, p. 39.
[23]*Ibid.*, p. 38.
[24]*Ibid.*, p. 39.

even a possible joint operation of a Baptist daily newspaper and Baptist radio station.

The Committee conceded that some of the proposals might be out of reach and said that the proposal of a high-powered radio station was being studied also by the Southern Baptist Convention and they had no intention of interfering with that study.[25]

The supplemental report ended with the suggestion that a Committee be named to study these possibilities and declared that ". . . we would be stupid to allow this age to pass without our having given our earnest and best thought to what could be done about making use of these instruments." [26]

Further evidence that Georgia Baptists were instrumental in at least working with the Southern Baptist Convention in the concept of a Radio Commission was that in this supplemental report the committee said that perhaps the best informed man on the subject was in Georgia. This was an evident reference to S. F. Lowe, who later was the first director for the SBC Radio Commission in Atlanta. The Committee indicated that there was another man, unnamed, who also was thoroughly conversant in the area of radio broadcasting.[27]

Clearly indicated was the fact that the weight of the Depression years was being lifted, and Georgia Baptists were making plans with an eye far into the future.

The report of the Social Service Commission to the Convention said:

> The following Christian principles should determine our attitudes and action with reference to the races:
>
> [1] The Fatherhood of God and the universal brotherhood of men;
> [2] The recognition of the principles of race;
> [3] The acknowledgement that Christianity aims to bring each to the highest possible development.

These races, especially the Negroes, have been unjustly

[25]*Loc. cit.*
[26]*Loc. cit.*
[27]*Ibid.*, p.p. 39-40.

discriminated against in our system of public schools, in the provision for their health, in recreational provisions, etc. Peonage or debt slavery has by no means disappeared from our land. There are more white people affected by this diabolical practice than were slaveholders; there are more Negroes held by these debt-slavers than were actually owned as slaves before the War Between the States. The method is the only thing which is changed. Lynching mobs still disgrace our land with their savage atrocities.[28]

This emphasis upon the need of consideration for Negroes in Georgia expresses again the concern which Georgia Baptists had historically for their Negro brethren, and evidenced growing desire on the part of the Convention to right what they considered to be wrongs in the area of social justice with regard to the Negro.

While the Committee of Seven was suggesting a study be made concerning the intensified use of communications media, the Radio Commission of the Georgia Baptist Convention had been making its own study and reported that a 1,000 watt transmitter could be built for between $15,000 and $20,000 and operated about four hours a day for $20,000 a year.[29] "A first class, high-powered station could be built for about $200,000 with operating costs at about $300,000 per year."[30] The Radio Commission said that endowment for such a station would need to be at least $15,000,000.[31]

The Radio Commission said also that many Baptist churches were broadcasting their services on local radio stations and that the meeting of the World Alliance in Atlanta during July had occasioned nearly 100 special programs. The Radio Commission co-operated actively in this special occasion and further that Baptist programs were being presented on several stations throughout the state. At the Convention in Augusta, in 1939, it was reported: "This Convention was presented to the listeners of WRDW [Augusta] and broadcast

[28]*Ibid.*, p. 45.
[29]*Ibid.*, p. 49.
[30]*Loc. cit.*
[31]*Loc. cit.*

direct from the Convention floor and studio programs." [32]

Giving trends were improving in Georgia during 1939. There were gains across the board, with Co-operative Program giving [Jan.-Oct.] of $166,582.51, a $9,176.33 increase, and designated gifts up by $7,338.55 for a total of $89,037.93. Miscellaneous contributions showed a large increase, $71,-526.70, for a total miscellaneous giving of $152,877.45, for a grand total for the 10 months of $408,497.89 an increase of $88,041.58 over the previous year.[33] Additionally, Mercer University received $20,591.42 from the General Education Board of New York.[34]

The Convention was told further that at the end of 1939, indebtedness was decreasing and the balance due on bonds for the Georgia Baptist Hospital had been reduced to $233,-000 with all payments being met. On April 1, 1930, the Convention's indebtedness was $535,051.33, the present debt figure being $233,000 for a reduction of $302,051.33 in less than ten years.[35] This was considered a giant step forward in light of the conditions of the Depression years.

The long awaited third volume *The Story of Georgia Baptists* by B. D. Ragsdale, was published between 1938 and 1939 and the Executive Committee reported it had distributed the volume. Five hundred copies of the volume were published, 300 of which were bound, and 221 copies were sold. Total cost of publication and distribution of Volume 3 was $505.53 and sales of the book had cared for all except $92.67 of the total.[36]

Miss Janice Singleton was elected in 1939 as Executive Secretary-Treasurer of the Woman's Missionary Union in Georgia to succeed Miss Mary Christian who had resigned June 1, 1939 to join the faculty of the W.M.U. Training School in Louisville, Ky.[37] As plans were made for the 1940

[32]*Ibid.,* p. 50.
[33]*Ibid.,* p. 74.
[34]*Loc. cit.*
[35]*Ibid.,* p. 75.
[36]*Ibid.,* p. 79.
[37]*Loc. cit.*

budget, it was set at a 60-40 ratio, still increasing the amount of funds allocated for Southwide causes with a total budget for 1940 of $213,666.67.[38]

B. D. Ragsdale was still listed as Convention historian for 1940, at a salary of $900 including expenses.[39]

In addition to renovation of the building for a residence for interns, the Hospital made other improvements during 1939, chief of which was completion of what came to be known as the Sheffield Cancer Clinic. I. M. Sheffield had contributed $27,000 for renovation of the old Glazer Memorial Church. The Sheffield Clinic not only was used as a cancer clinic, but the auditorium of this clinic was for many years used as a meeting place for the Executive Committee of the Georgia Baptist Convention. Purchase of new equipment and improvements to the hospital were accomplished also during 1939 with what was at the time a record gift on Hospital Day of $8,547.32.[40]

EXPANDED WORK WITH NEGROES

In the area of State Mission work, the Convention had begun in 1938 an expanded program of work with Negroes and this program consisted mainly of co-operating with Negro Baptists by providing funds to help maintain Negro Baptist headquarters and promoting training institutes in Georgia.[41]

The Mercer Church Efficiency School, as of 1940, came to be known as the Mercer Preachers' School. The 10th session of this efficiency school had been held in June, 1939, wth 300 ministers and 350 laymen and women enrolled.[42]

In this year also, Georgia had 2,575 Baptist churches with 2,281 Sunday Schools.[43] The Training Union work, proceeding under the leadership of Gainer Bryan, reported a

[38]*Ibid.*, p.p. 80, 81.
[39]*Ibid.*, p. 81.
[40]*Ibid.*, p.p. 122, 123.
[41]*Ibid.*, p. 93.
[42]*Loc. cit.*
[43]*Ibid.*, p. 98.

total of 1,005 churches having one or more unions which was an increase of 84 over the previous year and during 1939, up to the time of the report to the Convention, 14,907 study course awards had been issued.[44]

The student ministry, 14 years old by 1939, was reaching out into colleges other than Baptist. During 1938, a Baptist Student Union had been organized at the State College for Women at Milledgeville. During 1939, an organization was set up at LaGrange Female College [45] and the program for Baptist student unions was beginning to make its impact at the level of state colleges.

As of 1939, out of the $1,063,824.70 contributed through the Baptist Hundred Thousand Club, Georgia had contributed $132,035.39, which made it second among the states in the Convention in total gifts to the club.[46]

As a prelude to what was to develop within several years as a Baptist Brotherhood Department, for the second year, promotion of Baptist Brotherhood work among men in the churches was sponsored by the State Mission program and was assigned to a committee of seven laymen and the executive secretary of the Executive Committee. Primary emphasis in promotion of work among the laymen included distribution of literature and tracts and emphasis upon a laymen's day which was held in October.[47]

PROGRAMS DETAILED FOR ALLIANCE

In a statement of welcome to Baptists of the world the Convention's Executive Committee, in the World Alliance edition of *The Christian Index,* outlined in summary detail the scope of its work and under the program of State Missions included the activities of Evangelism, Stewardship Promotion, Sunday Schools, Training Union, Student Work, Laymen's Work, Support of Missionary Pastors through Pastoral Aid, Emergency Church Building Aid,

[44]*Ibid.,* p. 101.
[45]*Ibid.,* p. 105.
[46]*Ibid.,* p. 110.
[47]*Ibid.,* p. 92.

Regional Conferences, Enlistment Promotion of the Cooperative Program, and Work Among the Negroes. As of June,
1939, Merritt in this advertisement, reported 2,434 churches
with a total membership of 499,404 in 86 district associations.[48]

In an article on the work of Negro Baptists in Georgia,
prepared by D. D. Crawford for this same edition of *The
Index,* Crawford, Executive secretary-treasurer of the Negro
convention cited some Georgia "firsts." He said the first
Negro preacher on record, George Leile, although born in
Virginia, was sold into Georgia as a slave and baptized into
the membership of a white Baptist church and ordained by
that church; the first Negro Baptist church in history was organized three miles west of Savannah by Abraham Marshall;
the first four Negro churches known to history were organized on Georgia soil including the Springfield Church,
Augusta, the Second Baptist Church, Savannah, the Ogee-
chee Baptist Church, Savannah. Crawford gave Georgia
credit for organization of the first Negro Baptist sunday
school, and the first Negro district association, the Zion,
which, although organized at Hilton Head, South Carolina,
was comprised of a majority of churches from Georgia.[49]

Crawford's tracing of this history of Negro Baptist work in
Georgia is of significance because Georgia Baptists had been
instrumental in working with Negroes from earliest days to
the present time, and out of these efforts came the growth of
the Negro work as a separate entity, particularly after the
War Between the States. Crawford said in his account that
of the Negro Christians in Georgia 68 per cent were
Baptists.[50]

This was the year of the so-called "heresy trial" at Mercer
University. During the academic year 1938-39 thirteen of
sixty ministerial students at Mercer brought charges of heresy
against five faculty members. Three students preferred
charges against one professor, two against another and one

[48]*The Christian Index,* June 15, 1939, p. 38.
[49]*Ibid.,* p. 20.
[50]*Loc. cit.*

against each of three professors and the charges were grouped into one general statement. Dowell in his report on Mercer University to the Convention said that upon receiving the charges, the matter was brought to the attention of the Trustees and all parties were given opportunity to present their positions.[51] A special committee was appointed by the Executive Committee of the Trustees to conduct an investigation and this committee found that the charges were not sustained.[52]

This "heresy trial" had been brought about apparently by circumstances of some years standing on the Mercer campus. Dowell said that the Executive Committee of the Trustees received a group of representatives from the Macon Baptist Pastors' Union on March 20, 1939.[53]

The committee from the Macon Pastors' Union submitted a request for an investigation. The students had not gone through the administration of the university, but had made their petition to the Macon pastors and Dowell reported that the petition came from a group of ministerial students who called themselves the "Fellowship Group," a secret organization ". . . to protect the institution from heretical teaching." [54] The Fellowship Group read a letter of complaint apparently in conjunction with a meeting of the state Training Union Convention which was held that year at the Tabernacle Church in Macon.

The charges had centered primarily around John D. Freeman, along with John G. Harrison and Edwin M. Poteat, three members of the faculty in the Department of Christianity. J. Seaborn Winn, at the time president of the Macon Pastors Conference, along with Marshall Nelms and Grover Tyner, were named by the complaining students to serve as their counsel. The hearing was held in Roberts

[51]*Minutes, Georgia Baptist Convention,* 1939, p. 133.

[52]*Ibid.,* p.p. 133, 134.

[53]Dowell, Spright, *A History of Mercer University 1833-1953,* [Atlanta: Foote & Davies, Inc., 1958] 420 p.p., p. 322.

[54]*Ibid.,* p. 323.

chapel in the Theology Building March 30, 1939 beginning at 11 a.m. and concluding at 9:15 p.m., with no recess.[55]

The exoneration of the three was clear at every level of review. However, as a result of the charges, Freeman, at the time 75 years old, submitted his resignation to Dowell on August 3, 1939 and Freeman's retirement was accepted with provision made for a retirement income of $100 per month.[56]

While some form of controversy was not new, this event marked the only time in the illustrious history of Mercer University that a direct confrontation of this type was made. Dowell's handling of the situation, and his full and prompt report to the Convention concerning it, probably foredoomed other possible efforts of the same type in later years.

This was the only event during 1939 to mar one of the most progressive years the Convention had experienced. Recommendations of the Committee of Seven were so far reaching that over 30 years later the impact of some of the actions still was evident.

The impact of the meeting of the Baptist World Alliance was to be felt among Georgia Baptist churches for many years, and probably was a contributory factor behind the ready response by Georgia Baptists to appeal for world relief programs following World War Two. Actually, a year later, in 1940, the Promotion Committee reported, presenting the needs of the British Baptist Missionary Society Emergency Relief Fund, with a generous response by Georgia Baptists.[57]

[55]Ibid., p.p. 323, 324.
[56]Ibid., p.p. 326, 327.
[57]Minutes, Georgia Baptist Convention, 1940, p.p. 60-61.

CHAPTER 21

From Hardship Through War: Growth

With 1940, Georgia Baptists emerged into a period of growth, which in the main was to be sustained from that time until the present. In all of the Convention's organized history, it had not been called upon to exercise the wisdom and patience which it exhibited during the decade of the 1930's.

From the mid-1920's until 1930, financial trends had been difficult. From 1930 through 1936, they had been almost impossible. However, despite the economic situation, a witness for Christ had been sustained, debts had been paid, all Baptist interests promoted, and plans made for the future. Tift, Shorter, and Norman were included in the 1941 budget adopted by the convention in 1940.[1] Although the amounts were not large, they did signify the strengthened financial position of the convention.

The Constitution of the Convention was amended in 1940. B. D. Ragsdale had earlier given notice in *The Index* of a proposal to amend. The amendment was, as Ragsdale termed it, to correct an oversight in providing that the assistant secretary of the Convention be a member, ex-officio, of the Executive Committee. Ragsdale pointed out that for about 100 years the assistant secretary had been a member of the Executive Committee until the Constitution revision in 1919, at which time the provision which would include an assistant secretary on the Executive Committee was not included.

[1]*Minutes, Georgia Baptist Convention,* 1940, pp. 11, 12.

555

Therefore, the amendment, to Section I of Article VI, dealing with Executive Committee membership, said:

> . . . and shall consist of the officers of the Convention, ex-officio, including the Assistant Secretary of the Convention appointed by the Secretary, the president, . . .[2]

This situation was unique in that it allowed the recording secretary to name his assistant, permitting naming a member of the Executive Committee by an individual rather than by the Convention's nominating committee.

Georgia Baptist Hospital continued to grow, treating 6,274 patients between Jan. 1 and Oct. 31, 1940 and Hospital Day gifts totaled $11,049.75.[3]

A committee, named in 1939 to study further the proposed tender of the South Georgia Industrial Orphans' Home at Baxley, reported to the 1940 Convention that after consideration of the matter again they did not consider it expedient for the Convention to accept the property because of restrictions which had been placed upon it by donor of the property, E. L. Odum. The conditions would limit, according to the study committee, the Convention in appealing to its constituents for funds to equip and operate the institution adequately. However, the same committee said there was a need for extension of the care of orphans by Georgia Baptists and recommended that a Committee of Seven be named by the Convention to report in 1941 on consideration of establishment of such an extended ministry. This, to the committee, called for a home at some point south of Macon to be operated under a unified Board of Trustees.[4]

As had been the case when the Convention met in Augusta, upon meeting in Atlanta in 1940, arrangements had been made with Radio Station WSB for a brief program from the Convention floor.[5] Interest in promoting the work of Georgia Baptists through communications media continued

[2]*Ibid.*, p. 15.
[3]*Ibid.*, p. 22.
[4]*Ibid.*, p.p. 32-34.
[5]*Ibid.*, p. 23.

to be keen, and this was really a pioneer endeavor during the mid-thirties up through the 1940's.

The Committee of Seven, in making its report, said it considered it a paramount duty to establish an Education Commission. This commission, they believed, should be set up before any survey of Christian education conditions in Georgia would be made.[6] Acting under authority of the 1939 Convention, this had been accomplished. The Commission was approved by the Executive Committee in September.[7] In the report of the Committee of Seven, recommendations included minimum goals for endowment of $3,600,000 for Mercer, $600,000 for Tift, $400,000 for Shorter, $200,000 for Brewton-Parker and $200,000 for Norman.[8]

More significant was the suggestion that the name Georgia Baptist Education Commission be changed to Georgia Baptist Foundation.[9]

Searcy S. Garrison, in 1940, read the report of the Social Service Commission which included areas of study embracing the Lord's Day observance, law enforcement, and church and state. In the report of the Commission for this year, there was a request for the Convention to reaffirm its faith in the historic principle of complete separation of church and state, and the Commission called upon all faiths to resist all inclinations on the part of the state and of its officers to disregard the constitutional guarantee.

> We disapprove the action of the President of the United States in sending Mr. Myron C. Taylor as his special or personal representative to the Vatican, and assigning him the rank of ambassador, without consulting the Senate, as a violation of this cherished principle of our Baptist people, as well as a violation of the plain meaning of the Constitution.[10]

The report commended further an earlier resolution of the Southern Baptist Convention upon the same subject.[11]

[6] *Ibid.*, p.p. 25, 26.
[7] *Loc. cit.*
[8] *Ibid.*, p. 27.
[9] *Loc. cit.*
[10] *Ibid.*, p.p. 40, 41.
[11] *Ibid.*, p. 41.

The Social Service Commission in 1940 reported on spiritual needs in the military as preparations for National Defense were under way following the Conscription Bill, or Draft Law which had been passed earlier by the Congress of the United States. The Commission recommended to the churches and the denomination that they recognize their obligations to the young men who were leaving their home churches for military training and called upon the churches to be opened to the soldiers at all times, and called upon pastors and church leaders to make themselves available for ministry to these men in groups and as individuals especially where churches were located near training camps. The Commission suggested further that Bibles, religious tracts and issues of *The Christian Index* be distributed to servicemen and also encouraged some ministers to serve as chaplains and spiritual leaders for the military forces.[12]

A survey of radio programs in Georgia under Baptist auspices during the year, made by the Radio Commission, indicated that Athens, Atlanta, Augusta, Brunswick, Griffin, Macon, Moultrie, Rome, Savannah, Thomasville, and Waycross radio stations were using programs by Baptist churches and Baptist groups.[13]

Entering into the field of Foreign Relations, the Committee on Resolutions presented to the 1940 Convention a statement which said;

> The Baptists of Georgia, assembled in their annual Convention, pledge their loyal support to the President of the United States in his foreign program. We pray the guidance of Almighty God upon him and his advisors. We also pray that this country may be spared the blight of war and may be enabled to use its strength and influence for the establishment of good will among the nations of the earth.[14]

The Committee on Resolutions took cognizance of a suggestion of the Executive Board of Woman's Missionary Union in conveying to the Convention for its approval expressions of deep concern

[12]*Ibid.,* p.p. 42, 43.
[13]*Ibid.,* p.p. 44, 45.
[14]*Ibid.,* p. 46.

that our boys assembled in cantonments for military training shall be safeguarded in their moral and spiritual life and that the surroundings of the cantonments and the character of the hostesses and others who are employed in the cantonments shall contribute to this end. . .[15]

The Promotion Committee recognized the value of special days to be observed in Sunday Schools, and included as recognized emphases those upon Home and Foreign Missions in March, Hospital Day in May, Ministerial Education in June, State Missions in October, and Orphans' Home in November.[16]

Co-operative Program receipts continued to rise in Georgia during 1940. Total gifts for the ten-month period January to October were $511,977.84, with Co-operative Program receipts up to $174,003.25 for the same period.[17] And, the Convention was projecting for a 1941 budget of $234,366.67.[18] The allocation remained at the 60-40 ratio until the budget was covered, and then all undesignated receipts over and above that sum would be divided on a 50-50 basis.[19] For the first time in 1940, the Program Committee listed a complete schedule of meetings for the year, marking a pattern which was to continue annually.[20]

Growing interest in several areas of work was reflected in 1941. The Executive Committee at its November 10th meeting in 1941 approved a resolution authorizing the Executive Committee to borrow $190,000 from the First National Bank in Atlanta to refund hospital bonds. This was approved by the Convention.[21] The Convention appropriated $1,000 for helping place the Penfield Cemetery in a state of good repair.[22]

Activity of the Georgia Baptist Convention Radio Com-

[15]*Loc. cit.*
[16]*Ibid.,* p. 61.
[17]*Ibid.,* p. 63.
[18]*Ibid.,* p. 69.
[19]*Loc. cit.*
[20]*Ibid.,* p.p. 78-81.
[21]*Minutes, Georgia Baptist Convention,* 1941, p.p. 12, 14, 15.
[22]*Ibid.,* p. 17.

mission was reflected in its report. The Commission said that more than 150,000 hours of radio broadcasting was being done in Georgia each year with 28 stations located in 21 cities. Every station carried some religious program each week and, with few exceptions, all stations carried some Baptist message each week.[23]

EMPHASIS UPON DEFENSE EVIDENT

The emphasis upon national defense in the days prior to World War II was evident as much from the reports of the Social Service Commission as any other Convention source. In the Commission report for 1941, the National Defense effort was presented:

> The efforts of the national government toward making secure the liberties of our people and integrity of our country commend themselves to the constituency of the Georgia Baptist Convention. The Social Service Commission endorses the basic objectives of the national defense program, and approves the administration policy which calls for the defeat of such powers as challenge the security of America, the hemisphere, the democratic process, and the Christian way of life.

The Commission called upon Georgia Baptists to lend themselves and their fortunes to the national defense effort.[24]

In a statement on race relations, the Commission called upon the Baptist people in Georgia to pledge ". . . good will and Christian love to men of all races, with particular regard to members of the Negro race."[25] Continuing its report, the Commission called upon Baptists to manifest a Christian spirit and attitude in personal relations with members of the Negro race and urged

> . . . the churches, pastors and denominational leaders to exercise themselves to the end that (1) members of the Negro race be given civil, economic, and educational justice; (2) that Negro church and religious life be given the support of our interest, prayers, and practical help.[26]

[23]*Ibid.*, p. 27.
[24]*Ibid.*, p. 31.
[25]*Ibid.*, p. 32.
[26]*Ibid.*, p. 33.

L. P. Glass presented an amendment to the Social Service Commission report, approved by the Convention, which called upon Georgia Baptists and other Christian voters to vote only for those candidates for state and county offices who had declared that they would work and vote for the restoration and reenforcement of prohibition in Georgia.[27]

In reporting for a committee which had been named to consider establishment of a Baptist daily newspaper, Louie D. Newton, pastor of the Druid Hills Baptist Church, said that ". . . we see no possible hope of such undertaking at the present, and therefore request the Convention to dismiss the committee." [28]

Following the decision in 1940 to not accept the Orphans' Home at Baxley, and a decision to study further the need for a Convention-owned home south of Macon, the study committee in 1941 reported that action, in their judgment, should be deferred for two reasons. One, it would be unwise to undertake a new branch until the present home was filled to capacity. The committee said (two) that additional land had been provided for the Hapeville Home with the gift of 115 acres and a building about a mile from the Home, and, two, the Committee felt it would be unwise to begin at that time an enterprise which would ". . . eventually involve the spending of several hundreds of thousands of dollars for buildings and equipment." [29] This property, 115 acres, was used later as a farm and dairy, providing milk and food for the Hapeville campus of the Orphans' Home. With the ultimate acquisition of the Home in South Georgia, which became known as the Odum branch of the Georgia Baptist Children's Home, and the large farm operations at the Odum branch, the farm and dairy were done away with at the Hapeville branch and the property sold.

The Convention approved a resolution calling for the Executive Committee to give serious consideration to setting up a Department of Brotherhood work in the State Missions

[27]*Ibid.,* p. 34.
[28]*Loc. cit.*
[29]*Ibid.,* p.p. 34, 35.

program and employing a full time secretary by the time the 1942 Convention should meet.[30]

Spencer B. King, Sr., who was treasurer of the Convention, reported that no funds had been administered by him during the year, and no reports were made because all monies were being administered through the Executive Committee and the Executive Secretary-Treasurer.[31] Prior to that time, the Convention treasurer had handled small amounts of monies, primarily for ministerial aid, and had submitted an annual report to the Convention. Hereafter, all funds were to be channeled through the office of the Executive Secretary-Treasurer. As it had done in other years, the 1941 Convention asked the Social Service Commission to consider carefully and formulate a clear definition of what should be the proper aims, functions, scope, methods and activities of the ". . . Social Service Commission . . . in harmony with the primary, major and established objects and activities of the Convention itself." [32]

After discussion of the Baptist Foundation report by Arthur Jackson [the Committee on Baptist Foundation being successor to the Committee on Christian Education as of 1940], the report was amended to add the president of the Convention and Executive Secretary-Treasurer of the Executive Committee and a representative from each of the five schools to the Endowment Commission. Willis Howard made a motion that the report be referred to a committee to consist of the Foundation Special Endowment Committee, and others to study recommendations in the report and submit findings to the Executive Committee in December.[33] "After consideration for a full day by the Executive Committee at its December meeting no conclusion was reached." [34] Content of the Foundation report was not made a matter of Convention minute record. However, the discussion was lengthy. M. E. Dodd, Shreveport, a scheduled speaker, failed to arrive.

[30]Ibid., p. 35.
[31]Ibid., p. 40.
[32]Ibid., p. 41.
[33]Ibid., p. 42.
[34]Loc. cit.

The late Senator Walter F. George, scheduled to speak, was detained in Washington. The secretary reported succinctly: "Prolonged discussions of other matters consumed the time, and it was now one o'clock, and many were hungry.[35]

WAYS TO AID NEEDY PROBED

The Convention approved a resolution, again dealing with the Social Service Commission, calling upon this Commission to consider the advisability of bringing to the 1942 Convention session information which would be of value to pastors and others as they sought to administer more efficiently and economically aid to needy persons in their several committees. This was done in view of the fact that even by 1941, federal, state, county and city governments had entered extensively into the area of charity through welfare programs, and these governmental agencies were inviting the assistance of churches in their charitable programs.[36] The goal of Georgia Baptists unofficially had become a debtless denomination by 1945, as this goal had become a slogan of the Hundred Thousand Club,[37] and Merritt reported that a new area of state missions work had been opened in terms of ". . . service to communities adjacent to Army camps, military centers and defense project areas." [38]

The Regional Conferences for 1941, upon which program emphases had been placed in a co-ordinated manner, attracted some 500 pastors and 1,400 laymen to discuss the work of the Convention.[39] These Regional Conferences were to continue annually until they were replaced in 1962 by a Denominational Emphasis Program which was also to have a large impact upon the promotional program of the Convention in terms of the total number of people which it reached.[39a] The 1942 budget for the Cooperation Program, as

[35]*Ibid.*, p. 43.
[36]*Ibid.*, p.p. 42, 43.
[37]*Ibid.*, p. 65.
[38]*Ibid.*, p. 84.
[39]*Ibid.*, p. 85.
[39a]*Minutes, Georgia Baptist Convention,* 1962, p. 93.

adopted by the 1941 Convention, was $277,333.33.[40] When the Convention, with 600 messengers and attendants, met in Macon in November of 1942, Georgia Baptists were able to increase this budget for 1943 to $303,402.00, with a recommended goal of $315,000, still with a 60-40 ratio until the budget had been met.[41]

The Convention received a report that establishment of a Department of Brotherhood work had been postponed because of the war-time conditions which existed,[42] and changed further the structure upon which the Georgia Baptist Foundation was to be erected permanently by adopting in 1942 special recommendations of the Executive Committee providing for amendments to the charter of the Georgia Baptist Foundation. The amended section was to read:

> That in addition to the principle object and purpose of said corporation as set forth in paragraph 4 of this petition, the said corporation shall also have the right to receive any gifts or bequests from any person or persons to be administered and used or distributed for the benefit of any institution in Georgia owned or fostered by the Georgia Baptist Convention in accordance with the provisions of the gift or bequest as specified by the donor.[43]

A further amendment was to make the charter, in the first sentence of paragraph five, read: "The said net income shall be distributed by the Trustees to such schools and colleges as qualify to receive such funds, and as directed by the Georgia Baptist Convention.[44]

The report on education for 1942 included an item which dealt with Norman College, which item was challenged by Louie Newton. The college had worked out an arrangement with the Colquitt County Board of Education under which arrangement high school students in Norman Park went to the high school department of Norman Junior College and the college was paid a fixed fee per pupil by the Colquitt

[40]*Minutes, Georgia Baptist Convention*, 1941, p. 70.
[41]*Minutes, Georgia Baptist Convention*, 1942, p.p. 12, 13.
[42]*Ibid.*, p. 64.
[43]*Ibid.*, p. 15.
[44]*Loc. cit.*

County Board of Education.[45] It was this feature of Norman's report which Newton challenged on the basis of separation of church and state, and after considerable discussion, the matter was tabled.[46] However, although this arrangement worked apparently well from Norman's point of view, and provided operational revenues for the college which it would not have received otherwise, it was to become enough of a point of disagreement in later years for the college to do away with this phase of its high school program, and finally the entire high school. The paragraph questioned by Newton was withdrawn from Norman's report upon motion of Willis E. Howard, who moved that the question be referred to a committee studying the Baptist position in this area.[47]

Georgia Baptists continued their concern for the rural church. A special committee was named in 1942 to study the entire State Missions program with particular emphasis on how the State Missions program might be of more assistance in rural church problems.[48] During two years of pre-war anxiety and during the war, circulation of *The Christian Index* took a significant turn upward. In 1940 circulation of *The Index* was 11,500.[49] By 1942 *The Index* circulation was 21,250, a sizeable gain in a two-year period.[50] *The Index* was to grow consistently from that point on in circulation, by 1943 reporting over 24,500, and in 1944 reporting 32,000, for a circulation almost tripled in a four-year period.[51]

In the Foundation report for 1942, read by Arthur Jackson, there was contained a recommendation that $10,000 be appropriated to defray one year's expenses for an endowment campaign. An amendment offered by Louie Newton, which called for funds needed to be paid for out of funds raised in the campaign was lost. Then, a motion was made by O. M.

---

[45]Author's conversation with Norman officials in 1945.
[46]*Minutes, Georgia Baptist Convention,* 1942, p. 17.
[47]*Ibid.,* p.p. 20, 21.
[48]*Ibid.,* p.p. 18, 19.
[49]Lester, James Adams, "A History of *The Christian Index,* 1822-1954," [Unpublished Master's Thesis, 1955] p. 132.
[50]Minutes, *op. cit.,* p. 19.
[51]Lester, p. 132.

Seigler that the $10,000 for financing the endowment campaign be taken out of Georgia's part of the Co-operative Program receipts after division between the state and southern convention causes had been made. This motion was adopted. The budget which had already been adopted was changed to include this item.[52]

$5 MILLION CAMPAIGN LAUNCHED

In 1940 a campaign had been launched to raise $5 million for the schools. The Endowment Campaign Committee reaffirmed its faith in the unified program of Georgia Baptists to secure endowment, using the Foundation as the focal point for the raising of endowment. The Committee then requested

> ... that a suitable man for endowment secretary should be employed; that the Georgia Baptist Convention should give assurances of wholehearted co-operation and financial support for a minimum of five years.[53]

Having been requested to reassess its function by the 1941 Convention, the Social Service Commission, in making its 1942 report, suggested to the Convention that an independent Convention committee be appointed to define the duties and functions of the Commission and that adequate financial resources be placed at the committee's disposal to perform this function.[54] At the conclusion of the Social Service Commission report, T. F. Callaway moved that the Convention recognize the Anti-Saloon League as its medium for fighting the liquor traffic.[55] This motion, approved by the Convention, followed an earlier agreement by the Convention to give funds to this cause, put the Convention on record as endorsing and participating in the work of the Anti-Saloon League, out of which was later to come Convention co-operation in what became the Georgia Temperance League.[56]

The 1942 session of the Convention had been scheduled to

[52]*Minutes, Georgia Baptist Convention*, 1942, p. 27.
[53]*Ibid.*, p. 28.
[54]*Ibid.*, p. 35.
[55]*Ibid.*, p. 39.
[56]*Loc. cit.*

meet in Savannah but was moved to Macon because it was deemed inadvisable to meet on a seacoast city in war time bringing large crowds together with a possibility of blackouts handicapping attendance at night sessions.[57] At the meeting in Macon, of the 603 registered, 328 were ministers, 102 were laymen and 173 women were in attendance.

The average attendance between 1912 and 1921 at Convention sessions was 459. The high mark was in Macon in 1919 with 837 and the lowest attendance in Macon was in 1918, with 291 in attendance. Between 1922 and 1931, average attendance was 544 with the high at Gainesville in 1929 of 910 and a low attendance at Valdosta in 1926 of 356. Between 1932 and 1941 average attendance was 624 with the high in 1941 in Macon of 807 and a low attendance at Savannah in 1936 of 484.[58] For the ten month reportable period prior to the Convention in 1942, Co-operative Program gifts were up to $252,538.87 making total gifts for the ten-month period $616,229.41. This marked a $171,374.67 increase over the previous ten months. This figure included a total of $146,505.87 for the Orphans' Home.[59]

By 1942, the Georgia Baptist Convention was almost out of debt, the final item being the balance due on the Hospital bond obligation in the amount of $162,000.[60] Merritt said there were 631 pastors and 1,113 churches enrolled in the Ministers' Retirement Plan with the total amount paid to Georgia annuitants for both age retirement and disability up to October 31, 1942, being $25,488.20.

Georgia Baptists, their churches, agencies and institutions, and denomination co-operated to the fullest with the United States government during World War II. Gilbert, for example, as editor of *The Index,* cooperated with agencies set up by the Federal Government to promote savings of critical materials and with agencies furthering the interest of the United States at war in other ways. During the war years,

[57]*Ibid.,* p.p. 64, 65.
[58]*Ibid.,* p. 55.
[59]*Ibid.,* p. 60.
[60]*Ibid.,* p. 61.

Gilbert also made use of war time religious experiences, sent to him by Georgia Baptist chaplains and soldiers, through the columns of *The Index*.[61]

Mercer University, because of its size and educational stature, was in a position to co-operate in the setting up of programs for the training of servicemen during World War II. Mercer had been active in training the military for the government during World War I, and again, under Dowell's leadership, the University co-operated in training programs. In June of 1942, the program for national defense at Mercer was converted into War Training Service with seventy naval cadets enroled.[62]

The law building and Columbus Roberts Hall were used and Mercer trained 731 men in the Navy's V-5 Aviation Instruction Program in basic training. This program came to a close in 1944.[63] The V-5 students had their classes in the Ryals law building and flight training at Herbert Smart airport in Macon.[64] Additionally, Mercer participated in the Navy's V-12 program to provide officers for the Naval Reserve during World War II. The V-12 program existed at the same time at the V-5 program did for a time. It was established at Mercer July 1, 1943, and operated until October of 1945. The V-5 program was in the area of aviation. The servicemen were sent to Mercer for periods ranging from four to sixteen months. The V-12 students used Sherwood Hall for housing and Porter Stadium for drill grounds.[65]

During this period, the University went from the quarter system to the trimester system to provide continuous training. One of the nine institutions in the southeast named to give aviation instruction under the V-5 program, Mercer performed a commendable service academically as well as other-

[61]*Lester*, p.p. 117, 118.
[62]Spright Dowell, *A History of Mercer University, 1833-1953* [Atlanta: Foote & Davies, Inc., 1958], p. 339.
[63]*Loc. cit.*
[64]*Ibid.*, p.p. 339, 340.
[65]*Ibid.*, p.p. 340, 341.

wise.[66] Approximately 30 Mercer alumni served also as chaplains during the Second World War.[67]

The Convention's plans for an intensive endowment campaign had been stalled because of World War II. Tift College had been allowed the privilege of conducting a campaign for $100,000 and Mercer trustees were interested in having their own campaign in the light of the Convention's delay in an overall campaign to raise funds.[68]

A Campaign Committee was appointed for Mercer University on August 28, 1943, and the University was informed that the General Education Board in New York would give $200,000 on a million dollar campaign effort when a total of $800,000 in cash and good pledges had been received. The campaign organization was set up in January, 1944.[69] By June, 1944, the campaign was well under way. By the end of 1944, the campaign had been completed and the goal exceeded by some $200,000, resulting in

> . . . $1,200,000 of new endowment and the establishment in due time of twelve distinguished professorships. One of the most beneficial results of the campaign was the widespread publicity of Mercer University among Georgia Baptists and their favorable response. More people than ever before were personally interested in the Institution with the result that they became more familiar with its services and needs and were pleased to regard it as their very own.[70]

Little had been said publicly concerning any new offices for the Georgia Baptist Convention following removal of the Convention to the Luckie Street site in November, 1935. At a called meeting of the Administration Committee of the Executive Committee on February 4, 1943, the Committee gave authorization to make a contract for purchase of property at 70 Broad Street for a headquarters building at a price not to exceed $57,500.[71]

[66]*Ibid.*, p. 341.
[67]*Loc. cit.*
[68]*Ibid.*, p. 342.
[69]*Ibid.*, p. 343.
[70]*Ibid.*, p. 344.
[71]*Minutes, Administration Committee, Executive Committee, Georgia Baptist Convention*, February 4, 1943, p. 417.

After the Administration Committee made apparent agreement on the Broad Street property, the property at the corner of Peachtree and Baker Streets became available and the Executive Committee of the Convention, at a called meeting on August 17, 1943, made a decision to purchase a building at the corner of Peachtree and Baker Streets for a purchase price of $190,000. Of this amount, $100,000 was to be paid in cash, with the balance, $90,000, payable in equal monthly installments over a 20-year period at 4 per cent interest with deferred payments.[72] For the first time, the Georgia Baptist Convention was to have a permanent home of its own.

The building consisted of four floors with two basements on a lot 100 by 177 by 77.5 by 134 feet and contained approximately 50,000 square feet of space. Between 1952 and 1954, the building was modernized and remodeled with air conditioning, installation of a new elevator, and other improvements.[73] In 1956, 1959, and 1966, during the present administration, further extensive renovations were made to the building and offices were modernized. Additionally, property along Baker Street, behind the Baptist building, was purchased over a period of several years, and is in use as parking space.[74]

The Baptist Building, when purchased, was used not only for offices for the Convention but as income property for some years with one entire floor under lease for several years. The major portion of the first floor has been used by the Sunday School Board of the Southern Baptist Convention for a Baptist Book Store.[75] The building provided space for the work of the Executive Committee in the area of administration and promotion, for all departments of the State Missions program, for Woman's Missionary Union, the Georgia

[72]*Minutes, Executive Committee, Georgia Baptist Convention,* August 17, 1943.

[73]*Encyclopedia of Southern Baptists,* Volume I [Nashville: Broadman Press, 1958], p. 556, monograph by James W. Merritt.

[74]*Encyclopedia of Southern Baptists,* volume III [Nashville: Broadman Press, 1971], p. 1732, monograph by James A. Lester.

[75]*Georgia Baptist Digest* 1970, volume 30, p. 13. [For some years, the Georgia Convention shared in ownership of the book store.

Baptist Foundation, *The Christian Index,* the Georgia Baptist Children's Home, and offices for the Atlanta Baptist Association.[76]

The Endowment Committee elected Arthur Jackson as its first executive secretary on August 26, 1943. Jackson, who had served numerous churches in Georgia as pastor, including the First Baptist Church in Savannah, began his service on September 15, 1943. On January 1, 1944, offices were opened in the Baptist building in Atlanta.[77] The first significant gift to the Foundation was made by Columbus philanthropist, Columbus Roberts. By October 1, 1943, he had given the Foundation $50,000, directing that the income be used for ministerial students at Norman College and Brewton-Parker College in equal amounts. Roberts was later to give $25,000 to Truett-McConnell College for the same purpose and income from his final gift of $200,000 to the Georgia Baptist Foundation was to be divided between Georgia Baptist schools and colleges on a basis of the amount of endowment each had at the close of each calendar year.[78]

As he did upon many occasions, Dowell enunciated to the Convention principles of Christian Education applicable not only to Mercer University. The confidence which Georgia Baptists had in Dowell was a factor in the continuing interest in and support of Christian Education by the Convention. To the Convention in 1942, Dowell said:

> . . . Mercer University defines the Christian college as the agency of Christian education that in its set-up, facilities, courses of study, personnel, objectives, and atmosphere is motivated by and committed to the principles and the practices of Christianity as revealed and exemplified in Christ.[79]

At the meeting of the Georgia Baptist Convention in Atlanta, in November of 1943, Georgia Baptists approved a budget for the next year, 1944, of $372,402.00 to be divided on a 60-40 per cent ratio between Georgia and Southwide

[76]*Loc. cit.*
[77]*Encyclopedia of Southern Baptists,* Vol. I, p. 557; Volume III, p. 1782.
[78]*Encyclopedia of Southern Baptists,* Vol. I, p. 557.
[79]*Minutes, Georgia Baptist Convention,* 1942, p. 109.

causes.[80] The Georgia Baptist Hospital was granted authority
to begin a campaign for $1,000,000 on a planned new hos-
pital addition, with the provision that the campaign be continued through 1945, with appeals to individuals and
churches.[81] At the time the hospital requested the authority
to begin its campaign, property of the hospital was valued at
$771,686.69.[82]

The enlargement program essentially was a continuation
of a five-year program authorized in 1938 for $300,000.00.[83]

In 1943, a constitutional amendment was offered, affecting
Section I of Article V, making the amended constitution at
that point to read:

> The officers of this Convention shall be a President,
> four Vice-Presidents, a Secretary, and a Treasurer, who
> shall be elected at each annual meeting by a majority
> ballot of the duly-elected Messengers present and voting,
> and who shall hold their offices until their successors are
> elected. Their duties shall be those usually discharged
> by such officers. No person may serve as President . . .
> more than three years.[84]

The significance of the amendment was the inclusion of the
phrase "by a majority ballot of the duly-elected Messengers
present and voting," rather than the reading of the earlier
article which said simply ". . . shall be elected at each annual
meeting. . ." [85]

Still concerned about the use of communications media,
particularly radio during the early 1940's, the Radio Commission in its report, read by S. F. Lowe, said that the Convention and the Radio Commission had co-operated with the
Southern Baptist Radio Committee in presenting The Baptist
Hour over WSB radio in Atlanta and WTOC in Savannah.
Additionally, in co-operation with the Hospital Day leaders,
the Commission had transcribed a 15-minute Hospital Day

[80]*Minutes, Georgia Baptist Convention,* 1943, p.p. 11, 12.
[81]*Ibid.,* p. 15.
[82]*Ibid.,* p. 26.
[83]*Ibid.,* p. 15.
[84]*Ibid.,* p. 19.
[85]*Minutes, Georgia Baptist Convention,* 1942, p. 6, Constitution adopted
1919.

program ". . . which was presented by a radio station in almost every city in Georgia that has a radio station." [86]

One of the more significant tasks done by this Radio Commission was in 1942, when it helped plan a statewide network to present a series of messages by Dr. George W. Truett. Efforts to repeat this in 1943 were hindered because of the war effort.[87] Recommendations of the Radio Commission for that year included: "That the Radio Committee, in counsel with Secretary W. H. Faust of the Department of Evangelism, and Executive Secretary J. W. Merritt, be and is hereby instructed to study the feasibility of a series of evangelistic broadcasts with state-wide coverage. . . ." This carried with it authorization to effect such broadcast upon approval of the Executive Committee and from funds provided by the Executive Committee. Additionally, the Radio Commission said that

> . . . in view of the evident increasing power of radio as a medium of influencing people, and in view of the phenomenal advances in radio with the practical use of television, frequency modulation, and increased lattitude in air channels following the war, we, the Georgia Baptist Convention, at its regular session, memoralize the Southern Baptist Convention to substantially enlarge its radio service.[88]

A study of the actions of the Radio Committee of the Georgia Baptist Convention indicated clearly the far-reaching influence of the work of Georgia Baptists in this area.

Although 1943 was a crucial year for the United States in the War, and Georgia Baptists gave whole-hearted support to the War, the evidence of the Hand of God in the affairs of the churches which comprised the Denomination was evident.

---

[86]*Minutes, Georgia Baptist Convention,* 1943, p. 27.
[87]*Loc. cit.*
[88]*Ibid.,* p.p. 27, 28.

CHAPTER 22

Ministering Through World War II

Because of the Convention's all-out support of the war effort, both by statements of the Social Service Commission, action of the churches, by encouraging ministers to enter the chaplaincy, and by Mercer's participation in military training programs, a special report of a committee named in 1942 to report in 1943 on the matter of separation of church and state, is of interest.

This committee cited Baptists' firm belief in and defense of religious liberty and separation of church and state. The committee report said that changing conditions

> . . . do not alter the principle that religious liberty is a priceless doctrine which we today must faithfully support. The tendency toward centralization of governmental authority and governmental responsibility in the social, economic, cultural, and even religious life of our people should not dim our vision of the principle that we are to render unto Caesar the things that are Caesar's and unto God the things that are God's.[1]

The report cited what it considered to be a dangerous trend in that agencies such as the National Youth Administration had work involvements on Baptist school and college campuses and that in the present emergency, the colleges and hospitals and other denominational institutions were serving the Government in training soldiers and nurses. The committee said:

> In this situation, we are called upon to serve the Government, and it would seem to your committee that we

[1]Minutes, Georgia Baptist Convention, 1943, p. 31.

can do nothing less than we are asked to do in such an emergency; but we do strongly recommend that our Baptist institutions discontinue such cooperation when the emergency is ended.[2]

The committee also "fraternally" recommended that ". . . agencies of this convention hold themselves free of any participation in funds raised by taxation, whether local, state, or national."[3]

Even as Georgia Baptists were supporting the war effort, they expressed concern about the principle of religious liberty and separation of church and state, and disentanglement with any type of governmental alliance after the war. The Social Commission cited plans for a ministry after the war and in what it termed world wide peace. The Commission declared to Georgia Baptists that

> . . . as Christians we face the greatest challenge in the history of our denomination in planning a post-war program for our returning men and women. They are coming back with their outlook on life changed from the boundaries of local communities to that of world-wide vision.[4]

The report of the 1943 Social Service Commission is of especial interest not only in content, but in its optimism, considering the fact that it was delivered in November of 1943, prepared therefore prior to delivery at a time when the military fortunes of the United States of America in World War II were, to say the least, questionable. The assumption, implied, in this report, was indeed an assumption of faith in victory on the part of the United States.[5] The Commission recommended further official cooperation with the Georgia Temperance League which had been organized just shortly before the Convention met, October 1, 1943.[6]

Again, the ten-month figure for total income for the Convention, January to October, 1943, was $1,000,187.26. The Co-operative Program was up to a total of $329,360.87, a

[2]*Loc. cit.*
[3]*Ibid.,* p. 32.
[4]*Ibid.,* p. 33.
[5]*Loc. cit.*
[6]*Ibid.,* p. 34.

sizeable increase over the January to October, 1942, figure of $252,538.87.[7] Total gifts received by the Executive Committee for distribution January 1, 1943 through December 31, 1943 were $1,436,443.49. This was an increase of more than $526,000 over the 1942 totals. The twelve-month total for that year in co-operative program giving was $411,762.08.[8]

The Hundred Thousand Club still was moving strong in Georgia in 1943, with a total given that year of $84,002.10[9] State missions exhibited a healthy gain also during 1943 with a total contributed for this ministry of $55,006.95. Of the 1943 total, $477,678.40 consisted of miscellaneous funds and educational endowment.[10]

Georgia's total giving to the Hundred Thousand Club by 1943 was over one-third of a million dollars; $344,330.02 since the movement began in 1933. The Executive Committee came to the 1943 Convention therefore, requesting that upon completion of payment in full of all Southwide debts which they anticipated would be by the end of that year, Georgia would be asked to retain the Hundred Thousand Club until all Georgia debts were paid.[11] The recommendation concerning the continuation of the Hundred Thousand Club indicated that if this club were continued, Georgia debts to which the funds would be applied would be: Hospital bond obligation, $133,000, Baptist building fund obligation [balance due on purchase price], $70,000; Mercer University balance due on loans from endowment funds, $43,929.68; and Norman Junior College $4,000.[12]

The Christian Index continued to increase circulation with approximately 25,000 by this year.[13]

When the Executive Committee asked the Convention for ratification of the purchase of the Peachtree building at 291 Peachtree Street in Atlanta, it reported that the property was

[7]*Ibid.*, p. 56.
[8]*Ibid.*, p. 143.
[9]*Loc. cit.*
[10]*Loc. cit.*
[11]*Ibid.*, p. 58.
[12]*Ibid.*, p. 59.
[13]*Loc. cit.*

paid for with $100,000 in cash and the balance of $90,000 to be paid over a period of years. However, unwilling to let the matter rest, the Executive Committee urged a special appeal for gifts to apply on the new building in connection with the State Missions day offering in October.[14]

Actually, between the time the building was purchased and the end of the calendar year, the Baptist building debt had been reduced from $90,000 to $73,730.26.[15]

The Executive Committee stated in its report to the Convention, that until the building was paid in full, net returns from rental space and the Executive Committee's part of net returns from Book Store operations would apply to reduce the building fund obligation.[16]

CHAPLAIN NAMED AT ALTO SANITARIUM

In an expanding ministry, W. A. Trotman was named during 1943 to serve as a representative of the State Missions program in the capacity of Baptist chaplain at the state sanitarium in Alto, Ga. [tuberculosis hospital].[17] In October of 1944, the next year, the Administration Committee granted Trotman a three-months leave of absence at full salary to complete his studies at Baptist Bible Institute in New Orleans.[18] This marked the second time that the Convention was to make provision for a salaried employee of the Executive Committee to be granted a leave of absence for additional study.

In 1930, the Administration Committee had granted Edwin S. Preston, B. Y. P. U. secretary, a two-month leave of absence to complete work on a master's degree at Mercer University.[19]

In 1943, the Convention approved a request from the

[14]*Ibid.,* p. 57.
[15]*Ibid.,* p. 140.
[16]*Ibid.,* p. 57.
[17]*Ibid.,* p. 58.
[18]*Minutes, The Administration Committee, Executive Committee, Georgia Baptist Convention,* October 23, 1944, p. 472.
[19]*Minutes, Administration Committee, Executive Committee, Georgia Baptist Convention,* June 5, 1930, p. 8.

Board of Trustees of the Georgia Baptist Orphans' Home that the name of the intsitution be changed to Georgia Baptist Children's Home.[20] The Home has been known by that name since that time, and as it expanded to include at a later time the property at Baxley and still later property at Pine Mountain, the three campuses were to be designated as branches of the Georgia Baptist Children's Home, Incorporated.

For many years Georgia Baptists had annually a *Georgia Baptist Digest,* containing essentials of the Denomination's program for the year, and basic information concerning the work of Georgia Baptist institutions and agencies. This Georgia Baptist Digest grew out of the first report of the Program Committee in 1940 which announced that a handbook would be ". . . issued as early as possible." [21] By 1943, this had expanded into a 32-page booklet.[22] It has been issued annually to the present.

A statistical comparison for the mid-war year of 1943 is of interest. In that year, there were 87 associations in fellowship with the Convention, 14 associations not members of the Convention, and contributing little if anything to Convention causes, and nine associations known as Missionary Baptist associations but not contributing to the cause of the Baptist program nor having representation in the 1943 Georgia Baptist Convention. Of the 1943 totals, including the 87 associations in fellowship, and associations contributing but not members, there were a total, together with several miscellaneous churches, of 2,491 churches with a membership of 552,360 reporting 16,451 baptisms. There were 254,556 enrolled in Sunday Schools, 2,942 B. Y. P. U.'s, 2,932 W. M. U.'s and the value of all church property was listed at $21,040,256. The nine associations not in fellowship and not contributing were comprised of 123 churches listing total membership of 13,481.[23]

[20]*Minutes, Georgia Baptist Convention,* 1943, p. 65.
[21]*Minutes, Georgia Baptist Convention,* 1940, p. 78.
[22]*Minutes, Georgia Baptist Convention,* 1943, p. 71.
[23]*Ibid.,* p. 251.

A brief survey of the educational institutions at this time also is of value. In the report of the Endowment Committee to the Convention, which included reports of the educational institutions, Mercer University reported that despite the war, attendance was relatively large; actually more than during the past fifteen years, with nearly 400 in liberal arts college, 105 in the V-5 organization, and 250 in the V-12 division. During the year, Mercer received another $100,000 gift from Columbus Roberts for endowment, bringing his gifts to nearly $250,000.[24] C. L. McGinty, reporting for Tift, indicated that the 97th session had begun with ". . . a gratifying increase in new students," and the college had raised an additional $100,000 in endowment, for a total as of July 1 of $320,235.13.[25]

Shorter reported the 1942-'43 session as being progressive, but no students were enumerated.[26] Paul Carroll, in his report on Norman College marked in 1943 the end of his tenth year as president of the college. Carroll said that the college was on sound financial footing, with current notes and accounts due and payable amounting to $19,511.08 with current obligations amounting to $525.11. Carroll said that the college would be out of debt completely upon repayment of a $4,000 obligation to the Endowment Fund made when the academic building was destroyed by fire in 1934.[27] Additionally, Carroll reported that a new academic building had been constructed and furnished, the gymnasium enlarged, dormitories renovated.[28] Strangely enough, it was to be slightly over a year after Carroll's report concerning the progress at Norman and the indebtedness occasioned by the destruction by fire of the academic building, that the new academic building was destroyed by fire also in December of 1944.[28a]

[24]*Ibid.,* p.p. 110, 111.
[25]*Ibid.,* p. 117.
[26]*Ibid.,* p. 121.
[27]*Ibid.,* p. 123.
[28]*Ibid.,* pp. 123, 124.
[28a]Author was eye witness.

Brewton-Parker had an increase in attendance rather than a decrease for the year which ended in May of 1943.[29]

The overall trend of growth in the colleges could well be considered unusual in a war-time economy with the drain of manpower, especially college-age young men, for military service.

At the meeting of the Convention in Atlanta, November 14 and 15, 1944, the Hospital Commission reported that following approval in 1943 for an effort to raise $1,000,000 for the hospital approximately one-third of the amount had been raised; $265,738.00 in cash, and pledges totaling $60,000.00.[30]

The Convention amended its constitution to make provision for two assistant secretaries rather than one, after two assistant secretaries had been elected at the opening session.[31] To provide for this Article V, Section I was amended to insert after the word "secretary," the words "two assistant secretaries" so that the sentence of Article V, Section I read:

> The officers of this Convention shall be a President, four Vice-Presidents, a Secretary, two Assistant Secretaries and a Treasurer, who shall be elected at each annual meeting by a majority ballot of the duly elected Messengers present and voting, and who shall hold their offices until their successors are elected.[32]

It was necessary to change also Section I of Article VI which dealt with membership on the Executive Committee to make the wording read to include "two assistant secretaries of the Convention nominated by the secretary". This sentence then read in the Constitution:

> An Executive Committee of this Convention shall be chosen by the Convention, and shall consist of the officers of the Convention, ex-officio, including the two assistant secretaries of the Convention nominated by the secretary . . .[33]

Again, a unique situation was evident in that the recording

[29]*Ibid.,* p. 127.
[30]*Minutes, Georgia Baptist Convention,* 1944, p. 17.
[31]*Ibid.,* p. 10.
[32]*Ibid.,* p. 33.
[33]*Loc. cit.*

secretary was empowered to nominate two assistants, both of whom would hold positions on the Executive Committee by virtue of their office as assistant recording secretary.

TRUETT-McCONNELL COLLEGE LAUNCHED

The beginnings of the present Truett-McConnell College at Cleveland, Ga. were in the 1944 Convention session when a proposal by Leslie S. Williams requested the Convention to give its approval to the establishment of a George W. Truett Junior College in Northeast Georgia. The matter was referred to the Executive Committee with a request that the committee bring a recommendation to the Convention in 1945.[34]

In the report of the Social Service Commission, presented again by Searcy Garrison, and which dealt with Baptists ". . . and the coming peace, . . ." among other things, including the liquor traffic, race relations, and retirement income, there was this significant statement:

> We suggest that the Convention give serious thought to the matter of publicizing our denomination. We find many other groups using the daily press throughout our state to keep before the public their beliefs and practices. We believe that Baptists are losing an opportunity to render the same type of service. We believe the Convention would be wise in asking its executive committee to give this further thought, designating a responsible person to prepare such publicity, and provide funds to meet the necessary cost.[35]

The editor of *The Index*, John Jeter Hurt, was to provide some assistance in this area. Shortly after Garrison became Executive Secretary Jan. 1, 1955, part-time assistance was employed in this area. Twenty-six months later, March 1, 1957, the office of the Executive Secretary was expanded for a major emphasis in this area, with one person, James A. Lester, devoting full time to the area of stewardship and general promotion and public relations.

B. D. Ragsdale died on July 19, 1944 at the age of 83. He has served as recording secretary of the Georgia Baptist Con-

[34]*Ibid.*, p. 34.
[35]*Ibid.*, p. 37.

vention for the longest period of any man. Elected secretary in 1896, Ragsdale served 48 years, [49 Conventions because of two sessions in 1902], until the time of his death. In addition to his service as recording secretary of the Convention, Ragsdale had served several churches in Georgia as pastor, had occupied the chair of English Bible at Mercer and for about 14 years of his more than 23 years at Mercer served also as treasurer and business manager of the University. After his retirement at Mercer, he began compilation of his Story of Georgia Baptists, later writing the memoirs of P. D. Pollock.[36]

An important development during 1944 was inauguration of a program of associational field work and city missions work. In reporting to the Convention, the Executive Committee said: "Acting under instructions from the 1943 Convention the Executive Committee has worked out plans for mission work in the associations."[37] A committee on associational work was named early in 1944 and under authority of the Executive Committee

> . . . presented for the consideration of the associations a plan for grouping 10 or 12 associations into 'fields of work or unit areas of operation,' with every association in the state included in one of these groups.
> When it developed that this plan did not give promise of meeting the needs of the associations for an intensive program of development among the churches, the Committee on Associational Work recommended and the Executive Committee approved a plan to cooperate with individual associations or small groups of two or more associations in the employment of missionaries.[38]

Out of this came the present program of associational missions work on a co-operative basis between the local associations and the Georgia Baptist Convention through its program of State Missions.

A significant gain continued evident in contributions by Georgia Baptists for their work. From January through Oc-

[36]*Ibid.,* p. 59; Spright Dowell, *A History of Mercer University,* 1833-1953 [Atlanta: Foote and Davies, Inc., 1958], p. 345; *Encyclopedia of Southern Baptists,* Vol. II, [Nashville: Broadman Press, 1958], p. 1131.

[37]*Minutes, Georgia Baptist Convention,* 1944, p. 65.

[38]*Loc. cit.*

tober of 1944, a total amount of $416,094.69, an increase of
$86,733.82, was given through the Co-operative Program.
Total increases from January to October 1944 amounted to
$298,504.60.[39]

Although the Executive Committe had set up a plan to
pay the remainder of the amount due on the purchase of the
Baptist building over a period of years, at the March 17, 1944,
meeting the Committee said that authorization had been
given to use funds on hand to retire the mortgage on the
building, replacing the funds and at the same time saving
interest.[40] In projecting a budget for 1945, the Convention
set a 60-40 ratio until all funds in the budget were met and
then set a budget goal of $431,300 with a total goal of
$500,000.[41]

Sentiment had developed among Georgia Baptists against
the debenture allocation of $633,492.73 to Mercer University.
Therefore, in an effort to improve relations between Mercer
and the Convention the Board of Trustees of Mercer met at
First Baptist Church in Atlanta on Novmber 14, 1944. At
this special meeting, Dowell cited the history of the allocation in 1928 to save the school,

> . . . the dissatisfaction that resulted, and the need for
> removing the irritation. After discussion, the motion
> was made and carried that the trustees of Mercer Uni-
> versity give back to the Convention the Mercer deben-
> ture note for $633,492.73, and that the decision be re-
> ported to the Convention next day.[42]

On behalf of Mercer University, the next day Dowell surrendered the debenture note with explanation to the Convention and at the afternoon session, the note was burned.[43]

Georgia Baptists were disappointed in their plans to be
host to the 1945 Centennial session of the Southern Baptist
Convention because of ". . . emergencies incident to World
War II." [44]

[39]*Ibid.*, p. 63.
[40]*Ibid.*, p. 67.
[41]*Ibid.*, p.p. 69, 70.
[42]*Dowell*, p.p. 344, 345.
[43]*Loc. cit.; Minutes, Georgia Baptist Convention*, 1944, p. 32.
[44]*Minutes, Georgia Baptist Convention*, 1945, p. 34.

The Allied forces were victorious in Europe in May of 1945, in August of the same year the Imperial Japanese forces surrendered. For the United States as a nation, for Georgia as a state, and for Georgia Baptists as a denominational body, the victories in war meant a vast transition from a war time to a peace time economy. Plans which had been suggested in previous reports of the Social Service Commission now had an opportunity to fulfillment.

UNIQUE PROPOSAL FOR HOSPITAL

Less than month after the end of World War II there was presented to the Executive Committee of the Georgia Baptist Convention a unique proposal from its Hospital Commission with regard to a new building on hospital property to be known as the Georgia Baptist Professional Building. Louie D. Newton, pastor of Druid Hills Baptist Church in Atlanta, Dick H. Hall, Jr., pastor, First Baptist Church in Decatur, Wiley L. Moore, Atlanta businessman, W. D. Barker, superintendent of the hospital, and James W. Merritt, executive secretary-treasurer of the executive committee had banded together to present a proposal to incorporate themselves as a non-profit corporation to be known as the Georgia Baptist Professional Building, Incorporated.

Purpose of the proposed corporate structure was, in the words of the formal recommendation:

> 1. To erect a building at a cost of approximately $700,000 on following described property, to wit: . . . [corner of Forest Avenue and Boulevard];
> 2. To pay the cost of erecting and constructing said building out of: [a] Revenue from the operation of the co-operation of such kind or kinds of business in said building as will be helpful and beneficial to the operation of the Georgia Baptist Hospital or the patrons thereof in the judgment of the directors of the corporation; [b] Revenue from the rental of space in the building to be erected; [c] Contributions, donations and such other funds as may become available to the corporation;
> 3. To give and convey unto the 'Executive Committee of the Baptist Convention of the state of Georgia' free of all debts, liens, encumbrances, all the assets of the

corporation, including, but not by way of limitation, the buildings and improvements placed on the land herein before described: This conveyance to be made by proper deed or instrument forthwith after the cost of said building and improvements, together with any indebtedness owing by the corporation have been paid, and whereas it shall be necessary for the Executive Committee of the Baptist Convention of the state of Georgia to convey the land herein before described unto the Georgia Baptist Professional Building, Inc., in order that the last mentioned corporation can borrow the money thereon to erect said building, and,

Whereas it has been discussed and agreed that the deed of conveyance, if and when executed, shall contain a provision that the title to said land, together with all improvements placed thereon, shall automatically revert to and invest in the 'Executive Committee of the Baptist Convention of the State of Georgia,' upon the cost of said building being paid and the corporation becoming free of debt in its assets, clear of liens and the like, and whereas, it is the considered judgment of this committee that the transaction herein outlined should be submitted to the Baptist Convention of the state of Georgia for their consideration; and, that this committee should recommend its approval to the Convention, now,

Therefore, be it Resolved, That the Executive Committee of the Baptist Convention of the State of Georgia convey unto the Georgia Baptist Professional Building, Inc., when formed, the land herein before described by proper deed, with provision therein contained that the title thereto, and together with all improvements placed thereon, shall automatically revert to invest in the grantor upon the cost of the buildings and improvements being paid and the grantee becoming free of debt and its assets clear of all liens, and encumbrances, and the like; and, that the proper officers of the 'Executive Committee of the Baptist Convention of the State of Georgia' be and they are hereby authorized and directed to execute such a deed of conveyance, if and when the transaction herein outlined and recommended for approval, is approved by the Baptist Convention in its regular, annual meeting in November, 1945.[45]

Although never implemented in the form suggested, the matter was presented from the Executive Committee to the Georgia Baptist Convention meeting in Macon in November,

[45]*Minutes, Executive Committee, Georgia Baptist Convention*, September 11, 1945, p.p. 1, 2.

1945 and the Georgia Baptist Convention approved the recommendation of its Executive Committee.[46]

In 1944, the Convention had referred to the Executive Committee a proposal concerning the establishment of a junior college. The Executive Committee recommended in 1945:

> That the Georgia Baptist Convention commit itself to establishing as early as possible such junior college.
> Second: That the Georgia Baptist Convention include in its 1946 budget an appropriation of $25,000.00 for this school.
> Third: That a committee be appointed to recommend to the Executive Committee the best location and plans for securing additional financial support for such school; that the Executive Committee shall only pay the $25,000 appropriated to some group in north Georgia which has established the proper relation with the Georgia Baptist Convention on the part of this school in relation to the Georgia Baptist Convention's educational objectives; . . .[47]

The Executive Committee was left with the responsibility for determining when and to whom the $25,000 appropriation would be paid [48] and out of this proposal was to come the next year selection of a site for the college at Cleveland.

Following the 1945 session giving approval to the concept of a college in the mountain areas of North Georgia, a committee was appointed to make recommendations concerning the location and plans for financing the institution to the executive committee. At the March, 1946 meeting, the Executive Committee approved a report which recommended that Cleveland, Georgia would be the location,[49] and the name of the school would be Truett-McConnell Junior College.[50]

> The Executive Committee appointed the members of the Convention's committee to serve as interim trustees with authority to appoint others to serve with them, and

[46]*Minutes, Georgia Baptist Convention*, 1945, p.p. 15-17.

[47]*Ibid.*, p. 24.

[48]*Loc. cit.*

[49]*Minutes, Executive Committee, Georgia Baptist Convention*, March 12, 1946.

[50]*Minutes, Georgia Baptist Convention*, 1946, p. 67.

authorized this group to secure a charter and also authorized the raising of at least $300,000.00 for buildings and
equipment and $500,000.00 or the equivalent thereof for
endowment for the new institution.[51]

Throughout the lifetime of the Georgia Baptist Convention it had obtained by gift or purchase institutions of several
types. The junior colleges, Shorter, Tift, the Children's
Home, and the hospital, had all been in existence and functioning at the time the Convention assumed control and
ownership.

Therefore, the establishment of Truett-McConnell Junior
College at Cleveland, in 1946 marked the first time that the
Georgia Baptist Convention had established a completely
new institution, by Convention authority, since the establishment of Mercer Institute in 1833. The establishment of Baptist Village in Waycross some years later was to mark the
third completely new facility to be established by the Convention. To the present time, although other acquisitions
have been made, they were acquisitions of property, including the Georgia Baptist Assembly, which had been used for
similar purposes under different sponsoring groups, except
Peachtree-on-Peachtree Inn, Atlanta, used as a hotel. It was
therefore, an historic occasion for Georgia Baptists, although
not noted as such, when they established this completely new
institution in the mountains of north Georgia.

The Convention committee named in 1945 to select the
site and to make recommendations to the executive commit-
tee, which committee became the interim trustees, consisted
of Frederick S. Porter, E. C. Sheridan, Searcy S. Garrison,
Harvey R. Mitchell, Walter L. Moore, L. C. Cutts, George F.
Brown, W. A. Duncan, Henry J. Stokes, Jr., and Bunyan
Stephens.[52] To this interim group were added the following
until trustees could be named by the Convention: Oscar
Lilly, Claude C. Boynton, Cliff Kimsey, Clarence Barrett,
W. A. Taliaferro, James Tankersley, Bob Edge, J. C. Puett,
Lee Routh, and W. A. Bearden.[53]

[51]*Loc. cit.*
[52]*Loc. cit.*
[53]*Loc. cit.*

CLEVELAND CHOSEN AS SITE

Cleveland had been recommended by the Convention Committee at the location for the junior college for seven primary reasons. 1. The offer of a site of 442 acres, valued at the time at $88,400, just east of Cleveland. 2. A cash gift of $90,000. 3. Living endowments of $100,000. 4. Concrete building blocks and lumber at cost. 5. The city of Cleveland had agreed to provide for five years water with water main, lights and sewage installed to the construction property and grading of the property for $1.00 and other considerations. 6. Residents from four counties adjacent to White County had pledged $95,000, and 7. Identified only as a prominent citizen, this citizen pledged ". . . to pay to the school a tithe of his income from now on." [54]

With the location decided, and background materials out of the way, on July 23, 1946 there was held in Cleveland a meeting at which time the movement to build a college there was announced.

L. Clinton Cutts who had served at McCaysville Church in Copperhill, Tenn. was named president of the college and by the time of the Convention meeting in November had assumed his duties. Therefore, the Executive Committee authorized payment of the $25,000 appropriation for the 1946 budget to the treasurer of the school.[55]

Another significant event in Georgia Baptist life in 1945 was approval upon the part of the Convention for acceptance of the offer of the Southern Industrial Orphans' Home property near Baxley, to be transferred to the trustees of the Children's Home at Hapeville provided the lawyer for the Children's Home and lawyers for the Executive Committee found no flaw in title ". . . to the property, or restrictions, or contracts or reversions in deed or contract that would preclude the Convention's acceptance of the property, . . ." After postponing discussion of the offer at one session of the Convention, the Convention finally approved this recommenda-

[54]*Ibid.*, p.p. 67, 68.
[55]*Ibid.*, p. 68.

tion for acquisition of the property.[56] The recommendation was framed as late as the pre-Convention meeting of the Executive Committee in 1945.[57]

Following the Convention action in 1945, the Executive Committee, at a called meeting on January 25, 1946, made the final decision to accept the Industrial Home property at Baxley in the belief that the title was clear and that it was the intent of the Convention in 1945 that the property be accepted.[58]

The Administration Committee, in its meeting apparently on the same date as the Executive Committee meeting, noted the agreement between the Executive Committee and the Southern Industrial Home, with the understanding that the Executive Committee, upon receiving the deed to the property, would lease the property to the Home as it was being operated for a period of one year, at an annual rental of $1.00 to give time to insure that the title was clear for the property.[59]

Although the minutes show in March 1946 that the property was to be leased back for one year at fee of $1.00, title to the property was accepted by the Administration Committe of the Executive Committee on September 3, 1946. At this time, trustees of the Georgia Baptist Children's Home took over active management. The Executive Committee, meeting on September 10, 1946, authorized transfer of the title to the property to the trustees of the Georgia Baptist Children's Home. This had been done by the November meeting of the Convention, and the Home had begun operations as a branch of the Georgia Baptist Children's Home.[60]

At the time the Convention acquired the property at Bax-

[56]*Minutes, Georgia Baptist Convention,* 1945, p.p. 25, 38.

[57]*Minutes, Executive Committee, Georgia Baptist Convention,* Nov. 12, 1945, p. 10.

[58]*Executive Committee, Georgia Baptist Convention,* January 25, 1946; Minute Book 3, p. 21.

[59]*Minutes, Administration Committee, Executive Committee, Georgia Baptist Convention,* Jan. 25, 1946, p. 23.

[60]*Minutes, Georgia Baptist Convention,* 1946, p. 68.

ley it was carried in the auditor's report for the Children's Home as being valued at $161,686.64.[61]

Following approval by the Convention of the proposal for constructing a Baptist Professional Building, the Executive Committee on December 4, 1945, gave authority to officers of the Executive Committee to execute the deed to the land on which the professional building was to be erected to the corporation.[62] There is no minute evidence, that the transfer of the property took place. A professional building was constructed upon the site at a later time, under a different plan.

With the report made by Secretary Merritt that Georgia Bapists debts would be paid in all likelihood by the end of the year [and they were],[63] this marked the first time in many years that the Convention had been out of debt. For the ten-month reportable period January to October 1945, receipts for the Cooperative Program had climbed to $492,747.06 with two months of the fiscal year to go. However, for this period this was an increase of $76,652.37. Total gifts for that ten-month period in 1945 climbed nearly half a million dollars; an increase of $459,701.47 over the previous ten-month period for a total in contributions of $1,758,393.42.[64]

W. H. Faust, who had served as secretary of the Department of Evangelism since its restructuring, died July 15, 1945, after eight and one-half years in office.[65] The Executive Committee at its meeting on September 11, 1945, named H. C. Whitener as the new secretary of evangelism.[66] With the adoption of the budget for 1946 in 1945, the ratio for division between Georgia and Southwide causes had become 55-45, and a total Co-operative Program budget was set at $655,455.00.[67]

The years 1939 through 1945 were momentous for Georgia

[61]*Ibid.*, p. 111.
[62]*Minutes, Executive Committee, Georgia Baptist Convention*, Dec. 4, 1945, p. 13.
[63]*Minutes, Georgia Baptist Convention*, 1945, p. 72.
[64]*Ibid.*, p. 71.
[65]*Ibid.*, p. 75.
[66]*Loc. cit.*

Baptists. They had paid their debts. They had solidified their interests. They had moved ahead into the establishment of two new works for the year 1946; Truett-McConnell College and a branch of the Children's Home in Baxley.

The Convention was becoming stronger internally. Its administrative offices functioned well during the period which this chapter comprehends. The increased income from a war-time economy, some of it at least, found its way into Georgia Baptists' channels of stewardship in the local churches and in some direct gifts to agencies and institutions of the Georgia Baptist Convention.

As a result, therefore, by the end of 1945 and into 1946 Georgia Baptists had established a pattern of operation, a program of promotion, and a means of securing enlistment through conferences and other promotional emphases which were to pave the way for continued growth during the next three decades.

Ibid., p. 76.

CHAPTER 23

Era of Expansion

Baptist layman and philanthropist Columbus Roberts was elected president of the Georgia Baptist Convention at the meeting in Savannah in November of 1946. Roberts was elected by a unanimous standing vote of the Convention, marking the first time a layman had been chosen as president since W. J. Northen was elected in 1908.[1]

At the same time the Georgia Baptist Convention was meeting in Savannah, the Negro Baptist convention was in session in that city also. Fred Smith made a motion that a committee be named to confer with leaders of the Negro convention anticipating a joint session of the two conventions. This was done, with the joint session arranged for 5:00 p.m. on Tuesday afternoon in the City Auditorium in Savannah. Approximately 500 messengers from the Georgia Baptist Convention attended the joint session which was termed one wholesome and helpful for both groups.[2]

One of the recommendations from the Executive Committee to the Convention, approved by the Convention, was that authorization be given the Executive Committee to confer with the secretaries of the various departments

> . . . on the advisability and feasibility of working out plans for an assembly that will meet the needs of our many gatherings, and a practical plan for achieving such an assembly, and bring report to the 1947 session.[3]

[1]*Minutes, Georgia Baptist Convention*, 1946, p. 10.
[2]*Ibid.*, p. 11.
[3]*Ibid.*, p. 16.

Agitation for a Georgia Baptist assembly was periodic, but continuing. After the Georgia Baptist assembly property at Blue Ridge was deeded back to that city, [though in reality it was never really owned by the Convention], assemblies by the several State Missions departments were held on campuses of Georgia Baptist educational institutions throughout the state. During this time, for example, the Training Union assembly was being held on the campus of Mercer University in Macon. Regional meetings were being held at Brewton-Parker, Norman, Truett-McConnell, and the Sunday School Department and missionary conferences were being held on the campus of Tift College at Forsyth. Additionally, the Sunday School Department and other groups were making some use at that time of the Lake Louise Bible Conference grounds, at Toccoa, Ga., then owned by industrialist R. G. LeTourneau.

Earlier studies had evoked a favorable response to the idea for an assembly, but as was to be the case with the recommendation to be returned to the Convention, in 1947, no firm proposals were developed which would permit the establishment of such an assembly.

W. D. Barker had been superintendent of the hospital from 1931 until his death Jan. 14, 1946.[4] Merritt was named acting superintendent of the hospital during Baker's illness, and after his death until a new superintendent could be named.[5] Lee C. Gammill served several weeks as administrator, resigned, and Merritt continued to manage the hospital until Edwin B. Peel became administrator May 15, 1946.[6] Barker was paid tribute as having performed outstanding work during the time he was superintendent of the hospital.[7] By the end of 1946, net worth of the hospital was reported at $902,281.31.[8] Peel has served from 1946 to the present. He came from Southern Baptist Hospital, New Orleans.[9]

[4]*Ibid.*, p. 70.
[5]*Ibid.*, p.p. 70, 71.
[6]*Loc. cit.*
[7]*Ibid.*, p. 114.
[8]*Ibid.*, p. 118.
[9]*Ibid.*, p. 70.

When the Executive Committee presented its budget proposals to the Convention, the ratio was at 45 per cent for Southern Convention causes and 55 per cent for Georgia Baptist Convention causes for a total budget of $829,318.00 for 1947.[10]

The report of the Georgia Baptist Radio Commission for 1946 was far-reaching in its potential. The report was adopted by the Convention with the recommendations being referred to the executive committee for study. The Commission said that a new door was opening for religious broadcasting in the form of FM radio. The report then defined FM [frequency modulation broadcasting] and recommended that the Convention co-operate with local Christian men and groups and institutions in the state in ". . . promoting the establishment and operation of a state network of independent FM radio stations on a non-profit commercial basis, looking to complete and satisfactory state radio coverage." [11] The Commission said that Georgia Baptists had discovered to their dismay in 1944 their tardiness in entering the field of broadcasting on a network basis ". . . when the Radio Commission tried to build a state-wide hook-up and failed in doing so." [12]

The recommendation of The Commission, referred to the Executive Committee, called for a Committee of Five to be selected which committee in turn would select three men from each community where such a station might be located. Then the Executive Committee was requested to study the advisability of Baptists owning and operating an FM station in Atlanta, and if the Executive Committee deemed such an undertaking appropriate, that they be authorized to appropriate $25,000 for 1947

> . . . on condition that the Radio Commission, S. B. C. and the Baptists of Atlanta each invest a like amount in such station, provided that action by the Executive Committee be taken at the December meeting of 1946 in order that, if the vote is favorable, there will be time for application to be made to the Federal Communica-

[10]*Ibid.*, p. 14.
[11]*Ibid.*, p.p. 20, 21.
[12]*Ibid.*, p. 20.

tions Commission before all FM channels for Atlanta are closed.[18]

The concept embraced in the ideas of this Commission was that commercial profits from the independent stations in a state network could be applied to a program of audience building and that a minimum of 40 per cent of all time on such independent stations would be for public service and that a large share of sustaining time on these stations would be devoted to religious broadcasts.[14]

POST WAR COLLEGE BOOM

Georgia Baptist colleges were experiencing the beginning of the post-war boom. Student enrollment in the Convention's five schools had increased from 1,339 in 1942 to 2,544 at the beginning of the fall of 1946, an increase of 90 per cent.[15] In a year's time, Truett-McConnell College, had received $400,135.00 in property, cash, notes and pledges.[16] Most of this was in property and pledges inasmuch as the college treasurer's report as of Dec. 1, 1946 indicated a cash balance in two banks as $36,999.33.[17]

The Georgia Baptist Hospital during 1946 was promoting its campaign to secure the remaining $100,000 on its original building fund goal of $1,000,000. However, Hospital officials reported to the Convention that due to increased costs in construction and equipment, a minimum of now $2,000,000 would be required to build and complete the facility; double the original cost.[18] Therefore, plans had been approved by the Atlanta Chamber of Commerce for a city-wide campaign on behalf of the hospital seeking to raise during the first three months of 1947 $1,000,000 within the city of Atlanta. Moreover, the Executive Committee had approved a request from the hospital commission that the statewide

[13]*Ibid.*, p. 21.
[14]*Loc. cit.*
[15]*Ibid.*, p. 23.
[16]*Ibid.*, p.p. 23, 24.
[17]*Ibid.*, p. 151.
[18]*Ibid.*, p. 70.

building fund campaign be extended through March of 1947.[19]

PARTICIPATION IN RELIEF PROGRAMS

Georgia Baptists, following the Southern Baptist Convention session in Miami in May, 1946, participated generously in the World Emergency Relief and Rehabilitation program authorized by the Southern Baptist Convention. The months of July, August, and September were designated for the offering, the states were assigned minimum goals, with Georgia being assigned a goal of $282,800. The Georgia committee increased this amount to $300,000 and with apparent wholehearted cooperation throughout the state the relief gifts from Georgia totaled $308,489.60. The total amount reported for the Southern Convention was $3,636,157.[20]

After it became apparent that Georgia Baptists were going to require $2,000,000 to complete the proposed Hospital expansion program, James P. Wesberry presented a resolution to the Convention which was amended and adopted, recommending that in the light of the fact that the problem of alcoholism was a growing one, and that the hospital was planning to build, the Convention recommended "that special consideration be given by the Georgia Baptist Hospital Commission to the establishment of a clinic for alcoholics." [21]

With approval having been given to the Executive Committee for inauguration of a Brotherhood Department and the employment of a full-time Brotherhood secretary, the Brotherhood report to the Convention in 1946 reflected the growing interest in work with laymen. The report challenged the Convention to work with the Southern Baptist Convention in having a million tithers in 1947 and a million men back in the churches for that same year.[22] The Department

[19]*Loc. cit.*
[20]*Ibid.*, p. 71.
[21]*Ibid.*, p.p. 29, 30.
[22]*Ibid.*, p.p. 30, 31.

was inaugurated in July, 1947.[23]

Alert to any area of church-state involvement, the Social Service Commission said:

> We respectfully remind the municipal and county officials of Georgia of the unconstitutionality of granting materials or labor to churches and religious institutions. The granting of materials and labor in the building of churches in the state have been an occasion of considerable abuse. We deplore this custom and call upon city and county officials to desist from this illegal and ultimately harmful practice.[24]

This resolution was occasioned by the fact that for many years, many city and county governments had provided convict labor for cleaning church cemeteries, and making some road and parking lot repairs on property owned by churches, including Baptist churches.

For the first full year after the end of World War II Georgia Baptists gave a total of $2,170,319.13 for all causes. The Cooperative Program gifts were $695,122.75, an increase of $73,780.52 over the 1945 totals of $621,342.23. Foreign missions during 1946 showed a tremendous gain in gifts by Georgia Baptists. In 1945 foreign missions received $112,217.46 in designated giving and in 1946 the total had jumped to $456,576.08. Of all contributions for the twelve month period, $535,895.40 had been contributed by Baptist Woman's Missionary Union in Georgia.[25]

MISSION WORK WELL ESTABLISHED

The program of associational and city mission work was on a sound basis by 1946. Merritt, in his report to the Convention said that the field workers were responsible for the promotion of a well rounded program of development. The work of the field men was ". . . under the joint direction of a Committee of Five appointed by the executive committee and by committees appointed by the associations served

[23]*Minutes, Georgia Baptist Convention*, 1947, p. 67.
[24]*Ibid.*, p. 35.
[25]*Ibid.*, p. 163.

by the workers." [26] City mission programs were in operation in Atlanta, Columbus, Macon and Savannah.[27]

The Convention at the 1945 session had authorized the Widows Supplemental Annuity Plan to be administered by the Relief and Annuity Board. The enrollment for this supplemental plan had reached 269 pastors by the time Merritt's report was prepared, only nine short of the number required to inaugurate the plan. This plan was later completed and inaugurated.[28]

While the plan for the Convention to enter the field of frequency modulation broadcasting looked good apparently to a number of people in Georgia, the Executive Committee in 1947 reported it felt it would be unwise to enter this field by owning and operating a station because of probable initial cost and heavy expense.[29] The Executive Committee recommended that the proposal for establishment of an assembly be referred back to the committee for further study with a report back to the 1948 session of the Georgia Baptist Convention.[30]

O. P. Gilbert, editor of *The Christian Index* since January 15, 1930,[31] died April 6, 1947 while conducting a revival in Aiken, S. C. Gilbert was in his 18th year as editor of *The Index*.[32] From the time of his death in April, until the election of John Jeter Hurt, Jr., in June of 1947, and the assumption by Hurt of his duties on July 6, 1947, Louie D. Newton served as acting editor and Secretary Merritt assisted in the business management of the paper.[33] Hurt, when he came to the editorship of *The Christian Index*, was at the time living in Atlanta pending reassignment by the Associated Press. He had served previously as that agency's bureau chief in Mem-

[26]*Ibid.*, p. 90.
[27]*Ibid.*, p. 91.
[28]*Ibid.*, p.p. 119, 120.
[29]*Ibid.*, p. 16.
[30]*Loc. cit.*
[31]James Adams Lester, "A History of *The Christian Index*, 1822-1954," [Unpublished Master's Thesis, 1955], p. 111.
[32]*Ibid.*, p. 118.
[33]*Loc. cit.*

phis, Tenn.[34] *The Index* under Gilbert had survived declines in circulation to a low in 1940 of 11,500, and he had led in efforts to increase circulation to approximately 37,000 at the time of his death.[35] Gilbert had made many personal sacrifices to promote and sustain *The Christian Index*. In his 1945 report to the Georgia Baptist Convention, one of his last, he said:

> Moreover, we should strive to produce a better paper
> . . . better edited and more modern in content and struc-
> ture. This cannot be fully achieved until a larger
> revenue is received with sufficient income to purchase
> manuscript of a higher order and cuts of photographs.
> The *Index* can be improved.[36]

During the same year Bernard D. King, at the time a public school official in Dalton, Ga., and the son of Spencer B. King, Sr., was elected as the Convention's first Brotherhood secretary. King assumed his office on July 1, 1947.[37]

While the Georgia Baptist Convention was slow in making any plans for an assembly, Woman's Missionary Union had been busy at the task of securing a site and building a camp. A 39-acre site, gift of the citizens of Rabun county and the city of Clayton, was developed into Camp Pinnacle.[38] In June of 1947 Camp Pinnacle was dedicated with the dining hall, guest house and kitchen completed and an administration building under construction.[39] The camp was to continue to be developed, with a chapel dedicated in 1952.[40]

As plans were being considered by the Southern Baptist Convention for what would later become Southeastern Baptist Theological Seminary, the Convention in 1947 adopted a motion which in effect asked the Southern Convention's Seminary Committee to consider Atlanta as a site if a seminary were to be established, and asked the Seminary Com-

[34]*Loc. cit.*
[35]*Ibid.*, p. 132.
[36]*Ibid.*, p. 117.
[37]*Minutes, Georgia Baptist Convention*, 1947, p. 67.
[38]Mrs. Frank Burney, *Wrought of God—A History with Memories of the Baptist Woman's Missionary Union of Georgia, 1884-1959*, p. 43.
[39]*Ibid.*, p. 45.
[40]*Loc. cit.*

mittee to give terms upon which a seminary could be located in Atlanta.[41]

With the expanded facilities at Baxley, the Children's Home "dealt with" 537 children during 1947. They received 99 children, 67 were sent out. There were 367 children at the Hapeville branch and 113 at the Baxley branch. By 1947 total assets of the Home had risen to $1,910,000.00.[42]

The Hospital Commission reported to the Convention meeting in November in 1947 that: "Funds accumulated for the new building program now amounts to $1,007,041.42. Plans for a campaign in Greater Atlanta for an additional fund of $2,500,000.00 are progressing satisfactorily." [43]

Co-operative Program giving continued to increase and designated gifts and miscellaneous giving declined. For the first ten months of 1947, the Co-operative Program showed a gain of $105,177.70 for a total of $654,964.84. Designated gifts declined during that same period by $298,097.11.[44] The decline in total giving for the 10-month period was $281,543.37 over 1946.[45] For the year, total receipts were $1,998,298.23. In the two-month period, designated gifts jumped, for a year's total of $1,171,811.05, with $826,487.18 for the Co-operative Program.[46]

One new feature of the 1946 budget was that which included special allocations in the amount of $140,000. Of this amount, $100,000 was designated as endowment for the schools and colleges.[47] With the entire amount paid, the budget for 1948, adopted in 1947, included $160,000.00 in special allocations, with $120,000.00 for endowment.[48]

Work in the State Missions program was progressing. When Vacation Bible Schools were recorded beginning in 1934 there were 29 such schools. By 1947, there were 1,031

[41]*Minutes, Georgia Baptist Convention,* 1947, p. 20.
[42]*Ibid.,* p. 32.
[43]*Ibid.,* p. 33.
[44]*Ibid.,* p. 66.
[45]*Loc. cit.*
[46]*Ibid.,* p. 160.
[47]*Ibid.,* p. 69.
[48]*Loc. cit.*

schools.[49] Slightly more than 60,000 members of Woman's Missionary Union were reported in Georgia at the end of 1946 with total gifts of $535,895.[50]

PERMANENT BAPTIST HISTORY COMMITTEE

The Convention in 1947 set up a permanent Committee on Baptist History,[51] and named J. C. Wilkinson as chairman. This Committee was in succession to several efforts upon the part of Georgia Baptists to establish committees for the preservation of Baptist history under one name or another. The first such organization, set up in 1878, was called the Georgia Baptist Historical Society, and functioned until 1888. The Society was re-organized in 1899, and a Committee on Georgia Baptist History was appointed in 1910. The permanent committee created in 1947 continues to the present.[52] From the inauguration of this Committee it has been active in securing and preserving materials related to Georgia Baptist history, and in the placing of historic markers at strategic points of Baptist interest across the state of Georgia.

For the first time since the Depression, when the Executive Committee presented its 1949 budget for approval to the Convention meeting in Atlanta in 1948, the Co-operative Program allocation had returned to a 50-50 per cent figure for the Georgia and Southern Conventions after certain agreed upon expenses had been deducted.[53] The Convention approved also a $5,000 appropriation for restoration of the old Mercer chapel building at Penfield, then known as the Penfield Baptist Church.[54]

In 1948, two other significant actions were taken by the Convention. One was approval being given to the trustees of Bessie Tift College for a campaign to raise $1,000,000.[55] A

[49]Ibid., p. 90.
[50]Ibid., p. 97.
[51]Ibid., p. 73.
[52]Encyclopedia of Southern Baptists, Volume I, [Nashville: Broadman Press, 1958], p. 557.
[53]Minutes, Georgia Baptist Convention, 1948, p. 14.
[54]Loc. cit.
[55]Ibid., p. 17.

second significant action was granting permission to the Hospital to borrow against seventy-five per cent of what it considered to be valid pledges toward the building campaign.[56] The hospital was given permission to make a special appeal to the churches in 1949 also.[57]

The matter of a Georgia Baptist Assembly, which had been re-committed to the Executive Committee for study, brought from this Committee in 1948 a recommendation that the Convention look with favor upon locating the proposed Georgia Baptist assembly on the campus of Bessie Tift College at Forsyth when Tift could provide facilities and accommodations. The Executive Committee would determine what would be considered ". . . adequate facilities and accommodations." [58]

One action which was to be of lasting significance for ministers who were ordained in Georgia after this time, was adoption of a recommendation by the Convention that each man ordained by a church in Georgia to the Gospel Ministry be given a copy of the American Standard Version of the Bible, a copy of a book on Baptist doctrine and upon his ordination there would be printed a brief factual story together with a small picture in *The Christian Index*. Additionally, each newly-ordained minister was to be given a special invitation to attend the first session of the Convention following his ordination and would be presented to the Convention.[59]

The Extension Department of Mercer University has been in existence since 1948. It was inaugurated following a study of a similar program at Howard College [now Samford University] in Alabama and was set up to provide training in Biblical as well as practical areas for ministers who had not been privileged to attend college or seminary. Operated as a part of the program of Mercer University, the Extension Department was set up to be operated as a part of the

[56]*Ibid.*, p. 18.
[57]*Loc. cit.*
[58]*Ibid.*, p. 19.
[59]*Ibid.*, p.p. 19, 20.

Georgia Baptist Convention program, and each year allocations were made for operation of this Extension Department.

At its inauguration, the sum of $15,000 was to be appro-
priated to cover the cost of salaries of director, faculty and
staff members and for necessary expenses.[60] The Extension
Department of Mercer University was to accomplish many
goals in subsequent years. The method of operation was to
consist of a series of extension centers across the state of
Georgia which would operate two semesters each 15 weeks
in length, with classes meeting one night each week. Each
center had a local director, registrar, and faculty members
and courses were open to religious workers without regard
to age or academic training. At the completion of a course
of 24 semester hours, a student was awarded a "Special Mercer certificate". "Advanced Mercer certificate" and the "Certificate of Superior Achievement" were awarded for additional work.[61]

The basic idea behind the creation of the Extension Department meant that expenses were kept to a minimum and as
the program developed across the years, types of operation
were developed which included an individual plan and an
associational plan, with the association paying a fixed amount
per course per semester and the student paying a minimal
amount. The wife of a minister or ministerial student then
would be charged one-half of the fee paid if the husband
were enrolled.[62] In a summary statement concerning the Extension Program J. Aubrey Estes, director, said that: "Since
1949, centers have been operated one or more semesters in
91 areas with a net enrollment of 17,209 persons since the
beginning." [63] [up to 1971.]

Acceptance of a tender by the Trustees of Brewton-Parker
College of the college to the Convention was another feature
of the 1948 Convention year. The Convention voted to accept
the college upon the conditions that there would be no out-

[60]*Ibid.,* p.p. 21-22.
[61]*Georgia Baptist Digest,* 1971, p. 47.
[62]*Loc. cit.*
[63]*Loc. cit.*

standing indebtedness, with the Convention recommending that churches comprising the twenty associations in Southeast Georgia which had appointed trustees for the college to raise $44,000, and with the Executive Committee working out all legal requirements. Upon completion of this and the acceptance of the title to the property, the Convention then would elect trustees to assume responsibility for operation of the school.[64] In subsequent years, both Norman Junior College and Shorter College were to come back into the Convention family, in somewhat similar fashion.

By-laws of the Convention were changed. Section I had read:

> At each annual meeting of this Convention the President shall nominate a committee of ten, whose duty it shall be to nominate to the Convention all Boards, Commissions and Committees chosen by the Convention.

It was changed to read:

> At each annual meeting of this Convention, the President shall appoint a committee of ten, to report at the next annual meeting, whose duty it shall be to nominate to the Convention all Boards, Commissions and Committees chosen by the Convention.[65]

Significance of the change was that the Nominating Committee would have a year in which to perform its duties rather than having to make recommendations to the Convention then in session.

A change in the Constitution, to become effective in 1949, was made also. The change was in Article 6, Section I, which was made to read:

> 1. An Executive Committee of this Convention shall be chosen by the Convention and shall consist of the officers of the Convention, ex-officio, including the President of the Georgia Baptist Sunday School Convention, the President of the Georgia Baptist Training Union, the President of the Women's Missionary Union, the President of the Baptist Student Union, and the President of the Baptist Brotherhood, ex-officio, and one member to be chosen from the territory of each cooperating District Association, and twenty additional Members from

[64]*Minutes, Georgia Baptist Convention,* 1948, p. 23.
[65]*Ibid.,* p. 27.

the State at Large.

The members of the Executive Committee shall be elected to hold office for one year, one-fifth for two years, one-fifth for three years, one-fifth for four years, and one-fifth for five years. The vacancies as the terms expire shall be filled for terms of five years. No one connected in any way with any Institution, fostered by this Convention, shall be eligible for membership on this Committee. No member of the Committee shall be eligible for re-election after the expiration of the term of service until he has been in retirement from the Committee for at least one year whether he served ex-officio or for a specified term from the territory of the Associations.

2. That Section 2-b of Article 6 be changed to read: Any vacancy caused by the death, resignation, or removal from the association which said member represents, or for any other reason, shall be filled by the Convention at its next regular session.[66]

This Constitutional change provided for an increased membership on the Executive Committee, and insured representation from every association.

Difficulties in the management of the Children's Home, never explained publicly up to this time, were reflected in a rather terse announcement to the 1949 Convention. Z. E. Barron, Convention treasurer, reported to the Convention

... that the messengers and visitors had donated $500.00 for the purpose of sending Manager and Mrs. J. L. Fortney, of the Children's Home, on a vacation, and that this sum had been turned over to Mr. Fortney. No other funds had come into his hands.[67]

There were 550 children enrolled in the Home during this year.[68]

OFFER OF LAND FOR ASSEMBLY

Following earlier agreement that Bessie Tift College be selected as a site for the Georgia Baptist Assembly under certain conditions, J. R. Smith offered to give to the Convention 100 acres of land provided the Convention would build on it necessary buildings for assembly grounds. This offer was

[66]*Ibid.*, p. 28.
[67]*Ibid.*, p. 43.
[68]*Ibid.*, p. 38.

referred to the Executive Committee without instructions.[69]

In view of the fact that approval had been given for the Hospital commission to borrow up to seventy-five per cent aaginst what it considered valid pledges, and in light of the fact that the Hospital already had apparently in excess of $1,000,000 on hand to begin construction, ground was broken for the new Hospital building on August 27, 1948.[70]

In the report by Arthur Jackson on the Georgia Baptist Foundation, he said that for the Convention year, $149,008.29 had been raised for building purposes. Additionally, $255,076.54 had been raised during 1948 for endowment, bringing a total increase in permanent assets of the Foundation for the year to $404,084.83. Of this amount, $200,000 had been given by Columbus Roberts. This made a total endowment held for educational institutions by the Foundation of $3,791,963.96.[71]

Considerable growth therefore during the year was reflected in the actions of the Executive Committee and in actions of the Convention at the 1948 session.

Meeting at Augusta in 1949, the Convention formally did away with the Holding Commission by striking Article VI, Section III from the Constitution, which Article set up the Holding Commission and defined its duties. The official demise of the Commission followed completion of duties assigned to it by the Convention and marked the winding up of all legal affairs of the Commission.[72] This was one of the most important committees created by the Convention.

Following the appointment in 1947 of a permanent Committee on Baptist history, this Committee reported four recommendations to the Convention. One was that the Committee be authorized to establish and identify Baptist landmarks and incidents in Georgia. Another recommendation was authorized to seek the co-operation of the Associations, churches, and individuals in collecting old minutes and his-

[69]*Ibid.*, p. 51.
[70]*Ibid.*, p. 118.
[71]*Ibid.*, p. 130.
[72]*Minutes, Georgia Baptist Convention,* 1949, p. 21.

torical volumes, letters, photographs, and other valuable historical documents for deposit in the fireproof library at Mercer University. The third recommendation, from which this present work developed ultimately, was the recommendation that the committee be authorized to sponsor a comprehensive history of Georgia Baptists to be written and published as soon as possible with the final approval of such volume or volumes to be given by the Convention or its Executive Committee. A fourth request was that the Convention give the committee a thousand dollars for the next year to operate on.[73]

Following establishment of this committee, enough interest was aroused, primarily through the efforts of this Committee, to begin securing a collection of valuable historical documents at the library at Mercer University. The late Charles H. Stone, librarian for Mercer University for many years, participated actively in this effort of the Committee on Baptist History, by encouraging preservation of the materials as well as providing access to the materials for persons interested in doing research and study in Georgia Baptist history.

What came to be known as the Simultaneous Evangelistic Crusades were planned for 1951 by the Convention in 1949 under the leadership of the Department of Evangelism. These crusades were to be repeated periodically through the years with marked services.[74]

In a report on the Ministers Retirement Plan, the Convention was told that after eleven years in operation there were 1,450 churches co-operating in the plan with 977 pastors enrolled.[75]

On Sunday afternoon, Oct. 3, 1948, a rededication service for the old Penfield Cemetery was held. The cemetery, which began in the church on the old Mercer campus, and featured the late Senator Walter F. George for the formal address, Columbus Roberts, President, Georgia Baptist Convention,

[73]*Ibid.*, p.p. 28, 29.
[74]*Ibid.*, p. 31.
[75]*Ibid.*, p. 41.

presided, and President Dowell of Mercer presided over the final service in the cemetery.[76]

The next year, 1949, the closing session of the Georgia Baptist Convention was held at Penfield and marked the dedication service for the restoration of the old Mercer chapel which was then the Penfield Baptist Church.[77] The chapel building had been planned in 1844, erected in 1846 and had stood for over a century.[78] The Convention had provided funds for the renovation of this chapel and the bronze tablet unveiled on the occasion read:

> The Penfield Chapel Mercer University Erected 1846 Restored 1949. This Historic Building—one of the finest patterns of classic revival architecture in the south— cherished by Georgia Baptists as a symbol of the faith and vision of the founding fathers—was restored and rededicated by the Georgia Baptist Convention and the Penfield Baptist Church on November 17, 1949 on which occasion the closing period of the 128th annual session of the Convention was held in this building . . .[79]

In this year, the Executive Committee membership was increased significantly by virture of the constitutional amendment approved by the Convention in 1948. Membership rose from 45 to 108 elected members. Including those who served as ex-officio members, the Executive Committee membership for the year totaled 121[80], an all time high. This 1948 amendment did in effect, what T. C. Burrell had proposed to the Convention in 1920, and which the Convention had rejected;[80a] call for a member from every Association.

Recognizing the role which the First Baptist Church of Hapeville played in the spiritual welfare and growth of the residents of the Georgia Baptist Children's Home, the Convention in 1949 approved for allocation in 1950 the sum of $10,000 to the Hapeville church for aid in construction of an

[76]Spright Dowell, *A History of Mercer University, 1833-1953* [Atlanta: Foote and Davies, Inc., 1958], p. 357.

[77]*Ibid.*, p. 358.

[78]*Ibid.*, p. 351.

[79]*Ibid.*, p. 358.

[80]*Ibid.*, p. 84.

[80a]*Minutes, Georgia Baptist Convention*, 1920, p. 21.

educational unit.[81] By 1949, Co-operative Program receipts were $929,939.48, designated gifts were $1,302,813.06 for a total in receipts of $2,232,752.54[82]

At a meeting of the Executive Committee on March 8, 1949, Monroe S. Swilley suggested the establishment of a home for aged Baptists in Georgia. A committee was named to study the matter and to report to the Executive Committee.[83] The Executive Committee reported to the 1950 Convention that:

> The Executive Committee looks with favor upon the eventual establishment of a home for aged Baptists and, since the launching of such a project would require a minimum of $150,000.00, the Committee recommends that the establishment of the home and adoption of plans of operation be postponed until this amount is in hand, and that the Convention appoint a committee to acquaint our people with the need for this institution and to receive funds for this purpose.[84]

The 1951 budget, as approved in Savannah in 1950, called for a Co-operative Program budget of $1,276,700.00.[85] For the second successive year $10,000 was allocated to the Hapeville church, making a total of $20,000 set aside by the Convention to aid in construction of an educational facility.[86] This made the Hapeville church recipient of the largest sum of money ever allocated by the Convention to a single church. Also at the 1950 Convention, Georgia Baptists continued to make provision for paying the churches' share of the Ministers Retirement Plan for those who entered the military chaplaincy, and approved social security coverage for employees of the Executive Committee eligible for such coverage.[87]

[81]*Minutes, Georgia Baptist Convention,* 1949, p. 87.

[82]*Ibid.,* p. 189.

[83]*Minutes, Executive Committee, Georgia Baptist Convention,* March 8, 1949. Minute Book 3, p. 144.

[84]*Minutes, Georgia Baptist Convention,* 1950, p. 22.

[85]*Ibid.,* p. 19.

[86]*Ibid.,* p.p. 20, 21.

[87]*Ibid.,* p. 24.

28,571 BAPTISMS IN 1949

In 1949, 28,571 persons were baptized by churches in the Convention.[88] As plans were completed for the simultaneous crusade in 1951, these plans emphasized the role of state missions in retaining the usefulness of these converts.[89] Additionally, an effort was made to obtain a circulation of 50,000 for the *Christian Index* by the end of 1950 and as of the last week in October of that year a total of 48,451 subscriptions had been secured.[90] The *Index,* on January 4, 1951, reported a circulation of 55,409; the goal reached and exceeded.[91]

John C. Warr came to the Georgia Baptist Children's Home on January 15, 1950 as acting manager. He had been superintendent of the Floyd County public schools. Fortney had stated at the Georgia Baptist Convention session in 1949 in Augusta that because of his health he needed a period of rest. He and Mrs. Fortney were given a six months leave of absence.[92] It was this statement evidently that occasioned Barron's announcement to the 1949 Convention that $500 had been given to Mr. and Mrs. Fortney.[93] Warr became general manager of the Home May 14, 1950;[94] a position he held until his death in 1969. During 1950, 507 children were cared for by the Home for a daily average of 463.[95]

Norman Junior College had for a number of years operated a high school department which served not only boarding students at the college for the high school department, but students who would have attended the Norman Park public schools. Questions had been raised concerning possible violation of principles of separation of church and state. In the light of this, and for other reasons, including financial, President Cutts of Norman reported to the Convention in

[88]*Ibid.,* p. 26.
[89]*Loc. cit.*
[90]*Ibid.,* p. 28.
[91]Lester, p. 133.
[92]*Minutes, Georgia Baptist Convention,* 1950, p. 34.
[93]*Op. cit.*
[94]*Ibid.,* p. 78.
[95]*Ibid.,* p. 34.

1950 that the high school department at Norman College had been discontinued.[96]

At the 1950 Convention a budget of $1,276,700.00 was approved for 1951. This was to be divided 50-50 between Georgia and southwide causes after certain funds were deducted for joint undertakings.[97] The Convention therefore continued on its original plan of Co-operative distribution. It is, therefore, of significance, that at a meeting of the Convention's Executive Committee on September 11, 1951, there appeared a statement concerning the agreement between the Executive Committee of the Georgia Baptist Convention and the Executive Committee of the Southern Batpist Convention concerning the division of funds.[98] The Convention meeting in November of that year also reaffirmed the agreement.[99] This was the agreement of 1934, which the Southern Baptist Convention, meeting in San Francisco in June of 1951 had also reaffirmed with the following clarifying amendments:

> A. Since [the] Co-operative program is a joint enterprise of the various state conventions in the Southern Baptist Convention, through which the churches carry out their world-wide denominational program, and in the interest of clearness and understanding among our people, we suggest that expense chargeable to the whole Co-operative Program be cared for as follows:
> [1] That we share in the administration and promotional expenses directly related to the operation of the Co-operative Program and the Woman's Missionary Union.
> [2] We recognize that the Ministers Retirement Plan is an appropriate charge against the whole program.
> [3] That for the sake of uniformity and clarity in reporting the above, the Executive Secretary of the Executive Committee and the several state secretaries undertake to work out uniform systems of accounting and reporting.
> [4] That we fraternally urge in every state that expenses chargeable to the whole Co-operative Program

[96]*Ibid.*, p. 162.
[97]*Ibid.*, p.p. 79, 80.
[98]*Minutes, Executive Committee, Georgia Baptist Convention,* September 11, 1951, p. 231.
[99]*Minutes, Georgia Baptist Convention,* 1951, p. 86.

be kept at a minimum, holding ever before us the ideal of the 50-50 division for both state conventions and the Southern Baptist Convention, and it is our further conviction that the items to be deducted for distribution should be limited to those above set forth. [5] Since, in the rapidly changing conditions which affect our plans, it would seem wise for us to have as circumstances may direct, mutual consultations concerning our expanding programs, we respectfully recommend periodic conferences for this purpose.[100]

The year 1950 marked the 16th consecutive year that undesignated Co-operative Program funds had increased.[101]

The Executive Committee, in September, 1951, heard a report from the Hospital Commission that expenses for completing and furnishing the new hospital building would be $723,291.00 in excess of the original estimate. Therefore, the Executive Committee, in an emergency action, approved the execution of a loan in the amount of $750,000 by the Executive Secretary to provide for the necessary funds.[102] The report of the emergency action said that the new building, when completed and furnished, would represent a minimum investment of $4,809,910.43.[103] Reasons for approval of the emergency action as given by the Executive Committee included the fact that the contractors had a cancellation clause and could under certain conditions cancel the contract if obligations were not met, and the rising costs of construction made delay seem unwise.[104]

The Executive Committee made a further report in 1951 following a study of the matter of assemblies and encampments and citing outstanding Convention obligations, recommended:

1. That we do not at this time undertake to establish a central summer assembly on a statewide basis, since it does not at this time seem to be expedient.

[100]*Minutes, Executive Committee, Georgia Baptist Convention,* September 11, 1951, p. 231; Southern Baptist Convention annual, 1934, p.p. 48, 48, 1951, p. 40. *Minutes, Georgia Baptist Convention,* 1951, p. 25.

[101]*Minutes, Georgia Baptist Convention,* 1950, p. 73.

[102]*Minutes, Georgia Baptist Convention,* 1951, p.p. 24, 25.

[103]*Loc. cit.*

[104]*Ibid.,* p.p. 90, 91.

2. That existing facilities be more largely used.
3. That the holding of summer assemblies and encampments in various areas of the state be encouraged in order to reach as many people as possible.
4. That emphasis in these assemblies and encampments be placed upon leadership training so as to prepare those who attend for work in church, associational, and other denominational programs.[105]

Following this recommendation of the Executive Committee, which for eleven years tabled the matter of an asssmbly for all practical purposes, there was increasing emphasis in the associations upon the construction of encampments by the associations. These encampments were, practically speaking, to drain from Association and Convention funds, monies which otherwise might have gone toward a state encampment. Impetus for the development of these associational camps appeared to subside following purchase of the Georgia Baptist Assembly at Toccoa authorized at the 1963 session of the Georgia Baptist Convention.

Merritt, in his report to the Convention, indicated that special allocations in the Convention budget each year since 1946 which were primarily for endowment of educational institutions had yielded in five years the sum of $471,481.57. During this same time other objects in the state had received $137,219.57 for a total of $608,701.14 since 1946.[106] Another new Department of State Missions was begun Oct. 15, 1951, when the Department of Church Music was inaugurated. Dr. Paul McCommon, who had been pastor of the Jackson Hill Baptist Church in Atlanta, was elected by the Executive Committee as first secretary.[107]

20,000 MEN IN BROTHERHOODS

With the Brotherhood Department now five years old, King reported that there were 20,000 men in 600 churches as a result of activity expended in organization of church brotherhood units.[108]

[105]*Ibid.*, p.p. 26, 27.
[106]*Ibid.*, p. 86.
[107]*Ibid.*, p. 113.
[108]*Ibid.*, p. 32.

A rotating plan of membership on all boards of trustees to follow the same guide lines as those used by the Executive Committee, was approved by the Convention in 1951,[109] and during that year there were 1,074 pastors enrolled in the Retirement Plan and 1,527 churches participating. Also, 115 annuitants were receiving monthly checks totaling $5,555.43, and 308 pastors were participating in the Widows Supplemental Plan with seven widows receiving annuities.[110] In the same year, there were 131 ministers and widows of ministers who were on the relief beneficiary role of the Annuity Board receiving a total for the year of about $18,953.50.[111] For the first time in 1951, a specific sum of $15,000 was earmarked in the 1952 budget for application on the purchase on a student center for the Georgia Institute of Technology.[112] The budget approved for 1952 was $1,288,800, again on a 50-50 basis.[113]

On November 29, 1951, the new Hospital building was dedicated and the cornerstone was laid, marking another era of progress in a development of the Georgia Baptist Hospital.[114] At the meeting of the Executive Committee on September 9, 1952, another recommendation was made regarding a proposed Bapitst professional building.[115]

Authorization had been given by the Convention in 1945 for a proposed corporation to be formed for the purpose of erecting a Baptist professional building at a cost then estimated at $700,000.[116] The Convention had approved this proposal in 1945, and the same basic proposal was restudied by the executive committee in 1952 at this September meeting substituting some names for those previously listed in the 1945 approval for the project. The Executive Committee

[109]*Ibid.*, p. 42.
[110]*Ibid.*, p.p. 50, 51.
[111]*Ibid.*, p. 51.
[112]*Ibid.*, p. 22.
[113]*Ibid.*, p. 21.
[114]*Ibid.*, p. 137.
[115]*Minutes, Executive Committee, Georgia Baptist Convention*, Sept. 9, 1952, p. 271.
[116]*Minutes, Georgia Baptist Convention*, 1945, p.p. 15-17.

voted to recommend that a similar proposal for a private corporation be made to the Convention in 1952, setting as a cost figure an amount not to exceed $1,500,000.

Louie D. Newton, Dick H. Hall, Jr., Wiley L. Moore, Edwin B. Peel, James W. Merritt, Guy W. Rutland, Sr., and I. H. Sheffield, Jr., were named as proposed incorporators of the Georgia Baptist Professional Building, Incorporated.[117] The basic proposal was that the non-profit corporation would erect a building, and upon completion of payment for the building, deed to the building would be placed in the hands of the Executive Committee of the Convention. It was to be necessary to deed the land upon which the proposed building was to be placed at the corner of Boulevard and Forrest Avenues to the Georgia Baptist Professional Building, Incorporated upon incorporation of the group.

However, when the Convention met in Atlanta in November, 1952, the recommendation of the Executive Committee had been changed and the Convention did approve construction of a Baptist Professional Building but in a different manner.[118] The Executive Committee was given authority by the Convention, *as an Executive Committee,* to erect a professional building on the hospital property and to execute a loan of up to $1,400,000 for this purpose, with authority to give certain hospital propeties and the Baptist building at 291 Peachtree Street as security for the loan.[119] The proposal approved by the Convention was a substitute for the action of the Convention in 1945 and the proposed action taken by the Executive Committee in September.[120]

Another Executive Committee recommendation to the Convention, which was approved, called for creation of a Commission on Education for the Georgia Baptist Convention.[121] This recommendation was approved and the Education Commission was set up the following year.

[117]*Minutes, Executive Committee, Georgia Baptist Convention,* Sept. 9, 1952, p. 271.

[118]*Minutes, Georgia Baptist Convention,* 1952, p. 18.

[119]*Loc. cit.*

[120]*Ibid.,* p. 23.

[121]*Ibid.,* p. 17.

With the retirement of D. B. Nicholson Jan. 1, 1952, Aubrey L. Hawkins, at the time Student Secretary at the University of Georgia in Athens, was elected as Secretary of the Department of Student Work. He was elected on March 11, 1952.[122]

Nicholson had been the first and only student secretary since the creation of the department in 1925. He had retained his home in Athens during the entire period and operated from the Athens residence and an office in the Baptist building in Atlanta.

Searcy S. Garrison, pastor of the Bull Street Baptist Church, was elected president of the Georgia Baptist Convention in 1952. Garrison succeeded Louie D. Newton who had served a two-year term. From this point, Garrison was to be identified prominently in Convention leadership until the present. Upon completion of his two-year term as president of the convention, Garrison was to become executive secretary-treasurer, being elected September 7, 1954.[123]

At the September, 1952 meeting of the Executive Committee, a committee which had been appointed to make an in-depth study seeking means of providing support and a fair allocation of funds to Georgia Baptist schools and colleges, reported [124] the Executive Committee had called upon the services of R. Orin Cornett, then Executive Secretary of the Education Commission of the Southern Baptist Convention, to help establish a formula for distribution of funds. The Cornett report, far-reaching in its implications, was presented to the Executive Committee and to the Convention, and out of this report the following suggestions were made.[125] The report called for a survey of Baptist educational institutions in Georgia and to do what was necessary to carry out recommendations of the proposed study. The Convention

[122]*Ibid.*, p. 81.
[123]*Minutes, Georgia Bapitst Convention*, 1954, p. 90.
[124]*Minutes, Georgia Baptist Convention*, 1952, p. 87.
[125]*Ibid.*, p.p. 21, 22.

approved therefore a recommendation that a Commission on Education be established to make the survey.[126]

The Commission was to be composed of presidents of the schools with power to vote by proxy if necessary, seven members from the Convention at large, plus the Executive Secretary-Treasurer, the President of the Georgia Baptist Convention and the President of Woman's Missionary Union. This Commission was empowered to make recommendations to the Executive Committee but not directly to the Convention and under the strictures of organization, any recommendation made to the Executive Committee must have obtained

> ... a simple majority vote of the non-institutional members of the Commission plus a majority of the institutional representatives; and that it be required that a quorum of each to be in attendance in order for such recommendation to pass.[127]

This marked the beginning of the Education Commission of the Georgia Baptist Convention as it is now known.

In 1952 also, the Convention accepted an offer from the Sunday School Board of the Southern Baptist Convention to purchase the Georgia Convention's interest in the Baptist Book Store for $125,000.[128] Prior to this, for a number of years, the Book Store had been operated under joint ownership of the Georgia Baptist Convention and the Sunday School Board of the Southern Baptist Convention.

In February of 1952, the first Associational Officers Conference was held in Atlanta and this conference attracted 160 moderators, clerks, and other associational leaders.[129] This marked the beginning, again, of a series of associational promotional conferences which have continued in similar form to the present. By the end of 1952, gifts by Georgia Baptists to their convention causes, state and southwide, had climbed to near the $3,000,000 mark. Gifts for the Calendar year 1952 for the co-operative program were $1,325,289.98.

[126]*Ibid.*, p. 22.
[127]*Ibid.*, p.p. 22, 23.
[128]*Ibid.*, p.p. 25, 26.
[129]*Ibid.*, p. 112.

Designated gifts were $1,625,593.31, for a total in receipts of $2,950,883.29.[130]

With the planned survey of the needs of educational institutions, Georgia Baptists were preparing to launch their most extensive efforts to undergird Christian education.

[130]*Ibid.*, p. 203.

CHAPTER 24

Plans For The Future

Spright Dowell resigned as president of Mercer University January 14, 1953, effective August 31, 1953.[1] Dowell became president of Mercer in 1928,[2] and held the position for twenty-five years, the longest single term of any president of the University. During the years 1948 and 1949, Dowell served also as president of the Georgia Baptist Convention. A recognized educator of national esteem, Dowell contributed much to shaping the pattern of thought concerning Christian education among Georgia Baptists during his tenure at Mercer. His belief in the permanent value of Christian educational institutions as part of the Convention structure, reaffirmed regularly, provided impetus for the Convention in many ways. His leadership during the Depression years in sustaining an interest in and support for all educational institutions in Georgia is a matter of record.

The matter of a Georgia Baptist Assembly still arose upon occasion. At a meeting of the Administration Committee of the Executive Committee on May 26, 1953, Merritt read to the Committee a letter from Franklin Owen, then pastor of the First Baptist Church in Gainesville, regarding an approach made to Owen concerning sale of the Lake Louise

---

[1]Spright Dowell, *A History of Mercer University, 1833-1953* [Atlanta: Foote & Davies, Inc., 1958], p. 371.

[2]*Ibid.*, p. 296.

property to the Baptists of Georgia. No action was taken. Evidently, the information was received as such, and in the light of previous Convention action, no further study was made.[3]

At a meeting of the Executive Committee on November 16, 1953, Editor Hurt reported to the Committee that a History of *The Christian Index* was being written. This History of *The Christian Index,* completed in 1955, was the first documented history of *The Index* from its inception in 1822 as *The Columbian Star* through 1954.[4]

Earlier, the Executive Committee, at its September 4 meeting, voted to accept the Good Samaritan Clinic which had been operated on Alexander Street in Atlanta. Acceptance involved the property as well as some cash, and the Executive Committee agreed to assume responsibility for operation of this Clinic.[5]

The matter of a Home for the Aged was mentioned first to the Executive Committee by Monroe Swilley in 1949.[6] At the Convention session in 1953, a motion was made by Francis Stewart that the Executive Committee be requested to make ". . . a thorough study of the need for Georgia Baptists to establish a Home for the Aged, and report to the next Convention." [7]

Following this recommendation, the Executive Committee named a small committee to explore the matter.[8] The committee made a study concerning type of operation, maintenance, financing, possible location and the method of procedure in establishing such a Home. Apparently, a number of sites were offered for the Home and the committee

[3]Minutes, *the Administration Committee, Executive Committee, Georgia Baptist Convention,* May 26, 1953 .

[4]Minutes, *Executive Committee, Georgia Baptist Convention,* November 16, 1953, p. 25.

[5]*Ibid.,* September 4, 1953.

[6]*Minutes, Executive Committee, Georgia Baptist Convention,* March 8, 1949, Minute Book 3, p. 144.

[7]*Minutes, Georgia Baptist Convention,* 1953, p. 38.

[8]*Minutes, Georgia Baptist Convention,* 1954, p. 96.

ments not only of Convention attendance but visits in the cities, together with an increased emphasis upon the ministries and work of the Convention, all contributed to the larger attendance.

Additionally, the increased promotional efforts evident over the past two years, particularly in reaching all the churches and pastors with the program of the Convention, were making an impact reflected in this increased interest upon the part of Georgia Baptists in their program.

Following the decision of the Convention in 1954 to leave Truett-McConnell College at Cleveland and Brewton-Parker College at Mount Vernon, the Atlanta Association expressed growing interest in a Baptist college in the Atlanta area. Monroe F. Swilley, pastor of the Second Ponce de Leon Baptist Church in Atlanta, was chairman of a committee from the Atlanta Association named to consider establishment of a Baptist college. Swilley made an unofficial report to the Executive Committee in September and requested a recommendation from the Executive Committee to the Convention that the Education Commission be enlarged in scope so that it could study this and other proposals as they developed, inasmuch as the Education Commission was confined by structure to authority in dealing with the six "existing schools".[54] From this request came Convention approval of expansion of the responsibility of the Education Commission to provide for added studies, including the matter of a Baptist college in Atlanta.[55]

The Atlanta Baptist Association College Committee was from this point on to be in communication with the Executive Committee, and to first solicit help from Georgia Baptists, then to withdraw from any relation to the Convention in its projection, and finally to establish a college.

With the selection of Harvey Mitchell to head the Home for the Aged [Baptist Village,] Mitchell reported to Georgia Baptists that the doors of "Baptist Village" would be open in

[54]*The Christian Index*, Sept. 20, 1956, p. 3.
[55]*Minutes, Georgia Baptist Convention*, 1956, p. 97.

1957 with three applications for each room available in the initial unit. The Convention had marked its first Baptist Village day in June and had received approximately $16,000 for this Home. The year had been spent in extensive research concerning a building and services which could be offered. Mitchell had surveyed facilities of like nature across the nation and based upon the surveys made by him, a master construction plan was adopted finally by the Trustees for Baptist Village and the Executive Committee to develop over a period of time a home which could care for 300 residents.[56]

Allocation for the purchase of land in Waycross actually was for the purchase of land in addition to the 248.8 acres of land which had been given for Baptist Village to provide a total of 525 acres. During 1956, $50,000 had been contributed as endowment for the home, by the late Carey Vinson of Waynesboro.[57]

With the evident success of the Executive Committee's program of promotion, the calendar year 1955 had been a year in which Co-operative Program gifts increased seventeen per cent. This was increased an additional twenty per cent during the first ten months of 1956, marking a two-year increase in Cooperative Program gifts of thirty-seven per cent.[58] For January to October, 1956, the ten-month total reflected a gain of $791,885.94.[59] Therefore at the end of the year, $4,597,729.02 had been given by Georgia Baptists for all causes through the Co-operative Program and by designated gifts.[60] This marked an all-time record for any year in the Convention's history. Records were to continue to be made each year thereafter in support of Convention ministries through 1971. At the same time that increases were evident in the giving of money, there was evident also an increased interest in the work of State Missions. Georgia

[56]*Ibid.*, p.p. 147, 148.
[57]*Ibid.*, p. 43.
[58]*Ibid.*, p. 87.
[59]*Loc. cit.*
[60]*Ibid.*, p. 211.

had recorded 34,695 baptisms during 1955,[61] and 33,221 baptisms in 1956 with a net gain of 38 churches.[62]

Upon retirement, T. W. Tippett presented to the Convention a summary statement of his 22 years of service as Sunday School secretary. Enrollment had grown between 1934 and to the end of 1955 from 272,624 to 574,781. Bible schools had grown from 29 in number to 1,860. Bible School enrollment by 1955 was set at 213,670. Tippett estimated that during his tenure as Sunday School secretary, he had traveled 451,298 miles, delivered 5,835 addresses, made contact with 2,213 churches, had planned and promoted 417 state-wide assemblies, conferences and conventions.[63]

Following a gift of $3,000 through the Committee On Baptist History to the Kiokee Baptist Church,[64] the Georgia Association, on October 18, 1956, held a special session at the Kiokee Church in which leaders in the Convention participated to mark the renovation of the church.[65]

In 1956, the Hospital reported that students at the School of Nursing were able to receive credits to be applied toward a Bachelor of Science degree at Tift College because the School of Nursing was affiliated with the college. This arrangement provided that with an additional four or five quarters work, the degree could be secured by the student nurses.[66]

Truett-McConnell College had, since its beginning, met in an old building in downtown Cleveland. Dormitory space was also in the downtown area. In 1956, the new administration-classroom building was used first on the 410-acre campus, just east of the city. This building was constructed at a cost of $250,000 and dedicated September 5, 1956. Joe H.

[61]*Ibid.*, p. 57.
[62]*Ibid.*, p. 335.
[63]*Ibid.*, p. 119.
[64]*Minutes, Georgia Baptist Convention*, 1955, p. 122.
[65]*The Christian Index*, Oct. 11, 1956, p. 5; Oct. 25, 1956, p. 5.
[66]*Minutes, Georgia Baptist Convention*, 1956, p. 139.

Miller, then president of the college, said that by using all space available, the college could teach 500 students.[67]

The decision to leave Truett-McConnell in Northeast Georgia perhaps was due as much to the Convention's historic interest in a mountain mission ministry as anything else. This ministry was phased out during the 1930's and some of the schools were either closed or turned over to the Home Mission Board of the Southern Baptist Convention. However, the historic interest remained and sustained residents in that area in their firm support for keeping a college there once it had been established, and in providing financial assistance to it.

At a meeting of the Administration Committee of the Executive Committee in December, 1956, the Committee voted to recommend to the Executive Committee that a Secretary of Promotion be recommended at the March, 1957 meeting, and that the chairman of the Administration Committee and the Executive Secretary be authorized to consider possible nominations to be made by the Administration Committee.[68]

Arthur Hinson had come to the Convention in 1953 as Secretary of Promotion. There had not been up to this time a person employed full time in the promotion of the Ministers Retirement Program in Georgia. A need was felt to provide additional promotion of retirement plans in cooperation with the Annuity Board of the Southern Baptist Convention. Therefore, the authorization to secure a Secretary of Promotion was, in part, due to a planned shift in emphasis on the part of Hinson's work, as well as a deliberate move toward enlisting increased interest in and support of the program of Georgia Baptists by an intensified use of communications media in Georgia through a Secretary of Promotion.

The stewardship and Cooperative Program efforts of the

[67]*Ibid.*, p.p. 198, 199.

[68]*Minutes, Administration Committee, Executive Committee, Georgia Baptist Convention,* Dec. 18, 19, 1956, p. 180.

Executive Committee of the Southern Baptist Convention had been, for a number of years, coordinated by Merrill D. Moore. In 1955, the Southern Baptist Convention adopted a statement which recognized the need for an intensification of assistance given to churches on methods and techniques in the area of church finance, fund raising and budget preparation. This recommendation in essence called for creation of additional plans which would be of value to the Southern Convention and especially to the State Conventions in working with the churches.[69] Out of this recommendation there came in 1956 a series of meetings, from which meetings emerged what came to be known as the Forward Program of Church Finance. This far-reaching program, developed in consultation with leaders from the several states and the Southern Baptist Convention, was used on an experimental, limited basis in 1956 and by 1957 was ready for introduction throughout the states.

Therefore, when the Administration Committee met on January 15, 1957, the Committee elected James A. Lester, who had been on the staff of The Times-Picayune in New Orleans, and was a graduate student at New Orleans Baptist Theological Seminary, to be an associate to the Executive Secretary-treasurer in the area of Promotion and Public Relations.[70] On March 5, 1957, the Executive Committee approved the action of the Administration Committee in employing Lester as an associate to ". . . assist in public relations and the Forward Church Programs. . ."[71] Lester assumed the newly-created position in the area of Promotion and Public Relations with dual responsibilities which included statewide promotion of The Forward Program of Church Finance—introducing this program to churches in the state.

[69]*Minutes, Southern Baptist Convention*, 1955, p. 42.

[70]*Minutes, Administration Committee, Executive Committee, Georgia Baptist Convention*, Jan. 15, 1957, p. 181.

[71]*Minutes, Executive Committee, Georgia Baptist Convention*, March 5, 1957, p. 189.

At this point, Hinson's responsibilities as Secretary of Promotion were changed to provide additional service in the area of promoting the programs of the Relief and Annuity Board, as well as provide additional administrative assistance to the executive secretary.

This increased promotional emphasis was coincident with the beginning of active promotion of the 30,000 Movement in the Georgia Baptist Convention. This movement was begun by the Southern Baptist Convention in 1956, to culminate in 1964 upon the commemoration of the 150th anniversary of the organization of Baptist work on a national level [establishment of the Triennial Convention in 1812]. The 30,000 Movement had as its goal to double the number of Baptist preaching places by creation of 5,000 churches and 25,000 missions by 1964.[72]

To promote Georgia efforts in the 30,000 Movement, R. T. Russell, Secretary of Evangelism, was named to direct the State's participation in this expanded program of missions, churches, and preaching stations.[73] Preparation of a detailed survey of needs in the state was the first step in Georgia's participation in the 30,000 Movement.[74] During this year, therefore, emphases centering upon increased use of communications media, increased focus upon Christian Stewardship teachings in the Georgia Baptist churches, coupled with detailed studies looking toward establishment of goals and sites for new churches and missions in Georgia, provided for Georgia Baptists renewed opportunities to look closely at both mission opportunities and stewardship opportunities at the local church level. Out of these emphases, which began in 1957, and because of the promotion of all areas of work, Georgia Baptists were entering into yet another era of advance in organized work as evidenced by the continuing increase in support of the work throughout the Convention.

[72]*Encyclopedia of Southern Baptists,* Vol. III, [Nashville: Broadman Press, 1971], p. 2025.

[73]*The Christian Index,* May 2, 1957, p. 14.

[74]*Loc. cit.*

CHAPTER 26

Continuing To Reach Out

The Convention during 1957 created something of a communications problem for itself in an unplanned manner. With presentation of the Social Service Commission report, there were recommendations by the Commission including one which said that:

> [4] The Convention approve the use by the Social Service Commission, whenever it deems wise, of such agencies as newspapers, radio, television, and our own Georgia Baptist organ, *The Christian Index,* to present factual reports and studies which may help in alerting the public and in molding public opinion in the direction of Christian action and social righteousness.

The Convention approved this report,[1] and approved also a report from the Executive Committee recommending the establishment of a Committee on Public Affairs

> . . . for the purpose of giving voice of the convictions of The Baptist Convention of the State of Georgia concerning religious freedom and the Baptist and American principle of separation of Church and State; . . .[2]

The Social Service Commission's interpretation of its authority to use public media to communicate purposes and opinions of the commission, and establishment of the Committee on Public Affairs created some problem. The Social Service Commission was directing its thinking in areas of Christian action and social righteousness. The Public Affairs Committee dealt in areas concerning religious freedom and

---

[1]*Minutes, Georgia Baptist Convention,* 1957, p.p. 42, 43.
[2]*Ibid.,* p. 26.

the principle of separation of church and state, inevitable overlapping occurred with the Convention having two authorized voices, one a committee, and one a commission, for making statements in behalf of the Convention without Convention approval. Additionally, a third channel to communications media was through the Office of Public Relations, communicating news materials which were within the framework of official Convention action and action by the Executive Committee or the Administration Committee of the Executive Committee.

The on-again off-again relationship between Shorter College and the Georgia Baptist Convention was settled, apparently finally, by the 1957 Convention, when a resolution from the Executive Committee was approved which authorized the Convention to accept a proposal from Trustees of Shorter to turn the college over to the Convention. The College was to be fully-owned and controlled by the Convention upon amendment of the charter to make it conform with all of the provisions called for in charters of Convention institutions. The Convention approved a stipulation whereby the legal title to the property would remain in the present corporation and the then existing corporation and itself would be controlled by and operated on the same basis as other Convention institutions. The transfer was to become effective upon appropriate amendment of the Shorter charter.[3] While the Convention controlled and operated Shorter College from this point to the present, title to the property remained with the corporation which had held title to Shorter throughout the years.

In 1957, the Convention was to adopt yet another amendment to the Constitution, Article VI, Section I, to make that section read:

> An Executive Committee of this Convention shall be chosen by the Convention, and shall consist of the officers of the Convention, ex-officio, including the President of the Georgia Baptist Pastors' Conference, the President of the Georgia Baptist Educational Directors,

[3]*Ibid.*, p. 25.

the President of the Georgia Baptist Sunday School
Convention, the President of the Georgia Baptist Training Union, the President of the Woman's Missionary
Union, the President of the Baptist Brotherhood, the
President of the Baptist Student Union, the President of
the Georgia Baptist Music Conference, ex-officio, and one
member to be chosen from the territory of each co-
operating District Association, and twenty additional
members from the State at large.[4]

With the adoption of this amendment, the Executive Committee was structured to provide for sixteen ex-officio members together with elected members as prescribed in the
Constitution.

During 1957, gifts through the Georgia Baptist Convention
for all causes were $4,702,782.10.[5] The budget therefore for
1958, as approved by the Convention, was $2,770,300.00.[6]

Again, $350,000 was classed under special allocations for
the six Georgia Baptist Schools and colleges according to
the 1954 Georgia Baptist Convention action.[7] With reduction of the loan of the Georgia Baptist Hospital to a balance
of $515,500, from the original $1,400,000 in 1952, and with
a loan of $1,325,000 on the Professional Building being re-
tired from leasing of office space,[8] the Convention in 1957
approved a request from the Hospital Commission for
authority to begin construction on an educational building
for the School of Nursing which would provide an auditorium and classrooms. Of the $500,000 estimated cost,
$232,120.58 was at that time in hand as a grant from the
Ford Foundation, and the Hospital Commission had set
aside $250,000 on August 17 from a special hospital operat-
ing and building fund reserve for a total available of
$482,120.58.[9] The Convention, as it had done on several
occasions, held an adjourned session again in 1957 from the

[4]*Ibid.,* p.p. 31, 32.
[5]*Ibid.,* p. 204.
[6]*Ibid.,* p. 76.
[7]*Loc. cit.*
[8]*The Christian Index,* Nov. 14. 1957, p. 3.
[9]*Minutes, Georgia Baptist Convention,* 1957, p. 80.
[10]*The Christian Index,* Nov. 24, 1957, p. 3.

Valdosta meeting. The final session of the Convention was held on the grounds of Baptist Village in Waycross at which time the dedication of the first unit of the home was held. The first unit provided accommodations for 24 persons and was constructed at a cost of $238,000.[10]

As was to be the case for many years following the request by Mercer University for permission to borrow Federal funds, and the subsequent request by Shorter College, the Executive Committee and subsequently the Convention, in 1958 approved authority for Tift College to borrow $200,000 from the Housing and Home Finance Agency.[11] In 1957, Baptist Village had been authorized to borrow from any bank in Waycross an amount not to exceed appropriations in 1958.[12] This amounted to $110,000.00.[13] In 1958, the Convention approved another request by Baptist Village to borrow against 1959 allocations from any bank in Georgia.[14] This again was $110,000.00.[15] A new record was set when *The Christian Index* in May of 1958 reached 100,000 in circulation. This was an increase from 40,140 in December of 1947, the year Hurt became editor.[16]

PROPERTY ACQUIRED

The Executive Committee proposed during this year that property be purchased for parking facilities for the Baptist Building.[17] Up to $175,000 in State Mission Reserve Funds was authorized for the use, with the State Mission Reserve Fund to be replenished at the rate of $20,000 a year from subsequent budgets beginning in 1959.[18]

This allowed the Executive Committee to purchase property behind the Baptist Building, facing Baker Street, which

[11]*Minutes, Georgia Baptist Convention*, 1958, p. 27.
[12]*Minutes, Georgia Baptist Convention*, 1957, p. 24.
[13]*Ibid.*, p. 20.
[14]*Minutes, Georgia Baptist Convention*, 1958, p. 27.
[15]*Ibid.*, p. 21.
[16]*Minutes, Georgia Baptist Convention*, 1958, p. 28; James Adams Lester, "A History of *The Christian Index*, 1822-1954", [Unpublished Master's Thesis 1955] p. 133.
[17]*Minutes, Georgia Baptist Convention*, 1958, p. 25.
[18]*Loc. cit.*

property not only was to provide needed parking space for the Executive Committee but which was to become in time property of great value to Georgia Baptists as the evaluation of downtown Atlanta property increased.

After the Convention had given approval in 1958 to the Executive Committee to purchase property near the Baptist Building for parking, the Executive Committee, in three steps, accomplished this objective. First, the Executive Committee on April 25, 1959 purchased property at 288-290 Ivy Street, Atlanta for $40,000. This property was on a street intersecting Baker Street which street was alongside the Baptist Building. On April 17, 24 Baker Street property was leased for a 50-year period with an option to purchase for $50,000 when a clear title could be obtained. And, on August 10, 1959, property at 22 Baker Street was purchased for $45,000. A building on this property was under lease until 1963. By this triple move, ownership or control of property extending all the way from the Baptist Building to Ivy Street, covering the entire block of Baker Street between Peachtree and Ivy was assured.[19] These purchases were the result of extended negotiations by Garrison in behalf of the Executive Committee.

Yet another amendment to the much-amended Constitution of 1919 was added during 1958. The Convention approved an amendment added into Section I of Article VI, which said:

> 1. That members of the executive committee who miss 50 per cent of the meetings of the Committee during any current year, including the pre-Convention meeting, without being excused at the meeting from which the members are absent or at the succeeding meeting, shall forfeit their membership on the committee:
> 2. That all members elected to membership on the Committee as representatives of associations must reside in the territory of the associations they represent.[20]

This amendment, by W. M. Marshall, Jr. provided that those who were absent consistently from Committee meetings could be replaced, and insured that a heavy grouping of

[19]*Minutes, Georgia Baptist Convention,* 1959, p. 82.

[20]*Minutes, Georgia Baptist Convention,* 1958, p. 31.

Committee members did not develop in any particular area of the state occasioned by pastoral changes. However, this restriction was to be softened in 1959.[21]

The educational picture in Georgia continued to improve. The Georgia Baptist Foundation reported to the Convention trust funds for institutions totaling $3,089,000.00, an increase of 12 per cent for the Convention year. Shorter's endowment, except some local real estate and small funds, had been entrusted to the Foundation.

All of the endowment of Truett-McConnell, Brewton-Parker, Baptist Village, and most of the funds from Norman were in the hands of the Foundation.[22] The colleges were showing increases in enrollment. Mercer gained 106 over the previous year, Tift showed a 14 per cent increase, Shorter had a 16 per cent increase, Norman a 27 per cent increase, and Brewton-Parker a 26 per cent increase, with no report from Truett-McConnell on its enrollment status.[23]

Assets of the institutions were given:

> The reports show that the total assets of Mercer University are now $10,712,000.00; Tift College, $2,239,-000.00; Shorter College, [based on 1957 report] $1,414,000.00. The three junior colleges report assets as follows: Norman College, $1,246,000.00; Brewton Parker, $581,000.00 and Truett-McConnell, $852,000.00. Your committee desires to call to your attention the fact that of the institutional assets listed above the major portions are reported in property. Mercer reports the largest endowment, $3,793,000.00; Tift $980,-000.00; Shorter [based on 1957 report], $956,000.00; and the three junior colleges; Norman, Brewton-Parker, and Truett-McConnell, $337,000.00, $234,000.00 and $189,000.00 respectively.[24]

In the area of benevolent ministries, the Children's Home reported an average of 500 cared for during 1957 and 1958. Baptist Village reported 22 residents, and in the report on Retirement Plans and Ministerial Relief, 776 pastors and

[21]*Minutes, Georgia Baptist Convention*, 1959, p. 33.
[22]*Minutes, Georgia Baptist Convention*, 1958, p.p. 32, 33.
[23]*Ibid.*, p. 33.
[24]*Loc. cit.*

church leaders were active in the retirement program, 32 per cent of the total eligible number, with 140 pastors and 26 widows receiving for 1958 $112,000 in annuity benefits. Additionally, 48 ministers and 104 widows received $31,-816.60 in ministerial relief in 1957.[25]

The Capital Improvements Program of the Georgia Baptist Convention, launched January 1, 1955, had through the year 1957 provided $1,047,031.34 to the educational institutions, which monies, on a matching basis, meant that more than $2,000,000.00 had been apportioned for repairs and improvements in a four-year period by Georgia Baptist educational institutions.[26] The significance and importance of the Capital Improvements Program was by this time quite evident. All of the efforts for Capital Improvements and paying of indebtedness of earlier years, and all of the efforts of the $75,000,000 campaign over a five-year period had not yielded to any degree the amount of funds, yielded in a four-year period through the Capital Improvements Program, although economic conditions in the state were different.

30,000 MOVEMENT INAUGURATED

When the Georgia Baptist Convention approved co-operation with the Southern Baptist Convention in the 30,000 Movement, a survey was planned. Perhaps the most intensive study of mission needs and church locations ever undertaken in Georgia was begun in 1957 by Fred E. White, an associate in the Department of Evangelism.[27]

White surveyed meticulously each Association, made comparative studies on strength of co-operating Baptist churches, non-co-operating Baptist churches and churches of other denominations. White's survey included also detailed maps of each association pin-pointing churches in existence, co-operating churches and areas where new churches or missions

[25]*Ibid.*, p. 35.
[26]*Ibid.*, p. 77.
[27]*Ibid.*, p. 83.

should be established. [Author kept and updated maps for several years.] Out of White's survey came a recommendation to the Georgia Baptist Convention in 1958 that the goal for Georgia's part would be to seek to establish 282 new churches. There had been 65 new churches in co-operation with the work of the Convention organized since January 1, 1956[28] up to 1958.

The Georgia Baptist Convention had previously enlarged the responsibility of the Georgia Baptist Education Commission to permit that body to co-operate with the Atlanta Baptist Association in a survey of a proposed college for the Atlanta area. At the Executive Committee meeting on September 9, 1958, the proposal from the Education Commission was presented to the Executive Committee and a joint recommendation then came from the Commission and the Executive Committee to the Convention.

This was the first formal step taken in a 10-year road which was to lead to the beginning of classes on a campus for the Atlanta Baptist College. The Education Commission and the Executive Committee recommended to the Convention that the Convention approve establishment of a Baptist college in the city of Atlanta which was intended to be a co-ordinate college of Mercer University.

The Convention then approved a campaign by the Atlanta Baptist Association through that Association's College Committee to raise $3,000,000 from the metropolitan Atlanta area with the appeal being limited to individuals, foundations and business concerns but not to churches. Additionally, the College Committee of the Association was authorized to choose a site and funds raised in the campaign were to be held by the Executive Committee.

A provision was made that the goals would be reached within three years and if the goals needed for capital funds and endowment had not been reached, then the Convention would have authority to determine whether sufficient funds had been raised to justify establishment of a college.

[28]*Loc. cit.*

If the funds were insufficient to establish a college, then the amount raised would be deposited with the Georgia Baptist Foundation, and income would be used for Christian Education as the Convention deemed appropriate.[29]

While the Campaign Committee in the Atlanta area was not to solicit from churches, in ensuing years churches were solicited directly for contributions to the Atlanta Baptist College campaign and churches were requested to put the college campaign in their budgets, which some Atlanta churches did.[29a] As evidence of the growth of Georgia Baptist Convention agencies and institutions, James W. Merritt, who had been appointed Convention treasurer, reported in 1958 that a study of the 1957 audits showed combined net assets of all agencies of the Convention in excess of $25,000,000.[30] An almost pathetic footnote is a part of the report of the Social Service Commission for 1958, when it was recommended

> . . . that our denominational leadership charged with the responsibility of planning our calendar of activities give consideration to a 'Stay At Home Night' each week so that families may become better acquainted and have ample time to share ideals and moral concepts.[31]

By the end of 1958 there were 120 missionary pastors being assisted by the Pastoral Aid Program.[32] The Program of Negro Work, was securing, in an unusual manner, the co-operation of Negro Baptists in Georgia in extension centers. During 1958, the Program Work had touched 2,296 Negro Baptists with programs of assistance.[33] Sunday School enrollment continued to increase, and by the end of 1957 stood at 595,923.[34]

A record $5,061,139.94 was received through the offices

[29]*Ibid.*, p.p. 95, 96.
[29a][Correspondence from Committee to Atlanta Association churches; study of several Atlanta Association church budgets by author after 1958.]
[30]*Minutes, Georgia Baptist Convention,* 1958, p. 100.
[31]*Ibid.,* p. 103.
[32]*Ibid.,* p. 109.
[33]*Ibid.,* p. 112.
[34]*Ibid.,* p. 114.

670 / A History of The Georgia Baptist Convention

of the Georgia Baptist Convention in 1958, with Co-operative Program gifts near the $3,000,000 mark—a total of $2,937,091.15. Designated gifts for 1958 were $2,124,048.79.[35] As the Convention grew, this growth was reflected by some slight increase during 1958 in baptisms with 34,593, again of 1,570, reported by the 2,869 churches in fellowship with the Convention.[36]

Woman's Missionary Union in Georgia staged a spectacular at the Fox Theatre, Atlanta, on November 14, 1958, and began a celebration of the Diamond Jubilee year of Georgia W. M. U. Woman's Missionary Union had been in existence, beginning with the old W. M. U. central committee for 80 years, and as an organized group for 75 years.[37]

Final official action on the part of Georgia Baptists in 1958 transpired in Atlanta on December 18th when the Executive Committee, among other items, adopted a resolution giving the Convention control of Shorter College.[38] The amendments to the Shorter charter opened enrollment to male students officially, although the college had enrolled male students since 1954.[39] Action became final with the granting of charter changes by the Superior Court of Floyd County, July 30, 1959.[40]

This action followed Convention approval in November for Shorter to come into the Convention family. With this addition, Norman College was the only Baptist-supported institution not owned by the Convention. Norman's trustees were elected by the Convention, but were chosen legally from sixteen southwest Georgia associations which held title to the institution.[41]

WESBERRY RECOMMENDATIONS

James P. Wesberry ended a second term as president of

[35]*Ibid.*, p. 219.
[36]*Ibid.*, p. 342.
[37]*The Christian Index*, Nov. 13, 1958, p. 5.
[38]*The Christian Index*, Dec. 18, 1958, p. 8.
[39]*Loc. cit.*
[40]*Minutes, Georgia Baptist Convention*, 1959, p. 79.
[41]*The Christian Index*, Dec. 18, 1958, p. 8.

the Georgia Baptist Convention at the 1958 session. In his President's Address at the 1957 Convention, Wesberry called for several programs for Georgia Baptists. He urged construction of a new Baptist Building, more endowment for colleges, called for continuing emphasis upon evangelism, missions and stewardship, and suggested a possible second home for the aged, consideration of a "real Georgia Baptist Assembly," and a possible Children's Home in north Georgia. Some of Wesberry's 1957 suggestions were studied later by the Executive Committee.[42]

When he addressed the 1958 session of the Convention, he suggested again a new office building; a survey of the Convention's program; that personnel employed by the Executive Committee be named for an indefinite period instead of being elected annually; a summer assembly; and a Department to assist pastors in obtaining churches and churches in obtaining pastors. He suggested also a housing allowance for secretaries of the State Missions Departments.[43] The suggestion for indefinite tenure was adopted and put into effect by the Executive Committee at its meeting in December.[44]

Out of the suggestions made by Wesberry in his two presidential addresses, suggestions which were concerns of others in positions of leadership also, were to come over the years impetus for implementation of many of them.

The years 1957 and 1958 were important ones for Georgia Baptists. In the Convention sermon in 1957, R. J. Robinson, pastor of the First Baptist Church, Augusta, had challenged Baptist leadership to major on paramount matters, with sincerity, heeding the commandments of God.[45]

The Wesberry proposals were considered of sufficient importance for the Executive Committee at its December meeting to name a special committee to study and report back concerning them.[46]

[42]*The Christian Index,* Nov. 14, 1957, p.p. 17, 18.
[43]*The Christian Index,* Nov. 13, 1958, p.p. 19, 20.
[44]*The Christian Index,* Dec. 18, 1958, p. 8.
[45]*The Christian Index,* Nov. 14, 1957, p. 13.
[46]*The Christian Index,* Dec. 18, 1958, p. 8.

The new leadership within the Convention family, emerging over a five-year period, was alert to new methods for advancing the Kingdom of God. The man in the pew sensed this mood expressed in many ways. Out of this positive atmosphere came a united witness and an atmosphere which was to enable the Convention to move forward.

Following Convention acceptance of control of Shorter College in 1958, Guy N. Atkinson, president of Norman College, informed the Executive Committee on September 8, 1959, that Norman trustees had requested that the College be accepted by the Convention to be owned and operated as a Convention institution. The college trustees had agreed to a charter change and on October 22, 1959, the Norman trustees voted to authorize a charter change. Therefore, the final educational institution receiving Baptist monies was approved by the 1959 session of the Convention to be controlled by that body upon appropriate charter changes providing ownership and control by the Convention.[47]

CONNELL DIES; HARRIS ELECTED

George Boyce Connell had served Mercer University for five years and eight months as president when he died of a heart ailment April 21, 1959, at the age of 54. Connell had been vice-president of the University during the administration of Spright Dowell. Following Dowell's retirement in 1953, Connell was named president. Upon Connell's death, Dowell was named acting president,[48] which position he occupied from the time of Connell's death until Rufus Carrollton Harris assumed the office of president of Mercer University, coming from the presidency of Tulane University, in New Orleans, late in 1959.[49] Harris did not assume full control at Mercer until mid-year 1960. He held dual responsibilities at Tulane and Mercer during this time. Harris

---

[47]*Minutes, Georgia Baptist Convention,* 1959, p.p. 26-28.
[48]*The Christian Index,* April 30, 1959, p. 3.
[49]*The Christian Index,* Nov. 19, 1959, p. 4.; *Minutes, Georgia Baptist Convention,* 1959, p. 48.

was still referred to as president-elect during March of 1960.[50] Harris, who had been elected earlier by the Mercer Trustees, came to the Convention in Augusta to announce his decision publicly to accept the presidency.[51] During Connell's tenure as president of Mercer, the institution had expended nearly $2,000,000 in building renovations and had added $1,500,000 in endowment. Connell had a heart condition for two years prior to his death.[52]

Harris was a native of Monroe, and a graduate of Mercer. He served as a Professor of Law at Mercer from 1923 to 1927, and was Dean of the Law School 1925-1927.[53] On Jan. 17, 1927, he requested Mercer's trustees to release him from his contract to become Dean of the Law School at Tulane University.[54] Of his departure in 1927, Dowell said: "He was rendering excellent service at Mercer and it was with sincere regret that the request was granted." [55] He was Dean and Professor of Law at Tulane from 1927 to 1937, and served as president of Tulane from 1937 to 1960.[56]

In his announcement of his acceptance of the Mercer presidency to the Convention in Augusta, Harris said:

> Mercer University is owned by the Baptists of Georgia. I want the fullest opportunity to declare my profound appreciation of that ownership, and to express at the same time my earnest appeal for your understanding, prayer, confidence and support.
>
> There is magnificent opportunity at Mercer and great love in my heart for her. There is at the same time tremendous need in our world for her ministry in education.
>
> Through its Christian base and central purpose it offers our best hope that the minds and hearts of people may acquire understanding enough to save our time from

---

[50]*The Christian Index*, March 24, 1960, p. 5.

[51]*Minutes, Georgia Baptist Convention*, 1959, p. 48.

[52]*The Christian Index*, April 30, 1959, p. 3.

[53]*Who's Who In America*, Vol. 36, 1970-1971 [Chicago: Marquis Who's Who], p. 963.

[54]Dowell, Spright, *A History of Mercer University*, 1933-1953, [Atlanta: Foote & Davies, Inc.], p. 288.

[55]*Loc. cit.*

[56]*Who's Who In America*, Vol. 36, p. 963.

darkness and error and establish in the heart of the world the adequacy of the Gospel of Jesus Christ.[57]

Once again, the Convention approved an amendment to the oft-amended Article VI, Section I, of the constitution modifying action of the previous year. The amendment said:

> That the fourth paragraph of Article VI, Section I, of the Constitution of the Georgia Baptist Convention be changed to read as follows: 'All persons elected to membership on the Committee as representatives of the associations must reside in the territory of the associations they represent, unless the Convention should accept an association's suggestion of a non-resident as its representative.' [58]

With this amendment it was becoming apparent that the Constitution of the Convention was being amended more or less annually.

The year 1959 marked the 20th anniversary of the beginning of enrollment of members in the Ministers' Retirement Program administered by the Annuity Board of the Southern Baptist Convention. After twenty years of promotion and enlistment, only 850 pastors were participating as active members in the Ministers' Retirement Program. For Georgia, this meant only 35 per cent of the leaders were included and 65 per cent of Georgia Baptist pastors were without retirement protection.[59]

Following approval for a fund-raising drive for the Atlanta Baptist College in 1958, the Executive Committee, upon request of Atlanta College Committee, approved the request of the Atlanta College Committee. The Committee agreed that expenses of the campaign for the college, about $3,000 per month, and not exceeding a total of $68,300, would be paid from gifts received in the campaign. The Executive Committee authorized the Executive Secretary to pay monies from receipts of the Campaign in the amount of $690,475 for a proposed college site consisting of approximately 450

[57]*The Christian Index*, Nov. 19, 1959, p. 4.
[58]*Minutes, Georgia Baptist Convention*, 1959, p. 33.
[59]*Ibid.*, p. 51.

acres of land[60] adjacent to Interstate Highway 85 some ten miles Northeast of downtown Atlanta.

Between 1957 and 1958, according to Convention Treasurer Merritt, total assets of all of the agencies of the Georgia Baptist Convention increased $8,000,000 based upon a study of audits in each year. Merritt reported that for 1958 assets were over $33,000,000, with the agencies spending more than $7,000,000 during that year in support of their programs.[61]

The effective program of promotion by the Executive Secretary and the State Missions staff, as well as the general impetus given to Georgia Baptist work by the Capital Improvements Program, and by fairly stable economic conditions among Baptists in the state, reflected in the total receipts for 1959 of $5,404,887.21. Of this amount, $3,254,-244.43 was given through the Co-operative Program in undesignated gifts, for a new record.[62]

When Hospital Administrator Edwin B. Peel told the Convention in 1959 in Augusta that there was a pressing need for a student nurses dormitory and that Georgia Baptists must provide acceptable housing, the stage was set for yet another building program by the Hospital and another loan from a federal agency.[63] The Executive Committee met on March 15, 1960, and gave the hospital authority to make preliminary application for a $2,500,000 loan from the Housing and Home Finance Agency. The resolution, which asked for permission to make the application, was a preliminary only and details would be submitted later. Louie D. Newton, Chairman of the Hospital Commission, said that funds to repay the loan would be from revenue earned from the Hospital's Professional Building, parking pavilion and grill. The plans called for an 11-story building which when completed would house 500 student

[60]*Ibid.,* p.p. 86, 87.
[61]*Minutes, Georgia Baptist Convention,* 1958, p. 100; *Minutes, Georgia Baptist Convention,* 1959, p. 119.
[62]*Minutes, Georgia Baptist Convention,* 1959, p. 234.
[63]*Ibid.,* p. 153.

nurses. The first three floors of the building were completed in 1959 and housed the Nurses' Educational Building and an auditorium.[64] The loan as approved by the 1960 Convention was for construction of a $2,500,000 dormitory, with $1,750,000.00 of the cost to be in the form of a loan from the Housing and Home Finance Agency.[65]

STUDY ON HOME SUPPORT

In presenting its report on the Children's Home in 1959, the Committee on Benevolences requested:

> That as convenient as possible the Executive Committee of our Convention study the matter of a possibility of the inclusion of our Children's Home in the Cooperative Program with our people and the churches always understanding that designated giving is our privilege.[66]

The matter was referred to the Executive Committee, which Committee named a Study Committee.

On March 15, 1960, the Executive Committee reviewed and approved the report of the Study Committee.[67]

In making the study, information had been secured from 22 [23] Children's Homes across the Southern Baptist Convention. General Manager Warr and Executive Secretary Garrison had provided information, also. The committee reported that it felt at that time it would be unwise to include the Children's Home in the Co-operative Program. The committee instead recommended that sufficient support from Baptist churches to care for all of the needs of the children be given, and that sufficient endowment be raised to care for maintenance of the properties, with money through wills and special gifts being raised to construct new buildings.[68]

The Children's Home had earlier, by request, withdrawn from the Co-operative Program, during the Depression years. This was done with the blessings of the Executive Com-

[64]*The Christian Index*, March 24, 1960, p. 5.

[65]*Minutes, Georgia Baptist Convention*, 1960, p. 91.

[66]*Minutes, Georgia Baptist Convention*, 1959, p. 52.

[67]*The Christian Index*, March 24, 1960, p. 5.

[68]*Minutes, Executive Committee, Georgia Baptist Convention*, March 15, 1960, p. 84; *Minutes, Georgia Baptist Convention*, 1960, p.p. 74, 75.

mittee. From that time, officials of the Home had made it clear that of its own choosing the Home was not included in the Co-operative Program when it made direct appeals to the churches and individuals.

While the Benevolence Committee in its 1959 recommendation believed that inclusion of the Children's Home would be helpful in view of increasing costs, these very cost increases were factors which would have prohibited effective implementation of the suggestion.

A picture of the problem is gained from noting that total expenses for the Children's Home for the year 1960 amounted to $864,122.14.[69] With the exception of the special allocations in 1960 for the Colleges, Baptist Village and the Baptist Student Center at the University of Georgia, which amounted to $433,030,[70] the amount required for the operation of the Children's Home was almost as much as the total for the entire Georgia section of the 1960 budget.[71] If the Children's Home had been included in the budget of the Convention, there would have been no way for the Convention to allocate funds necessary for operation of the Home in the amounts necessary. Therefore, the recommendation by the Executive Committee that the Home continue under its present plan of operation.

Two more requests were to come to the 1960 Convention through the Executive Committee for borrowing funds from the Housing and Home Finance Agency. One request came from Norman to borrow $120,000. A second request was from Baptist Village to borrow 98 per cent of $265,000 for construction of a third unit at Waycross. These requests were granted.[72]

However, the continued requests from the institutions for permission to borrow from federal agencies were beginning to be met with some reservation on the part of some members of the Executive Committee and Georgia Baptists as a

[69]*Minutes, Georgia Baptist Convention,* 1960, p. 135.
[70]*Minutes, Georgia Baptist Convention,* 1959, p. 24.
[71]*Loc. cit.*
[72]*Minutes, Georgia Baptist Convention,* 1960, p. 27.

whole. These requests, although approved, were soon to come to an end when the Convention went on record in 1966 as being against acceptance of any further loans from government agencies on the basis of the principle of separation of church and state and government subsidy in the form of low interest loans.[73]

The warning flag was raised in 1965. Action by the Convention came in the form of approval of a study by the Education Commission, submitted to the Executive Committee, and through the Executive Committee to the Convention. The Education Commission was required to submit any recommendation to the Convention through the Executive Committee.[74] In the same set of recommendations was one, approved by the Executive Committee also, requesting Convention approval of a request from Mercer University to borrow $500,000 under provisions of the Government's Higher Education Facilities Act of 1963.[75] Mercer was given approval to borrow the money from a commercial lending agency.[76] [The Education Commission concluded that it was unwise for the Convention to approve borrowing of monies from governmental agencies.] [77]

The report of the Social Service Commission in 1960 was rejected by the Convention after extended discussion, and a one-paragraph substitute was offered in place of the entire report. The report was primarily in the area of race relations, and the Commission recommended that Georgia Baptists give prayerful thought to the matter in the light of biblical teaching; that local churches attempt to repair the goodwill between the races which had been damaged in recent years; and 3. that Baptists as individuals seek to harmonize their religious convictions with federal court rulings on the subject and if the two were irreconcilable then to seek some alternative ". . . that will conform to faith and

[73]*Minutes, Georgia Baptist Convention*, 1966, p. 25.
[74]*Op. cit.*
[75]*Minutes, Georgia Baptist Convention*, 1965, p. 111.
[76]*Ibid.*, p.p. 23, 116-118.
[77]*Ibid.*, p.p. 116-118.

continues our position as law-abiding citizens." [78] Following lengthy discussion upon these basic concepts in the Social Service Commission report, a substitute for the entire report was offered by Louie D. Newton, and adopted.[79]

The substitute report said:

> Believing that our public schools are essential in the preservation of our democratic way of life, we, . . . do hereby earnestly and respectfully petition the Governor and the General Assembly, and all other responsible state, county, municipal and district officials to take such steps as will, in their wisdom, insure the continuing ministry of our public school system to the children and young people of our state; and we hereby pledge our prayerful, sympathetic cooperation.[80]

COMMISSION ABOLISHED

Following this report of the Social Service Commission, and adoption of the substitute on Tuesday evening, at the Wednesday morning session a motion was made by Joe S. Holliday that the Commission be discontinued and the motion carried by ". . . a standing count." [81]

Through 1959, $2,025,816.10 had been made available on a matching basis to the six colleges from Cooperative Program receipts. From the 1959 budget alone $541,767.88 was made available to the colleges,[82] meaning that in a five-year period, 1955 through 1959, more than $4,000,000 had gone to the institutions through Cooperative Program funds matched by these institutions for Capital Improvements and repairs.

In September, 1959, the Executive Committee gave its endorsement to a proposed Chapel of All Faiths to be erected at Milledgeville State Hospital.[83]

[78]*Minutes, Georgia Baptist Convention*, 1960, p. 105.

[79]*Ibid.*, p. 33.

[80]*Loc. cit.*

[81]*Ibid.*, p. 35.

[82]*Ibid.*, p. 73.

[83]*The Christian Index*, September 17, 1959, p. 3.

The resolution was reaffirmed by the Executive Committee in September, 1960.[84]

In reporting to the Convention in 1960 on actions between Convention sessions, this resolution was cited along with a report that through September, 1960, designated gifts from Georgia Baptist churches in the amount of $56,860.85 had been received toward construction of the Chapel of All Faiths.[85]

Georgia Baptists had historically expressed interest in projects which could have a meaningful, Spiritual impact upon people within the state, whether Baptist or not. The support of the fund drive for the Chapel of All Faiths indicated the readiness of the churches to continue in this tradition.

Moreover, the Convention in 1960 approved a request from the Colorado Convention asking that the state of Wyoming be adopted by Georgia as an area in which Georgia churches could cooperate in mission work and encouraged Georgia churches to assist in direct mission gifts to missions and new churches in the state of Wyoming.[86]

Following 1958 approval by the Convention of the fund raising effort for the proposed Atlanta Baptist College, the Convention returned to the matter in 1960; adopting recommendations which were an amendment to the original agreement with the Convention.

There was some disagreement as to the ultimate common objective if Mercer was to serve as a parent to the Atlanta college, which would be a coordinate campus of Mercer. The recommendations, therefore, included provisions that the college would be a college of Mercer University and would be staffed, operated, and administered by the Board of Mercer University, with eight members of the Mercer Trustees to be chosen from the Atlanta Association. These eight Trustees would become a standing committee of the

[84]*Minutes, Georgia Baptist Convention,* 1960, p. 79.
[85]*Loc. cit.*
[86]*Ibid.,* p. 27; *The Christian Index,* Nov. 24, 1960, p. 8.

Corporation of Mercer University to give especial oversight to the Atlanta College.

Additionally, the Atlanta Association would have responsibility for raising capital funds necessary to procure a land site and construct an administration and classroom building. At that time, the cost for such a building was estimated at $1,000,000 with the building and construction under the direction of Mercer Trustees.[87]

The college then would begin with a Freshman year, to be followed by a Sophomore year, with the junior and senior years added on the basis of need and resources available, to be determined by the Mercer trustees and approved by the Georgia Baptist Convention. It was agreed at that time that resident facilities for boarding students would not be erected until the college had operated long enough to demonstrate a need for such facilities.

Finally, Mercer Trustees would expect the Atlanta Association to raise an initial $600,000 for endowment and to pledge to raise an additional $500,000 at a later date, depositing $100,000 in cash to cover any operating deficit during the first years of operation.[88]

The original Capital Improvements program was nearing completion. The Executive Committee, early in 1960, learned that at the rate of attainment, the Capital Improvements Program would be completed during 1961. Therefore, a study was made by the Executive Committee, out of which study came a recommendation for a Capital Improvements and Endowment Program to begin immediately upon completion of the current Capital Improvements program. Goal for the future Capital Improvements and Endowment Program was to be $5,710,000, with efforts made to complete the program within six years. The matching provision of the Capital Improvements Program was to be continued. Areas which had been included in the Capital Improvements Program, such as the Baptist Student Center project at the

[87]*Minutes, Georgia Baptist Convention*, 1960, p.p. 92, 93.
[88]*Ibid.*, p.p. 93, 94.

University of Georgia, and *The Christian Index* would not be required to match monies allocated to them. This second program was approved by the Convention,[89] and got under way in 1961.[90]

State Missions programs continued to grow. During 1960, 199 workers had served in the various State Missions programs. Included in the number were 104 mission pastors, 32 associational missionaries, two area missionaries, and five superintendents of city missions, who had received salary supplements from State Mission funds. The State Mission budget for the year had been $469,300.00, of which $360,000 had been provided from the Cooperative Program budget. Special offerings by Woman's Missionary Union during the State Missions season of prayer, and by the Sunday Schools on State Missions day provided additional operational income for the State Missions program.[91]

By 1960, the Georgia Baptist Hospital was the second largest private hospital in the state and for several years more patients had been hospitalized, excluding new born infants, than at any other hospital in Georgia.[92] Contributions for all causes in Georgia rose again during 1960, with total receipts of $5,610,445.54, of which amount $3,333,526.87 was for the Cooperative Program undesignated.[93]

The year 1960 marked a six-year period of unparalleled growth upon the part of Georgia Baptist institutions, programs and ministries. There was a "new wave" of enthusiasm, and a new period of cooperative ministries which to this point was marred only by some dissension concerning the role of the Social Service Commission and the pronouncements which that Commission made in the area of race relations.

During this time, the internal organization of the Executive Committee's staff was being strengthened. Upon his

[89]*Ibid.*, p.p. 94, 95.
[90]*Minutes, Georgia Baptist Convention,* 1962, p. 84.
[91]*Minutes, Georgia Baptist Convention,* 1960, p. 109.
[92]*Ibid.*, p. 136.
[93]*Ibid.*, p. 199.

election as executive secretary, Garrison had organized the departmental secretaries into a staff, with scheduled monthly meetings for evaluations of the assigned programs of work and for suggestions and planning sessions of future endeavors. The areas of associational and city missions were being given not only intensive co-operation, but were being strengthened with increased funds, and by increased support from the State Missions Departments.

The Capital Improvements Program, begun with the 1955 budget year, had provided monies for educational institutions beyond that which was anticipated when the campaign was begun on January 1, 1955. This Capital Improvements program had the effect of providing additional motivation to the institutional heads to seek from private foundations, corporations, and individuals, especially from alumni, monies to match the allocations from the Convention.

Moving into 1961, therefore, the Georgia Baptist Convention entered into a new decade of advance.

CHAPTER 27

Problems Concerning Use of Federal Funds

During the first half of the 1960's two problems especially were vexatious to Georgia Baptists, and defied easy solution. One was that of acceptance of loans from governmental agencies for construction of buildings on property of institutions owned by the Georgia Baptist Convention. The second was that of seeking to steer a course in the area of work of the Christian Life Commission in order that Biblical teachings might be underscored and upheld and at the same time not create a climate of dissolution and strife in an area where there was wide disagreement upon the part of many Baptists in fellowship with the churches in the Convention.

While Georgia Baptists were, during this time, upon occasion, accused of being more concerned with the Co-operative Program dollar than speaking out on "vital" issues, such was not, as a matter of record, the case at all.

The primary concerns of the Georgia Baptist Convention during the 1960's was unchanged basically from primary concerns of preceding generations going back to the Convention's beginnings in 1822; that of providing an effective channel of witness and service to advance the Kingdom of God. Therefore, with a basic recognition of the principal purpose for organized work, Convention leadership sought diligently to create and maintain an atmosphere of harmony and unity in which progress in every area might be maintained, and at the same time speak with Christian boldness—yet with compassion—to the needs of a people in a changing and rapidly segmenting society. For, it was recognized that if a strong witness was to be maintained and continued, then the co-operation of the churches and the associations must be focused on the great basic principles upon which the Georgia Baptist Convention had stood historically.

Evident, therefore, in the record of this decade was the caution which accompanied the boldness of the Convention in plans for continued outreach. Evident also during this period was the fact that in the main, Georgia Baptists were determined that a heritage, then 140 years old, would not be splintered by dissension.

Questions which revolved around the matter of use of loans from the Federal Government were not, in the final analysis, centered in the matter of church-state relations alone. The very fact that Georgia Baptists, over a seven-year period approved such loans, documents this point. The larger question, as indicated in reports and minute records, was the underlying concern for Christian education, and providing the means to support this area of ministry in the light of changing economic conditions, and inflationary trends. The Capital Improvements Program from 1955 through 1960 had demonstrated amply that Georgia Baptists could, when challenged, provide increased support for their institutions. However, even with the increase for capital improvements, and subsequently, for endowment, on a matching basis, the matter of institutional support still was one of grave concern.

This particular problem was complicated further by the increased emphasis upon the establishment of community state colleges throughout Georgia, which colleges were able to offer tuition and board at costs far less, upon the surface, than at denominationally-owned institutions.

There were other large programs of activity to be under way during the period 1961-1965. These included the establishment of an entirely new campus for the Hapeville branch of the Georgia Baptist Children's Home; the acquisition in

1963 of the Lake Louise Bible Conference Grounds for development as a Georgia Baptist Assembly, settling a question which had been discussed off and on for 54 years.

Baptist Village, at Waycross, was continuing to seek means of an enlarged ministry, and this effort also was to cross the line and enter into the discussion regarding loans from the Federal Government. Complicating further the structure for growth was the increased emphasis during the early 1960's in the Atlanta area for establishment of a Baptist college.

During World War II, many Georgia Baptist churches wanted to build new facilities, and could not do so because of war-time restrictions upon construction. The boom in building by Georgia Baptist churches which followed the end of the war in 1945, and the consequent availability of materials, continued through the 1950's and into the 1960's, creating a growing preoccupation with needs of the local church which left less time for preoccupation with the affairs of the Convention, and less money to be channeled into denominational efforts. The churches not only were increasing their buildings, but they were adding staffs at a record rate during the 1960's.

Further, the Georgia Baptist Hospital, in need of providing necessary facilities, was in a continuous program of expansion, either in actuality or in the planning stages. In the light of these factors, therefore, the denominational leadership was constrained to exercise astute leadership in keeping the channels of cooperation open and providing opportunity for continued growth.

A growing move toward independent churches was another factor during the decade of the 1960's which must be kept in focus. With the sentiment of the times one of independence and at times isolation, churches and church leadership upon occasion declined in their historic cooperation with the denomination.

Two other forces were at work among Georgia Baptists which made difficult the sustained advance which was accomplished, which forces had existed at no other time in the history of the Convention: Frustration over the rapidly changing public school system, or threats thereof, which could not be expressed in terms of action to reverse the trends, expressed itself in denominational life. Not since the reconstruction days of the 1870's had Georgia Baptists—and Georgians as a whole, reacted against governmental authority —if not overtly, in terms of resentment, which resentment carried over into other areas of their lives. The hand of authority, which independent congregations had resented historically, was evident from governmental levels. This resulted in a spirit which expressed freedom—and one area alone in which this expression could continue unchallenged, was in the area of religious expression, and denominational life. Georgia Baptists—and the Convention—had weathered in unity the early days of indecision following the decision of the Supreme Court on integration in the public schools, largely because no time element was set. As orders at the Lower Court levels began to spell out the growing curbs and the coming events, this too, evidently had its impact upon attitudes by Georgia Baptists. Actions concerning acceptance of federal loans, therefore, may not be linked exclusively to the matter of a principle of separation of church and state. They were, based upon observation of the decade, linked to resentment at what was considered unwarranted government intrusion into state and county and local affairs.

A second force was that the denominational press as well as the secular press during the 1960's indicated clearly that there was a growing concern over what was termed increasing liberalism within the traditionally conservative denomination. Georgia, in the heart of the original Southern states forming the Convention in 1845, had been considered conservative theologically, and properly so. Therefore, as shifts in emphases in literature and programs at the Southern Convention level became obvious, these shifts were met by some Georgians with opposition. Having abolished its own Social Service Commission in 1960, and the next year setting up a Christian Life Commission with several fences around it, some Georgia churches were disenchanted with statements and declarations enunciated at the Southwide level. This further complicated the problem of keeping the state Convention united and progressing.

It is in the light of these complex trends that Georgia Baptists made their significant gains during the 1960's and into the first part of the 1970's. These trends related to the events of the period, lend themselves to presentation in a manner different than the previous 140 years of the history are treated. These are recounted by areas of interest.

EDUCATIONAL TRENDS

Educational life in Georgia was affected by educational trends, inflation and the issue of separation of church and state from 1958 to the present. The issues were interwoven, and the complexities of the educational picture began in 1958 when both Mercer University and Bessie Tift college obtained direct loans from the Federal government with the endorsement of the Executive Committee and with Convention approval.[1] Mercer borrowed $750,000.00 for campus construction, and Tift secured $200,000 to erect a dormitory.[2]

In 1960, the trend continued, with the Executive Committee securing a loan of $1,750,000.00 for its hospital; Norman securing $120,000.00 for a cafeteria, and Baptist Village, $260,000.00 for a housing unit; all from Federal lending agencies.[3] The Convention in 1960 expressed commendation to President-Elect John F. Kennedy for his declared ". . . position of his support of the historic and established principle of separation of Church And State, . . .",[4] but said nothing against the borrowing of money from the government, rather granting authorization for such loans.[5]

Again, in 1961, the Executive Committee and the Convention authorized applications for government loans. These

[1]*Minutes, Georgia Baptist Convention,* 1964, p. 132.
[2]*Loc. cit.*
[3]*Loc. cit.; Georgia Baptist Convention Minutes,* 1960, p.p. 27, 91.
[4]*Minutes, Georgia Baptist Convention,* 1960, p. 45.
[5]*Op. cit., Minutes, Georgia Baptist Convention,* 1960.

were for Shorter College, $650,000.00; Tift College, $200,000.00; Norman College, $300,000.00; Mercer University, $604,000.00; and Baptist Village, $600,000.00.[6]

HELD NOT IN VIOLATION

At this session [1961] the matter of borrowing government money was questioned from the floor. In reply, Executive Secretary Garrison declared that:

> . . . in the judgment of those making the recommendation the principle of separation of church and state was not violated since the Federal Government makes no grant, but makes it possible to secure money at a low rate of interest.[7]

No motion was made concerning the matter, but it was not to be quiescent. In this year, the indebtedness of Georgia Baptist institutions was $3,437,000.00 as of September 1; and this did not include the $2,500,000.00, authorized in 1960 for the dormitory for the School of Nursing at the Hospital. [The action on the hospital loan was not completed until after the September 1 report.][8] By the end of the year, however, the total indebtedness, including $1,750,000.00 for the Hospital, was $4,187,000.00.[9]

Georgia Baptist institutions, during the period when monies were borrowed from the Federal government, were, from a business standpoint, saving money in that the loans carried rates of interest about half that of commercial lending agencies. By 1966, the matter was clearly a major problem for Georgia Baptists. Extent of the problem was reflected in action taken at the Pre-Convention meeting of the Executive Commitee. Citing previous loans authorized, and noting that other institutions were making requests for authority to borrow money from the government, the Executive Committee came to the Convention with recommendations that a policy

[6]*Minutes, Georgia Baptist Convention,* 1961, p.p. 34, 82-83, 95.

[7]*Ibid.,* p.p. 29, 30.

[8]*Ibid.,* p. 79.

[9]*Ibid.,* p. 78.

be adopted by the Convention in the matter.[10] The recommendations were:

> 1. That the Georgia Baptist Convention as a policy approve the securing of long-term, low interest loans from public funds for construction of buildings by Georgia Baptist institutions provided the rate of interest paid is equal to the cost of the government in making the loan plus one-fourth of one per cent per annum for administrative costs.
> 2. That should the interest paid by any Georgia Baptist institution in any year be less than the Treasury Department Estimate of Cost, plus one-fourth of one per cent, that the institution pay the government at the close of the year an amount equal to the deficiency.[11]

The report of the Executive Committee was the principal item of business for the first full day's session in Columbus. Recommendation eight from the Executive Committee was the request for a statement of policy in the matter. It was deferred until the afternoon session during Miscellaneous Business, at which time it was voted upon by secret ballot, and was defeated by a vote of 761 to 388.[12]

Between the time the matter was questioned first on the Convention floor and the action by the Convention in 1966, the issue was to be one which was a constant irritant in the life of the Convention. The colleges were troubled increasingly by inflation. The Cornett study for the Education Commission and that Commission's report had set guide lines for proper financing and administration of the Convention's educational institutions, with ratios suggested for operational costs, among other things.[13] Discussion upon the motion to decide upon a policy was lengthy,[14] and at times acrimonious. By this year, total indebtedness of Convention institutions was $7,421,621.45, with repayment scheduled into the 21st century for some of the loans. Of the total indebtedness, $5,922,000.00 was to the Federal Government.[15]

[10]*Minutes, Georgia Baptist Convention,* 1966, p. 34.
[11]*Ibid.,* p. 35.
[12]*Ibid.,* p. 25.
[13]*Op. cit.*
[14]*Minutes, Georgia Baptist Convention,* 1966, p. 36.
[15]*Ibid.,* p.p. 102-103.

The years between 1961 and this action were years of expansion for all Convention institutions. They were being aided in an unparalleled manner by funds from the Capital Improvements and Endowments programs, and some of this money was being applied by the institutions toward repayment of their loans. In 1962, the Convention met in the sanctuary of the Mabel White Baptist church in Macon. At the morning session of the first full day, William Anglin, who questioned the matter in 1961, raised the issue again. This time, he was joined by others who voiced objection also. The matter was deferred for consideration until the night session.[16] At the evening session, William R. Anglin moved that the action authorizing colleges to borrow money at low interest rates be rescinded, the motion received several seconds. The minutes of the proceedings do not indicate the Hospital and Baptist Village as being included in the motion, although at the time the Hospital had a loan in the amount of $1,750,000.00 from the Housing and Home Finance Agency, and Baptist Village had authorizations for similar loans from the 1960 and the 1961 conventions.

The discussion on the matter lasted until nearly midnight, at which time a vote sustained the policy of the Executive Commitee ". . . by a substantial majority".[17] After the matter was raised in 1961, the Executive Committee, at its March, 1962 session, appointed a Committee of Five to make a study of the matter. Included on this committee were Louie D. Newton and Dick H. Hall, Jr., both long-time advocates of the principle of complete separation of church and state. The report of the Committee of Five was approved by the Executive Committee in September, 1962.[18]

The Committee based its study upon existing conditions and the enabling act, the College Housing Program, Title IV, Housing Acts of 1950, as amended. The Committee report sustained the judgment of the Executive Committee in the policy of permitting loans, and included in its report

[16]*Minutes, Georgia Baptist Convention,* 1962, p. 25.
[17]*Ibid.,* p. 33.
[18]*Ibid.,* p. 94.

suggestions made by the organization Protestants and Other Americans United For Separation of Church And State to safeguard principles of separation while executing loans.[19] The Executive Committee report to the Convention for 1962 contained information about the study as well as reports of authorization for loans of a similar nature to Truett-McConnell College, Brewton-Parker College and Mercer University, the amount totalling $2,000,000.00.[20]

The picture became somewhat more complicated by 1963, especially with regard to Mercer University, which by then had become an object of some vocal attack upon the part of some Georgia Baptists, as had been the case historically. Several factors entered into the matter. One, Mercer in 1963 had become integrated racially. There was criticism at this point. Major changes were occurring as a new administration was reshaping the internal affairs at the University. Enrolment of ministerial students had declined. And, Mercer had secured authorization for loans in amounts greater than all other institutions, as might be expected because of its size.

Therefore, three factors were involved, but nothing was done about the matter at the Convention meeting at the Bull Street Baptist church in Savannah in 1963. A motion by W. M. Marshall—an amendment to the budget—which called for elimination of the $105,345.00 allocation in the 1964 budget for Mercer, was defeated.[21] A motion urging Mercer's trustees and administration to reconsider the advisability of securing loans from a federal agency "at this time" was referred to the Committee on Resolutions.[22] The Resolutions Committee reported later that the loan in question had been consummated, and the essence of the motion was conveyed to Mercer authorities.[23]

The report on Christian Education for that year contained two observations which applied to the situation. The Com-

[19]*Ibid.*, p. 95.
[20]*Ibid.*, p.p. 95-96.
[21]*Minutes, Georgia Baptist Convention,* 1963, p. 25.
[22]*Ibid.*, p. 32.
[23]*Ibid.*, p.p. 47, 48.

mittee making that report said that for the present, the institutions were meeting their financial obligations and were solvent. However, the report declared

> . . . the time has come when we, as a Convention, must realistically appraise our entire educational program and make whatever changes that will insure the future of Georgia Baptists as a factor in providing a Christian atmosphere for our young people to acquire a quicker grasp of experience which we call education.[24]

By 1964, the picture had changed somewhat. The Christian Life Commission for that year made a study in the area of "Religious Liberty And Separation of Church and State." As one area of its report, the Commission dealt with the historic position of the Convention in the area of church-state relations. The report, received as information by the Convention, requiring neither approval nor disapproval, and dealing in the area of national problems, said in part:

> (2) In recent years, the Federal Government has made large grants to church and religious institutions. The 1963 Higher Education Facilities Act, Public Law 88-204, briefly stated, makes available matching grants from the federal government for construction, rehabilitation, or improvement of needed academic facilities. The Separation of Church and State is involved and our problem is that of the principle and not the details of the act.[25]

Provisions of the Higher Education Facilities Act were, as indicated, provisions for grants. Loans came through other programs.

Concluding observations of this Commission were:

> (1) It is the opinion of the Christian Life Commission that we should be willing to uphold the principle of separation of church and state and should continue to apply it as we undertake to make decisions which could directly or indirectly adversely affect the religious liberty of our people or of any people.
> (3) This Commission also holds the opinion that the acceptance by local churches and associations of gratuities from local units of government is a violation of the historic principle of separation of church and state.
> (4) Your Commission believes that we are in danger of

[24]*Ibid.*, p. 34.
[25]*Minutes, Georgia Baptist Convention*, 1964, p. 133.

sacrificing our historic principles of separation of church
and state due to pressures to accept governmental sub-
sidies.

(6) Also, the acceptance of federal funds will blind our
people to their responsibility to provide for their own
needs.[26]

While dealing in the area, the report of the Christian Life
Commission skirted in specific wording the issue of acceptance of loans, dealing rather with provisions for grants.

PUBLIC HEARINGS CONDUCTED

Sentiment against the matter, had, therefore, been building
for several years. In 1965, Mercer University was the only
institution seeking authority to secure a loan from the Federal Government. This was in a recommendation from the
Executive Committee that the Convention grant Mercer
approval to execute a $500,000.00 loan under provisions of
the Higher Education Facilities Act of 1963.[27] This recommendation was not approved, and instead, Mercer was
granted authority to borrow the money from a commercial
lending agency.[28] Other institutions, looking obviously into
the future, during 1964 and 1965 completed loans authorized
by earlier Conventions. Truett-McConnell advised the Executive Committee in March of 1965 that it was exercising
authority to negotiate a loan authorized in 1962.[29]

During 1965, the Education Commission had taken the
unusual step of holding public hearings at four strategic
centers in Georgia. These hearings, afternoon and evening
sessions, were devoted to obtaining views from all areas of
Convention life concerning the matter of federal loans and
grants to Convention institutions. These hearings, well attended, together with information obtained from several

[26]*Ibid.,* p.p. 133, 134. [Note: the report of this Commission for this year
traces the actions of the Convention in the area of church and state to a
limited degree, and the complete study, contained in the minutes of the
Convention for 1964, p.p. 126-134, provides basic study material.]

[27]*Minutes, Georgia Baptist Convention,* 1965, p. 111.

[28]*Loc. cit.*

[29]*Ibid.,* p. 88.

sources, provided the Education Commission with materials and information for a report submitted to the Administration Committee of the Executive Committee in October, 1965.[30]

Substance of the opinion of the Education Commission was that prevailing sentiment among Georgia Baptists was such that the Commission felt it

> is not wise in view of prevailing opinion for the Georgia Baptist Convention to approve acceptance of grants from the Federal Government by Georgia Baptist colleges. . . .[31]

These hearings marked the first time since the Convention held similar meetings in the 1830's at Forsyth to discuss with the Primitive Baptists their respective positions, that there had been such public hearings on a matter, in-so-far as records indicate.

These hearings, at Cartersville, Madison, Cordele and Statesboro, drew a total attendance of about 415, with 73 speakers opposing grants and eight in favor of grants at the hearings.[32] The week after they ended, Hurt declared editorially in *The Christian Index* that the then new Capital Improvements program provided part of the answer, and that "We will sell Georgia Baptists on their six Georgia schools or we fail. We should start now." [33] Sentiment of Georgia Baptists in this area was crystalizing rapidly. The word "grant" rather than the word "loan" was used frequently at the hearings, although the matter of loans was actually the matter under primary discussion. The lines of delineation had merged.

One other factor was the reply during 1965 to a memorial to the 1964 Convention from the Noonday Association, referred to the resolutions Committee, and subsequently to the

[30]*Ibid.*, p. 116. [Note: Tape recordings were made of the positions of many Baptists speaking at these hearings and were deposited with the Education Commission following the hearings, for future reference and study; the author having made the recordings at the request of the Commission.]

[31]*Ibid.*, p. 118.

[32]*The Christian Index*, September 23, 1965, p. 5; September 30, 1965, p. 3.

[33]*The Christian Index*, October 7, 1965, p. 6.

college presidents. The memorial from the Noonday requested the colleges to state doctrinal positions and the type of textbooks used.[34]

This memorial, in essence, was a request for the colleges to assert their loyalty to historic Baptist doctrine and polity. At the September hearings by the Education Commission, the issue of doctrinal loyalty was injected upon more than one occasion into the matter of federal grants [loans.][35] The assertion of loyalty to Baptist doctrine by all of the colleges, in detailed reports to the Convention,[36] together with Education Commission hearings, had the effect of quieting to some extent the more vocal opposition to the colleges. However, the stage was set clearly for the Executive Committee to ask for a statement of policy from the 1966 Convention, which Convention rejected the idea of acceptance of further government loans.[37]

The Convention's action in November, 1966, rejecting the Executive Committee's recommendation of continued approval for loans from the Government, was to be followed in less than a month by a proposal from the Board of Trustees of Mercer University [December 3, 1966] requesting the Executive Committee to name a study committee of pastors and laymen to consider ". . . the future financing of Christian education in Georgia Baptist Colleges, . . ." and asked that the committee report its findings to a special called session of the Convention.[38] The Education Commission and the Administration Committee of The Executive Committee considered the proposal, made a study, and presented recommendations to the Exectuive Committee, which that Com-

[34]*Minutes, Georgia Baptist Convention,* 1965, pp. 138-141; *Minutes, Georgia Baptist Convention,* 1964, p.p. 31, 47.

[35]*The Christian Index,* November 18, 1965, p. 3.

[36]*Minutes, Georgia Baptist Convention,* 1965, p.p. 139-146; *The Christian Index,* November 18, 1965, p. 3.

[37]*Minutes, Georgia Baptist Convention,* 1966, p. 25.

[38]*Minutes, Georgia Baptist Convention,* 1967, p. 131.

[39]*Loc. cit.*

mittee accepted,[39] and which the Convention approved in 1967.[40]

Essentials of the study called for recognition of the needs of the colleges for immediate, increased assistance from Georgia Baptists; encouraged churches and individuals to make direct contributions to the colleges; recommended cooperation with the Best Education Study Task, then under way and sponsored by the Education Commission of the Southern Baptist Convention; and suggested that there was no need for a special session of the convention. It was recommended further that studies of methods of future support be left with the Executive Committee and the Education Commission, to which groups the responsibility was assigned already.[41] Out of a study made by the Education Commission, and a request to the Budget Committee, came a recommendation from the Budget Committee which called for a 24 per cent increase in appropriations for operating expenses for the colleges for the year 1968. This amounted to $97,000,000,[42] and was approved along with other budgeted amounts. Further consideration of the BEST study was on the Convention's agenda for January, 1968.[43]

The matter was not yet closed. With rejection of its request of December, 1966, for a special called session of the Convention, and with the report of the Education Commission adopted by the Convention in 1967, the Mercer trustees on January 25, 1968, adopted a resolution. The action cited Convention actions in past years, and also an amendment to Standard Two of the Commission on Colleges Standards of Accreditation of the Southern Association of Colleges and Schools, declared:

> That the Board of Trustees of the Corporation of Mercer University does hereby resolve that . . . this Board of Trustees will exercise fully its independent judgment in all matters of institutional policy and corporate decision. It further resolves to declare to the aforesaid

[40]*Ibid.*, p. 37.
[41]*Ibid.*, p.p. 131, 132.
[42]*Ibid.*, p. 133.
[43]*Loc. cit.*

Southern Association that while it will welcome the expression of any wish, opinion, or judgment of any person or body of persons on any matters, yet after having considered these the Mercer Trustees as a body will make the decisions on them in accord with their conscience and responsibility as trustees.[44]

Also in January, 1968, Mercer trustees instructed their Executive Committee to consider seeking ". . . all available federal funds and aids, . . ." and report on their study by April.[45] A week prior to the Mercer action, the Atlanta Baptist Association authorized trustees of the Atlanta Baptist college, at a special called meeting of the Association, to seek and accept federal funds. The action, by vote of 487-370, was made prior to opening of the college, scheduled in September, and did not distinguish between federal loans and grants.[46] Action by the Atlanta Association caused some repercussions. Dick H. Hall, Jr., resigned as vice-president of the college the day after the vote by the Association, in protest of the action.[47]

In response to the statement of the Mercer Trustees, the Executive Committee, meeting in March, 1968, adopted a lengthy statement which had the effect of reminding the Mercer trustees that the Convention still elected the Trustees of the institution, which was established by the Convention, and would coninue to do so.[48] Allen B. Comish, Columbus, at that time chairman of the Executive Committee, said: ". . . this resolution is friendly, a reminder of our historic relationship with Mercer."[49]

HISTORIC TIES CITED

The resolution cited the historic ties between the Convention and its University, the support accorded the institution over the years, and the fact that neither the Executive Com-

[44]Copy of Resolution, author's possession, dated February 7, 1968.
[45]*The Christian Index*, February 1, 1968, p. 3.
[46]*The Christian Index*, January 25, 1968, p. 3.
[47]*Loc. cit.*
[48]*The Christian Index*, March 28, 1968, p. 3; Copy of resolution, author's possession.
[49]*Loc. cit.*

mittee nor the Convention had sought to prevent the trustees from exercising their rights and responsibilities. It concluded by stating that the Executive Committee reaffirmed its desire ". . . to strengthen Mercer University for the purpose for which it was established, and for the ministry for which it is supported by Georgia Baptist people through the convention." [50] The Mercer trustees, meeting in April, deferred any decision on seeking and accepting federal funds until the Convention completed a study of the educational needs of the convention.[51] The study referred to was a study authorized by the Executive Committee in September, 1967,[52] and made by the Associated Consultants in Education, Inc., Tallahassee, Florida, headed by Doak S. Campbell.[53] The study was presented to the Education Commission and the Administration Committee in July, 1968.[54]

Guide lines of the Campbell report included:

A. The Baptists of Georgia are committed to the proposition that higher education is an integral part of the Christian witness.
B. Expenditures for the current operation of the Baptist colleges will increase from 5 to 7% each year until 1975-1976.
C. The minimum of productive endowment funds should be at least $4,000.00 per equivalent full-time student.[55]

A special committee was set up to evaluate the Campbell report. This committee then made recommendations, endorsed by the Executive Committee and approved by the Convention with one amendment.[56]

Recommendations to the Convention included recognition of the Capital Improvements and Endowment Program, in operation in Georgia for nearly 14 years, which most states did not have. It recommended increased support by Baptists,

[50]Copy of Document, author's possession.
[51]*The Christian Index*, April 25, 1968, p. 3.
[52]*Minutes, Georgia Baptist Convention*, 1968, p. 111.
[53]*Ibid.*, p. 133.
[54]*Ibid.*, p. 111.
[55]*Ibid.*, p. 113.
[56]*Ibid.*, p.p. 111, 112.

and the three guide lines of the Campbell report which are listed above.[57] The recommendation, which included one paragraph concerning seeking monies, was amended from the floor to insure that ". . . no monies shall be sought or accepted from Government tax funds." [58]

There still was more to come upon the subject. During this period when relations between the Convention and Mercer appeared strained, the matter occupied much interest, attention and discussion by Georgia Baptists.

In the light of the continuing actions in the field of education, the Executive Committee on September 10, 1968, approved a study of its Education Commission by a committee which would ". . . bring back to the Executive Committee any recommendations which the committee might find necessary." [59] This Study Committee presented the conclusions that the Commission was rendering service

> . . . in harmony with the organizational structure of the Convention and the colleges. It is the considered opinion of the Committee that administrative authority over the Baptist Colleges is neither desirable nor practical.

The report reaffirmed that the Commission remain as currently structured.[60] The Convention confirmed this study[61]

By this time, the matter of institutional control by the Convention had developed into a major issue. At a meeting held at the Georgia Baptist Assembly, Toccoa, on March 31, 1969, Searcy S. Garrison, Executive Secretary, presented a document to the 1969 conference for institutional trustees and members of the Executive Committee. Entitled *Institutions In The Work of Georgia Baptists,* and in the fashion of some circular letters by Jesse Mercer on the subject of education, Garrison traced the historic concept of Christian education, Baptist concepts of cooperative work, characteristics of Baptist institutions, and concluded by declaring:

[57]*Ibid.,* p. 113.
[58]*Ibid.,* p. 30.
[59]*Document, Report of Committee, Author's Possession.*
[60]*Loc. cit.*
[61]*Minutes, Georgia Baptist Convention,* 1969, p. 95.

In recent years Baptist institutions have been the subject of considerable discussion and disagreement. The debate has the potential of becoming conflict which will certainly disturb the fellowship, adversely affect our cooperative work, and compromise our Baptist witness. Such results would be tragic beyond words to describe, and must be avoided by all who share concern for the ministries, good name and institutional life of the denomination. . . .

Baptists must understand and accept the organizational structure of their institutions:

Baptist institutions are not churches, or Sunday schools, or mission societies, even though they receive support from these organizations and contribute to their strength and progress.

Denominational institutions are not subject to the direct management of the churches or associations, nor of the Convention.

Denominational institutions are quasi-public corporations which must be operated in accord with the provision of the charter granted by the state, by the laws and public policy of the state, as well as under policies and for objectives established by the parent body and sustaining constituency.

To fail to recognize this basic organizational concept will result ultimately in the loss of all Baptist institutions, and retirement to our churches for educational and benevolent work as well as for worship and fellowship activities. A failure to accept institutions for what they are in fact and law will restrict even mission operations as now conducted by Baptists [schools and hospitals are operated in mission programs at home and abroad]. To understand the quasi-public character of these institutions is to provide a basis for resolving the problems which currently trouble our Baptist people.

Let all who share responsibility for the operation of Baptist institutions realize that they are stewards and servants, and as such, responsible to many persons, groups, and organizations who share interest, concern, and rights in these institutions.

A responsible officer of a Baptist convention or institution, whether president, secretary, or executive officer, or whether trustee, or administrator, or employee, can not do always what he wants to do—when he wants to do it—even though he may think it desirable at the time. Responsible action requires consideration for the interests and rights of all who share in the operation and support of institutions, and the well-being of the whole enterprise of which the institution is a part.

> Let us realize that while many, with sometimes conflict-
> ing points of view and with a complex organizational
> structure, we Georgia Baptists are yet one body, and the
> health and well-being of the whole denomination de-
> pends upon the proper function and well-being of each
> institution.[62]

Garrison's address followed less than two months a vote by the Mercer trustees [February 7, 1969] that the University would seek grants from agencies of the Federal Government in the amount of $570,000.00.[63]

The Administration Committee, in a document dated April 1, 1969, and presented to the Executive Committee the day after Garrison's address to the institutional Trustees and Executive Committee members, said:

> 1. The circumstances in which Georgia Baptists find
> themselves require patience, thoughtful consideration,
> prayer and restraint on the part of all responsible per-
> sons, boards and committees.
> 2. The action of the Board of Trustees of Mercer Uni-
> versity in voting to accept grants . . . is not considered
> to be in the best interests of the fellowship, interests and
> total program of the work of the Georgia Baptist Con-
> vention.[64]

The paper, adopted by the Executive Committee, then recommended that the Mercer trustees be prepared to report to the Convention in 1969 concerning the application for grants from the Government.[65]

At the 1969 Convention in Atlanta, the Board of Trustees of Mercer University, through W. Chas Smith, III, a trustee, presented a printed report to the Convention. In this state-ment, the trustees cited their action concerning application for federal grants; the past history of acceptance of grants by Georgia Baptist institutions; the role of trustees in decision

[62]*Document,* address delivered March 31, 1969, Author's Possession.

[63]Document; Statement of Administration Committee In Reply; *Minutes, Georgia Baptist Convention,* 1969, p.p. 97-102.

[64]*Document,* Author's Possession, pp. 3, 4, *Concerning the Action of the Board of Trustees of Mercer University In Voting to Accept Grants From Federal Government Agencies; Minutes Georgia Baptist Convention,* 1969, p. 100.

[65]*Ibid.,* p. 5; *Minutes, Georgia Baptist Convention,* 1969, p. 102.

making; and said: "Many people either do not realize or refuse to admit that Mercer is confronted with a serious financial crisis." [66]

The trustees denied in the report that their action was "defiant," and denied further that Mercer wished to be separated from the convention.

> "The trustees do *not* want Mercer to be divorced from the Convention, for they take pride in the splendid historic connection between the Georgia Baptist Convention and the University. Mercer is a fine, dedicated Baptist college." [67]

The report expressed gratitude for financial assistance rendered by the Convention, and stated Mercer's purpose, which included the sentence: "Every Baptist college was founded as something of a joint enterprise of church and state. Mercer is not a Baptist church, and should not be expected to operate as a church." [68] The report concluded with the statement which said, in part: "We have sought only to assume the full measure of our responsibilities and duties as trustees. We prayerfully and earnestly solicit your understanding and your support." [69] The report listed 48 Baptist schools in Georgia which had died or were no longer affiliated with Baptists.[70]

Following the reading of the statement, a motion was approved which said that the messengers

> ... reaffirm the principle of the autonomy of the boards of trustees of our institutions, at the same time reminding them that they are officers of this Convention, that we have placed in their keeping these sacred trusts, and that we depend upon them to fulfill their stewardship to the best of their abilities, remembering their commitment to Baptist principles, and to the well-being of our total task of which the institution is a part.[71]

A later motion that the Convention appoint a committee

[66]Printed report, copy in Author's Possession.
[67]*Loc. cit.*
[68]*Loc. cit.*
[69]*Loc. cit.*
[70]*Loc. cit.*
[71]*Minutes, Georgia Baptist Convention,* 1969, p. 28.

of eleven members to begin a special drive to raise $3,000,000.00 in a two year period, after discussion, was referred to the Executive Committee upon a second substitute motion by Allen B. Comish.[72] The Convention then approved by a standing vote a motion that the Convention request trustees of Mercer to delay their application for grants until the Executive Committee reported in 1970 concerning any conclusions on a special fund drive.[73]

STATEMENT OF PURPOSE ISSUED

The Education Commission in 1969 issued a Statement of Purpose of Georgia Baptists in Providing Support for Baptist Colleges. Included in this document of the Committee on Purpose of the Georgia Baptist Convention In Giving Support to Baptist Colleges is the statement:

> Baptists support colleges in the conviction that Christian higher education is essential to providing adequate leadership for the churches and denomination, and in assisting in the education and training of community, state and national leaders.[74]

With the actions of the 1969 Convention, the matter became quiescent. Tensions in this area had begun to dispel by the 1970 Convention. The position paper which Garrison had presented to trustees and members of the Executive Committee in the spring of 1969 had, according to observers, served to create a climate of lessening tensions. The Mercer position paper presented to the Convention, together with the resolution approved by that body, ameloriated attitudes toward the University.

While the controversies swirled around Federal monies, and focused particularly upon Mercer University, the Georgia Baptist Convention had, during these years, been active in a program of Mission endeavor and advance in missions. Every area of activity had advanced, despite the tensions. In

[72]*Ibid.*, 1969, p.p. 35, 36.

[73]*Ibid.*, p.p. 46, 47.

[74]*Ibid.*, p. 121. [Note: Detailed information upon the subject may be found in the Minutes of the Georgia Baptist Convention for 1969, pp. 97-102, 119-121.]

1961, total indebtedness of Georgia Baptist institutions, as of September 1, was $3,437,000.00.[75] As of August 1, 1970, indebtedness had climbed to $7,843,875.46, of which $5,699,-087.03 was for loans secured from the Federal Government.[76]

The Executive Committee considered the proposal for a special fund drive for the educational institutions and reported, in effect, that special appeals were not very productive, were expensive, and that the Capital Improvement and Endowment Programs were ". . . a better way." [77]

Tracing of the difficulties surrounding disagreements on acceptance of federal loans or grants points out two historic facts. 1—The Georgia Baptist Convention and Mercer University were linked so closely by historic ties that the issue was one involving not only a principle but evidencing the proprietary interest which Georgia Baptists had in the University. 2—The action demonstrated again that when matters related to education were being studied, other Georgia Baptist educational institutions remained in the wings, as it were, waiting for the basic issues to be resolved between Mercer and the Convention. It was almost as if the shadow of the Mercer System of Colleges lingered still, and to a degree it did.

When the Convention met on Jekyll Island in 1971, there was no issue dealing with education as controversy. The only action concerning an institution was Convention approval of acceptance of Norman College as a South Georgia assembly.

CAPITAL IMPROVEMENTS AND ENDOWMENT PROGRAMS

While Georgia Baptist institutions were seeking additional means of financing their work, a program which began in 1955, and which continues to the present, was, in a unique manner, providing support for these institutions in amounts which had not previously been afforded these causes.

[75]*Minutes, Georgia Baptist Convention,* 1961, p. 79.
[76]*Minutes, Georgia Baptist Convention,* 1970, p. 90.
[77]*Ibid.,* p.p. 91-93.

It all began with a report from the Education Commission to the Convention in 1954, the last year Garrison served as president of the Convention, and the last year Merritt served as executive secretary. A detailed study of the needs of the institutions revealed at the time that $5,562,969.00 was required for capital needs. With this information came the recommendation that $350,000.00 be allocated in the 1956 budget to be used on a matching basis to meet these needs.[78] By 1961, $2,606,805.16 had been made available through this Capital Improvement Program.[79]

> Including funds raised by the colleges and funds made available from Cooperative Program receipts, approximately $5,110,567.64 has been spent on repairs and improvements included in the program adopted by the Convention in 1954.[80]

The program was amended in 1959 to include Baptist Village and Baptist Student Centers.[81]

Response to this challenge had been sufficient to warrant approval by the Convention in 1960 of a new program, to be called the Capital Improvements And Endowment Program, and to be implemented upon completion of the Capital Improvements Program, anticipated during 1961.[82] This second program called for a goal of $5,710,000.00, with the provision that the funds be applied on a matching basis except for limited amounts for *The Christian Index,* and Baptist Student Center Projects.[83] Of the total amount proposed in the new program, $2,680,000.00 was to be for capital improvements, and $3,030,000.00 for endowment [colleges] and construction at the Hospital, Baptist Village, Student Center, and for *Index* reserve.[84] The original goal for the first program was completed before the end of 1961, and the new pro-

[78]*Minutes, Georgia Baptist Convention,* 1954, p. 106. [A full report may be found in Minutes, Georgia Baptist Convention, 1956, p.p. 97-107].

[79]*Minutes, Georgia Baptist Convention,* 1961, p. 77.

[80]*Ibid.,* p. 76.

[81]*Minutes, Georgia Baptist Convention,* 1962, p. 127.

[28]*Minutes, Georgia Baptist Convention,* 1961, p. 76; *Minutes, Georgia Baption Convention,* 1960, p.p. 94-96.

[83]*Minutes, Georgia Baptist Convention,* 1960, p. 95.

[84]*Ibid.,* p. 96.

gram became operative near the end of that year.[85] The
amount of $274,227.84 was applied on the new program out
of 1961 receipts, and $723,814.05 out of 1962 receipts, for a
total of $998,041.80 in about 15 months.[86]

By the end of 1963, $1,795,147.46 had been raised through
the Cooperative Program on this second stage, and the Executive Committee, anticipating conclusion of the program
authorized in 1960, presented to the Convention in 1964 a
recommendation that a new Capital Improvements and
Endowment Program be authorized to begin upon completion of the then current program.[87]

The Convention in 1965 did approve a new program with
a goal of $10,000,000.00, $5,475,000.00 from the Cooperative
Program, with the plan that it be completed in eight years.
This new program was to be a matching one, except for the
same exclusions of the second program, which by this time
included the Georgia Baptist Assembly.[88] This program set
specific objects for use of the money as allocated on a matching basis—dollar for dollar.[89] Still ahead of its goal, the
Capital Improvements and Endowment Program authorized
in 1960 and operative in 1961 was completed before the end
of 1965, with a total of $3,030,000.00 made available on a
matching basis, and $361,787.98 was available during the
year for the new $10 million program.[90] Through 1967,
more than half of the Convention's share of the program,
$2,645,409.04, had been paid in two years.[91] At the end of
1968, $3,697,372.03 had been allocated from Cooperative
Program Funds.[92]

FOURTH PROGRAM AUTHORIZED

Again, in 1970, with completion of the Convention's part

[85]*Minutes, Georgia Baptist Convention,* 1962, p. 127.
[86]*Minutes, Georgia Baptist Convention,* 1963, p.p. 84, 85.
[87]*Minutes, Georgia Baptist Convention,* 1964, p. 117.
[88]*Minutes, Georgia Baptist Convention,* 1965, p. 106.
[89]*Ibid.,* p.p. 108-109.
[90]*Minutes, Georgia Baptist Convention,* 1966, p.p. 99-101.
[91]*Minutes, Georgia Baptist Convention,* 1968, p.p. 86, 87.
[92]*Minutes, Georgia Baptist Convention,* 1969, p. 90.

in the third program nearing, Georgia Baptists authorized a fourth such program, calling for a goal of $13,056,250.00, with a target of six years for completion of the program which would follow the 1965 program.[93] This program as approved by the Convention listed approved projects, and followed the same basic structure as previous programs. The 1965 program, was completed in 1970, the total amount being made available from the Cooperative Program for assistance to Georgia Baptist institutions on a matching basis was $5,475,000.00.[94] This meant, that in 16 years, in three programs, with $315,988.98 on a fourth program,[95] with funds raised by the institutions, a grand total of $21,985,-213.00 had been channeled into support of Convention ministries; $11,373,742.35 from the Cooperative Program. Additionally, $315,988.98 was available from 1970 funds, after completion of the 1965 program, to apply on the 1970 program.[96] During 1971, $1,407,568.52 was applied toward this program from Cooperative Program funds.[97]

These programs had as their basic concept the belief that Georgia Baptists could and would provide support for their institutions through the regularly-established channels of the Cooperative Program. The difficulties with special fund drives had been evident for many years. With all of the emphasis upon the $75 Million Campaign, and other emphases, including the plan set up prior to the $75 Million Campaign by Georgia Baptists for providing extra monies for institutions, nothing had done what these programs did in the way of providing funds in excess of allocations for operational needs.

If L. R. Scarbrough could write of the $75 Million Campaign in terms of *Miracles of Divine Leadership,* Georgia Baptists could write their own chapter also under the same

[93]*Minutes, Georgia Baptist Convention,* 1970, p.p. 112, 113.

[94]*Book of Reports,* Executive Committee, Georgia Baptist Convention, 1971, p. 10.

[95]*Ibid.,* p. 11.

[96]*Loc. cit.,* Business Office, Georgia Baptist Convention, Records.

[97]Business Office, Georgia Baptist Convention, Records.

directive. However, despite the generous support of the Convention, both in operating funds and Capital Improvement and Endowment Funds, Norman College was in trouble.

This college, begun in 1900 as Norman Institute, and sponsored originally by the Mell Association,[98] had, during the years following World War II, made consistent progress. Enrollment of veterans had swelled income as well as enrollment. But on June 6, 1971, Norman closed its doors as a college, a part of the Convention's program of education, and became a South Georgia Baptist Assembly.[99]

It became Norman Baptist Assembly officially when the Convention in 1971 gave unanimous approval to acceptance of the former college.[100] The Executive Committee on March 23, 1971, accepted responsibility for liabilities and assets of the college, and agreed that July 1, 1971, would be the date for acceptance.[101] Garnie A. Brand, who had served as Vice President and Business Manager for Norman, was elected manager,[102] all subject to Convention approval. Brand had served as Secretary of the Church Training Department for the Convention. Prior to that time, he had served as pastor of the Norman Park Baptist Church and teacher of Bible at the college. He had served also as acting president.

At the time of Convention acceptance, the college had assets of $4,013,423.00, including $819,063.00 in endowment held by the Georgia Baptist Foundation, and liabilities of $958,523.00.[103] Major portion of the liabilities was indebtedness on a Student Center and two dormitories, in the amount of $830,024.00.[104] It was estimated that the facilities could be converted to assembly use for $500,000.00.[105]

---

[98]B. D. Ragsdale, *Story of Georgia Baptists,* Volume Two [Macon: Mercer University, 1935], p.p. 354-356.

[99]*The Christian Index,* June 3, 1971, p. 4.

[100]*The Christian Index,* November 18, 1971, p. 3.

[101]Book of Reports, *Executive Committee, Georgia Baptist Convention,* 1971, p. 19.

[102]*Loc. cit.*

[103]*Ibid.,* p. 22.

[104]*Loc. cit.*

[105]*Loc. cit.*

One factor behind the unanimous approval given to the project by the Convention was the long-felt need by many South Georgia Baptists for a facility such as this. Another factor was the wide and enthusiastic use which had been made of the Georgia Baptist Assembly at Toccoa.

The facilities were used for assembly purposes from June, 1971, through the year.[106] Norman had come into the Convention family from ownership by 16 Southwest Georgia Baptist Associations late in 1959,[107] for the second time.[108] The College Trustees had approved on Sept. 8, 1959, a resolution asking the Convention to assume ownership of the college. This was approved subject to completion of necessary legal steps.[109] The Executive Committee reported that transfer had been completed Dec. 17, 1959.[110] In 1960, the first year following transfer, the College had an enrolment of 346, with nearly half of the students coming from within a 30-mile radius.[111] Audit reports of the college from the mid-1960's on revealed a picture of declining funds, high costs, and a decrease in student enrolment.[112] By 1967, Norman's operational deficit was $29,645.00.[113] By June 30, 1968, an audit revealed that the college had a deficit in operations of $151,698.00, and that a loan of $12,000.00 had to be made in October to meet payrolls. The cumulative deficit for the 1968-69 academic year, by November, 1968, was projected at $221,261.00.[114]

Trustees of the college and the college president had requested from the 1968 Convention authority to borrow an additional $120,568.00 to meet deficits in the Fall quarter of operations ,and requested further permission from the Convention to use ". . . approximately one-third of the en-

[106]*The Christian Index*, June 3, 1971.
[107]*Minutes, Georgia Baptist Convention*, 1960, p. 75.
[108]*Loc. cit.*
[109]*Minutes, Georgia Baptist Convention*, 1959, p.p. 26, 27.
[110]*Minutes, Georgia Baptist Convention*, 1960, p. 75.
[111]*Ibid.*, p. 177.
[112]See *Minutes, Georgia Baptist Convention*, 1965-1970.
[113]*Minutes, Georgia Baptist Convention*, 1967, p. 218.
[114]*Minutes, Georgia Baptist Convention*, 1968, p. 31.

dowment now held by the Georgia Baptist Convention for Norman College . . ." to pay off accumulated deficits.[115] The Executive Committee recommended to the Convention that in addition to the $12,000.00 loan, authorization be granted for loans not in excess of $67,434.00, and called for a complete study of the financial condition of Norman for report to the Executive Committee in December, 1968. Further, the Convention granted Norman permission for direct appeals to the churches for financial assistance for one year.[116] An audit substantiated the deficit estimate.[117] By the fiscal year ending June 30, 1969, Norman was showing a deficit of $159,128.58.[118]

Finally, in 1971, college officials announced that Norman would close, and the facilities were offered to the Executive Committee of the Georgia Baptist Convention.

All Georgia Baptist interests benefited from the Capital Improvements and Endowment Program during this period; Convention internal life began to stabilize, and Norman was well on the way to being another useful addition in the Assembly program, which, once begun in 1963, by 1971 had become a multi-million dollar enterprise.

[115]*Loc. cit.*
[116]*Ibid.*, p. 32.
[117]*The Christian Index,* December 19, 1968, p. 3.
[118]*Minutes, Georgia Baptist Convention,* 1969, p. 229.

CHAPTER 28

Expanding Ministries

The question of a Georgia Baptist Assembly was one which was raised periodically from the beginning of the 20th century until such as assembly was established finally. In addressing the Georgia Baptist Convention in 1958, James P. Wesberry, then president, suggested again that Baptists consider the idea of owning a statewide assembly.

The matter was referred to the Executive Committee which recommended back to the Convention that in the light of the established policy of the Convention, approved in 1951, and in the light of Convention commitments, no Assembly building program be undertaken at this time. Embraced in the suggestion was the fact that properties of the colleges were available and being used for Summer Assembly Programs.

Facilities owned by Woman's Missionary Union at Camp Pinnacle and Camp Glynn were being utilized also for camp and Assembly programs and the Rock Eagle 4-H Center, a state-owned facility was being used also for denominational programs.[1] The Convention's policy at this point had been to encourage the Associations to develop their own assembly programs and assembly facilities as the Associations deemed wise.[2]

For many years, the Lake Louise Bible Conference Grounds at Toccoa, owned by industrialist R. G. LeTourneau, had been used by some Georgia Baptist groups, especi-

[1]*Minutes, Georgia Baptist Convention*, 1959, p. 110.
[2]*Loc. cit.*

ally for Sunday School conventions. The Department of Student Work had, upon occasion, used these facilities for the annual International Student Retreat. The Lake Louise property had been used by the United States Government during World War II as an Army Hospital.

The matter of an Assembly had remained dormant from the recommendation in 1959 until 1963. The minutes of the 1963 Convention state:

> The recommendation of the Executive Committee to purchase Lake Louise Conference Grounds was discussed at length. Most of the discussion was in the form of questions about the property and its suitability for assembly programs. Time was extended for discussion, and the recommendation was approved.[3]

Behind this single paragraph, there had been a fast-moving series of developments which for the first time placed the Convention into an Assembly ministry as an integral part of the Program of State Missions. Informal conversations had been held by Channing P. Hayes, manager of the Conference Grounds for LeTourneau, and one time B. Y. P. U. Secretary for Georgia, with several leaders of the Denomination in the Executive Committee offices in Atlanta.

Sometime during the summer of 1963, Hayes conferred with Searcy S. Garrison, executive secretary-treasurer, expressing to Garrison LeTourneau's interest in selling the Bible Conference grounds, and particularly his interest in insuring that Georgia Baptists had an opportunity to purchase it if they so desired. From this conversation, there came subsequent meetings with the Administration Committee and at the September, 1963 meeting of the Executive Committee, the Administration Committee was authorized to explore the possibilities of purchase of the Lake Louise property as a Baptist Assembly.[4]

The Administration Committee presented a proposal to the Executive Committee which proposal was adopted by that Committee at the pre-Convention meeting, and in turn

[3]*Minutes, Georgia Baptist Convention*, 1963, p. 25.
[4]*The Christian Index*, Sept. 19, 1963, p. 3.

presented to the Convention which approved the proposal.[5] LeTourneau had invested over a period of years several millions of dollars in the Lake Louise property.[6] Through the LeTourneau Foundation, an offer came to sell the property to the Convention for the sum of $195,000.[7]

After study by the Administration Committee, State Missions Department Secretaries, and the architect for many Baptist projects, Henry Whitehead, the Administration Committee reported its belief that ownership of this property would make possible an enlarged ministry to the associations and churches co-operating in the work of the Convention. The report said that the property was well suited for development of such an assembly, because it was on a tract of land including 300 acres of timber, and improved land and a lake covering 200 acres, near Interstate Highway 85, and near the Toccoa airport.

The recommendation called for purchase of additional property in the amount of 155 acres in one tract, and 33 acres in another tract to provide control of the shoreline of the lake. Options on the purchase of these pieces of property had been obtained for $29,857. It was indicated that extensive renovations and repairs would be required to place the existing buildings in a usable condition, calling for a minimum of $250,000 as an initial outlay. The Administration Committee had concluded that once a program was established, it would develop into a larger operation requiring additional capital investments. LeTourneau had offered to make a personal contribution of $10,000, Hayes and his wife had offered $1,000. Another offer from W. H. Hunt of $500 was considered in the recommendation to purchase.

Therefore, the Administration Committee recommended authorization of purchase of the property from the LeTourneau Foundation and that the Georgia Baptist Convention enlarge its State Missions Program to include an Assembly ministry utilizing this property with authorization for the

[5]*Minutes, Georgia Baptist Convention,* 1963, p.p. 25, 30.
[6]Author's conversations with Channing Hayes, then Manager of the property.
[7]*Minutes, Georgia Baptist Convention,* 1963, p. 111.

Executive Committee to secure funds not to exceed $500,000 for development of the property. The recommendation suggested further that the Executive Committee make provision that funds in excess of $80,000 in the State Missions offering for 1964 be applied on indebtedness incurred.[8]

The November Executive Committee approved the proposal.[9] Title to the property was acquired December 20, 1963 and Channing Hayes who had managed the property for LeTourneau was named interim manager of the Conference Grounds, renamed Georgia Baptist Assembly. During 1964 a chapel had been made out of an old barracks building and refurnished and dedication for the facilities was held at the Assembly as part of the September meeting of the Executive Committee.[10] At this September meeting, Clifton A. Forrester, who had been pastor of the Tattnall Square Baptist Church in Macon, was named manager for the Assembly. The dedication service was presided over by R. J. Robinson, pastor of the First Baptist Church in Augusta, and chairman of the Convention's Administration Committee.[11]

After the Convention purchased the Assembly, Bernard D. King, Brotherhood Secretary, was designated as an assistant to Garrison in helping organize and develop the new State Missions ministry. The Assembly was operated throughout the year 1964, almost from the time it was acquired by the Convention, and Garrison reported that for this first year of operation the operating costs were met by charges for Assembly use, permitting funds appropriated from the State Mission budget to be invested in repairs and new equipment and improvements.[12] By 1965, the Assembly property consisted of approximately 1,000 acres and during 1964 there were 3,204 who registered for attendance at some session at

[8]Document of Administration Committee presented to Executive Committee, November, 1963, Author's possession.
[9]*Minutes, Georgia Baptist Convention*, 1963, p.p. 111, 112.
[10]*Minutes, Georgia Baptist Convenion*, 1964, p. 92.
[11]*The Christian Index*, Sept. 17, 1964, p. 3; *Minutes, Georgia Baptist Convention*, 1964, p. 99.
[12]*Minutes, Georgia Baptist Convention*, 1964, p. 98.

the Assembly. It was evident that Assembly earnings would sustain operational costs.[13]

Woman's Missionary Union had dedicated Camp Pinnacle at Clayton June 8, 1947. By 1952, the Camp Pinnacle property had expanded until there were 13 buildings, constructed at a cost of approximately $250,000.[14] Woman's Missionary Union was still active in camp support and in the early 1950's, when Royal Ambassadors still were under the sponsorship of W. M. U., Glendon McCullough, Royal Ambassador secretary, proposed a camp for boys.

Out of this suggestion for a camp, along with a suggested location in South Georgia, interested parties in Brunswick suggested Hillary Island [Blue Herron] near that city. This island was purchased October 13, 1953 for $12,000. There were 14 acres of land on a large island, 2.8 acres on a small island, and 255 acres of marshland. Facilities were constructed, and in 1956 Camp Glynn was dedicated by Woman's Missionary Union.[15]

With the transition of Royal Ambassador work from Woman's Missionary Union to sponsorship by the Brotherhood Department, Woman's Missionary Union found decreasing use for Camp Glynn. In March of 1965, the Executive Committee voted to receive as a gift from Georgia Baptist Woman's Missionary Union the Camp Glynn property, which would be assigned as a State Mission facility, and which would be operated along with the Georgia Baptist Assembly as part of the Assembly program with Forrester supervising both the Toccoa and Brunswick properties. The land with buildings and improvements was valued at about $222,000 at the time it was given to the Convention. This camp continued operations under its original design as a part of the Assembly program.[16]

By the end of 1965, $660,172 had been invested in the

[13]*Minutes, Georgia Baptist Convention,* 1965, p.p. 163, 164.
[14]Mrs. Frank Burney, *Wrought of God—A History with Memories of the Baptist Woman's Missionary Union of Georgia,* 1884-1959, p. 72.
[15]*Ibid.,* p. 75.
[16]*Minutes, Georgia Baptist Convention,* 1965, p.p. 87, 88.

Toccoa property, including purchase cost and improvements with only $77,210.52 indebtedness upon the facilities. Improvements in 1966 amounted to $255,043.59.[17] Attendance at functions held on Assembly grounds by 1966 had increased to 5,128 registered guests [18] and the State Missions departments, which had been accorded priority in scheduling of meetings, had made extensive use of the property. The main building on the property was featured in earlier years as the world's only all steel hotel from the time it was constructed of one-quarter inch boiler plate steel in 8' x 4' sections welded together. It was renovated with second floor additions made on several of the wings, providing by 1966 facilities for up to 300 persons.[19]

During 1967, houses were constructed and Camp Tugalo, a boys' camp near the main Assembly grounds, was in the process of development. During 1967, $191,279.51 had been invested in Assembly improvements, bringing a total investment in the Assembly as of October 1, 1967, including the original purchase price, to $1,382,905.51. The indebtedness at the time on the property was $425,228.64 and with gifts from the State Missions offering and provision in the Capital Improvements and Endowment Program, the indebtedness was scheduled to be reduced by at least $100,000.[20]

With the report to the Convention in 1970, the Assembly had been expanded to provide care for about 350 to 400 people [21] with the ultimate objective being accommodations for 1,200 people. Operated as a year-round facility, the Assembly was serving as a meeting place not only for denominational groups but for meetings by individual churches and in some instances non-Baptist groups.

By 1971 a new motel-type building had been constructed with space for an additional 80 people [22] providing capacity

[17]*Minutes, Georgia Baptist Convention*, 1966, p. 105.
[18]*Ibid.*, p. 159.
[19]*Ibid.*, p. 160.
[20]*Minutes, Georgia Baptist Convention*, 1967, p. 98.
[21]*Minutes, Georgia Baptist Convention*, 1970, p. 147.
[22]Book of Reports, Executive Committee, Georgia Baptist Convention, 1971, Atlanta, p. 78.

for 500 visitors at one time.[23] A summer campground had been developed also with facilities for 20 campers for those who wished to bring their camping trailers or camping trucks to Toccoa.[24]

In 1971, Forrester reported that 203 different groups used the Assembly, 16 groups used Camp Tugalo, and 14 groups held meetings at Camp Glynn. The concept of a Convention Assembly had become a reality. Over 13,000 guests registered at the Toccoa Assembly for 1970-1971.[25] Evaluation of the property at Toccoa and Camp Glynn was near the $2,000,000 mark. At this point in the Assembly development, Norman Junior College became a south Georgia assembly and with its facilities valued in excess of $4,000,000 by mid-1971, Georgia Baptists had a full-grown assembly program with property valued at nearly $6,000,000, providing year-round accommodations for over 1,000 people at the three Assembly locations and providing a ministry as a phase of the State Missions program, which had been desired for 70 years. And while Georgia Baptists had been seeking to provide adequately for Christian Education, and had developed an Assembly program, they had not been idle in other areas of interest.

HOSPITAL EXPANSION

Georgia Baptists continued to maintain an extensive, first class Hospital ministry. Net worth of the Hospital as of December 31, 1961, was $9,065,489.36.[26] During that year, 27,819 patients had been admitted to the hospital and 4,409 babies had been born there.[27] Of the number admitted, approximately half were Baptists and the great majority of patients were from Georgia with 137 countries represented.[28] Total gross earnings for the year were $5,297,682.16, and net income from patients was $4,832,398.21.[29]

[23]*Minutes, Georgia Baptist Convention,* 1970, p. 147.
[24]*Loc. cit.; Book of Reports,* 1971, p. 78.
[25]*Book of Reports,* 1971, p. 78.
[26]*Minutes, Georgia Baptist Convention,* 1961, p. 146.
[27]*Ibid.,* p. 139.
[28]*Ibid.,* p. 141.
[29]*Ibid.,* p. 144.

The Convention in 1960 had given authority to the Hospital Commission and the Executive Committee to construct a dormitory for the School of Nursing and construction was begun in August of 1961.[30] The Nurses' Building was occupied March 5, 1963.[31] The Hospital Commission decided that the old Nurses' dormitory would not be suitable for Hospital services or auxiliary programs, and the Executive Committee concurred with the Commission in plans to demolish the building, and use the space for a new building needed by the hospital.[32]

During this same year, the Hospital Commission made a study of the ministry and long range needs of the Hospital with the help of professional consultants, and out of this study came a statement of needs in order of priority. This was approved by the Hospital Commission and presented to the Executive Committee for its approval as a guide in planning hospital developments for the future.

The needs were in three areas. One area was that of Auxiliary Services, which included Clinical Laboratories, Pathology and Histology, X-ray, elevators, pharmacy, and a supply unit. The second need was for In-patient Facilities, including an intensive care unit, additional facilities for obstetrical uses, a section for Orthopedics and Neurosurgery, Medicine, and Surgery.

The third long-range proposal looked toward an Open Psychiatric Unit for intensive therapy over a period of eight to twenty-eight days. This facility was not contemplated as a substitute for existing or planned state mental health facilities.[33]

As the Hospital took a look at its long-range needs, and established priorities, it reported also in 1963 the 10th anniversary of utilization of the greater Georgia Baptist Hospital. Edwin B. Peel reported to the Convention that in more than 50 years of hospital service free and part-free charity medical

[30]*Ibid.,* p. 78.
[31]*Minutes, Georgia Baptist Convention,* 1963, p. 86.
[32]*Ibid.,* p. 93.
[33]*Ibid.,* p. 94.

care totaling $5,000,000 had been rendered. During this 10 year period, 1953-1963, the Hospital had provided more patient admissions and more charity service than during the entire previous 40 years under Convention ownership.[34]

In 1967 the Convention accepted recommendations made through the Executive Committee by the Hospital Commission on a planned expansion program for the Hospital which, among other items, called for a new Hospital building with 250 beds, space for x-ray equipment and other ancilliary operations. This projected program was based upon the development program which the Convention approved in 1963. Cost of the proposed new building was estimated at $6,000,000 and the Hospital Commission believed that at least $2,000,000 could be raised in gifts, with the balance being financed by commercial loan.[35]

The Hospital had, from its earliest days, a Board of Trustees elected by the Convention. However, since 1922 the Executive Committee had operated the hospital through a Commission which the Executive Committee elected, four from its membership and four from the Board of Trustees for the Hospital, elected by the Convention, and the Executive Secretary-Treasurer.

Inasmuch as the Board of Trustees elected by the convention had no responsibility for the hospital operation and management, it was decided by the Convention in 1967 that the Board of Trustees be discontinued after the 1967 session. However, since the Hospital Commission named four of its nine members from trustees elected by the Convention, provision then had to be made for election of these members of the Commission upon abolishment of the Board of Trustees.

It was decided, therefore, that with the expiration of the terms of those chosen for the Commission from the Trustees, that the Executive Committee elect from the Convention at large persons to serve as their successors. Other members of the Hospital Commission would be elected by the Executive Committee as provided for by action of the Convention

[34]*Ibid.*, p. 162.

[35]*Minutes, Georgia Baptist Convention*, 1967, p. 112.

in 1922 and in 1958. The Convention's policy on rotation of membership on boards was to apply to the Commission.[36]

In 1967, the Hospital Commission reported that it was proceeding with plans for a new building. The recommendation was that the Convention approve the effort now being made by the Hosptial Commission to raise funds to be used in the construction of a new building and commending these efforts to friends of the hospital.[37] However, actual authorization for construction of the hospital building, and the renovations, was left to the Convention session in 1968.[38]

As of September 8, 1968, $2,300,000 had been pledged on the new hospital building program by physicians, friends, Foundations and others in the Atlanta area. Therefore, approval for the actual construction project was for renovation of 23,000 square feet of space at the ground floor and first floor levels of the existing building, and a new building containing 120,000 square feet at a cost estimated to be $9,369,000.[39] This was for the same basic construction for which costs had been estimated previously to be $6,000,000.[40] Authorization for a loan not to exceed $6,000,000 was provided. The recommendation called for submission to the Executive Committee of plans and terms of the loan, for Exectuive Committee approval on behalf of the convention if arranged before the 1969 session.[41]

By 1969, inflation had again caught up with the 1967 estimates on the cost of a building. The original estimate, increased in 1968 to $9,369,000, had been increased to $11,800,000 by the Convention session in 1969. By this time, however, $3,000,000 had been pledged or given on the new building and authority was given to the Executive Committee to arrange a loan not to exceed $6,000,000.[42] Architects were

[36]*Ibid.*, p.p. 112, 113.
[37]*Ibid.*, p. 112.
[38]*Minutes, Georgia Baptist Convention*, 1968, p. 109.
[39]*Loc. cit.*
[40]*Minutes, Georgia Baptist Convention*, 1967, p. 112.
[41]*Minutes, Georgia Baptist Convention*, 1968, p. 109.
[42]*Minutes, Georgia Baptist Convention*, 1969, p.p. 118, 119.

completing plans for the building by 1970, estimated then to cost $11,000,000.[43]

Final hurdles were cleared in 1971. By the summer of that year: "With refinements and improvements in plans for the new hospital building and facilities, the cost of construction is now estimated at approximately $16,000,000." [44]

Under authority from the Convention in 1969, the Hospital did begin a renovation project, estimated to cost $600,000.[45]

An important consideration also was need for a new Professional Building to serve an expanded hospital.[46] Therefore, the 1971 Convention approved construction of a $16,000,000 Hospital building, and a $4,000,000 Professional Building, authorizing negotiations for a loan up to $10,000,000 for the Hospital, and up to $4,000,000 for the Professional Building.[47]

CHILDREN'S HOME

With the Assembly program established firmly, and the Hospital in an extensive building program, providing services to a record number of patients, there were yet other areas of Georgia Baptist life where distinct progress was evident.

The Baxley branch of the Georgia Baptist Children's Home, Incorporated had been developed extensively during the 1960's. The operations of the branch had become a model in farm-type operations for a Children's Home, with extensive landholdings, farming, cattle raising, and also with the addition of several buildings and improvement of others. The biggest problem faced by Georgia Baptists in the operation of their Children's Home branches was in the continued

---

[43]*Minutes, Georgia Baptist Convention*, 1970, p. 89.

[44]*Book of Reports, Executive Committee, Georgia Baptist Convention*, 1971, p. 12.

[45]*Ibid.*, p. 44.

[46]*Ibid.*, p. 45.

[47]Book of Reports, *Executive Committee, Georgia Baptist Convention*, 1971, p. 45; *The Christian Index*, Nov. 18, 1971, p. 3.

effective operation of the Hapeville branch at its historic site.

As Atlanta became the air hub for the South, with several hundred airliners landing and taking off each day, the Children's Home, on adjoining property, became daily less desirable. With the advent of the use of jet airplanes commercially by the 1960's, the noise level at the Children's Home had at times become almost unbearable, because the home property was in the path of one of the runways for take-offs and landings at the airport.

Additionally, the buildings were old and the cost of repairs was a prohibitive item. Further, the property itself at the Hapeville location had increased in value to a considerable degree during the 1950's and into the 1960's. Manager John C. Warr had for several years declared that the time would come when the Children's Home would need to be moved to another location because of the factors cited.[48]

The Convention granted authority at its session in 1965 in Augusta to the Board of Trustees of the Children's Home to sell the campus at Hapeville at a price and on terms that the Board of Trustees deemed advisable.[49] About a month after the Convention had given authority to relocate, the Children's Home purchased a 400-acre tract in Fulton County for $250,000. The area was located near Palmetto, and included a 35-acre lake and 4,000 feet of frontage on a paved road.[50] Warr had indicated in his report to the Convention in November, 1965, that property in Hapeville at the time was selling for $40,000 to $50,000 an acre and that the Home had 79.8 acres there.[51] The property was sold to the city of Atlanta for $3,500,000, which evidently was the largest single real estate transaction in Convention history. The property was to be used for expansion of runways at the Atlanta airport.[52]

[48]Conversations with John C. Warr; Minutes, Executive Committee meetings, Georgia Baptist Convention, 1960's.

[49]*Minutes, Georgia Baptist Convention*, 1965, p. 27.

[50]*The Christian Index*, Dec. 16, 1965, p. 3.

[51]*Loc. cit.*

[52]*The Christian Index*, Nov. 17, 1966, p. 3.

Warr had estimated it would require two years to build a new campus, contemplating facilities to accommodate 220 or 230 children, which would have been a ten per cent increase over the Hapeville capacity. The purchase price for the new property was paid out of funds held in reserve from the sale earlier of the farm in Clayton county.[53] In 1966, the Executive Committee at its March meeting, authorized the Children's Home to borrow up to $2,500,000 on a two year open unsecured note to begin construction of new buildings near Palmetto while the property at Hapeville was being sold.[54]

The new campus, described as Georgia Baptists' largest "all at one time" building project, was dedicated October 27, 1968. The Children's Home had, by that time, completed an entirely new child-care facility comprised of 23 buildings located upon 400 acres of land.[55] By the time of the move to Palmetto, total Children's Home property was valued at $9,000,000, including some 3,800 acres of land belonging to the Home, with endowment of approximately $1,250,000. During the year 581 children had been cared for by a staff comprised of 160 men and women.[56]

John Warr died on June 9, 1969, having served as General Manager nearly 19 years. Following Warr's death, Clarence F. Sessions served as acting general manager [57] until the election of O. L. Pedigo as general manager of the Home in 1970. He assumed his duties April 1, 1970.[58]

Pedigo came to the Children's Home from a nine-year tenure as pastor of the First Baptist Church in Stone Mountain. In 1970, the Convention heard a motion requesting the manager and trustees of the Home to implement an admissions policy of openness to children of all races.[59] The motion was referred to the Resolutions Committee.

[53]*The Christian Index*, Dec. 16, 1965, p. 3.
[54]*Minutes, Georgia Baptist Convention*, 1966, p. 104.
[55]*The Christian Index*, Oct. 17, 1968, p. 5.
[56]*Minutes, Georgia Baptist Convention*, 1968, p. 157.
[57]*Children's Messenger*, Vol. 45, No. 3, March, 1970, unnumbered page 3; *Minutes, Georgia Baptist Convention*, 1969, p. 165.
[58]*Minutes, Georgia Baptist Convention*, 1970, p. 155.
[59]*Ibid.*, p. 33.

When the report of the Committee on Resolutions was read, the report included the statement that the Committee had given consideration to the recommendation concerning admission policies of the Children's Home. The Committee had examined the charter and said that by 1968 action, the Georgia Baptist Convention had removed race as a factor in admissions policies. The Committee in its resolution, therefore, said implementation of this policy was a matter for the Children's Home Trustees.[60] After the report of the Committee on Resolutions was presented for adoption, a motion was made to amend the report to read:

> That this session of the Georgia Baptist Convention go on record as requesting that the General Manager and Trustees of the Georgia Baptist Children's Home begin to implement an open policy of admissions to all races.

This amendment was discussed and lost.[61]

At the 1971 Convention, John Nichol, Decatur, who had presented the motion in 1970, brought the matter before the Convention again. Messengers refused to extend time during a miscellaneous business session to hear Nichol's motion to implement an open-door policy for children of all races. Later, Nichol sought to amend the official report of the Children's Home to add a paragraph stating ". . . that we go on record that it is our will and intention to operate a Children's Home for children of all races." Nichol's amendment was ". . . defeated by about a two-to-one margin." [62]

The Convention still left the matter in the hands of the Trustees.

CARE FOR ELDERLY

As Georgia Baptists were completing an expanded child-care ministry and utilizing the new facilities at Palmetto, they were expanding two other ministries and preparing to add a third. As indicated earlier, the Georgia Baptist Assembly was in a program of expansion almost continually from 1964. Additionally, Baptist Village at Waycross continued to move

[60]*Ibid.*, p. 51; *Minutes, Georgia Baptist Convention*, 1968, p.p. 113-114.
[61]*Minutes, Georgia Baptist Convention*, 1970, p. 49.
[62]*The Christian Index*, Nov. 18, 1971, p. 5.

toward its ultimate goal of 300 residents with facilities including hospital type care facilities.

On Sept. 1, 1963, there were 50 people being cared for at Baptist Village.[63] On June 4, 1964, the facilities at Baptist Village were dedicated. By that time, the plant consisted of a central service area, an administration building, and 120 private apartments. Harvey R. Mitchell, Administrator, was then projecting plans to build an infirmary for 50 people and ultimate nursing care provisions for 100 people or one-third of the planned capacity for Baptist Village.[64]

Total plant fund assets by July 31, 1964 were listed at $1,851,496.07, for a net gain of $377,042.02 during the year. Mitchell's audit report listed total assets at $2,006,268.06.[65]

During 1967, a new building was under way which was designed to increase the capacity at the Village to 216.[66] The building was completed in 1968 and provided space for 84 additional people, along with offices and treatment rooms for high quality nursing care.[67] In 1968, total income for Baptist Village was $573,087.65 with $216,238.81 listed as excess of income over expenses.[68]

By 1969, Baptist Village reported total income of $746,752.33, with total expenses of $472,712.96, for an excess of income over expenses of $274,039.37.[69] As Baptist Village became established not only in physical facilities but in the life of the Convention, a new development was pending.

Searcy S. Garrison, who had been chief negotiator in a series of meetings for some months prior to the Georgia Baptist Convention session in Columbus in 1966, paved the way for recommendations from the Administration Committee and the Executive Committee to the pre-Convention meeting of the Executive Committee which laid the ground-

[63]*Minutes, Georgia Baptist Convention,* 1963, p. 173.
[64]*Minutes, Georgia Baptist Convention,* 1964, p. 176.
[65]*Ibid.,* p. 178.
[66]*Minutes, Georgia Baptist Conevntion,* 1967, p. 175.
[67]*Minutes, Georgia Baptist Convention,* 1968, p. 174.
[68]*Ibid.,* p. 177.
[69]*Minutes, Georgia Baptist Convention,* 1969, p. 187.

work for yet another home for elderly men and women, this time in Atlanta.

The Executive Committee at this meeting approved for recommendation to the Convention an offer made by the Beazley Foundation to the Georgia Baptist Convention of property at 176 Peachtree St., N. W., which had been known at Peachtree on Peachtree Hotel, together with $50,000 in cash for use as a home for ". . . elderly people of modest means." The resolution from the Executive Committee was that this offer be accepted and that in accordance with terms of the offer, a corporation known as Peachtree on Pearchtree Inn, be incorporated to operate the facility.[70]

The Convention approved ". . . by a standing vote of gratitude" [71a] the offer of the Beazley Foundation incorporated of Portsmouth, Virginia. The benefactor was Fred W. Beazley of Portsmouth, a retired Atlanta businessman. The property, earlier known as the Winecoff Hotel, was valued at the time of $2,000,000, making it the largest single gift in Convention history and the facilities, readily adaptable for a home for elderly people, were equipped to provide residence for 175 persons.[71] The Executive Committee of the Convention, at its December, 1966, meeting, authorized the trustees of Peachtree on Peachtree Inn to secure a loan of $250,000 for renovating the property.[72]

W. L. Rainwater was named first administrator of Peachtree on Peachtree Inn,[73] and remained in this position for about a year before returning to service as a pastor. Cecil T. Underwood, then pastor of the Morningside Baptist Church, Savannah, succeeded Rainwater as administrator and in his

[70]*The Christian Index*, Nov. 24, 1966, p. 3; *Minutes, Georgia Baptist Convention,* 1966, p.p. 29, 30.

[71]*The Christian Index,* Nov. 24, 1966, p. 3. [Full details on the Convention action may be found in the minutes for 1966, p.p. 29-34, including the charter approved by the Convention.]

[71a]*Minutes, Georgia Baptist Convention,* 1966, p. 25.

[72]*Minutes, Georgia Baptist Convention,* 1967, p. 93.

[73]*Ibid.,* p. 179.

first report to the Convention in 1968, said that the institution, in its second year of operation, had 128 residents.[74]

By 1970, Peachtree on Peachtree Inn was operating in the black with income of $7,187.04 in excess of expenses,[75] and had 165 residents.[76]

This Convention ministry served residents of the Atlanta area primarily, and between 1967 and 1971 had been developed into a first-class facility for ambulatory residents. It did not have facilities for care of non-ambulatory patients as did Baptist Village.

SOCIAL SERVICE COMMISSION

The Social Service Commission of the Georgia Baptist Convention was abolished in 1960.[77]

The 1961 Convention created in its place a Christian Life Commission. The original motion was to restore the Social Service Commission as an active committee of the Convention, and that the committee be composed of five members. The motion was amended to change the name of the proposed commission to that of the Christian Life Commission.[78]

A motion was made later that a committee from the Executive Committee be appointed to define the areas of the Public Affairs Committee and the Christian Life Commission.[79] Thus, the Social Service Commission, which in a period of several years had dealt with the race issue, among other things, and which owed its demise to this issue as much as any other item, was resurrected by a different name but with initial safeguards to define clearly its assigned responsibility. However, a move to define the role of this particular commission was not new. This had been done intermittently since the creation of the first Social Service Commission many years earlier.

[74]*Minutes, Georgia Baptist Convention*, 1968, p. 179.
[75]*Minutes, Georgia Baptist Convention*, 1970, p. 182.
[76]*Ibid.*, p. 179.
[77]*Minutes, Georgia Baptist Convention*, 1960, p. 34.
[78]*Minutes, Georgia Baptist Convention*, 1961, p. 26.
[79]*Ibid.*, p. 28.

This was done also by the Executive Committee at the March, 1962 meeting. The responsibilities of the Christian Life Commission as set forth by the Executive Committee were that it would assist Baptists in propagating the Gospel, by helping them to become more aware of the ethical implications of the Christian Gospel with regard to such aspects of daily living as family life, human relations, moral issues, economic life, citizenship, etc. The Commission was to help create a moral and social climate in which the Georgia Baptist witness would be most effective.[80]

To accomplish these objectives, the Commission was to make studies in areas of its assigned responsibility and to cooperate with the Christian Life Commission of the Southern Baptist Convention in certain areas of agreement, as well as with Christian Life Committees in associations and churches, and by annual report to the Convention.[81] The Commission report was then submitted as information, and not for Convention approval.

The 1961 motion to define the area of responsibility of the Christian Life Commission was also a motion to define the area of the Public Affairs Committee's responsibility. Therefore, when the Executive Committee made its study, it indicated the areas of responsibility for the Christian Life Commission and indicated as this Commission's channel to the Convention the annual report to be published in the Book or Reports, which meant inclusion in the Minutes of the Convention.

Responsibility of the Public Affairs Committee was indicated as that of articulating the position of the Convention on public issues upon which the Convention had declared itself in reports and resolutions as well as to act in the field of public affairs wherever the interest of Georgia Baptists required conferences or negotiations with governmental bodies.[82]

In 1963, the Christian Life Commission's report had as

[80]*Minutes, Georgia Baptist Convention,* 1962, p. 118.
[81]*Ibid.,* p.p. 89, 118.
[82]*Ibid.,* p.p. 89, 90.

Section III an area dealing with race relations, citing the increasing perplexity and seriousness in this area. The Commission cited, among other things, its belief that Georgia Baptists could continue to contribute toward the relief of social tensions by seeking as individuals to live as Jesus admonished; by seeking to apply the mind and spirit of Christ to the problems of racial conflict which were developing; by pastors and church leaders seeking to improve and strengthen channels of communication with Negro pastors and community leaders; and also by strengthening the Program of Negro Work in the Georgia Baptist Convention State Missions Program.[83]

The Resolutions Committee, in its report which was adopted by the Convention, endorsed the recommendations contained in Section III dealing with race relations. These recommendations were issued by a joint meeting June 27, 1963 of the Administration Committee, the Public Affairs Committee and the Christian Life Commission, the essence of which was contained in the section on race relations in the report of the Christian Life Commission.[84]

The statement was therefore a position statement of the Convention when it was adopted upon recommendation of the Committee on Resolutions. Therefore, the Commission was to make in depth studies dealing with specific areas, including principles of separation of church and state, areas of religious liberty, abortion, crime, race relations, gambling and other issues which the Commission felt should come to the attention of Georgia Baptists.

The Commission ceased really to be controversial following its re-establishment along different lines of responsibility by the 1961 convention and the delineation of responsibility by the Executive Committee in March of 1962. The influence of the Christian Life Commission, however, made itself felt throughout Georgia. For example, the study of the Commission in 1965 which dealt with the subject of marriage practices and actually aimed at a tightening

[83]*Minutes, Georgia Baptist Convention,* 1963, p.p. 127, 128.
[84]*Ibid.,* p.p. 45, 46.

of laws in Georgia concerning "quickie marriages," focused attention upon yet another area where changes were needed in state law. By making copies of such reports available to the members of the State Legislature, the Commission felt that the voice of Georgia Baptists would be heard.

In 1968, the Commission used as its study area that of Baptists working with other Christian groups. For this study, the Commission held a two-day session devoted to conversations with other Christian bodies, black and white. The strongest statement dealing in the matter of race relations in several years appeared out of this study when the Commission, noting the historic fact of membership by Negroes in white churches before and after the War Between the States, suggested that ministers cross denomination and racial lines in co-operative worship services and encouraged churches to observe annual race relations Sunday.

The Commission suggested also that fraternal messengers from other Christian groups and Negro Conventions be invited to attend the Georgia Baptist Convention sessions and suggested that an invitation could be extended to a Negro Baptist preacher to preach to the Convention.[85] While this report did not call for Convention approval, it was accepted by the Convention as information. An analysis of the content of the 1960 report of the Social Service Commission which was rejected, and the 1968 study indicates that the 1968 study was more forceful than the 1960 study which, in part, occasioned the demise of the Social Service Commission.

Allied to this subject was the report in 1970 of the Public Affairs Committee which was a statement on public and private schools. The Public Affairs Committee reported that the Executive Committee voted on the statement and 13 members of the Committee were in opposition to the report and requested that a record be made of the opposition.

The report said that the Georgia and Southern Conventions had voiced support consistently of a system of public education and urged Georgia Baptists to resist efforts of those

[85]*Minutes, Georgia Baptist Convention*, 1968, p.p. 126-131.

who would risk, as the Committee termed it, destruction of a successful system of public education in order to resist integration. In effect, the statement on public and private schools by the Public Affairs Committee was one of caution to the churches against establishment of private schools to avoid integration.[86] The statement cited 1970 Federal Court rulings to sustain its warning.[87]

In areas covered in this chapter, Georgia Baptists had made solid, effective gains, and other areas were to reflect the Convention's mature, deliberate progress.

---

[86]*Minutes, Georgia Baptist Convention,* 1970, p.p. 94, 95.
[87]*Ibid.,* p. 95.

CHAPTER 29

Expansion In All Areas

By 1961, the Constitution and By-Laws adopted by the 1919 Convention, and much amended since that time, was an unwieldy document. Motions were made during the 1940's and 1950's to amend the Contsitution to add members to the Executive Committee as organizations developed. By 1961, supplemental reports were giving authority to the Executive Committee to fill unexpired terms or to fill vacancies in at least two situations. This was actually in violation of the wording of the Constitution. However, it was approved by the Convention.[1]

Additionally, the By-Laws were becoming increasingly lengthy. In 1962, upon recommendation of the Executive Committee, the Convention approved an addition to the By-Laws, Section 7, which stated:

> Sec. 7. No new enterprise, involving expenditure of money, shall be authorized by the Convention except upon favorable action by the Convention in two succeeding annual meetings; provided, however, that this restriction shall not apply to a recommendation of an agency of the Convention concerning its own work; and provided further, that notice of creation of new enterprises or discontinuance of existing agencies must be published in *The Christian Index* at least thirty days before the annual meetings of the Convention; and, provided further, that no agency of the Convention shall be discontinued without a majority vote at two successive Conventions.

Section 7 as then listed became Section 8.[2] This had apparent

[1]*Minutes, Georgia Baptist Convention,* 1961, p. 47.
[2]*Minutes, Georgia Baptist Convention,* 1962, p. 108.

reference to the elimination of the Social Service Commission in 1960 and the creation of the Christian Life Commission in 1961.

Again, in 1964, two changes were made in the Constitution. One, affecting Section One of Article Three added the phrase: "The dates and places of meetings shall be planned two years in advance." The revised section read:

> The Convention shall meet at least once each year, the time and place to be fixed by the Convention or the Executive Committee. The dates and places of meetings shall be planned two years in advance.[3]

Again, the Executive Committee in that year recommended amending the Constitution by insertion of a paragraph in Division Six of Section One concerning Boards and Commissions. This was to bring the Boards and Commissions section in line with previous action concerning the Executive Committee. It said:

> Members of boards of trustees of Convention institutions and commissions who do not attend fifty [50] per cent of the meetings of these bodies during any current year, without being excused at the meeting from which the members are absent, or at the next succeeding meeting, shall forfeit membership on the board of trustees or commission to which they have been elected. Vacancies are to be reported to the Executive Committee, and the Convention will follow its regular procedure in electing persons to fill unexpired terms.[4]

A proposed amendment in 1967 which would have dealt with officers of the Convention and procedures to be followed upon death, resignation or removal from the state of the president or vice-president was withdrawn from Convention consideration.[5]

In 1968 Convention parliamentarian H. Tucker Singleton suggested to the Convention that a complete study be made of the Constitution with the purpose of reviewing and clarifying all phases of that document. This was referred to the Administration Committee for study. At the same time, a

[3]*Minutes, Georgia Baptist Convention,* 1964, p.p. 14, 136.
[4]*Ibid.,* pp. 15, 115
[5]*Minutes, Georgia Baptist Convention,* 1967, p.p. 29, 30, 121-122.
[6]*Minutes, Georgia Batpist Convention,* 1968, p.p. 47, 48.

notice of a proposed amendment dealing with election of a president, to be presented in 1969, was read.[6] The Executive Committee came to the 1969 Convention with proposed amendments to the Constitution which amendments were voted on individually and approved as changed. The amended Constitution and By-Laws of 1969, follow:

CONSTITUTION

Adopted 1919. [Including changes approved by the Convention in 1969.]

I. Name and Object

Sec. 1. The name of this body shall be the Baptist Convention of the State of Georgia.

Sec. 2. The object of this Convention shall be to furnish a medium of Cooperation for the Baptist Churches of Georgia in their divinely commissioned work of missions, education, and benevolence.

II. Membership

Sec. 1. This body shall be composed of messengers from Baptist churches in harmony and cooperation with the work and purpose of this convention.

Sec. 2. Each church shall be entitled to two messengers and one additional messenger for each $500 contributed to Convention causes, but in no case shall any church have more than 15 messengers.

III. Meeting

Sec. 1. The Convention shall meet at least once each year, the time and place to be fixed by the Convention or the Executive Committee. The dates and places of meetings shall be planned two years in advance.

IV. Powers

Sec. 1. This Convention shall never attempt to exercise authority over any church, but shall always cheerfully recognize and uphold the church's sovereignty under Christ.

Sec. 2. All funds entrusted to the Convention or to any of its boards or agents shall be strictly applied according to the expressed will and direction of the donors.

V. Officers

Sec. 1. The officers of this Convention shall be a president, four vice-presidents, a secretary, two assistant secretaries and a treasurer, who shall be elected at each an-

738 / *A History of The Georgia Baptist Convention*

nual meeting by a majority ballot of the duly elected messengers present and voting, and who shall hold their offices until their successors are elected and installed. Their duties shall be those usually discharged by such officers. No person shall serve as president more than two years, and thereafter he shall not be eligible for re-election to this office.

No person shall be nominated and elected as an officer who is not a registered messenger of the Convention.

VI. Boards and Commissions

Sec. 1. An Executive Committee of this Convention shall be chosen by the Convention, and shall consist of the officers of the Convention, ex-officio, including the president of the Georgia Baptist Pastors' Conference, the president of the Georgia Baptist Religious Education Association, the president of the Georgia Baptist Woman's Missionary Union, the president of the Georgia Baptist Student Union and the president of the Georgia Baptist Music Conference, ex-officio, and one member to be chosen from the territory of each cooperating association, and 20 additional members from the state at large.

The members of the Executive Committee shall be elected to hold office one fifth for one year, one fifth for two years, one fifth for three years, one fifth for four years, and one fifth for five years. The vacancies as the terms expire shall be filled for terms of five years. No one connected in any way with any Institution fostered by this Convention shall be eligible for election to membership on this Committee. No member of the Committee shall be eligible for re-eleciton after the expiration of his term of service until he has been in retirement from the Committee for at least one year, whether he served ex officio or for a specified term from the territory of the Associations.

The members of the Exectuive Committee who miss 50 per cent of the meetings of the Committee during any current year, including the pre-Convention meeting, without being excused at the meeting from which the members are absent or the next succeeding meeting, shall forfeit their membership on the Committee.

All members elected to membership on the Committee as representatives of associations must reside in the territory of the associations they represent, unless the Convention should accept an association's suggestion of a non-resident as its representative.

Members of boards of trustees of Convention institutions and commissions who do not attend fifty [50] per cent of the meetings of these bodies during any current year, without being excused at the meeting from which the members are absent, or at the next succeeding meeting, shall forfeit membership on the board of trustees or commission to which they have been elected. Vacancies are to be reported to the Executive Committee, and the Convention will follow its regular procedure in electing persons to fill unexpired terms.

At least ninety days before each annual session of this Convention the Committee on Nominations for the year shall publish in the Organ of the Convention the names of the Associations from which Executive Committee members will be elected at the next session of this body, and it shall at the same time remind the constituency of the Convention within the Fellowship of such Associations that they may offer suggestions to the Committee on Nominations concerning the Executive Committee members to be elected from within their respective Associations.

Sec. 2. The Executive Committee shall have charge and control, except when otherwise directed by the Convention, of all work of the Convention including missions, education and benevolence, in the interim between sessions of the Convention. No member of the Executive Committee shall have any official connection with any of the institutions whose work it fosters.

[a] When an unforeseen emergency occurs in any of the affairs of the Convention, or in any of the interest it controls, that, in the judgment of the Executive Committee, requires action before the next session of the Convention, the Executive Committee in that case shall have full authority to take such action as it thinks will be best in the interim, and all parties will be bound by its action, provided [1] that it must report to the next session of the Convention all the facts in each case and what action it took; and provided [2] that whatever action it takes in such cases will be binding only until the next session of the Convention; and provided [3] that nothing in this article shall be construed as giving the Executive Committee authority over any matters already committed by the Convention to any of its Boards of Trustees, unless such boards decline to act.

[b] Any vacancy occurring in the membership of the Executive Committee, caused by death, resignation, removal from the Association represented, or for any other reason, shall be filled by the Convention at its next regular session.

[c] Rotation of membership on all Boards and Commissions, except the Trustees of the Georgia Baptist foun-

dation, shall be on the same basis as that of the Executive Committee. All vacancies occurring on Boards and Commissions during the year shall be filled by the next Convention, with no interim appointments being made.

VII. Amendments

Sec. 1. This constitution may be amended at any regular session by the vote of two-thirds of the messengers present and voting at the time; provided, that no amendment shall be made later than the second day of the Convention, and further, that notice of the proposed change has been given in writing to the Convention or in the State paper ninety days before its meeting.

BY-LAWS

Sec. 1. At each annual meting of this Convention, the President shall appoint a committee of ten, to report at the next annual meeting, whose duty it shall be to nominate to the Convention, all Boards, Commissions and Committees chosen by the Convention, and the President of the Convention shall be a member of the Committee on Order of Business for the next annual session of the Convention.

Sec. 2. All boards, commissions and committees of the Convention shall cause to be embraced in their reports of finance the usual "Balance Sheet" accompanied by an unqualified audit prepared by a certified public accountant, and a budget of estimated income and expenditures for the ensuing year.

Sec. 3. The Boards and other like bodies belonging to the Convention and under its control shall have their Treasurers placed under bond. Every Auditing Committee of a Treasurer's account shall report as to the validity of his bond.

Sec. 4. No recommendation shall ever be embodied in any reports made to this Convention by any agent, secretary, or other officer of any Board or like body, which, if received and adopted, will modify or amend any item of the Constitution, By-Laws or Standing Resolutions of the Convention.

Sec. 5. It shall be the duty of the Committee on Order of Business to provide for the consideration of any proposed amendment to the Constitution.

Sec. 6. No new enterprise, involving expenditure of money, shall be authorized by the Convention except upon favorable action by the Convention in two succeeding annual meetings; provided, however, that this restriction shall not apply to a recommendation of an agency of the Convention concerning its own work; and, provided further, that notice of creation of new enterprises or discontinuance of existing agencies must be published in *The Christian Index* at least thirty days before the annual meeting of the Convention; and, provided further, that no agency of the Convention shall be discontinued without a majority vote at two successive Conventions.

Sec. 7. These By-Laws may be altered at any annual meeting by a majority vote of the members present and voting, notice of the proposed change having been given in the State paper at least thirty days before the Convention.[7]

However, despite the extensive changes in the Constitution approved in 1969, yet another amendment was adopted by the Convention in 1970, which was an addition to Article VI, Section I. The amendment said:

No one regularly employed by any institution or agency fostered by the Convention shall be eligible for election or appointment to membership on the governing or supervisory body of the institution or agency by which such person is employed.[8]

The reports of the Radio Committee of the 1940's and 1950's had been reports of work done by Georgia Baptists. By the mid-1950's, and from that point on, reports were of the activities of the Radio and Television Commission of the Southern Baptist Convention. And, although Georgia Baptists were doing some work in the area of radio programming and news presentation, this work was not included as a part of the report of Georgia Convention's Radio and Television Committee.

STATE MISSIONS

In an expanded ministry of State Missions, the Executive Committee recommended in 1961 that the Georgia Baptist Conference of the Deaf be recognized as one supporting the objectives and program of the Convention, and commended the work of this Conference to the churches, suggesting that the Administration Committee give such assistance as possi-

[7]*Minutes, Georgia Baptist Convention,* 1969, p.p. 30, 121-127.
[8]*Minutes, Georgia Baptist Convention,* 1970, p. 33.

742 / A History of The Georgia Baptist Convention

ble to the Conference as a phase of its ministry to silent people.[9] This action followed a request by the Convention in 1960 that the Executive Committee consider the possibility of establishing such a relationship.[10] While the emphasis had been changed with regard to cooperative support between the Home Mission Board and the Georgia Baptist Convention in programs of City Mission Work, and in states with well-established programs, the Convention continued to expand in its own program of mission work.

By 1961 there were 32 associational missionaries, two area missionaries, five city missions superintendents, and 96 mission pastors whose salaries were supplemented from State Mission funds.[11] The State Missions budget for 1961 provided for ministries costing $498,652.[12] The State Mission program was to expand in a decade to ministries costing $1,118,312 for 1972.[13]

A ten-month consolidated report for 1961 indicated ministries of "Pastoral Aid" missionaries showed a total of 4,485 weeks of services, with 12,124 sermons preached, 82,094 visits and conferences with a total for this ten-month period of 1,207,212 miles travelled. These missionaries had received 1,942 members by baptism, 7,737 by letter, and 336 by restoration for a total of 4,015.[14] The program of Associational Missions had expanded to include work in 55 of the 94 associations under one of the several programs.[15]

The Convention still maintained its interest in a ministry to patients at Battey Hospital in Rome, providing a chaplain there, and continued with the Emergency Church Building fund which, though small, had proven to be of value when emergencies occurred in a church.[16]

[9]Minutes, Georgia Baptist Convention, 1961, p. 79.
[10]Loc. cit.
[11]Ibid., p. 109.
[12]Loc. cit.
[13]Book of Reports, Executive Committee, Georgia Baptist Convention, Nov. 8-10, 1971, Atlanta, p. 66.
[14]Minutes, Georgia Baptist Convention, 1961, p. 110.
[15]Ibid., p. 111.
[16]Ibid., p. 113.

The Department of Church Music observed its tenth anniversary on October 15, 1961. A ten-year comparison revealed that the Associational organizations had increased from one in 1951 to 89 in 1961, and Georgia had remained in first place in the number of church training awards for seven years and had never been lower than second place in the Department's history. In 1951, there were 12 full-time ministers of music in the state. In 1961 the number had increased to 132.[17]

The Program of Negro Work continued to be effective despite mounting racial tensions. During this year 6,689 National Baptists had enrolled in some type of training program within the Convention's ministry in this area,[18] and assistance had been rendered in construction of an associational assembly and Durwood V. Cason, Sr., had led in an effort to secure land near Swainsboro for the Negro convention.

Woman's Missionary Union continued to progress. Georgia Baptist women had been active not only in camps at Pinnacle and Glynn, but they had cooperated in sponsoring camps for Negroes at Camp John Hope near Fort Valley.[19]

The ministry of the Extension Department of Christian Education at Mercer University, a Convention-supported ministry, had during 1960 and 1961, 42 centers in operation with 173 classes being taught, and a total enrollment of 2,002. Certificates had been awarded to 21 students and Advanced Certificates to four students June 4, 1961. This program, which had been authorized by the 1948 Convention, had from the first been administered by Mercer University, with P. Harris Anderson at that time dean of Denominational Extension Services. A study syllabus, *The Witness and Work of Georgia Baptists,* referred to earlier, was by 1961 being taught in more than 20 centers across the state.[20]

Gainer E. Bryan, Sr., for 25 years secretary of the Training Union Department of the Convention, and for 15 years prior to that time an associate in the Sunday School Department,

[17]*Ibid.,* p. 121.
[18]*Ibid.,* p.p. 122-123.
[19]*Ibid.,* p.p. 124, 125.
[20]*Ibid.,* p. 165.

retired at the end of 1962.[21] Bryan had led in Training Union development, which included the promotion of M Night beginning in the early 1940's. Mobilization Night became subsequently a standard event in Southern Baptist Convention life for many years. Bryan had promoted Training Union assemblies for many years, which provided a channel for presentation of Georgia Baptist ministries to all age groups. These assemblies were held on the campus of Mercer University and prior to that on the campus of Shorter College.

Bryan, in his final report to the Convention, indicated that churches with one or more training unions had grown during his tenure in number from 958 to 2,216 churches, and that enrollment had increased from 50,004 to 220,514.[22]

Garnie A. Brand, then pastor of the First Baptist Church of Fitzgerald, was elected to succeed Bryan.[23] Brand served until September, 1969, at which time he resigned to become vice president of Norman College.[24]

Georgia Baptists became active during 1962 in providing assistance and cooperation with other State Conventions to Cuban refugees. The Executive Committee, in September, heard a report from Bernard King, who had been named chairman of the Cuban Relief Committee, that 330 churches in 23 associations had provided approximately 50,000 pounds of food to be shipped to the Miami, Fla. area, the heaviest concentration area for refugees, together with $7,776.04 in cash. Additionally, through efforts coordinated by King and Garrison, six Georgia Baptist churches had accepted responsibility for relocating refugee families, providing homes for 24 persons.[25]

During 1957, the program of Associational Mission work was studied carefully.[26] Out of this study came a plan for programs in which

[21]*Minutes, Georgia Baptist Convention,* 1962, p. 32.
[22]*Ibid.,* p. 138.
[23]*Ibid.,* p. 90.
[24]*Minutes, Georgia Baptist Convention,* 1969, p.p. 103, 104.
[25]*Minutes, Georgia Baptist Convention,* 1962, p. 86.
[26]*Minutes, Georgia Baptist Convention,* 1957, p. 73.

. . . two or more associations cooperated with each other and with the Convention in an associational group mission program. These programs have been encouraging and studies led the Executive Committee to approve the plan of the Administration Committee . . . to encourage associations now without a mission program to cooperate with one or more neighboring associations, and with the Convention, in a group program of associational mission work. [26a]

Under this plan a number of associations cooperate with the State Mission Program in supporting a mission and promotional work in the area of the cooperating associations. The missionary is employed as a State Mission worker, and is directed by the Administration Committee, with the cooperation of an area committee composed of the moderators and members of the Georgia Baptist Convention's Executive Committee from the cooperating associations. The financial support for the missionary and his work under the group plan is provided jointly by the cooperating associations and from State Mission funds.[26b]

On March 1, 1957, Homer A. Morris, formerly a missionary in the Chattahoochee Association began service to five associations in Northeast Georgia under this plan.[26d]

In 1958, a second such program was initiated for the Southeast Georgia area, with Roy E. Russell as missionary.[26e]

During this time, five cities, in Georgia were operating under City Mission programs, joint programs of the Georgia Baptist Convention, the Associations, and the Home Mission Board of the Southern Baptist Convention. They were Atlanta, Augusta, Columbus, Macon and Savannah.[26f]

By 1961, T. M. Underwood had been named to serve in an area of six associations in Northeast Georgia, under what had by that time had some to be called an Area Missions Program.[26g]

As the concept of associational work developed, the State

[26a]*Loc. cit.*

[26b]*Ibid.*, p. 100.

[26c]*The Christian Index*, February 14, 1957, p. 5.

[26d]*Minutes, Georgia Baptist Convention*, 1958, p. 381.

[26e]*Ibid.*, p. 111.

[26f]*Minutes, Georgia Baptist Convention*, 1962, p. 91; Minutes, Georgia Baptist Convention, 1961, p. 370.

746 / A History of The Georgia Baptist Convention

Missions program of the Convention, along with participating associations, assumed increased responsibility for the support of the missionaries.

The program of area mission work expanded from this time, along with continuing participation in the associational mission programs as well as the city missions programs.

The 30,000 Movement, which had as its goal 200 new churches for Georgia in 1963, continued to move forward. With cooperation from the executive secretary, his office staff, and The *Christian Index,* Woman's Missionary Union and the Department of Evangelism, 173 new churches and 269 new missions had been established by 1962, since the beginning of the program in June, 1956.[27] It was also in this year that Georgia Baptists moved into an accelerated program of ministries to students at campuses other than Baptist.

The Executive Committee in March, 1962, authorized the Administration Committee to plan the construction and equipping of a new Student Center Building for the University of Georgia students at Athens. This facility was estimated then to cost approximately $350,000.[28] From this point on heavy investments were made by the Convention in sites and buildings at state-owned colleges or adjacent to state-owned colleges for a ministry to students.

By the end of 1971, Georgia Baptists had invested $1,183,682 in facilities for ministries to students at state colleges in Athens, Valdosta, Statesboro, Tifton, Carrollton, Milledgeville, and Atlanta [Georgia Tech].[29]

ATLANTA COLLEGE AND THE CONVENTION

Details of the proposed Atlanta Baptist College had been indicated earlier.[30]

The projected three-year campaign required an extension.

---

[27]*Minutes, Georgia Baptist Convention,* 1962, p. 92.
[28]*Ibid.,* p. 96.
[29]Book of Reports Executive Committee, *Georgia Baptist Convention,* 1971, p. 178.
[30]*Minutes, Georgia Baptist Convention,* 1958, p.p. 95, 96; 1959, p.p. 86-88; 1960, p.p. 93-94.

The Executive Committee and the Education Commission recommended to the Convention in 1962 that a one-year extension of time be granted to the Atlanta Baptist Association for the college campaign project, and that conferences be held during 1963 to appraise the status of the project and present additional recommendations.[31]

The picture had changed by 1963. The Association reported in July in a conference with the Education Commission of the Convention, that 464 acres of land had been secured at a purchase price of $750,000, which had been paid. The committee reported further that $100,000 for possible operating deficit had been raised, and that $700,000 in pledges were on hand toward an agreed endowment of $600,000.[32] The Education Commission, in meetings in July and September of 1963, agreed to make a recommendation to the Executive Committee in September of 1963, and to the Convention in the same year, which called for the Convention to reaffirm its agreement and extend the time again one year from the 1963 session.[33]

The report called for parties to the agreements of 1958 and 1960 to recognize that rising costs would mean that funds considerably higher than the original appraisal would be needed.[34] However, at the September 3, 1963 meeting, representatives of Atlanta College campaign stated that in their judgment it would be better if the Convention would release the Association from the agreements of 1958, 1960 and 1962.

Therefore, at the September 10, 1963 meeting, the Education Commission received a resolution from the Executive Committee of the Atlanta association, which indicated that the association believed it to be in the best interest of Christian Education for the Convention to release the Association from its agreement, and called for establishment of a Baptist college in the Atlanta area to be the responsibility of the

[31]*Minutes, Georgia Baptist Convention*, 1962, p.p. 107, 108.
[32]*Minutes, Georgia Baptist Convention*, 1963, p. 106.
[33]*Ibid.*, p. 107.
[34]*Loc. cit.*

Association alone with this request superseding all previous agreements.[35]

The Executive Committee concurred with the Education Commission in agreeing to this proposal,[36] and the action was approved subsequently by the Convention.[37]

From this point, the Atlanta Baptist College, as a college, ceased to be a matter of Convention concern. In essence, the Atlanta Baptist Association representatives informed the Executive Committee they believed they could do better in promoting a Baptist college in Atlanta without the assistance of the Georgia Baptist Convention than being linked organically and by name to the Convention.[38]

Shortly before the Convention met in Augusta in 1970, the Atlanta Baptist College entered the Convention picture again; this time in a different manner. At that time, the college was in is third year of operation. Trustees had sold 60 acres of the property sometime in the Fall of 1970 to pay then current indebtedness of the college. With the sale of this land, indebtedness was paid and a balance in excess of $400,000 was reported. It was anticipated then that the College could, with this balance and other resources, operate through the term ending June 1, 1971.[39]

Earlier in 1970, the Atlanta Association had discussed the matter of college operation, and despite warnings from President Monroe F. Swilley that the college was in serious trouble, the association had instructed Swilley to continue operating the college. However, the Trustees of the Atlanta Baptist College began negotiations with the Administration Committee and the Executive Committee of the Convention. Following these negotiations the board of trustees of the college voted to tender through the Executive Committee to the Convention title to the Atlanta Baptist College property and

[35]*Ibid.*, p.p. 106-108.
[36]*Ibid.*, p. 108.
[37]*Ibid.*, p. 25.
[38]Personal conversations with leaders in Atlanta Association, statements made at Executive Committee, September 1963.
[39]*Minutes, Georgia Baptist Convention*, 1970, p. 34.

its assets, then estimated at $8,000,000 in value, for use in development of a Baptist Center.[40]

The offer was conditioned upon the Convention arranging for one of the senior colleges owned by the Convention to sponsor college operation the remainder of the 1970-1971 academic year in order that students enrolled in the college could complete their work toward a degree.[41]

The trustees recognized that it would be impossible to provide sufficient funds for the operation of the college through the Cooperative Program of the Convention and also that the Convention had no endowment funds available for that purpose. They agreed further that operation of the college after June, 1971, would be contingent upon funds available for operations. The Board of Trustees of the College indicated they would do their best to raise funds, but in the offer it was understood the Executive Committee would not be responsible for continued operation of the college after June, 1971, if monies were not available to cushion the budget deficit.

The proposed tender of the property was conditioned further upon the fact that if the Executive Committee found it evident that resources were not available for continued operation of a college, the property and assets conveyed to the Convention would be used in continued development of the center.[42]

Along with this recommendation, there was a recommendation from the Executive Committee to the Convention requesting the Convention to authorize the Executive Committee to lease or sell the Baptist Building properties at Peachtree, Baker and Ivy Streets in Atlanta. The Executive Committee had been offered a 99-year lease at an annual rental of $115,000 for three years, and beyond that escalation at one and one-half per cent compounded for the remainder of the 96 years of the lease with taxes, insurance, maintenance,

[40]*Minutes, Georgia Baptist Convention,* 1968, p. 34; *The Christian Index,* Nov. 19, 1970, p. 5.
[41]*Ibid.,* p. 35.
[42]*Minutes, Georgia Baptist Convention,* 1970, p.p. 34, 35.

and other expenses on the property to be born by the leasee, in addition to the rental, and that the interest of the convention would not be subordinated to any loan made by the leasee.[43]

Therefore, the Convention in 1970, with little advance notice, was faced with a tentative, conditioned offer of property valued at $8,000,000 for development, as well as with a lateral proposition to sell or lease the Baptist Building propeties in Atlanta in anticipation of a move of the Georgia Baptist Convention office building to the campus site, if it were developed into a Baptist Center.[44]

Authorization was granted to the Executive Committee to consumate a longe term lease on the downtown property at its discretion.[45] The Convention rejected a proposed amendment that the property be regarded as an endowment of the Atlanta Baptist College to insure continuation of the college as an integral and vital part of the proposed Baptist center and also it would be recognized that the Atlanta Baptist college would be considered a vital segment in the Convention's interest in higher education.[46]

The Convention, by its action, gave the Executive Committee authority to assume the property and a degree of discretion as to what to do with it conditioned upon decisions made by the Trustees of the college, and ability of the college to pay its way as a college if control were assumed by the Convention. There followed a year of indecision concerning the matter. The tentative proposal to the Convention in 1970 had occasioned plans for a Baptist center which would involve several denominational institutions and ministries.[47]

Late in December, 1970, the Trustees of the College voted to recommend that title be transferred to the Convention, with the stipulation that the Convention "make every possible effort to keep the school in operation." [48] The Atlanta Associ-

[43]*Ibid.,* pp. 35, 36.

[44]*Loc. cit.; The Christian Index,* Nov. 19, 1970, p. 5.

[45]*Minutes, Georgia Baptist Convention,* 1970, p. 35.

[46]*Ibid.,* p. 30.

[47]Book of Reports, *The Executive Committee, Georgia Baptist Convention,* 1971, p. 14.

ation Executive Committee, meeting early in January, 1971, refused to accept the 21-8 recommendation of the Trustees, and voted instead that

> . . . the Atlanta Baptist Association retain sponsorship of the college and that the college be continued, even though this may require a severe reduction in expense in order to match income, and a re-organization of the administration and the trustees of the college.[49]

The matter was complicated further by a suit brought against trustees of the college by a group of students.[50] In the suit, the students alleged that the trustees, who had sold 59 acres to the Gulf Life Insurance Co., and Kroger Properties, Inc., of Jacksonville, in leasing another 230 acres of land to these firms had agreements restricting sale of the property to anyone except the two specific firms for 10 years.[51] The suit alleged that a "restrictive covenant" had been invoked which required that any college property sold or leased within 10 years be used for office buildings only.[52]

Earlier in the year, following decision of the Association Executive Committee to retain the college, the Board of Trustees of the College voted on Feb. 26, 1971,

> . . . to express continued interest in the Georgia Baptist Convention establishing an administration center on the Atlanta Baptist College site. The Trustees offered unanimously to sell to the Executive Committee of the Convention 25 acres of its choice land at $2,000 per acre for use in relocating the Convention's administration offices. In response to this offer, the Executive Committee voted to purchase from the Atlanta Baptist College Board of Trustees approximately twenty-five [25] acres of land at a price of $2,000 per acre as a site for a Georgia Baptist Convention administration center. It was understood that fee simple title to the property would be conveyed by the College to the Executive Committee.[53]

This action was delayed by the suit, which was dismissed

[48]*The Christian Index*, Jan. 7, 1971, p. 4.
[49]*The Christian Index*, Jan. 21, 1971, p. 3.
[50]*The Christian Index*, March 25, 1971, p. 3.
[51]*Loc. cit.*
[52]*Loc. cit.*
[53]Book of Reports, *The Executive Committee, Georgia Baptist Convention,* 1971, p. 15.

by the Supreme Court of Georgia, Sept. 28, 1971, thus removing this cause of delay.[54]

At this point, the Executive Committee, approving the relocation of the Convention offices to the College site, authorized the Administration Committee and the Executive Secretary ". . . to proceed with plans and preparations for the construction . . ." of a center.[55] At the end of 1971, the matter rested with plans under way for a new Baptist Building, and expectations of development of a unique center upon this 25-acre site. The Convention purchased the 25 acres early in 1972.

By March, 1972, College President Monroe Swilley declared that the institution was ". . . on its feet and walking with assurance." There were 221 full time students and 19 part-time students.[56]

GENERAL GROWTH

In 1962, an all time record was set by the Children's Home when more than 700 children had lived on one of the three campuses during the year with the average number in care at 593.[57]

The work of the Georgia Baptist Foundation continued to grow. Corpus of trust funds held on June 30, 1962 were $4,062,635.95, an increase for that year of $329,317.99. The Foundation had from its beginnings exercised influential leadership in assisting Georgia Baptists in the making of wills and in the encouragement of setting up bequests to benefit agencies, institutions, and mission causes fostered by the Georgia Baptist Convention.[58] It was moving into an even stronger factor as Endowment funds from the Capital Improvements and Endowment programs were added annually.

In 1963, the Convention through its Resolutions Com-

[54]*Loc. cit.*
[55]*Loc. cit.*
[56]*The Christian Index*, March 9, 1972, p. 7.
[57]*Minutes, Georgia Baptist Convention,* 1962, p. 152.
[58]*Ibid.,* p. 176.

mittee endorsed the 1963 Southern Baptist Convention's statement of faith and message and urged that the approval which it expressed as a body be conveyed by circulation of the document among the churches and by publication of it in an attempt to strengthen the doctrinal understanding and position of Baptists in fellowship with the Convention.[59]

In its expanding program, the Convention added an associate to the Department of Evangelism, Andrew L. Miles, and stationed him as Baptist chaplain at the Reidsville State Prison.[60] An expanded service was offered also which included a ministry to patients at Milledgeville State Hospital. During 1963, scholarships were granted to eight pastors for a three-month study service program and counselling at the State Hospital. Of these scholarships, three were available for study programs for an entire year, with the programs being directed by the Department of Religious Services at the State Hospital, and the scholarships being administered by the Administration Committee of the Executive Committee. The sum of $5,000 was established in the budget in 1963 for this new ministry.[61]

R. T. Russell, Secretary of Evangelism for the Convention for nine years, and prior to that an associate for ten years, retired in 1963. Elected to succeed him in leading the Convention's evangelistic efforts was O. M. Cates, at the time pastor of the Cherokee Heights Church in Macon.[62]

For many years, the Regional Conferences on Denominational Ministries had been held throughout Georgia. These continued through 1961. In 1962 an emphasis known as the Denominational Emphasis Visitation Program, later called the Denominational Emphasis Program, was launched. This promotional program sought to focus attention upon the ministries of the entire Convention by saturation of a given associational grouping of churches on a Sunday for emphasis upon Convention ministries by servants from every area of

[59]*Minutes, Georgia Baptist Convention*, 1963, p. 47.
[60]*Ibid.*, p. 89.
[61]*Loc. cit.*
[62]*Ibid.*, p. 88.

denominational life. This program was designed to reach four to five areas of three to four associations each during each calendar year.[63] With the beginning of the Denominational Emphasis Program, some 50,000 people have been reached each year until the present.

The Program of Negro Work continued to grow also, with over 33,000 enrolled during 1963 in some phase of the training program.[64] In the same year, Woman's Missionary Union observed its 75th anniversary.[65]

In 1964, the Convention joined in celebration of the Baptist Jubilee Year, marking the beginning of organized Baptist work in the United States with a formation of the "Triennial Convention" in 1812. To commemorate this event, a pageant was presented depicting Baptist history. The pageant, entitled, "For Our Lord", was prepared and directed by Dr. Helen Thornton of Mercer University.[66]

In 1958, the Executive Committee had urged the churches to participate in a fund-raising drive for Chapels of Faiths at Milledgeville State Hospital. Work was undertaken on three chapels, with costs to be raised by public subscriptions. The chapels were constructed and dedicated early in 1964, and for these, Georgia Baptists had contributed $97,690.98 to the project, which cost over $922,404.21.[67]

Following approval earlier of cooperation with the Georgia Baptist Conference on the Deaf, the Convention's Administrative Committee named Charles A. Fanshaw to live at Cave Spring and serve in a ministry to students at the School for the deaf. This was a program supported from State Missions funds, as well as funds from the Home Mission Board of the Southern Baptist Convention. Fanshaw had worked with the deaf in a church in Savannah earlier.[68]

Another expansion of the State Missions ministry during 1964 was the naming of a Baptist minister to the University

[63]*Minutes, Georgia Baptist Convention*, 1962, p. 93.
[64]*Minutes, Georgia Baptist Convention*, 1963, p. 146.
[65]*Ibid.*, p. 147.
[66]*Minutes, Georgia Baptist Convention*, 1964, p. 20.
[67]*Ibid.*, p. 89.
[68]*Ibid.*, p. 100.

of Georgia community. B. Carroll Carter, who had been pastor of the First Baptist Church in College Park, enrolled at the University to complete work on a doctor's degree, and at the same time served as Baptist minister to assist in counselling and other ministries to students and faculty at the University of Georgia.[69] Carter was later to become a professor at Tift College.

On July 10, 1964, seventy-six persons assembled on the campus of Mercer University and formed the Georgia Baptist Historical Society, electing Arthur Jackson president, J. Emmett Henderson, vice president, Edgar M. Crosby, secretary and treasurer, and Spencer B. King, Jr., curator. The Mercer University library was designated as depository of historical materials.[70]

Commenting editorially, Editor John J. Hurt, of *The Christian Index*, extended congratulations to the newest denominational organization and said:

> It is our major hope to correct one of our greatest deficiencies.
> Georgia Baptists have done comparatively little to preserve their history. Our depository is at Mercer University where it is somewhat of a step-child in operation of the library. The neglect is not the fault of Mercer but the shame of the Georgia Baptist Convention.

In his editorial, Hurt cited the fact that the 150th anniversary of the Convention would be in eight years, and called for a new history of the Convention to be written.[71]

Hurt said:

> We must agree now that an excellent Georgia Baptist history book will be a part of our 150th anniversary or content ourselves with another book which fails to tell the story.[72]

This society was in a line of continuity of a similar body

[69]*Ibid.*, p. 101.
[70]*Ibid.*, p. 122.
[71]*The Christian Index*, July 16, 1964, p. 6.
[72]*Loc. cit.*

begun in 1878, and which had continued sporadically, with an active society at times.[73]

From this point on, the Historical Society as well as the Committee on Baptist History of the Georgia Baptist Convention worked together closely. Actually, the History Committee announced to the Convention formation of the Historical Society. Subsequently, reports of the Historical Society were to be carried in the minutes of the convention. The annual appropriation for work by the Committee on Baptist History was set at $1,600 for 1965.[74] The Committee on Baptist History began about this time to present citations to distinguished Georgia Baptists on behalf of the Convention, enumerating the accomplishments of those so honored at each session of the Convention. The continued cooperation between the Committee on Baptist History and the Historical Society was marked by a joint meeting of the two groups at Toccoa in 1965 and also in 1966.[75]

Beginning with the 1967 Minutes, the report of the Historical Society was printed following the report of the Committee on Baptist history. The Historical Society took note of the collection of history which was being expanded at the Stetson Memorial Library at Mercer, and by 1967, Mrs. Mary Overby was curator of the materials at Macon.[76]

During 1968 the Committee on Baptist History provided work grants to students in cooperation with the Historical Society and with the Stetson Library at Mercer to index and classify materials in the Baptist history section of the library.[77]

Viewpoints-Georgia Baptist History, Volume I, was published in 1968, the first such publication by the Historical Society, and was dedicated to the memory of Arthur Jackson,

[73]*Encyclopedia of Southern Baptists,* Vol. III [Nashville: Broadman Press, 1971], p. 1735.

[74]*Minutes, Georgia Baptist Convention,* 1964, p.p. 23, 122, 123.

[75]*Minutes, Georgia Baptist Convention,* 1965, p. 124.

[76]*Minutes, Georgia Baptist Convention,* 1967, p.p. 118, 121.

[77]*Minutes, Georgia Baptist Convention,* 1968, p. 122.

first president of the current society, and retired executive secretary-treasurer of the Georgia Baptist Foundation.[78]

The Committee on Baptist History for the Convention cooperated with the Executive Committee in laying groundwork for a proposed history of the Georgia Baptist Convention to be prepared in time for the 1972 150th Anniversary celebration.[79]

Mrs. Overby, who had been assigned by Mercer as a member of the Mercer staff to work full time in the Baptist historical section of the library in 1964, had cooperated with assoications, churches, and individuals, and also with the Georgia Department of Archives and History in microfilming church, association, and college records.[80]

RETIREMENT PROGRAMS

The year 1964 marked the 25th year in which the Ministers Retirement Program had been in operation in the state. Arthur Hinson in his report to the Convention, said that more than 2,100 churches had at one time participated in the program and more than 1,500 pastors and staff members had participated. As of September 1, 1964, there were 1,134 Georgia Baptist churches paying membership dues, and pastors and staff members participating as of September 1, 1964 numbered 1,227.[81]

Activities of the Georgia Baptist Foundation had continued to grow. The Foundation by 1964 reported a corpus of funds in excess of $5,500,000 for permanent investments. Trust funds for the year increased by approximately $600,000.[82]

In response to a request from the Laurens County Association for an opinion as to whether or not the Convention held legal title to Mercer University, the attorney for the Executive Committee, John J. Poole, gave as his opinion the

[78]*Ibid.*, p.p. 124, 125.
[79]*Minutes, Georgia Baptist Convention*, 1969, p. 133.
[80]*Minutes, Georgia Baptist Convention*, 1970, p. 127.
[81]*Minutes, Georgia Baptist Convention*, 1964, p. 181.
[82]*Ibid.*, p. 183.

fact that although Mercer was a separate corporation, with its own Board of Trustees, that since the Convention elected all of the members of the Board of Trustees

> . . . It is proper to say that Mercer University is owned and controlled by the Baptist Convention of the State of Georgia.
>
> In this connection, two limitations are contained in the charter. First, future amendments to the charter must be approved, before being granted, by a majority of those present at a regular meeting of the Baptist Convention of the State of Georgia and by a two-thirds vote of all members of the Board of Trustees of Mercer University then in office. Second, in regular elections of trustees each year four shall be nominated by the remaining members of the Board of Trustees and two shall be nominated by the alumni of Mercer University. In this connection, the charter specifically provides that in the case of disapproval of any nomination, the Board of Trustees or the alumni shall submit another name or names until an acceptable name is submitted and that the Convention shall fill all vacancies only from names thus nominated to it.[83]

In his report to the Convention in 1965, the year that the general offices were scheduled to be moved to the Baptist Building, Manager John C. Warr reported the average number of children in care at 582, with the cost of $3.22 per child per day and the cost of administration for the year at $1.00 per day per child.[84]

During 1965, gifts for Georgia causes totaled $5,293,-139.32.[85] Georgia Baptists gave for all causes through their denominational offices in that year $9,411,514.21. Cooperative Program gifts for the year amounted to $4,709,293.36, and Designated Gifts were $4,702,220.85.[86]

Approval having been given several years earlier for construction of a Baptist Student Center to serve the University of Georgia, construction began in August of 1965 on the building.[87] This building was completed at a cost of $375,000

[83]*Minutes, Georgia Baptist Convention*, 1965, p.p. 88, 89.
[84]*Ibid.*, p. 173.
[85]*Ibid.*, p. 252.
[86]*Ibid.*, p. 251.
[87]*Ibid.*, p. 92.

and was dedicated September 25, 1966, debt free.[88] Plans at that time were under way for construction of a new Baptist Student Center to serve Georgia Southern College in Statesboro, and plans were being made for a Student Center Building at Georgia Tech. The Savannah Association had purchased a lot for $10,000 for a Student Center when funds were available. A lot had been purchased for future development of a student center at West Georgia College. Land for a Baptist Student Center had been purchased in Tifton for future development. Additionally, a residence had been secured in Milledgeville for the director of Student Work at the Woman's College in order to have the lot available for building of a student center.[89] With these construction plans, and with the University of Georgia Center already completed, Georgia Baptists were expanding into what would become a multimillion dollar Student Center operation on campuses other than Baptist owned.

NEW EDITOR OF THE CHRISTIAN INDEX

In November, 1966, Jack U. Harwell, who for nine years had been associated with The *Christian Index,* was named 28th editor of the religious journal, succeeding John J. Hurt. Hurt, who had served as editor for 19 years, had resigned earlier to become editor of the *Baptist Standard,* the organ of the Baptist General Convention of Texas.[90]

For the first time in 1965 the closing session of the Convention was a Youth Night, with emphasis upon the role which young people could have in the ministries of the Georgia Baptist Convention. The Youth Night feature was to continue as a part of the annual Convention program.[91] In 1966, Searcy S. Garrison completed preparation of a Book of Charters, authorized by the Convention at its 1958 session.[92]

[88]*Minutes, Georgia Baptist Convention,* 1966, p. 154.
[89]*Loc. cit.*
[90]*The Christian Index,* November 24, 1966, p. 7; *Minutes, Georgia Baptist Convention,* 1966, p. 36.
[91]*Minutes, Georgia Baptist Convention,* 1965, p. 79.
[92]*Minutes, Georgia Baptist Convention,* 1966, p. 103.

This Book of Charters was the second such book in the history of the Convention, the first one having been completed in 1903 and revised several years later.

In an expanding ministry, the State Mission budget had allocated during 1965 and 1966 $10,000 toward construction of a house of worship and educational building for the Jekyll Island Baptist Church. Although sufficient funds had not been raised for construction, the ministry at the state-owned resort island was an expanding one by this time.[93]

Another new ministry of the Georgia Baptist Convention —really not new but re-established—was that of a New Church Site Fund, which provided that at the close of 1966

> . . . any available funds up to $5,000 from the State Missions budget will be used to begin this fund, and the State Missions budget committee is requested to make provisions for increasing the fund with gifts from the special State Missions offerings in 1967.[94]

The policy for use of $1,500 toward the purchase of a site for location of a new church, provided that a church or association invest an equal amount in the purchase of the site. The Executive Committee would then take a lien on the property in the amount of the gift from the fund, to be cancelled when the church had contributed a total of 10 times the amount of the loan to denominational causes through the Co-operative Program. This program was activated after January 1, 1967.[95]

Georgia Baptists committed themselves to participating in The Crusade of the Americas, and during 1968 and 1969 preparation was being made by the several departments of State Missions led by O. M. Cates, secretary of the Department of Evangelism. Cates assured priority for this Crusade effort in the churches. The Crusade revivals were held in March and April of 1969, with January, 1968 through March, 1969 as a period of prayer and preparation for this effort.[96]

By 1967, permanent assets of the Georgia Baptist Founda-

[93]*Ibid.,* p. 106.
[94]*Ibid.,* p. 107.
[95]*Loc. cit.*
[96]*Minutes, Georgia Baptist Convention,* 1967, p. 140.

tion exceeded the $8,000,000 mark, earnings were at the $300,000 level for the year, and Charles C. Duncan had been named as Assistant Secretary of the Foundation in the program of expansion.[97]

PASTOR–CHURCH PROGRAM

Two proposals dealing with pastors and churches were introduced to Georgia Baptists in 1968. A recommendation from the Executive Committee was for adoption of a report concerning a service in the area of church and pastor relationships. The Executive Committee at its meeting in March, 1968, asked the president of the Convention to appoint a committee of twelve to study the matter of church-pastor relationships and report to the Executive Committee in September.[98]

At the September meeting, the special committee made its report, and the Exectuive Committee joined in recommendations to the Convention. The report cited problems in the area of pastor-church relationships, and said that changes in pastorates ". . . are of sufficient gravity to merit the thoughtful and prayerful study of pastors, churches, associations, pastors conferences and the convention."

The recommendation carried a request that authorization be given for establishment of a committee on church-pastor relations, and also calling for an enlargement of the State Missions program to include such a service to churches and pastors with care being exercised so that there would be no intrusion upon the affairs of the churches.[99] This proposal, presented by James N. Griffith for the Committee, was defeated.[100] This was similar to a proposal made by James P. Wesberry in his Presidential address in 1958.[101]

The 1970 Convention heard a similar proposal. A special committee, headed by James W. Waters, to study church-

[97]*Ibid.*, p. 185.
[98]*Minutes, Georgia Baptist Convention*, 1968, p. 110.
[99]*Ibid.*, pp. 110-111.
[100]*Ibid.*, p. 27.
[101]*The Christian Index*, Nov. 13, 1958, p. 20.

minister relations, again presented a report, essentially the same as in 1968, in calling for an expansion of the State Missions program to include a service to churches and ministers in the area of church-minister relations. This would be operated as a phase of the State Missions program under policies established by the Executive Committee and supervised by the Administration Committee.

The proposed service, if established, would be available upon a request basis only.[102] With the presentation in 1970, the proposal was approved by ballot vote of 651 for and 356 against.[103] Implementation of this program was begun with the election in September, 1971, of Roy N. Hinchey, pastor of the Jefferson Avenue Baptist Church in East Point, as first secretary. The program was designated Church-Minister Relations Service of the Georgia Baptist Convention.[104] Hinchey assumed his duities November 1, 1971.[105]

Allied to this growing concern for a ministry in this area, was a motion made and carried at the 1968 Convention that the Executive Committee consider providing a counselling service for Georgia Baptist ministers and their families.[106] Following the motion by John Bledsoe,[107] The Executive Committee referred the matter to its Administration Committee. Upon studying the situation, facts were presented that professional counselling service was available to ministers through the chaplain of the Georgia Baptist Hospital and his assistants, and through the chaplain at Central State Hospital in Milledgeville.

It was noted further that the Georgia Baptist Hospital and the Central State Hospital provided clinical educational programs for pastors and the services of the leaders of these programs were available to ministers on an individual basis.[108] Other sources for counselling were cited, and the Con-

[102]*Minutes, Georgia Baptist Convention,* 1970, p.p. 27-30.
[103]*Ibid.,* p. 27.
[104]*The Christian Index,* Sept. 23, 1971, p. 5.
[105]*Loc. cit.*
[106]*Minutes, Georgia Baptist Convention,* 1968, p. 39.
[107]*Loc. cit.*

vention adopted a recommendation which said in essence that recognition was taken of the fact that pastors and members of their families at times had need of counselling service, and that those who needed such service be advised to communicate with the chaplain of the Georgia Baptist Hospital. The Hospital Commission and administration were requested to consider the possibility of expanding its program to include a counselling ministry to pastors.[109]

The September, 1970, meeting of the Executive Committee received a report that counselling service to pastors, staff members, and members of their families had been established as a phase of the counselling service of the Georgia Baptist Hospital.[110]

As a follow-up to the plans for construction of student centers, early in 1968 the Baptist Center Building at Georgia Southern College in Statesboro was dedicated debt free, and the contract was signed in October of 1968 in the amount of $430,000 for construction of a Baptist Student Center to serve the students at the Georgia Institute of Technology.[111]

The Convention in 1969 approved the action of the Committee on Baptist History and Administration Committee in making plans for a publication of a history of the Georgia Baptist Convention. James A. Lester, who had served for eleven and one-half years as Secretary of Promotion and Public Relations for the Convention, and who was serving at the time as editor of *Baptist and Reflector*, the news journal of the Tennessee Baptist Convention, was commissioned to write the manuscript.[112]

In a first for a Georgia Baptist College, Trustees of Tift College, in Forsyth, were authorized to borrow money to construct a motel at the intersection of Interstate Highway 75 and Tift College Drive. The college instead chose to lease

[108]*Minutes, Georgia Baptist Convention,* 1969, p. 93.
[109]*Loc. cit.*
[110]*Minutes, Georgia Baptist Convention,* 1970, p.p. 27, 28.
[111]*Minutes, Georgia Baptist Convention,* 1968, p. 92.
[112]*Minutes, Georgia Baptist Convention,* 1969, p. 94.

the land to a private group for development of a motel.[113] The year 1970 was a first in several ways. For the first time in the history of the Georgia Baptist Convention, the state mission budget for a single year exceeded $1,000,000. The budget for 1970 was $1,062,165.[114]

This was a year of changes. Garnie A. Brand had resigned in 1969 to become vice president of Norman College, and Waldo Woodcock was named to succeed Brand as secretary of the Church Training Department.[115]

A Judson Burrell, long-time pastor of the Rose Hill Baptist Church, Columbus, was elected in 1969 as Secretary of Stewardship Promotion. On Jan. 1, 1970 he assumed responsibility also for the Convention's Annuity Ministries following the retirement of Arthur Hinson on Dec. 31, 1969.[115a]

Harold Sangster, who had been an associate in the Department of Evangelism for four years, resigned to become a pastor at Tallapoosa,[116] and Julian P. Snyder, who had served in the Department of Church Training for 26 years, retired on July 15.[117] Additionally, Harry V. Smith, Sr., retired as Executive Secretary-Treasurer of the Georgia Baptist Foundation, and was succeeded by Charles C. Duncan.[118]

Georgia Baptists during 1970 gave through their Convention offices $10,742,040.00 for all causes. Of this amount, $4,687,346 was designated and $6,054,694.00 was for the Cooperative Program.[119] With this background of giving, the budget adopted for 1971 was $5,872,200.[120]

When the Georgia Baptist Convention met for its 150th session on Jekyll Island in November, 1971, it reviewed a year of accomplishments, finalized plans for a year-long observance of the Sesquicentennial of the Georgia Baptist

[113]*Ibid.,* p. 96.
[114]*Minutes, Georgia Baptist Convention,* 1970, p. 134.
[115]*Ibid.,* p. 96.
[115a]*Minutes, Georgia Baptist Convention,* 1969, p. —; 1970, p. —.
[116]*Ibid.,* p. 97.
[117]*Ibid.,* p. 96.
[118]*Ibid.,* p. 32.
[119]*Ibid.,* p. 248.
[120]*Ibid.,* p. 103.

Convention in 1972, and was at the time entered into yet another era of growth and expansion of ministries.

The stage was set for this expanded era earlier and was enunciated well in 1971. The newly-elected president of the Convention, R. J. Robinson, pastor of the historic First Baptist Church in Augusta, where the Southern Baptist Convention was born in 1845, said:

> To be creative in the coming year we must have confidence in ourselves. My plea is that we not allow ourselves to be swallowed up in an age of conformity, following each other, instead of being ourselves and following almighty God. . . . The struggles of 1971 are to be fought by contemporary Georgia Baptists under the leadership of God's spirit in the arena of competitive secularism. . . .
> Surely we Georgia Baptists ought to get past pitting liberals against conservatives, evangelism against social concern, and schools against churches, for one-million Georgia Baptists need to realize that we live under the shadow of God's judgment.[121]

Within the framework of this concept, a Convention which had matured theologically and organizationally many years earlier, during 1971 experienced a time of consistent growth.

Having grown through the years upon a strong base of State Missions and education, a summary of progress in these areas to the 150th session of the Convention is given.

Objectives of the State Mission Program were unchanged basically. They were:

> [1] . . . to win the lost people of Georgia to faith in Christ; [2] to establish new missions and churches where needed; [3] to strengthen the churches, both small and large, so they can realize their divinely-commissioned work and world-wide mission; [4] to extend the ministries and witness to our churches to unreached and needy people; [5] to develop in Georgia a spiritual climate which will be favorable to Christian life and the development of a Christian social order.[122]

Within this concept, and with a budget for 1971 of $1,118,312, the State Mission Program included Associational Missions work in 81 of the 93 associations; ten de-

---

[121]*The Christian Index*, Jan. 7, 1971, p. 3.
[122]Book of Reports, The Executive Committee 1971, p. 66.

partmental areas of work, supported also through the work of Woman's Missionary Union; ministries in language missions, weekday programs, mission centers, summer mission programs, chaplaincy ministries, juvenile rehabilitation, and a ministry to the hippie community in Atlanta.

Additionally, the program of promotion included conferences for associational officers, continuation of the Denominational Emphasis Program, schools of missions, stewardship development, Emergency Church Building Fund, and related activities.[123]

For the year June 1, 1970-June 1, 1971, Georgia Baptist Hospital had discharged 25,562 patients.[124] Baptist Village had 200 residents,[125] and Peachtree-On-Peachtree Inn reported 166 residents.[126]

Participation in retirement programs grew, with 1,394 churches and 1,405 pastors, 46 associational and area missionaries, and 249 church staff members participating.[127]

The Children's Home had provided care for 519 children, and had assisted in placement of over 100 others.[128]

Charles C. Duncan reported to the 1971 Convention session that assets of the Georgia Baptist Foundation stood at $10,162,064.[129] The Endowments section of the Capital Improvements and Endowment Program continued to provide large amounts of money for future welfare of the institutions.

As of August 1, 1971, indebtedness upon the institutions owned by the Convention was $7,975,678.14.[130] The Capital Improvements and Endowment Program of 1965, completed in 1970, provided $5,475,000 from Cooperative Program Funds, and the Capital Improvements and Endowment Program of 1970 was implemented, with $315,988.98 made

[123]*Ibid.*, p.p. 66-70.
[124]*Ibid.*, p. 97.
[125]*Ibid.*, p. 104.
[126]*Ibid.*, p. 109.
[127]*Ibid.*, p. 114.
[128]*Ibid.*, p. 88.
[129]*Ibid.*, p. 121.
[130]*Ibid.* p. 13.

available in this year for the new program.[131] By the end of 1971, $1,407,568.52 had been applied on the new program, of which amount $1,091,579.54 was from the 1971 budget.[132]

Enrollment at Mercer University was nearing the 2,000-student mark,[133] and Tift, Shorter, Brewton-Parker and Truett-McConnell colleges continued to provide a ministry of Christian education.

During 1971, a total of $6,317,345.39 was given by Georgia Baptists through their Cooperation Program, and total gifts for the year were $11,270,175.04, an all-time record.[134]

[131]*Ibid.*, p.p. 10-11.
[132]*Georgia Baptist Digest*, Vol. 32, 1972, p. 29.
[133]Book of Reports, the Executive Committee, 1971, p. 66.
[134]*Georgia Baptist Digest*, Vol. 32, 1972, p. 12.

CHAPTER 30

The Sesquicentennial Year—1972

The Georgia Baptist Convention entered into its Sesquicentennial year of celebration with 93 associations, 2,952 churches, and total membership of 1,018,052. There were 30,076 baptisms recorded during 1971 and at the end of 1971 there were 2,605 pastors serving churches in fellowship with the Convention and 2,623 full-time churches, 285 half-time churches, and 44 quarter-time churches.[1]

The Georgia Baptist Convention presently is engaged in a program of ministry through ten State Missions departments, one of which includes the assembly programs, five educational institutions, a hospital, two Homes for the Aged, a Children's Home with three campuses, and active programs of promotion of the entire work of the Convention through the Executive Committee and its administrative officer, Searcy S. Garrison.

Additionally, Woman's Missionary Union is an auxiliary to the Georgia Baptist Convention and the Convention is ministering in the associations through assistance to missionaries in 37 associational missions programs and in ten area missions programs which embrace 37 associations.

With Garrison as administrator, the State Missions program is one of three major areas of Convention work; the others being education and benevolent ministries. State Missions departments include Evangelism, Sunday School, Church Training, Brotherhood, Church Music, Student

[1]Georgia Baptist Digest, Vol. 32, 1972, p. 11.

work, assemblies, Church Minister Relations, and a Program of work with National Baptists. Additionally, the Cooperative Missions work is a part of this program. There are approximately 150 persons employed in the State Mission ministries, including thirteen mission pastors and other missionaries named, several part time and summer workers and the Executive Committee staff in the Baptist Building in Atlanta.

For 1972, the State Mission budget was $1,221,004 with $834,000 of this amount allocated from the Cooperative Program in special gifts during the State Mission emphasis expected to provide the remainder of the budget. Other State Mission ministeries continued to include a pastoral aid ministry, emergency church building aid, a new church site bond, the Denominational Emphasis Program, and the annual Associational Officers' Conference, together with the Study Service Ministry being carried out at Central State Hospital in Milledgeville. Earnest Kelley, an assistant to the Executive Secretary-Treasurer, has responsibility for the administration of the Cooperative Missions work, which includes associational and area Missions program, together with other administrative functions.

When the Georgia Baptist Convention assumed Norman College at its meeting in November, 1971, it provided an expanded assembly ministry with Garnie A. Brand, a former Vice-President of Norman and a former secretary of the Church Training department of the Georgia Baptist Convention as Assembly manager.

Clifton Forrester continued to serve as manager of the Georgia Baptist Assembly and under Forrester's management also was Camp Tugalo for boys located on the Assembly grounds at Toccoa and Camp Glenn located near Brunswick, Georgia. During 1971 the Georgia Baptist Assembly registered 13,177 guests, representing 203 church groups and Conventions sponsored retreats.

The newest ministry, Church-Minister Relation Services was established in 1971 with Roy W. Hinchey as secretary.

Other state mission programs included the Department of Evangelism with O. M. Cates as secretary, the Sunday School department with Julian T. Pipkin as secretary, the Church Training department with Waldo M. Woodcock as secretary, the Brotherhood department with Bernard D. King as secretary, the Department of Church Music with Paul Mc-Common as secretary, the Department of Student work with Aubrey L. Hawkins as secretary, and the Program of Work with National Baptists with Earle F. Stirewalt as secretary.

Benevolent ministries included Georgia Baptist Hospital, Edwin B. Peel, administrator; Georgia Baptist Children's Home Inc., O. Leonard Pedigo, Jr., administrator, Baptist Village, Waycross, Harvey R. Mitchell, administrator, and Peachtree Inn in Atlanta, Cecil T. Underwood, administrator.

For the fiscal year July 1, 1970, through June 30, 1971, the Georgia Baptist Hospital had cared for 25,562 patients with 149,896 patients with 149,896 patient days involved. During 1971, for the fiscal year ending June 30, the Children's Home had provided care for 519 boys and girls on campuses at Baxley, the Odum branch, the Palmetto campus and the Pine Mountain campus at Meansville. Additionally, the Children's Home provided care through a foster home program and a ministry to the families of the children. At the close of 1971, there were 200 residents of Baptist Village with capacity in the Nursing Department of Baptist Village for 132 and Peachtree on Peachtree Inn at the end of 1971 had 166 residents.

Under the area of benevolent ministries, A. Judson Burrell serves as secretary of Annuity and Protection Programs, a ministry operated in cooperation with the Annuity Board of the Southern Baptist Convention. Burrell serves also as secretary of Stewardship.

The Christian Index continued to serve as the official organ of the Georgia Baptist Convention, owned by the Executive Committee, administered through a Board of Directors elected by the Convention upon recommendation of the Convention Nominating Committee. Jack U. Harwell is editor of *The Christian Index* with George J. Sheridan, associate editor and R. L. Duke, promotion associate.

The auxiliary to the Georgia Baptist Convention Woman's Missionary Union continued to be led by Miss Dorothy Pryor, Executive Secretary-Treasurer of Woman's Missionary Union.

During 1971, Georgia Baptists gave $2,564,348 for Christian Education causes. The Georgia Baptist Foundation Inc. and Endowment Committee of the Georgia Baptist Convention, with Charles C. Duncan as Executive Secretary-Treasurer serves as the trust agency to receive and administer funds from wills, bequests, and other sources.

Mercer University, under the leadership of Dr. Rufus Carrollton Harris, president, enrolled for 1970 1,929 students. The facilities of the main campus of Mercer consists of 75 acres adjacent to Macon's Tatenal Square Park. The University observed in 1971 its Centennial Year in Macon. Mercer University administer also the extension program of Christian Education for the Georgia Baptist Convention under the direction of J. Aubrey Estes. The Extension Centers provide training for pastors, their families, and other interested persons throughout the state. Robert W. Jackson served as president of Tift College, which in 1972 was in its 123rd year of 4 years liberal arts college for women. Randall H. Minor was president of Shorter College at Rome, which was founded in 1873 and which in 1972 was offering majors in 14 fields of study.

J. Theodore Phillips served as president of Brewton-Parker college, Mount Vernon. Brewton-Parker, as of 1972, was the oldest of the junior colleges established under Baptist auspices and Convention patronage. Truett-McConnell College was led by Warner Earle Fusselle as president.

Additionally, the Georgia Baptist Hospital School of Nursing was directed by Mrs. Kathryn Ransbotham. In addition to the School of Nursing the Hospital was operating a Pastoral Care program, residencies in six specialties for physicians, rotating internships for physicians, a school of anesthesia for nurses, and a school of medical technology. The Hospital is the largest, private medical center hospital in Georgia. For the fall quarter of 1971 a total of 4,593 students were enrolled in the three senior colleges, the two junior colleges, and the Georgia Baptist Hospital School of Nursing program.[2]

In May, 1972, Harold L. Sangster was named assistant manager of the Georgia Baptist Assembly, Toccoa. Sangster had served the Convention earlier as an associate in the Department of Evangelism.[3] Finally, by mid 1972, The Georgia Baptist Children's Home had acquired a "group home" facility in Savannah, with an initial capacity of eight teen-age girls, purpose of the home was to assist older teen-agers in making a ". . . transition from rural institutional life to adulthood in an urban setting." [4]

[2]*Ibid.*, Entire Digest; Book of Reports, 1971, the Executive Committee, The Baptist Convention of the State of Georgia. [Both sources used for general compilation of materials in this brief chapter.]

[3]*The Christian Index*, May 4, 1972, p. 1.

[4]*The Christian Index*, June 1, 1972, p. 1.

Epilogue

An epilogue cannot, in actuality, embrace the historical-critical approach. *A History of the Georgia Baptist Convention: 1822-1972* is a studied, careful effort to present an accurate, documented portrayal. History, however, flows in a continuing stream, and continues to be enacted.

Georgia Baptists looked toward 1972 with growing enthusiasm for the commemoration of the 150th anniversary of the founding of the Georgia Baptist Convention. Even as they did this, however, there was continued progress. R. J. Robinson was elected to a second term as president of the Convention in 1971, and would serve in this capacity through the Sesquicentennial observance. In his President's Address to the 1971 Convention, Robinson said: "I believe that the church of Jesus Christ is neither senile nor arthritic. We just may be suffering temporarily from the paralysis of analysis." [1] Citing adverse criticisms from within and without the church, Robinson continued in his address to assert: "But I still insist that while the church and her ministers have many foibles, faithful servants of God proclaiming 'the Kerygma' are Almighty God's instruments of redemption for our day." [2]

Concerning 1972, Robinson declared:

> Also, in the 150th year of organized Baptist life in Georgia, I want us to go beyond recalling historical events with colorful pageantry. Let us re-discover the convictions and commitments of our Baptist forbears, which made them strong and useful in the kingdom enterprise. With renewed personal and corporate commitment to Jesus Christ, we should proceed with our

[1] Document, President's Address, p. 5, Author's Possession.
[2] *Ibid.*, p. 6.

775

work—confident of God's blessings and sure of success according to his purpose.[3]

In these statements, Robinson articulated well the apparent sentiment of the great majority of Georgia Baptists.

Georgia Baptists have produced great Christian statesmen, and have been led by great Christian staesmen for more than 150 years. Current leadership at every level of Georgia Baptist life; the local church, the association, the state convention, is in the finest tradition of the Convention's long history. Few men have given of themselves in courageous, effective leadership as have Searcy S. Garrison and the dedicated staff with whom he serves. Leaders at every level of Convention life are men dedicated to the cause of Christ and the advancement of the Kingdom of God.

Behind each church and in every association, and concerning every leader in the ministry of Christ, there is a story of courage, sacrifice and devotion. It is to the author's regret that there was not space to recount some of these stories.

Even as Georgia Baptists prepared to mark 150 years of service, they laid the groundwork in 1971 for a record of advance in 1972. Authorization of a $16 million addition to the Georgia Baptist Hospital, and construction of a $4 million Baptist Professional Building speaks for itself. Statesmanship in the handling of the transfer of Norman College property, making it an Assembly, again, speaks for itself, when, in the report from the Executive Committee to the Convention, in recommending the action, is found the statement.

> It is the studied conclusion of the Administration Committee that: 1. Georgia Baptists will not allow a debt on any Georgia Baptist institution to remain unpaid and will accept responsibility for retiring the debts of Norman College.[4]

Decisions to construct a Convention Administrative Center indicate again the progress of Georgia Baptists, just as the

[3]*Ibid.*, p. 2.
[4]Book of Reports, 1971, p. 22.

statement concerning Norman identifies an historic attitude of Christian stewardship upon the part of the Convention.

This then, is the record. It speaks for itself.

James Adams Lester,
Brentwood, Tennessee,
May, 1972

Appendix A

Baptist Beginnings,
The Heritage of Georgia Baptists

They marched across the pages of history in growing numbers. Facing persecution, imprisonment, hardship, deprivation, and the onus of anti-establishmentarianism, Baptists have been a part of and leaders in Georgia life from the earliest days of the settlement of this state.

By Baptist, we mean that group of people, identifiable as a part of the mainstream of Evangelical Christianity, who took the Bible to be the inspired Word of God—many taking literally the King James version of that Word—declaring their belief in a Triune God, the Lordship of Christ, and the presence and continuous working of the Holy Spirit in the hearts and lives of men on earth.

Many of them were poor, lacking in many instances higher education, and the refinements of a comfortable civilization and culture, and making their appearance historically as a part of the mainstream of the Protestant heritage.

What they lacked in temporal comforts, they made up for with a zest for life, an uncluttered belief in the goodness of God, tinctured with a liberal dose of strict Calvinism, and cured in the day-by-day difficulties of helping conquer a new world.

Baptists, from their earliest beginnings, placed emphasis upon the Lordship of Christ, the direct access of the believer to God, without intermediary of any type; and they expressed

779

their complete agreement with the congregational form of church polity. Taking as their ordinances the Lord's Supper and Believer's baptism, these Baptists grew numerically despite persecution; they grew in influence despite opposition, and their witness made itself felt from their earliest recorded beginnings in Europe. They were part of their day and age—whatever that day and age—and their oft-times rigid orthodoxy, never-the-less earned for them the right to be called sincere children of God, and the respect, ultimately, of their contemporaries.

These Baptists emerged historically in the early years of the 17th century.

Despite the efforts of many writers to trace lineal descent of Baptists to John the Baptist, historic fact does not support that presupposition. Baptists were dissenters; dissenters from an established, authoritarian church.[1]

Three schools of thought are accepted by modern historians concerning their emergence. Baptists as we know them today, with their distinct beliefs and practice in church polity, have been some 20 centuries in development. One body of thought as exemplified by Orchard's *Baptist History,* was that they started at the River Jordan, and have been the only group of importance since that time.[3] This concept is based upon the theory that visual continuity from Jesus Christ to the present day is a necessity to insure Biblical succession.[4]

A second school of thought is that Baptists were, in effect, a foam washed up during the period of Protestant revolt in the 16th century. This is based upon a concept that Luther, Huss, Wycliff, and others spawned a sect or group of sects, one of which would ultimately be called Baptists. However,

[1]Robert G. Torbet, *A History of the Baptists* [Philadelphia: The Judson Press, 1950], p.p. 24-31.

[3]G. H. Orchard, *A Concise History of Foreign Baptists* [New York: Sheldon, Lamport & Co., 1855], p. 22.

[3]*Loc. cit.,* see also, Torbet, p.p. 59-60.

[4]*Ibid.,* Sections I, II, III, p.p. 1-37.

nothing is spawned full grown. There must be antecedents. Walker traces well these antecedents.[5]

The third school of thought is that we should assume a mediating position between the two extremes, allowing room for the historic emergence of an entity based upon centuries of theological formulation.[6]

It is safe to assert that the spirit and ideas of the present-day Baptists, embraced, for example, in the New Hampshire Confession of Faith, and other similar confessions, can be traced directly to the teachings of our Lord. A reasonable, historic statement is that there have been throughout history, since New Testament times, a group of people who believed in the Bible as the Word of God, and who sought to order their lives and religious efforts around the teachings of this Word. Baptist thought and theology had antecedents in the teachings of Menno Simons, the Waldensians of another century, and in the thinking of all those who stood behind the Word of God and man's right of direct access to God, believing in the substitutionary atonement of Jesus Christ.[7] As well known a historian of the 19th century as Thomas Armitage, in his *Edition Deluxe,* devoted more than 300 pages to tracing of Baptists in theological, if not historic, succession from the New Testament times to the emergence in the late 16th and early 17th centuries as an identifiable entity.[8]

In the midst of the Protestant Reformation, in the early part of the 16th century, men like Conrad Grebel, Balthasar Hubmaier, and others led in what was termed "a radical wing of dissent" which produced small "gathered churches" on the continent, and a Baptist movement in England. Continental Baptists have been identified as "Pelagian." Pela-

---

[5]Williston Walker, *A History of the Christian Church* [New York: Charles Scribner's Sons, 1947], p.p. 457-467.

[6]Torbet, p.p. 15-31

[7]*Loc. cit.*

[8]Thomas Armitage, *A History of the Baptists,* Volume I [New York: Bryan, Taylor, and Co., 1887], covering first 300 pages.

gius, a British or Irish monk, representing many older views theologically [around 400 A.D.], held to the freedom of the human will. "If I ought, I can;" an attitude popular also with stoic ethics.[9] He denied original sin as an inheritance from Adam, and "affirmed that all men now have the power not to sin." [10] His teachings are traceable historically up to the Reformation.

British dissenting thought centered to a large degree around the teachings of John Calvin, born in Noyon, France, in 1509, and Jacob Arminius, who directed his thinking on more "practical aspects of religion, a disinclination toward sharp creedal definitions, and a more tolerant attitude." [11] Calvin promulgated the concept of unconditional predestination, and Arminius ascribed to man a freedom of choice absent in the rigid predestinarian concepts of Calvin.[12]

Whatever the earlier identification, at the time the name Baptist began to emerge historically in the early days of the 17th century, identifications developed which made evident distinctions in Baptist life in this country under the terms General Baptists, and Particular Baptists.

Against this background of emerging diverse theological views, the political situation in England created a climate out of which arose what were then identified as the Separatist movements. This growing body of "non-conformists" in England became the object of attack first by Elizabeth I, and then by James I, of England. Following the rather strong attacks against those who disapproved of the state church, James I having said: "I will make them conform, or I will hurry them out of the land," dissenters fled from England to Holland.[13]

The word "Baptists", as we know it today, was used first in English literature in the year 1644, in the First Confession

[9]Walker, p. 185.
[10]Loc. cit.
[11]Ibid., p. 454.
[12]Loc. cit.
[13]Henry C. Vedder, A Short History of the Baptists [Philadelphia: The American Baptist Publication Society, 1907], p. 20.

of Faith issued by Particular Baptists. Those who issued this confession described themselves "as commonly, [but unjustly], called 'Anabaptists.' " While they repudiated the name Anabaptist, they did not for some time claim the new name of Baptists, seeming to prefer "Baptized believers," or, as in the Assembly's Confession of 1654, "Christians baptized upon profession of their faith." [14]

Osiander, a historian of the 17th century in Tubingen, Germany, said: "Our modern Anabaptists are the same as the Donatists of old." [15] Christian says, however, that "these rigid moralists, however, did not count themselves Anabaptists; . . ." [16]

A summary statement of the beginnings of Baptist churches in Modern times may well follow this listing:

I. General Baptists. 1606—John Smyth left the Church of England to join a group of Separatists in Gainesborough.[17] 1607—Smyth left Gainesborough to join and lead a group in Amsterdam. 1608—Scrooby Manor Church, led by John Robinson, goes to Amsterdam.[18] 1608—Smyth, Thomas Helwys and others left this "second English church at Amsterdam" to found a church based upon Believer's Baptism; became an Anabaptist.[19] 1609—Robinson, most of congregation, move to Leyden.[20] 1610—Helwys, Smyth split.[21] 1611 or 1612—Helwys and others returned to England, and formed the first General Baptist church of this type in England.

II. Particular Baptists. 1616—A group of dissenters, led

[14]*Ibid.*, p. 3.
[15]John T. Christian, *A History of the Baptists*, Vol. I [Nashville: Baptist Sunday School Board, Southern Baptist Convention, 1922], p. 46. [Note: For further information on the history of these sects and groups, the reader may refer to Ayer, *A Source Book for Ancient Church History*, Vedder, Torbet, Walker.]
[16]*Loc. cit.*
[17]Torbet, p. 63.
[18]*Loc. cit.*
[19]*Loc. cit.*
[20]*Ibid.*, p.p. 63, 64.
[21]*Ibid.*, p. 65.

by Henry Jacob, organized in London.[22] 1633—Division within this congregation created formation of a new church with some members holding Anabaptist views.[23] 1640—The original Jacob church divided again, with a group being led by Richard Blunt and Henry Jessey, holding to immersion. Blunt baptized one Blacklock, then Blacklock baptized Blunt; then the two baptized the rest of the congregation.[24] 1644— Seven of these churches issued a confession of faith specifying immersion, and known as the First London Confession.[25]

Baptists have, therefore, been in the stream of religious thought which placed priority upon the direct access of man to God, which placed emphases upon Believer's baptism, The Lord's Supper as a "memorial" and the congregational form of church government.[26]

[22]Ibid., p. 69.
[23]Ibid., p. 70.
[24]Ibid., p.p. 71, 72.
[25]Ibid., p. 74.
[26]See further Torbet, especially Chapter III.

Appendix B

Baptist Beginnings In The United States

The stage was set, historically, for the emergence of Baptists in this country as in the words of Backus: "The light of revelation, and the superstitions and persecutions of the Church of England, were the causes of the first planting of New England."[27] "The heritage and background of American Baptists is chiefly British." [28]

There were two groups of Baptists who made their impact upon the settlement of Baptists in the colony of Georgia. There was the group indicated by Backus as coming first to New England, and the natural course of geographic development in this country moved them down the Eastern Seaboard from the New England states. Historically, then, the emergence of Baptists into the stream of religious history was in effect a synthesis of religious thought which centered around believer's baptism, the centrality of the word of God, the right of self-government, and the privilege of religious freedom, denied Christians under an authoritarian church.

Roger Williams is credited with founding the first Baptist church in America at Providence, R. I., in 1639. Although Williams was not to remain with this church, the congregation did continue Baptist.[29] The great principles of religious liberty expounded by Williams live both in Baptist life and in the framework of laws governing this constitutional democracy. The First Baptist Church in Newport,

[27]Isaac Backus, *Church History of New England from 1620 to 1804* [Philadelphia: Baptist Tract Depository, 1839], p. 19.
[28]Torbet, p. 219.
[29]Backus, p.p. 50, 51.

Rhode Island, was founded by John Clarke at least by 1648,[30] and played a significant role in Baptist beginnings in America.

[30]Vedder, p. 295; Torbet, p.p. 220 221

Appendix C

Significant Dates In Georgia Baptist History

1733—Arrival of General James Edward Oglethorpe, Yama-craw Bluff, with at least two Baptists aboard the Good Ship Anne.

1751—Nicholas Bedgewood [Bedgegood] First Baptist minister who proclaimed the gospel in Georgia.

1759—First observance of The Lord's Supper by a group of Seventh Day Baptists who settled near Tuckaseeking, in what is now Effingham county.

1771—Edmund Botsford preaches first sermon at Tuckaseeking, June 27.

1771—Daniel Marshall moves to Georgia.

1772 [1]—Kioka Baptist Church founded by Daniel Marshall, First Baptist church in Georgia.

1784—First Association, the Georgia, organized.

1801—First of three conferences at Powelton, germ of later Convention organization. Two other conferences, 1802, 1803.

1802—Analytical Repository established, Savannah; first Georgia Baptist paper, by Henry Holcombe.

1813—Formation of a Baptist Foreign Mission Society in Savannah, first Georgia associational organization for missionary purposes.

1821—Georgia, Ocmulgee Associations appoint messengers, name place for organizational meeting of Convention.

1822—The General Baptist Association of the State of

Georgia constituted June 29.

1822—*The Columbian Star,* later *The Christian Index,* first issued in Washington, D.C., February.

1830—Executive Committee of Baptist Convention of the State of Georgia chartered.

1833—Mercer Institute organized, Penfield.

1833—*The Christian Index* moved to Washington, Georgia, Jesse Mercer, owner.

1836—The year of the final, permanent breach, organizationally, between Missionary and Primitive Baptists.

1840—*The Christian Index* offered to, accepted by Georgia Baptist Convention, Jesse Mercer, donor.

1841—Jesse Mercer died, Sept. 6, in Butts county, Georgia.

1845—Southern Baptist Convention, Domestic Mission and Foreign Mission Boards of that Convention, organized, Augusta, May 8-12.

1871—Orphan's Home work begun.

1873—Mercer University moved to Macon from Penfield.

1874—Sunday School Department authorized; First such Department.

1877—State Mission Board constituted; basis for present work of State Missions.

1913—Georgia Baptist Hospital enterprise launched.

1919—Constitution rewritten, Executive Committee created, $75 Million Campaign, authorization for purchases of *The Christian Index.*

1920—*The Christian Index* becomes Convention property again.

1925—Unified United Kingdom Budget Plan promoted [later called the Cooperative Program].

1941—Georgia Baptist Foundation chartered.

1955—First Capital Improvements and Endowment Program.

1956—Baptist Village—first Home for Aged begun.

1963—Georgia Baptist Assembly, Toccoa, purchase authorized.

1966—Peachtree-on-Peachtree Inn established.

1971—Norman College becomes Norman Assembly.

1972—Convention observes Sesquicentennial

Appendix D

The College That Failed
Before Starting; Making of
Mercer Institute A University

This is a background of the proposed Southern Baptist College at Washington. Out of the failure to begin this college, Georgia Baptists decided to make a university of Mercer Institute. Therefore, this statement is of historic value. [The remainder of this appendix is quoted material.]

"To The Trustees of The Mercer University

At the meeting of the Baptist Convention of the State of Georgia, held at Augusta, April, 1857, the following Resolution was adopted:

> Resolved, That the Board of Trustees be instructed to inquire into the propriety of engaging some competent person to collect the materials for a history, in detail, of the inception of subscriptions, foundation, and endowment of Mercer University, and all other such details and facts, incidents and anecdotes, which it will be interesting and valuable to preserve, and have the same at least reduced to manuscript for the use of the Convention.[1]

To aid in carrying out the design of this Resolution, the subscriber has been requested to furnish some materials, and with special reference to two points, viz:

> 1. Were any of the subscriptions for the Washington location considered available for Penfield before they were transferred by the consent of the Donors?

[1] *Minutes, Georgia Baptist Convention,* 1857, p. 10.

789

2. Were any subscriptions taken by you that had not reference to Penfield as the location?

As some other person, or persons, will probably furnish an account of the Institution in its Academic character, I shall confine myself to its history especially as to the endowment in its collegiate character.

In the year 1835, there was an effort made by a portion of the Presbyterian Denomination to establish a College under their auspices, at Washington, Wilkes County. A considerable subscription was made up for the enterprise, but the Washington project failed, and their Institution was located at Midway, near Milledgeville, and is now known as the Oglethorpe University. In the meantime the inquiry was propounded, "why may not the Baptists have a College at Washington?" To use the language of the venerable Mercer, "The notion took like wild-fire." Large portions of the first subscription were transferred, and new amounts were added. The Rev. Wm. H. Stokes, now of Texas, and Dr. Wm. H. Pope, were particularly active in forwarding the enterprise—the latter performing much voluntary service as agent in getting up the subscription.

In October of the same year, the project was brought to the notice of the Georgia Association, at its annual session in Augusta, and was favorably entertained by that body.

The next year the plan was submitted to the Convention at its session in Talbotton, in May, 1836. A subscription of some forty or fifty thousand dollars was tendered to the Denomination, on condition that a College should be established at Washington. The plan was adopted, and it was agreed that the Institution should be known by the name of "The Southern Baptist College." Agents were sent out to increase the subscription; a charter was obtained from the Legislature; and at the next meeting of the Convention, held at Ruckersville, Elbert County, a subscription of $100,000 was reported as having been made up, this being the amount agreed on as essential to justify the commencement of the enterprise. Of this amount, I think about $40,000 were subscribed in Wilkes County, Jesse Mercer increasing his first subscription of *three thousand,* to the liberal amount of *ten thousand* dollars.

In the meantime a great pecuniary pressure came on, and many of the friends of the College enterprise began to fear that it could not well be carried out, in connection with that aid which it was necessary still to render to the Mercer Institute. Many at last strongly urged the abandonment of the Washington location, and concentration on the Institute. This produced some warm discussions in the Board of Trustees; Sanders and Cooper leading in the project of giving up Washington [though the latter was not particularly partial to Penfield], and Mercer with some others, strongly opposing any change. As the Convention Resolution at the head of this communication calls for anecdotes, I would state that at the discussion in the meeting of Trustees in Washington, [I think it was in June,] the venerable Mercer manifested more feeling than I recollect ever to have witnessed in him. He opposed the discussion of the question of change. He said they had been appointed under the charter to perform a certain work, and if any could not agree to help in carrying it forward, it was their duty at once to resign and give place to others.

Still the discussion went on, till Brother Mercer became so much warmed up, that he left his seat as Chairman, and refused to preside. Cooling at length, and kindly urged by his brethren, he went back to the Chair. Nothing definite, however, was agreed on at that meeting, but at an adjourned meeting held in Athens, the following August, [1837,] the project, so far as the then existing Board of Trustees was concerned, was abandoned by a considerable majority, five or six, as well as I remember, voting in the negative; to whom should be added Brother Mercer, who was in the Chair. The following Resolutions, drawn up and presented by Brother Mark A. Cooper, were adopted on the occasion:

> Resolved, That the important business of raising and organizing a Southern Baptist College in Georgia, en-

trusted to the care of this Board, has been maturely examined and enquired into. They have duly considered the means and resources required therefor, and are of opinion that it is inexpedient to undertake the building of a College under present circumstances. The reasons that have brought the Board to this conclusion, are in part the following: First, the embarrassment of the times. Secondly, the differing views of brethren in regard to the plan proposed. Lastly, the inadequacy of the means in hand.

Be it therefore Resolved further, That the whole subject be referred to the Executive Committee of the Baptist Convention for the State of Georgia, with the recommendation of this Board, that they surrender the present charter, and abandon the enterprise, or seek to set on footing a plan that will command the resources demanded for the accomplishment of the great undertaking.

By virtue of this movement, the Washington plan was virtually dead, though the Executive Committee went through the form of surrendering up by Resolution, the charter and project to the Convention. This was done August 25th, 1837.

The question then arose, shall the important design of establishing a Baptist College in Georgia, be abandoned? The Executive Committee, [with many others], felt that it must not be given up, and at once resolved to carry out the main design, or make a serious attempt to do so, by connecting a Collegiate Department with the Mercer Institute, still continuing the Academic feature of the Seminary. This they believed they had the power to do, inasmuch as "the ultimate and conclusive direction of all the interests and operations of the Institution," had been vested "in the Executive Committee as Agents of the Convention," and that they had been "left at liberty to alter or amend, as expediency might seem to require."

And here may be the proper place to notice particularly the first question above stated: "were any of the subscriptions for the Washington location considered available for Penfield, before they were transferred by the consent of the donors?

As far as I know, the giving up of the location was considered by the Agents, the Executive Committee, and subscribers themselves, as a forfeiture of the original subscription. It is true there were many of the subscribers that had no particular choice as to location, and others that from the first preferred Penfield; but the consent of the subscribers in all cases was considered necessary to render their subscription binding, and in no single instance to my knowledge, was there an attempt made to force the collection of a subscription not transferred. No subscriptions were taken up before the abandonment of Washington for any other location. The work had to be done over again. A large portion of the original subscription, say $35,000, was not transferred at all. The larger portion of the Wilkes County subscription was lost, say upwards of $28,000, something less than $12,000 only being transferred. Jesse Mercer reduced his subscription from $10,000 to $5,000; Dr. Wm. H. Pope reduced his from $2,000 to $1,250. Some amounts had been paid over to the Treasurer of the Washington project; amongst the rest a subscription from the late James Lockett of Clinton, of $1,000. Brother Lockett transferred and I think the others who had paid; but they were not held bond to do so. My recollection as to this is confirmed by an entry made by me in one of my Books when acting as Agent of the University. Under a memorandum of money that had been paid over to Wm. H. Pope, Treasurer of the College at Washington, for which he gave his note, and afterwards transferred to B. M. Sanders, Treasurer of Mercer University. I find the following entry made at the time. "A few of these subscribers have not been consulted with reference to the transfer of their subscriptions to the Mercer University; if any are unwilling to transfer, the money will be refunded."

That a transfer was necessary to bind the subscriptions, was, I think, the universal impression, at least amongst those who best knew the facts of the case. I was present at the Central Association, when the plan of elevating the Mercer

Institute to a College was considered; the Association passed Resolutions expressive of their concurrence with the views of their Executive Committee, and recommended a transfer of subscriptions in their bounds to the Mercer Institute, "upon condition that the contemplated plan is carried out."

The subscribers in the bounds of the Central Association were consulted; nearly all agreed to transfer, and some increased their subscriptions. Brother John B. Walker increased his subscription from $1,250 to $1,800. The subscriptions in the bounds of the Central Association amounted to about $20,000. In October of the same year, the subject was before the Georgia Association, when the following Resolutions were passed:

> Resolved, That the plan of establishing a respectable Collegiate Institution in the State, with the ample means we possess for carrying it into successful operation, should by no means be abandoned.
>
> Resolved, That the abandonment of the location at Washington, though to many a matter of disappointment and regret, should not be allowed to alienate the minds of our brethren from a noble and useful enterprise, but should rather stimulate to more vigorous exertion, impress us with the importance of union and friendly compromise, and of surrendering up all such predilections and prejudices as might tend to mar the prospect of success.
>
> Resolved, That from the best information that can be obtained, we are inclined to the opinion that no other location in the State, than the Mercer Institute, in Green County, could be selected, which would harmonize, to any desirable extent, the views and efforts of the denomination.
>
> Resolved, That we approve of the plan adopted by the Executive Committee of the Georgia Baptist Convention, for connecting with the Mercer Institute a Collegiate Department, and that we recommend the transfer of the old subscriptions within our bounds to the Mercer University.

As already intimated, the amount of the old subscription transferred, [I do not pretend to perfect accuracy] was about $65,000. Of this, however, a portion was lost from death, removal and other causes. The new subscriptions, amounted at first, nominally, to about $30,000; though on this amount also considerable losses have been sustained.

And here I will speak to the second question propounded, "were any subscriptions taken by you that had not reference to Penfield as the location?" After the transfer of the project to Penfield, I answer, not a single subscription, and all taken before had reference to Washington. No other location, as a practical one, ever entered my mind. It was generally considered that if we failed at the Mercer Institute, our failure would be a serious and protracted one. In a circular issued by the Executive Committee in October, 1837, they thus express themselves: "Under present circumstances, the Committee feels well assured that no other location in the State would command the resources demanded for the accomplishment of the great undertaking." This, I believe, was the general feeling entertained by the most efficient friends of the project, and hence as one of the Agents, I did not feel inclined nor at liberty to discuss the merits of other places, much less to take up subscriptions for them, and I think this was the case with other Agents.

An incident with reference to the very liberal subscription of Dr. Cullen Battle, of Alabama, may here be stated. When the brethren were first agitating the College project, he said, "if you will make the Mercer Institute a College, I will give you $5,000." I do not know that he pledged a single dollar to the Washington location. After this location was given up, and we had fallen upon his favorite scheme, I happened to meet him, I think in Powelton, and reminded him of his promise. "Oh," said he, "you have got me now," or words to this effect, and immediately executed a $5,000 note to the Mercer University. He had not then, nor has he since, to my knowledge, had an eye to any other location.

The whole permanent endowment, as appears from the Treasurer's Reports, is about $120,000. Of this I suppose the sum of about $80,000 was raised by subscription. The balance, being about $40,000 [a little more or less,] is the proceeds of the legacies of Jesse Mercer. The tenor of Mr.

Mercer's will, under which the Institution holds this amount, will, I suppose, best explain the conditions connected with this part of the endowment. I will here quote such passages of his will as have relation to this matter, leaving it for those versed in the science of law to determine their legal bearing.

"I give and devise to the Trustees of the Mercer University, Penfield, Green County, Georgia, one hundred and twenty-five shares of capital stock in the Georgia Railroad and Banking Company, for the support of the Faculty of said Institution, and such other purposes as the said Trustees may find necessary; the dividends or annual income only to be used.

* * * * *

"I make the further bequests: "I give and devise to the Trustees of the Mercer University, at Penfield, Georgia, one hundred shares of the capital stock of the Bank of the State of Georgia, and the whole residuary of my Estate, which may remain after the payment of my just debts, and necessary claims thereon, and what may hereafter be bequeathed. This amount to constitute, with the sum of the Professorship made by the Central Association, a Professorship of Sacred Biblical Literature, or Theological Learning. The annual income of which only to be used.

"My Library I wish also to be turned over to the University, and all other books which may remain undisposed of at the time of my decease, to be disposed of as the Trustees may direct."

To the above I would add a statement, which, though possessing probably no legal force, should have some moral bearing on a religious body.

There is probably no person living that better knew the private feelings of Mr. Mercer in relation to the University, than myself. I am fully confident, that there was no other location than Penfield, [his favorite Washington scheme being abandoned] which would have conciliated his anxious and disturbed feelings, and secured his munificent bequests. The Institution at Penfield bore his honored name; he had already expended large amounts of money, and much anxious solicitude upon it, and when his fondly cherished plan of building up a College at Washington failed, he found himself at liberty to turn the main current of his beneficence towards the next dearest enterprise. To have hinted at any other College location, as a claimant upon large bequests, I think would have been offensive to him.

A word about the Orphan fund [now about $3,000,] may not be out of place, as that may be considered indirectly a part of the College Endowment. It was designed to aid the education of young men at the Mercer University, as now established, and I am pretty confident that it was so explained to the Treasurer of the Convention, when it was handed over. The donor is yet living, and to my certain knowledge, he is unwilling that the proceeds should be expended anywhere else. Should the Institution be removed from Penfield, he feels at liberty [and might feel it to be his duty] to require the Convention to return the funds.

The above are the principal facts that now occur to me with reference to the endowment of the Mercer University. I could have gone more into details, but I suppose that this might not be needful. I would add, however, that subscriptions were taken up in nearly seventy counties of Georgia, besides a few in South Carolina and Florida, and Brother Battle's [already spoken of] in Alabama. The following twenty-five counties were the most liberal contributors, and as to their respective amounts, about in the order named: Wilkes, Green, Taliaferro, Morgan, Putnam, Hancock, Richmond, Muscogee, Twiggs, Houston, Baldwin, Columbia, Warren, Harris, Lee, Pulaski, Lincoln, Bibb, Walton, Burke, Elbert, Troup, Chatham, and Talbot. In several of the other counties there were, however, a number of very liberal individual subscriptions. All of which is respectfully submitted. C. D. Mallary. New Albany, Dougherty County, Feb., 1858." [2]

[2]From the minutes of the Georgia Baptist Convention, April 15, 1858, beginning on page 27 [all quoted material, printed in body type for convenience of the reader, because of length of the quotation.]

Other Baptist Conventions In Georgia

During the organizational span of the Georgia Baptist Convention, three other conventions were formed which had some influence upon Baptist life in Georgia; and upon the Georgia Baptist Convention. These organizations did not embrace groups which had separated into Primitive Baptist organizations, nor did they embrace the many separate missionary societies which existed at one time or another. The three conventions were: The Cherokee Georgia Baptist Convention; the South Georgia Convention; and The General Missionary Baptist Association of North Georgia.

In each instance, the cause of missions and education were focal points of organization, and loose ties to the Georgia Baptist Convention were specific. While seeking to promote specific regional interests, the North Georgia and South Georgia Conventions sought also to promote, in varying degree, the ministries of the Convention. The Cherokee Convention, although not hostile openly, was not very sympathetic with Convention ministries.

THE CHEROKEE GEORGIA
BAPTIST CONVENTION

This Convention was organized November 23-24 in Cassville, and grew out of a movement in 1853 to establish a Cherokee Baptist College in Cassville. Cherokee Georgia was identifiable as a geographic area, which by 1860 was a section north and west of the Chattahoochee River, with about 200,531 residents in twenty-six counties.[1] A board of trustees was named for the Cherokee College late in 1853,[2] and Baptists in Cherokee Georgia—a geographic area—were invited to meet in Cassville in 1854. Two associations, the Coosa, which reached from Dade County to Cedartown, and the State Line, which embraced churches in southeast Tennessee and Northwest Georgia, responded to a call from the Middle Cherokee Association, which extended from Dalton south to Cartersville.[3]

The constitution adopted by this convention outlined purposes of the group.

> 1. To unite the friends of education and to combine their efforts for the establishment and promotion of Institutions of Learning, where the young of both sexes may be thoroughly educated on the cheapest practical terms.
> 2. To foster and cherish the spirit of missions, and to facilitate missionary operations in any and every laudable way.[4]

During its 10 years of existence, this convention published a paper entitled the *Landmark Banner* and *Cherokee Baptist*, and owned and supported two colleges.

> For varying lengths of time, then, probably eight associations, representing churches in Georgia, Tennessee, and Alabama participated. At its height about 1860, the Convention was comprised of more than 250 churches, having a total membership of about 15,540 and being led by about 190 ordained and licensed ministers.[5]

The Convention took control of the Cherokee Baptist College in May, 1856, and in July of that year assumed re-

[1]*The Quarterly Review*, April, May, June, 1971, Nashville; Sunday School Board, Southern Baptist Convention, Article by Robert G. Gardner on "The Cherokee Georgia Baptist Convention," p. 56.

[2]*Ibid.*, p. 57.

[3]*Loc. cit.*, quoting Middle Cherokee Baptist Association, 1854, p. 5; Minutes, State Line Baptist Association, 1854, p. 6; Minutes, Coosa Baptist Association, 1854, p.p. 5-6.

[4]Minutes, Middle Cherokee Baptist Association, 1854, p. 5; B. D. Ragsdale, *Story of Georgia Baptists* Vol. III [Atlanta: The Executive Committee of Georgia Baptist Convention, 1938], p. 106.

[5]Gardner in *The Quarterly Review*, p. 58.

sponsibility for the Woodland Female College, which opened in 1851 at Cedartown.[6] It supported a missionary to the Cherokee Indians on a part-time basis until about 1863 or 1864.[7]

This convention was oriented strongly toward the landmark movement, and ". . . J. R. Graves virtually dominated the 1858 meeting in Rome. . ."[8] The Convention died about the time of the end of the War Between The States.[9]

Twice in later years, in 1898, and in 1925, suggestions were made for reviving this convention, both within the Middle Cherokee Association. In 1898, the Association proposed a college to be called the Cherokee College.

> In 1901 the Cherokee Baptist High School was opened, the trustees of which in 1905 recommended formation of the 'Cherokee Georgia Baptist Convention; which convention shall be organized for educational purposes only.' "[10]

The Association itself made the suggestion in 1925, which apparently was futile.[11]

As late as 1939-1940, and 1947-1948

> . . . the Convention was once more an object of attention by the Middle Cherokee Association . . .[12] Hope was expressed that federal money might be forthcoming as reimbursement for the Cassville college building. Recognizing that the institution had been owned by the Convention, and not by any one local association, an investigating committee in 1948 formally recommended dismissal of the entire proposition. In a discussion on the floor of the association, opposition to the report was voiced in the form of a suggestion that a skeleton Convention might be formed.[13]

Hope for federal reimbursement stemmed evidently from the

[6]*Ibid.*, p. 60.
[7]*Ibid.*, p. 61.
[8]*Ibid.*, p. 59.
[9]Detailed information on this Convention is included in Gardner's article in *The Quarterly Review*, pages 56-63, and Ragsdale, Vol. III, pages 105-108.
[10]*Ibid.*, p. 63.
[11]*Ibid.*, p.p., 62, 63.
[12]*Ibid.*, p. 63.
[13]*Loc. cit.*

apparent fact that the college was destroyed by Union forces during the War Between the States.

THE GENERAL MISSIONARY BAPTIST
ASSOCIATION OF NORTH GEORGIA

This body was organized July 25, 1878, at the Hopewell Baptist church in Hall county.[14] It lasted until 1894. This convention met in Lawrenceville in that year, set the 1895 session for Gainesville, but there was no record of a meeting in 1895 or later.[15]

Objects in the constitution of the Association included: "To unite the labors of Baptists in preaching everywhere; To assist weak churches in our own bounds, and To aid young men in preparing for the ministry." Fraternal relations were to be sought with the Georgia Baptist Convention.[16]

The Chattahoochee Association sent out a call for the organizational meeting,[17] and this body did send C. W. Pruitt as a missionary to China three years after the Convention was formed.[18] This convention received, apparently gladly, representatives from the Georgia Baptist Convention.[19]

At the organizational meeting, there were representatives from ". . . 42 churches of the Chattahoochee, Lawrenceville, Hightower, Clarkesville, Sarepta, and Tugalo associations."[20] At one time, the group held titles to Hiawassee High School and Hollingsworth High School.[21]

SOUTH GEORGIA BAPTIST CONVENTION

The motive behind the formation of this convention dif-

[14]*The Christian Index and Southwestern Baptist,* August 1, 1878.
[15]Ragsdale, Vol. III, p. 110.
[16]*Ibid.,* p. 109.
[17]*Ibid.,* p. 108.
[18]*Ibid.,* p. 109.
[19]*Ibid.,* p. 110.
[20]*Encyclopedia of Southern Baptists,* Vol. II [Nashville: Broadman Press, 1958], p. 1020.
[21]Ragsdale, Vol. III, p. 110.

fered markedly from motivation for organization of the Cherokee Georgia and North Georgia Conventions. This Convention was planned

> . . . to effect a permanent organization for the more successful co-operation among ourselves and the better aiding of the Georgia Baptist Convention and its Mission Board to meet the wants of this section of the State.[22]

The concluding resolution of the organizational statement was: "Resolved, That this organization is in no wise to sever or to embarrass our connection with any existing organization whatever." [23]

Guiding spirit behind organization of this Convention was P. A. Jessup, then pastor at Eastman. Ten associations met in McRae in November, 1890, with about 27 messengers to organize.[24]

Jessup is credited with leading in formation of the New Ebenezer College at Cochran, Freddie Shipp College at Cordele, and Norman College, Norman Park, because of his interest in Christian education, and the esteem in which he was held throughout South Georgia.[25]

This Convention sought evidently to bolster the work of the Georgia Baptist Convention in the South Georgia area. In 1898, speaking concerning the future of the Convention, which had been in question for about a year, Jessup declared:

> My answer is, 'It has none,' Having helped to bring a needy field and needy people in touch with the needed help and encouragement, together with its own people becoming able to stand alone, what was known as the South Georgia Convention can afford to retire, giving place to stronger and better things.[26]

It dissolved apparently about that time.

[22]*Ibid.*, p. 112.
[23]*Loc. cit.*
[24]*Ibid.*, p. 111.
[25]*Loc. cit.*; B. D. Ragsdale, *Story of Georgia Baptists*, [Macon: Mercer University, 1905] Vol. II, p.p. 351, 353, 354.
[26]*The Christian Index*, November 24, 1898.

Religious Papers Published In Georgia

During the history of the Georgia Baptist Convention several papers were published under Baptist auspices. These include the *Analytical Repository*, by Henry Holcombe, 1802, 1803 in Savannah. The Analytical Repository ranks as the first religious periodical in Georgia and perhaps the first in the nation.

The *Temperance Banner* was published at Washington beginning in 1834 by Jesse Mercer and W. H. Stokes.

The *Southern Baptist Review* was published at Penfield by J. S. Baker, who was also editor of *The Index*. It lasted only a brief time. The *Georgia Illustrated* was published for one year and the *Orion* for about two years by a William Gary Richards, apparently from Penfield.

The *Landmark Banner* and *Cherokee Baptist* was published, as indicated, by the Cherokee Baptist Convention, later moving to Atlanta. The *Baptist Banner* was published at Cumming and apparently was issued periodically from 1878 to 1883. The *Baptist Leader* at Cumming was published 1891 until 1897 and sold to A. E. Booth who was for a time president of the Hightower Institute. The *North Georgia Baptist* was published at Cumming apparently, according to Ragsdale, a new name given to the *Baptist Leader* after it was purchased by Booth and continued until 1901. These appeared to be limited in denominational emphasis. The *Baptist Sun* was published at Gainesville, 1887, 1888. The *Baptist Reporter* was published at Excelsior, 1886-87 and at Guyton, 1889 and the *Central Georgia Baptist* was published in Macon, 1889.

Church and School was published in Rome sometime during the 1870's and 1880's apparently. The *Cherokee Messenger,* at Rome, was published in the last part of the 19th century. Sometime around 1888, the *Gospel Expositor* was published in Atlanta. E. R. Carswell, Jr., was listed as editor.

The *Bible Baptist* was published at Waycross, again by E. R. Carswell. The *Baptist Mirror* was published at Cuthbert and apparently at Macon, edited by E. Z. F. Golden. Ragsdale says it was discontinued in January of 1900 for financial reasons and subscription list was turned over to the Texas *Baptist Standard.*

H. R. Bernard, long time auditor for the Convention, published *The Religious Forum* for two or three years in Atlanta, beginning about 1905 as a monthly journal. The *South Georgia Messenger,* at Cochran, was published by B. J. W. Graham from 1897 until he became associated with *The Christian Index* in 1900 at which time it was discontinued. The *Georgia Baptist* was published at Vidalia around 1905.[1]

[1]Information on these publications in Georgia from B. D. Ragsdale, *Story of Georgia Baptists* Vol. III [Atlanta: The Executive Committee of Georgia Baptist Convention, 1938], p.p. 181, 184.

Appendix G

Historical Points of Interest

GEORGIA BAPTIST
POINTS OF INTEREST

HIAWASSEE · 33   34 · CLAYTON

CLEVELAND · 32
35 · TOCCOA

ROME · 31
30   29 · CARTERSVILLE ·   26 · RUCKERSVILLE
CAVE SPRING

28 · ATLANTA
PENFIELD · 25 23 22 · WASHINGTON
BETHESDA CHURCH · 24   · PHILLIPS MILL CHURCH
27 · PALMETTO   21 · FICKLIN   1 · APPLING

17 · LOCUST GROVE   3 · AUGUSTA
18 · JACKSON 19   20 · POWELTON 2 · MT. ENON
16 · MEANSVILLE   · EATONTON
15 · FORSYTH   · WAYNESBORO
4 · BOTSFORD CHURCH

14 · MACON   5 · BIG BUCKHEAD CHURCH

6 · TUCKASEE KING
· CLYO

13 · MT. VERNON
7 · SAVANNAH

12 · BAXLEY   8 · SUNBURY

11 · NORMAN PARK   10 · WAYCROSS   9 · BRUNSWICK

Established 1822
SERVING WITNESSING
GEORGIA BAPTIST CONVENTION

807

1. APPLING: (1) Kiokee Church (1772), the first Baptist church in Georgia, is located here. The currently used building is in the town; the old building (1811) is two and a half miles out. (2) A monument to Daniel Marshall (1706-1784), founder and first pastor of Kiokee Church, stands in the town in the middle of US Highway 221.

2. MOUNT ENON: The village of Mount Enon was laid out as the location of Mount Enon Academy (1807-c.1812), which was the first cooperative project of the Baptists of Georgia. This school was established by the General Committee of Georgia Baptists, a forerunner of the Georgia Baptist Convention. The site is fourteen miles from Augusta on US Highway 1.

3. AUGUSTA: (1) The First Baptist Church (1817), at Greene and 7th Streets, was host to the first session of the Southern Baptist Convention (1845). (2) In Augusta (c.1770) Daniel Marshall, early Baptist preacher (See 1), stood trial for preaching in St. Paul's Parish (now Richmond County) without a license from the authorities. The exact place of trial is not now known.

4. BOTSFORD CHURCH: Named for Edmund Botsford, founder and first pastor, Botsford Church was the second Baptist church (1773) established in Georgia. It was about twelve miles east of Waynesboro.

5. BIG BUCKHEAD CHURCH: Big Buckhead Baptist Church (1787-1923) was host to the 1831 session of the Georgia Baptist Convention, in which decision was made to establish Mercer Institute (now Mercer University). (See 14 and 25). The church was dissolved in 1923. The building stands three and a half miles west of Perkins on US Highway 25.

6. TUCKASEE KING: This was a center of Baptist activity from about 1767 to 1772. Benjamin Stirk and Edmund Botsford preached here regularly, but no church seems to have been established. A marker is located one mile north of Clyo on Georgia Highway 119.

7. SAVANNAH: (1) The site of the first baptism by Baptists in Georgia (1763) is at Bethesda Home for Boys, on the site of George Whitefield's Orphan House (1740), on Ferguson Avenue ten miles south of the city. A marker is on the location. (2) The First Baptist Church (1800) is noteworthy. Henry Holcombe, the first pastor (1800-1811), was the main support of Mount Enon Academy (See 2). Also he published the first Baptist paper in the South, the *Analytical Repository* (1802-03). W. B. Johnson, the second pastor (1811-14), was the first president of the Southern Baptist Convention (1845). (3) At 20-22 Broughton Street, West, is the building used as a residence and jewelry shop by Josiah Penfield, deacon of the Savannah First Church, and first benefactor (1825) of Mercer University. (See 25). A plaque is in the sidewalk next to the building. (4) The first Negro Baptist church in Georgia, said to be the oldest in North America, was constituted here in 1788 by Andrew Bryan and Abraham Marshall. The first site, at 575 Bryan Street, West, is occupied by the First Bryan Baptist Church. A later site, at 23 Montgomery Street, is occupied by the First African Baptist Church. (5) The Baptist Book Store (1954) is located at 153 Barnard Street.

8. SUNBURY: (1) This former coastal town was the location of the earliest known Baptist woman's missionary society in the state. Known as the Sunbury Female Mite Society, it sent $101.00 on June 23, 1817, to the Baptist Board of Foreign Missions at Philadelphia. (2) Sunbury was also the home of Edward A. Stevens (1814-?), the first native of Georgia to become a Baptist foreign missionary. (See 26). Take Georgia Highway 38 at Midway for Sunbury.

9. BRUNSWICK: Camp Glynn (1955), Royal Ambassador camp, is owned and operated by the Georgia Baptist Convention. It was given to the Convention by Georgia Baptist Woman's Missionary Union. The camp is located seven miles from Brunswick on Blue Heron Island.

10. WAYCROSS: Baptist Village (1958), a Georgia Baptist home for retired people, is three miles west of the city.

11. NORMAN PARK: Norman Baptist Assembly (1971) was created as a phase of the Convention's state missions program. It is on the campus of the former Norman College, Baptist junior college (1900-1971).

12. BAXLEY: The Odum Branch (1946) of the Georgia Baptist Children's Home occupies an extensive campus and farm 11 miles south of the city on Georgia Highway 121.

13. MOUNT VERNON: Brewton-Parker College (1904), a Georgia Baptist junior college, faces US Highway 280, half way between Mount Vernon and Ailey.

14: MACON: (1) Mercer University (1833), the oldest and largest institution of Georgia Baptists, has been located here since 1871. (See 25). (2) The First Baptist church was the place of ordination (1878) of R. J. Willingham, corresponding secretary of the Southern Baptist Foregin Mission Board (1893-1914). It was also the donor of Warren Memorial Hospital (1903), Hwangshien, China, the first Southern Baptist hospital in a foreign country. It was named for E. W. Warren (1820-1893), a former pastor of this church. The first location of the church is marked by a plaque on the east wall of the Bibb County courthouse.

15. FORSYTH: Tift College (1849) Georgia Baptist senior college for women, faces Interstate Highway 75.

16. MEANSVILLE: The Pine Mountain Branch (1957) of the Georgia Baptist Children's Home is located on US Highway 19 six miles south of Zebulon.

17. LOCUST GROVE: Locust Grove Institute (1894-1928) was a Baptist secondary school. The building is now used by the local public high school. A marker is on the location.

18. JACKSON: The house where Jesse Mercer died on September 6, 1841, is near the village of Stark, six miles from Jackson. Mercer was an early Baptist leader of prominence in Georgia. (See 21, 22, 23, 25.)

19. EATONTON: (1) The home and the private school (1832-36) of Adiel Sherwood (1791-1879) were located here. A granite marker is located one mile north of the city on the west side of US Highway 441. (2) The site of the church where Sherwood preached (1826-36) faces Church Street at the rear of the public library. (See 24). Sherwood was one of the early Georgia Baptist leaders.

20. POWELTON: In the Baptist church here the "Powelton Conferences" were held (1801, 1802, 1803), out of which came the General Committee of Georgia Baptists. (See 2.) In this church in 1822, the Georgia Baptist Convention was organized. Powelton is on Georgia Highway 22, between Sparta and Crawfordville.

21. FICKLIN: The burial place of Silas Mercer (1745-1796), father of Jesse Mercer, is at this village. Here also (c.1790) Silas Mercer founded Salem Academy, the first known school operated in Georgia by a Baptist. (See 22, 23). Ficklin is on Georgia Highway 47, seven miles south of Washington.

22. WASHINGTON: (1) The site of Jesse Mercer's home is identified with a metal marker at the junction of US Highway 78 and Georgia Highway 44. (2) The First Baptist Church

(1827) was founded by Jesse Mercer. The grave of Nancy Mills Simons, Mercer's second wife, is on the church property; the grave slab is set in the wall of a classroom. A picture of Mercer is in the corridor. (3) Next door to the church is the Tupper House, home of Henry Allen Tupper (1828-1902), Washington pastor (1853-1872) who became corresponding secretary of the Southern Baptist Foreign Mission Board (1872-1893). (4) The building where Mercer published *The Christian Index* from 1833 to 1840 and financed the first temperance paper in the south, *The Temperance Banner* (1834-36), was located at the corner of West Toombs Avenue and Depot Street. (5) The house, Holly Court, was the site of the marriage of James Pettigru Boyce, first faculty chairman of the Southern Baptist Theological Seminary.

23. PHILLIPS MILL CHURCH: Established by Silas Mercer in 1785, Jesse Mercer, Silas' son, was baptized (1787) and ordained (1789) here. (See 21.) It is about ten miles west of Washington on Georgia Highway 44.

24. BETHESDA CHURCH: In 1820 Adiel Sherwood (1791-1879) was ordained in this church, which was established in 1785. The present building was erected in 1818. It is one mile north of a point on Georgia Highway 44 five miles east of Union Point. (See 19.)

25. PENFIELD: The first campus (1833-71) of Mercer University (see 14) is located here. The village was named for Josiah Penfield. (See 7). The brick chapel building is now used by the Penfield Baptist Church. The president's home still stands. The cemetery nearby contains the graves of Jesse Mercer, Billington Sanders, and other Baptists of note. Penfield is about seven miles north of Greensboro.

26. RUCKERSVILLE: (1) At the annual session of the Georgia Baptist Convention here, May 6, 1837, Edward A. Stevens was ordained to the ministry. (See 8). (2) The Van's Creek Baptist Church (1785) here was established by Dozier Thornton (1755-1843), Revolutionary War soldier and pioneer Baptist preacher. At Van's Creek Church, in the 1820 Sarepta Baptist Association meeting, Adiel Sherwood made a motion which led to the formation of the Georgia Baptist Association.

27. PALMETTO: The main campus of the Georgia Baptist Children's Home is located here, having moved from Hapeville in 1968. Started privately in 1872, the home came under Convention control in 1898.

28. ATLANTA: (1) The Georgia Baptist Convention Administration Building is at 291 Peachtree Street, NE. (2) The Baptist Book Store is in the GBC office building. (3) The Georgia Baptist Hospital (1901) is at 300 Boulevard. Its School of Nursing is the largest in the state. (4) At 1350 Spring Street NW is the office building of the Southern Baptist Home Mission Board. (5) Peachtree-On-Peachtree Inn, Inc. (1967), a home for retired persons, is located at 176 Peachtree Street NW. The hotel facility was given to the Georgia Baptist Convention by the Beazley Foundation. (6) Atlanta Baptist College (1964) was chartered by the Atlanta Baptist Association. It is located at 3000 Flowers Road, Chamblee.

29. CARTERSVILLE: (1) In the First Baptist Church here in February, 1873, Lottie Moon surrendered for Southern Baptist foreign missionary service. A native of Virginia, she was teaching school here at the time. She served in China from 1873 to 1912. The Southern Baptist Christmas offering for foreign missions is named for her. (2) Cartersville was the birthplace of Mrs. W. J. Neel, president of Georgia Baptist Woman's Missionary Union, 1911-1932.

30. CAVE SPRING: (1) The Hearn Manual Labor School (1839-1923), a Baptist secondary school, was formerly located here. (2) Cave Springs Female Seminary, also a Baptist school, functioned here from 1849 to 1883.

31. ROME: On one of the seven hills of this city stands Shorter College (1873), Georgia Baptist senior college.

32. CLEVELAND: Truett-McConnell College (1946), Georgia Baptist junior college, perpetuates here the names of George W. Truett and F. C. McConnell, eminent Southern Baptist preachers of a generation ago. (See 34).

33. HIAWASSEE: Hiawassee High School (1887–c.1926), former Baptist school located here, was founded with the encouragement of F. C. McConnell (1856-1929) by George W. Truett (1867-1944), the first principal (Jan., 1887—June, 1889). (See 33). A commemorative tablet stands before the present county high school building.

34. CLAYTON: Camp Pinnacle (1947), youth camp owned and operated by Georgia Baptist Woman's Missionary Union, is located two miles east of the town.

35. TOCCOA: Georgia Baptist Assembly (1963) was created as a phase of the Convention's state missions program when a 1,000 acre conference center was purchased from Christian Industrialist R. G. LeTourneau.

Appendix H

ORGANIZATIONAL STRUCTURE, GEORGIA BAPTIST CONVENTION

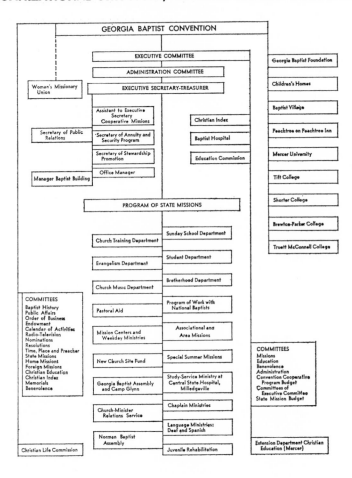

GEORGIA BAPTIST STATISTICS, 1971

Number of Associations	93
Number of Churches	2,952
Total Membership	1,018,052
Number Baptisms	30,076
Number of Pastors	2,605
Number of Full Time Churches	2,623
Number of Half Time Churches	285
Number of Quarter Time Churches	44
Number of Sunday Schools	2,816
Enrolment in Sunday Schools	585,050
Number of Vacation Bible Schools	2,038
Enrolment in Vacation Bible Schools	237,683
Number of Church Training Departments	1,951
Enrolment in Church Training Departments	172,166
Number of Churches with WMU Organizations	1,902
Enrollment in WMU Organizations	107,024
Number of Student Union Organizations	39
Number of Churches with Brotherhood Organizations	1,366
Enrolment in Brotherhood Organizations	49,958
Number of Churches with Graded Choir Programs	1,311
Total Choir Enrolment	98,047
Number of Churches in Southern Baptist Protection Program	1,375
Number of Churches with The Christian Index in Budget	1,216
Circulation of The Christian Index	132,357
Endowment Funds held in Trust Georgia Baptist Foundation, Inc. (Approx.)	$10,100,000.00

Appendix J
DIRECTORY OF ASSOCIATIONS — 1972

Association	Moderator and Address	Clerk and Address	Chairman of Executive Committee and Address
Altamaha	Mr. Jackie D. Anderson, Route 1, Screven 31560	Rev. James E. Bacon, 292 Hickory St., Jesup 31545	Mr. Eugene D. Campbell, 642 Younce, Jesup 31545
Appalachee	Rev. Robert Allen, P. O. Box 325, Bogart 30622	Mr. W. A. Wagner, Route 2, Watkinsville 30677	Rev. Derris Davenport, 205 N. Broad St., Winder 30680
Atlanta	Rev. W. Norris Wilkerson, 4741 Covington Rd., Decatur 30032	Mr. Milton L. Holcombe, 462 Bryan St., S. E., Atlanta 30312	Rev. W. Norris Wilkerson, 4741 Covington Rd., Decatur 30032
Augusta	Rev. James L. Adkins, 1556 Walton Way, Augusta 30904	Rev. W. H. Barfield, 2130 East Side Court, Augusta 30906	Rev. James L. Adkins, 1556 Walton Way, Augusta 30904
Ben Hill-Irwin	Mr. J. D. Hawkins, Irwinville 31760	Mrs. Davis C. Sims, P. O. Box 367, Fitzgerald 31750	Mr. J. D. Hawkins, Irwinville 31760
Bethel	Rev. Eugene Brock, P. O. Box 296, Edison 31746	Mrs. Ruel Everson, Edison 31746	Rev. Eugene Brock, P. O. Box 296, Edison 31746
Bowen	Rev. Ralph Norman, Jr., 263 East Pine St., Colquitt 31737	Mr. Marvin Reed, 1103 East Evans St., Bainbridge 31717	Rev. Ralph Norman, 263 East Pine St., Colquitt 31737
Carrollton	Rev. J. Howard Cobble, Tabernacle, Bradley at W. Ctr., Carrollton 30117	Mr. Marion Harris, Route 3, Carrollton 30117	Rev. J. Howard Cobble, Tabernacle, Bradley at W. Ctr., Carrollton 30117
Catoosa	Rev. David Hudson, Sr., Route 1, Ringgold 30736	Mrs. Dewey E. Boyd, P. O. Box 100, Ringgold 30736	Rev. David Hudson, Sr., Route 1, Ringgold 30736
Centennial	Rev. Robert E. Blackburn, 109 Springdale Dr., Thomaston 30286	Rev. H. Allen Redd, P. O. Box 446, Molena 30258	Rev. Robert E. Blackburn, 109 Springdale Dr., Thomaston 30286
Central	Rev. Walter A. Brown, Route 2, Box 41, Eatonton 31024	Mr. Jessie Moore, Haddock 31033	Rev. Walter A. Brown, Route 2, Box 41, Eatonton 31024
Chattahoochee	Rev. Ed Sisson, Route 1, Flowery Branch 30542	Mr. James L. Maddox, Gillsville 30543	Mr. LeRoy Whiting, Route 1, Flowery Branch 30542
Chattooga	Rev. Hilton C. Garrett, 9 Kirby St., Summerville 30747	Rev. L. Frank Welch, P. O. Box 219, Trion 30753	Rev. Hilton C. Garrett, 9 Kirby St., Summerville 30747
Colquitt County	Rev. Kenneth Kicklighter, Route 5, Moultrie 31768	Mrs. Betty Shiflett, Route 1, Camilla Hgts., Moultrie 31768	Rev. Kenneth Kicklighter, Route 5, Moultrie 31768
Columbus	Rev. Richard Hearn, 4117 St. Mary's Rd., Columbus 31907	Mrs. R. M. Wall. 1931 Springdale Dr., Columbus 31906	Rev. Richard Hearn, 4117 St. Mary's Rd., Columbus 31907
Concord	Rev. Claude Rainwater, Clarkdale 30020	Mr. Herman Daniell, 493 Floyd Rd., Mableton 30059	Rev. Claude Rainwater, Clarkdale 30020
Consolation	Rev. Raymond Walden, Lumber City 31549	Mrs. Theo Wilcox, Route 3, Hazlehurst 31539	Rev. David Howle, First Church, P. O. Box 323, Baxley 31513
Coosa	Rev. R. V. Wells, Jr., Route 1, Rock Springs 30739	Mr. Farrell Brown, Route 2, LaFayette 30728	Rev. R. V. Wells, Jr., Route 1, Rock Springs 30739
Daniell	Rev. Gene Brooks, P. O. Box 25, Soperton 30457	Rev. Ray Simpson, 503 Smith St., Vidalia 30474	Rev. Gene Brooks, P. O. Box 25, Soperton 30457
Dodge County	Mr. Billy McLeod, P. O. Box 146, Chester 31012	Mr. W. Ray Stuckey, Route 6, Box 270, Eastman 31023	Mr. Billy McLeod, P. O. Box 146, Chester 31012
Ebenezer	Mr. A. T. Wimberly, Box 192, Jeffersonville 31044	Mr. B. W. Jones. Dry Branch 31020	Mr. A. T. Wimberly, Box 192, Jeffersonville 31044
Emanuel	Rev. Albert W. Huyck, Jr., P. O. Box 828, Swainsboro 30401	Mrs. Atelia S. Hopkins, P. O. Box 123, Swainsboro 30401	Rev. H. E. Keel, Route 2, Twin City 30471
Enon	Rev. Lloyd E. Free, Route 1, Cornelia 30531	Mr. Idus Harrison, Route 1, Box 231, Cornelia 30531	
Etowah	Mr. A. B. Allred, Sr., Tate 30177	Rev. J. R. Huddleston, Route 1, Waleska 30183	Mr. A. B. Allred, Sr., Tate 30177
Fairburn	Rev. Frank Brown, 3692 Tampa Trail S. W., Atlanta 30331	Mrs. Sterling Sexton, Box 40, Red Oak 30272	Rev. Frank Brown, 3692 Tampa Trail, S. W., Atlanta 30331
Flint River	Rev. Paul E. Wade, P. O. Box 408, Griffin 30223	Rev. Jack Bridges, 100 College St., McDonough 30253	Rev. Paul E. Wade, P. O. Box 408, Griffin 30223
Floyd County	Mr. Maurice Newman, P. O. Box 1642, Rome 30161	Mr. Vernon Stephens, Route 4, Rome 30161	Mr. Maurice Newman, P. O. Box 1642, Rome 30161
Friendship	Rev. John T. Simmons, Plains 31780	Rev. E. W. Dupree, 311 S. Lee St., Americus 31709	Rev. John T. Simmons, Plains 31780
Georgia	Rev. Harold Tice, P. O. Box 28, Greensboro 30643	Mr. Ben O. Teasley, P. O. Box 592, Washington 30673	Rev. Harold Tice, P. O. Box 28, Greensboro 30643
Gilmer-Fannin	Rev. Fred Stahl, Jr., Route 4, Box 140, Ellijay 30540	Mr. Guinn Williamson, Route 1, Box 123, Blue Ridge 30513	
Gordon County	Rev. J. W. Wallis, 35 College St., Calhoun 30701	Mr. Clarence Garren, Route 2, Calhoun 30701	Rev. John O'Neal, P. O. Box 503, Calhoun 30701
Grady County	Rev. Robert L. Franklin, 120 6th Ave., N. W., Cairo 31728	Mr. Melvin Knight, Jr., Route 1, Whigham 31797	Rev. Robert L. Franklin, 120 6th Ave., N. W., Cairo 31728
Habersham County	Rev. Ed L. Aiken, P. O. Box 67, Baldwin 30511	Mrs. E. O. Bonnette, Route 1, Demorest 30535	Rev. Billy A. Burrell, Route 1, Mt. Airy 30563
Haralson County	Rev. Grant Finnell, Route 1, Highway 120, Bremen 30110	Mrs. Detrice T. Mahler, Route 2, Box 229-B, Bremen 30110	Rev. Doyle Hollingsworth, James St., Tallapoosa 30176
Hebron	Rev. Edward Sayer, Route 3, Elberton 30635	Mr. Guy W. Wilson, Route 2, Elberton 30635	Rev. Edward Sayer, Route 3, Elberton 30635

Association	Moderator and Address	Clerk and Address	Chairman of Executive Committee and Address
Hephzibah	Rev. Stanley R. Hendricks, Stapleton 30823	Rev. William G. Deakins, P. O. Box 217, Wrens 30833	Rev. W. R. Shaw, Box 203, Alexander 30801
Hiawassee	Mr. Robert W. Gibby, Young Harris 30582	Mr. E. G. Jones, Route 3, Box 146, Hiawassee 30546	Mr. Robert W. Gibby, Young Harris 30582
Hightower	Rev. Roy Bailey, Route 3, Cumming 30130	Mr. A. M. Sosebee, Route 6, Cumming 30130	Rev. Ralph O'Bryant, 3983 Tilly Mill Rd., Doraville 30340
Houston	Rev. J. Reuben Johnson, Route 3, Box 117, Vienna 31092	Miss Nell Bond, Route 2, Cordele 31015	Rev. J. Reuben Johnson, Route 3, Box 117, Vienna 31092
Kilpatrick	Rev. Harold Eubanks, Route 1, Appling 30802	Mr. Lon L. Fleming, P. O. Box 224, Thomson 30824	Rev. Harold Eubanks, Route 1, Appling 30802
Kimbell	Rev. R. W. Jenkins, RFD 2, Jackson 30233	Mr. B. Y. Lunceford, 280 S. Harkness St., Jackson 30233	Rev. R. W. Jenkins, RFD 2, Jackson 30233
Laurens County	Rev. J. C. Nalls, Route 2, East Dublin 31021	Mr. Tyrus F. Gaillard, 206 N. Elm St., Dublin 31021	Rev. Bill Weeks, 514 Cardinal Dr., Dublin 31021
Lawrenceville	Mr. Ferd F. Dowis, Jr., 229 Pine Forest Dr., Lawrenceville 30245	Rev. Fred Musser, Grayson 30221	Mr. Ferd F. Dowis, Jr., 229 Pine Forest Dr., Lawrenceville 30245
Liberty	Rev. W. A. Trotman, Sr., Route 1, Baldwin 30511	Mr. Lewis Meeks, Route 3, Box 150, Toccoa 30577	Rev. W. A. Trotman, Sr., Route 1, Baldwin 30511
Little River	Rev. Jack Dowdy, Pitts 31072	Mr. J. L. Faircloth, Abbeville 31001	Rev. Jack Dowdy, Pitts 31072
Lookout Valley	Rev. A. D. Phillips, P. O. Box 2005, Ft. Oglethorpe 30742	Mrs. June Wilson, Route 2, Trenton 30752	Rev. A. D. Phillips, P. O. Box 2005, Ft. Oglethorpe 30742
Macon	Rev. Kenneth Youmans, 3805 Napier Ave., Macon 31204	Rev. William S. Saloom, 2142 Montpelier Ave., Macon 31204	Rev. Kenneth Youmans, 3805 Napier Ave., Macon 31204
Mallary	Rev. Malvin Miller, P. O. Box 66, Poulan 31781	Rev. Caley R. Nichols, 1534 E. Broad Ave., Albany 31705	Rev. Malvin Miller, P. O. Box 66, Poulan 31781
Mell	Rev. J. Terrell Ruis, Box 368, Omega 31775	Miss Virginia Garrick, 616 N. Central Ave., Tifton 31794	Rev. J. Terrell Ruis, Box 368, Omega 31775
Memorial	Rev. Winford Casey, Route 3, Calhoun 30701	Mr. John D. Sweat, 1362 U. S. 41 North, Calhoun 30701	Rev. Winford Casey, Route 3, Calhoun 30701
Mercer	Mr. L. V. Graham, Route 1, Barney 31625	Mr. M. H. Belcher, Route 2, Quitman 31643	Mr. L. V. Graham, Route 1, Barney 31625
Merritt	Rev. Ron Weadon, Box 26, Talbotton 31827	Rev. Jimmy Chapman, Route 1, Manchester 31816	Rev. Ron Weadon, Box 26, Talbotton 31827
Middle	Rev. A. Maurice Crowder, P. O. Box 827, Millen 30442	Mrs. Nina Cash Ernest, P. O. Box 14, Rocky Ford 30455	Rev. A. Maurice Crowder, P. O. Box 827, Millen 30442
Middle Cherokee	Rev. John W. Wilson, 19 W. Iron Belt Rd., Cartersville 30120	Rev. James T. Hatcher, Jr., 21 Goodyear Ave., Cartersville 30120	Rev. Herb Gibson, 114 Gilmer St., Cartersville 30120
Morgan County	Mr. E. W. Armour, 105 S. Main St., Madison 30650	Mr. Tom Riden, 921 S. Main St., Madison 30650	Mr. E. W. Armour, 105 S. Main St., Madison 30650
Morganton	Rev. A. E. Harper, Hemp 30561	Miss LuAnn Weeks, Route 1, Box 45, Copperhill, Tenn. 37317	Rev. A. E. Harper, Hemp 30561
Mountaintown	Rev. James Holt, First Church, 24 Dalton St., Ellijay 30540	Mr. C. F. Owen, Ellijay 30540	Mr. Gomer Gibson, Route A, Ellijay 30540
Mount Vernon	Rev. Oscar T. Cope, 110 S. Valley St., Wrightsville 31096	Mr. H. Z. Josey, Route 1, Box 162, Bartow 30413	Rev. Inman Gerrald, Box 293, Adrian 31002
Mulberry	Mr. Billy Ray Banks, Box 27, Carl 30203	Rev. J. O. McNeal, Box 21, Braselton 30517	Rev. James Hall, Route 1, Bethlehem 30620
Murray County	Rev. B. F. Babb, 622 Fort St., Chatsworth 30705	Mr. Paul R. Huddleston, Route 3, Chatsworth 30705	Rev. B. F. Babb, 622 Fort St., Chatsworth 30705
New Sunbury	Dr. Charles H. Pollock, 109 Bradwell St., Hinesville 31313	Mr. Clyde L. Chapman, P. O. Box 212, Ludowici 31316	Rev. Norman E. Beverly, Route 2, Box 35, Ludowici 31316
New Union	Mr. Taylor Dowdy, Route 2, Dahlonega 30533	Mrs. Jim Bailey, Route 1, Box 193, Murrayville 30564	Mr. Taylor Dowdy, Route 2, Dahlonega 30533
Noonday	Rev. Francis W. Gibson, P. O. Box 388, Kennesaw 30144	Rev. W. L. MacMillan, 1422 Shiloh Trail East, Kennesaw 30144	Rev. Francis W. Gibson, P. O. Box 388, Kennesaw 30144
North Georgia	Rev. Leonard Cordle, Westbrook Rd., Dalton 30720	Mr. Dewey E. Hughes, 1208 Vanderbilt Dr., Dalton 30720	Rev. Leonard Cordle, Westbrook Rd., Dalton 30720
Notla River	Rev. B. A. Buchanan, First Church, Blairsville 30512	Mrs. Joe Straner, Hwy. 180 N., Suches 30572	Rev. Joe Straner, Hwy. 180 N., Suches 30572
Ogeechee River	Rev. Gordon A. Hunter, P. O. Box 457, Pembroke 31321	Rev. Ted Callahan, P. O. Box 306, Brooklet 30415	Rev. Bill Brown, Route 1, Statesboro 30458
Piedmont-Okefenokee	Rev. Carl Ledbetter, 505 Bibb St., Waycross 31501	Rev. Brooks Hampton, McGregor St., Blackshear 31516	Dr. Harold Withers, 1404 Satilla Blvd., Waycross 31501
Pine Mountain	Mr. Charles Story, N. College St., Hamilton 31811	Mrs. Mabry Collins, P. O. Box 124, Hamilton 31811	Mr. Charles Story, N. College St., Hamilton 31811
Polk County	Rev. Carl Johnson, 705 Hogue Ave., Rockmart 30153	Mr. Curtis Brown, 1219 Brooks St., Cedartown 30125	Rev. Rufus Morman, Route 3, Cedartown 30125
Pulaski-Bleckley	Rev. Jearl Fordham, Route 1, Cochran 31014	Rev. Guy Kelly, Cochran 31014	Rev. H. M. Hawkins, Route 1, Eastman 31023

Association	Moderator and Address	Clerk and Address	Chairman of Executive Committee and Address
Rabun County	Rev. Lowell McElroy, P. O. Box 36, Lakemont 30552	Rev. Malcolm Chapman, Box 52, Clayton 30525	Rev. Lowell McElroy, P. O. Box 36, Lakemont 30552
Rehoboth	Dr. Billy H. Adams, P. O. Drawer 838, Warner Robins 31093	Mr. W. Howard Brown, Route 1, Byron 31008	Dr. Billy H. Adams, P. O. Drawer 838, Warner Robins 31093
Roswell	Rev. James A. Price, Route 1, Woodstock Rd., Roswell 30075	Mr. Robert Jackson, 2568 Laurelwood Rd., Doraville 30340	Rev. James A. Price, Route 1, Woodstock Rd., Roswell 30075
Sarepta	Rev. R. T. Williams, 289 Forest Rd., Athens 30601	Dr. Frederick W. Bennett, 410 University Dr., Athens 30601	Rev. Don Fuller, P. O. Box 227, Colbert 30628
Savannah	Rev. Joseph T. Greene, 2602 13th St., Savannah 31408	Mr. J. A. Tomlinson, 26 Nancy Place, Savannah 31406	Rev. Thomas D. Austin, Box 9551 Savannah 31402
Smyrna	Rev. Frank N. Bearden, Jr., P. O. Box 65, Nicholls 31554	Rev. Charles E. Bagent, 1410 E. Ward St., Douglas 31533	Rev. Frank N. Bearden, Jr., P. O. Box 65, Nicholls 31554
Southeast	Rev. Frank Haynes, First Church, Kingsland 31548	Rev. Robert Hoffman, 3105 Wildwood Dr., Brunswick 31520	Rev. Frank Haynes, First Church, Kingsland 31548
South Metro	Rev. Jack Overton, Box 135, Fayetteville 30214	Mrs. Milton Faglier, 6074 Ledgewood Dr., Forest Park 30050	Dr. Joe Brown, 6634 Pleasant Valley Dr., Morrow 30260
South River	Rev. Vernon Smith, 1773 Hollyhock Terrace, Decatur 30032	Mr. Linton Ray, Route 5, Conyers 30207	Rev. S. R. Jones, 1174 Panola Rd., Stone Mountain 30083
Stone Mountain	Rev. Charles W. Drake, First Church, 6616 Hillandale Dr., Lithonia 30058	Rev. Charles Elder, P. O. Box 119, Conyers 30207	Rev. Charles W. Drake, First Church, 6616 Hillandale Dr., Lithonia 30058
Summerhill	Mr. B. J. Goodwin, Weston 31832	Mrs. Ross Jones, Box 26, Weston 31832	Rev. George Deadwyler, Dawson 31742
Tallapoosa	Rev. Clarence G. Cole, 202 E. Memorial Dr., Dallas 30132	Mr. Kenneth Hammond, Route 2, Hiram 30141	Rev. Clarence G. Cole, 202 E. Memorial Dr., Dallas 30132
Tattnall-Evans	Mr. J. Herbert Rogers, Manassas 30438	Mrs. Betty L. Bazemore, Collins 30421	Rev. W. H. Oellerich, 202 S. Claxton Ave., Claxton 30417
Telfair	Rev. James E. McClain, P. O. Box 484, McRae 31055	Mr. Grady Saunders, P. O. Box 157, Helena 31037	Mr. R. Guy Thomas, P. O. Box 185, Milan 31060
Thomas County	Rev. T. J. Davis, Boston 31626	Mrs. Leon Harrison, 426 Glen Arven Dr., Thomasville 31792	Rev. T. J. Davis, Boston 31626
Troup County	Rev. Fred Buchanan, 1301 Washington St., LaGrange 30240	Mrs. Allen Teasley, 101 Marchman Dr., LaGrange 30240	Rev. Harry Chafin, 604 Hill St., LaGrange 30240
Tucker	Rev. O. A. Collins, P. O. Box 105, Newton 31770	Miss Annie Ellis, Camilla 31730	Rev. Thomas Thorne, Route 4, Camilla 31730
Tugalo	Rev. Gerald Bearden, Route 2, Toccoa 30577	Rev. C. Ray Black, Route 1, Homer 30547	Rev. W. I. Pritchett, Route 2, Martin 30557
Turner	Mr. Gilbert Branch, Ashburn 31714	Mr. Wallace Beard, Route 1, Sycamore 31790	Mr. Gilbert Branch, Ashburn 31714
Valdosta	Rev. James Pitts, First Church, P. O. Box 670, Valdosta 31601	Mrs. Clyde Stokes, 419 Canna Dr., Valdosta 31601	Rev. James Pitts, First Church, P. O. Box 670, Valdosta 31601
Washington	Rev. Milton L. Wood, Route 1, Box 26, Sandersville 31082	Dr. T. E. Smith, 411 Forest Rd., Milledgeville 31061	Rev. Milton L. Wood, Route 1, Box 26, Sandersville 31082
Western	Rev. Douglas Johnson, First Church, Hogansville 30230	Rev. Woodrow W. Wall, Box 458, Greenville 30222	Rev. Shuford M. Jones, Jr., Route 5, Box 434, Newnan 30263
White	Rev. C. C. Harper, Route 4, Cleveland 30528	Mrs. Guy L. Palmer, Route 1, Sautee-Nacoochee 30571	Rev. Verner London, Route 1, Cleveland 30528

817

Statistical Information
on
Georgia Baptist Convention

Statistical information on the following pages is taken from sources indicated, and from material compiled from selected minutes of the Georgia Baptist Convention. Information included, not identified otherwise, was prepared and furnished by Lawrence E. Webb, Secretary of Public Relations, Georgia Baptist Convention.

Year	Associations	Churches	Members	Baptisms	Ministers Ordained	Ministers Licensed	Sunday School Members	Mission Gifts	Gifts Convention Causes
1822	----	----	----	----	----	----	----	----	----
1823	----	----	----	----	----	----	----	----	----
1824	10	264	18,108	----	115	25	----	----	----
1825	10	260	18,484	----	110	23	----	----	----
1826	----	----	----	----	----	----	----	----	----
1827	----	----	----	----	----	----	----	----	----
1828	16	356	28,268	----	115	25	----	----	----
1829	----	----	----	----	----	----	----	----	----
1830	----	----	----	----	----	----	----	Education Fund	1186.24
								General Purpose Mission Fund	304.58½
									961.97¾
1831	17 year (constituent)	506	37,490	------	271	----	----	----	----

Breakdown By Associations

Year	Associations	Churches	Members	Baptisms	Ministers Ordained	Ministers Licensed
1832	Georgia	50	7162	951	23	8
1832	Sunbury (1784)	18	6918	843	8	--
1832	Sarepta (1798)	33	2668	302	11	5
1832	Ichoconaugh	32	1915	----	18	--

819

Breakdown By Associations

Year	Associations	Churches	Members	Members (net +gain —loss)	Baptisms	Ministers Ordained	Ministers Licensed	Sunday School Members	Mission Gifts	Gifts Convention Causes
1832	Ebenezer	30	1349		184	8	3			
1832	Flint River (1824)	38	2494			11	9			
1832	Yellow River (1810)	43	2670			14	5			
1832	Oemulgee	35	2821			11	2			
1832	Columbus	25	1093			10				
1832	Western	39	1518			14	4			
1832	Ocklocknee	21	684			7	3			
1832	Canoochie	16	365		39	8				
1832	Chattahoochee, Al	7	89			1				
1832	Houston	11	365			3	5			
1832	Tugalo	32	1604			13				
1832	Washington	9	533			7				
1832	Piedmont	11	267			5	4			
1832	Hephzibah (1757)	36	1757			17				
1832	Total (18)	486	37,072		2319	189	44			

I. M. Allen, U. S. Baptist Annual Register for 1832.

Year	Associations	Churches	Members	Members (net +gain —loss)	Baptisms	Ministers Ordained	Ministers Licensed	Sunday School Members	Mission Gifts	Gifts Convention Causes
1833	--									
1834	--									
1835	21	583	41,810			298				

Year	Associations	Churches	Members	Members (net +gain —loss)	Baptisms	Ministers Ordained	Ministers Licensed	Sunday School Members	Mission Gifts	Gifts Convention Causes
1836	Bethel (1832)	34	1037	+232	106	10	3			
1836	Canoochie	16	365			8				
1836	Central (1834)	11	798	+107		4	1			
1836	Chattahoochee (1824)	17	848	+110	51	9	1			
1836	Chattahooch Riv (1825)	5	86			1	4			
1836	Columbus (1829)	29	2521	+83	222	11				
1836	Coosa (1835)	10	122	+48	44	3	3			
1836	Ebenezer (1814)	29	1405	+119	211	10	4			
1836	Flint River (1824)	41	2464	+16	109	18	12			
1836	Georgia (1784)	49	6987	+96	478	21	5			
1836	Hephzibah (1796)	23	1766	+26	45	7	2			
1836	Hightower (1835)	11	320		37	3				
1836	Houston (1830)	14	387			3	2			
1836	Ichaconna (1829)	27	1924	+268	278	18	8			
1836	Mountain (1833)	15	557			9	3			
1836	Ocklocknee	21	684			10	3			
1836	Oemulgee (1810)	32	2274	+101	197	10				
1836	Piedmont	11	267			5	5			
1836	Sarepta (1798)	33	2770			16	2			
1836	Sunbury (1818)	20	5158	+117	198	10				

Year	Association	(Founded)						
1836	Tugalo	(1817)	17	917	-112	29	7	3
1836	Washington	(1829)	9	533			7	-2
1836	Western	(1829)	45	2648			14	-2
1836	Yellow River	(1824)	45	2730	132		15	4
1836	Other Churches		8	3381	10		7	2
1836	Total	24	572	42,949	2370	236	69	

The foregoing Summary shows that there are in Georgia, 572 churches, and only 236 ordained ministers. It is probable that there are several unassociated churches, not included in that number, of which we have no information. It is also probable that the tabular view does not contain the names of all the ordained ministers in the State. The Minutes from which the tables are made, in general, contain the names of such ministers only as were appointed messengers to the Associations; and although the ministers are generally included in this delegation, it sometimes happens that a few are not. The whole number of this class in Georgia will not exceed probably twenty-five. Let this number be added to 236, and we have only 261 ministers for 572 churches, leaving 311 churches without pastors, unless they are supplied by such as have two or more charges.
I. M. Allen, the Triennial Register, No. 2, 1836.

Year							$	G B C gifts
1837								
1838								
1839								
1840								
1841								
1842								
1843								
1844								
1845	46	971	58,388	4561	464	142	$1,148.41	G B C gifts *Minutes
1846	50	1004	59,467		505	166	5,946.77	G B C gifts 1846 pg 27
1847	54	1060	63,097		549	204	9,885.73	36,423.82
1848	56	1105	67,098		583	292	8,714.24	44,417.82
1849	57	1132	69,869		628	177	7,392.49	46,914.50
1850	57	1183	71,879	5579	615	296	10,181.86	51,559.75
1851	58	1213	75,540		674	192		
1852	61	1242	77,962	4951	681	200	14,057.63	48,881.94
1853	53	1252	81,043	5040	709	208	11,791.79	48,442.83
1854	59	1240	82,307	5505	706	206	17,021.52	48,315.09
1855	60	1333	86,701	4984	711	220	16,823.03	48,642.53
1856	63	1373	89,989		710	209		
1857	63	1350	85,113	5008	689	177	18,093.35	
1858	64	1406	93,447		769	211		49,454.74
1859	65	1429	95,727		737	211		49,692.86
1860	65	1435	99,149		757	229		51,130.10
1861		1015			540	141		52,128.12

Year	Associations	Church	Members	Baptisms	Ministers Ordained	Ministers Licensed	Sunday School Members (see note)	Mission Gifts	Total Gifts	Notes
1862										
1863										
1864										
1865										
1866	65	1435	99,149		757	229				
1867	66	1454	97,345		800	211				
1868	69	1218	115,198		760	194				
1869										
1870	72	1745	131,642	4,657*	836	259		12,026.10		1870-G C Min
1871										
1872	86	1973	146,407		1056	210				
1873	87	2001	164,292		902	241	3,325			
1874	107	2201	183,435		811	216	3,689			
1875	107	2307	193,662	5,775*	956	292	6,639			1875-G B C Min
1876	107	2392	202,356		725	326	6,104			
1877	107	2532	209,790		762	279	26,267			
1878	107	2636	219,000		694	217	10,289			
1879	107	2636	210,900		762	219	13,155			
1880	110	2680	217,041		809	278	15,246	17,942.72	32,402.90	
1881		1063	84,732							Dem in Ga.)
1882		1076	83,759							
1883		1091	85,372							
1884		1126	88,281							181+ Reason for drop in churches and Assoc. Harrison figures incl Anti colored etc.
1885	41	1101	85,183	6,288					29,697.05	
1886		1135	90,935							
1887		1169	90,664							
1888		1190	103,232							
1889		1207	105,188							
1890	45	1288	108,917	5,514			2,055 teachers			
1891		1283	113,050						85,706.11	
1892		1303	111,795				30,503			

Samuel Boykin History of Georgia Baptists with Biographical Compendium, p. 243 (Chart from 1862-1880 do not include baptisms, mission gifts and gifts, Convention causes. These came from material secured from Minutes, G. B. C.

Reason for drop in number of churches and Associations beginning in 1880 is that Boykin's figures included Anti, Neutral, colored, etc: through 1880.

Samuel Boykin History of Georgia Baptists with Biographical Compendium, Atlanta: Jas. P. Harrison Co. 1881, p. 243 chart 1845-1880.

Year						
1893	1378	---	-----	115,587	59,255	---------
1894	1402	55	-----	124,311	30,815	---------
1895	1527	---	-----	127,665	------	---------
1896	1558	---	7,882	139,273	------	---------
1897	1666	---	-----	154,589	46,954	---------
1898	1743	---	-----	164,005	40,466	---------
1899	1758	---	-----	167,559	40,810	73,742.19

History of Georgia Baptists with Biographical Compendium, by Samuel Boykin p. 243 (Chart from 1845-1861 do not include baptisms, mission gifts and gifts, convention causes. These came from material furnished by 22 of the 57 Associations constituent members of the Convention (Minutes, GBC 1851).

1972

150th ANNIVERSARY
GEORGIA BAPTIST CONVENTION

Thanksgiving - Commitment - Achievement

Established 1822
SERVING — WITNESSING
GEORGIA BAPTIST CONVENTION

Year	Association	Churches	Members	Baptisms	Sunday School Members	Church Training (B.T.U)	W.M.U.	Brotherhood Royal Ambassador	Mission Gifts	Total Gifts
1900	66	1815	171,417	8,324	36,214	—	—	—	—	—
1901	—	1,840	175,369	7,765	45,278	—	—	—	—	—
1902	—	1,850	178,644	8,771	—	—	—	—	—	—
1903	—	2,079	202,724	13,123	72,822	—	—	—	—	—
1904	—	2,098	208,886	13,057	74,779	—	—	—	$ 104,607.35	—
1905	—	2,120	213,325	13,325	78,137	—	—	—	—	—
1906	—	2,170	224,921	13,721	81,249	—	—	—	—	—
1907	—	2,186	230,397	12,381	—	—	—	—	—	—
1908	86	2,218	237,271	12,960	—	—	—	—	—	—
1909	85	2,248	244,223	16,031	134,005	—	—	—	$ 206,941.21	—
1910	87	2,293	256,515	14,503	120,842	—	—	—	—	—
1911	88	2,335	261,416	14,203	123,020	—	—	—	—	—
1912	91				148,155	—	—	—	—	—
1913	91	2,399	279,175	13,623	154,671	—	—	—	—	—
1914	92	2,423	287,079	14,753	151,500	—	—	—	211,652.33	—
1915	94	2,426	293,244	15,306	152,285	—	—	—	—	—
1916		2,422	299,691	15,829	180,225	—	—	—	—	—
1917	—	2,473	311,341	15,440	184,499	—	—	—	—	—
1918	95	2,473	315,801	14,694	226,268	—	—	—	—	—
1919	94	2,506	331,846	13,132	—	—	—	—	1,774,399.74	—
1920	—	2,469	330,307	16,716	—	—	—	—	—	—
1921		2,532	349,009	26,556	—	—	—	—	—	—
1922	97	2,504	368,481	20,220	—	—	—	—	—	—
1923	97	2,514	383,202	17,756	—	—	—	—	565,170.79	—
1924	97	2,542	390,844	17,773	—	—	—	—	—	—
1925	97	2,553	399,640	19,611	—	—	—	—	—	$ 1,017,880.00
1926	95	2,528	404,559	15,767	242,736	—	—	—	—	2,845,393.18
1927	90	2,371	408,673	16,340	237,008	—	—	—	—	2,863,807.67
1928	88	2,423	413,815	15,062	208,328	—	—	—	—	2,902,691.63
1929	88	2,407	418,565	17,030	230,762	—	—	—	411,414.95	2,806,054.79
1930	88	2,410	427,874	19,119	251,189	—	—	—	—	2,722,397.45
1931	89	2,430	441,756	20,400	264,459	—	—	—	—	2,358,278.95
1932	85	2,376	450,610	21,553	269,766	—	—	—	—	1,975,135.01
1933	84	2,408	457,941	18,424	260,670	—	—	—	—	1,751,064.74
1934	84	2,392	462,849	18,988	250,741	—	—	—	—	2,002,323.88
1935	84	2,407	470,362	16,669	250,418	—	—	—	392,111.60	2,148,880.33
1936	85	2,414	481,206	16,510	252,870	—	—	—	—	2,419,987.43
1937				18,307		—	—	—	—	2,568,017.72

Note It will be noticed that the total number of churches reported this year is 28 less than last year. This is accounted for partially by the fact that heretofor we have listed some of the schools and mission stations which brought the total for last year to 2432 (G B C minutes. 1921)

Year										
1938	86	2,434	499,404	24,111	263,456	—	—	—	—	2,891,544.92
1939	86	2,421	505,839	22,276	268,987	—	—	—	—	3,039,423.82
1940	86	2,428	520,546	22,427	278,525	—	—	—	—	3,408,583.40
1941	86	2,459	530,952	17,268	269,070	—	—	—	—	3,495,355.58
1942	86	2,476	539,617	17,562	259,231	—	—	—	—	4,112,505.52
1943	87	2,491	552,360	16,451	254,556	—	—	—	667,161.37	5,140,282.72
1944	87	2,511	566,231	18,664	259,731	—	—	—	—	5,339,825.03
1945	88	2,531	581,599	21,057	286,311	—	—	—	—	8,651,563.54
1946	88	2,559	598,728	20,798	293,845	—	—	—	—	9,428,703.52
1947	88	2,588	615,854	23,781	318,771	—	—	—	2,265,245.06	10,736,469.23
1948	87	2,567	629,491	26,192	350,114	—	—	—	—	12,331,026.61
1949	88	2,584	651,265	28,571	387,309	—	—	—	—	13,608,751.98
1950	90	2,614	675,305	31,280	426,175	—	—	—	—	15,821,214.80
1951	90	2,654	701,821	32,670	446,461	—	—	—	—	19,104,568.28
1952	—	—	718,808	27,027	467,165	—	—	—	—	17,983,637.87
1953	92	2,684	738,250	29,956	486,536	—	—	—	—	21,214,046.65
1954	93	2,720	760,024	33,379	549,962	—	—	—	—	24,429,877.70
1955	94	2,748	786,086	34,605	573,032	111,463	97,159	17,229	2,803,566.14	27,765,179.83
1956	94	2,819	805,241	33,221	587,455	177,577	116,313	42,831	3,937,221.93	30,980,711.59
1957	94	2,848	824,555	33,023	593,687	184,568	124,223	48,100	4,597,729.02	31,400,970.58
1958	94	2,869	843,828	34,593	602,450	192,735	130,980	54,167	4,702,782.10	33,373,132.45
1959	94	2,907	865,198	36,793	613,917	203,195	134,867	54,676	5,061,139.94	35,933,544.34
1960	94	2,940	885,376	33,287	620,015	211,360	137,086	53,922	5,404,887.21	38,674,741.56
1961	94	2,950	903,404	34,270	630,188	214,480	135,102	55,245	5,610,445.54	40,385,952.59
1962	94	2,981	918,163	31,966	632,884	218,790	134,663	62,355	5,923,879.33	43,037,279.68
1963	94	2,994	935,768	28,573	635,135	219,282	134,601	55,357	6,837,279.68	45,530,317.92
1964	94	3,004	950,704	30,079	636,669	217,694	141,185	52,893	7,094,397.77	48,564,546.13
1965	94	3,010	964,672	29,430	637,834	211,376	135,956	50,463	7,914,564.53	52,760,904.88
1966	94	3,008	980,758	30,568	639,684	208,803	137,912	51,384	10,722,054.95	57,078,788.00
1967	94	3,015	990,948	29,839	636,453	208,055	134,735	49,834	9,787,772.91	61,332,195.00
1968	95	3,011	995,973	28,975	628,975	219,670	131,915	49,973	9,971,052.29	68,105,606.75
1969	93	2,998	1,007,400	27,886	617,124	214,580	119,054	47,645	10,948,173.05	72,998,486.33
1970	93	2,974	1,007,856	28,458	600,239	204,177	113,372	47,168	10,745,665.94	76,103,542.00
1971	93	2,952	1,018,052	30,076	585,050	172,166	107,024	49,958	11,270,175.04	83,517,369.00

STATISTICS Indicating Relative Membership By Races 1852-1895. *

"Convention" Churches Only

Year	Churches	Members White	Members Colored
1852	730	34,711	16,817
1853	739	34,545	19,927
1854	770	34,884	21,010
1855	781	36,130	20,310
1856	773	35,847	22,605
1857	785	36,002	23,720
1858	---	---	---
1859	---	---	---
1860	---	---	---
1861	---	---	---
1862	---	---	---
1863	---	---	---
1864	---	---	---
1865	---	---	---
1866	---	---	---
1867	---	---	---
1868	---	---	---
1869	---	---	---
1870	706	37,560	9,705
1871	---	40,618	5,745
1872	792	47,237	5,849
1873	852	48,814	4,661
1874	854	65,114	3,539
1875	943	71,250	3,295
1876	950	76,677	2,100
1877	942	78,794	1,906
1878	1037	81,610	1,594
1879	1028	80,790	1,400
1880	1066	84,196	1,051
1881	1063	84,035	697
1882	1076	83,125	634
1883	1091	85,150	222
1884	1126	88,160	121
1885	1101	84,942	241
1886	1135	90,774	161
1887	1169	90,573	91
1888	1190	103,177	55
1889	1207	105,188	124
1890	1288	108,809	108
1891	1283	112,958	92
1892	1303	111,717	78
1893	1378	115,126	22
1894	1402	124,286	25
1895	1527	127,652	13
1896	1558	139,273	---
1897	1666	154,589	---
1898	1743	164,000	---
1899	1758	167,559	---

*Material furnished by Lawrence E. Webb, Secretary of Public Relations, Georgia Baptist Convention.

Bibliography

SINGLE-VOLUME WORKS

Anderson, P. Harris, General Editor, *The Witness and Work of Georgia Baptists*, Mercer University, Macon, Georgia, 1961.

Armitage, Thomas, *A History of the Baptists*, Volume I, New York: Bryan, Taylor, and Co., 1887, 492 p.p.

_____, *A History of the Baptists*, Volume II, New York: Bryan, Taylor, and Co., 1887, 493-978 p.p.

Backus, A. M., Isaac, *Church History of New England from 1620 to 1804*, Philadelphia: Baptist Tract Depository 1839, 250 p.p.

Barnes, William Wright, *The Southern Baptist Convention 1845-1953*, Broadman Press, Nashville, Tennessee, 1954, 330 p.p.

Benedict, David, *A General History of the Baptist Denomination In America, etc.*, New York: Lewis Colby and Company, 1848, 970 p.p.

Boykin, Samuel, *History of Georgia Baptists With Biographical Compendium*, Atlanta, Georgia: Jas. P. Harrison and Co., 1881, History, 274 p.p., Compendium, 613 p.p.

Burney, Mrs. Frank, *Wrought of God—A History with Memories of the Baptist Woman's Missionary Union of Georgia, 1884-1959*, 117 p.p.

Campbell, Jesse H., 1807-1888, *Georgia Baptists: Historical and Biographical*, Richmond, H. K. Ellyson, 1847. 288, [2] p. 19½ cm.

Cathcart, William, *The Baptist Encyclopedia*, Philadelphia: Louis H. Everts, 1886, 1324 p.p.

Coleman, Kenneth, *The American Revolution In Georgia*, 1763-1789, Athens: University of Georgia Press, 1958, 352 p.p.

Dowell, Spright, *A History of Mercer University 1833-1953*, Foote & Davies, Inc., Atlanta, 1958, 420 p.p.

Franklin, Benjamin, *Autobiography of*, New York: The Macmillan Company, 1911, 249 p.p.

Gillies, John, *Memoirs of Rev. George Whitefield*, Middletown, Conn.: Hunt & Noyes, 1838, 648 p.p.

Kilpatrick, W. L., *The Hephzibah Association Centennial, 1794-1894.*

King, Joe M., *A History of South Carolina Baptists*, The General Board of the South Carolina Baptist Convention, 1964, 494 p.p.

King, Spencer B., *Georgia, A Mission Field*, Executive Committee, Baptist Convention of the State of Georgia, Atlanta, 1928, 167 p.p.

Knight, Lucian Lamar, *Georgia's Bi-Centennial Memoirs and Memories*, First Series, Volume IV, Published by the author for private distribution: 1933, 432 p.p.

Lawton, James S., *The Baptist Centennial Volume*, containing the addresses delivered at the 100th anniversary of the Georgia Baptist Association, Washington. Atlanta: James P. Harrison and Co., 1885.

Mallary, Charles D., *Memoirs of Elder Edmund Botsford.* Charleston: W. Riley, 1832, 240 p.p.

——————, *Memoirs of Elder Jesse Mercer*, New York: John Gray, 1844, 455 p.p.

——————, *Memoir of Elder Billington M. Sanders and Funeral Discourse*, Charleston: Southern Baptist Publication Society, 1854, 108 p.p.

Marshall, Jabez P., *Memoirs of the late Abraham Marshall.*

Mercer, Jesse, *A History of the Georgia Baptist Association*, Washington, Georgia, 1838, 419 p.p.

Miller, Alexander Lee—Editor, *History of Bethel Association Including Centennial Meeting, 1909-1934.*

Mosteller, James Donovan, *A History of the Kiokee Baptist*

Church in Georgia, Ann Arbor, Michigan: Edwards Brothers, Inc., 1952, 275 p.p.

Neel, Mrs. W. J., *His Story in Georgia W.M.U.* History W. M. U., Georgia Baptist Convention, 1939.

Orchard, G. H., *A Concise History of Foreign Baptists,* New York: Sheldon, Lamport & Co., 1855, 382 p.p.

Paschal, George Washington, *History of North Carolina Baptists, 1663-1805.* Raleigh: The General Board of the North Carolina Baptist State Convention, 1930.

Pollard, Edward B. and Stevens, Daniel Gurden, *Luther Rice: Pioneer In Missions and Education.* Philadelphia: The Judson Press, 1928.

Robinson, R. L., *History of the Georgia Baptist Association,* 1928, 263 p.p.

Rutledge, Arthur B., *Mission To America,* Nashville: Broadman Press, 1969, 271 p.p.

Scarborough, L. R., *Marvels of Divine Leadership,* Nashville: Sunday School Board, 1920, 245 p.p.

Semple, Robert B., *Semple's History of the Rise and Progress of the Baptists in Virginia,* Revised by G. W. Beale, 1894.

Sherwood, Julia L., *Memoirs of Adiel Sherwood D. D.,* Philadelphia: Grant and Faires, 1884, 416 p.p.

Stevens, Daniel Gurden, *The First Hundred Years of The American Baptist Publication Society,* The American Baptist Publication Society, 120 p.p.

Stone, Eugenia Wootten, *Yesterday at Tift,* Doraville, Georgia: Foote and Davies, 1969, 291 p.p.

Sweet, William Warren, *The Story of Religion in America,* New York: Harper and Brothers, 1950, 492 p.p.

Torbet, Robert G., *A History of the Baptists,* Philadelphia: The Judson Press, 1950, 540 p.p.

Vedder, Henry C., *A Short History of the Baptists,* Philadelphia: The American Baptist Publication Society, 1907, 431 p.p.

Walker, Williston, *A History of the Christian Church,* New York: Charles Scribner's Sons, 1947, 624 p.p.

Wayland. Francis, *A Memoir of the Life and Labors of the*

Reverend Adoniram Judson D. D., Volume I, Boston: Phillips, Sampson, and Company, 1853.

White, Rev. George, *Historical Collections of Georgia*. New York: Pudney and Russell, 1855, 688 p.p.

Williams, Leslie Spencer, *Youth's Fifty Years*, Baptist Training Union Department of Georgia Baptist Convention, 1945.

Who's Who In America, Vol. 36, 1970-1971. Chicago, Marquis Who's Who, 2785 p.p.

MULTIVOLUME WORKS AND SERIES

Book of Reports, Executive Committee, Georgia Baptist Convention, 1957-1971.

Christian, John T., *A History of The Baptists*, Nashville: Atlanta: Sunday School Board of the Southern Baptist Convention, Volume I, 1922, 408 p.p.

Encyclopedia of Southern Baptists, Volume I, Nashville: Broadman Press, 1958, 748 p.p.

Encyclopedia of Southern Baptists, Volume II, Nashville: Broadman Press, 1958, 749-1,555 p.

Encyclopedia of Southern Baptists, Volume III, Nashville: Broadman Press, 1971. 1553-2,065 p.

Minutes, Georgia Baptist Convention, 1822-1971 [microfilmed copies 1822-1952; Bound Volumes 1953-1970; None for 1865].

Owens, Loulie Latimer, "Oliver Hart, 1723-1795, A Brief Biography," *Baptist History and Heritage*, Volume I, Number 2 [July, 1966], 1945.

Ragsdale, B. D., *Story of Georgia Baptists* Volume One, The Executive Committee of Georgia Baptist Convention, 1932, Atlanta, Georgia.

_____, *Story of Georgia Baptists* Volume Two, Mercer University, Macon, Georgia, 1935.

_____, *Story of Georgia Baptists* Volume Three, The Executive Committee of Georgia Baptist Convention, Atlanta, 1938.

Saye, Albert B., "Georgia, /History of/," the *World Book Encyclopedia*, Volume VII, p.p. 122-135, Field Enterprises Corporation, Merchandise Mart Plaza, Chicago, Illinois, 1962.

The World Book Encyclopedia, volumes 7, 15, Field Enterprises Educational Corporation, Chicago, Illinois, 1962. Periodicals

The Analytical Repository, Henry Holcombe, Editor, Volumes I and II, 1802-1803, Savannah, [microfilm].

The Christian Index, 1822-May 25, 1972, especially the following issues: *The Christian Index*, June 15, 1939; *The Christian Index*, June 1, 1922; *The Christian Index*, December 25, 1920. [Microfilm 1822-1953; Bound Volumes 1954-1970; Loose Issues, 1971.]

The Quarterly Review, April, May, June, 1971, Nashville: Sunday School Board, Southern Baptist Convention, 98 p.p. Article by Robert G. Gardner on "The Cherokee Georgia Baptist Convention."

UNPUBLISHED WORKS

Act of Incorporation, Mount Enon Academy, W. P. A., transcript De Renne Collection, University of Georgia Library, Athens.

Akins, Billy Lee, *Georgians and the War of 1812.* Typed Master's thesis, Georgia Southern College, Statesboro, Georgia, 1968.

"Boston Baptist Church Manuscript Sketch," 6 p.p.

Brewton-Parker College, A Brief History of [unpublished, undated, typewritten manuscript provided by the college.]

Carswell, W. J., *Source Materials on Mount Enon Academy*, [listing of primary sources of information,] Savannah, 14 p.p.

"Concerning the Action of the Board of Trustees of Mercer University to Accept Grants for Federal Government Agencies," Executive Committee, The Baptist Convention of the State of Georgia, mimeographed.

Edwards, Morgan, *Materials Toward A History of the Baptists in South Carolina.* Furman Collection.

_____, Materials Toward A History of the Baptist in Georgia.

Garrison, Searcy S., "*Institutions in the Work of Georgia Baptists*," Executive Committee, The Baptist Convention of the State of Georgia, Atlanta, mimeographed, 1969.

Johnston, Edwin B., *A History of the South Georgia Baptist Convention.*

——————, A History of the General Missionary Baptist Association of North Georgia.

Lee, Walter M., "A Little Visit to the Baptist Church on the Kioka," 317-330, *Review and Expositer*, Volume 20, No. 3, July, 1923, Louisville: The Seminary Press.

Lester, James Adams, "A History of *The Christian Index*, 1822-1954," Unpublished Master's Thesis, 1955.

——————, "A Short History of the Baptists: A brief investigation of Christian thought relative to the Baptist denomination and a historical survey," unpublished essay.

Minutes, The Administration Committee, Executive Committee, Georgia Baptist Convention, 1919-1971.

Minutes, Charleston, South Carolina, Association, 1775, 1777, 1778, 1779, 1785-1792.

Minutes, The Executive Committee, [First], Georgia Baptist Convention [scattered], 1830-1919.

Minutes, The Executive Committee, The Georgia Baptist Convention, 1919-1971.

Minutes, Georgia Baptist Association, 1803-1905.

Minutes, Hephzibah Association, 1808-1836.

Minutes, Kiokee Baptist Church, Columbia County, Georgia, 1790-1955.

Minutes, Savannah River Association, 1813.

Minutes, State Mission Board and Executive Committee. State Mission Board, Georgia Baptist Convention, [originals], 1905-1919. [None known to be in existence in original form 1877-1904.]

Minutes, Sunbury Association, 1818-1824.

Proctor, Emerson, *Georgia Baptist Organization and Division, 1772-1848*, Georgia Southern College, Statesboro, unpublished thesis, 1969.

"Report of Committee Named to Study Structure of the

Education Commission of the Georgia Baptist Convention," Executive Committee, Baptist Convention of the State of Georgia, Atlanta, mimeographed.

"Report of Committee on Purpose of the Georgia Baptist Convention in Giving Support to Baptist Colleges," Executive Committee, Baptist Convention of the State of Georgia, Atlanta, mimeographed.

"Report Concerning Lake Louise Assembly Property," Executive Committee, The Baptist Convention of the State of Georgia, Atlanta, mimeographed.

"Report to the Executive Committee, Georgia Baptist Convention, Concerning Ministry in the Area of Church/ Minister Relations," mimeographed.

"Report and Recommendations Concerning Georgia Baptist Hospital Development Programs," Executive Committee, The Baptist Convention of the State of Georgia, Atlanta, mimeographed.

"Resolution Adopted by the Board of Trustees of Mercer University," January 25, 1968, Executive Committee of the Baptist Convention of the State of Georgia, mimeographed.

"Resolution Concerning Counseling Service for Ministers and Their Families," Executive Committee, The Baptist Convention of the State of Georgia, Atlanta, mimeographed.

"A Resolution of the Executive Committee of the Baptist Convention of the State of Georgia in Response to a Resolution of the Board of Trustees of Mercer University," mimeographed.

"Special report of Mercer Trustees to Georgia Baptist Convention, 1969," November 11, 1969.

OTHER SOURCES

Allen, I. M., *The Triennial Baptist Register*, Philadelphia: Baptist General Tract Society, 1836.

_____, *The United States Baptist Annual Register for 1832*, Philadelphia: Printed by T. W. Ustick, 1833.

Asplund, John, *The Annual Register of the Baptist Denomination in North America, 1790.*

—————, *The Annual Register of the Baptist Denomination in North America, 1791.*

Duke, R. L., *History of Phillips Mill Baptist Church,* 1960, taken from church minutes.

Jernigan, Paul M., *History of Powelton Baptist Church,* Nashville, Dargan-Carver Library, Item 76, Georgia Collection.

Robinson, Robert Jackson, President's Address to Georgia Baptist Convention, 1971. Mimeographed copy, 6 p.p.

Standard, Janet Harvill, *This Certain Shepherd, A Profile of Elder Jesse Mercer,* Washington, Georgia, 1968, 20 p.p.

The Baptist Church in Savannah, historical sketch of, no date, title page, Archives, Stetson Memorial Library, Mercer University, Macon. 27 p.p.

"The Progress of Higher Education Under the Control of Georgia Baptists," Archives, Stetson Memorial Library, Mercer University, Macon, pamphlet, 1922, 22 p.p.

Selected Index

Singleton, G. Gordon, 508.
Singleton, H. Tucker, parliamentarian, 736.
Slack, William, 1, 2.
Smith, Charles Lee, 319.
Smith, Harry V., Sr., 642, 764.
Smith, Peter, 33.
Smith, R. H., 277.
Snyder, Julian P., 764.
Social Service Commission, 341, 347, 352, 386, 471, 495, 512, 563, 566, 576, 582, 634, 650, 661, 678, 729; Commission abolished, 679.
South Carolina Convention, 61.
South Carolina, members in, 159.
South Georgia Convention, 802.
South Georgia Messenger, 354.
South Georgia mission work, 108.
Southeastern Printing Company, 403.
Southern Baptist College, 119.
Southern Baptist College, proposed, 789.
Southern Baptist College for Young Women, 263.
Southern Baptist College in Washington, 118, 121, 122.
Southern Baptist Convention, 205, 390, 517.
Southern Baptist Domestic Mission Board, 148.
Southern Baptist Education Committee, 386.
Southern Baptist Preacher, 133.
Southern Baptist Publication Convention, 154.
Southern Baptist Publication Convention Society, 155, 160, 161, 164.
Southern Baptist Theological Seminary, 259, 282.
Southern Baptist University, 426.
Southern Bible Board, 164.
Southern Bible Board, suspended, 183.
Southern Convention organized, 146.
Southern Female College, 259, 307.
Southern Industrial Orphans' Home, 540, 589.
"Southern" Slant, 143.
Southern Seminary, 196.
Southern Watchman, 83.
Southwestern Baptist Home Mission Society, 139, 143.
Spalding, A. T., 226.

Spanish-American War, 272.
Springer, Rev. Mr., 51.
St. Simons Island, 7.
Standige, William, 58.
Standing Resolutions, compiled, 472.
State Mission Board, 212, 289, 366, 367; idea for, 204; financial channel, 227; indebtedness, 277; report trends, 241; work of, 233.
State Mission Fund, 158.
State Missions, 164, 528.
State Missions Day, 534.
State Missions department, 170.
State Missions, Jubilee of, 473.
State Missions program, 221, 226, 228, 234, 255, 272; expansion, 626; programs grow, 682.
State Sanitarium, Chaplain, 578.
State Superintendent, 329.
Stearnes, Martha, 36.
Stearnes, Shubal, 6, 7, 23.
Stevens, Edward A., ordination by Convention, 119.
Stevens, Paul M., 634.
Stewardship promotion, 113.
Stewart, A. H., 422.
Stirk, Benjamin, 13.
Stocks, Thomas, 442.
"Student Activities" department, 459.
Student Center, Statesboro, 759.
Student Center, Georgia Tech, 759.
Student Centers, 746.
Student work, Department of, 449.
Sunbury, 29, 134.
Sunbury Association, 58, 59, 157, 173, 174.
Sunbury, missionary serving that Association, 147.
Sunbury, (Old Savannah River) , 64.
Sunday School, 193, 330.
Sunday School Board, 466.
Sunday School Convention, 256.
Sunday School Department, 214, 234, 277.
Sunday School and Young People's Movement, 271.
Sunday School work, 304; summary of growth, 657.
Supplemental Appeal Plan, 494.
Surgical Building dedicated, 469.
Swilley, Monroe S., 610.

Tabernacle Baptist Church, 333, 419.